A SHEARWATER BOOK

ALDO

❃

LEOPOLD'S

❃

ODYSSEY

ALDO LEOPOLD'S ODYSSEY

JULIANNE LUTZ NEWTON

ISLANDPRESS / SHEARWATER BOOKS

Washington • Covelo • London

The Library of Congress has cataloged the hardcover edition as follows:
Newton, Julianne Lutz.
Aldo Leopold's odyssey / Julianne Lutz Newton.
p. cm.
Includes bibliographical references and index.
ISBN-13: 978-1-59726-045-9 (alk. paper)
ISBN-10: 1-59726-045-2 (alk. paper)
1. Leopold, Aldo, 1886–1948. 2. Naturalists—Wisconsin—Biography.
3. Conservationists—Wisconsin—Biography.
4. Nature conservation—United States—History—20th century. I. Title.
QH31.L618N49 2006
508.092—dc22[B]   2006028102

ISBN-13: 978-1-59726-442-6
ISBN-10: 1-59726-442-3

British Cataloguing-in-Publication data available.

For the apple tree

Contents

Preface

I first heard of Aldo Leopold when I was a graduate student in wildlife ecology at the University of Illinois. One day, in the midst of a conversation about some research questions, a colleague at the Illinois Natural History Survey pulled from his shelf a copy of *A Sand County Almanac*, offering me my first discovery of its author. I read it and found the book interesting, but I did not at the time grasp Leopold's significance.

I continued with my education, doing fieldwork, collecting and analyzing data, attending classes in wildlife science, statistics, and as many 'ologies as I could fit in. I loved what I was learning, but I began to feel increasingly unsettled. Science could go far in helping people understand the world, but in its objectivity it could never go far enough in making the modern world a more pleasant and healthier place in which to live. For that, something else was needed. At this point I happened into a class on conservation literature, and it was here that I rediscovered Leopold. I learned about Leopold in the context of the history and philosophies of the conservation and environmental movements. And I began to see him not just as a careful observer of nature but as something more—as someone uniquely insightful and clear minded and as an artist with an unusual gift for lyrical prose. Here, too, like many others, I began to see in Leopold's work what might be needed, in addition to good science, to help promote the beauty of nature.

Leopold has become something of a household icon of the

conservation movement, perhaps most recognized for his "land ethic," expressed succinctly in his oft-quoted phrase "A thing is right when it tends to preserve the integrity, stability, and beauty of the biotic community. It is wrong when it tends otherwise." But how, I wondered, did Leopold come to call for a land ethic in the first place; what did Leopold mean by those words; and, practically speaking, what did he think it might take for humans to dwell on the land yet at the same time preserve its integrity, stability, and beauty? And what did he mean by his less talked about though central idea—what he came to call "land health"—an evolving vision that included human-inhabited places?

Pursuing answers to these questions seemed just the sort of project that not only would allow me to investigate Leopold's provocative thinking but also had relevance to contemporary environmental concerns and to the search for more positive versions of modern, civilized life than the prevailing one. My work began as simply a study of Leopold's thinking about land health; I soon found, however, that his concept of land health was such a rich and integrated one that to comprehend it required probing his scientific understandings—what Leopold meant by "land"—his critiques of human culture and values, and how he brought them together.

Tracking along with Leopold's intellectual journey, rediscovering his life's work, can help us to think more clearly and, ultimately, to act more compassionately toward the land—and by land, I soon understood, Leopold meant not only fields and forests but the whole of nature. This was Leopold's hope, and it seems even more vital today, when the dangers of not doing so are even more pressing and the pleasures of doing so are as great as ever.

Leopold's way of thinking, in the words of one of his former students, Albert Hochbaum, was not "that of an inspired genius, but that of any other ordinary fellow trying to put two and two together." "Because you have added up your sums better than most of us," Hochbaum told his old professor, "it is important that you let fall a hint [in your writings] that in the process of reaching the end result of your thinking you have sometimes followed trails like anyone else that lead you up the wrong alleys."[1] Leopold was an extraordinary ordinary man; like any of us, sometimes he followed wrong trails, which twisted and turned, in his pursuit of a vision and means to healthy lands. But his compass was set on this goal, and once he found that he had headed astray, he retraced his steps and tried a different path. In Leopold's words, he made many excursions from "a single starting-point"—the longing for truth and beauty—"to which man returns again and again to organize yet another search for a durable scale of values."[2] To follow along on that journey is to share in many discoveries; it is to get to know the deeper thinking of Leopold and, indeed, to encounter provocative yet realistic ideas for a more ecologically enlightened and prosperous civilization, as relevant today as they were during his lifetime.

No person can ever know fully the mind of another. It can indeed be a fearful thing to try. Fearful, in my case, in the sense that I wanted to give as complete and honest a picture of Leopold and his thinking and experiences as possible, yet I recognized that whatever I saw inevitably would be colored by my own ignorance, ideas, and experiences. Nonetheless, drawing on a wealth of archival materials, on his vast opus of published and unpublished writings, on interviews, and on the critical work of others, I have tried to give as objective a portrait as I could of Leopold's intellectual journey.

Aldo Leopold's Odyssey portrays Leopold's multifaceted adult intellectual journey. It is not a full biography of Leopold; rather, it is an account of the maturation of his thinking, which builds in part, as detailed in the notes, on much fine Leopold scholarship that has come before it. Curt Meine's remarkable *Aldo Leopold: His Life and Work* remains the standard biography, chronicling Leopold's life from birth to death, and Meine's more recent *Correction Lines: Essays on Land, Leopold, and Conservation* provides probing commentary on Leopold's legacy. Susan L. Flader's *Thinking Like a Mountain: Aldo Leopold and the Evolution of an Ecological Attitude toward Deer, Wolves, and Forests* insightfully traces the evolution of Leopold's thinking through study of a representative ecological and land management puzzle, the relationship between deer, their predators, the forest, and land-use attitudes and practices. J. Baird Callicott was largely responsible for drawing attention to Leopold's now famous land ethic. Callicott's seminal philosophic essays on Leopold are collected in two volumes: *In Defense of the Land Ethic:*

Essays in Environmental Philosophy and *Beyond the Land Ethic: More Essays in Environmental Philosophy*; he also edited *A Companion to "A Sand County Almanac": Interpretive and Critical Essays*, a very helpful guide for serious readers of Leopold's most well-known work. Legal scholar and conservation historian Eric Freyfogle has shown the central importance in Leopold's thinking of conservation on private lands and the land health concept, most recently in *The Land We Share: Private Property and the Common Good* and *Why Conservation Is Failing and How It Can Regain Ground*. Philosopher Bryan Norton has perceptively examined Leopold's philosophic ideas and has applied them in *Sustainability: A Philosophy of Adaptive Ecosystem Management*. Marybeth Lorbiecki has written a fine summary biography of Leopold's life, *Aldo Leopold: A Fierce Green Fire*, and Richard Knight and Suzanne Riedel have edited a helpful book of essays connecting some of Leopold's ideas to contemporary issues, *Aldo Leopold and the Ecological Conscience*.

Aldo Leopold was also an avid photographer, and many of the photographs in this book are ones he took himself. Leopold purchased a camera while on a research trip to Germany in 1935. He bought the camera for his son, he said, yet he imagined it would serve all of his family "as a field glass for a long time."[3] Leopold, in fact, used it himself to take thousands of black-and-white lantern slides, documenting the landscapes he studied and incorporating many images into his lectures. Technical photography became to him an important enough facet of conservation work that he believed land management professionals should be trained in it.[4]

Aldo Leopold's Odyssey also could not have been written without the help and guidance of numerous colleagues and friends. This book began as a dissertation written for a PhD degree taken in the Department of Natural Resources and Environmental Sciences at the University of Illinois at Urbana-Champaign and fulfilled that role. I thank University of Illinois ecologists Richard Warner, Ed Heske, Tim Van Deelen, Jeff Brawn, Scott Robinson, Pat Brown, Gary Rolfe, and Wes Jarrell for their intelligent guidance in fieldwork and as graduate committee members while I was studying at the University of Illinois. I thank Richard Warner and his wife, Zöe, for their enduring support, friendship, and patient and wise guidance of inestimable value through two degrees and beyond. And I thank Richard Warner, too, for orienting me in the field of wildlife ecology. Mary Lowry—always alert and helpful—guided me through the mazes of graduate school requirements and paperwork. I am grateful to Bill Sullivan, director of the Environmental Council, who generously provided postgraduate research support, which allowed me the valuable opportunity to explore new fields and to finish this work. Todd Wildermuth, characteristically generous, has been an insightful friend and colleague from the start and helped gather many secondary sources on Leopold. Also, at the University of Illinois, I thank Carol Augspurger in the Department of Plant Biology, who read and commented on parts of this manuscript and, in her graduate class in plant ecology, helped teach me to think. Val Beasley, in the College of Veterinary Medicine, helped point me in the direction I needed to go some years ago. It was Eric Freyfogle, in the College of Law, who first suggested I undertake this exploration and who guided its progress. Through sharing of his own understandings, numerous thoughtful discussions, rigorous and skillful editorial suggestions, and intellectual encouragement, he contributed substantially to the genesis, development, and content of this work.

In addition to his scholarship and writings about Leopold, I am also indebted to Curt Meine for his help as a graduate committee member and for stimulating postdegree conversations about Leopold, for his careful and insightful comments on the manuscript at various stages, and for his example as both a thoughtful and a practical conservationist. I also thank Dave Foreman, executive director of the Rewilding Institute, and Volker Radeloff of the UW Department of Forest Ecology and Management for helpful conversations about conservation and Leopold. Courtney White, founder of the Quivira Coalition and an inspirational practitioner and promoter of land health, was also a helpful reader of parts of the manuscript.

I am personally and professionally grateful to Nina Leopold Bradley for sharing her knowledge and for her warm kindness, hospitality, and friendship, kindled over many an evening fire. I thank

Carl Leopold, Estella Leopold, and the late Luna Leopold, too, for taking time to correspond and talk with me about themselves, their own work, and their father.

I thank the Aldo Leopold Foundation of Baraboo, Wisconsin (http://www.aldoleopold.org, which promotes Leopold's legacy), and especially executive director Buddy Huffaker, for their generosity and their support of this work. Buddy at the Aldo Leopold Foundation, Bernie Schermetzler, curator of the University of Wisconsin (UW) Leopold archives, and Scott Craven, chair of the UW Department of Wildlife Ecology, in addition to their encouragement, also kindly gave permission to read and copy Leopold materials and to reproduce photographs from their collections. And thanks go to Laurie Ballentine, also in the UW wildlife department, for her always gracious administrative help. Susan Flader's prior work in organizing and cataloguing the Leopold papers at the University of Wisconsin made my archival work approachable and pleasant.

I thank New Englanders Peter Forbes and Helen Whybrow of Knoll Farm and Connie Kousman, Janice Orion, and Suzanne Lupien for teaching me about practical conservation work, good farming, and how to eat. Ashley Ravestein, in hiking solo up the Pacific Crest Trail, has taught me much about foresight and courage, and through her loyal friendship I have been much encouraged.

I thank the board of The Burroughs Institute at Woodchuck Lodge, Inc.—Tom Alworth, Diane Galusha, Karen Rauter, Joe Farleigh, and John McDaniel—for their enthusiasm and hard work. And I am grateful to Chuck and Ann Tompkins and Mary Anne and Terry Murphy for their patience, friendship, and encouragement.

My parents, John and Una Lutz, my brother, John Burroughs Lutz, and my sister, Rebecca Cross, have loved me relentlessly. They are a family of grace.

I am grateful to Tim, a man of honor, who loved, supported, and encouraged me through many years.

It has been a pleasure to work with Island Press at every step of the way. I am grateful to Barbara Dean for her supportive influence and kind friendship. Emily Davis and Jessica Heise have worked skillfully on the production of this book. Pat Harris' wonderful attention to detail and sensitivity to the text during copyediting have helped smooth the reader's path. This book has been shaped by many thoughtful comments and probing questions by my editor, Jonathan Cobb. He is one of a rare and special breed of editors who I hope will never die out; and, one of a kind, he is an insightful friend.

For any errors, omissions, and misrepresentations in the text, I take full responsibility.

ALDO
LEOPOLD'S
ODYSSEY

Introduction

Launching Out

Launch out on his story, Muse . . . start from where you will—
sing for our time too.   Homer, *The Odyssey*

Aldo Leopold landed in Casas Grandes, in the northern Mexican
state of Chihuahua, three days before Christmas 1937, just two and
half weeks shy of his fifty-first birthday. The flight, his first ever, had
taken him over winding streams and arroyos, rocky hills covered
with twisted oaks and junipers, and canyons abounding with white-
tailed deer and wild turkeys. It brought him into a region once
inhabited by great thirteenth- through fifteenth-century Mexican
civilizations and several even older ones. Within a short distance
of the modern-day Hotel Regis, boasting the local distinction of
flushing bathroom fixtures, lay a broad labyrinth of smooth-walled
rooms of pink clay, ruins of the sophisticated city of the ancient
Pacquime people. Leopold, staying in town for the night, took a
black-and-white photograph, documenting that, at least in this moment in the 1930s Casas Grandes, no priests, traders, artisans, or
farmers ambled by as in centuries past; only a few men with cowboy
hats and a woman in a long, dark coat picked their way along the
muddy main street after a recent snowy rain. The throbbing drums
and tinkling copper bells of former Mesoamerican religious rituals
no longer sounded under the clouded sky. But a horse pulling a
wooden buckboard over the rutted road rattled by the flat white
fronts of the local grocery store, barbershop, and two cantinas.

Leopold had come to Casas Grandes on vacation from his work as professor of game management at the University of Wisconsin. It was the starting point for a second annual two-week hunting and pack trip that would see him into 1938 and what would be the final decade of his life. Accompanied by his brother, his eldest son, and a few loaded burros, he would soon enter the interior recesses of the Sierra Madre Occidental, traveling along the trout-inhabited Rio Gavilan.

The greater southwestern region was divided into two nations by the U.S.-Mexico boundary line, creating a landscape of similarities and contrasts in time and in space. Its juxtapositions were not lost on Leopold. In climate and form the mountains of the Sierra Madre in Mexico resembled the nearby terrain where, nearly a quarter of a century earlier, he had begun his career. In 1909 the twenty-two-year-old Ivy League kid from Iowa had entered the ranks of professional life as a forest ranger. With enthusiasm he took up his position in one of the new USDA Forest Service's most rugged, least populated districts. District 3 included the forests in Southwestern Arizona and New Mexico — not far across the border from Casas Grandes. Leopold served this district for fifteen years before returning to the Midwest to settle down with his growing family.

On that Arizona–New Mexico frontier, Leopold had met the noble Spanish woman who became his wife and fathered the first four of their five children. He had traipsed the mountainous terrain on the U.S. side of the border on foot and by horseback, mapping the location, quantity, and quality of timber. Then he worked as a forest supervisor, inspecting forest conditions while observing the spread of new ranches and the growth of towns scattered within and around the area's public lands. Traveling the region, Leopold witnessed the ideal of pioneering technological progress in action: the expansion of railroads, telephone wires, automobiles, mines, dams, and reservoirs. He observed firsthand the spread of plowing and cropping into the region. He watched the unfolding of all this rapid economic development — what he would later term the "industrial Juggernaut" — and witnessed its ill effects on these fragile, arid lands.

The Mexican side of the mountainous landscape, in contrast with District 3, still remained largely unmapped, unowned, and unsettled in 1937. The Mexican government was implementing a development policy that would promote road building, agriculture, towns, and tourism. In years past, however, settlers had shied away from the Sierra Madre—most recently because of lack of development funds for local services; in the 1910s because the Mexican rebel hero Pancho Villa roamed there; and before that because of peril presented by warring Apache Indians. The region's lack of settlement gave Leopold the opportunity to move back in time by simply crossing a political boundary line. By visiting Mexico's Sierra Madre he could "feast his eyes on what his own mountains were like before the Juggernaut." The contrast with the U. S. Southwest was great. On the Mexican side of the border, Leopold observed,

> these live oak-dotted hills fat with side oats grama, these pine-clad mesas spangled with flowers, these lazy trout streams burbling along under great sycamores and cottonwoods, come near to being the cream of creation. But on our [the U.S.] side of the line the grama is mostly gone, the mesas are spangled with snakeweed,[1] the trout streams are now cobble-bars.[2]

The Mexican Sierra Madre was comfortably familiar yet strikingly new to Leopold. His year-end visit on the eve of his fifty-second year thus allowed him not only to savor the present moment but also to reflect on the past and consider the future of "the land"—Leopold's inclusive term for soils, waters, plants, animals, and people collectively. Years later Leopold recorded[3] his observations in a lyrical, penetrating essay, "Song of the Gavilan,"[4] which appeared in his final and best-known work, *A Sand County Almanac*. In this essay Leopold reflected on what he had learned as he explored the territory belonging to this dancing, riffled river.

→- -←

"Start from where you will, Muse," Homer's narrator commands in book I of his *Odyssey*: sing of the adventuring "man of twists and turns," tell the tale of the man who was "fighting to save his life and bring his comrades home." Aldo Leopold's years were not spent fighting to bring anyone home from a dangerous voyage over "wine-dark seas," as Odysseus' were. His struggles were less violent yet no less challenging. Leopold fought to save lands from human recklessness and to help people prosper, generation upon generation.

The Gavilan River in Chihuahua, Mexico, January 1938. Leopold later wrote an essay about the river, "The Song of the Gavilan," which appeared in A Sand County Almanac.

Motivating his career was an elementary, lofty hope: that a rising population of modern, technologically powerful humans would learn and practice ways of living that met their various needs yet at the same time kept the land healthy. To raise such a high hope in the face of increasing land-use-related problems—severe soil erosion, looming timber shortage, increasingly destructive floods, water pollution, and the loss of plant and animal species—was to begin an intellectually adventurous journey involving its own twists and turns.

On Christmas Eve 1937, the morning after their arrival in northern Mexico, Leopold and his companions departed Casas Grandes for the wilds. A few evenings later found the men comfortably weary and the campfire low. An arrow had struck well, and they feasted on venison and biscuits with gravy while imbibing cherry bounce. As the others turned in, Leopold sat silently in the still night, watching the stars climb high over the rimrock that edged the river Gavilan. A lone wolf howled far off. Leopold thought about all he had seen and had tried to understand in years past. He contemplated the night sky hanging over the mountainous terrain on both sides of the Mexican-American border—the one spangled with flowers, the other with snakeweed. And rising like the moon in the darkness was an insistent question demanding his attention, the question that had guided his work over the past quarter century and that would continue to guide it for the next decade until his death: how might today's civilization inhabit lands in ways prosperous to it and good for the whole of nature?

Leopold listened in the night air to the quiet rustle of leaves and the rippling waters. Here was a river that had not yet witnessed the American ideal of progress in action—the ideas, as Leopold later expressed it, "that every river needs more people, and all people need more inventions" and that "the good life depends on the indefinite extension of this chain of logic."[5] What did the "good" in good life mean, Leopold wondered. And where did human inventiveness and power cross the line between positive creativity and destructiveness? Progress to most Americans was defined in a way quite different from the vision slowly developing and gathering cohesion in Leopold's mind.

Leopold appreciated the many goods that civilization had wrought from the land, goods that made a two-week trip into the wilds an adventurous vacation rather than simply an exercise in outdoor survival. By now much of the nation, the Leopold family included, benefited from the comforts of indoor plumbing and electricity, railways and automobiles, square meals and warm beds, enameled bathtubs and radios, sliced bread and cake mixes. Leopold's life began with the first Ball-Mason canning jars in 1887, stretched to the 1910 tea bag and to Wonder Bread in 1921, and ended in the year of Nestlé's Quik, in 1948. Human population, too, had risen between 1909 and 1948, from 95 million to more than 146 million people eager to live well and prosper, putting increasing pressure on the productivity of the land.

*Leopold's photograph of Casas Grandes, the Mexican town where he and
his traveling companions stayed overnight in late 1937 before embarking
on a two-week trip along the Gavilan River.*

Human creativity mixed with the land's fruitfulness had brought
many benefits indeed. Yet these had come with costs that increasingly were demanding payment. Leopold had witnessed the unhappy
consequences of ignoring nature's charges—first in national forests
of the New Mexico and Arizona territories covered by USDA Forest
Service District 3, and then repeatedly over the course of his career
and in landscapes across the country. Such consequences jointly
affected man and the rest of nature. Leopold watched as human
settlements literally eroded away under the feet of pioneers in the
Southwest following insensitive livestock grazing, dam building,
irrigation, and plowing. He saw the same thing happening to farms in
the Midwest. Overgrazing was a particular problem because it
destroyed the vegetation that held the soil and moderated water
flows. Heavy rains melted away vulnerable stream banks and cut

into fertile valley lands. As the soil washed away it silted rivers and newly built reservoirs, to the harm of fish and human users alike. Damage also came when settlers and government officials eliminated wolves, bears, and other large predators. With predators gone, deer populations rose, leading to overbrowsing, degraded lands, and starving deer. Meanwhile, farmers across the nation were busy replacing millions of acres of diverse native vegetation with wide expanses of wheat, corn, and other kinds of crop monocultures. Along with the high crop productivity came explosions of plant and animal pests, which brought problems of their own.

And then there were the dust storms—perhaps the most dramatic evidence of land misuse. The year 1937, coming to a close now as Leopold listened to the Gavilan sing, recorded the most frequent and intense Dust Bowl storms. Winds carried black clouds of prairie soil—recently plowed, sodless, now drought parched and barren—across the Great Plains states and on to the Midwest and the East Coast, darkening the sun day after day. Multitudes of people were made homeless, poor, and desperate as a result. The misused land had evicted its human inhabitants.

Many communities newly established across the American landscape, in sum, were suffering because of unwise land-use practices. So were the soil's fertility and native species diversity. Watersheds and human livelihoods alike in many places were degraded and destroyed. Leopold's difficult questions were far from theoretical ones. They had to do with the well-being and survival of families and neighborhoods and, ultimately—as the productive capacity and habitability of lands declined—with the endurance and strength of the country itself.

Leopold, of course, was far from the first American to worry about land misuse. Explorer John Wesley Powell had worried before him, as had linguist and diplomat George Perkins Marsh, writer Henry David Thoreau, and naturalist Mabel Osgood Wright. The Forest Service that Leopold entered in 1909, led by Gifford Pinchot under President Theodore Roosevelt, was specifically charged with reforming America's unwise forestry practices. And Leopold's career overlapped with those of nature lover John Muir, agrarian essayist John Burroughs, anthropologist George Bird Grinnell, sportsman and game scientist Herbert Stoddard, forester P. S. Lovejoy, ornithologist William Vogt, soil scientist H. H. Bennett, educator and horticulturist Liberty Hyde Bailey, wildlife advocate William T. Hornaday, ecologist Paul Sears, zoologist Rachel Carson, and political cartoonist Jay "Ding" Darling—all interested, like Leopold, in calling land troubles to the attention of American citizens and working for positive change.

Many others, indeed, had noticed the degradation of nature and labored hard to halt it. Yet few of them, perhaps none, would travel as far or range as widely as Leopold in probing the root causes of land degradation and in figuring out what needed to change. In his quest after the hope of harmony between humans and land, Leopold pursued two main intellectual paths. One line of inquiry turned to the land itself, seeking to learn how it worked and what land-use practices would promote intact, fertile soils; clean, well-flowing waters; and diversity of native species. The second line of inquiry turned to people and culture, trying to understand human motives and behaviors—particularly how people could be encouraged to *want* to promote lands in good condition and follow through in practice. The first path carried Leopold to discoveries arising from ecological and evolutionary sciences. The second brought him face to face with considerations of prevailing economic, social, political, and cultural values. As he explored both paths, Leopold discovered that they ultimately converged, and that conservation's work must take place at their confluence.[6]

When Leopold began his career in 1909, the science of ecology—the study of organisms in relation to their environments—was, as a formal science, yet a fledgling. To the popular mind land was still understood as a collection of individual resources—timber, minerals, water flows, and fish and game species—not an integrated whole. Responding to signs of resource shortages, conservationists of the day resolved to promote more careful use of America's raw materials. Early twentieth-century conservation was both a prudential and a moral effort aiming to increase efficiency of resource use, decrease waste, and leave an ample supply for present and future generations.

As the new science of ecology matured through the first half of the twentieth century, however, a growing number of botanists, zoologists, and aquatic scientists, Leopold eventually among them, began to see significance in the vast and dynamic intricacies of nature's interrelationships. Leopold and others were coming to understand land not merely as a collection of discrete parts but as an integrated, dynamic community of plant and animal life. Living organisms were linked with their environments—soils, waters, climate—and flows of circulating energy bound them together. No part of nature was independent of the other parts, and humans, too, were included in the complexly woven web of life.[7] Changes to one part of the land community triggered ripple effects that spread elsewhere, for good or ill. When a hillside woodlot was clear-cut for timber, for instance, soil and soil nutrients washed off the land and into nearby creeks and rivers, creating problems far from their origin. Indiscriminant cutting disrupted relationships among the soils, waters, plants, and animals. Many resident species could no longer survive and different ones took their places. Waterways experienced changes in temperature, flow pattern, and water level and clarity that disrupted fish and other aquatic life. In extreme cases land-use disruption could render lands unfit for human habitation. In short, the land's productivity could suffer from ecological derangement as well as from resource exhaustion. Ecologically informed conservationists needed to pay attention to nature's organization and functioning and not just to particular resource flows.

Leopold took naturally to the ideas developing within the new field of ecology—the "science of communities,"[8] as he understood it—and he played an important role in shaping them. From an early age he displayed a bent for piecing together stories of land interrelationships. While a teenager, he spent a week on his own traipsing through marshes to test his theory that phoebes congregated around early-blooming skunk cabbage because the cabbage attracted the season's first emerging insects—prey for the birds. Through research and observation he would spend his lifetime trying to understand such stories—the "biotic dramas" of the land's workings—and how human activities were affecting them. Not long after his Gavilan trip, Leopold declared that ecology had revealed the "outstanding discovery of the 20th century"—the immense complexity of the collective interactions and organizations of nature.[9]

In time Leopold came to conceptualize nature's ways as a kind of odyssey—in two dimensions. Accumulating scientific information was indicating that, across the earth, not only humans but all forms of life were creatures of "twists and turns" involved in a great drama: the age-old tale of "[dust] unto dust."[10] All organisms fought continually for their places in the sun, side by side, living and dying, eating and being eaten. As they did so they participated collectively in an ecological "odyssey," as members of integrated systems bound together by energy flows into a web of life. Food was a primary force of connectivity: the root of a tree nudged free a nutrient atom from a limestone ledge, which became part of the soil, which grew a tuft of bluestem, which hoarded the sunlight in its leaves until, nibbled by a deer mouse, it fed the eagle flying overhead or the wolf howling on the mountain, which in time died and returned the nutrient atom to the soil, where it was picked up by a spiderwort, which was eaten by a rabbit, which was eaten by a man. In general, Leopold surmised, the greater the diversity within a community of life, the longer it could keep nutrients circulating among its members, and thus the more fertile and productive of life it was. Humans misused land when they diminished native diversity, shortened food cycles, disrupted energy flows, and sent nutrients more rapidly downstream and onward to the bottom of the sea.

This ecological odyssey taking place in the present in particular places intersected, as Leopold put it, at a "right angle"[11] to the other natural odyssey—an evolutionary one.[12] The evolutionary odyssey was historical, beginning in the slow reaches of time and extending into an unknown future. This enterprise of life unfolded for the most part beyond the sight of mortal beings but was recorded in its living creations. Along the way it offered the ultimate test of survival. With their "fellow voyagers,"[13] in Leopold's words, humans were part of this succession of life, sharing in the possibilities of both re-creation and extinction.

As characters in ecological and evolutionary stories, humans were interdependent organisms integral to the whole community of life, Leopold understood. But humans over the centuries, unlike any other creature, had learned to make powerful tools that aided them in their comfort, expansion, and endurance as a species. They had

Leopold, age fifty, on his 1937–1938 Gavilan trip, an experience that would significantly shape his understanding of land.

invented technologies that could destroy competitors and greatly increase their take from the land. At the same time humans had the capacity to choose how and where they wielded their tools and whether and how they limited their take. It was at this concourse — where what was possible met what was ideal — that Leopold faced conservation's toughest practical challenges, challenges that have not yet been overcome. Here it was, in other words, that Leopold would confront both the scientific questions about how land was organized and functioned and the set of questions bound up with his other path of inquiry about people and culture: Could humans recognize their role in promoting or destroying the health of the land? What would it take to induce them to care for the land?

As Leopold probed the human predicament in nature he identified three cultural attitudes that posed grave obstacles to conservation and ultimately to an enduring and prosperous civilization: individualism, a get-rich-quick mentality, and the commodification of nature.[14]

Individualism. Prevailing in American culture was the view that people were free to pursue their individual self-interest as isolated actors as long as they did not cause overt harm to other human individuals. Some of this presumed autonomy of individuals clashed with basic lessons of ecological and evolutionary sciences, which taught that humans were interconnected with intricately organized soils, waters, plants, and animals and their life processes, as well as with their human neighbors. No action happened in isolation. A land-use practice occurring in one spot resulted in rippling effects in other places. Conduct that seemed inconsequential when carried out by one person could cause grave communal damage when undertaken by many people, whereas keeping the land healthy often could not be accomplished by individual landowners but required neighbors working together across a landscape. The ethic of individualism largely failed to take interconnection and cumulative community effects into account.

Get-rich-quick mentality. The rapid accumulation of cash and manufactured goods was the prevailing yardstick of American well-being. As people pursued wealth in the short term they often pushed the land hard, in ways that exhausted or otherwise damaged its self-organization and functional capacities over the longer term. Ecological and evolutionary sciences were teaching that land had limits, both in the quantities of resources that could be removed before exhaustion occurred and in the extent to which land could be disturbed (e.g., by agricultural techniques or settlement patterns) without derangement. These limits were neither readily nor immediately apparent. The get-rich-quick mentality failed to give due weight to nature's capacities and limits and human ignorance in regard to them.

Commodification of nature. Finally, a third obstacle to conservation was the dominant cultural tendency to view nature as a warehouse of distinct commodities. Most Americans imagined that nature was divisible into individual parts directly useful to themselves—timber, water, soil, game, fish. Humans could live and thrive only by consuming parts of nature. But nature's parts were intricately woven into whole communities, and the land's productivity depended upon the ability of the community as such to function. Community functioning depended, in often unknown ways, upon the presence of many parts that humans did not directly value. The commodification impulse thus was doubly flawed: it fragmented nature in defiance of ecological interconnections, and it employed a grossly incomplete measure of nature.

Conservation and long-term human prosperity, Leopold ultimately concluded, required a scientific understanding of land and the emergence of a new set of cultural values—what he termed an "ecological conscience." Just as ecology was the science of communities, an ecological conscience incorporated an ethics of community life, a community that included as its members not only humans but also soils, waters, plants, and other animals.

"When god-like Odysseus returned from the wars in Troy," Leopold wrote, in the midst of his own life's journey,

> he hanged all on one rope a dozen slave-girls of his household whom he suspected of misbehavior during his absence.
>
> This hanging involved no question of propriety. The girls were property. The disposal of property was then, as now, a matter of expediency, not of right and wrong.
>
> Concepts of right and wrong were not lacking from Odysseus' Greece: witness the fidelity of his wife through the long years before at last his black-prowed galleys clove the wine-dark seas for home. The ethical structure of that day covered wives, but had not yet been extended to human chattels. During the three thousand years which have since elapsed, ethical criteria have been extended to many fields of conduct, with corresponding shrinkages in those judged by expediency only.[15]

The keeping and hanging of human chattels in America had been outlawed. But land, like Odysseus' slave girls, was still a matter of property, and conventions of ownership still allowed people to degrade what they owned. To "sing for our time too," Homer's Muse would need to be updated and enlightened with ecological and evolutionary understandings. An ethical attitude—a common understanding of right and wrong ways to treat nature—needed to be extended "to man's relation to land and to the animals and plants which grow upon it."[16]

Considering again the ecological consequences of modern culture, in the spring after his Gavilan trip Leopold wrote:

> We end, I think, at what might be called the standard paradox of the twentieth century: our tools are better than we are, and grow better faster than we do. They suffice to crack the atom, to command the tides. But they do not suffice for the oldest task in human history: to live on a piece of land without spoiling it.[17]

This was to Leopold not merely the end of the matter but also the beginning. This never-ending challenge served as the "single starting point"[18] for practical land experiments and for successive intellectual journeys, as important for our time as for his own: how then shall we live prosperously within nature and keep it healthy, too?

Chapter 1

Seed Plots

The conservation of our natural resources and their proper use constitute the fundamental problem which underlies almost every other problem of our national life.

President Theodore Roosevelt, June 10, 1907

By 1909—the start of Aldo Leopold's professional career—the United States had traveled far on a journey toward material prosperity within its continent of natural bounty. The New World was a cornucopia of land products. Already it had fed industrial revolutions in western Europe and in America, helping to transform the world. Its natural wealth also had stimulated the emergence of a new, multiethnic civilization—a capitalist industrial one characterized by individualism, faith in science and technology, democracy, and economic growth. Most Americans were engaged in a hopeful quest for progress,[1] and they were working hard at it, in a pulsing combination of people, land, and dreams. Fresh out of forestry school and assigned to America's southwestern frontier, Leopold was caught up in the exciting bustle of the times, though doubts would soon arise in his mind about where the country was heading.

Progress in America was calculated largely in expanding ciphers. If emerging costs of growing prosperity were beginning to cast a shadow, for more than a hundred years the general trend on the development side of the national ledger had been upward. The geographic expansion of the nation itself, for example, had been extraordinary. The thirteen original states covered 210 million acres of land and water; by the early twentieth century the territory of the United States had swelled to nearly 2 billion acres with the addition of the Louisiana Purchase and the annexing of new states and territories.[2] From the beginning of the nineteenth century the U.S. population rose from 5 million people, with an average density of 7 people per square mile, to 88 million people, averaging 30 people per square mile by 1909.[3] Homestead entries, too, continued to rise as more new settlers spread westward across the continent—1909 saw more than 12 million acres claimed, double the amount registered just a decade earlier.[4]

Many Americans evidently believed that decent lives might still be built by farming the land, and one-third of the 1909 laboring population, more than 12 million workers (including 6 million farmers), was engaged in agricultural pursuits, including dairying, lumbering, forestry, stock raising, and crop growing. Stocks of cattle, horses, sheep, mules, and swine had risen within a half century from 53 million to 206 million animals by 1909.[5] The two largest cereal crops—corn and wheat—alone covered 57.5 million acres in 1870, and within forty years the acreage had nearly tripled.[6] By then irrigation had allowed 10 million additional acres of dry, agriculturally unproductive land to grow grains, fruits, and vegetables.[7]

Just as agriculture was expanding and transforming the landscape, so, too, were industry and commerce. By the time Leopold began his career there were almost as many manufacturing workers in the nation as there were agricultural workers,[8] and between 1850 and 1909 the combined value of manufactured products had risen from $1 billion to more than $20 billion, more than twice the value generated by the nation's farms at the time.[9] To distribute foods and manufactured goods—grains, cotton, livestock, coal, railroad ties, groceries, fabrics, ladies' hats, linseed oil, and axle grease—and to boost overseas trade, an elaborate network of transportation and communication also was developing. In 1909 trains carried close to 1 billion passengers and more than 1.5 billion short tons of freight over 240,000 miles of rail lines.[10] More than 2 million miles of public roads crossed the nation[11] and millions of short tons of commodities were floated on the country's inland rivers.[12] By 1909, too, more than 8 million miles of telephone and telegraph wires knitted the countryside.[13]

The materials to develop America's landscapes largely came from the land itself. If conventional indicators of national progress were showing steep upward trends, on the other side of the ledger the supplies of nature's raw materials needed for such growth—minerals, timber, fish, soils—were noticeably declining. The nation's forests, for example, had been heavily used to build America's homes, farms, industries, and expanding networks. By the first decade of the twentieth century the forest products industry was the nation's fourth largest (behind food products, textiles, and iron and steel industries), valued at more than $1 billion annually.[14] In 1909 alone, for example, the steam and electric railroad industries purchased nearly 124 million hewed and sawed railroad ties—of oak, southern pine, cedar, chestnut, Douglas fir, tamarack, cypress, hemlock, and western yellow pine.[15] The same year, railroads and other utilities together purchased 4 million wooden poles, mostly of cedar, chestnut, oak, pine, and cypress.[16] Fifteen billion roofing shingles were cut,[17] and private mills produced 44 million M ft. of lumber[18] that year for a multitude of building projects.[19] Pine trees in southern states yielded 29 million gallons of turpentine for use in paint thinners, cleaners, electrical insulation, soaps, and sizing.[20] Before European arrival, forests covered nearly half the country—around 1 billion acres.[21] In the 250 years between 1600 and 1850 new settlers had deforested 173 million acres of the country. In the following half century almost twice that amount—an additional 323 million acres of forest—fell to the axe and saw. Barely 500 million acres of forest remained by 1909, when Leopold began his career as a forest ranger, and the cutting continued.[22]

By the late nineteenth century pressures on the forests had prompted efforts to promote their more efficient use. In 1905 the nation's 60 forest reserves regulated activities on 56 million acres.[23] Four years later, as Leopold began his career, these numbers, thanks largely to presidential proclamations made by Theodore Roosevelt,[24] had risen sharply, to 150 national forests covering 172 million acres—all the responsibility of the USDA Forest Service, by then four years old.[25]

The national forests were created to protect the natural resources within them. They were to do this, however, not by *preventing* all uses but by *managing* forest resources better so that America's progress could be ongoing. In fact, some of these forestlands remained open for homesteading and private settlement. The national forests also offered free timber to individual home owners for firewood and home-building projects. In 1909, under the program 33,431 citizens cut 105,205 M ft. of timber for private use.[26] Commercial timber sales took an additional 352,000 M ft. that year,[27] while leased grazing lands within national forests added up to 130 million acres and supported more than 9 million cattle, goats, hogs, horses, and sheep.[28] Forest-use pressures were intense, and juggling all the demands on forest's while keeping their productive capacities operative for present and future generations was the challenging task presented to the mostly young, all-male troupe of professional foresters.[29]

A photograph in Leopold's collection. By 1909, when Leopold began his Forest Service career, the forest products industry was the country's fourth largest, and about half of the nation's 1 billion acres of forest had already been cut to help meet the growing demands of development.

OF MEN AND TREES

Aldo Leopold of Burlington, Iowa, at age twenty-two, received his Master of Forestry degree from the Yale Forest School in 1909 and immediately began work with the USDA Forest Service in Arizona. He was proud to be counted among the first of the nation's scientifically trained foresters, and he dreamed of one day being supervisor of a public forest covering thousands, even millions, of acres. Just before graduation, a classmate had remarked, "I'd rather be a Supervisor than be the King of England." Leopold heartily agreed.[30] Forestry was heady work, given what forests had meant—and still meant—in the nation's history. It was also sobering work, given the alarms raised about the decline in the nation's available timber.

Among those showing the greatest concern about shrinking forests was Gifford Pinchot, founder of the Yale school and first chief of the Forest Service.[31] By Pinchot's estimate, with at least half of the nation's timber already gone, the nation's forests retained only a twenty-year supply of timber at the annual rate of use as the twentieth century began.[32] Every year Americans were cutting at a rate up to two-thirds faster than the forests could grow. A timber famine was looming, Pinchot asserted, and it would "touch every man, woman, and child in all the land."[33] Pinchot's warning echoed widely across the country, casting a shadow on the nation's future and giving force to the conservation impulse.[34] It added urgency to the labors of his young, developing Service, which was challenged to apply scientific management to keep timber flowing.

Worries about the nation's declining forests extended to the cultural and political values that forests were said to promote. Writing in 1896, the influential historian Frederick Jackson Turner proclaimed forest clearings "the seed plots of American character."[35] Forests challenged pioneers one by one, family by family, to turn dense vegetation into gardens and groves for human habitation, in the process gaining self-reliance and fortitude—"a forest-change,"[36] Turner called it. Forest clearing, that is, forged a new national type, the self-made man, free and equal—bearing the hope of a better future for himself and his community. This typical settler, Turner contended, displayed "faith in man, hope for democracy, belief in America's destiny, [and] unbounded confidence in his ability to make his dreams come true."[37] The forest-forged man of action was quick to call on the national government "to break down the mountain barrier by internal improvements"[38] so that no obstacle might frustrate his or his neighbors' opportunities for economic prosperity. America's aggressive forces of democracy and nationalism, Turner concluded, came "stark and strong and full of life."[39] And they emerged out of America's forests.

These links between forests and America's pioneering, self-reliant culture were later echoed in a 1940 novel, *The Trees*, by Conrad Richter. In Richter's story a late eighteenth-century family, the Lucketts, headed west to Ohio from their home in Pennsylvania, which suffered from a "woods famine" and lack of reliable game. Arriving in Ohio's unbroken forest, the Lucketts felt both the allure of natural abundance and the dark foreboding of land not yet refashioned by human hands:

> They rounded a high ridge . . . for a moment Sayward reckoned that her father had fetched them unbeknownst to the Western ocean and what lay beneath was the late sun glittering on green-black water. Then she saw that what they looked down on was a dark, illimitable expanse of wilderness. It was a sea of solid treetops broken only by some gash where deep beneath the foliage an unknown stream made its way. . . . Though they waited here till night, the girl knew that no light of human habitation would appear except the solitary spark of some Delaware or Shawanee campfire. . . . This is the way it was, she would say to herself. Nowhere else but in the American wilderness could it have been. . . . "You can smell the game!" [Father said]. . . . "We mought even get rich and have shoes!" Sulie [the youngest] spoke out.[40]

The fictional Lucketts would face a host of struggles and griefs as their lives unfolded. Yet, because they and real settlers like them managed to endure, the generations that followed had not only shoes but a great deal more. Somehow the first crudely equipped settlers cleared a vast land, giving rise to a striving, energetic culture—first carving out simple and lonely dwellings, then creating forest neighborhoods with dirt paths and cartways. In time small settlements grew into towns linked by carriage roads and then railways. And at

A photograph taken by Leopold near Plainfield, Wisconsin, around 1939. Tree stumps remained for years after a settler carved out a farm from the wilderness; the process, repeated by millions of people, transformed the country's landscape.

each step of development, forest products played a role. Timber formed and warmed houses, stores, churches, and courthouses. Shaped into logs and boards, it provided foundations for rail ties and supplied structure for iron and coal mines. Forest trees, forest clearings: from the beginning they played leading roles in America's civilization-building story.

SETTLING IN

Aldo Leopold's first post with the Forest Service was as an assistant forester in a district containing some of the wildest landscapes remaining in the United States. Nothing could have pleased him more. Arriving in Springerville, Arizona, in July 1909, Leopold found grama grass underfoot and an endless sky overhead. Giving character to Forest District 3 were hollows fragrant with junipers and filled with the chatter of piñon jays. To the southwest were the alpine-tipped White Mountains and the Mogollon Rim; to the southeast, the tangled canyons of Blue River, full of wild cattle, wild turkeys, white-tailed deer, and mallards on the river flats. Looming large on the southern horizon was Escudilla, the "far blue mountain," home still to stray grizzlies, wolves, and mountain lions. Spread across it all was the Apache National Forest. Here on the Apache, Forest Assistant Leopold laid aside his Ivy League apparel and outfitted himself with boots, chaps, bandanna, and a tall, very broadbrimmed hat. He took up pipe smoking, found himself a good horse—"Jiminy Hicks"—and was issued his regulation set of pistols. Fitted with a new saddle and given a few roping lessons, Leopold set out, only a month after his arrival, on his first and none too successful assignment. In spite of (or maybe because of) his zeal for his work, Leopold botched the job of leading a reconnaissance crew on a mission to map the unfamiliar landscape of the Blue Range and to inventory its standing trees. Not only did he make serious computational errors; Leopold also mismanaged and offended his men with an overconfident attitude. When he was offered another reconnaissance assignment the next summer, Leopold had a chance to redeem himself. This time—having gained in both humility and experience while losing none of his vibrancy—he successfully led his crew into the White Mountain Plateau, "some of the most breathtaking country on the Apache."[41]

Leopold (second from the right) and his men on their second, and this time successful, reconnaissance assignment to map and inventory the White Mountain Plateau on the Apache National Forest, 1910.

The Apache National Forest was in the drainage basin of the Gila River—the headwaters of which rose from the high forested areas along the western slope of the American Continental Divide. The region had long been occupied by people—tillers of the soil and builders of irrigation works, traces of whose ancient ruins could still be found. Later much of the region became the hunting grounds of the Apache Indians. Then came Jesuit missionaries, as early as 1539. Spanish occupation and development of the area kept pace with the growth of the mission. When the Jesuits were expelled in 1776, a general exodus of Spaniards followed. The Apache Indians would retain their land claim longer, until the Treaty of Guadalupe Hidalgo in 1848. The treaty ended the Mexican War and ceded to the United States the territory north of the Gila River, the region's major watercourse; later the Gadsden Purchase of 1854 would add the territory south of the Gila. Immediately Americans began arriving in the newly acquired lands, but fear of Apache hostilities kept farmers out of the upper reaches of the Gila until the 1870s. From the 1880s on, settlement of the area quickened,[42] particularly in the region's broad and fertile valleys.

Fertile soils, souls in need of converting, and abundant game were not the only treasures that lured settlers to the region. Somewhere nearby lay the fabled Seven Cities, said to overflow with gold, silver, and precious jewels.[43] No gold and silver ever turned up, but copper deposits awaited just beyond the southern border of the Apache Forest, around Clifton, Arizona. Mines required timber, and these would make the first large-scale demand on the nearby forest.[44] Bursting with the entrepreneurial spirit of the times, Leopold, in October 1909, explained in a letter home that he loved his work because "it deals with *big* things. Millions of acres, billions of feet of timber, all vast amounts of capital." "Why it's fun to twiddle them around in your fingers," he admitted. "I want to handle these 15-million [board feet] a year sales when they come. That would *be* something."[45] Leopold's enthusiasm at the time for the Forest Service mission to help keep up America's progress was waxing. Two years later he declared in another letter home that "[t]he Service is more than mere work or a mere livelihood." It was "*[s]ervice* and *glorious* service too."[46]

For Leopold there were additional allures in this new land. High among them was the dark and beautiful Estella Bergere of Santa Fe, whom Leopold first met while on temporary detail in Albuquerque. He described Estella as a wonder on a horse, slender, elegant, with a low voice and an adventuresome spirit. She captured him completely. Around the same time—less than two years after arriving in District 3—Leopold was promoted to deputy supervisor and transferred to the Carson National Forest, seventy miles north of Santa Fe. From his new station in Tres Piedras, New Mexico, he could make occasional visits to the Bergere home, traveling down the Rio Grande on the burro-slow train to Santa Fe. Leopold's letters made more frequent appearances. His skillful pen and lyrical, passionate prose soon won Estella's agreement to his marriage proposal.[47]

A few months before the wedding, Leopold was promoted twice more. In March he was appointed acting supervisor of the Carson, and on August 10, 1912, Leopold became that forest's full-fledged supervisor—the first of his Yale class to receive so high a position.[48] Although still rugged and beautiful, the Carson had been used by people longer and harder than had the more wild and remote Apache National Forest. The upper Rio Grande, in fact, was perhaps the most heavily grazed watershed in the country, mostly by cattle and sheep of large-scale ranchers. Vegetative cover in many parts was sparse and degraded. The forests were depleted and unregenerate, and soil erosion was gullying the range and muddying the waters. The Forest Service staff in the Carson, furthermore, had a history of high turnover and dishonorable practices, and few of its members spoke Spanish. Plenty of challenges awaited the young Leopold.[49]

But first there were family matters to attend to. As Leopold wrote proudly to his fiancée, the Forest Service appropriated "six-hundred-and-fifty large round silver dollars, coin of the realm,"[50] to construct a new supervisor's home at Tres Piedras. Aided by Estella's advice, Leopold drew up blueprints, and construction of the home began in May. Set among piñons and granite boulders—visited by their own wandering mountain lion—the structure was to face east over the thirty-mile-wide Rio Grande Valley to the snow-tipped Sangre de Cristo Mountains. Cozy and simple, the house would have an ample front porch where Aldo and Estella could rest on pleasant, starlit

*Aldo and Estella courting on the railroad tracks near her
family's home, circa 1912.*

evenings. Inside would be a great fireplace for cool days. There
they could sit and read to each other while Leopold puffed on his
pipe.[51]

Aldo and Estella married in Santa Fe on October 9, 1912, and hon-
eymooned in their new little house, which they named Mia Casita.
Soon Estella began tramping with her husband through the woods,
hunting, catching, and skinning rabbits for dinner, much to Leopold's delight. At some point during this time Leopold copied down
lines from a Vachel Lindsay poem that captured his own amorous

feelings: "And I would sing you of her beauty now . . . / And I will kiss her in the waterfalls / And at the rainbow's end, and in the incense / That curls about the feet of sleeping gods."[52] By spring Estella knew she was pregnant with their first child.

"I was made to live on and work on my *own* land," a twenty-two-year-old Leopold wrote to his mother on November 17, 1909, four months after arriving in District 3. "Whether it's a 100-acre farm or a 1,700,000-acre Forest doesn't matter—it's all the same principle, and I don't think I'll ever change my mind about it."[53] Here he was, three years later, already realizing his dream of being a supervisor responsible for a vast forest. In his outdoor freedom he could gaze at the sky and build his life into rugged soil. He possessed all the "necessaries of life": work, love, food, air, sunshine, and adventure.[54] The future was bright indeed. He was a happy man, living on the land and infused with the pioneer spirit.

Leopold's forestry work helped further the nation's ongoing expansion, using scientific principles of management. Yet, even as he vigorously plotted timber cuts in the forests and enjoyed his new home life, Leopold became increasingly aware of the tension between the limits to the land's bounty and the march of civilization. New settlers were rapidly changing the land. He could see it happening all around. Soon after his arrival on the Carson, Leopold was struck by its poor condition in comparison with the Apache. Overgrazing was clearly a grave problem. Cavernous gullies were evident, and game, he began to notice, was scarce. "If ever a country needed radical constructive protection," he declared, "that's it!"[55] After a year on the Carson, Leopold was having disturbing dreams about land problems and his responsibility to do well by both the forest he managed and the people who depended on it. To Estella, a few months before their wedding, he wrote, "I dreamed you and I were listening to [a mockingbird] singing, and that we walked down to where he was and that—when we came to 'The River' somebody said—'please'—and . . . the river was very, very wide, and deep, and . . . dry. It wasn't *my* fault that the river was dry, though—was it?"[56]

What would happen to wild nature and to the land's beauty if human demands continued to expand without limit? And would the land-use practices of the growing population produce settlements that could survive for generations? The United States was a land of great beauty. It was also a land of natural wealth and opportunity. Could Americans come to enjoy wild beauty in harmony with expanding civilization—and if so, for how long? The tension had existed for decades. For Leopold it was becoming a professional challenge.

THE SLEEPING TENSION

For the visitor from the East first viewing the Great Plains and semi-arid grasslands—the visitor, that is, whose sense of beauty was not confined to green mountains and brook-fed forests—the West that Leopold inhabited offered sweeping vistas, stunning and inspiring. Among such receptive travelers to this West, late in his life and after the rail lines were laid down, was Walt Whitman, a uniquely American poet, distiller of the ideals of his age. Whitman wore clothes of bright hope and drank intoxicating draughts of home-brewed liberty. The vigorous American of Whitman's poems was not the isolated loner so much as he was the hearty comrade, the hale fellow who was at once a free individual and a reliable citizen of the communities of men and nature. Whitman's American was attached to all that was around him. He was part of things bigger than himself, and all that he took in he gave out to others freely.

Born in 1819 and raised in the East, Whitman first saw the plains in 1879 while traveling by train to Colorado. He imbibed the colors and winds, observed the flora, fauna, and people, and wrote about what he called "America's characteristic landscape."[57] If forest clearings were the seed plots of American character, as Turner later put it, the prairies and grasslands of the West fed the American spirit. Impressed by the "capacity and sure future destiny of that plain and prairie area (larger than any European kingdom)," Whitman could imagine the entire region transformed by the human touch:

> It is the inexhaustible land of wheat, maize, wool, flax, coal, iron, beef and pork, butter and cheese, apples and grapes—land of ten million virgin farms—to the eye at present wild and unproductive—yet experts say that upon it when irrigated may easily be grown enough wheat to feed the world.[58]

It was not just the productive capacity of the region that impressed Whitman so strongly. There was an aura to it all, an aesthetic presence, an intangible force that seemed to arise from nature itself:

> While I know the standard claim is that Yosemite, Niagara falls, the upper Yellowstone and the like, afford the greatest natural shows, I am not so sure but the Prairies and Plains, while less stunning at first sight, last longer, fill the esthetic sense fuller, precede all the rest, and make North America's characteristic landscape.... I have again been most impress'd, I say, and shall remain for the rest of my life most impress'd, with that feature of the topography of your western central world—that vast Something, stretching out on its own unbounded scale, unconfined, which there is in these prairies, combining the real and ideal, and beautiful as dreams.[59]

Writing in 1879 Whitman failed to see, or at least here did not comment on, the sleeping tension that lay within this land of dreams, so lush with prairie grasses yet so sensitive when humans dug into it— the tension between civilizing the land's humming productivity in order to "feed the world" and respecting its wild beauty. As the century turned—as more train track was laid, as mines were built with new timber, as water was diverted onto new lands, and as Henry Ford emerged in Detroit—America's "characteristic landscape" would show its natural limits. To Whitman and many others the new land still seemed inexhaustible: 10 million farms, wheat for the world, beef and pork, wool and flax, apples and butter, if tamed and irrigated. Yet what would be the future of the land's most impressive feature: its wildness, that "vast Something," unbounded, untamed, both "real and ideal, and beautiful as dreams"? Was it possible to have both—the farms *and* the intangible essences, nature's wild beauty *and* expanding wealth? If the question earlier went unasked within Whitman's musings, Leopold would address it in earnest.

INTERDEPENDENCE

In Whitman's youth another observer of America, the Frenchman Alexis de Tocqueville, crossed the ocean to see what Americans were doing on their continent. Traversing the country in 1831 and again in 1832, Tocqueville saw clearly enough how Americans had altered the country's newly settled regions. A land-wasting civilization had triumphed over natural beauty in many parts of the East, and pioneers were spreading it westward in hillsides stripped of trees and in polluted waterways. "The Americans arrived but yesterday in the land where they live," Tocqueville recorded, "and they have already turned the whole order of nature upside down."[60] Tocqueville's note of caution gained strength over the decades. In 1864 Vermonter George Perkins Marsh, in *Man and Nature; or, Physical Geography as Modified by Human Action*, issued a particularly forceful warning to Americans about the destructive ways in which their actions were transforming the natural world.[61] Not quite twenty years later, explorer John Wesley Powell pointed to the ecological limits of western drylands and urged the nation to revise its land practices to take into account nature's sensitive realities.[62]

"Look at my wealth!" the prototypical pioneer cried proudly in 1800. "Look at this continent of mine, fairest of created worlds, as she lies turning up to the sun's never failing caress of her broad and exuberant breasts, overflowing with milk for her hundred million children." This was pioneer optimism in its purest, strongest form, according to historian Henry Adams, writing near the close of the nineteenth century.[63] And it expressed one of America's most influential myths—inexhaustible resources. Yet it was a fool's optimism, Adams complained. Although the continent might be bountiful, the land's milk did not always flow, not when settlers pressed it too hard or for too long.

Such earlier warnings went largely unheeded until the decade in which Leopold stepped into the Forest Service. The ills of rampant deforestation first registered in national policy during the administration of President Theodore Roosevelt (1901–1909). An avid big game hunter, Roosevelt had served as first president of one of the first national conservation organizations, the Boone and Crockett Club, which included among its members Gifford Pinchot and other prominent political and industrial men. All were dedicated to the preservation of big game and high standards of sportsmanship, both of which were apparently waning. All were committed, too, to conservation of the nation's natural resources, which were linked to one another and critical in making up homes for game species.

The problem that the Roosevelt-Pinchot era could see, ever more unavoidably than the generations of the Lucketts, Tocqueville, Whitman, Marsh, and Adams, was that the cutting of trees came with costs. Beginning in the Northeast, settlers had shown a seemingly insatiable appetite for trees and tree cutting. Entire hillsides and mountains, all but the most rugged elevations, were stripped bare of hardwoods and hemlocks, both for the wood itself—to build mines, railroads, and homes and supply tannins for tanneries—and to clear the land for crops and livestock. In Michigan, Wisconsin, and Minnesota towering white pines clogged rivers as huge log masses were floated downstream to sawmills. Left behind were landscapes denuded of virgin timber and soon scarred by raging fires. Long-term residents claimed that heavy timber cutting even changed local climate in harmful ways. Winters seemed colder and summers hotter and drier. Water for irrigation became more limited.

By the late nineteenth century, the connections between forests and waterways were becoming increasingly clear.[64] Intact forests covered soils, preventing them from eroding into waterways. Living trees helped maintain the clear, flowing rivers that were indispensable for internal navigation. On the other side, timber-cutting and timber-related industries, such as tanneries and pulp-making operations, polluted rivers and disrupted the catches of fishermen. And heavy deforestation allowed large amounts of soil to slide downhill, silting rivers and making navigation difficult.

Recognition of the interdependence of intact woodlands and clear, navigable waterways provided the background for an unprecedented national conservation conference convened by President Roosevelt in 1908, as Leopold was finishing up at Yale. A Governors' Conference it would be termed, though its list of participants was far longer. Roosevelt's call went out to leaders of the states, to organizations grappling with resource problems, to natural-resource experts, to members of Congress and the Supreme Court, and to journalists. The time had come to think about America's resource problems in a coordinated manner, Roosevelt proclaimed. It was time to rethink America's laissez-faire attitude toward land use and to usher in a new management era, more bureaucratic and scientific.

In his opening address Roosevelt gave the conference its focus and set its tone. Two national needs would dominate the agenda, he announced. One was keeping waterways free for commerce. The other was conserving natural resources, "the great fundamental sources of wealth of this Nation."[65] Roosevelt linked these two issues to the story of America's founding:

> It was in Philadelphia that the representatives of all the States met for what was in its original conception merely a waterways conference; but when they had closed their deliberations the outcome was the Constitution which made the States into a nation.... The Constitution of the United States thus grew in large part out of the necessity for united action in the wise use of one of our natural resources. The wise use of all our natural resources, which are our national resources as well, is the great material question of today.[66]

Almost from its inception the Roosevelt administration believed that (in the words of forester R. A. Long) "[t]he forest problem"— linked as it was to soil and waterways resources—was "the most vital internal problem before the American public."[67] The Governors' Conference emphasized what had already become clear to those with eyes to see. The nation needed to manage its forests with more foresight and wisdom, not just so that future Americans would have trees to use but so that the future of the entire nation would remain bright. The nation needed to find ways of inhabiting the land that could endure for generations.

If forests posed the most obvious resource problem, the assembled governors in Washington soon heard about other matters as serious or worse. According to geologist Thomas Chamberlin, soil loss, not timber famine, was the "*key* problem" of the day.[68] If it could be addressed, if soil erosion could be halted, the nation would at the same time solve a "whole complex of problems," including problems with navigation.[69] The nation's soil, Chamberlin reported, was wasting away at an alarming rate. The upper rate of soil formation from rock substrate was around one foot per 10,000 years. Yet foot after foot, a billion or more tons of the "richest soil-matter" were being carried annually down the rivers into the seas.[70] It was a loss not just to the landowners involved but to the nation as a whole.

As for the nation's mineral ores, which also drew the governors' attention, it was difficult to forecast when supplies might come to an end. Americans were consuming basic minerals at astounding rates of increase. Between 1883 and 1907 production rates for gold increased by 63 percent, for lead by 150 percent, and for zinc by 537 percent.[71] In 1856 U.S. coal production was just over 12 million tons; by 1907 it was 429 million tons and rising.[72] Charles Van Hise, president of the University of Wisconsin, warned that "even the most sanguine calculations can not hold out the hope that the available high-grade ores . . . at the present rate of exploitation, will last for many centuries into the future."[73]

Then there was the country's water resource—arguably the "most valuable of all assets."[74] "Water is power. Water is strength. Water is health," former senator Joseph Carey told the conference audience.[75] And of the nation's 2 billion acres, fully one-third were economically unproductive and uninhabited by reason of insufficient rainfall, according to Dr. W. J. McGee, who was in charge of soil erosion investigations for the U.S. Department of Agriculture.[76] Even in the remaining two-thirds, rainfall was often inadequate for crop growing and industrial use. In many regions residents sustained water-use patterns by drawing recklessly on groundwater stores. In at least half a dozen states water tables already had fallen by ten to thirty feet.[77]

Water shortages were most apparent in the West, where it was clear to many that aridity imposed grave limits on growth. The governors were encouraged to think of America's vast western places, not yet occupied, in practical rather than mythical terms. In the Great Plains, devastating droughts in the 1890s had pushed thousands of farmers off the land. The land's milk, indeed, did not always flow reliably. As farmers departed, cattlemen appeared in their wake, until overproduction and overgrazing diminished the industry's profitability. Government-expanded homesteading opportunities and government-endorsed advertisements lured new settlers to the semi-arid and arid regions as the twentieth century dawned. But pioneers and prairie grass had trouble coexisting. The coming of the farms typically brought an end to the soil-protecting grass. Ranchers and plowmen had come west to turn grass into meat and wheat. Too often their gains came at the expense of the soil, turned up by the plow and exposed overgrazing. Indeed, the soil—the foundation of America's prosperity, as Chamberlin phrased it[78]—was rapidly moving downstream, sapping the land's fertility and clogging waterways. To those who paid attention, Leopold among them, the myth of resource inexhaustibility was losing its force.

NATIONAL EXPANSION

In spite of the Governors' Conference and warning figures and forecasts, the expansive spirit retained its hold on the nation, and the dream of having it all—Whitman's "vast Something" plus rising prosperity—remained the stronger cultural vision. Vacant public land, still available for homesteading, beckoned the eager, restless, and unemployed. Railroads drew settlers from the East and from Europe, offering small pieces of their vast government land grants at low prices. Failing ranchers and speculators, some with vast acreages of now overgrazed land, also were prepared to sell cheaply to newcomers. The welcome signs remained out.

Only by claiming territory and mixing labor with it, only by mining its wealth and connecting the country with roads and markets, could the nation become great, many Americans believed. Revised versions of the 1862 Homestead Act in 1909 and 1912 encouraged continuing settlement, particularly in arid lands, by doubling the acreage of allowable homesteads there and reducing the number of years of residency required to gain land titles.[79] Other laws promoted the rapid building of railroads with government loans and land grants. To the Progressive-era mind, strong, scientifically informed conservation efforts could nevertheless overcome the dangers of resource exhaustion that development entailed, allowing the nation's physical expansion to roll on.

Roosevelt himself believed that conservation meant development as much as it did protection.[80] He recognized the right and duty of Americans to use the natural resources of their land. Yet he decried resource wastage, believing that the right to use implied not merely looking out for one's self-interest but also being responsible to neighbors and to future generations:

> We are coming to realize as never before the right of the Nation to guard its own future in the essential matter of natural resources. In the past we have admitted the right of the individual to injure the future of the Republic for his own present profit. In fact there has

been a good deal of demand for unrestricted individualism, for the right of the individual to injure the future of all of us for his own temporary and immediate profit. The time has come for a change. As a people we have the right and duty . . . of requiring and doing justice, to protect ourselves and our children against the wasteful development of our natural resources, whether the waste is caused by the actual destruction of such resources or by making them impossible of development hereafter.[81]

SEEKING EQUILIBRIUM

The Forest Service's work was part of a larger national undertaking, and Teddy Roosevelt's "New Nationalism" provided the backdrop for Leopold's early career. New Nationalism embodied the Progressive-era conflict between expansion and conservation. It brought together and sought to contain a combination of strong cultural and biological forces—democracy, capitalism, immigration, reproductive increase, and the unforeseen but increasingly recognizable limits of nature. Individual opportunity remained a strong element of it, but it was an individualism linked to civic engagement, the common welfare, and good citizenship.[82] One part of this vital mix, according to Roosevelt, was the American democratic ideal—the Jeffersonian dream that every family might live and work independently on its own land. There was also the American promise, the vision of self-advancement and a perpetually better future, typically defined by greater income and wealth.[83] And there was the American nation as the mighty "Mother of Exiles," beckoning the "huddled masses" and their many children to the "gold door."[84] These three elements largely coexisted peacefully as long as the frontier remained open. But how could the nation ensure its founding ideals of landownership, independence, and prosperity to a rising population when its territory became full? To historian Turner, the nation's predicament was plain: the time finally had come for restless Americans to learn to live where they were, to find ways of living in peaceful equilibrium with one another and with the land. A new season of national life seemed to be turning, from pioneering to the establishment of a permanent civilization:

This, then, is the real situation: a people composed of heterogeneous materials, with diverse and conflicting ideals and social interests, having passed from the task of filling up the vacant spaces of the continent, is now thrown back upon itself, and is seeking an equilibrium. The diverse elements are being fused into national unity.[85]

But how could this fusing be done? Was it possible to hold on to the democratic ideal of landowner independence and the American promise of economic opportunity while dealing with human population growth and down-to-earth nature-imposed limits? One idea was for the nation to buy more land, keeping the frontier open. Jefferson had taken this tack a century earlier, with his Louisiana Purchase. The land-buying idea, though, had run its course on the continent. No good land was left to take. A second idea was to look inward, adding new farms by irrigating more drylands. This was the job assigned to the federal Reclamation Service, established in 1902 under the U.S. Geological Survey and five years later made an independent bureau within the Department of Interior. On the surface it appeared to hold more promise.

The May 1909 volume of *National Geographic* included an extraordinary article that illustrated and promoted this second strand of nationalistic sentiment. Prepared on behalf of the new Reclamation Service, it appeared with full-page photographs that portrayed visions of the new, irrigated prosperity of the West. There were pictures of grapes heavy on vines, reminding readers of Caleb's Old Testament reconnaissance report on the milk-and-honey land of Canaan. There were beehives, apple groves, and cows knee-high in alfalfa with proud farmers standing nearby. There were melon fields, orange groves, and contentedly grazing sheep. Pumpkins, peaches, pears, plums, cherries, apples: all spilled out of a cornucopia of drylands watered by human ingenuity. And there were the expected new schools, churches, homes, flower gardens, pastures, and roads—whole communities, it seemed, springing up overnight. All of this was made possible by towering concrete dams and irrigation systems, a source of immense engineering pride for the American government. Conservation and the American dream walked hand in hand.

C. J. Blanchard, statistician and spokesman for the Reclamation Service, wrote the article accompanying these photographs, titled "The Call of the West."[86] "The Great Plains invite the scientific farmer," Blanchard wrote, "to overcome the lack of rain by intelligent methods of cultivation and wisdom in seed-production."[87] Even farther West, in the region too arid for dryland cultivation, there was the "desert—mysterious, silent, expectant, quivering under cloudless skies."[88] It, too, held a promise of freedom and independence, Blanchard attested, for the careworn and the discouraged.

> Untouched by plow, unleached by rain, the desert holds fast the accumulated fertility of ages. It awaits the quickening kiss of canal-borne water to yield abundant harvests and to provide homes for millions of our people. No national work is of more importance today than that of reclaiming for home-builders an empire which in its present state is uninhabited and worthless.[89]

The third idea for addressing the expansion-conservation tension was to apply scientific methods to enhance the productivity of renewable resources—such as forests, ranges, and fisheries—and to minimize resource waste. Scientific management could extend, perhaps indefinitely, the time that future generations could live on their own lands. It was chiefly to implement this third option—conservation of natural resources—that the Forest Service was founded. Leopold's employer thus was charged with more than growing trees and keeping waterways clear. It was entrusted with perpetuating American dreams and ideals through science and wise management. This vision provided the starting point for Leopold's lifetime of conservation work, for his quest to find some way to harmonize nature and a demanding American culture.

The Common Wealth

Conservation, in Roosevelt's mind, loomed as "a great moral issue" involving "the patriotic duty of insuring the safety and continuance of the nation."[90] The obvious aims of conservation were to stop wasteful resource use and to plan for a prosperous future. Conservation was also, in the eyes of national Progressives, about driving out special interests from politics and fairly distributing wealth.[91] As the final bells tolled on the Gilded Age, resource monopolization carried a particular worry. It was critical to American democracy, Chief Forester Pinchot cautioned, to keep control of vital resources in public hands.[92] Natural resources should profit the entire country in ways that met needs and spread wealth fairly. One way both to limit waste and to prevent monopoly, Pinchot thought, was to foster multiple uses of a single resource. A stream, for example, was valuable not only for navigation and irrigation but also for water power. Forests not only supplied timber but also helped utilize rainfall, protected stream banks and water flows, were home to game and other wildlife, and offered opportunities for recreation. Multiple uses provided a system of checks and balances on excessive pressure on any particular use. Developing all uses together could maximize resources' benefits and diminish waste while guarding the commonweal from takeover by overweening private interests. In short, multiple use—considering "not one resource, but all resources together"[93]—could hopefully help achieve the conservation ideal of promoting the maximum good for the maximum number of people over the long term.

For the nation to challenge the cupidity and special interests of Pinchot's day it had to recognize forests, waters, minerals, and soils as distinct, exhaustible resources. These resources needed identifying and naming, Pinchot urged, before they could be regulated and managed scientifically by government. Yet to sever the resources from their connections to one another, considering them only discretely, paradoxically was itself wasteful and inefficient. Forests helped keep rainfall in the soil, soil on the land, and waters flowing in their channels. Uses of particular resources, in short, were interconnected with uses of other resources. To think seriously about the multiple-use ideal one had to understand how the use of one resource affected the uses of other resources.

The trouble was, even conservationists tended to view the nation's land-use challenges merely in terms of separate resources. W. J. McGee, in charge of soil erosion investigations, opined, "without disparaging the other resources, that water ranks first as the prime requisite of life."[94] Geologist Thomas Chamberlin countered that "[t]he solution of the soil problem . . . may thus prove to be the *Key* problem."[95] And forester R. A. Long, though recognizing soil as a fundamental resource, nonetheless regarded the forest as most nearly "supplying the every want of man."[96] Still the idea of multiple and coordinated resource uses itself remained strong. Even Congress had caught a glimpse of it when it set the purposes of the national forests. The national forests, Congress announced, would have three interrelated aims: to improve and protect the forests, to secure favorable conditions for water flows, and to furnish a continuous supply of timber.[97]

The Effect on the Forest

As Aldo Leopold traipsed the forest, contemplating its management, he was swept along by these powerful cultural currents. Like his fellow rangers, and now as forest supervisor, Leopold thrived on panting up canyons to count and qualify trees, standing on ridges in cold wind to survey stretches of wildland, and suffering locust thorns and deerfly bites to bag wild turkeys. Like other conservation workers he believed that America would be strong if—guided by a rational conservation policy that limited waste, resisted money power, and guarded the nation's future welfare[98]—it built the new railroads, mined the ores, and diverted its rivers onto drylands to grow the meat and wheat needed for an expanding population. Leopold thrived on knowing that he was contributing to it all.

Less than a year after he and Estella moved into Mia Casita, however, Leopold's forest outran him. Even though he had felt sick a couple of days earlier, on April 7, 1913, Leopold began a trip to the Jicarilla district, home to some of the worst overgrazing in District 3. He hoped to iron out conflicts between the Forest Service and local sheepmen. While camping out he was caught in a rainstorm. Then, already wet through, he endured a hailstorm that lasted two days. On the way home he got lost taking a shortcut, failing to reach camp until April 23, amazingly upbeat but with body and knees so swollen that he had to cut open his riding boots to get them off. He was severely ill. The doctor in Santa Fe diagnosed nephritis, a life-threatening kidney condition, and prescribed bed rest. After a few weeks Leopold still had not regained his strength. The doctor ordered him back to Iowa, where the lower altitude might aid his health. Estella and Leopold boarded the train for Burlington on June 6.[99]

Leopold had spent many months roaming the Southwest's rocky ravines and flowing rivers, filled with a sense of mission. At day's end he would then return to his warm hearth and his view of the sunrise over the Sangre de Cristo Mountains. But as an invalid in Iowa he now faced long, sedentary days in his parents' home. It was a hard pill to swallow, even as he enjoyed familiar surroundings and family members. Restless but obedient to doctors' orders — and with Estella and the little one on the way to give him hope — Leopold began a slow recovery. He took advantage of the enforced rest and fresh environment to gain perspective on his Forest Service efforts. From his resting chair on the east-side porch and with pipe in mouth, he reviewed back issues of *Atlantic Monthly* and *National Geographic.* He plowed through important books, including works by Henry David Thoreau, Theodore Roosevelt, William Temple Hornaday, and Stewart Edward White, as well as a new volume by Will Barnes on western grazing and forests.[100] From the family porch perched high above the Mississippi River, Leopold's eyes took in the Flint Hills and the city of Burlington below. Yet his mind remained in the Southwest, back in the Carson, and with his coworkers on the land.

Aldo's childhood home in Burlington, Iowa, to which he returned from the Southwest in 1913 and 1914 to recuperate from his illness.

On July 15, 1913, Leopold penned a lengthy letter to his fellow forest officers of the Carson, a letter that soon appeared in an issue of "The Carson Pine Cone," a monthly circular that Leopold had started after his arrival at the forest. In his letter Leopold's thoughts ranged as expansively as his physical activity was narrow, and evident now was a fresh emphasis on land itself as the measure of Forest Service progress. Taking an overall view of the Service's work, he contemplated foresters' standards of success. The objective of his contemplations, he admitted, was "arriving at, and pinning down, what seems to me a final, specific truth."[101] "We ride," Leopold asked of the Carson's officers, "but are we getting anywhere?"[102] To leave this question hanging, as busy Service officers were apt to do, was to expose the Service to debilitating confusion over means and ends, Leopold believed.

Operational efficiency was a popular concept in the day of Frederick Winslow Taylor's *Principles of Scientific Management* and the assembly-line innovations of "Henry Fordism." Efficiency was a principle that the Service actively promoted, and Leopold generally agreed about its importance. But "in actual practice," he wrote,

> we are confronted, surrounded, and perhaps sometimes swamped, with problems, policies, ideas, decisions, precedents, and details. We ride in a thicket. We grapple with difficulties; we are in a maze of routine. Letters, circulars, reports, and special cases beset our path as the logs, gullies, rocks, and bog-holes and mosquitoes beset us in the hills.[103]

The sole *task* of the Service, Leopold clarified, was to increase the efficiency of forest operations. But a policy of operational efficiency was not the *object* of the Service, Leopold argued. Long-run administrative efficiency might be the Service's task, but it should not be confused with its principled conservation aim.

The aim of the Forest Service was to concretely apply "the well known principles of conservation, to the resources within the National Forests." The Service was "entrusted with the protection and development, through wise use and constructive study of the Timber, water, forage, farm, recreative, game, fish, and esthetic resources of the areas under our jurisdiction," Leopold explained; "I will call these resources for short, 'The Forest.'"[104] And, he continued, "the sole measure of our success is the *effect* . . . on *the Forest.*" "My measure," he repeated, this time in capital letters, "is THE EFFECT ON THE FOREST. . . . Effects are good and doubtful, the 'doubtful' ones being cases where we can not easily tell that the *net* result is beneficial."[105] For foresters to do their jobs well, they needed to keep their eyes on this overall land-use aim, considering each action in terms of the forest itself. It was mostly to convey this "final specific truth," as Leopold termed it, that he had dispatched his letter.

This 1913 letter contained many seeds that would grow and flower in Leopold's developing thoughts and ultimately spread far beyond the forest. Leopold's chief point was that land managers needed some way to determine whether the effects of their separate daily actions were "good or doubtful," on the forests as a whole, and to make improvements as necessary. To answer the question of whether foresters were "getting anywhere" they needed to experiment with how to apply broader conservation principles to actual forests. They needed to think independently about their work in unique locales in relation to more general, overarching conservation aims. Leopold urged his fellow foresters to think out loud and critically about means and ends in their conservation work.

→- -←

As Leopold talked about the forest at the time, he did so still in terms of resources. His 1913 letter in that regard would be for him only a half step. Yet in the years ahead, even as he focused in on aesthetics and became increasingly ecological in his thought, he remained attentive to visions of enduring, flourishing human settlements. Landscapes should provide not merely raw materials to harvest but also places for families to live, thrive, work, and play.

Yet what did it take for a landscape to provide a good home for generations? If conservation was judged by its effect on the land itself, as Leopold said, how did one evaluate those effects? Leopold would return to these questions repeatedly, slowly constructing answers and gaining confidence in them. How did the land's many resources all fit together, and how did beauty come in? How could people use land to meet their needs and keep that "vast Something," too?

Even as Leopold's thoughts churned, his body rested and his health slowly returned. In February 1914, his doctor in Iowa agreed that Leopold could return to the Southwest, but he was not yet well enough to work. Aldo, Estella, and their four-month-old son, Starker, traveled back to the Bergere home in Santa Fe, where Leopold continued his recuperation. He still harbored hopes that he would soon be restored as Carson's supervisor. In June, however, a relapse of illness sent him back to Burlington for several months. Finally, on September 14, 1914, after sixteen and a half months on medical leave, Leopold was back in the Southwest, reinstated by the Forest Service, and given a desk job in the Office of Grazing in Albuquerque. Leopold packed up Mia Casita in Tres Piedras and got ready to move his family to their new town the next month. Although still not reconciled with his inability to return to the forest, he was glad to be back at work. "It will be a great relief," wrote Leopold to his father that October, "to have a roof of our own, and makes me feel pretty near like a U.S. citizen again."[106]

Chapter 2

Written on the Hills

*Air, water, fire, soil, give us our strength and our growth; they
also destroy us if we fail to keep right relations with them.*

John Burroughs, "The Good Devils"

*In the presence of these characteristic catastrophes which dev-
astate civilization, one hesitates to judge their details. To
blame or praise men on account of the result is almost like
praising or blaming ciphers on account of the total.*

Victor Hugo, *Ninety-Three*

Leopold returned to the Forest Service in September 1914 after his
recuperative leave of absence, which had stretched well over a year.
Still weak from his illness, he was assigned to paperwork in the Albuquerque Office of Grazing, where he served as assistant to the district
supervisor. The administrative position gave him technical knowledge of range management matters and brought to his focused attention the question of how to determine a range's "carrying capacity"
— the number of livestock a given grazing area could support without that degrading.[1] This question would set in motion in Leopold's
mind a cascade of other questions about interconnections between
soils and waters, as well as plants and animals, which he would pursue back out in the field and, with remarkable results, over the course
of his career.

Nine months after Leopold's reinstatement, with his vigor

returning and his frustration with being confined to an office mounting, the region's head forester put Leopold in charge of District 3's new recreational policy. He would also oversee publicity work and coordinate a new fish and game program.[2] Leopold's new assignment took him on investigative and speaking tours across the region to drum up support for game conservation. At the same time his travels enabled him to observe how new settlers were changing the landscape —its rangelands and its forests—and the problems that often resulted.

As Leopold's health returned and he began this new phase of his work, Europe was sinking into war. "Life is a chaplet of little miseries which the philosopher unstrings with a smile,"[3] Leopold copied into his personal journal. As turbulence was rising across the ocean, President Woodrow Wilson urged an attitude of neutrality toward the European belligerents. The United States, he proclaimed, would be the "one great nation at peace,"[4] available when needed to play the part of impartial mediator and international peacemaker. Like most Americans, though, Leopold was worried. And as much as may have been hoped otherwise, America hardly could remain unaffected, connected as it was to Europe economically, historically, and sentimentally.

In fact, in December 1914, only four months after the war began, Wilson urged legislators in Congress to consider America's "common duty" in this crisis as a great people of influence and power.[5] Part of this duty, Wilson believed, was to share the country's plentiful natural resources with other nations. For that to happen Congress would need to promote transatlantic trade and increase shipbuilding. Although officially the United States was economically neutral, between 1914 and 1916 commerce with Germany and Austria fell from $169 million to $1 million and trade with the Allies jumped from $825 million to more than $3 billion, intertwining the success of the Allied cause and American economic prosperity.[6]

Importantly for conservation, Wilson asked Congress to "unlock" the vast natural resources of the public domain. "We have," argued Wilson,

> year after year debated . . . the best policy to pursue with regard to the use of the ores and forests and water powers of our national domain in the rich States of the West. . . . The key is still turned upon them, the door shut fast at which thousands of vigorous men, full of

initiative, knock clamorously for admittance. The water power of our navigable streams outside the national domain also . . . is still not used as it might be . . . because the laws we have made do not intelligently balance encouragement against restraint.[7]

To achieve such a balance was the hope of the national conservation movement. Now, however, new international pressures taunted prudence and added weight to the "use" side of the scales. What degree of economic resource development was appropriate, given war needs? In his first inaugural address, Wilson critiqued the nation for its "inexcusable waste" of resources. The nation had "not stopped to conserve the exceeding bounty of nature" and had failed to count the cost of industrial achievements.[8] But now war was casting its shadow, and as 1914 ended sixteen European countries were engaged in it. To many, war made conservation seem less important than extracting resources to help supply potential allies.

Leopold himself was disturbed by the confusion the war was bringing on. Eleven days after Wilson's December speech, Leopold wrote home, "I am still amazed at the astounding unintelligence of the American comment on the war. I am not referring to its trend of sympathy, but [to] the general lack of understanding."[9] Contemporary philosophers—German ones included, he felt sorry to write to his German-descended parents—all were making fools of themselves. "The most sensible comment I have read," Leopold confessed, "is Bernard Shaw's."

The war commentary that Leopold endorsed appeared, in the closing weeks of November 1914, in both the *New York Times* and London's *New Statesman*. "Common Sense about the War," a three-part article by British playwright and essayist George Bernard Shaw, posed a hard-hitting critique that blamed the war on competing groups of self-interested plutocrats. In Shaw's view the pursuit of individualistic wealth for its own sake and the building of a just civilization ran toward opposite poles. Shaw hoped that the citizens of the countries involved would come to their democratic senses and move in a different direction.

Considering the effects the pursuit of wealth had on United States landscapes, Leopold apparently agreed. The passion for "Money, and money quick!" was an underlying cause of careless and unnecessary resource destruction, Leopold had concluded early on.[10]

Civilized progress required the incorporation of many noneconomic values, including implied obligations to perpetuate forests and wildlife.[11] An enduring civilization did not rush to "unlock" all of nature and convert it to economic use; rather, it took time to consider what the long-term effects of such use might be and acted wisely.

The Forest Service existed to protect resources from abuse by wealth-hungry speculators and monopolizing industries so that plain American citizens could benefit from them. The intent was to keep forest resources available for domestic and commercial use far into the future.[12] Wilson's plea to Congress pushed against this restraint and temporarily shifted Forest Service priorities. Timber demands increased and cattle were added to already degraded ranges to meet wartime demands. While the United States was still on the sidelines the Forest Service was directed to produce walnut timber for 3 million rifle stocks.[13] In the Pacific Northwest the call went out for light, resilient Sitka spruce to build fleets of airplanes. Across the country, as the United States entered the war, the private lumber industry was prodded to cut "Uncle Sam's lumber" ahead of more lucrative civilian orders.[14] By the war's end, the forests of America had contributed to the effort as much as a full year of peacetime timber consumption, with more to come in the postwar building boom.[15] Meanwhile, the stocking of cattle on national forest grasslands more than doubled, from 1,627,321 head in 1915 to 2,137,854 in 1918.[16]

While his Forest Service colleagues labored to meet these demands, Leopold worked relentlessly at his new game conservation duties, traveling across the southwestern region to encourage sportsmen to organize new local and state game protective associations (GPAs), the aim of which was to "promote the protection and enjoyment of wild things."[17] He was busy, too, surveying newly approved recreational lots in the district for anticipated postwar use by returning soldiers.[18] In June 1915 Leopold made the first of several visits to the Grand Canyon to report on conditions.[19] In 1916 his surveys took him to Flagstaff and the Coconino National Forest, to Silver City and the wild Gila River, and to the Apache and Sitgreaves national forests. That September Leopold set up new GPAs in Tucson and Payson and surveyed grazing lands leased to private stockmen in the

Crook and Tonto national forests.[20] A minor recurrence of nephritis that fall, however, forced him to ease up on his arduous schedule and return to work in the Albuquerque office for several weeks.[21]

When the United States formally entered the war in the spring of 1917, Congress adopted the Selective Draft Act. Because of his age, ill health, and work and family situation, Leopold was exempt.[22] Instead he worked with Albuquerque civic groups on war-related activities, particularly the Albuquerque Chamber of Commerce.[23] The chamber was struck by his clear-sightedness and his skills in organizing and communicating and offered him the paid position of secretary. Although he had little interest in promoting commerce and was no fan of "society" and "all the forty 'leven kinds of tommyrot that includes,"[24] he took the job, beginning early in 1918. Forest Service salaries were low, and the chamber job came with a raise. His growing family could use it: in August 1917 Aldo and Estella's third child, Adelina, was born. In addition, Leopold hoped that in the chamber job he could continue his game protection work without being diverted to work on the Service's wartime priorities of lumbering and raising livestock.

Leopold viewed his new responsibilities broadly. He promptly pushed the chamber to go beyond promoting local business interests and become the "common center—the clearing house . . . of all public spirited effort in Albuquerque."[25] The chamber of commerce should work to unify fragmented sections of society, he proposed, while highlighting the distinctive history and culture of Albuquerque. Leopold urged builders to feature indigenous Spanish architecture in new projects and asked the city to employ a professional planner. He invited labor groups to get involved in chamber activities. And he voiced support for draining the Rio Grande Valley to aid agriculture in the area—another means, he hoped, to promote the common good.[26]

One civic project that united Leopold's many aims was a city tree-planting campaign. The campaign, Leopold hoped, would both add greenery to the city and get private landowners and businesses working together. Leopold threw himself into it. He identified people who knew something about trees and brought them together to set specifications for appropriate tree species and the timing and care of

Estella with the first three of their five children—Luna, Starker, and Nina (left to right)—in Albuquerque, 1919.

local plantings. The specifications were published in the newspaper, and private bids were invited. Reasonable bidders that passed committee review (agreeing to subject future work to inspection by a trained forester) then solicited interest from property owners in the city, aided by a citywide chamber advertising campaign. To Leopold's delight, the response was exceptional. More than 1,000 trees were planted in a single year, and 95 percent of them thrived. The public and the contractors were pleased, the city looked better, and civic spirit increased.[27]

While acting as chamber of commerce secretary, Leopold never left off studying the natural world around him. He submitted several pieces for publication in the well-respected ornithological journal *The Condor*. Some of these came from his detailed hunting journal: on the relative abundance of ducks in the Rio Grande Valley, the weights and plumages of ducks in New Mexico, and the behavior of pintail ducks in a hailstorm.[28] Other pieces were on nongame species, particularly the red-headed woodpecker. In a February 1918 note Leopold reported that the woodpeckers moved across the treeless plains following railway lines and telegraph poles, apparently using them in lieu of trees.[29] The following spring Leopold reported that he and two friends had been first witnesses of the birds' breeding in New Mexico.[30]

Leopold also continued writing on national forest issues[31] and grabbed what time he could to promote game protective associations and to draft ideas for a system of game protection,* parallel to scientific forestry. Overall, though, he was able to fit in less wildlife work than he had hoped, and he was disappointed also in the level of support for his more idealistic civic experiments. Some movement toward conservation was taking place, but it was proving difficult to muster among the citizens of Albuquerque a broader than economic attitude.[32]

By early 1919 the Great War was winding down. Teddy Roosevelt died suddenly in his sleep, ending another era. From Washington, word came that the Service was returning to peacetime plans. As the year progressed Leopold was offered and accepted the position of assistant district forester in charge of operations, the second highest position in a district that spanned 20 million acres in central and southern Arizona and New Mexico.[33] His responsibilities would be many—including everything from handling personnel issues to forging good relationships between the Forest Service and private landowners to carrying out law enforcement and education work, in addition to evaluating the ways conservation was being carried out on the district's lands. To fulfill these duties he needed to make

---

*Leopold generally used the term "game" when talking about animals hunted for sport or as a natural resource, a subset of the broader category "wild life," which also included nongame species. Sometime in the mid-1930s, at least by 1936, "wild life" became "wildlife" for Leopold and others. In the 1930s, too, a shift occurred within the conservation movement from usage of "game" in organizational names to the more inclusive term "wildlife," tracking with the broadening concerns of the times. When discussing matters relevant to sport species, I use the term "game," and when referring to the more inclusive category, I use the one-word term in current usage, "wildlife."

regular inspection tours of the district's forests, reporting on his observations and recommending improvements.

Forest inspections covered all of the forest resource uses—particularly timber, watersheds, grazing, and recreation—as well as the physical conditions of the forests themselves. They also addressed mundane aspects of forest management, from the treatment and feeding of work stock to the accuracy of office records. Leopold attended to these details with increasing rigor, eventually initiating a new districtwide system of report making.[34] If foresters could become more efficient in keeping records, he hoped, they could attend more to the substance of their tasks.

What drew Leopold's particular attention, though, were the larger issues of land-use patterns and their consequences. To evaluate them successfully he had to gain a better understanding of forests themselves and had to learn to identify the ripple effects of various land-use practices—as he put it, "namely *Diagnosis* of evidence supplied by nature."[35] If a few years earlier Leopold had challenged his fellow officers always to evaluate their work in terms of its "effect on the Forest,"[36] now he was having to flesh out what that meant. What was the best way to judge the effects of human actions on the forest? When was a forest overall in good condition? The questions were not easy.

Leopold visited and revisited forests throughout his district in 1919 and 1920, taking particular note in the Prescott National Forest of the severe soil erosion there.[37] In the spring of 1921 he inspected the Sitgreaves and Lincoln national forests as well as the Apache, which included the Blue Range. There, where he had begun his Forest Service career more than a decade earlier, Leopold saw how people in the intervening years had damaged the forest watershed—eroding soils, silting streams, and spreading weeds—in the years he had been absent. Evidence of degradation was stark, and it stuck with him.[38]

No job could have better positioned Assistant District Forester Leopold to think seriously about human-used landscapes in their entirety. As he traversed the Southwest, setting up GPAs and surveying and later inspecting forests, Leopold had ample opportunity to witness the condition of new human settlements and ranches scattered within and around the region's public forests. The picture was

This spreading, water-carved gully, one of many extensive ones in the region, drained and destroyed a grassland in Arizona—a result of land misuse.

often discouraging. Through the war years and beyond, into the 1920s, Leopold was developing a deeper concern. The federal government, through an array of acts and incentives, continued to respond supportively to the relentless national desire for private landownership. Thousands of Wilson's vigorous men—full of initiative and clamoring for admittance—were arriving on the scene and gaining access to the "unlocked" resources. Who could predict the full effects as these hope-filled, industrious citizens claimed their individual lands; built their mines, railroads, churches, schools, storefronts, and homes; plowed and irrigated drylands for crops; and unleashed their livestock to graze on the open ranges? Would room be left for wild plants and animals, and what about the soils and waterways?

As Leopold undertook to unravel the causes and effects of recent land-settlement failures, he soon realized the magnitude of the task. To find the underlying causes he first needed to understand better the ecology of the region.[39] To go further and prescribe enduring remedies, deep understanding was needed. And conservation required coordination among public and private land users in pursuit of a common land-use goal. This meant coming up with one and then finding the most appropriate means to reach it consistent with America's democratic ideals.

Forests in the post–World War I years were threatened by a surge of building demands. The greater than ever pressure on the nation's forest resources revived fears of timber shortage, and the pressure was not only on public forests. Attention also was turned on the 75 percent of America's forests in private ownership.[40] What, though, would encourage private forest owners to operate in a way that would preserve the nation's forests for the future? Former chief Gifford Pinchot, leading one faction, called for direct federal regulation of private timber harvesting. The American Forestry Association and other conservationists urged instead that the federal government promote education and use incentives to stimulate voluntary compliance with minimal forestry requirements. Both views appeared in competing bills introduced in Congress. How to promote conservation on private as well as public lands was a matter that hardly could be avoided, Leopold could see.

The national forests had been established in the first place to protect the public interest in land from abuse by enterprising private citizens and commercial interests. Yet many public forests were interspersed with private landholdings, and forests often suffered degradation because of what private owners were doing. Ownership boundaries or not, real lands were interconnected and a land use in one place often affected lands downstream, with no regard for political or ownership boundaries. It was an awkward situation, raising questions about the obligations of private land users to protect the public interest in multiple land values. In various reports and articles Leopold called upon the officers of the Forest Service, even though it was not technically their responsibility, to exercise leadership in encouraging private owners to use their lands more responsibly.[41]

Leopold's travels throughout District 3 gave him abundant opportunities to observe and contemplate the complex tangles of causes and effects of land-settlement failures within a landscape matrix that included publicly and privately owned and managed forestlands and rangelands. And his firsthand experiences motivated him to find solutions that worked—ecologically and democratically. Leopold was particularly disturbed by the failings of small agricultural settlements in the Southwest. Why had they failed? One representative degraded community particularly drew his attention—involving the lands along the Blue River in Arizona's Blue Range. If he could figure out what had gone wrong there, perhaps he could identify a solution.

THE BLUE RIVER COMMUNITY

American settlements in the Southwest were relatively new when World War I ended, yet their defects already were becoming apparent. As new homes, farms, and villages were built in one place, recently established ones elsewhere were deteriorating. Entire communities—private homes and barns, gardens, orchards, and crop fields, some hardly a decade old—were literally crumbling away. Soils were eroding under the feet of farmers and ranchers in the mountain-creek areas of the Southwest—the cream of agricultural lands in the region—carrying off with them the livelihoods of the people. Creek bottoms—relatively level sites with deep, productive soils—were among the few places where agriculture was possible. Only here—where water was easily had simply by diverting it—could families raise hay for milk cows and plant orchards and gardens. These areas also were natural sites for ranch headquarters and the only feasible sites for building roads. "[T]hese creek bottoms, by and large, are the key not only to the prosperity of Forest industries, but to decent social conditions and the building up of Forest homes," Leopold commented in the early 1920s.[42] Only by taking care of these could humans inhabit and prosper in this rugged, dry landscape.

In May and June 1921 Leopold inspected the Blue Range and along the wild Blue River, running through the Apache National Forest. This had been the area covered by his first reconnaissance trip as a green forest ranger twelve years earlier, and he remembered enough from his earlier work there to identify the disturbing changes that had occurred.[43]

By the mid-1880s the Blue River valley, a reliably watered and relatively broad land, had been well settled by American pioneers. The Blue River—its headwaters rising in the high forests of the White Mountains and Blue Range—flowed into the San Francisco River, which was in turn the largest tributary of the Gila River watershed. Nearly four thousand acres along the Blue River's course were under cultivation, mostly as hay meadows, pastures, alfalfa fields, peach orchards, and flower and vegetable gardens. In 1900 the land had supported some three hundred people on forty-five family ranches. The bottomlands, averaging 700 feet wide, were lined with tall pines and cottonwoods, while willows hung over the banks. Across the open country cattle feasted on white grama grass, which grew luxuriantly to a height of thirty inches.

With its clear water and abundant trout tumbling over red and white cobblestones, the Blue River was generally a peacefully flowing watercourse, though it was known to display changeable widths and intermittent flooding. Floods typically were caused by rains of unusually long duration, resulting in the river spreading out over wide areas. Pima Indians had recorded floods of this sort in 1833, 1869, and 1884.[44] Yet the landscape showed no apparent signs that those earlier floods had caused heavy erosion, either on the lower river or in the mountains.

By the first decade of the twentieth century, however, barely a generation after initial European settlement, flash flooding and widespread erosion were taking place. The new arrivals had cut down trees, grazed their livestock, and plowed and planted crops. They had also diverted water flows for irrigation, taking the water from Pima Indians, who had successfully inhabited the area for centuries. In combination these activities, grazing in particular, it seemed, quickly brought disastrous effects.[45] Between 1909 and 1919 the entire agricultural area of the upper San Francisco River, including the land along the Blue River, was swept away by flash flooding of a kind not known in the region's history.[46] A storm in October 1916 created an unprecedented deluge, degrading river bottoms already torn up by the earlier intense floods. By 1917 the area was a wide wash.[47] Soils and entire livelihoods disappeared under roaring torrents. Forty years earlier the bottomland had been well sodded and grassy, the river lined with cottonwoods and tall pines. In 1921, Leopold recorded soberly, the same place was "mostly boulders, with a few shelves of original bottom land left high and dry between rocky points"; less than 8 percent of its arable area remained.[48]

By the time he made this description Leopold had already begun refining his thinking about the dry southwestern land and the effects that particular human uses were having upon it. He had made the fruits of this thought public the previous winter, in an address delivered at the University of Arizona's Farmers' Week. In the talk he emphasized the fundamental importance of soil to the land's productivity and the work of conservation.[49] The Southwest's conservation problem had to do with the greater landscape, Leopold realized; it was not just about trees. And at the base of that landscape the fount of terrestrial life was the soil. "All civilization," Leopold proclaimed to his Arizona audience,

> is basically dependant upon natural resources. All natural resources, except only subterranean minerals, are soil or derivatives of soil. Farms, ranges, crops, and livestock, forests, irrigation water, and even water power resolve themselves into questions of soil. Soil is therefore the basic natural resource.

This was a new emphasis for Leopold, and he pushed it hard, connecting its importance to other natural resources:

> It follows that the destruction of soil is the most fundamental kind of economic loss which the human race can suffer. With enough time and money, a neglected farm can be put back on its feet—if the soil is still there. With enough patience and scientific knowledge, an overgrazed range can be restored—if the soil is still there. By expensive replanting and with a generation or two of waiting, a ruined forest can again be made productive—if the soil is still there. With infinitely expensive works, a ruined watershed may again fill our ditches or turn our mills—if the soil is still there. But if the soil is gone, the loss is absolute and irrevocable.[50]

The case of the Blue River area vividly illustrated Leopold's point. In 1900, according to Leopold's figures, the valley had boasted 4,000 acres of tillable land and 300 people on forty-five ranches. By the early 1920s, 3,600 acres had been lost through erosion, leaving only 400 acres and a mere 90 people on twenty-one ranches. "Not only were 34 established homes destroyed," summarized Leopold, "but the land carried away was a 'key' resource, necessary for the proper utilization of the range, timber, and recreational values on half a million acres of adjacent mountains. There is no other land in the region suitable for homes, stock-ranches, mills, roads, and schools."[51] Regardless of the profit of the agricultural and rangeland businesses, as things stood these were unsocial institutions,[52] wasting away entire communities.

The sad truth was that insensitive land use also had largely destroyed the profit of the area's ranching business, along with the homes of families and the stability of communities. Without bottomlands for crops, hayfields, and pastures, food both for livestock and for people had to be packed in from the nearest railroad, sixty miles away. In one studied case, the loss of sixty acres of farmland to erosion increased the stockman's production costs by $6.50 a head for 850 cattle and reduced his gross income by 24 percent. Building a new road through this country—over rocks and hills rather than level bottomland—was costing half a million dollars and because of erosion would not even be connectable with the remains of the Blue River community. The estimated value of the land lost to erosion along the Blue River was $324,400, enough, noted Leopold, to have paid for a small reclamation project.[53]

Leopold was stuck by the incongruity and waste of it all. It was absurd, he complained, for the nation to "bring new land under irrigation by the construction of huge and expensive works," while "floods are tearing away, in small parcels, here and there, an aggregate of old land, much of it already irrigated, at least comparable to the new land in area and value."[54] And the Blue River area was only one example of widely spreading conditions. By January 1921 Leopold had tallied his observations of thirteen similar agricultural creek valleys in Arizona, only two of which had no significant damage.[55] By 1923 Leopold had added to his survey tally nineteen additional valleys in the national forests of District 3. Of the thirty-two total, four valleys were ruined by erosion. Nineteen were partly ruined or had the beginnings of erosion. The remaining nine had only slight erosion or none.[56] By Leopold's estimate the agricultural lands in Arizona and New Mexico lost to erosion by 1923 approached 100,000 acres. In comparison, the total irrigable acreage of U.S. reclamation projects—involving dam construction and diversion of water from streams and rivers onto drylands—in the two states was 430,000 acres. Comparing the estimates, "it would appear," Leopold wrote, "that erosion has destroyed somewhere around a fourth as much farmland as reclamation has created."[57] Erosion also was degrading the region's reservoirs, upon which much agriculture depended. Water-storage capacity was being lost to silting faster than engineers had calculated. "We, the community," Leopold lamented, "are saving at the spigot and wasting at the bunghole."[58] At best, progress overall was mixed. The wasteful ways in which his countrymen approached reclamation, land use, and erosion reminded Leopold of a favorite line of the popular literary naturalist John Burroughs. At work was the misguided "genius" of the potato bug, Leopold asserted, which, "by exterminating the potato, thereby exterminates itself."[59] "The opening of these great reclamation projects we celebrate by oratory and monuments," Leopold wrote in 1924,

[b]ut the loss of our existing farms we dismiss as an act of God—like the storm or the earthquake, inevitable. But it is not an act of God; on the contrary, it is the direct result of our own misuse of the country we are trying to improve.[60]

The devastation in the Blue River lands made a powerful impression on Leopold. The test of true civilization, he was realizing, was whether it could endure, whether its citizens could prosper for generations in a place. By this measure the settlement along the Blue River had failed. Yet to call the settlement a failure was merely to prompt new questions—about the land, about the nation's institutions and values, and about the conservation ideas he had been taught.

Some of Leopold's questions had to do with the land's functioning. Much of the erosion was evidentally initiated by overgrazing. But was the problem a matter of exceeding the carrying capacity of a range's forage by grazing too many animals, or was it something else? In addition, erosion was only one of several obvious landscape changes going on. Were the changes all related? And how were uses in one place affecting land conditions in another? Halting "the ravages of erosion and restoring our organic resources to a productive condition," Leopold was coming to understand, "is so intricate and difficult a problem that we must know something about causes before we can well consider remedies."[61]

The Blue River settlement failures also prompted Leopold to think more critically about American culture. The land-use troubles there apparently were expressions of the new settlers' dominant attitude toward land. Ancient peoples had found ways to live in the region for generations, Leopold understood. What, then, was wrong with American ways now that led to such a disaster within a single generation? Much of the harm in the valley had taken place on privately owned land. Was the common understanding of private property itself part of the problem? "Thus far," Leopold complained, "we have considered the problem of conservation of land purely as an economic issue."[62] A broader view was required, he realized, one that considered all of the social forces affecting land uses.[63]

In the end the Blue River's primary lesson for Leopold may have involved the clash between ignorance and action. Americans were settling the Southwest with precious little knowledge of how it worked. In time science might unravel its ecological processes, which could lead to more informed decisions about the land. But what was the nation to do in the meantime? How were land-use decisions to be made in the face of ignorance? Inevitably people had to make choices about the land based upon values and pragmatic concerns that extended well beyond science's reach. Who was to make those decisions, and on what bases would they be made? "The world has become a picture puzzle," Leopold had copied from a 1914 *Atlantic Monthly* article onto the first page of his personal journal. "When we have put together the few pieces that science has given us, we are often too pleased with our success to be impressed by the result."[64] But, as Leopold understood, the proof was in the result. And in the ecologically sensitive Southwest the results often were not good.

On the ecological issues posed by the Blue River disaster Leopold would make substantial progress before he departed the Southwest for Wisconsin a few years later. On the human cultural issues he also would entertain theories. But they would remain tentative and speculative ones, some of them so far removed from the assumptions of his Forest Service colleagues that he was reluctant to speak of them openly.[65]

Private Homes and the Public Good

As Leopold surveyed erosion damage in his region's national forests, it became all apparent to him that grazing was erosion's chief and proximate cause. In the eroded creek valleys that he had observed, the damage seemed "to have started since the range began to be used for stock, and the case of the Blue River indicates that an entire valley can be ruined within a decade."[66] Leopold was far from the first observer to recognize this connection. Some of the first public forest reserves had been created at the request of towns and cities for watershed protection because livestock grazing was silting up their water supplies.[67] In 1913 Will Barnes of the Forest Service, in his *Western Grazing Grounds and Forest Ranges*—a book Leopold read and recommended to other foresters in his district—described how the small community of Manti, Utah, had learned to connect livestock grazing in mountainous headwater areas to increased flooding and erosion.[68] Rainwater cutting into livestock-worn passageways, for example, within a decade could drain a wet, grassy meadow, producing a gaping, barren hole as dry as a dusty road and as long as a mile, fifty feet wide and fifteen feet deep.[69] Grazing, in short, was a resource use that could undercut a forest's ability to serve other uses. The Forest Service's ideal of using an area for multiple purposes— managing timber, water flows, and forage—sometimes worked better in theory than on the land.

Much of the Southwest's grazing had taken place on private lands in and around the national forests. One of Leopold's first considerations, then, as a forest supervisor was to determine how public and private use might best fit together in forest watersheds. For the Service this issue was an old one. National forests owed their origins to the failure of private parties to use lands well. Timber and watershed resources were being degraded by reckless cutting and fire, often on private land. From its inception the nation had turned public lands over to private owners, as quickly and completely as possible. Now some observers were having second thoughts: given the degradation on private lands, perhaps remaining federal lands should stay in public hands. Critics of reserves had long claimed that they "locked up" resources, but the intent, at least, was plainly otherwise.[70] Forest resources were set aside with "suitable protection"[71] for future use. Private parties would use the forestlands under rules that would keep them productive over the long term. Timber harvesting, grazing, mining, and other extractive activities all would be undertaken by private entities, not by the government itself. The prevailing policies for national forests, in short, were intended to blend the public and private in ways that would keep resources flowing indefinitely.

Public and private came together in the forest reserves in another, contentious way as a result of the interspersion of public and private lands. Most timberland in the West was interspersed with good livestock range.[72] When the national forests were designated, sections of range were included simply because of the difficulty of excluding them. The Forest Service fully supported leased grazing and had no desire to end it. But it was determined to protect the ranges from "being burned up or from being overcrowded and overgrazed."[73] The Service also wanted to devote rangelands to their highest-valued uses. In that calculation private home owners ranked higher than large-scale grazing operations. Complicating matters was that some of these rangelands, even though in national forests, remained open to homesteaders. At any time these lands within the forests could be settled, passing from public to private hands. The whole arrangement was fraught with tension, as Leopold and others could see.[74]

Homesteading in the forests could take place under the Forest Reserve Homestead Act,[75] passed in 1906 to meet the clamor of complaints that forest reserves were locking up land from private use. This act made homesteading possible on nontimbered land classified as suitable for farming so long as the homesteads would not threaten the well-being of the forests. The Forest Service was under pressure to open lands to settlers, yet it was reluctant to allow homesteading because of the fire threat farmers posed to the nearby forests.[76] Nevertheless, between 1906 and 1915 the U.S. Department of Agriculture approved 13,000 forest homestead entries, and by 1915 almost 2 million acres of national forest land had been opened to entry—enough for 18,000 settlers.[77]

The theory behind this homestead policy was set forth in the 1907 *Use Book*, in a defensive tone:

> When a National Forest is created the home maker is not interfered with in the least. . . . The home seeker can travel all through a Forest, pick out the agricultural land he wants for a home, apply for it, have it listed, settle upon it when listed, enter it, build his home, cultivate his fields, patent it, and spend the rest of his days there.[78]

A man could spend his days there, that is, if he figured out how to fit his land use together with the realities of the arid landscape. But it was by no means clear that homesteaders would do this.[79] Private owners were degrading their lands and endangering the forests in the process. Congress, though, had set the governing policy: the individual home owner would receive special consideration—not just in getting land but also in getting free timber for domestic use; also, the man with a home in or near a forest even had priority on nearby grazing rights.

An agreement of the secretaries of agriculture and the interior on February 7, 1910, hinted at conflicts that were arising among the various forest resource priorities even as it reemphasized the watershed protection mission of the forests. The Forest Service's statutory charter to protect favorable water flows, according to the new interagency agreement, would extend to "erosion prevention on any watershed important to irrigation, water power, or water supply."[80] Between the lines of the agreement was an implicit warning of looming trouble: the preference Congress was giving to private home owners was causing conflicts with efforts to protect federal lands, given the questionable practices of private owners.

The truth was, individual liberty and private property had an ecological dark side in the Southwest. And Leopold was seeing it. Indeed, as he looked out on the watersheds that private owners had degraded, he wondered openly about how people understood the rights and responsibilities of private landownership. How feasible was unregulated private ownership in such ecologically sensitive terrain? Perhaps the public-interest impulse of the National Forest System needed to be extended further, he mused. Perhaps the federal government should inspect and manage nonforested land that was also subject to private misuse. Such public oversight would not supplant private enterprise, any more than it did in national forests. All of the safeguarded resources in the forests were regularly made available to private users in the form of legally protected private rights. But the living forest itself, including its waters and wildlife, remained in public hands. In this way public and private were mixed. Leopold carried this reasoning even further. Had the time come, he wondered provocatively, to apply the same mix of public and private control to the soil itself? Should the law allow private use of soil but restrict that use to protect the public good? "The long and the short of the matter," he wrote,

> is that semiarid countries cannot be occupied and used by man, and their resources acquired as private property, without serious damage to their ultimate capacity to support man and hence without serious damage to the public interest. . . . This is the fundamental reason why the nation retains ownership of the mountain forests and why the nation builds and regulates reclamation projects. But while partial provision has been made, through the Forest Service and Reclamation Service, to conserve the forests and the water supply, no provision has been made to conserve that fundamental resource, land.[81]

The possibility of expanded federal ownership or regulatory control, Leopold recognized, would be an issue for the future. In the meantime action was needed to address privately caused erosion. Private grazing was seriously harming public interests in watersheds. It was the job of the Forest Service to take action, or so Leopold emphasized in his 1922 inspection report on the Prescott National Forest. The control of private-lands erosion was essential

> to the success of watershed conservation and to the welfare of all Forest industries and uses, including grazing, timber, and recreation, as well as to the development of roads and trails. While technically we are not responsible for it, we are forced to secure its conservation.[82]

Two years earlier Leopold had inspected that same forest. "Erosion of agricultural creek valleys is serious throughout the Prescott division," he had written in his 1920 report.[83] Actual erosion-control work was urgently needed, Leopold asserted. Further studies alone were not enough:

> The erosion of range lands is also starting in many places. The prevalence of soft granite soils makes it impossible to check the process without artificial works. . . . I consider *actual work* on erosion as a major problem on this Forest, and further "investigative work" of the kind previously done by our office as a waste of time. What is needed is a series of actual demonstrations, to test and improve technique and to serve as examples to private interests.[84]

The problem in the early 1920s was the same one that had prevailed in 1913 when Leopold penned his instructive letter to the forest officers of the Carson. It was hard to get Service offices to shift from mere investigative and administrative work to actual beneficial work on the ground. It was particularly difficult in this case because the Forest Service, rightfully proud of its success in range improvement, found it hard to acknowledge that grazing was still causing erosion. Leopold urged a hard look at the truth.[85] In his 1920 "Report on the Prescott" he recommended two types of essential demonstration projects. The preventive aim of the first type would be to "demonstrate and develop technique in the saving of agricultural valley lands from creek erosion."[86] The restorative object of the second type would be to "demonstrate and develop technique in checking gullies"[87] in places where they had already started. Model projects, Leopold proposed, should be constructed on each publicly owned ranger station. Private landowners could then see clearly the value of such measures. Perhaps they might even organize themselves voluntarily into erosion-control ventures to address regional degradation.

Leopold spoke frankly to his fellow professionals about the failure of the Forest Service to recognize the necessity for artificial erosion-control works such as check dams, gully plugging, fencing, and vegetation plantings along banks.[88]

> There has been a widespread assumption among foresters that such works are unnecessary and impracticable. I have even heard it said, by experts on watershed problems, that *to admit the necessity of artificial control works would be admitting the failure of our range control system.* I take strong exception to any such viewpoint. Our function is not to prove the infallibility of our initial forest policies, but to conserve the Forests.
>
> I have stated that any system of grazing, no matter how conservative, induces erosion. The proof of this statement can not be set down in print, but may be seen almost anywhere in the hills.[89]

By 1922 Leopold found himself entertaining numerous policy positions more demanding than those of his Forest Service colleagues. The multiple uses of the forest conflicted quite sharply with one another, Leopold believed, at least on ecologically sensitive lands. Grazing was a particular problem. In arid landscapes it undercut other resource values and produced erosion almost everywhere it took place. Even sharper was Leopold's mounting critique of private landownership in places where insensitive land use harmed the public. Private ownership as it was construed, he suggested, not only permitted land misuse but almost inevitably produced it in grazing areas with little rain. In any event, the basic principles of ecological interconnection were such that the public had a legitimate interest in the way private lands were used.

WRITTEN ON THE HILLS

On the day he submitted his 1920 report on the Prescott, Leopold sent a letter home to Burlington. "I have a new hobby," he explained:

> I am seriously thinking of specializing in erosion control. The problem is perfectly tremendous here in the Southwest, and I seem to be the only one who has any faith in the possibilities of tackling it successfully. Don't you think one more hobby would help keep me out of mischief?[90]

Despite his lighthearted comment, Leopold was both worried and perplexed by erosion and took seriously his obligation as a forester to do something about it in and around national forest lands. His worry had grown as his inspections had proceeded.[91] "Erosion," he observed,

> eats into our hills like a contagion, and floods bring down the loosened soil upon our valleys like a scourge. Water, soil, animals, and plants—the very fabric of prosperity—react to destroy each other and us. Science can and must unravel those reactions, and government must enforce the findings of science.[92]

"A diagnosis of the process of destruction," Leopold believed, "gives the most reliable pointers as to the best process of prevention and cure."[93] Carefully he began to piece together the ecological story of grazing and erosion as it was written in the hills.

One investigative lead handed to Leopold was a tale repeatedly told by ranchers in the southern Arizona foothills about how brush had taken over the country, replacing many formerly grassy and wooded areas. Old-timers could remember when an area that now hardly carried one cow had supported up to thirty.[94] As grazing had increased, changes had taken place in the distribution of vegetation.

These changes suggested that the climate had become drier, but tree-ring studies showed no increase or decrease in aridity during the past three thousand years.[95] Why, then, was uphill woodland changing to brush species, and why was woody growth increasingly moving downhill to enter formerly grassy areas?[96] As he thought about these questions Leopold paid attention also to other, less apparent landscape changes. In one area on the Prescott, the land now was about half covered in oak brush, with about one-tenth in grama grass and side oats. It also contained old, fire-killed junipers—about three burned two-foot-diameter stumps per acre. A ring count of the new growth of woody species revealed an average age of thirty-five to forty years. From this Leopold guessed that the brush had grown out since the last fire, around the time of first settlement. Given the area's current vegetation, he knew that it would not sustain a fire. So how had the junipers burned? What vegetation had fueled a fire severe enough to burn the widely spaced junipers forty or so years earlier?[97]

Somewhat heavier grass and piñons may have previously grown in this area, according to the theory offered by forester Wales, in charge of the Prescott National Forest. He surmised that such vegetation, not too different from what had grown in the past, had since been consumed by decay and then possibly by a light fire.[98] Leopold's theory, much different, was that extremely heavy grass had once covered the land, thick enough to sustain a very hot fire and to spread it from one juniper to another. Overgrazing had then destroyed the grass.[99] With the grass eaten, intense fires could no longer spread. And with no fires and no grass to compete with the brush, the brush had taken over the area. "These theories," noted Leopold in his report,

> would carry with them two widely different objectives for grazing management and watershed protection. The first theory must [approve] the present vegetation as measurably close to satisfactory. The second theory must regard the present vegetation as a state of denudation.
>
> Granted such an important bearing on practical present problems, is it not important to get the best available skill to diagnose such indicator-areas and recommend, for administrative approval, pretty definite objectives or ultimate standards of conservation?[100]

Foresters could manage rangelands to achieve a variety of different objectives in terms of desired types of vegetation, but the methods of reaching these objectives would differ radically in each case. To promote tree growth, Leopold observed, grazing should remain or perhaps even be increased to keep down grass and brush; to restore grass cover, in contrast, grazing would need to be reduced or eliminated. Two forest administrators, both eager to conserve, could come to "opposite ideas as to what most needed conserving, and hence with opposite plans of administration."[101] How, then, could a forester administer his area without knowing which objective to work toward?[102] And how would a person decide which objective was most appropriate?

Before Leopold's days as forest inspector the success of grazing had largely been judged by its effects on forage and on the amount of grass it grew to support live stock. Stocking levels were deemed proper as long as the stock's grazing did not exceed the forage carrying capacity. As Leopold surveyed the southwestern landscapes, he began to doubt this wisdom. For livestock rearing, Leopold suggested, the carrying capacity of the land itself might be less than that of the land's forage considered separately. In other words, "the forage will carry more stock than the land."[103] Livestock might survive adequately on a range's vegetation even while the capacity of the range for future habitability—its soils and waters—was nonetheless being degraded. In economic terms, cows and sheep were eating not only the land's interest but also its principal—the very source of the nation's wealth. Ranchers and government institutions, paying attention only to the forage, had been measuring the annual rate of interest while the land itself, the principal, was dwindling.[104]

Step by step Leopold worked out his erosion-grazing theory on the basis of evidence on the ground, figuring out the roles of grass, fire, timber, and moving water. Here was one big puzzle. He continued to seek out clues, reading the land as a detective might, making careful notes and diagrams of his observations as he carried out his many inspections. He mapped occurrences of erosion, counted tree rings, examined fire scars on trees, and took notes on types of new vegetative reproduction taking place and on the condition and placement of surviving species. In his 1923 report on the Tonto

National Forest Leopold brought many of his observations together into a "grass-fire-brush-erosion theory" of land change as it applied to pine and woodland landscapes.[105] By 1924 he felt confident enough in his overall theory to go public with it in an article published in the *Journal of Forestry*.

Before European-American settlement of the country, Leopold thought, fires had been started by lightning and by Indians and had kept brush thin. With grass as its fuel, hot-burning fires killed the junipers and other tree species, allowing the quick-growing grass to retain the upper hand. The grass sod prevented erosion in spite of periodic fires, which bared the soil from time to time. Then came new settlers with their livestock. The animals grazed the grass intensively and trampled it, giving it little chance to resprout or reproduce, eventually killing it. As the grass decreased, the once widespread fires no longer had adequate fuel to burn. And without grass roots to compete with, brush species could move into the soils and grow. Soon young oak, pine, and juniper began invading also. It was evident from this, Leopold concluded, that the conditions of soil and climate were suited to grow vigorous woodland, as long as fire was kept out.[106] That is, the thick grass and thin brush before new settlement had remained dominant only because periodic fires had swept across large regions. The substitution of grazing for fire had brought on a vegetational transition type of thin grass and thick brush, which eventually gave way to woodland. Remarkably, then, it was fire—considered forestry's number one enemy—that had conserved soil, watershed values, and the land's ability to support carefully managed homesteads. And it had done so by promoting grass, not trees.[107]

To accept Leopold's theory as to the "ecology of these brush-fields"[108] was to conclude that grass could sometimes be better at conserving watersheds than foresters had been willing to admit. The theory also explained what had been relatively obvious, that grazing was the prime factor destroying watershed values. As livestock ate and trampled vegetation, the original forage plants declined, giving way to vegetation that was less successful in protecting soil. Particularly in places near water holes, where livestock inevitably gathered, gullies could begin even when surrounding landscapes remained well covered in vegetation. With fire and no grazing, erosion had been minimal. With no fire and severe grazing, erosion took hold.

Leopold had thus pieced together a supportable story about conditions in the watershed before European-American settlement. He had pulled together evidence of when, how, and why the present conditions had developed. Now the question that arose was a matter of objectives. If the purpose of the forest was to produce wood, then heavy grazing alongside fire suppression was acceptable (though that choice had its own perils).[109] Grazing helped the forest expand by keeping down grass and allowing woody species to come in, in time producing more timber. But if the prime objective instead was to protect watershed values—to minimize erosion, flooding, and silting—then it would be better to promote grass. With its firm policy of suppressing fire the Forest Service had made a choice and was inadvertently experimenting with the land. Fire suppression and grazing were allowing trees to take over the grasslands. The full ripple effects of this landscape change were not known, but its effects on the watershed were not at all promising.

What Is the Goal?

As Leopold continued to work out the details of the grass-fire-timber-grazing-erosion story, he also was refining his views about the role of science in managing lands. Science might be able to explain how landscapes worked and how landscape change in one place affected natural conditions elsewhere. But something other than science was needed to determine whether or not the end results were desirable. To judge the results the forester had to take that extra step, deciding on the ground what was beneficial. But what criteria should be used? What would a good result look like?

These questions had been implicit in Leopold's 1913 letter wherein he urged foresters to use the "effect on the forest" as their measure of management success. They needed to distinguish clearly between means and ends and then to think very clearly about the ends. In 1922 Leopold returned to the question in a manuscript titled "Standards of Conservation,"[110] never completed and not published in his lifetime.[111] In it he probed the differences between what he called *machinery* standards and *conservation* standards:

At the outset, it may be well to give examples of the two classes of standards. When an administrative officer is directed to spend at least 40 days a year on grazing work or to make at least two general inspections per year of each unit of range, there is set up a *machinery standard* (heretofore vaguely called administrative standard, or standard of performance). On the other hand when there is set up as an objective of administration that a certain unit of range shall be brought to an .8 density of grama grass capable of carrying 1 head per 20 acres, there is established a *standard of conservation* for that unit.[112]

Leopold's measure of success remained its effect on the land itself, on the forest. As for administrative Forest Service efficiency, it was a desirable trait of the *means* used to achieve a beneficial land-use effect, but it was not and could not be the *objective* of that work. Nor was it enough, Leopold could see, merely to claim that the proper goal was "conservation," given the ambiguities and vagueness of that word. Forest Service men and others assumed that every resource should be conserved as far as possible. But the on-the-ground meaning of conservation was itself vague. "It can be safely said," wrote Leopold, "that when it comes to actual work on the ground, the objects of conservation are never axiomatic or obvious but always complex and usually conflicting."[113]

In Leopold's mind, the protection of watersheds and thus of soil simply could neither sensibly nor officially be a subordinate part of the Service's mission. Every acre of forest in the Southwest drained into rivers or basins important to irrigation.[114] In some settings the importance of watershed protection was clearly prescribed by law. For instance, most of the Tonto National Forest and parts of the Prescott and Crook national forests had been established particularly for watershed conservation; other uses on these forests were expressly subordinate to watershed values. On other forests in the region, in contrast, the priority of watershed conservation was not clear in law. It had to be determined by the principle of highest use, drawing upon all relevant policy considerations. Everywhere foresters needed clear standards of conservation—"a clearly defined ultimate goal"[115]—to guide their work. If they possessed such a goal, they would have far less need for machinery standards.

In 1923, after nearly fifteen years in the Southwest, Leopold assembled the Forest Service's first *Watershed Handbook*—a striking accomplishment—to help guide the Service's work on erosion. The discussion in the *Handbook* was an important measure of how far he had come in his thinking, not just about the land's functioning but also about the essential need for sound policy and sound science to come together.

NATURE'S STANDARD

Leopold's assessment of the situation in the Southwest, particularly his harsh judgment about erosion, cut against the optimism that had long permeated the American West. The rain-follows-the-plow mentality, which insisted that nature would bend to human desires, had hardly disappeared. It was unsurprising, then, when colleagues questioned his conclusions about grazing and erosion. In spite of Leopold's detailed evidence from the Blue River area and elsewhere, one reviewer of his 1923 manuscript, "Some Fundamentals of Conservation in the Southwest," directly challenged his warnings about an erosion problem:

> The world's most outstanding example of the benefits of erosion is the valley of the Nile, the wonderful fertility of which is due to a silt deposit each year of alluvial soil which, of course, could not occur without erosion in the higher reaches. The soil is removed from its location of rough and comparatively worthless inaccessibility to the valley of convenient utilization by the process which you entirely condemn. I am not sure that we yet know what erosion is harmful and what is beneficial.[116]

Leopold was well aware that certain levels of erosion were natural, sometimes even beneficial. But much of it, to his observation, was neither. What kind and degree of erosion was human caused, and how much erosion was too much and should be controlled? The questions were difficult, and scientists in the 1920s were unable to answer them exactly. But precision was not needed to see clearly that erosion was destroying large portions of formerly habitable land[117]—of key importance to Leopold the forester, who had to think about human-related problems in human temporal and spatial scales.[118] From this perspective the matter simply had to be addressed, even as scientists labored to learn more.

Leopold tackled the issue in the first section of his *Watershed Handbook*.[119] Over geologic time, he asserted, certain kinds and rates of erosion existed in every place and wrought significant changes.[120] It thus made sense to distinguish "normal" erosion from the "abnormal." Erosion was normal when the configuration of a landscape did not change materially over the course of a human generation. This kind of erosion, as in the Nile River Valley, could prove beneficial to agriculture. Abnormal erosion, on the other hand, visibly rearranged some part of the country within a period of months, years, or a few decades. A series of cloudbursts, for instance, might wash away creek bottoms or lead to the gullying of hillslopes. This type of erosion often produced floods, gullies, silting of waterways, and decreases in the land's productivity. Erosion like this had occurred before European-American settlement. Leopold nonetheless labeled it abnormal because it typically was a local and temporary condition— an exception to the more widespread and self-adjusting process of normal erosion.

Both types of erosion, normal and abnormal, could be explained mechanistically by the interplay of two forces, Leopold suggested. The first force was resistance, defined as the capacity of a given land to remain physically secure. Resistance depended on the types of vegetation and the geologic formations involved.[121] The second force was disintegration—the various powers that could disrupt soil, including water flows, rainfall, the actions of freezing and thawing, and wind.[122] When the forces of resistance and disintegration approximately balanced, the land was in equilibrium and no erosion took place. When the force of resistance was greater, soils had opportunity to build; when the opposite occurred and disintegration was greater, erosion occurred.

In Leopold's view, many people misunderstood erosion mostly because they did not distinguish between normal and abnormal erosion and failed to consider the important changes in erosion patterns occurring after their arrival. The coming of livestock, irrigation, and modern agriculture had brought new forces of disintegration. These new forces—including concentrated and widespread trampling and grazing of domestic animals, plowing, and cropping—brought an increase in abnormal erosion. Before new settlement the forces initiating abnormal erosion—bursts of wind and rain—had been local and temporary. The land typically had time to regain equilibrium between resistance and disintegration before another disruptive event. Grazing and plowing, in contrast, affected wider areas and were of more continual duration: their ongoing impacts weakened the land's resistance, making soil more susceptible to erosion from other forces. Land had less opportunity for "self-healing"[123] through the regrowth of soil-protecting vegetation. The extent of the resulting destruction varied from place to place on the basis of climate and local vegetation.

Grazing in a humid, flat region, for instance, might cause little erosion. Nature here did not become "disorganized but adjust[ed] herself to the changes wrought by man and continue[d], by and large, to be beneficent to his use of her resources."[124] However, the same grazing in the semi-arid Southwest could bring about destruction. In all landscapes, though, the destruction would ultimately end when the land found a new condition of equilibrium. At some point, that is, even abnormal erosion would cease of its own accord. But this might occur only after soil had eroded down to rock and cobbles. This new state of balance would be quite an unproductive one from the economic standpoint, Leopold pointed out.[125] The Blue River valley was a reminder that it also would be quite an uninhabitable one.

There was no simple formula for remediation of grazing damage and every locale was different, Leopold realized, but he was beginning to develop some general principles. The immediate, practical lesson to be drawn from all of this study, he urged, was for the Forest Service to move fast to build up the forces of resistance in the land, which grazing and plowing had so weakened. The Forest Service should become a model in such efforts and should urge private landowners to follow its lead.[126] Leopold recognized the importance of the livestock industry to the West and rarely suggested that grazing be halted entirely. Nevertheless, it was time to act. So much destructive erosion now was taking place that there was little danger, thought Leopold, of control work being so successful that it would interfere with normal or beneficial erosion. If humans wanted to inhabit the Southwest for the long term, there was little choice but to adjust their land uses and conservation techniques to the sensitivities of the landscape—to the "most delicate ecological balance."[127]

Leopold realized that in this matter Americans were dealing with the fundamental question of whether "we are here to 'skin' the Southwest and then get out, or whether we are here to found a permanent civilized community with room to grow and improve."[128] Once again, the desired end would determine the necessary prescription for land use. And, once again, determining and bringing about that end would involve cultural as well as ecological insights.

In the final section of his *Handbook* Leopold brought up the ultimate question of a land-use goal. He did so by posing a hypothetical but practical question that forest officers would find familiar. "Where a conflict exists between watershed conservation and other uses, what are the local Forest officers expected to know and do toward applying the principle of highest use?"[129] The first step, Leopold proposed, was for the officer to learn "what was the virgin condition of the watershed." Next, he must identify "when, how, and why the present condition resulted." Finally, there was the need to understand and bring together the various relevant policy values and to execute a plan of action. On this final point of policy and action, it was essential to "weigh the public service values of the conflicting uses, and to know the extent and manner in which the one having the lesser value should be controlled to the point where it will not destroy greater values than it creates."[130] All of this was, of course, much easier said than done. These four investigative steps for a landscape—identifying what *was*, what *is*, the reasons behind changes, and what *should be*—went beyond identifying the physical considerations. They presented a particular way of analyzing and evaluating land based on its past, its present, the agents of change, and a desired future. It was a sound investigative approach, Leopold thought, and over the years he would use it many times. Leopold particularly liked the approach because it separated facts from values, insofar as they could be separated, and gave science the role appropriate to it. Most of all, it got people to consider separately the desired aim of land management— a far more complex issue than the Service realized.

Something to Go By

Leopold's investigative work in the semi-arid Southwest was producing more questions than answers. The more he looked, the more he realized both the gaps in his knowledge and the difficulty of making sound judgments. In the meantime, though, land-use decisions had to be made. So what was the best way to make them in the face of factual ignorance and vague goals? Leopold addressed these issues in two manuscripts, written in 1922 and 1923, neither of which was published. The ideas in both went beyond anything foresters had learned in school.

Leopold's earlier manuscript explored what he viewed as the natural "skill" that certain people had in making judgments based on experience and intuition.[131] Leopold illustrated this innate skill with a forest example involving two men, one a scientific tree specialist, the other a natural woodsman. Independently each man had published an article on the factors determining the reproduction of western yellow pine, and both had come to the same "new and different" conclusions. The silviculturist spent ten years and $25,000 to deliver his conclusions. The lumberman's judgment, based on observation and intuition, "cost the use of a pair of sharp eyes and some spare time, and became available upon utterance." It was a curious situation.

> Granting the former class of truth to be in every way a more valuable asset to forestry, the fact remains that if there were a way to discover and test the latter class, it would give us "something to go by" in a multitude of questions wherein we now flounder about, without the means to even start a scientific analysis, much less to finish and use it.[132]

What if foresters with good judgment of this type could be identified and allowed to make decisions, Leopold asked. Would not the results be far better than if people without such skill merely went by the book or made decisions based on fragmentary knowledge? The evidence of science remained essential, and its conclusions, when arrived at, were more reliable. But Leopold was intrigued by the idea that some people seemed to know things that others did not. Maybe the best way to address ignorance was to find and cultivate natural skill:

> Who, for instance, has set down the laws governing erosion in the Southwest? And when will they be set down? Maybe our grandsons will have them, but by that time the best parts of the Southwest bid

fair to repose in the Gulf of California. We must have "something to go by" now.[133] Natural skill, Leopold believed, was typically quite specialized within a person when it existed at all. A person could have skill in cattle and cattle management but know little or nothing about range conditions or erosion. Indeed, Leopold contended, there was no such thing as a "good all-around forester" because good forestry required natural skill in too many subjects.[134] But where skill existed it was wise to put it to use. The negative comments that Leopold received on the manuscript prompted him to set it aside. But he could not set aside the underlying challenge of making good decisions despite ignorance. If a personnel management system that graded employees on their natural skill was not the answer, then he needed to keep looking.

Leopold's 1923 manuscript, "Some Fundamentals of Conservation in the Southwest," was a more wide-ranging one—and one of the most revealing that he would ever write. More strongly than in his published papers, Leopold pointed an accusative finger at prevailing American culture. He particularly criticized that "system of competitive destruction inherited from frontier days," which was being "perpetuated by the archaic land policy of the government and some of the several states."[135] The ongoing destruction of land was a direct manifestation of the narrow view that nature was merely the raw material of wealth, that America's natural resources were essentially unlimited, and that profit making was so desirable as to make it legitimate as an overall national vision regardless of the consequences. With these attitudes had come a certain unwillingness to adapt to the Southwest's natural conditions, leaving the erosion problem unchecked. Settlers were failing, in particular, to attend to the predictable cycles of drought and to adjust their stocking levels accordingly. This failure to plan for drought was "cause for astonishment":

[A]nd, when drouth come, the stock eat up the range, ruin the watershed, ruin the stockman, wreck the banks, get credits from the treasury of the United States, and then die. And the silt of their dying moves on down into our reservoirs to someday dry up the irrigated valleys—the only live thing left![136]

Leopold may have decided that his criticisms of America's economic habits were simply too strident to put into print. Perhaps, though, it was the final section of his paper and his uncertainties about it that led him to return his essay to his desk drawer. In that final section he proposed consideration of "conservation as a moral issue." His was a less unusual way to understand the subject, he admitted, but appropriate nonetheless:

> A false front of exclusively economic determinism is so habitual to Americans in discussing public questions that one must speak in the language of compound interest to get a hearing. In my opinion, however, one can not round out a real understanding of the situation in the Southwest without likewise considering its moral aspects.[137]

One place Leopold looked for moral guidance was the Bible, which he had begun studying while a student at Yale University. He seemed particularly fond of the Old Testament and copied passages from it into his personal journal. The epitome of the moral question, Leopold believed, was summed up by a passage from the book of Ezekiel:

> Seemeth it a small thing unto you to have fed upon the good pasture, but ye must tread down with your feet the residue of your pasture? And to have drunk of the clear waters, but ye must foul the residue with your feet?[138]

"It is possible," Leopold wrote, "that Ezekiel respected the soil, not only as a craftsman respects his material, but as a moral being respects a living thing."[139] Also influencing him was a unique volume he picked up sometime in 1922 or 1923 — *Tertium Organum*, by Russian philosopher Piotr Ouspensky.[140] Ouspensky's philosophy dealt with the limits of human perception, and he conceived of the earth as a living organism. Whether or not this was an apt conception, Leopold found the perspective provocative. "Many of the world's most penetrating minds," Leopold added to his 1923 manuscript,

> have regarded our so-called "inanimate nature" as a living thing, and probably many of us who have neither the time nor the ability to reason out conclusions on such matters by logical processes have felt intuitively that there existed between man and the earth a closer and deeper relation than would necessarily follow the mechanistic conception of the earth as our physical provider and abiding place.[141]

Having raised Ouspensky's idea, Leopold proceeded to draw directly upon his thesis:

[I]t is at least not impossible to regard the earth's parts—soil, mountains, rivers, atmosphere, etc.—as organs, or parts of organs, of a coordinated whole, each part with a definite function. . . . In such a case we would have all the visible attributes of a living thing, which we do not now realize to be such because it is too big, and its life processes, too slow. And there would also follow that invisible attribute—a soul, or consciousness—which not only Ouspensky, but many philosophers of all ages, ascribe to all living things and aggregations thereof, including the "dead" earth.[142]

If this was true, Leopold asserted—if the earth was best understood as "an organism possessing a certain kind and degree of life" that humans might "intuitively respect"—then it followed that humans could not "destroy the earth with moral impunity."[143] In any case, the essential thing to recognize was "the interdependent functions of the elements."[144] Perhaps this interdependence itself was sufficient for the earth to deserve moral status:

Possibly, in our intuitive perceptions, which may be truer than our science and less impeded by words than our philosophies, we realize the indivisibility of the earth—its soil, mountains, rivers, forests, climate, plants, and animals, and respect it collectively not only as a useful servant but as a living being, vastly less alive than our selves in degree, but vastly greater than ourselves in time and space.[145]

To view the earth this way was to pose fundamental questions about the human predicament: "[W]as the earth made for man's use," Leopold wondered, "or has man merely the privilege of temporarily possessing an earth made for other and inscrutable purposes?" The question of what he can properly do with it must necessarily be affected by this question."[146] Even if the earth were made for man, Leopold pushed, there was the question, "What man?"[147] Was it past races, present Americans, future generations? Surely it was not only for the present, but also for the future, he urged; surely living humans bore "the responsibility of passing it on, the better for our use, not only to immediate posterity, but to the Unknown Future."[148]

→→ ←←

For years, even after leaving the Southwest, Leopold would continue to unravel the twisting and turning intrigues of the region's erosion story. Along the way he would develop new insights into the great drama of the land, what he would come to perceive as an ecological "odyssey." On returning to the Midwest in 1924, Leopold would study similar land problems there. In Wisconsin, though, his attention would first largely turn to wildlife as a resource and as an essential part of the land community—work that similarly build upon experiences and activities in the Southwest.

Chapter 3

The Middle Border

*Let Americans turn to America, and to that very America
which has been rejected and almost annihilated. Do they
want to draw sustenance for the future? ... Now is the day
when Americans must become fully self-reliantly conscious of
their own inner responsibility. They must be ready for a new
act, a new extension of life.*

D. H. Lawrence, December 15, 1920

As Leopold was piecing together the erosion story in the Southwest
and beginning his professional game protection work—between
1914 and the mid-1920s—the world was changing rapidly around
him. Millions died in the Great War and from an influenza pandemic,
and political boundaries in Europe were redrawn. On the American
plains farmers plowed millions of acres of land, transforming much
of the vast, fertile American prairie. In the fall of 1917, 42,170,000
acres were planted in wheat, 1 million more than in any preceding
year and 7 million more than the preceding five-year average.[1] Meanwhile, agricultural prices fluctuated widely. Wheat, corn, and livestock prices nearly doubled between 1914 and 1919, only to drop
precipitously after the war.[2] As prices fell, hundreds of thousands of
struggling farmers lost their farms—450,000 farmers in 1920 and 1921
alone went bankrupt.[3] By 1920 more than half the land area of the
United States was taken up by farms,[4] yet rural people increasingly

were moving into cities—by that year half the country's roughly 100 million people were urban dwellers.[5] Meanwhile, millions of automobiles were rolling off assembly lines, and to carry these cars, hundreds of thousands of miles of public roads were transecting the country.[6] Trade unions formed and fractured, labor riots erupted, and the population became increasingly diverse in ethnic background as nearly 3 million immigrants entered the country between 1914 and 1920.[7] For many it became ever harder to make sense of the world. The 1914 comments of Walter Lippman, essayist and editor of the *New Republic*, seemed even more apt after the war: "We are unsettled to the very roots of our being."[8] A social radical, John Reed, summed up the postwar times similarly, from the view of a man turning thirty:

> Sometimes it seems to me the end of the world's youth. Certainly the Great War has done something to us all. But it is also the beginning of a new phase of life, and the world we live in is so full of swift change and color and meaning that I can hardly keep from imagining the splendid and terrible possibilities of the time to come.[9]

America's promise had been an ever better future; the Progressive-era reformers had taught that a better future could be had only by sound planning and self-construction.[10]

The postwar years in America were characterized by an unsettling internal tension between moral disillusionment—a disappointed faith in the rising goodness of civilized humanity and people's ability to control their future—and the headiness of stepping now into the spotlight of world power. "The world broke in two in 1922 or thereabouts,"[11] wrote Great Plains novelist Willa Cather, lamenting the loss of the more ordered world of the prewar era. Henry James was even more somber: "The plunge of civilization into this abyss of blood and horror," he wrote,

> so gives away the whole long age during which we have supposed the world to be, with whatever abatement, gradually bettering, that to have to take it all now for what the treacherous years were really making for and *meaning* is too tragic for any words . . . [the war] was an unspeakable giveaway of the whole fool's paradise of our past.[12]

A far different view was offered by Henry Ford, who, not surprisingly, foresaw a bright industrial future. Machinery was "binding the world together," he explained. Airplanes, radios, motion pictures "know no boundary." "These soon," Ford said, would "bring the world to a complete understanding. Thus may be visioned a United States of the World."[13]

Leopold's own vision for a modern world was broader than Ford's and more optimistic than James'. "Is it too much to hope," Leopold wrote, "that our future standard of civic values may even exclude quantity, obtained at the expense of quality, as not worthwhile? When this is accomplished shall we vindicate the truth that 'the virtue of a living democracy consists not in its ability to avoid mistakes, but in its ability to profit from them.'"[14] One mistake Leopold believed people had made was in thinking that economic progress and development spelled the inevitable "disappearance of wild life."[15] Wildlife, he believed, was "absolutely essential" to the highest development of civilization.[16] And civilized progress, he felt strongly, was no excuse for destruction of native animals and birds.[17] Gradually Leopold would merge this worry with his concerns about degraded farms and settlements. In the process he would forge a more comprehensive picture of how land functioned ecologically and deepen his understanding of the common cultural attitudes he saw at the root of the nation's land problems. Into the 1920s sagging wildlife populations would increasingly become a national worry and, like so many issues of the era, would prove to be fractious. In understanding and addressing this worry, Leopold within a decade would become the nation's leading expert.

PROGRESS FOR WILDLIFE

The plight of America's game species first gained visibility in the mid-nineteenth century. In 1857, seven years before he published his well-known *Man and Nature*, George Perkins Marsh expressed alarm that Vermont's fisheries were being ruined by unwise forest cutting, soil erosion, dams, and industrial pollution. His worry echoed that of concerned citizens who were pushing states to enact laws and create game and fish commissions.[18] A group of scientific birders established the American Ornithologists' Union, which formed its bird protection committee in 1884. In 1887, the year of Leopold's birth, Theodore Roosevelt and other hunters founded the

Boone and Crockett Club to conserve North America's big game animals and their habitats. A year earlier George Bird Grinnell had formed the first Audubon Society "to protect wild birds and their eggs," particularly from the plume trade and other collectors; in 1905 it expanded nationwide.

By the turn of the century the federal government also was getting involved in wildlife conservation. In the U.S. federal system individual states had jurisdiction over game and other wild animals. Migrating animals, however, ignored political boundaries, and there was little interstate cooperation on their behalf until 1900. In that year the federal Lacey Act gave the USDA Biological Survey jurisdiction over interstate commerce in game and fur animals and over the importation of wild animals from foreign countries. In 1913 the federal Migratory Bird Act cut off hunting seasons on most songbirds and shortened seasons on waterfowl migrating across state boundaries, in response to estimates that, in a mere half century, the wildfowl supply of the United States had dropped by more than 90 percent.[19] And in 1918 the Migratory Bird Treaty Act extended protection to birds that traveled regularly between the United States and Canada.

In 1918, as he began his employment with the Albuquerque Chamber of Commerce, Leopold sketched a broad view of wildlife conservation. He did so in an article that characterized as a fallacy the notion that progress of industrial civilization must inevitably eliminate wildlife. The nation had learned that extensive forests were compatible with, if not necessary to, the highest development of civilization, doing away with "[a] stump [as] our symbol of progress." Unfortunately, millions of people still assumed that "the abundance of game must bear an inverse ratio to degree of settlement." In Leopold's view this assumption was exerting "an incalculably mischievous influence against the progress of the movement for wild life conservation." "To let the people think," he explained, "that economic progress spells the disappearance of wild life, is to let them believe that wild life conservation is ultimately hopeless."[20]

Wildlife had been an interest of Leopold's since his youth in Burlington, Iowa. From his father, Carl, he learned woodsmanship and ethical sportsmanship while hunting waterfowl along both banks of

*Commercial hunters carry waterfowl to market, 1912. By the first decade of
the twentieth century, it was estimated that the country's waterfowl population
had dropped by more than 90 percent over the previous fifty years, in part because
of such hunting pressure. Leopold retained this photograph in his collection.*

the Mississippi River and game birds in choice upland spots. Leopold
thrilled at a well-placed shot to a duck or a quail. On family nature
outings he and his younger sister and brother learned about trees and
bushes, birds and swamp animals. Their father would open up a
decaying log to reveal the mice or large insects in it, point out signs of
mink occupation in an old tree snag, and identify the contents of a
raccoon's droppings to diagnose its dinner.[21]

Leopold caught on quickly. By the time he was fifteen his interest
in songbirds had gone beyond identification and description to the
experience of deep aesthetic pleasure. Although he was capable of the
boyish ambition of shooting a flock of crows, he was also intimately
aware of wildflowers and the dazzling colors of a Blackburnian
warbler. While a teenager attending The Lawrenceville School in
New Jersey and preparing to enter Yale University, Leopold spent
one March week observing the habits of the plain-looking phoebe.

He learned that the birds gathered in spring around foul-smelling skunk cabbage, one of the first blooming plants in the area. In perhaps his first ecological theory he guessed that phoebes congregated this way because skunk cabbage attracted the earliest emerging insects from surrounding wetlands, prey for the birds. He corroborated his theory by wading through springheads and bogs for several days.[22]

Sentiment for wildlife ran deep in Leopold and took a firm, practical hold. As a seventeen-year-old, in the spring of 1904, he expressed dismay about rampant waterfowl destruction in a letter he wrote home from Lawrenceville. Upon receiving family news of that season's ruthless hunts back in Iowa, he promptly offered comment:

> I am very sorry that the ducks are being slaughtered as usual, but of course could expect nothing else. When my turn comes to have something to say and do against it and other related matters, I am sure that nothing in my power will be lacking to the good cause.[23]

Leopold's formal assignment in 1915 to the new Forest Service fish and game work gave him opportunity to prove the sincerity of good intentions. He quickly prepared his *Fish and Game Handbook*, his first substantial work on game conservation. Like his *Watershed Handbook* a few years later, it was a first in the Forest Service. Leopold's work also took him on travels across New Mexico and Albuquerque, "stirring up enthusiasm for conservation." He helped to establish numerous local and state game protective associations under the nationwide umbrella of the American Game Protective Association (AGPA). He also served personally as secretary of both the Albuquerque GPA and the New Mexico GPA (NMGPA). Working with the NMGPA, Leopold helped push for better enforcement of existing game laws and encouraged the state to depoliticize the process of appointing game wardens. He also urged that game refuges be established in the national forests and supported the killing of wolves, falcons, and other predators that seemed to threaten game populations.

Leopold was fired up by his success with his *Fish and Game Handbook*, the GPA groups, and progress in game law enforcement. He was filled with zeal for the cause. Leopold related his passion in a submission to the Yale class alumni record for 1916:

We have about twenty million acres of Forest in this District, part of which is unfit for livestock, and on these waste lands I ultimately plan to raise enough game and fish to provide recreation for twenty thousand people and bring $25,000,000 a year into the country. This is an ambitious project but I know it can be done and I have got the public to where they are about ready to believe me. I am organizing game protective associations over both states [AZ and NM], securing the reintroduction of locally extinct species, stocking hundreds of waters with trout, fighting suits for violation of the game laws, giving illustrated lectures to the public, hammering on game protection through the newspapers, raising a fight on predatory animals, and have written a book outlining plans, ways, and means. While making good progress I think the job will last me the rest of my life.[24]

In a way, it would indeed.

In January 1917 Leopold received a personal note of congratulation from Teddy Roosevelt for his Albuquerque GPA game enforcement work,[25] and in July the Albuquerque GPA received the Gold Medal of the Permanent Wild Life Protection Fund, established by game protectionist William Temple Hornaday. In his "Address before the Albuquerque Rotary Club" on the occasion of the award, Leopold painted in vivid colors the grand aims of the wildlife cause and the practical role of the NMGPA:

We have hitched our wagon to a star, but we are using just ordinary axle grease to speed it on its stony way. Let me illustrate what I mean. The G. P. A. ideal is to "restore to every citizen his inalienable right to know and love the wild things of his native land." We conceive of these wild things as an integral part of our national environment, and are striving to protect, restore, and develop them not as so many pounds of meat, nor as so many live things to shoot at, but as a tremendous social asset, as a source of democratic and healthful recreation to the millions of today and the tens of millions tomorrow. . . . We go to the common man and say: "Here if you want to have anything left for your kid to shoot at, it's time to get busy."[26]

Leopold showed no discomfort in working specifically to promote game species, being an avid hunter himself and knowing that sportsmen were his prime audience. But he regularly slipped into his remarks incidental comments about wildlife generally, as in his

Albuquerque address, with its references to "the wild things of the land." Writing for professional foresters in 1918, Leopold took a broader view than most: "[G]ame management should always prescribe a mixed stand—that is, the perpetuation of every indigenous species."[27] He repeated this stance in a contribution to the bulletin of the Albuquerque GPA in which he described a growing rift between "game farmers" and "wild lifers."[28] Game farmers and wildlifers both were determined to tackle the problem of dwindling game. The game farmers, concerned mainly with producing something to shoot, proposed to do so using market devices—creating businesses in game propagation under artificially regulated conditions—and opposed more restrictive hunting laws. The wildlifers, by contrast, supported strict laws when game was scarce, shuddered at the thought of a wide-open game market, and sought to perpetuate at least "a sample of all wild life, game and non-game."[29] "[T]he Wild Lifer," explained Leopold, "regards the perpetuation of native species as an end in itself, equal if not greater in importance than the perpetuation of 'something to shoot.' It may be safely concluded that as to this point the Wild Lifer enjoys the advantage of an ethical as well as of a utilitarian objective."[30]

Leopold supported hunting as a democratic form of vigorous outdoor recreation, and he was dismayed by the mounting evidence that citizens were losing the chance to engage in it. Farm owners were increasingly posting their lands to keep off roaming hunters. Game conditions were so degraded in many places that winter feeding,

Leopold duck hunting in New Mexico, November 1920.

warden patrols, vermin control, and habitat maintenance were necessary to sustain populations and were costly. Inevitably, he feared, hunting privileges would be commercialized. Meanwhile, the number of hunters was on the rise: licensed hunters would increase nearly sixfold between 1911 and 1929.[31] In combination these trends put greater than ever pressure on managers of public lands, particularly foresters of national forests, to protect the public's interest in wild animals and free hunting.

VANISHING WILDLIFE

The person who helped stimulate Leopold's early work on wildlife was the man behind the 1917 Gold Medal awarded to the NMGPA — the fiery conservationist William T. Hornaday. His first conservation book appeared in 1889, before the National Audubon Society existed, the Lacey Act was written, or the USDA Forest Service was established. Anyone seriously involved in wildlife protection was bound to run into Hornaday's bold opinions and influence. Leopold listened to Hornaday respectfully and retained many of his ideas. Yet Hornaday's law-based, combative approaches would serve only as intermediate steps in Leopold's conservation philosophy. Soon he would head in his own, much different direction.

While on a speaking tour of the West, the sixty-one-year-old Hornaday visited Albuquerque and met Leopold, on October 13, 1915. The visit was perfectly timed for Leopold, who recently had received his fish and game assignment. Hornaday gave an impassioned speech to the sportsmen of the city, and they responded enthusiastically. Within a week, led by Leopold, they had formed the Albuquerque GPA. Before leaving town, Hornaday inscribed to Leopold a copy of his latest book, *Wild Life Conservation in Theory and Practice*, based on lectures he had delivered to the Yale forestry school, Leopold's alma mater.[32] "It is my desire to offer to the Yale Forest School," said Hornaday,

> a foundation on which may be erected a structure of useful knowledge pertaining to the extermination and preservation of the wild life of North America. . . . We hold that toward our remnant of wild life, every forest ranger, every teacher of forestry and every intelligent American in general, has a solemn duty which no conscientious man can evade.[33]

At least as provocative were ideas that Hornaday had expressed earlier in 1915 in an article titled "The Seamy Side of the Protection of Wild Game," published in the *New York Times*. Among the conditions that he felt needed "quick and radical treatment" Hornaday included "the deplorable conditions in the national forests," where many large game species were on the brink of extermination.[34] National forests encompassed many of the last remaining blocks of habitat suitable for large game species and should be turned into game reserves, Hornaday urged, with severe restrictions on hunting most wild creatures.[35] Foresters could see firsthand the shrinkage in populations; they were the people, Hornaday hoped, who might have the interest and sympathy to speak out on the matter—to "raise the flag of conservation higher than ever before."[36]

These conservation ideas, so engaging to Leopold and others, emerged out of Hornaday's own participation in the demise of wildlife. Hornaday had studied under renowned botanist Charles Bessey and then under taxidermist Henry Ward before going to work in Ward's biological specimen–collecting company. Soon he was traveling to India, Egypt, Ceylon, and Borneo, hunting and stuffing rare, disappearing animals to add to leading museum collections. It was back in the United States, in Montana, though, while on the last federally sponsored scientific bison hunt in 1886, that Hornaday was stirred to action in the wildlife cause. The bison slaughter that was taking place on the American plains hit him hard. It was possible, he realized, to hunt even a huge population of large mammals to near extinction.[37]

When the trip was over, Hornaday undertook an inquiry into the rapid decline of the great ungulate. The conclusions he came to would thereafter shape his views on conservation policies and issues.[38] Early bison hunting, Hornaday argued, had sometimes reduced herds significantly, but it had been necessary to feed hungry pioneers. By the 1830s, however, systematic slaughter was taking place and market hunting had become dominant.[39] The demise of a number of great American bison herds, Hornaday concluded, had what to his mind were disgraceful causes: increasing commercial greed, improved firearm power, and a lack of stringent hunting regulations. If these causes undercut the bison population, he theorized, perhaps they also accounted for other wildlife declines. Hornaday responded to the bison crisis by writing a book that became a best seller, *The Extermination of the American Bison*, and by founding in 1889 the National Zoo in Washington, D.C., where imperiled North American species could be protected and propagated. Hornaday gave comprehensive coverage of the American wildlife situation in his 1913 book, *Our Vanishing Wild Life.*[40] Leopold, then recuperating from nephritis at his parents' Iowa home, purchased a copy as a gift for his father as soon as it came out.[41] Two years later Leopold arranged to sell to local GPA members quantities of the volume—"the most convincing argument for game protection ever written," he pronounced.[42] At the moment, Hornaday loomed big in Leopold's understanding.

Our Vanishing Wild Life outlined for the common man the lay of the wildlife conservation battlefield and Hornaday's strategy for protection. "We are weary of witnessing the greed, selfishness and cruelty of 'civilized man' toward the wild creatures of the earth,"[43] Hornaday wrote in his preface. "It is time for a sweeping Reformation." Chapter 1 opened with an account of wildlife's former abundance in America. "Nature gave to each square mile and to each acre," Hornaday claimed, "a generous quota of wild creatures, according to its ability to maintain living things."[44]

Hornaday had trouble attaching exact numbers to this abundance and thus to the extent of loss, however. Board feet of timber were easier to calculate than numbers and kinds of wild animals, and few sound animal censuses had been conducted. Accounts of wild animals that had been present before European settlers pushed through with axes, plows, and cows were recorded not in pounds of animal flesh but as descriptive testimonials written by naturalists, explorers and early pioneers such as James Audubon and Lewis and Clark. The Norwegian O. E. Rölvaag was one pioneer who recounted his personal experiences of the late 1870s frontier in his novel *Giants in the Earth.*[45] The story was told through the eyes of fictional character Per Hansa, who with his family and earthly possessions had moved west from Minnesota to the Dakota territory:

One Sunday evening the boys had come home wild with excitement. They had made a long trip westward on the prairie to some big swamps which lay out there, with tall grass growing from them, and long stretches of open water in between. They told of thousands upon thousands of ducks, so tame that you could almost take them in your hand.[46]

Just as much as Hornaday, Leopold was intrigued by early accounts of wildlife. He compiled notes on them from his readings, particularly on game in the Southwest.[47] From various works— James Pattie's personal narrative of 1824; S. W. Cozzens' *The Marvellous Country* (1876); *The Daring Adventures of Kit Carson and Frémont* (1887)—Leopold retrieved data on the locations, numbers, ranges, and types of wild animals found in the lands of District 3. The Tularosa abounded in trout, Leopold recorded; wild turkey was eaten at Tubac, Arizona; a new kind of wild oxen was observed four leagues east of the Indian pueblo Acoina; grizzlies, mountain sheep, beavers, antelopes and elk, deer, prairie dogs, wild horses, wolves, jaguars, panthers, white bears, wild geese—all numbered among the inhabitants of the canyons and coves, the rivers and valleys, and the mountain slopes and ravines of the Southwest. The first thing Spanish conquistador Francisco Coronado had "mentioned in his diary when he crossed the present border" of New Mexico, wrote Leopold, was "'great herds of wild sheep, with horns the girth of a man's thigh.' . . . Today [in 1917] there are less than 200 left in the entire State."[48] Leopold noted, too, that in Arizona by 1916, in addition to mountain sheep, three other big game species—the antelope, the javelina, and the Sonora deer—were hovering on the verge of extinction.[49] And by this year he had begun keeping records of game killed, preliminary game censuses, and data on rare species within and around the national forests of District 3.[50]

Like the fictional Luckett family portrayed in Conrad Richter's novel *The Trees*, eighteenth- and nineteenth-century pioneers found themselves moving westward to follow the game, which had disappeared along with the fallen trees: "It was the game that had fetched the Lucketts out of Pennsylvania" and across the Ohio River.[51] Hamlin Garland, a novelist of the nineteenth-century western pioneer, gave his own firsthand account in his autobiography, *A Son of the Middle Border*.[52] The "middle border" was Garland's culturally symbolic name for the Missouri River Valley—where late nineteenth-century homesteaders heading west met failed ranchers heading back east. Across the landscape Garland recalled sharp declines in prairie chickens and other wild animals from the 1880s onward, as cattle and the plow took over the plains. He remembered even earlier, too, the antlers and bones that he and others had found, lying bleached and bare, reminders of the elk and bison herds that once fed in the flowery savannas. The early 1870s, wrote Garland, were years of swift change on the Middle Border. Day by day the settlement thickened. Section by section the prairie was blackened by the plow. . . . Groves of Lombardy poplar and European larch replaced the tow-heads of aspen and hazel through which we had pursued the wolf and fox.[53]

Although his facts were fragmentary, Hornaday tried to catalogue and explain America's wildlife declines, such as those noted by Hamlin Garland. In the second chapter of *Our Vanishing Wild Life* Hornaday focused particularly on the North American birds that had gone extinct. This was a somewhat easier task, since birds were among the animals most noticed by humans, in their presence and their absence. His list was more than a "roll call of the dead species of American birds," including the great auk, Pallas cormorant, Labrador duck, and passenger pigeon—"all exterminated by civilized Man" between 1840 and 1910.[54] He wanted it to stand as a monument for all missing species and for the deep dishonor that had descended upon "civilized man . . . the shameless destroyer of Nature's gifts":[55]

To-day, the thing that stares me in the face every waking hour, like a grisly spectre with bloody fang and claw, is the *extermination of species*. To me, that is a horrible thing. It is wholesale murder, no less. It is capital crime, and a black disgrace to the races of civilized mankind.[56]

Hornaday went on to identify, in addition to the natural causes of extermination, the "guerrillas of destruction" and the "unseen foes" destroying species. In his lists of villains Hornaday left out no one. Sportsmen of various types came in for attack, as did market hunters, game breeders, ornithologist-collectors, businessmen, fashionable ladies, domestic cats, telegraph and telephone wires, Italians, southern Negroes, poor whites, wild animal predators ("vermin"), and introduced species that had become pests. In addition he issued a call for a new shooting ethic—for the sportsman to purposefully limit the rising power of his artillery to the defenses of his prey. And again he laid out plans for even stricter game laws and more game preserves. Hornaday concluded pragmatically by calling also for cash, "the duty of the hour" — "to pay workers [in the wildlife conservation cause]; to publish things to arouse the American people; to sting sportsmen into action; to hire wardens; to prosecute game-hogs and buy refuges for wild life."[57]

Leopold's *Game and Fish Handbook*, published by the Forest Service in 1915 as a supplement to the regular Service manual, showed the early influence of *Our Vanishing Wild Life*. The *Handbook* ranged widely, covering the values of game and fish resources, state and national game laws, Service regulations and instructions, refuge policies, fish planting, censusing, maps, and the natural history of game, with a final section titled "Six Rules for Sportsmen in the National Forests." In his introductory comments on the "biological value" of wild animals, Leopold directly echoed Hornaday's words and his combative tone:

> North America, in its natural state, possessed the richest fauna in the world. Its stock of game has been reduced 98%. Eleven species have been already exterminated, and twenty-five more are now candidates for oblivion. Nature was a million years, or more, in developing a species. There are occasions when a refusal to heed lessons of the past becomes a crime. If it is a crime to steal $25, what shall we say of the extermination of a valuable species? Man, with all his wisdom, has not evolved so much as a ground squirrel, a sparrow, or a clam.[58]

Leopold would remain firm in his belief in the goodness of life and in the wisdom of protecting it. On these points he supported Hornaday, and the two men remained friends. On the best means of protecting wildlife, though, they were parting ways. The reasons for the bison's decline did not apply to all declining species, Leopold was seeing. Other factors were at work, and they required different responses.

ZEAL WITHOUT KNOWLEDGE

Hornaday's zealous, protectionist view toward wildlife enjoyed favor for much of a generation. To save wildlife it relied upon captive propagation of game species, greater limits on hunting, predator control, and additional refuges, defined as areas off-limits to shooting. Once a sportsman himself,[59] Hornaday now believed that only greater cuts in game harvesting could succeed in conserving game — even though, he predicted grimly, they would not suffice to turn things around. By the 1920s conservationists of various sorts, Leopold included, were resisting Hornaday's approach and his pessimism.[60] The protectionist view simply overlooked too many causes of population decline. Roads, growing urban areas, new settlements, wetland drainage, and modernized agricultural cropping all were shrinking wildlife habitat. Major groups such as the National Audubon Society and the national AGPA, initially cooperative with Hornaday's views, were countering with the reality that wildlife species required suitable food and cover to thrive, on both public and private lands. In any case, many conservationists hoped for more than a "strung-out" game supply; many wanted game and nongame populations of wildlife to thrive. Was this possible, though, and what would it take to achieve it? No one really knew, and the required scientific facts were largely absent. The bottom line for both sides was that too few facts — such as wildlife demographic information comparing shot areas with unshot areas and ploughed, drained, dammed, grazed, or cutover lands with similar virgin ones — were available to back up either viewpoint. Such data would be difficult to come by, yet without them clashes of largely unsubstantiated opinion would continue to rule the day.

Differences of opinion among wildlife advocates showed up clearly over the roles of refuges, one of the major planks of the AGPA.[61] Hornaday's motive for refuges had been to protect game *from* hunters, thereby cutting harvesting rates. In Leopold's view refuges should protect areas to build up game *for* hunting.[62] Refuges should have hunting grounds surrounding them. "A refuge is not a refuge unless it is surrounded by hunting grounds," he would argue.[63] Leopold flatly rejected Hornaday's proposal to shut off entire national forests to hunting. Refuges should be much smaller, he proposed. These areas could be fenced in or posted and patrolled, with feed or extra cover provided and predators cleared out.[64] In due course rising game populations would overflow refuge boundaries, thereby supplying game to areas where hunting was legal.[65] Wildlife would benefit, and so would hunters. With hunting already disallowed in national parks, the national forest lands were virtually the last vast public areas in which hunters could freely roam.[66] To Leopold it was vital that they remain open.

By 1918 Leopold already was outlining a new, positive plan for game protection, going far beyond refuges. As it took shape through the 1920s and into the 1930s, his approach would entail collecting scientific facts, using those facts to make management decisions, and educating citizens. Most of all it would view wildlife as a distinct crop and try to promote that crop along with others. In an article published in the *Journal of Forestry*[67] Leopold identified three reasons for the "lack of an aggressive game policy on the National Forests."[68] There was the handicap of dual authority over national forest game—the federal government owned the land while the state owned the wild animals. There was the lack of strong local demand for better game administration. And there was the fear that "a real crop of game might interfere with both grazing and silviculture, as if grazing and silviculture might not also interfere with each other!"[69] None of the obstacles was insurmountable, he urged. The first two could change, and as far as the third—it seemed possible that timber, grazing, and game production policies could be "dovetailed," coordinated such that the achievement of all three could stand as the forest's "highest use."[70] The only true difficulty—indeed, the greatest single obstacle to progress in game conservation—was simply the "lack of constructive thought."[71] "The time has come," Leopold stressed,

> for *science* to take the floor, *prepared to cope with the situation*. . . . If it is true that the country is confronted with the eleventh hour necessity of developing the science of game management, what can the new science borrow from the science of forestry? In the opinion of the writer, a great deal.[72]

Leopold supported his proposal with an extended analogy between forest science and the science of game management. As he did so he catalogued the many facts needed to make sound judgments about regulating the numbers and distribution of particular species. The first step in scientific game management would be the game census, similar in purpose to the forest reconnaissance or the timber

estimate. The census would include the numbers of game (stand estimates), their distribution (type map), data on predator damage (fire
and insect damage) and on water, cover, and food (soils and site qualities), and information on past annual kills per unit area (old cut-
tings). Next in line was to safeguard breeding stock (growing stock)
by patrolling against killing and predator damage (timber-trespass
and fire damage). Leopold assumed here an unlimited demand for
hunting—a plausible assumption, given the rapidly rising numbers
of hunting licenses—and therefore perceived a need to regulate the
annual kill (annual cut), with the aim of achieving a sustained annual
kill (sustained annual yield). Accomplishing these various steps in
game management would be a difficult job. But foresters—who had
regular, intimate contact with the land and already had the needed
scientific training—were qualified to perform the work and very
much needed to do so.

The ultimate goal of game management would be to limit the
annual kill to protect the productive *capacity* of the wild breeding
stock, enabling it to thrive generation after generation. In achieving
that goal the key informational needs were to formulate "kill factors"[73] and then to determine the allowable annual kill. The kill
factor was an index of the productive capacity of a given wild population, that is, the ratio between the number of breeding animals on
the range and the number that hunters could kill without decreasing
the breeding stock (analogous to forestry yield tables).[74]

In 1922 Leopold began gathering for publication in book form his
by then copious notes on game and game management.[75] He titled
the manuscript "Southwestern Game Fields" and enlisted as coauthors two fellow conservationists—J. Stokley Ligon of the USDA
Biological Survey and R. Fred Pettit, an Albuquerque dentist.[76] As he
worked on this project, which continued through 1929 but never
came to publication, Leopold began comparing the new game management field not only to forestry but also to animal husbandry and
agriculture, while noting important points of contrast. He considered replacing the concept of highest use with the idea of dovetailing
a wide range of uses. Most of all, he discussed not only limiting kill
but also promoting conditions amicable to the increased productivity of game. This could be done, he asserted, by manipulating various

environmental factors, including cover, food and water, and number of predators. It was simple enough. Well-designed environments would produce more game. Yet there remained a knotty two-part question: what types of species should inhabit a range, and what was the proper population level of each?

As he proceeded with his wildlife work Leopold identified the vast gaps in the biological knowledge needed to carry out effectively even simple management tasks. Even basic data were missing, inconclusive, or unreliable. This ignorance posed the biggest obstacle to game management. Leopold's recurring refrain—"We don't know"—appearing in various forms, was above all a challenge to find out. Yet he understood that land-use decisions in wildlife management as well as in forestry still had to be made in the present. Human ignorance was not going to end soon. In the meantime, decision-making processes somehow had to take that into account.

Getting to What Should Be

In his draft of "Southwestern Game Fields" Leopold focused on what it took to make good land-use decisions involving game. To begin with, he urged, "[w]e must know something of the Southwest as an environment; what it was, what it is, and why."[77] It was, for Leopold, a familiar litany, for he had proposed a similar learning process in his *Watershed Handbook*. Begin by figuring out what the land used to be like; then compare that with the present; then identify what had changed and why.

What made his new project different and harder was that wild animals now were included in the ecological mix, along with soils, waters, livestock, trees, grasses, and humans. When all components were considered, the resulting pictures of the land would show even more variation over time and place. The complexity led Leopold to wonder whether this land was "too complex for its inhabitants to understand; maybe too complex for any competitive economic system to develop successfully. For the white man to live in real harmony with it seems to require either a degree of public regulation he would not tolerate or a degree of enlightenment he does not possess."[78]

Leopold applied his pattern of investigative questions to the

Southwest's deer: What had been historical conditions before new settlements had arisen? What were current conditions? And what were the possible causes behind any changes occurring over time? He was able to offer a few generalizations, but he quickly ran out of evidence.

> This riddle of [deer population] distribution is intensely interesting to science, and its solution is probably vastly important to game management. As we shall see later, there are other riddles in the distribution of quail, turkey, and blue grouse. All of them fling down the glove to research. All of them present the challenge: "Tell us *why!*" When we can tell why a species cleaves to this country and not to that, then we shall probably know what to do to make it thrive there.[79]

Reliable census numbers were simply not available. Without a clear idea even of "what is," it was not possible to figure out with any precision what had changed and why. To get at the "what was" for deer, Leopold and his coauthors combed through early written accounts. Where were deer in "the old days," and how many were there? Deer died and disappeared, unlike "certain gnarled and ancient Junipers," which were "chronographs of ecological revolution." So Leopold returned to the early accounts of Coronado and other explorers, searching for clues. Again he was able to draw only a few generalizations before his evidence ran out:

> By and large, the following is the best guess we can make about the old days: (1) Deer were not uniformly abundant; (2) the cream of deer country then is the cream now, only the present cream is thinner; (3) certain poorly watered country is possibly better now than it ever was; (4) certain southern brushfields are probably as good now as they ever were; (5) a very large amount of northern country is much poorer now than it was in the old days; (6) some low altitude country has been permanently lost to deer.[80]

Changes in deer numbers and distribution were linked to the landscape changes wrought by overgrazing, fire control, irrigation, and agriculture, it seemed. But the fundamental reality, once again, was that little was really known.[81] A few minor questions could be answered, but the authors were forced to "leave the rest for the future."[82]

If determining the past and present was hard, it was every bit as challenging for Leopold and his coauthors to determine what ought to be in the Southwest, in terms of desirable deer populations.[83] "Any and all attempts at game management," they asserted, "must begin with two questions: 'Is the area properly stocked? Is the stock productive?'"[84] Or, more simply, "What is proper stocking?"[85]

Game management was like farming, Leopold believed, in the sense that it involved cultivation of a crop. Yet there was a difference. "Farming, except in haymeadows and pastures, does not employ natural species."[86] Farming by its nature was a process of "artificialization." Not so in the case of hunting. "The good sense (or good taste) of the average American sportsman," Leopold asserted,

> revolts at the thought of an unlimited intensification of game culture. The prospect of an abundant game supply produced by intensive game farming is to him only slightly less dreary than the prospect of a gameless continent due to no culture at all.[87]

A better comparison, then, was between game stocking and forestry, which also dealt with crops of wild species in situ. The techniques of foresters therefore provided a useful place to start. A forester would consider a tract of timber "properly" or "normally" stocked if, in comparison with the most productive area of the same soil type, it contained approximately the same number, species, and sizes of trees. Normal stocking, that is, was equated with maximum stocking observed in any environmentally similar area. The same idea could apply to game, Leopold contended. Normal stocking of game could be defined as when "the consensus and the kill factor" of a game species was "the same as that of the most productive similar range."[88]

Leopold and his coauthors chose the Gila National Forest as the best range to serve as a yardstick for what was normal in the Southwest. An alternative, the Kaibab National Forest, north of the Grand Canyon—not hunted until recent years and mostly cleared of large predators—was already becoming renowned for *over*stocking, which was leading to reduced vegetative productivity and winter deer starvation. Overabundance was a relatively new concept in an age that worried about too little game, but would take on great significance. The Kaibab was also unsuitable because the needed vital statistics on deer populations did not exist. The same was true of the

Apache National Forest, the only other large area in the Southwest of "typically deer country."[89] The Gila, in contrast, had continuous statistics beginning with 1923, although even there no formal census data had been compiled. Without good census data the kill factor could not be established with any confidence. This gap in data forced the authors to find an alternative. As a substitute they suggested an index based on the total number of bucks killed per square mile per year.[90] Left open, too, was the composition of a "normal deer herd." What were normal ratios of bucks to does, of bearing to barren does, and of fawns to bearing does? This would be important information for management, but the authors did not yet have it.[91] The information gaps were increasing. Nonetheless, the authors continued their work, even if chiefly to identify the critical factors and to catalogue the unanswered questions.[92]

East Meets West

Leopold began writing "Southwestern Game Fields" while in the Southwest, as President Warren G. Harding preached his postwar politics of normalcy and as his business-oriented administration swindled the nation, profiteering and accepting bribes. Leopold would perform most of his work on the manuscript, however, in Wisconsin and would continue developing his game management ideas there.

Prompted by a specific request from William Greeley,[93] the Forest Service's chief, Leopold became assistant director of the Forest Products Laboratory in Madison. Its mission was to contribute to forest conservation through better use and preservation of wood. Greeley valued this work and sought to fill the open job with "one of the outstanding leaders of the country in forest research."[94] Although Leopold had no experience with forest products work, Greeley was impressed by his leadership and investigative abilities. The job offered was coequal in status with those of district foresters and thus one step up from Leopold's position as assistant district forester.[95] Plus, Greeley hinted that the current director would move on "sooner or later" and that Leopold might take over the directorship.[96] Leopold had never wanted to become a "[railroad] tie pickler,"[97] as he had put it in his youth. And he had serious reservations both about leaving the field and about severing himself and his family from the land and from his wife's family in the Southwest. Still, for reasons he never fully explained, he accepted the position in April and left for Wisconsin a few weeks later.

The Leopolds—now six in number—settled in a campus neighborhood in Madison. A nearby neighbor coincidentally was Wisconsin native Frederick Jackson Turner, historian of the American West. "Wisconsin, now much like parts of the State of New York," Turner had written in 1896,

> was at an earlier period like the State of Nebraska of to-day. . . .
> Thus the old Northwest [today's Ohio, Indiana, Illinois, Michigan, Wisconsin, and parts of Minnesota] is a region where the older frontier conditions survive in parts, and where the inherited ways of looking at things are largely to be traced to its frontier days. At the same time it is a region in many ways assimilated to the East. It understands both sections. It is not entirely content with the existing structure of economic society in the sections where wealth has accumulated and corporate organizations are powerful; but neither has it seemed to feel that its interests lie in supporting the programme of the prairies and the South. . . . It is still affected by the ideal of the self-made man, rather than by the ideal of industrial nationalism. It is more American, but less cosmopolitan than the seaboard. . . . Moreover, the old Northwest holds the balance of power, and is the battlefield on which these issues of American development are to be settled.[98]

The lives of "middle border" author Hamlin Garland and his family poetically symbolized Turner's theory about cultural change near the turn of the twentieth century, as would the Leopolds' a generation later—their respective stories varying in detail, of course, and with the times, but telling a classic American tale that was repeated and enlarged in the life of the nation as a whole. Garland was born in 1860 in Wisconsin and later succeeded as a writer in the East. In the meantime his father, full of pioneer spirit, carried his family step by step farther west, homesteading and moving on through the final decades of the nineteenth century. Garland's mother, longing for deeper roots and a place to stay, had endured many hardships. Her children also had suffered, and two were dead. Now, at the end of

Leopold's Madison, Wisconsin, home, at 2222 Van Hise Avenue.

their lives and with wheat crops failing, Garland decided to move his parents from the Dakota plains and himself from Boston together back to Wisconsin, seeking to win the struggle for stability. The West and the East would meet there, and stay:

> As May deepened I went on up to Wisconsin, full of my plan for a homestead, and the green and luscious slopes of the old valley gave me a new delight, a kind of proprietary delight. I began to think of it as home. It seemed not only a natural deed but a dutiful deed, this return to the land of my birth, it was the beginning of a more settled order of life.[99]

Leopold returned to the center of the country in 1924, as the nation itself, in the midst of tumultuous times, sought healing from fractures and a more unified sense of its self. Likewise, the wildlife conservation movement was increasingly in need of establishing common ground among its often warring members. A few months after the Leopolds' move to Wisconsin, the *New York Times* ran a short article titled "Quarrel among Game Conservationists." Hornaday, it reported, was criticizing gun manufacturers for promoting weaponry far too powerful for sport, while gun interests were chastising Hornaday for excessively blaming overhunting for game declines.[100] A few months later, in another article in the *Times*, George Bennett, author of "Our Game Protectors at War," portrayed the "paramount national question" of game protection as a battle between eastern and western states. Western states were revolting against "Roosevelt conservationist policy" on the ground that it locked up too much western land under public management. Bennett urged conservationists of the East and Midwest, who had been bickering over Hornaday's ideas, to join forces in preventing western interests from undoing "the conservation work of half a lifetime."[101]

More troubling for Leopold was the conservation movement's factiousness according to specific resource interests. For sportsmen and game breeders, it seemed, the vision of conservation success was game behind every bush; for the forester, success meant more trees than bushes; for the fisherman, perpetually heavy nets and a fish on every hook; for the nationalist, expanding prosperity and security; for the nature lover, songbirds and wildflowers; for the recreationist and prophet, wilderness; for the farmer, abundant, well-watered crops and everlasting soil fertility; for the home builder, resources for comfortable life at an affordable cost; for the capitalist, endlessly increasing wealth. What Leopold and a few others were beginning to see was how interconnected and interdependent all of these interests and ideals were. They were also seeing how futile it was to try to manage them separately, even with the best of intentions.

Leopold had already displayed an urge to find middle ground among competing land-use factions. Back in 1915 he suggested smoothing over antagonism between game protectors and the livestock industry by focusing on predator control, a problem of concern to both.[102] A few years later he suggested how and why settlements and wildlife might be mutually beneficial rather than mutually exclusive.[103] By 1918 he was regularly writing about the ways forestry and game conservation could fit together.[104] Even mining men and foresters in the Southwest, he argued, shared an interest in preventing forest fires,[105] as did foresters and game protectionists.[106]

Now Leopold wanted to broaden these areas of overlap. He wanted to get all resource users to stop thinking only about their particular resources and instead consider all of the land's possible products together. They should cease thinking about production in the "limited industrial sense" of single commodities—"boards, meat, dollars, or even tourists"[107]—and develop instead a more comprehensive definition that included "a certain ability to see that a landscape, a covey of grouse, or a saw-log all represent production and may be—nay, must be—all grown on the same forest land."[108] Morals and beauty should also enter into this new vision of land use. Conservation should include "a fundamental respect for living things and that fundamental aversion to unjustifiable killing and to unnecessary ugliness which in all lands and all times has been a necessary foundation for good morals and good taste."[109]

Leopold's hope was that land-use factions would think less about their individual pocketbooks and more about the common good. It was a high ideal, showing his own community-mindedness, his wide-ranging experiences in land use, and his Progressive faith in enlightened scientific management. Yet even as he offered his vision Leopold very likely knew that it fit poorly with the temper of the age. The old Progressive push for the common good and moral reform, so strong two decades earlier, had lost much of its strength. Harding had ushered in a new age, more comfortable with self-centered behavior and individualistic morals.

The political conflict between old and new was particularly clear in Wisconsin at the time the Leopolds arrived from the Southwest. A central element of the Progressive ideology had been the "Wisconsin idea" of expert administrative management in the public interest. No one was more associated with the idea than Wisconsin's governor turned senator, Robert M. "Fighting Bob" La Follette. Now, with the presidential race of 1924, La Follette was leading the charge to revive the populist spirit of Progressivism. From his central vantage point in Madison, Leopold could follow events closely.

Shunned by both political parties and running as an independent against Calvin Coolidge, who contended that "wealth is the chief end of man,"[110] La Follette reiterated Progressive themes that had carried the day two decades earlier—the paramount issue remained "to break the combined power of the private monopoly system over the political and economic life of the American people."[111] He criticized the ill effects of concentrated wealth and urged farmers and workers to organize and resist. Like many Americans, La Follette was incensed by the Teapot Dome scandal and other instances of fraud in the Harding administration, many having to do with the management of public lands. He called for greater public control over resources that were vital to the public welfare.

Leopold did not reveal his opinion of La Follette's campaign, but La Follette's record of effective public service was one Leopold supported.[112] Leopold, too, was calling for better management of public and private lands for the common good. La Follette's plea for all working people to unite was similar to Leopold's hope that resource users could rally behind a shared vision of good land use, well grounded in morality. And, like La Follette, Leopold kept his faith in skilled experts. La Follette's campaign, though, was out of touch with the times. Farm and labor interest groups were not inclined to work together toward shared goals; they would go it alone, using their separate organizations to work within the system for their own economic gain. Few showed interest in pushing for fundamental political or cultural change. La Follette's messages furthermore sounded radical to many audiences of the 1920s, and he was frequently attacked.[113] Under the slogan "Coolidge or Chaos," Republican leaders accused La Follette of communist sympathies, predicted an economic depression if La Follette won, and called for confidence in the nation's established economic leaders.

On election day La Follette received a record number of votes for a third-party candidate, but it still was only 16.5 percent of the total, to Coolidge's 54 percent and 28.8 percent for the Democratic candidate, Wall Street lawyer and southern native John W. Davis. For the moment, regulatory-style Progressivism had come to an end on the national political scene. Only months later, on June 18, 1925, La Follette died in Washington after a heart attack; the next day his casket rolled into Madison, where thousands awaited. La Follette's death came during a period of little more than a year that also saw the deaths of Eugene Debs, William Jennings Bryan, Samuel Gompers, and Woodrow Wilson, as if to punctuate the nation's transition to a new era. An aloof and dignified Coolidge was in charge, happy to give a free hand to the open market and its ethic of competition.

Leopold may have been dismayed by the fading away of old-style

Progressivism, but he had shown little interest in political philosophy. He was coming to believe that, in terms of conservation, public policies were best determined from the ground up. Public forestry was best when it had good effects on forests. Conditions of game populations themselves provided the measure of successful game conservation. This was a pragmatic view that potentially avoided many ideological conflicts, especially between public and private interests.[114] Yet it was also an ambitious view. Ideology aside, how could land managers produce good results overall without a clear vision of good land use? And what would it take to get groups that were interested only in specific resources to elevate their sights, merging their economic goals into a larger, coordinated-resource goal that considered a wider constellation of values?

FROM PUBLIC SERVANT TO PRIVATE CITIZEN

Between 1924 and 1928 Leopold continued to write articles on game management and its links to forestry, grazing, and agriculture. Progress on "Southwestern Game Fields," though, was slow. Moreover, his work at the Forest Products Laboratory was not bringing satisfaction. The director had not left and Leopold's expected promotion had not come through. Leopold had put to good use his skills in organizing and composed characteristically penetrating articles about wood products and timber conservation,[115] but his passions were plainly confined. In April 1928 Leopold announced his intent to leave.[116]

Once Leopold publicized his interest in new work, job opportunities arose. The contract that Leopold seized and signed came the next month from an industry trade group—the Sporting Arms and Ammunition Manufacturers' Institute (SAAMI). SAAMI hoped to resolve the conflict between Hornaday-type game protectionists, who continued to blame hunting for game declines, and those who believed that better land management could raise game numbers, including members of the National Association of Audubon Societies, members of the American Game Protective Association (AGPA), and the USDA Biological Survey. Without solid facts only opinions could be volleyed, and the volleys were hurting the conservation cause. In part to clear itself from the conflict, arms and ammunitions companies withdrew their direct financial support from the AGPA; SAAMI would cooperate above board with the AGPA instead.[117] And SAAMI would look into the issue by funding a nationwide survey of game conditions by an acknowledged expert. The game survey, it was hoped, would find the relevant facts and produce the basis for sound answers. Leopold was chosen for the job. On July 8, 1928, the *New York Times* took note of the appointment:

> Mr. Leopold's first private undertaking will be an assignment from the Sporting Arms and Ammunition Manufacturers' Institute to make a survey of American game resources. The purpose of the survey is to collect the experience and ideas of sportsmen and other conservation agencies as to the best ways and means for inducing the sustained production of game crops. By assembling the facts and making them available to sportsmen, the sponsors of the survey hope to stimulate the formulation of an effective program of game restoration.[118]

One of Leopold's first steps in preparing for the survey, before the national announcement of his appointment, was to pay a respectful visit to Hornaday. On June 7, 1928, he journeyed to see his old mentor, now seventy-three and confined to bed in Stamford, Connecticut. "I told him," wrote Leopold in his first game survey report,

> that I wanted him to know first hand about my intended connection with the Game Survey. . . . I told him that I was not asking for his advance approval of the findings of the Survey; I was asking that in the event anything came up which met with his disapproval that he give me a chance to come and see him before making his disapproval public.[119]

Hornaday was adamant that tighter restrictions on hunting offered the only solution to game shortages,[120] but he held respect for Leopold and agreed to his request.[121]

Meanwhile, sportsmen would be waiting for information, surrounded by mostly sobering news. Prairie chickens had disappeared almost entirely from large regions, including Dane County, Wisconsin, where Leopold lived.[122] Leopold's native Iowa was among the several states that had rising numbers of hunters along with year-long closings on bobwhite quail. And everywhere, it seemed, private landowners were putting up No Trespassing signs to ward off frustrated shooters seeking out the few remaining game animals.[123] Hunting was in danger of becoming a rare recreation unless something was done.

THE MEAT OF THE PROBLEM

By six months after the start of the survey Leopold had compiled data from five midwestern states,[124] and at the fifteenth annual American Game Conference in December 1928 he presented a report on his progress. In it Leopold summarized his appraisal of the state of upland game (e.g., partridges, prairie chickens, quail, grouse, pheasants, hares, squirrels) and of game research efforts. Some trends, he noted, were positive, particularly in methods of artificial propagation and in the training of skilled men. Less progress was being made, though, in understanding where and when to release or "plant" farmbred pheasants and other artificially raised species. Leopold wondered: Was there something fundamental about the land that might have led to various outcomes? And where would it be most prudent to plant game in the future?[125] Until more was known, propagation could prove wasteful.

Leopold's questions were good ones, and his survey work already was highly visible among game officials and conservationists. Although hardly as well known as Hornaday, Leopold already was widely recognized and respected in the game field. One mark of respect came with his appointment by the American Game Conference, at the December 1928 meeting, to head a small committee of professionals to draft a national game policy. The conference had no legal authority—it was convened by various conservation interests —and its policy would have no legal effect, but it was the leading annual forum for wildlife discussions. A conference-backed policy would carry weight. Leopold accepted the unpaid post and worked on the policy alongside his survey work.

At the close of the 1928 conference Leopold also met with his SAAMI sponsors. After discussing his progress they decided to scale back the national survey to concentrate on the north-central block of states: Ohio, Indiana, Michigan, Illinois, Wisconsin, Minnesota,

Iowa, and Missouri. A countrywide survey was simply not feasible. After covering this smaller region Leopold was to publish a full report.[126]

By the end of 1929 Leopold had visited all eight states and was beginning to envision a book that would draw together the information he had gathered on game populations, on ongoing research, and on land-use practices that affected game.[127] He looked into public sentiment toward game and its conservation and compiled data on game administration. And he paid attention to private landowners and their organized efforts, if any, to remedy local game problems. All of this was to appraise in each state the prospects for the "sustained production of game crops."[128] During the year, crisscrossing the region, he had collected a mountain of information from direct observation and from conservation officials, sportsmen, and naturalists. In his 1929 report presented at the sixteenth American Game Conference he summarized three findings "outstanding in size and significance" for policy making. These were his important conclusions, and he did not want them lost:

1. All game crops in the agricultural belt were shrinking, Leopold stated, and "clean farming" (which encouraged removal of tree rows, roadside mowing, wetland drainage, stream straightening, and planting of monocultures of machine-harvestable crops) was the principal culprit. Intensive farming methods were depriving game animals of food and cover. Overgrazing was a further contributing factor, as was the absence of sound forestry on private farm woodlots. These habitat declines were grave enough to offset even closed hunting seasons.[129]

2. Game population cycles—episodically waxing and waning numbers of animals—also played a role in game scarcity. And they were not at all well understood. In the forest belt several small game species could be hunted only one year in three because of low numbers. From year to year populations of species such as ruffed grouse and showshoe hares fluctuated violently and regularly. The reasons for such fluctuations were mysterious, thus far impossible to control. More research was needed.

3. Finally, conservation efforts were being wasted in planting non-
   native, or "exotic," species on lands not well suited to them.
   Wherever possible it was preferable to have native species,[130]
   but many intensively used landscapes could no longer support
   them. It was in such cases, Leopold thought, that sportsmen
   might turn reasonably to exotics (e.g., Hungarian partridges
   and pheasants as substitutes for quail, ruffed grouse, and prairie
   chickens), if their habits and requirements enabled them to
   thrive in the altered landscapes. But finding a match between
   exotic species and altered landscapes was not easy. Many plantings had failed and populations had quickly died out. Again,
   research was needed.

Less than two years from the start of the game survey Leopold
was able to point strongly to unfavorable environmental factors—
especially food, cover, predators, and disease,[131] in addition to hunting in some cases—as chief causes of declines in upland game. Particularly to blame were midwestern farmers and the agricultural
agents who advised them:

> Game coverts in the agricultural belt are shrinking by reason of clean
> farming and the absence of forestry practice in farm woodlots. . . .
> The physical manifestations of the covert shrinkage are plain to any-
> one who can look out of a train window: woodlots are grazed clean
> of reproduction and undergrowth, there is less and less cover on
> fencerows and drainage channels, hedges are uprooted to make
> room for metal fences, swamps are increasingly drained or burned to
> make new pasture or tillage, and in many regions corn is no longer
> left standing over winter, but shocked or gathered in fall. . . . All
> species are adversely affected, including quail, rabbits, prairie chick-
> ens, pheasants, Hungarian partridges, and squirrels. . . . The decline
> is taking place regardless of whether the game is overshot or not shot
> at all.[132]

The ill effects of these farm practices, Leopold concluded, were
great. All upland game species were affected. At least in the case of
midwestern game, then, Hornaday was wrong and his critics were
right. Overhunting alone was not to blame, and greater restrictions
on it would not go far enough to aid game populations. Research was

needed to make sense of game cycles and to ensure sensible uses of exotic species—items two and three on Leopold's list. But needed fundamentally was a change in rural land-use practices. Modern farming was bringing down game. Incorporating these conclusions and building on further survey work, Leopold's game policy committee was ready, by the time of the seventeenth American Game Conference in 1930, to present to conference members their draft of an "American Game Policy," in response to the problems they had identified.[133] "Something new must be done," Leopold stressed in a brief summary of it. "Radical changes" were in order; a more "positive program" was needed.[134] Needed, in other words, was a positive form of game management that would seek to make land so attractive for game that populations would thrive by virtue of their own reproductive powers rather than by continual artificial restocking. After discussion and haggling, mostly over the idea of landowner compensation for hunting privileges, the group's American Game Policy, authored by Leopold, was adopted by the conference as submitted.[135] It provided the country's first comprehensive national strategy, offering common ground for sportsmen, resource managers, policy makers, researchers, and, Leopold and others hoped, private landowners. It would remain the guiding statement of the wildlife management profession until the 1970s.[136]

At the core of the 1930 policy were recommendations for actions to aid game and other wildlife. Several of these were obvious and uncontroversial, but others were certainly not. The policy proposed to increase the public's ownership and management of high-quality game lands, both to protect wildlife and to support public hunting. On private lands it proposed to recognize the landowner as custodian of the game, even though wildlife under American law was owned by the public generally, with states acting as trustees. Private landowners simply had to get involved in promoting game or little could happen. Yet while the landowner would gain recognition as custodian of public game, responsibility for promoting wildlife in general would rest more widely: joint responsibility would lie with the nonshooting protectionist, the scientist, the sportsman, and the landowner. The policy called for a comprehensive conservation program based on a recognition of joint "responsibility for conservation of wild life as a whole,"[137] of which game restoration was only one part. Also, a greater number of well-trained professionals were plainly required, along with extensive wildlife research. Money had to be raised, both privately and, the policy proposed, by means of sporting-related taxes. In the end, though, it was the call to experiment that stood as a key recommendation. In some manner landowners, sportsmen, and the public needed to cooperate and find mutually beneficial ways to promote game and the environmental conditions that game required. Experiments could help find ways to do that.

Of all of the policy's recommendations, the most controversial was its call to give private landowners a major role in producing game crops. They would most likely do that only if they could benefit in some way. And that could mean public or private compensations, including the right to post their private lands against outside hunters and perhaps charge hunters for access. To some this seemed in contravention of the long-standing American ideal of free public hunting. The idea rubbed many people the wrong way, but Leopold and his committee came to view it as essential. Without incentives, there would likely be little to shoot. In addition the policy urged as big a program of free public shooting as had ever been discussed at an American game meeting.[138]

Leopold urged those who cared about wildlife to rise above the disputes of the past decade. It was time to quit arguing and start experimenting:

> We conservationists are the doctors of our game supply. We have many ideas as to what needs to be done, and these ideas quite naturally conflict. We are in danger of pounding the table about them, instead of going out on the land and giving them a trial. The only really new thing which this game policy suggests is that we quit arguing over abstract ideas, and instead go out and try them.[139]

Leopold was eager to take his own advice and would press on throughout the rest of his career actively doing so, as he continued to hone his ideas of how to go about it. By 1931 Leopold had published his comprehensive *Report on a Game Survey of the North Central States*,[140] which amply supported the 1930 American Game Policy. He also had published the first chapter of *Game Management*, which would become the standard text in the field, shaping it for decades.[141] *Game Management* would incorporate material from his now abandoned manuscript "Southwestern Game Fields" and draw extensively upon the results of his game survey. As the survey ended, this text became his primary project. He worked on it steadily, readying it for publication by the end of that year.[142] The book project also provided him with a sense of sure purpose amid the uncertainties of the early Depression. By mid-1931 SAAMI was looking to curtail the survey. Leopold's support from that source would soon end, and his future income would become uncertain.

A PRICELESS OPPORTUNITY

"The agricultural depression," Leopold had written optimistically the year after the stock market crash, "represents a priceless opportunity to plant the idea of game as a secondary farm crop, wholly free from any foreseeable overproduction."[143] More than half of the country's land area at the time was in private farm ownership. Thus, as Leopold stressed in the introduction to his 1931 survey report, "the crux of the game problem [was] on the farm."[144] Game supply was dwindling largely for the same fundamental reasons that other land crops were flooding the market, pressing prices down and kicking up dust across the plains: too much slick-and-clean farming, which pursued cash as its primary end. More intensive farming was a powerful economic trend. For the individual farmer it made sense to grow more and more; for the nation as a whole it did not. "The effects of devegetation," Leopold had written in his 1929 interim survey report,

> extend into fields of conservation even more important than game. A part of the erosion which is undermining the fertility of farm lands and choking rivers and harbors with silt is due to the same devegetation of gullies, creek banks, and drainage·channels which is undermining the game crop.[145]

The loss of game, in short, was not an isolated problem but part and parcel of a larger derangement of the landscape. At the root of it was a dominant economic approach to land that was degrading and destroying not only game but whole landscapes.[146] Leopold saw serious dangers in this approach, yet if landowners were chiefly interested in producing crops, then perhaps it made sense to talk about game that way. He could talk about game using crop production language. As a discrete land crop, however, game presented a particular economic challenge that distinguished it from other crops. "In the case of ordinary economic products," wrote Leopold in his 1930 conference report,

> the free play of economic forces automatically adjusts supply to demand. Game production, however, is not so simple. Irreplaceable species may be destroyed before these forces become operative. Moreover, game is not a primary crop, but a secondary by-product of farm and forest lands, obtainable only when the farming and forestry cropping methods are suitably modified in favor of the game. Economic forces must act through these primary land uses, rather than directly.[147]

Without question this economic conundrum had no simple or quick remedy. The main thing, Leopold would reiterate, was to start trying out any idea that offered potential. It was time to *do* something. And one of the first things that needed doing was to extend "positive recognition to the farmer," who with the right educational, social, regulatory, and compensatory incentives might just participate in building up game on his land.[148]

→- -←

Leopold was anxious to try out his own advice and experiment with new management ideas in the field—particularly on private lands. Even as he looked forward to field testing, though, he recognized the still vast gaps in his understanding of nature's ways. Two problems seemed to loom above all others in the attempt to come up with a management formula: What were the causes of the wide, inexplicable swings that took place in the numbers of many animal populations? And what about the role of predators and their effects on game production and on population numbers generally? Without these key pieces his management formula could only be tentative.

The predator problem soon would resolve itself with solid answers. The cycle problem, on the other hand, would not. In the meantime, Leopold found himself spending even more time thinking about another old matter—soil erosion—and about the centrality of soil fertility to the durability of the entire natural order. Soon

Leopold would enter the academy as one of the nation's first professors of game management. There he would forge important ties with professional scientists around the world, including leading ecologists. In his new position he would continue gathering facts about the land, and he would begin weaving together a mental picture of how its parts fit together into a whole.

Chapter 4

Interpreting Pharaoh's Dream

It is just as I said to Pharaoh: God has shown Pharaoh what he is about to do. Seven years of great abundance are coming throughout the land of Egypt, but seven years of famine will follow them. . . . So Pharaoh said to Joseph, "I hereby put you in charge of the whole land of Egypt."

Genesis 41: 28–29, 41

By 1931, two years after the stock market crash, millions of Americans were jobless, homeless, and destitute. "Hoovervilles" arose on the edges of large cities—crude shelters built of packing crates, cardboard, and old metal—while lines of hungry men waited for soup and bread. Families dug through garbage dumps in St. Louis and sought table scraps outside Chicago's restaurants. In New York City hundreds suffering from malnutrition or starvation were admitted to hospitals. Across the country thousands of people were on the move, migrating in quest of relief or for a simple sense of motion.[1]

THE LEAN AND THE FAT

During late July 1931, far from the breadlines of America's cities, Copley Amory of Boston hosted the Matamek Conference on Biological Cycles at his summer home in Labrador, Canada, three hundred miles east of Quebec, where the Matamek River flows into the Gulf of St. Lawrence. About thirty prominent scientists from various specialties, Aldo Leopold among them, assembled at Amory's personal expense to discuss population fluctuations and cycles of wild animals and to consider their possible links to human prosperity. For Leopold, this meeting connected ideas, raised questions, and stimulated his thinking in ways that would ripple through the rest of his career.

With the Depression then in its third year, social and economic instability provided the conference's subtext, if not its rationale. "What then, is our chief need?" Johan Hjort, a Norwegian fisheries scientist, rhetorically asked the assembled group. It was "[s]ecurity for the future,"[2] he responded. In a similar vein, Amory explained his goal for the conference in his welcoming speech:

> The vast resources of this Canadian sea have presented us with strange periods of rich abundance and disconcerting scarcity. Our gulf fishermen, I am sorry to say, are now tasting the bitterness of the lean years. No subject could find worthier place for discussion at this table. . . . Any one who has lived in Labrador during the last twenty-five years is painfully struck by the many evidences of vanishing wild life. . . . While one of the purposes of this Conference is the consideration of the fluctuations which are the cause of the present economic depression in this region so far as it is due to a diminished bounty from nature in fur-bearers, food game and fish, the primary goal of our investigations and discussions should, in my opinion, cover the wider range of world-wide biological conditions.[3]

Amory's hope was not merely for scientific progress. It was for practical help for the economy and for land conservation:

> It is . . . a justifiable hope that the information so gained may pave the way for a steady advance which in time may allow the prediction of the periods of fluctuation, thus aiding the economic life of peoples, the stabilizing of certain industries, and the conservation of our natural resources.[4]

The conference's scope was visibly displayed for all in a flowchart, prepared by Yale economic geographer Ellsworth Huntington, that diagrammed relationships among humans, wildlife, and general environmental factors.[5] Humans were in the picture, front and center, yet their well-being was attached to nature's parts and forces. A box at the top contained the words "Fluctuations in human prosperity in part dependant upon variations."[6] The box was connected by lines to fishes, nonmigratory birds, agriculture, fur, and forests, which in turn were connected to their various food supplies and other life factors, including ocean currents, temperature, plants, pests, and soil organisms. All of these, finally, were linked with disease and climate. Huntington's diagram displayed what the Matamek discussion was all about: making sense of these interconnections, influences, and factors so as to be able to predict and control fluctuations in animal numbers.

The conference was widely reported in the media and in scientific venues. Huntington's summary of highlights appeared in the September issue of *Science*,[7] while more popular outlets stressed the possible links between economic ups and downs and the ebbs and flows of animal populations. A *New York Times* report carried the title "Find Hidden Forces Run Animal Cycles . . . Strange Outside Influence Dominates Man, Beast and Plant—Great Laws Link All."[8] *American Weekly*'s article of November 1, replete with provocative photographs and artwork, was equally vivid: "Science Finds Everything Goes Up and Goes Down Once Every 10 Years: Birds, Beasts, Fishes, Insects and Even Trees and Plants Have Regular Cycles of Abundance and Hardship, Similar to Man's Prosperity and Panics; and Perhaps Sunspots Are to Blame for It All."[9] Accompanying the article was a portrayal of the biblical story of Joseph, interpreting Pharaoh's dream of the lean and fat cattle and the ears of wheat. The dream allowed Joseph to predict the seven prosperous years followed by the seven lean ones, and to plan accordingly.

If the *American Weekly*'s account was a sensationalized version of the sober proceeding, it exaggerated only modestly the hopes of the participants. To discover and substantiate any such "hidden forces" or "great laws"—perhaps the keys to human well-being—was a dream of many scientists present. To do that, according to Donald Roy Cameron, associate director of the Canadian Forest Service, the group had to stay focused:

In all these studies of cycles, if we are to get anything out of them and learn enough so we can predict the course of events which is our main objective, we must come down to the simplest fundamentals.[10]

A major theme of the conference was the possible influence of sunspots on animal populations. A number of animal cycles occurred simultaneously across continents, apparently synchronized. What fundamental force could exert an influence so broad? Sunspots flared up in cycles of approximately 11 years, with releases of ultraviolet light peaking once during each period. Sunspot effects were complicated, however, by the interaction of sunspot cycles with climate. Also occurring was a tidal cycle of 18.6 years, thought to be connected to the moon and to climate and storm cycles, with tree-ring evidence pointing to their biological effects. And that was just the beginning.

At the microscopic end of the size scale there was the disease theory of Robert Green, professor of bacteriology and immunology at the University of Minnesota.[11] Green was studying the disease tularemia, which he discovered in a great number of species— including ground squirrels, game birds, rabbits, foxes, coyotes, opossums, woodchucks, voles, sheep, cats, and humans. The disease was found in all parts of the United States and in Canada, Russia, and elsewhere. Because of its distribution and the number of infected species the disease was a candidate for "fundamental principle" status. Green's work suggested that tularemia corresponded in its prevalence to the approximately ten-year cycle of rabbit and grouse population numbers. He suspected that the disease might display a corresponding variation in virulence, killing more animals at its peak strength than at its lows.

Linking the cosmic to the microscopic, Ralph DeLury, of the Dominion Observatory of Ottawa and missionary for the sunspot theory,[12] commented, "Green has made out a strong case for what seems to be a very serious factor in cycles. At the same time, I think it is grand sunspot material. . . . This cycle of virulence also links up well with the sunspots."[13] In years of greater ultraviolet light, organisms were able to produce more vitamin D than in years of lesser light. Virulence of microorganisms could therefore be related to nutrition, which declined when clouds came out.

Not everyone waxed enthusiastic over such blanket theories to explain the many cycles. Archibald Huntsman, professor of marine biology at the University of Toronto, addressed an abrupt question to Green: "Does Dr. Green believe he could find a tularemic fish and explain the disappearance of the salmon as well as the rabbit?"[14] Perhaps not, Green suggested; the disease theory was best understood as describing one of several factors. Ecologist Charles Elton of Oxford University, founder and director of its Bureau of Animal Population,[15] called for greater attention to multifactor explanations:

> About seven years ago I started an idea; which I think many other people started in other countries—namely sunspots. Since then I have had the satisfaction of proving myself wrong. The average length of the [wildlife population] cycle is something less than ten years—(9.7), not 11.2 as in the sunspot cycle. You can not predict whether it will be 9 or 10 years. That suggests there may be more than one periodicity at work.[16]

Plainly, this was a tricky business. "We are forgetting how extremely complex these problems are," Huntington observed, midway through the conference:

> We have insects and trees affecting each other and the parasites affecting both the tree and the insect. All three may have different cycles. There are also temperature, rainfall and local conditions. . . . Put ten variables together and you will find how unreliable a theory may become. . . . We should not come to hasty conclusions.[17]

It was clearly critical not to settle upon false fundamentals. At the same time, all participants longed to find common ground. Two days into the conference Green challenged attendees to reach agreement: "I am therefore hoping that it will be possible for the Conference to outline some conclusions we can consider definite enough to carry back with us."[18] Aldo Leopold readily agreed:

> I would like to second Dr. Green's plea for a definite and concrete outcome of this Conference. It might be well to set forth not only the fields of work which need to be pushed for evidence to deal with this phenomenon of cycles but also the ways and means.
> The people with whom I am associated have started to finance research work to cover the ground where cycles impinge upon their interests. The ammunition industry in addition to providing

fellowships in agricultural colleges have set up a fellowship [that of Ralph T. King] to cooperate with Dr. Green in the University of Minnesota in studying [ruffed grouse] cycles.[19]

Leopold had been invited to the Matamek Conference to talk about his work on game bird cycles. His reports on his game survey had highlighted the need to study these cycles, and he had recently produced (with coauthor John Ball) two provocative articles on the subject.[20] Even so, Leopold had trouble getting leave to attend the conference from his employer, the Sporting Arms and Ammunition Manufacturers' Institute (SAAMI). On May 4, 1931, Leopold wrote to John Olin, his supervisor, seeking approval to be gone for two weeks. "I do not think we can afford to absent ourselves from this recognition of game research and of our part in it," Leopold coaxed. "This trip will of course constitute an interruption to the work on the game management text, but a very welcome one from my viewpoint, since continuous writing is more or less a self-destructive activity."[21]

Three days later, Olin responded:

[E]ven assuming as the result of the conference a clear definition of the facts which underly cycling performance can be ascertained, I should like to know what can be done about it after this information is developed. . . . I am asking you to tell me as frankly as you are able what commercial benefit will accrue to the Sporting Arms and Ammunition Manufacturers' Institute as a result of your attendance at the Labrador conference.[22]

Leopold's response was coy but ultimately convincing to his employer. "I appreciate your leaving the matter of the Matamek conference to my discretion," he wrote, at the same time outlining for him four practical values that research on cycles might have for SAAMI's sponsors: (1) If the cycle were determined to be hitched to some permanent cause, such as sunspots, it would enable prediction and aid game administration and ammunition production, even if the cause were not controllable. (2) Whatever the ultimate cause, it must work through some environmental factor, which might be subject to control. (3) Knowledge was itself a good thing and might become useful in unforeseen ways. (4) It was a good strategy to keep game research in the scientific picture and to demonstrate to the scientific community the goodwill of SAAMI's supporters.[23]

After he returned home, Leopold submitted an upbeat report. "I am extremely glad that I took a chance and went to the conference, because it was the most significant thing of its kind which I have ever attended."[24]

These presentations piled up overwhelming evidence of the fact that grouse, rabbits, fur bearers, and fish all share the same 10-year cycle, that the cycle fits the variations in solar radiation, and that the probable mechanism whereby solar radiation affects wild life is the varying virulence of bacterial diseases as recently discovered by Green.[25] If further work substantiated present beliefs about cycle causations, Leopold went on, then the grouse cycle on managed areas perhaps could be controlled by "the wholesale liberation of ticks carrying low-virulence bacteria"[26]—a possibility, he hoped, that Olin would find appealing.

Leopold himself would continue his own fact-finding attack on the mystery of game cycles. In an August 6, 1934, letter to Amory, Leopold noted King's recent theory that solar radiation caused vitamin fluctuations in foods, which in turn interacted with the size of grouse clutches and population density.[27] Two months later he wrote to Amory that a fellowship student of his, Leonard Wing, had discovered that the migration dates of many birds also fluctuated with the solar cycle.[28] In March 1943 Leopold reported to Ellsworth Huntington that he and Paul Errington had completed a paper[29] dealing with animal cycles and on-the-ground environmental factors.

Even with these and other factual findings, however, game cycle research overall produced inconclusive answers year after year. As the problem continued to resist research it became for Leopold more than merely a topic of inquiry. Cycles symbolized nature's complexity and humanity's ignorance of it. Even so, Leopold's curiosity led him to continue to pursue various leads as to cycle mechanisms, from sunspots to disease; to soil fertility; to ranges on the edges of optimum soils, climate, or habitat; to violent human impacts; and to combinations of these. In a 1945 paper Leopold proposed that pheasant declines were very likely due to "the cycle," only to add that "no one knows what the cycle is, so that isn't saying much."[30]

PICKING UP THE MARCH

In March 1932 Leopold's funding from SAAMI came to an end. He worked out a deal for individual states temporarily to share expenses for the survey, but by June his survey work was over.[31] That January Leopold had signed a book contract with Charles Scribner's Sons for publication of his book *Game Management*. For the rest of the year he worked on it, in consultation with many of the nation's best wildlife experts. He also hung out his shingle as a "consulting forester" and gained intermittent work with the Wisconsin Conservation Commission setting up game management demonstration projects. Intent on keeping his family in Madison with his two eldest boys enrolled at the university, Leopold largely provided for them from a $7,000 inheritance from his father, returns on stock from his father's successful Leopold Desk Company, and modest personal savings.[32]

The months between Franklin D. Roosevelt's election and his inauguration as the thirty-second U.S. president in March, 1933 were the toughest part of the Depression for most in the nation. "That historically cruel winter of 1932–33," penned one writer, "chilled so many of us like a world's end. . . . It was like a raw wind; the very houses we lived in seemed to be shrinking, hopeless of real comfort."[33] Roosevelt intended to turn matters around. "I pledge you, I pledge myself," Roosevelt had declared in his presidential nomination speech at the Democratic National Convention, "to a new deal for the American people."[34] The day after the speech an alert cartoonist plucked out the words "new deal" and made them the banner of the Roosevelt administration.

Roosevelt's New Deal vision included ideas about land conservation. In his nomination speech he proposed a massive effort to reforest cutover and marginally useful lands. The work would provide relief while helping the country to resume its "interrupted march along the path of real progress":

> We know that a very hopeful and immediate means of relief, both for the unemployed and for agriculture, will come from a wide plan of the converting of many millions of acres of marginal and unused land into timberland through reforestation. There are tens of millions of acres east of the Mississippi River alone in abandoned farms,

in cut-over land, now growing up in worthless brush. Why, every European nation has a definite land policy, and has had one for generations. We have none. Having none, we face a future of soil erosion and timber famine. It is clear that economic foresight and immediate employment march hand in hand in the call for reforestation of these vast areas.[35]

Roosevelt had experienced success in creating jobs for the unemployed by organizing public work on reforestation and other conservation-related projects as governor of New York. Now he would extend a similar program to the nation. By the end of March Congress had authorized the Civilian Conservation Corps (CCC). Its first inductee was enrolled in April 1933, and by September 1935 more than five hundred thousand unemployed men were working in

Leopold returned to the Southwest for a few months in 1933 to oversee government erosion control work, including the construction of check dams — structures built to plug gullies and prevent their spread. In this photograph, taken in New Mexico a few years later, a gully is showing signs of healing, supporting a good growth of grass.

CCC camps across the country. Their tasks were diverse: a new "tree army" would plant trees and battle soil erosion; stock fish; build wildlife shelters, fire trails, and roads; wage war against destructive insect pests; and string telephone lines. Still without consistent work, Leopold was invited back to his old southwestern haunts in New Mexico and Arizona to help in this effort. He returned there at the end of April and stayed through the summer, overseeing CCC erosion-control work and revising the *Watershed Handbook*, already ten years old.[36]

In April 1933, too, *Game Management* finally rolled off the presses. "My whole venture into this field," Leopold wrote to William Hornaday, "dates from your visit to Albuquerque in 1915 and subsequent encouragement to stay in it."[37] On April 28 the *New York Times* announced the publication:

> Aldo Leopold, consulting forester, wrote "Game Management," decorated with drawings by Allan Brooks and published by the Scribner's today. The book describes "the art of cropping land for game and points the way toward its integration for other land uses."[38]

Meanwhile, behind-the-scenes discussions had been going on regarding Leopold's future. Since 1927 Harry L. Russell, dean of the University of Wisconsin's College of Agriculture, had wanted to establish a game management program under Leopold's guidance. In June 1933 the Wisconsin Alumni Foundation, directed by Russell, agreed to fund the program. The university hired Leopold on a five-year trial basis, ending his trauma of unemployment and making him one of the nation's first professors of game management. The appointment, too, drew a brief notice in the *New York Times*.[39] And William Hornaday wrote to Leopold saluting "the University of Wisconsin, for its foresight and enterprise" and congratulating "the Wisconsin Alumni Foundation on its correct initiative" in choosing Leopold for the job. He also complimented Leopold on his talents, which he knew would help in the "struggle to save American game and sport from finally going over the precipice, A. D. 1940."[40]

One of the painful anomalies of the early 1930s was the juxtaposition of farm surpluses and widespread hunger. In the West ranchers who could neither feed nor market their sheep because of low prices

Aldo Leopold, professor of game management, circa 1935.

slit their animals' throats and hurled them into canyons.[41] In the Great Plains states, the people in "breadlines marched under grain elevators heaped high with wheat."[42] Back in 1909 the Reclamation Service had advertised new lands by showing glossy photographs of heavy-laden grapevines, fat cattle, and luxurious orange groves. One observer in 1932 offered a dismal contrast: "Beginning in the Carolinas and extending clear into New Mexico are fields of un-picked cotton that tell a mute story of more cotton than could be sold for enough, even, to pay the cost of picking. Vineyards with grapes still unpicked, orchards of olive trees hanging full of rotting fruits and oranges being sold at less than the cost of production."[43] The irony was savage — of want amid plenty, of poor people starving in a rich, overproductive nation.

The persistence of the Depression raised fundamental questions, some reaching to the efficacy and goodness of capitalism itself. The Roosevelt administration's "Brain Trust" — an advisory group of college professors — believed that the days of "small proprietors, corner grocers, and smithies under spreading Chestnut trees" were gone forever.[44] Needed now, they claimed, were structural reforms to stabilize the economy. Effective reforms required business-government cooperation, yet what that meant was not entirely clear — widespread national planning or perhaps much less. Maybe what was needed was not radical change but only a wiser combination of elements to keep various powers in check and stabilize the country. No one knew. The word that appeared most frequently in New Deal writings was "balance."[45]

Leopold's own contribution to the search for balance was game management. In 1931 he proposed a new definition of the activity: "It consists in keeping the range 'in balance,' and limiting the kill on each farm to its productive capacity. . . . 'Balancing' our range means providing on each unit of land what our various species need to get through that season in a thrifty condition."[46] Game management's job, thought Leopold, would be to balance theory and practice, science and use, biology and sport, conservation and utilization. It was in the field and on the ground where everything came together. Wrote Leopold, "There is no stabilizer like a piece of land."[47]

PULLING LEVERS

Observers of nature had long recognized that landscapes were constantly in flux. At the same time one could walk in the woods or fields, day after day, and recognize the natural surroundings—there was a sense that things were the same. Nature, that is, kept its character in a readily identifiable way even while alive and ever changing. Nineteenth-century naturalist John Burroughs offered an explanation of the phenomenon:

Nature does not balance her books in a day or in ten thousand days, but some sort of balance is kept in the course of the ages, else life would not be here. Disruption and decay bring about their opposites. Conflicting forces get adjusted and peace reigns. If all forces found the equilibrium to which they tend, we should have a dead world—a dead level of lifeless forces. But the play of forces is so complex, the factors that enter into our weather system even, are so many and so subtle and far-reaching, that we experience but little monotony. There is a perpetual see-saw everywhere, and this means life and motion.[48]

What was new in the modern era was the intensity with which humanity was disrupting this natural dynamism and now was trying to predict and control it for more reliable human benefit. To do so, humans would need to understand the mechanisms of the land so that they would know, as Leopold put it, "which levers to pull."[49]

Also changing with the times were the perceptions people were forming of their own powers. Shaken by recent disasters and emboldened by new inventions and grand engineering feats, many people rallied with hope that future tragedies indeed might be prevented by humanity's collective ability to figure out what nature's levers were and how to pull them. It was hopeful confidence of this sort—as people peered into the vast storehouse of knowledge made accessible by turning the key of science—that had encouraged the development of professional forestry, the gathering of the Matamek Conference on Biological Cycles, and Leopold's new ideas of game management. Fresh from Labrador, Leopold was impressed more than ever with the great complexities of nature, yet he also shared this hopeful zeal:

The mechanisms of nature, like any other engine, can be driven, if we know which levers to pull. Only science can tell us which levers and why. . . . Scientists are beginning to understand their responsibilities to wild life conservation, and . . . conservationists are beginning to realize that their further progress in one field after another is being blocked by lack of knowledge.[50]

The scientists assembled at the Matamek Conference had focused on fluctuations that took cyclic form.[51] Cycles of animal abundance, however, hardly could be understood unless scientists also could make sense of wildlife populations that were more numerically stable. What mechanisms kept them that way? This was similar to the question Thomas Malthus had so influentially considered more than a century earlier—with the welfare of human societies in mind.[52] In the late 1920s Leopold and his coauthors of "Southwestern Game Fields," their never published book manuscript, tried to get at the larger principles and mechanisms that brought relative stability to most animal populations.[53] Even earlier, in his *Watershed Handbook*, Leopold had explored stability in the context of soil, defining it as the balance of positive and negative erosion forces.[54] A similar balance, he sensed, was at work in the case of animals. Populations that remained fairly constant in number over a given time period in a given place appeared to do so because the various "disintegrating forces" or "decimating factors"[55] influencing game populations—such as predators, hunters, and disease—and the various limiting "welfare factors"— such as food, cover, and water—were all at work, thwarting the inherent tendency of any given population to increase geometrically in number.[56] It was important, Leopold sensed, for people to appreciate the larger scheme of these contending forces and not get lost in the details. "This survey of the breeding habits of deer in relation to the mechanism of productivity is necessarily intricate," Leopold wrote in one draft of "Southwestern Game Fields"; however,

> [t]he reader should also fix in his mind that in any stable [deer] herd the forces making for unimpeded increase and the factors of environment are in equilibrium, and that the net effects of the particular combination of variables operating on a given herd may be expressed in the form of ratios or constants. These serve as standards

for comparison with other herds, and for setting up in each region criteria of normal or satisfactory productivity.[57]

In the case of a deer population, for example, stability meant the tendency of its numbers to vary within a given range. That stability was brought about in nature by the dynamic and "collective effect of all the factors on deer populations." It was evident that the downward-pulling forces were powerful because they were able "almost always" to "pull the soaring curve of unimpeded increase down to the horizontal of stable population."[58] Upward and downward forces were largely offset. "We may conceive . . . of a population," Leopold suggested in his 1933 *Game Management*, "as a flexible curved steel spring which, by its inherent force of natural increase, is constantly striving (so to speak) to bend upward toward the theoretical maximum, but which the various factors are at the same time constantly striving to pull down."[59] In his textbook Leopold explored these countervailing forces in detail, considered their practical implications, and expanded his ideas to multiple populations interacting as communities,[60] explaining that

[t]he so-called "balance of nature" is simply a name for the assumed tendency of the population curves of various species in an undisturbed plant and animal community to keep each other horizontal. The growth of biological knowledge trends strongly to show that while population curves may oscillate about a horizontal median, a single curve seldom or never stays horizontal from year to year even in virgin terrain. Fluctuation in numbers is nearly universal.

A state of undisturbed nature is, of course, no longer found in countries facing the necessity of game management; civilization has upset every factor of productivity for better or for worse. Game management proposes to substitute a new and objective equilibrium for any natural one which civilization may have destroyed.[61]

The concept of opposing natural forces affecting a population—a natural tendency toward reproductive increase versus limiting factors—was central to the new science of game management. If a game manager could figure out which factor or factors were pulling down the curve, he might release the population's growth potential by softening or removing the limiting factor or factors—by

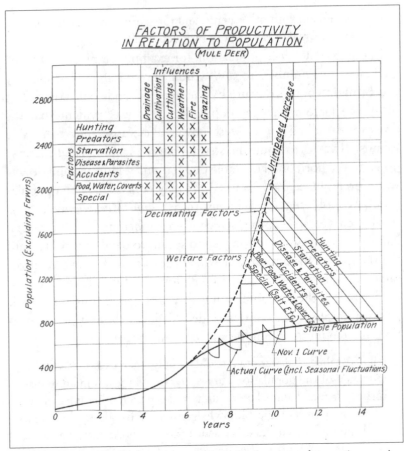

Controlling the tension between a population's inherent tendency to increase in number (creating the theoretical upward curve) and limiting environmental factors—for example, hunting, predators, disease, food, cover—that prevent the population's continual increase (resulting in the horizontal curve) was at the heart of Leopold's early game management technique. This graph appeared in a draft of "Southwestern Game Fields" and, later, in Leopold's text Game Management.

restricting hunting, for instance, removing predators, preventing diseases, or adding more food, water, or cover to the environment. He would know, in other words, which levers to pull to increase a game population. The professional forester, Leopold reminded his readers, had never been content to limit his harvest to the productivity of unaided nature. His aim instead was to "make nature outdo herself in productivity."[62] This, wrote Leopold, is also "the very heart of game management."[63] A scientifically trained, observant game manager could do much more than merely string out the dwindling game supply, as protectionists envisioned. The hope was that he could build up game populations by adjusting the operative factors in nature.

THINKING ABOUT POPULATIONS

As Leopold sought to make sense of game populations he drew extensively upon the work of field ecologists. Particularly important was the research that Herbert Stoddard based on a comprehensive, multiyear study of bobwhite quail in a region around Thomasville, Georgia, and nearby Tallahassee, Florida. The first real study of management of a game population, Stoddard's project was sponsored by a group of "public-spirited sportsmen"[64] who were concerned about declines in quail numbers, in cooperation with the USDA Biological Survey. Out of it eventually came a lengthy, elegant illustrated book about the bird.[65]

Stoddard's investigation, which was conducted between March 1924 and June 1929, covered the types and qualities of the quail's southeastern territory, its life history, its voice, its food habits and its movements, its patterns of mortality and disease, its relation to agricultural activities, preserve development and management,[66] control of natural enemies, methods and techniques for quail study and for artificial propagation, and popular attitudes and beliefs about the bird. No stone was unturned. It was a model field study, and it set a high standard for Leopold's and others' research.[67] Its influence on Leopold was great.

Stoddard's work supported Leopold's conclusions that changing land-use practices were the key to control of game bird populations. Although bobwhites could be depleted by unregulated shooting even in the most favorable environment, they could disappear just as surely under the pressure of adverse agricultural tendencies that exhausted soil fertility[68] and destroyed bird habitat, without the firing of a shot:

> The well-founded belief that agriculture favors the quail is true only of agriculture of a primitive type. . . . [N]ot only are modern agricultural practices seriously curtailing the food supply of quail, but

the recent tendency to clean up thickets, hedges, and fence rows serves both to expose the birds to attack of natural enemies and to isolate coveys in widely separated "islands" of thicket cover, or even to extirpate the birds from great areas.[69]

Animals of all kinds were hard to count, and quail were no exception. Stoddard's chapter on quail populations[70] explored techniques for census taking. Unlike grouse, quail were not visibly cyclic in population size: their fluctuations seldom exceeded 50 percent. Quail populations also seemed to have a "saturation point," a maximum number of birds per unit of area. In many places the saturation point seemed to hover around one bird per acre. Using a concept Leopold also had applied to animal studies earlier in the 1920s (i.e. the "kill factor"), Stoddard explored the "annual yield" of the quail, the number of birds that could be killed without depleting the population, which supplied a measure of the land's productivity. Stoddard's conclusion: it was safe in some places to shoot one-fourth to one-half of the quail crop annually. Stoddard acknowledged that different soils and regions varied in their "carrying capacity"—the ability of a given piece of land to support a population without degradation.[71] Among Stoddard's provocative conclusions was that under natural conditions bobwhite predators did not lower population numbers:

> Where cover and food supply are adequate, great reproductive powers usually enable the bobwhites to maintain themselves against their natural enemies. When man enters into the equation, however, [and hunts the birds and clears their habitat] . . . it soon becomes evident that control of enemies is required to offset this unnatural drain.[72]

This suggestive conclusion, together with Stoddard's observation that good cover could protect quail from enemies, would take on vital importance in the work of Paul Errington, one of the first SAAMI fellows. Under Leopold's oversight, Errington began work in July 1929 on the restoration of quail coverts in the dairy region of southern Wisconsin, where, as in Georgia, modern agricultural practices were reducing the birds' habitat. He combined this work with a PhD program at the University of Wisconsin, submitting his thesis on the northern bobwhite[73] in May 1932, a year before Leopold formally joined the faculty.[74] Errington's research was more narrowly focused than Stoddard's. Errington had set two specific tasks for his work: to determine winter quail mortality (quail in Wisconsin were on the extreme edges of their range) and to evaluate predators as a factor in the quail environment.[75]

As Errington set out to determine the causes of cold weather bobwhite losses he paid particular attention to the influences of food, cover, and predators on mortality. Quail populations with sufficient food and cover, he found, typically survived the winter, the most trying time for quail, without serious loss. If quail were well fed, in strong "physical and psychic" condition, and with ample cover, they could survive the cold and escape their enemies. "The best way to protect bobwhite from predators," he concluded from this,

> is to provide cover in which the birds can seek their own safety and to provide food which enables them to reach that cover when they have to. . . . Much can be accomplished in quail management merely by manipulation of the food factor.[76]

In general, whatever the season, when food and cover were readily available, predators had little discernible effect on the bird's numbers over time:

> Where native predator and strong native prey species cohabit a given area, the adjustment between them seems sufficiently close yet sufficiently elastic that the prey species—given proper living conditions otherwise—are capable of maintaining themselves satisfactorily despite the predator pressure. . . . It is quite unlikely, in short, that the ordinary depredations of native predators upon native prey . . . effect more than the removal of the surplus from the species preyed upon.[77]

Predators might also cull unfit animals, helping quail populations to stay healthy. More generally they could help keep populations in check. Quail did not maintain a steady condition in any sense; population numbers were always subject to fluctuations. But "the fact remains," Errington noted,

> that the two [predator and prey] were co-existent in a tolerable if not harmonious ecological state when the white man invaded the new world. . . . It is immaterial that we cannot express as an equation the full role of predators or that even were we capable of so doing we

probably could not understand it. Whatever function our native predators do or do not perform, their existence is sanctioned by thousands or hundreds of thousands of years of Nature's experimentation. . . . . They *belonged* in the original fauna which in salient essentials we are fighting to preserve.[78]

Leopold took to heart these conclusions about the long-term relationships between predator, prey, and environment, integrating them into his thinking about game management and other conservation issues. In the field they had broad and critical ramifications, most visibly in raising doubts about popular predator-control policies. One of the primary jobs of the U. S. Bureau of Biological Survey was to kill predators in order to protect game and livestock. Even Hornaday had advocated control to protect game species.[79] Leopold had accepted the prevailing wisdom and at one time had enthusiastically participated in control efforts. Now, in light of new facts, control seemed problematic even when the aim was to maximize game. Adequate cover and food were more important, a conclusion that added to the mounting indictment of slick-and-clean farm practices.[80]

As Leopold absorbed these various ideas from Stoddard and Errington, he combined them with other ideas, including some that came to him from a more distant correspondent, Charles Elton of England. The two had begun a friendship at the Matamek Conference, warming to each other immediately. Elton had written to Leopold promptly upon his return to Oxford:

> In returning here I found the volume of your Game Survey awaiting me. . . . I wish I had seen it before coming to the Conference. I was in any case impressed by the work you described there, but had hardly grasped the scale on which you had been doing it.[81]

In a reply a few weeks later Leopold responded, "I find many individuals with whom I can pleasurably discuss some one little compartment of things, but not things in general,"[82] as he would with Elton. Leopold in this letter also exchanged some ideas regarding a hypothesis of Elton's and urged him to read Stoddard's 1931 book on quail.[83] Elton, in turn, after *Game Management* was out, later in 1933 praised it with high enthusiasm.[84]

Leopold found particular value in Elton's understandings of how coexisting populations formed complex societies or communities,

*Matamek Conference on Biological Cycles, July 1931. Left to right:
University of Alberta waterfowl expert William Rowan and Oxford
University professor of zoology Charles Elton, who became Leopold's
lifelong friends, and Leopold.*

which in effect regulated animal numbers from the top down. Elton portrayed the animals (and plants) living together in a given place as linked by food interdependencies into food chains and these various food chains in turn linked into dynamic community food cycles. Matters of food supply—predators eating prey—structured animal societies into pyramids of numbers based on food size, with smaller, more abundant herbivorous animals at the bottom and the larger carnivores, relatively small in number, at the apex. Animals, in other words, found their places within the pyramid of numbers on the basis of their food habits and the food habits of those around them.[85] This was a pattern of arrangement found all over the world, and it comported with Stoddard's conclusion that managers could adjust bobwhite populations by manipulating food factors.[86]

Leopold, in *Game Management*, used Elton's conceptualization of the pyramid as the starting point for considering predator-caused game mortality. Animal abundance tables, once developed for given locales (and none yet had been developed completely, though Leopold provided a sketch of one based on estimates for a southern

Arizona quail range) might allow managers to estimate predator-prey ratios and to determine whether predator control would or would not increase a particular game population.[87] Elton's pyramid concept would in fact remain a centerpiece of Leopold's thinking about land for the rest of his career.

Elton, in his works, paid particular attention to animal number fluctuations and to the mechanisms that brought them about. "A great many of the phenomena connected with [animal] numbers," Elton concluded, "owe their origin to the way in which animal communities are arranged and organised, and to various processes going on in the environment of the animals."[88] Elton spoke the language of descriptive ecology, yet the factors and processes of interest to him were the same ones that Leopold the game manager had found so critical. For Leopold the central question was about proper stocking levels; for Elton the question was "What is the desirable density of numbers for different animals?" "It will be seen," Elton contended,

> that the whole question of the optimum number for a species is affected by the unstable nature of the environment, which is always changing, and furthermore by the fact that practically no animals remain constant in numbers for any length of time. We have further to inquire into the effects of variations in numbers of animals, and into the means by which numbers are regulated in animal communities.[89]

Elton began his own discussion of nature's means of controlling animal numbers by illustrating how abundant many species could naturally become if populations were unchecked. "Almost everywhere," he reminded readers, Leopold among them, "the same tale is told—former vast numbers, now no longer existing owing to the greed of individual pirates or to the more excusable clash with the advance of agricultural settlement."[90] By way of evidence Elton cited documented scenes of African zebra herds covering two miles in extent, American buffalo as far as the eye could reach, and eight hundred thousand earthworms in an acre of arable land. Elton posed the rhetorical question "What would happen if any one species were allowed to multiply unchecked for several years?"[91] Beyond the fanciful image of elephants packed together so closely they could only sit on one another's knees, there were plenty of real-life instances of smaller animals—English mice and African springboks, for instance—that had increased to immense abundance. The examples illustrated the "tremendous powers of increase possessed by them and by all animals":

> Any species, if given the opportunity, is capable of increasing in the same alarming way as the mice, the locusts, or the *Gonyaulax*; and as a matter of fact most species probably do so occasionally, producing plagues which are rather sudden in onset. . . . It is not a rare or exceptional thing for a species to break out of control of its normal checks . . . "plagues" of animals are an inevitable consequence of the way in which animal communities are arranged and of the great instability of the environment.[92]

The most striking incidences of sudden increase, Elton remarked, came about when a new species was introduced "into a country strange to it, in which it does not at first fit harmoniously, often with disastrous results to itself or to mankind."[93] When this happened a characteristic sequence of events often followed. First the new animal went unnoticed. Then came the appearance of plague. Then, perhaps years later, the plague died down, a result not of any control efforts by people but apparently of the species itself having struck a new balance with its surroundings and acquired a new set of population checks.[94]

Leopold was paying careful attention to Elton's comments about mechanisms behind species outbreaks, and Elton's idea that disturbed populations found new balances resonated with him. It paralleled his own writing about the progress of erosion in the Southwest, which sometimes continued to occur, washing away the soil until harder rocks were exposed and the erosion slowed or ended. In most cases, Leopold had observed, watercourses proceeded to revegetate, thereby restoring a new equilibrium. But the new equilibrium, he concluded, was "a relatively unproductive one from the economic standpoint."[95] Errington echoed the point in his 1931 thesis. Mankind's changes might eventually come to a new equilibrium, but whether humanity would end up ahead was far from certain. Leopold attempted to draw from the evidence a general conclusion. Man, he agreed in 1934, can never fully destroy the balance of opposing natural forces, any more than he can prevent the conservation of energy. The new balance may be more to his liking, or it may be extremely harmful to him. It is man's job to understand the balance well enough to be sure, when he changes it, that the new . . . will be to his advantage.[96]

When a new balance did emerge, bringing to an end a population gyration, it gave evidence that some further mechanism existed to keep populations in check. And it added to the evidence that there existed, for each species in each place, an appropriate range for the size of its population. Elton was inclined to discuss the issue in terms of a species' "desirable density," the word

"desirable" being used in the teleological sense of that density which will in the long run give the best chances of survival for the species. . . . If we go into the question carefully, it soon becomes clear that there is an optimum density in numbers for any one species at any one place and time. This optimum number is not always the same and it is not always achieved, but in a broad way there is a tendency for all animals to strike some kind of mean between becoming too scarce and too abundant.[97]

The principle Leopold and his colleagues were closing in on went something like this: The world contained vast numbers of coexisting animal populations, all with a high power of population increase. This power of increase, though it may become temporarily "unchecked," is constantly tending to an "optimum density," which varies with time and place. How, though, did this regulation take place, and by what means, and what constituted optimum density? Recent research had added much, but wide gaps remained. The discussions at Matamek, quantitative population theories, Stoddard's and Errington's studies on quail, Elton's *Animal Ecology*, Leopold's *Game Management*—all were concerned with these fundamental questions. In an undated lecture titled "Theories of Population," probably written in the early 1940s, Leopold drew comparisons between population studies and other scientific endeavors:

The constitution of animal populations is a problem comparable in some respects to the constitution of matter. Both deal with aggregations of units, held together by an unstable equilibrium between invisible forces. . . . In animals we see units but must largely infer the aggregation; in physics we see the aggregation but must infer the unit. . . . [E]xperimental verification of hypotheses [in ecology vs. physics] is beset with peculiar difficulties . . . [but] what would the physicist give to band an atom?[98]

Leopold's own efforts to make sense of things illustrated both his openness to ideas and his willingness to toss out those that did not stand up. Particularly on the most knotty issues such as cycle mechanisms, no idea was too preposterous to be excluded without inquiry, yet no idea was so sacrosanct that it could retain respect without evidence. Leopold saw benefit in much of the work then taking place, particularly of the many various types of scientists tackling specific parts of the larger population-mechanism problem.[99] All of the work, Leopold emphasized, was aimed at a common problem. If it seemed appropriate to talk about cycles, carrying capacity, and territory as separate issues, it was only because separate groups were exploring them. Understanding populations was the common problem, and synthesis of all applicable work—the essence of Leopold's method—was required to make sense of it.[100]

Leopold's own strength was not in quantitative studies;[101] he was, however, interested in the rising work of the mathematical ecologists, including that of Alexander J. Nicholson of CSIRO Australia's Division of Economic Entomology—one of that nation's top population scientists.[102]

Nicholson's 1933 article titled "The Balance of Animal Populations"[103] offered an overview of why the author understood competition as fundamentally important in limiting animal populations. Nicholson noted that scientists sometimes argued against the existence of a balance of animal populations with their environment because populations did not maintain constant densities. For Nicholson the argument was illogical. A population density that did not change with the environment could not be in a state of balance with the environment, he asserted, but must be fixed independently from it. Population fluxes, that is, were actually indications of animals in balance with a changing physical, chemical, and biological environment. "Let us take a simple analogy," Nicholson wrote:

> A balloon rises until the weight of air displaced exactly balances the weight of the balloon, but if ballast be then discarded the balloon again rises until it reaches a new position of balance. Because a

balloon in the air is a balanced system, there is a relation between the weight it carries and the height it reaches; without balance, the height reached would be indeterminate.

The balance of animal populations is similar. . . . The balloon is continually in a state of tending towards a position of stationary balance, but continues to rise and fall because the position of stationary balance is changing all the time. . . .

The observed fact that there is a relation between the population densities of animals and environmental conditions can be explained only in terms of balance, just as the relation between the weight carried and the height reached by a balloon can be explained only in this way. Without balance the population densities of animals would be indeterminate, and so could not bear a relation to anything.[104]

It was competition that played the central role, Nicholson urged, in limiting animal populations and thus bringing about balance:

Indeed, any factor that produces balance is almost necessarily some form of competition, for balance can be produced only if increasing density decreases the chance of survival of an average individual. . . . [Diminishing quality of a population's environment due to increasing density of that population] appears to be of major importance in the control of plants and micro-organisms, and not only limits the densities of species but also plays an important part in determining what other species may exist in the same environment. . . . Thus the alteration of the physical qualities of the environment by the activities of animals may be of the utmost importance in determining what kinds of animals can live together in any given environment.[105]

Competition, in short, sometimes operated indirectly and in complex ways, according to Nicholson. Population numbers, for instance, interacted with environmental factors to determine the numbers and kinds of species that inhabited a given local community. Nicholson's point bore similarities with Elton's vivid concepts of the pyramid of numbers, food chains, and food cycles, all based on animal size and food habits in relation to animal numbers.

Leopold would pick up and incorporate Nicholson's points in his work, just as he would draw ideas from Stoddard, Errington, Elton, and other scientists at the Matamek Conference. Leopold was a synthesizer,[106] willing to draw ideas from any and all reliable sources to compile an understanding of how nature worked. And it was a particularly interesting time to do so.

Between the time Leopold began his career, in 1909, and the early 1930s, the young field of ecology had matured into a full-fledged professional science. In the early 1900s Victor Shelford—soon to become one of America's most rigorous community ecologists—was advised by a top biologist that he ought to redirect his efforts to a more productive field because ecology was "ignis fatuus"—a foolish endeavor.[107] Yet the British Ecological Society was formed in 1913, and two years later the Ecological Society of America was established. By 1920, according to W. C. Allee, ecology had become a fully "self-conscious" discipline, with several texts at its disposal.[108] By the 1920s, too, the need for organization of the facts that had piled up over the past decades had become widely recognized within the field. Some plant and animal ecologists, bothered that their fields were developing separately, worked to bring about better coordination of their ideas and some turned their attention to making sense of populations and their fluctuating numbers, focusing on quantitative experimental and laboratory studies and developing ecological theory. Such studies became earnest in the 1920s, and mathematical theoretical ecology—which eventually was extended from populations to the more complex communities of populations—developed as a special effort to bring integration to the field and identify general principles within the new science.

In the 1920s and 1930s a number of ecologists and others hoped to discover general principles to use in predicting and balancing not only game populations but also a human world that for many seemed an insecure and unstable place. The Matamek Conference of 1931 had been motivated by such hope. By the early 1930s the Depression had brought high unemployment rates and considerable despair. Barely a decade earlier great numbers of people had died in fighting a war among members of the world's most industrially advanced civilizations and in the 1918–1919 influenza pandemic. It was becoming easy to believe that powerful forces, beyond any individual's control, were at work in the world—having drastic effects on human populations.[109] Understanding nature with an eye toward predicting and controlling its activities and outcomes was certainly not easy. But ecology, as Elton put it, was "perhaps more able to offer immediate practical help to mankind than any of the other [zoological fields]."[110] Leopold was coming to agree. From the beginning, as a conservationist indoctrinated into the Progressive-era faith in science, Leopold studied nature as a means of helping people live better. His aspiration was to make sense of landscapes, including those that had people in them. To do so he increasingly turned to ecology as a tool to understand nature and the human place in it, drawing upon the work of the quantitative population ecologists but increasingly attracted by the rising stars of energetics and economics in ecology, including his new friend Charles Elton. In the early 1930s Leopold's ecological work had only just begun.

Meanwhile, as scientists, Leopold among them, were trying to make sense of population mechanisms and natural cycles, the cause of conservation in the United States was again receiving national attention. The national enterprise had gone spectacularly awry, and the economy was still stumbling. So grave were the problems that a suite of new ideas was open for discussion, or so it seemed. Was it time to reconsider the nation's commitment to individualism in relation to social and ecological interdependencies? Should organized planning rather than individual autonomy provide the framework of the new age? And in an age of massive soil erosion, rising dust clouds, and declining wildlife populations, should unrestricted private property rights be rethought?

As millions looked to Washington for answers Leopold would be among those on the margins calling for caution and careful attention to detail. The questions for the New Deal administration, he urged, were in fact the ones that had been around all along: How should people live on land? What were the best mechanisms for integrating resource values on individual parcels of land? Fellow conservationists asked loudly about the conservation needs of the entire nation, and Leopold was involved in federal policy making. Yet increasingly he was apt to look to the land-use attitudes and behaviors of individual landowners. As Leopold considered the questions involved in bringing about good land use, his ecological ideas about land and his understanding of human attitudes and systems would continue to develop and intertwine.

Chapter 5

An American System

Maybe we thought because the land went on
Liberty went with the land: there was always liberty:
There was all outdoors to be liberty . . .
There was always the grass ahead of us and on and on . . .
We wonder if the liberty was grass . . .
Or if there's liberty a man can mean that's
Men: not land.

Archibald MacLeish, Land of the Free

By 1933, as Franklin Delano Roosevelt took office as president and initiated the relief programs of his dizzying first 100 days, the American home-building dream had gone in reverse. Home foreclosures were taking place at the rate of more than a thousand per day.[1] New farm technology made farming more efficient and sent countless unneeded agricultural workers drifting into cities[2] while at the same time the amount of land in farms rose to more than a billion acres, covering more than half the land area of the continental United States.[3] With crop production high and crop prices low, farm bankruptcies increased, also pushing many rural dwellers out of their homes. More than 5 percent of the nation's farms were subject to forced sales in 1933 — a national high.[4]

Contributing to these reversals of fortune was a severe drought, beginning in the spring and summer of 1930 and spreading westward over a band from Maryland and Virginia to Missouri and Arkansas.

By 1931 the drought was threatening communities in a greater part of the country, its center having shifted to the Great Plains—particularly parts of Kansas, Colorado, New Mexico, Oklahoma, and Texas.[5] At harvest time in 1934 close to one-fifth of planted crop-lands had failed.[6] Through the rest of the decade drought and high winds would continue to sap the agricultural southern plains in par-ticular, helping to kick up heavy clouds of dust and chase from their farms multitudes of people—this occurring across the region Walt Whitman a half century earlier had proudly called "America's charac-teristic landscape."

THE MOON WAS BORN

The moon, they say, was born when some mighty planet, zooming aimlessly through the firmament, happened to pass so near the earth as to lift off a piece of its substance and hurl it forth into space as a new and separate entity in the galaxy of heavenly bodies.

Conservation, I think, was "born" in somewhat this same manner in the year A.D. 1933. A mighty force, consisting of the pent-up desires and frustrated dreams of two generations of conservation-ists, passed near the national money-bags whilst opened wide for post-depression relief. Something large and heavy was lifted off and hurled forth into the galaxy of the alphabets. It is still moving too fast to be sure how big it is, or what cosmic forces draw rein on its career.[7]

Hardly any development in American conservation would cause Leopold to feel more out of step than the whirlwind conservation effort of the New Deal. On the surface the opportunity for progress was appealing. Not since the administration of FDR's cousin Theo-dore Roosevelt had conservation enjoyed such visibility. Leopold, however, sensed that action was taking place ahead of clear thinking. People did not really understand the causes of land degradation or how to address them. With so little preparation, how could the nation's leaders seize the moment (and the money) to develop con-servation programs that would succeed? Indeed, was it even clear that a massive infusion of money and effort would make the land better rather than worse?

Many early New Deal programs, intending to help both urban

and rural people get back to work and into homes, were conservation related or had land-use related components.[8] Some were concerned with moving people off lands ill suited for agricultural crops and into better situations. Others sought to check erosion, agricultural overproduction, and poor timber management while promoting reforestation, recreation, and better cropping methods and drainage. The Agricultural Adjustment Act (AAA), signed into law on May 12, 1933, provided subsidies and price supports to farmers to retire unneeded croplands and to supplement low crop prices. A major program—the Federal Emergency Relief Administration—was given $25 million to identify and buy up "submarginal" or even "marginal" farmlands that owners had misused and that were not economically productive.[9] Then there was the Civilian Conservation Corps (CCC), designed to put hundreds of thousands of unemployed to work rebuilding degraded lands[10]—including Aldo Leopold, who spent the summer of 1933 in the Southwest overseeing soil conservation efforts. Nearly all of the programs were narrowly focused on specific land-use ills and dealt with problems one by one.

Leopold's CCC opportunity allowed him a chance to think further about his erosion theory[11] and to observe the consequences of multiple single-track government land-use programs—trying to serve simultaneously, for example, forestry, watersheds, wildlife, and recreation—as they were implemented on the same piece of ground. On the basis of their effects on land, how well were these government efforts working? The multiple-use ideal was at least as old as the USDA Forest Service. That ideal, Leopold concluded, had taken "the open money bags of 1933, however, to demonstrate what a disparity still exists between this paper ideal"[12] and what actually happened on the land.

In a penetrating article from early 1934, "Conservation Economics," Leopold offered a sober assessment based on his observations of New Deal conservation programs at work.[13] "When applied to the soil," he asserted, single-track "measures frequently clash, or at best, fail to dovetail with each other."[14] A roadside cleanup crew might fell trees and shrubs that were essential for game and then burn the downed wood, which could have fueled fireplaces in campgrounds being built by recreation crews. Meanwhile a road-building crew might go to work cutting a grade along a clay bank, which would roil the trout stream below it that another crew was improving with dams and shelters. Worsening this lack of land-use integration was the failure of New Deal programs to reform the land-use practices that had caused the problems in the first place. In the same 1934 essay Leopold asked readers to imagine a hypothetical Wisconsin farm.[15] The AAA paid a farmer to take his land out of corn or tobacco production but did not encourage him to shift to less destructive land uses. The CCC built check dams for a farmer to stop his gullies but did not address the cause of the erosion by requiring him to move his grazing cows off steep slopes. The government's well-meaning efforts, in sum, were lacking in two ways: the various conservation measures were not dovetailed, and remedial measures typically addressed symptoms, not root causes, of land problems.

As Leopold thought about these deficiencies in conservation programs he returned to his earlier questions from the Blue River settlement failure about private versus public ownership.[16] In Wisconsin, as in the Southwest, private landowners often used their lands in ways that degraded them. In addition to the consequences of lost fertility and depleted resources, such land misuse was *actually creating a cash liability against the taxpayer.*[17] It imposed economic burdens on citizens when private land owners depended on public help to repair or make up for ruined land or when misused land was abandoned with unpaid taxes, as it often was, and the costs of government ownership and restoration shifted onto taxpayers' shoulders. Leopold did not challenge the need for governments to acquire lands for conservation: this was in fact much needed, and on a large scale, he believed.[18] The government should develop more proactive land-acquisition programs, he thought. It should not continue allowing land misuse only to take possession of abandoned lands after the fact.[19] Instead it should plan ahead to buy lands best suited for public ownership after careful consideration of the land's physical features—its soils, waters, and characteristic plants and animals—and the human uses that they could sustain. Such lands also could reasonably include samples of many types of habitats to be set aside as parks and preserves for wildlife, scientific study, and recreation. Migratory waterfowl required networks of widely dispersed marshes and waters for feeding and breeding; these lands, too, were suited for federal ownership and management.

Many conservation goals, however, could not be achieved merely on scattered tracts of publicly owned lands. Private landowners also had to promote them, over entire landscapes. Many wild species had "an inherent intolerance of concentration"[20] and thus required wide, well-dispersed areas of habitat to survive. To thrive, in other words, many species had to spread out across the countryside, sharing lands that were also prime areas for human agriculture and human neighborhoods. This was true for bobwhite quail and other upland game birds, many mammals, wildflowers, amphibians and reptiles, and songbirds. The only way to protect them was to manage *"all suitable land,"*[21] Leopold calculated—lands that also produced economic crops. Public ownership was simply not enough to "assure the physical integrity of America in A. D. 2000, or even A. D. 1950," Leopold concluded. Conservative land use would need to involve *"every acre on every watershed in America* whether it be farm or forest, public or private."[22]

Leopold's statement carried with it a critical implication. Conservation, to be successful, would require both programs of public land acquisition *and* the cooperation of private landowners. The former were under way but, even if thoughtfully executed, could carry conservation success only part of the distance. The need for cooperation from private landowners, Leopold thought, was a neglected and in the end unavoidable reality and perhaps the toughest and most critical conservation challenge. The public needed to come up with ways to protect its interest in private lands—better ways than the New Deal had so far developed. The matter of private land conservation would occupy Leopold for the rest of his life. It would ultimately lead him, when other measures failed to yield results, to insist on the need for a social conscience in land use, a "land ethic": a culturally agreed upon, cooperatively practiced idea that there was a moral right and wrong in land use, reaching beyond individual economic profit.[23]

Leopold had been developing his idea of "land use as a moral issue" since at least the early 1920s, as we saw in chapter 2.[24] A decade later, in 1933, he published an essay on the subject titled "The Conservation Ethic."[25] By 1934 Leopold had made use of the term "land-ethic"[26]—for which he would become well known. Moral change was at best a long-term solution, though, and land problems were urgent. In the meantime, other measures were needed. Thus, even while he developed his idea of extending an ethical relationship to land, Leopold continued searching for economic vehicles and political arrangements that might prompt more immediate conservation action by landowners:

> The crux of the [conservation] problem is that every landowner is the custodian of two interests, not always identical, the public interest and his own. What we need is a positive inducement or reward for the landowner who respects both interests in his actual land practice. All conservation problems—erosion, forestry, game, wild flowers, landscapes, or what not—ultimately boil down to this. What should this reward or inducement be? What is a practical vehicle for it? These are the two basic questions in American conservation. An answer seems to require the collaboration of economists, jurists, regional planners, ecologists and esthetes.[27]

What was needed to make conservation successful at every scale and in every realm—from land concept to policy to management and land-use practice—was the cooperation of private landowners and the coordination of public land programs toward a clear, geographically comprehensive conservation goal. But what mechanisms could bring this about? How could the nation get its private landowners to use their lands better, given nature's complexities, human ignorance, and America's commitment to individual liberty?

PASSING THROUGH REFORM

Leopold's mounting questions about private and public landownership challenged the allocation of power in America. Where various conservation concerns were at stake, where should power lie, he implicitly asked—more in private hands or in public? At the federal level or in government closer to the people? The issues seemed particularly pressing in the early days of the New Deal, with the nation's economy in disarray. And for the moment major reform seemed possible. Should the national government and big business become working partners in the implementation of centralized national planning? Instead, was big business so economically powerful and socially dangerous that it needed to be broken up? Or, as a third choice, did the economic system merely need to cleanse itself of excessive optimism and allow the stern discipline of the market to restore order in a way that would ultimately be beneficial to land conservation?

Although few may have recognized it at the time, the New Deal narrowed its course between the first and second halves of the 1930s as the initial round of lawmaking gave way to what appeared to some as a "Second New Deal."[28] In the process reform ideas narrowed and the most radical ones were dropped. The first New Deal had carried forward influential ideals from the era of reform progressivism early in the century. It had sought to rebuild America by reforming national economic institutions, primarily banking and the stock market. It embraced a liberal conviction that government ought to play a direct role in the economy, keeping people free in the sense of protecting them from domination by corporate economic power.[29] The Second New Deal was based largely on the popular laissez-faire model of the market and the belief that it should remain dominant in ordering the nation. The liberalism of this second phase focused less on national needs and more on increasing "individual liberties" for people to act in their private interest, economic or otherwise.[30] By the late 1930s the "capitalists"—with ideals of open competition for individual wealth and power—had largely conquered "the planners"—who proposed to use government more actively to protect people from corporate economic power, to guarantee some basic standard of living, and to promote better land uses, even as on the surface talk of planning continued. In any case, whatever the mechanisms the nation deployed to secure a just and stable society and under whatever banners they were promoted, they would continue to build upon a foundation of market capitalism and individual liberty—nothing more radical. Nor would the policy of the nation significantly amend its desired end, which had changed little since the century began. It was, in the words of one planner,

> the bringing about in an orderly, democratic manner of the highest possible standard of living, the greatest amount of security, and the maximum possible measure of well-being for the people of the Nation.[31]

LAND PATHOLOGY

In addition to urgent economic questions, Americans had a pressing physical crisis to address, a natural disaster soon termed the Dust Bowl. Centered in the western ends of Kansas and Oklahoma, it darkened, literally and figuratively, the whole nation. Many would interpret the catastrophe as an act of God, caused by nature rather than human folly. But sober minds of the day could see what historians would later make clear: the Dust Bowl had as much to do with ill-considered land-use practices as with drought and wind patterns.

Beginning in 1931 high temperatures, low rainfall, and stiff winds set upon the lands of the Great Plains, once held in place by the natural short-grass prairie sod. Before the plow the prairie comprised a diverse community of plant and animal species—grama and buffalo grasses, wire grass, bluestem grass, bunchgrass, sand grass and sand sage, brown snakeweed, yellow sunflowers, sundrops, poppy mallow, bee balm, jackrabbits, grasshoppers, mice, pocket gophers, kangaroo rats, prairie dogs, moles and badgers, ferrets and skunks, coyotes and wolves, lesser prairie chickens, horned larks, and great white cranes, among hundreds and thousands of other species. All of these had been well adapted to the region's climatic extremes—its predictably unpredictable periods of dryness and high winds. In place of the prairie humans had created farms that grew little more than wheat,[32] which was not particularly well adapted to the climate. Wheat was subject to wilting and burning in heat and dryness and was susceptible to disease and insect plagues. Once destroyed, wheat left nothing behind that would hold down the soil—nothing to hold the earth together.[33]

Wheat, though, was one of the nation's top staple crops and highest-yielding exports. For farmers it was a crop that quickly maximized short-term farm productivity and cash profits. To help cultivate it, new tractors arrived on the southern plains as early as 1900 along with other innovations in farm machinery, including the one-way disk plow and combines that both harvested and threshed the wheat. With this popular new technology, purchased by many in spite of drought and economic depression,[34] farmers remade in their culture's own likeness the face of the earth and their rural life.

Mechanization put many farmhands and tenants out of work and homes. It was not simply dust storms after all but also what was underlying them—the machines, one-crop specialization, tenant insecurity, disease (particularly tuberculosis), and soil misuse—that evicted the residents of the Dust Bowl territory.[35] Yet the dust storms blew in drama and great suffering of their own—in degree and kind ample enough to get the attention of the whole country.[36] For the better part of a decade dust was part of life: "day after day, year after year, of sand rattling against the window, of fine powder caking one's lips, of springtime turned to despair, of poverty eating into self-confidence."[37] A few small storms appeared in 1932. In the next year 179 occurred in April alone. In November 1933 a dust storm carried soil from the plains all the way to Georgia and New York. But it was the storm of May 9–12, 1934, that riveted the nation. Dirt from Montana, Wyoming, and the Dakotas blew in dark, dense clouds to Chicago, where 12 million tons fell on the evening of May 9. On the following day the blizzard turned afternoon into night in Buffalo. On May 11 dust settled over Boston, New York, Washington, and Atlanta, and by the twelfth Savannah's skies had become hazy. Ships three hundred miles off the Atlantic coast found dust on their decks. Such storms, of varying ranges and intensities, would continue into 1941.[38]

In the memories of many plains residents, the blackest year, though, was 1935. For six weeks between February and mid-March there were no clear days. Then came what became known as "Black Sunday," April 14, 1935—the day that one of the greatest dust blizzards arose suddenly and spread across the plains. The next day Leopold had occasion to speak publicly to a group of scientist-colleagues about the unfolding tragedy. Now heavily equipped with machines, Americans had accelerated "the velocity of [land] destructive interactions" in ways "unmistakable and probably unprecedented."[39] Conservation, he explained, was a "protest" against this type of "destructive land use."[40] To remedy existing harms and prevent future ones, Americans needed to better adjust their land uses, bringing them into alignment with the realities of nature. This crisis, too, emphasized the pressing conservation need, Leopold explained, to formulate "mechanisms for protecting the public interest in private land."[41]

One of the most catastrophic dust blizzards of the 1930s arose on April 14, 1935, which became known as "Black Sunday." It swept south from western Kansas and Oklahoma, approaching the small town of Stratford, Texas (pictured here).

With dust clouding the air the New Deal had dawned with an intense concern not only about putting millions of people back to work and into homes but also about conserving soil—that "fundamental resource."[42] The Soil Erosion Service (SES) was formed in the U.S. Department of the Interior, with soil crusader Hugh Hammond Bennett named head in October 1933 (the agency in 1935 was renamed the Soil Conservation Service and transferred to the U.S. Department of Agriculture). The Taylor Grazing Act of 1934 subjected grazing on the western public domain to national regulation in an effort to control erosion caused by livestock. In 1935 Congress enacted the Soil Conservation and Domestic Allotment Act, which gave farmers money for sowing grasses and legumes instead of wheat and other soil-depleting crops. The importance of combating erosion was accentuated by *Fortune* magazine: "It is conceivable that when the history of our generation comes to be written in the perspective of a hundred years the saving of the broken lands will stand out as the great and most enduring achievement of the time."[43] It was a hopeful observation.

To Leopold's mind it was some of the work of the new Soil

Erosion Service under Bennett that gave particular cause for hope. It was one of the few government-sponsored projects that addressed both of Leopold's major questions: how to integrate multiple land uses on a single piece of land and how to get private landowners to work for the public interest on their own land. The SES received $5 million to demonstrate how farmers could plan farming operations that promoted the long-term productivity of the soil.[44]

In October 1933 the SES officially designated the hilly Coon Creek watershed in southwestern Wisconsin its first soil conservation demonstration area. Coon Valley farmers, beset with widening gullies and increasingly frequent and intense flooding, were enthusiastic about participating in the project. More than half of them joined up, signing five-year cooperative agreements with the government. The government would supply fertilizer, lime, and seed. Farmers would follow recommendations for soil-conserving farming techniques.[45] Demonstration work on the land began in the spring of 1934 and continued until it was phased out in 1935. From his position at the University of Wisconsin, Leopold served as extension advisor to these efforts, which aimed at formulating a "'regional plan' for the stabilization of the watershed and of the agricultural community which it supports." Coon Valley would involve private farmers in voluntarily growing crops and grazing livestock while promoting woodlots, wildlife, and wildflowers and protecting streams and watersheds from soil erosion and flooding—all on the same piece of land.[46] No project seemed closer to Leopold's ideal, and he was enthusiastic about it. "We have almost a plethora of conservation demonstrations," he explained, "but these [of the Soil Erosion Service] differ from the common run in one very important respect: They propose to show how *all kinds* of conservation can be *combined* on a single piece of *private* land, rather than to show that some one particular kind is the sole road to salvation."[47] Coon Valley was one of the few projects that would address the "crux of the land problem" and show "that integrated land use is possible on private farms, and that such integration is mutually advantageous both to the owner and the public."[48]

The Coon Valley project today is still held up as a success story by what is now the USDA Natural Resources Conservation Service.

*The Civilian Conservation Corps (CCC) camp in Coon Valley,
Wisconsin, an army of help for farmers interested in implementing
soil conservation measures.*

After the demonstration closed, farmers voluntarily continued to
follow some soil conserving farm practices. In 1982 scientists calculated that erosion in Coon Valley had been reduced by at least 75 percent since 1934, to the economic good of farmers, who were still
making a living on their lands, and to the good of the entire community, members of which could again fish for trout in Coon Creek.[49]

Yet when he looked back from the 1940s Leopold did not believe
that enough had been accomplished by such government projects.[50]
After the five-year government contracts ended, farmers may have
continued certain soil-saving measures, such as strip-cropping
(planting alternating rows of cultivated and sod-forming crops
following the land's contour), that were economically profitable to
them individually, but they continued little else in terms of wildlife,
marshland, and woodlot restoration and management. And while
they indeed had slowed erosion, a decade later there would still be
less soil on the land. Government payments, it appeared, changed
behavior as long as the money flowed. When the money stopped, old
habits often returned. Many landowners appeared to be guided by
money, not ideals of good land use.

Through the 1930s and 1940s Leopold could see that private land

A widening gully caused by land misuse on a farm in Coon Valley, Wisconsin, similar to what Leopold witnessed in the Southwest.

use and conservation posed challenges that economists of the day were ill suited to address. According to prevailing economic theory, the individual pursuit of self-interest would automatically promote the common good. But this theory did not work when it came to land use, especially in ecologically sensitive places. Self-interested landowners often acted in ways that harmed the land, with consequences that extended beyond their property boundaries. When all landowners practiced conservation in concert all might benefit. But conservation by one landowner acting alone could prove costly to the individual. The profit of conservation, that is, often accrued *to the community* as a whole working together, not to individuals working in isolation. Many parts of nature could not be conserved by individuals working alone (e.g., a landscape's soils, waters, wideranging wildlife, scenery), and many parts of nature were not economically profitable to conserve (e.g., songbirds and other wildlife, wildflowers, small fisheries) in the first place but were parts of well-functioning and beautiful landscapes.[51] Given these economic realities, what could be done? Could the factors affecting land use somehow be manipulated so as to prompt individuals to act better? Could the economic system be adjusted so that landowners found it profitable to use their lands conservatively?

ECONOMIC TOOLS

A first step in addressing these questions, Leopold believed, was to apply scientific research to them. In a proposal prepared in 1934 he invited his colleagues at the University of Wisconsin to join him in an interdisciplinary project.[52] Leopold's reasoned justification for the proposed study was that the present trend of substituting government initiative for private initiative was unsound because the tax base could not carry the load and also because only a person who lived on the land, in many cases, could properly manage it. Government could not buy *all* land; therefore, private individuals must participate for conservation to be successful. The common assumption, Leopold asserted, was that the conservation toolbox included three economic tools: the individual profit motive, public land purchase, and public subsidy. But, he pointed out, "no thorough appraisal of the comparative economy and effectiveness of the three vehicles, as applied to particular local [land] problems, has ever been made."[53] Moreover, the frugality of preventing abuse in the first place had not been weighed. What was needed to help society move beyond inadequate measures, he urged, was a comparative testing of new mechanisms that had potential to promote good land use.[54]

Leopold's proposed interdisciplinary study remained unfunded, but he nonetheless continued to think over possible economic remedies for rampant land misuse.[55] An obvious tool was land-use regulation—some form of rural zoning that curtailed bad land-use practices. Zoning had the merit of being local and flexible in its administration, Leopold noted, but was limited in being a negative rather than a positive measure (e.g., it told people what they could not do, not what would be beneficial to do). It was, therefore, in and of itself insufficient.[56] Legislative compulsion would not help in situations in which conservation required positive, locally applied skill and not merely abstention or rote rules in the use of land and, in any case, seemed not preferable. Another tool, not yet tried, was "consumer discrimination." This would involve putting "green" or "clean" labels on products that came from well-managed lands to express approval for conservative land use. It could also include boycotts to express disapproval for poor land use and its products—for example, "erosion butter" and "exploitation milk."[57] Plying purchasing and investment power for conservation would work by using economic incentives or disincentives to pressure producers and advertisers. Consumers might have to pay more for a "green" product, Leopold realized, but might they not be willing, he suggested, to buy wool from sheep grazed on "greener pastures" or to buy paper for their children's textbooks produced in ways that had not polluted rivers?

A second proposal for a new kind of economic vehicle appeared in Leopold's richly woven 1934 "Conservation Economics"—which Jay "Ding" Darling, conservationist, two-time Pulitzer Prize-winning cartoonist, and new chief of the USDA Biological Survey, claimed was full of ideas good enough that they ought to make Leopold president of the United States.[58] "It seems likely," as Leopold explained matters, "that really sound [land-use related] remedial forces will have to deal in some way with the problem of motivating individual landowners to act for their joint rather than individual benefit."[59] As far as Leopold could tell, the "existing legal and economic structure" did not contain "the vehicle for exerting economic pressure of this kind. If not, a vehicle must be built *de novo*."[60] In "Conservation Economics" Leopold began such an effort, raising the possibility of a "sweeping simplification of conservation law"[61] that would reorient the overall focus of economically based decision making. His idea might qualify him for the "asylum for political and ecological dreamers,"[62] Leopold confessed, but what if landowners were rewarded for good land use? Instead of subsidizing landowners' efforts to restore damaged lands, why not put money into the *prevention* of land destruction by aiding the integration of land uses? What about some conservation law, he proposed,

which sets up for each parcel of land a single criterion of land-use: "Has the public interest in *all* its resources been protected?" which motivates that criterion by a single incentive, such as the differential tax, and which delegates the function of judging compliance to some single and highly trained administrative field-inspector, subject to review by the courts. Such a man would have to be a composite tax assessor, county agent, and conservation ecologist. Such a man is hard to build, but easier, I think, than to build a law specifying in cold print the hundreds of alternative ways of handling the land resources of even a single farm.[63]

It would be a difficult job, though, to build a composite conservation man.[64] Added to that was the challenge of deciding how good and bad land uses would be judged. "I have administered land too long to have any illusion, or to wish to create one," Leopold wrote,

> that this idea of preventive subsidy is as simple as it sounds, but I doubt if it would be as complicated as the cures on which we are now embarked. Differential taxes, I realize, must reach far enough back into national finance to forestall the mere local shifting of the tax burden, and must be based on some workable criterion of good vs. bad land use. How to define it? Who to define it?[65]

As dust from the Great Plains flew, Leopold's questions begged answers.

SERVING THE NATION

Leopold and other conservationists in the 1930s sensed a need not only for new economic mechanisms but also for political remedies imposed at the national level, particularly land planning from above. Localized private actions alone would not suffice to solve land-use problems that were broad in cultural and geographic scope any more than government programs would be sufficient to attend to the infinite local social and ecological peculiarities that existed across landscapes. Nor would local or even state government actions be enough, even though when applied appropriately they were critical. The political puzzle, like the economic one, involved identifying the best way to blend public and private powers together into a coherent, countrywide system of good land use.

Problems such as the Dust Bowl and declining wildlife populations were nationwide political problems. They called for nationwide responses, to the same degree as did stock market crashes, banking failures, and widespread poverty. Only a national land-management plan could protect flowing water, migratory birds, and other wide-ranging animals that crossed political and private-public boundaries. Only a national plan could identify and protect the public's interest in all the country's lands, including privately owned ones. Only sound agricultural policies at the national level would enable widely dispersed local farmers to consider wildlife's needs and keep soils well protected.

Throughout the 1930s the call for coordinated political action had produced a string of national committees and administrative agencies, all trying to bring order to the nation's resource uses and its institutions. One result of the push for land-use planning was the National Resources Committee, which divided the country into eleven districts, with a chairman, a consultant, and legislative liaisons for each. Focused primarily on agricultural lands was the U.S. Department of Agriculture's Agricultural Extension Service, which was tapped to help administer some of the New Deal's AAA programs. The Resettlement Administration, led by brain truster Rexford Tugwell, had the particular mission of withdrawing unprofitable or submarginal lands from cultivation and moving the farmers to more fertile places that were better able to sustain families. Cooperating with these programs, on paper at least, were the National Park Service, the Bureau of Indian Affairs, the Division of Grazing, the Soil Conservation Service, the Biological Survey, and the Forest Service, along with the recently established Tennessee Valley Authority. Within their spheres these agencies were intended to add coordination to the national system. But their sheer number and overlapping jurisdictions created yet another need for coordination, among the agencies themselves. Particularly for people close to the ground, worried about detailed land-use issues, this alphabetical proliferation brought as much worry as it did solace.[66]

Leopold's attitude about national planning and political life in general revealed ambivalence—national leadership was necessary but usually ineffective—and it included disdain for bureaucracy. Part of his response seemed simply a matter of personal preference. Leopold was reluctant to get into situations that meant he would have to "fight politics" or defend "the intellectual rut of two generations."[67] But his ambivalence through the 1930s and beyond also reflected considerable thought about the best way to accomplish conservation. In one sense Leopold's dissatisfaction with top-down schemes was a more developed expression of his 1913 claim that efficiency in the Forest Service was not an end but a means to an end. The real measure of conservation success remained to Leopold's mind not organizational efficiency but conservation's effect on land. Sound conservation needed to start with the land itself, in other words, and with people who understood the land and how to use it. It needed to begin with a firm foundation at the bottom, rather than at the top with human schemes based largely on power plays.

A letter from Leopold to John H. Baker, executive director of the National Association of Audubon Societies, revealed elements of Leopold's experience and thinking about bureaucracy. To Baker Leopold expressed his opposition to a proposed government plan to regroup federal agencies.[68] His objection, Leopold explained, was "purely a psychological one":

> Any moving of bureaus is seized upon by the public mind as in itself constituting reform. I do not believe it is a reform, and I believe this is the proper moment for the public to begin to realize that reform is a much deeper question than that, hence my vote.

In a postscript Leopold added:

> Perhaps the briefest way for me to express my doubts about reorganization bills is this: Such bills are a manifestation of the basic political fallacy, "There ought to be a law." I do not deny that laws are important, but in the conservation field the passage of new laws has continually served as a substitute for thought. We are now about to again defer, by same old method, the needed processes of cerebration.[69]

Leopold did not particularly trust the conservation knowledge of the leaders who had been, by the mid-1930s, pushing for some type of reorganization for twenty years. What was needed was a real shift of ideas, not merely a shift of seats.[70] Conservation, Leopold urged, was more than a sum of physical acts of government. It was more than bureaus, laws, land purchases, road building, fire prevention, grazing permits, timber sales, and hunting regulations. Conservation required a deeper-sprung national philosophy toward land and the ways people used it.

Among the bureaucratic planning efforts initiated during the early New Deal years that particularly frustrated Leopold was a little-noted national committee on which he served that dealt with wildlife.

On the first working day of 1934 Secretary of Agriculture Henry A. Wallace announced the appointment of a committee, eventually called the President's Committee on Wild Life Restoration, to "develop and supervise a nation-wide plan for promoting and protecting wild life."[71] Thomas Beck, editor of *Collier's* magazine and the man who suggested the idea to FDR, was appointed chairman; Leopold and Ding Darling were the two other members. The committee's ultimate plan, it was hoped, could be coordinated with the efforts of the "National Recovery and the Agricultural Adjustment Acts" in a way that aided economic recovery, agriculture, and wildlife all at once.[72]

Scarcely three weeks later the committee outlined its program for game preservation at the annual American Game Conference. Chairman Beck, rising to the occasion, declared that "the time for conservation has passed, the time for restoration has come."[73] The committee recommended that one-third of the 50 million acres of marginal land, earmarked for purchase by the USDA under its national farm rehabilitation program, be set aside chiefly to benefit migratory waterfowl. The committee also called for a nationwide restoration program for upland game (including turkeys, quail, grouse, rabbits, and other native species) and public acquisition of habitat for various game and nongame species, particularly for species becoming increasingly scarce. Overseeing these measures and others like them should be a "coordinated and businesslike administration to carry the plan into successful operation."[74] Authority over wildlife, which was scattered through several agencies, should be orchestrated in order better to achieve conservation and restoration of wildlife.[75]

The committee's proposal encountered stiff resistance in gaining legislative and executive approval.[76] For money to flow the proposed expenditures would have to be "drafted as a public works project providing employment."[77] The president sensed that it would appear inconsistent to spend money on wildlife when families were in need. The committee promptly revised its plan, to include a call for the employment of 45,000 men for six months. According to an unofficial source reported in the *New York Times* on June 7, the White

A cartoon drawn by Pulitzer Prize–winning Jay "Ding" Darling. Darling was a member—along with Leopold—of the federal-level "Beck Committee," charged with forming a plan to restore the nation's wildlife. The cartoon was page 2 of the committee's report to President Roosevelt.

House approved a budget request of $3.5 million for the plan.[78] At this point, though, matters stalled. Wildlife was not a priority, given the nation's other needs.

Realizing that such a major federal program would not emerge from the White House or Congress without greater public demand,

Ding Darling put the challenge to the wildlife conservation community. In a speech in October 1935 to the National Association of Audubon Societies, Darling complained that the various outdoor organizations—consisting of birders, hunters, game breeders, wildlifers, the ammunition industry, and so on—still seemed unable to subordinate their special interests to the common cause.[79] Conservation as a whole had no "single, unified program backed by an organization representing all interests and strong enough to make a fight before Congress and win its demands."[80] Until it did, and until public pressure on the federal government mounted, there would very likely be no national wildlife program.[81] For his part Leopold distrusted committee work that did not emphasize skilled, on-the-ground policy administration. At decade's end, looking back on his small role in the national planning effort, he offered a somber assessment: "I am not at all proud of the work of the President's Committee."[82]

PLANNING DRESSES FOR ANOTHER MAN'S WIFE

The fight over the national wildlife program continued in the midst of bureaucratic frustrations. FDR supported wildlife efforts but needed other supporters to confront the opposition. To elevate the issue and stimulate greater public unity, he called a North American Wildlife Conference, to be held in lieu of the annual American Game Conference. "It has long been my feeling," FDR wrote in remarks prepared for the conference,

> that there has been lack of a full and complete public realization of our wildlife plight, of the urgency of it, and of the many social and economic values that wildlife has to our people. This, and my firm belief in the ability of the American people to face facts, to analyze problems, and to work out a program which might remedy the situation, is what impelled me to call the North American Wildlife Conference.[83]

As planning for the gathering began, conference organizer Seth Gordon solicited ideas from Leopold about the subjects that should be covered. Leopold answered Gordon's letter from a hotel in Berlin, where he and five other American forestry experts were engaged in a study of German practices.[84] His response to Gordon went on for six pages. The main obstacle to conservation, Leopold contended, was a deeply rooted one—the "basic assumption that land is a merely economic commodity" and "that land-use is governed wholly by economic forces."[85] For conservation measures to succeed, they "must be premised first of all on a revision of the national attitude toward land, its life, and its products."[86] Somehow landowners had to be motivated to keep their lands in good shape ecologically. This was the only way to protect the public interest in its private lands and resources. "The ownership and use of land," he wrote, "entails obligations and opportunities of transeconomic value and importance, just as the establishment of a family does. Until this concept of land becomes an integral part of the national philosophy, conservation can be nothing but makeshift." "Economic forces," Leopold continued,

> especially the forces of mechanized society, tend constantly to obstruct and defeat such an attitude toward land. To this extent economic development has become, from the viewpoint of conservation, a pathological process. The ways and means to conservation, then, must deal primarily with arresting these pathological tendencies, and with the removal of economic obstacles to better land use.[87]

Leopold's ideas drew prompt comment from Ding Darling, who had received a copy of Leopold's suggestions from Gordon. Darling wrote to Leopold pointing out to him how far his suggestions were drifting from those of the dominant national culture, which accepted as a matter of fact the goodness of pioneering individualism and economic resource development.[88] Groups as well as individuals could misuse land, Darling reminded him. Socialist or democratic, any government could view nature as a collection of inexhaustible resources available for economic exploitation, with the same harmful effects on the land itself.[89] Darling admitted that poor government organization was perhaps not the most significant challenge facing conservation. But if bureaucratic reform had to wait until a new scientifically informed, public-spirited attitude toward land emerged and if people's attitudes resisted such change, where did that leave conservation? Landscape planning made little sense given the independence of landowners. Why prepare plans for private lands over which the public had little managerial control?

Darling had no answers, but he was not sure Leopold did either. "I agree with you as to the desired objective of a new national wildlife policy," Darling wrote. Both Leopold and Darling agreed on the basic importance of enriching "the national life through contacts with nature"[90] and agreed that this would require a change in "the national attitude." In his experience, though, Darling pointed out, government leaders often pronounced upon use of private lands without private landholders being present. Understandably, landowners were "singularly unimpressed by . . . philosophies and conclusions" made by distant bureaucrats. In other words, "we have been planning dresses for another man's wife," Darling observed wryly. Leopold's hope was that landowners would eventually come to embrace a new, community-based idea of good land use and that social pressures would help prompt it. Darling could imagine a man coming to "wish for his land to be popular with his neighbors as he wishes his wife and children to be smart and useful citizens,"[91] but it was a utopian ideal, he warned, and would be long in coming if it ever did. In the meantime, Leopold's call for a new orientation toward land sounded, to Darling's ear, a troubling note:

> I can't get away from the idea that you are getting us out into water over our depth by your new philosophy of wildlife environment. The end of that road leads to socialization of property which I could only tolerate willingly if I could be shown that it would work. . . . One of the most terrifying spectacles in modern *socialized states* is the rape of natural resources to raise the level of an otherwise low standard of living. . . . The Napoleonic law, under which Germany operates its wildlife program and on which rests the ownership of wildlife in the government seems to me to be as near an approach to socialistic control as is practical at this period of progress in civilization. I had looked for some expression from you on this subject upon your return from your trip into Germany.[92]

Leopold was well aware of this tension regarding governing ideals, yet he had also observed some of the conservation successes of Germany's more centralized system. He wrote on the subject in a 1936 report, "Notes on Game Administration in Germany." With a much denser population than that of the United States, Germany had organized farm game administration efficiently. Leopold, pondering the situation, observed:

[The] whole system is manifestly a surrender of individualism to the community. There is no real distinction between government (organized from the top-down) and the popular voice (organized from the bottom-up). . . . The combined spread of the system of law, administration, ethics, customs, and procedures is incredibly complete and internally harmonious.[93]

Leopold firmly believed in the need for an American form of game administration that delivered at least equally good results. To accomplish this, however, fresh ideas were needed.[94] As he mused over his German experience, Leopold wondered if the appropriate form of national game administration might be determined by human population density.[95] Perhaps top-down controls were more needed in crowded places. Perhaps proper forms of governance might be related to some balance between hunting and development demands and the amount of game and game territory. Germans were ahead of Americans in their biological understanding of game cropping, their system delivered results with a much higher ratio of people to land than in the United States, and they had achieved these results on the basis of field experience rather than scientific study. Perhaps with good science, more land, and a lower human density America could achieve equally good outcomes with a less controlled system. "Is it a rosy dream," Leopold asked,

> to envisage the ultimate emergence of an American system, founded upon ecological science, unencumbered by too much history, utilizing to the utmost our basic advantage of elbow-room, and so integrated with our sociology and economics as to perpetuate indefinitely the opportunity for contact with natural beauty?[96]

It seemed to Leopold "not a dream, but a challenge."[97]

Plainly Leopold was wrestling with the enigma of fitting private individuals who valued their liberties into larger economic and political systems in ways that successfully promoted conservation.[98] How could the individual parts fit together into harmonious wholes, particularly in the cases of individual landowners? What measures might motivate private individuals to embrace conservative land practices for the good of their community, state, and country? More generally, how should negative personal freedom—the liberty of individuals to act as they pleased as long as they did not harm one another—be balanced with positive collective freedom—the liberty of people to work together to achieve shared landscape goals? The issues, Leopold knew, lodged at the center of the conservation predicament.

Many of Leopold's writings were touching upon these questions, and at least a few observant readers could see the struggles Leopold was having with them. Particularly attentive during the 1930s and 1940s was a former student, Douglas Wade. In a 1944 letter to his former teacher, Wade recounted a recent discussion he had had with Eleanor King, editor of *Audubon Magazine* and publisher of a number of Leopold's articles. "Several months ago," wrote Wade on September 30,

> I had an opportunity to chat with [Eleanor] King. . . . As far as I can recall, she felt that your articles stopped short of conclusions that would show where we were headed. . . . I have wondered if you felt this way about some of your essays? . . . Now I believe that I have hit on something that might be of interest to you and Miss King. I have just finished reading a review of [Friedrich A. von] Hayek's book THE ROAD TO SERFDOM. . . . Hayek, like many of the great political thinkers of the past, apparently believes that socialism and national planning (perhaps a modern form of socialism) lead to "slavery." Socialism and national planning are probably successful only as they progressively remove all freedom of choice from the individual. I believe that you have sensed this pull and have battled against it. In other words you have wanted to be a "liberalist" but have been unable to conclude many of your essays because they point in the direction of socialism or national planning; at least this is what I seem to get from your essays.[99]

After taking note of Hayek's book—in time a libertarian classic— Wade summarized eight of Leopold's articles that illustrated his point. Each article left unclear the proper roles of private initiative and government action on land-use issues. The articles, Wade suggested, revealed the battle in Leopold's mind between liberal individualism and a more coercive, socialist-type order. Wade complimented Leopold, though, for wrestling with the tension. "Impatience," concluded Wade,

> breeds contempt for the slower but perhaps safer ways of private initiative. We are impatient because we believe that many plants and animals will be extirpated and that landscape changes will be so

radical as to destroy forever certain values. Hence we fall easy victims to national planning and socialism. We need some philosophies to guide us. So far, you are one of the few wildlife men who has attempted to give us some guideposts. We are in need of some more guideposts; or, at least, some thoughts that will disturb our complacency.[100]

Leopold was clear, however, on one related point, particularly in his recent writing: all conservation work, whether undertaken from the top down or the bottom up, soon encountered the obstacle of popular attitudes and understandings about nature. But to Leopold's mind, while both remained important, working from the bottom up held distinctly more democratic promise in accomplishing conservation's two interrelated priorities: positive effects on the land itself and positive effects on people.

Leopold replied to Wade in a brief letter addressing the tension that Wade had perceived. As he had in earlier letters to Seth Gordon and Ding Darling, he focused on the role of cultural attitudes as foundations for economic and political organizations. He had been reticent to discuss these matters publicly, but he could see clearly enough that his own developing conservation philosophy required deep changes in the American people:

> The subject you bring up is one that interests me greatly, but I am not sure that we can discuss it satisfactorily by letter. I'd like very much to talk it out with you. As far as I know the thing that is lacking in my papers arises from my realization that nothing can be done about them [conservation problems] without creating a new kind of people. Rules and recipes are useless for those who can't understand what's behind them. I am not aware of a conflict between liberalism and social planning in my mind because I am thoroughly convinced that social planning in the degree apparently favored by me is thoroughly no good. Things that are done wholly by government are really not done, because any decent land-use is worthwhile, not only for its effect on the land, but for its effect on the owner. If the owner is an impersonal government, nobody is benefited except the government employee.
>
> Please don't consider this as a real reply to your very important letter. Will you bring the matter up the next time we can have a beer together, or better still, two or three beers?[101]

To Leopold's mind conservation needed to take place from the ground up, both literally, in terms of physical effects on the land, and in human terms, measured qualitatively in attitudes and values. Conservation, in other words, would require not merely new political and economic mechanisms and vehicles but also changes in the human values and attitudes that ultimately shaped economic and political systems. Perhaps "'democracy,' 'communism,' and 'fascism'" were not the only three possible modern political alternatives, he mused in a brief, uncompleted essay.[102] All three embraced industrial economies and rested on innate human behavior patterns. None promoted an ethical understanding toward the land. Perhaps a new kind of government could emerge in the light of new conservation-related discoveries. "The conservation professions," Leopold wrote, "occupy a peculiar and interesting position":

> They are something like the frog in a railroad switch, which "started out in life," so to speak, to be just a plain and humble piece of steel, but which later, by accident of placement, finds itself responsible for routing the world's traffic.[103]

Whatever its form, government was needed in conservation to fulfill particular functions, including to help further much-needed research. And government's work would become "real and important" if and when conservation did rise up from below:

> Government is the tester of fact vs. fiction, the umpire of bogus vs. genuine, the sponsor of research, the guardian of technical standards, and, I hasten to add, the proper custodian of land, which, for one reason or another, is not suited to private husbandry. These functions will become real and important as soon as conservation begins to grow from the bottom up, instead of from the top down, as is now the case.[104]

To help create "a new kind of people" and better policies real facts were required, based on well-designed scientific experiments that considered local conditions.[105] Until more local facts were gathered, even basic understandings about land would remain tentative.

From the Ground Up

After Leopold returned from Germany in November 1935 he pulled together materials dealing with his own bottom-up land-use experiments, for presentation at the North American Wildlife Conference.

Taking place at the Mayflower Hotel in Washington, D.C., on February 3–7, 1936, the conference included a broad gathering of conservation concerns. The primary purpose was to assemble national leaders in conservation and allied fields to draw up "a program for restoration of our wildlife resources."[106] Conference participants were looking to share new facts about wildlife and to develop a national and international wildlife program, making "real progress toward a common goal."[107] A third, more focused objective, indicative of the continuing demand for greater cooperation, was to form a national federation of wildlife interests. The federation ideally would include sportsmen's clubs, farm organizations, nature leagues, bird societies, and other conservation associations. Once united, the groups would be better able to speak with authority. Out of the conference, its organizers hoped, would come the concrete national wildlife plan for which FDR was still calling.[108]

Leopold spoke twice at the conference. In one talk he stressed the importance of conserving private lands: "[N]o rounded program for wildlife is possible unless it is applied on private as well as public lands,"[109] he declared. His other talk was delivered at a special session on farmer-sportsman cooperatives—a promising form of bottom-up conservation. Cooperatives were local, voluntary organizations of farmers and nonfarming hunters who came together to make farmlands produce more game.[110] A great variety of organizational arrangements were being tried out across the country. Members typically pooled acreages and delegated responsibilities among landowners and city-based hunters. As Leopold had recommended in his 1931 game report, many cooperatives were experimenting with various forms of farmer incentives—cash, service, or protection of farm property—in exchange for use of their lands by hunters and specific land-use measures to increase game populations. Leopold was active in organizing such cooperative ventures in Wisconsin,[111] just as he had helped to establish game protective associations, promote associations of livestock owners, and encourage community efforts to plant trees in Albuquerque. Leopold understood that cooperatives were one way for people and their neighbors to "help themselves," to do their own work in improving their farms and shared landscapes and to reap the shared pleasures.[112]

A feeding trough set up with a protective cover to determine which foods game birds preferred during cold months. Leopold and his students planned to use the results to help sportsmen and farmers better manage habitat for game.

Leopold concluded his talk on cooperatives by explaining their vital significance despite their small size. In terms of acreage cooperatives so far encompassed relatively few "microscopic specks on a state map." Still, they were more important than "our more comprehensive strokes of propaganda which sweep in graceful arcs [across the country]." "It is the difference," as Leopold put it, "between vertical and horizontal planning." When a distant government agency tried to promote any single type of conservation, he explained, it was "trying to spread an idea over an infinite horizontal expanse." This did not work sufficiently because every spot on the map was unique. When the government tried to dovetail two or more such ideas over the same expanse ("together with sermons on bureaucracy and blue prints for reorganization of departments"), the outcome was confusing, to say the least. "If we could focus the minds of a whole battery of conservation experts simultaneously on one spot," Leopold suggested instead, the experts would "often reach an agreement on its condition, its properties, and its needs" and its best and most enduring uses. "It may take a long time to cover the country," Leopold admitted, but such "vertical planning" was "preferable to a smear."[113]

Conservation problems became too theoretical when viewed from a distance. Successful work arose from the ground up. It involved real places, with soils, waters, wild plants, animals, and real people who lived on their lands. Without a firm foundation, top-down planning for conservation made little sense and could even do significant harm. When it came to conservation, sound planning needed to start with specific lands and the wild creatures that were parts of them:

> I also doubt, as a matter of hindsight, whether anything but ultimate discredit can come to the wildlife movement if it encourages or participates in orgies of incontinent public expenditure on half baked plans for wildlife betterment.... Perhaps a sounder start can be made by beginning at the bottom-end of the problem, and building programs on the specific needs of particular birds and mammals, rather than on the desires, ambitions, and prerogatives of bureaus, departments, and public groups.[114]

Leopold reiterated his insistence on a bottom-up perspective in a 1935 exchange with Ding Darling on the subject of getting game management advice into landowners' hands.[115] Darling was anxious to prepare a simple game management guide to distribute to landowners throughout the country. He wrote to ask for Leopold's help in preparing the guide:

> Farm Bureau directors and county agents together with many State game officials have written in to know where a simplified plan of applied game management could be had. I have cited your volume and the works and articles by Stoddard, etc. But almost invariably the request has come back for something boiled down to A.B.C. simplicity.[116]

Leopold's response was sympathetic yet firm. The sentiment was a worthy one, but the project was unsound:

I thoroughly share your conviction that there is pressing need at this moment for published game material in ABC form suitable for laymen.

I am certain, however, that this material must be compiled by regions, or preferably by states. In other words, any attempt to compile it nationally would automatically contain so many "ifs and ands" as to destroy its simplicity, and if these "ifs and ands" were omitted, it would no longer be true. Accordingly I have [been] thinking in terms of state or regional farmers' handbooks, and for the last two years I have been preparing to get one out for Wisconsin. . . .

If the Biological Survey can stimulate the compilation of such handbooks region by region or state by state, it is one of the most important new steps which the Bureau could possibly undertake. In many regions, of course, the material does not yet exist due to the absence of local research and the absence of local demonstration areas from which local techniques could be derived.[117]

By the late 1930s, Leopold could write hopefully, at least, that "the day has passed when it is necessary to justify research."[118] Yet the picture was not as rosy when one understood how little had been accomplished relative to need and with what little tangible support. Thinking back over the course of the decade, Leopold continued:

Half a dozen New Deal Bureaus are spending a score of millions on wildlife work, but not a red penny for research. They [the bureaus] [come] to some research Unit whose total budget would not pay their office boys and say: "Please give us the facts on which to build our program." Naturally we can't. Nor could we if we stood with them under the financial cloudburst. Facts, like pine trees, take not only rain, but time.[119]

In 1933 Leopold had compared conservation to the birth of the moon—something heavy hurled forth into space, traveling rapidly through the galaxy of the alphabets and passing near the open moneybags of post-Depression relief. Near the end of the decade a frustrated Leopold concluded, "At the present moment, however, it is easier to get help for the problems of the moon than the problems of the Earth."[120]

➤➤ ◄◄

Leopold would spend the latter part of his life imagining and trying out ways to bring America's complex social, political, economic, and cultural forces into a cohesive national vision and practice of good land use. With increasing clarity he was seeing that a sound vision of good land use was not possible until people gained a more comprehensive understanding of how the land itself was organized and functioned. Near the bottom of all of Leopold's thinking was a growing collection of facts and observations about real land. From the late 1930s into the 1940s and until his death, Leopold's thinking about scientific research and the meaning of gathered facts would increasingly cohere and mature. He would continually work with those facts and observations, synthesizing them, attempting ceaselessly to give conservation the soundest ecological foundation.

Chapter 6

A Common Concept of Land

I hardly think it necessary to argue the importance of analogy before a group of ecologists. . . . What homology is to the geneticist, analogy is to the ecologist.

Alfred E. Emerson, *Plant and Animal Communities*

Conservation, to Leopold's mind, was about the relationship between human thoughts and actions and their effects on the land. A civilization functioning in concert with the land's conservation, he believed, would be not only good for land but also more productive of rich human lives, which were interwoven with it. To best integrate human ways with nature's, however, would first require understanding how the parts of the land—its soils, waters, plants, and animals—interacted to sustain life. Nature was vastly complex. Understanding its workings was much easier said than done.

Leopold was not alone in recognizing the need for this kind of ecological understanding. By the 1930s the demand for new ecologists had exceeded the supply, particularly of ecologists with a broad practical knowledge of the field, capable of advising a nation in ecological trouble.[1] In their studies of nature's dynamic interrelationships, ecologists were dealing with vast intricacies—oftentimes difficult to probe experimentally or to develop into general principles.[2] So far ecologists had done better at collecting facts than at connecting them into useful packages of information. "Ecology," pioneering ecologist Charles C. Adams lamented in 1913, was "a science with its facts all out of proportion to their organization or integration."[3] More than a quarter of a century later the mismatch remained, prominent University of Chicago ecologist Thomas Park emphasized:

> Ecology appears to stand in great need of coordination and synthesis. That the field [in both population and community ecology] has produced an abundance of factual material in the last thirty years is indisputable. However, the facts have not been adequately assembled into principles and concepts.[4]

Ecology in the early decades of the twentieth century was also struggling toward professional recognition as a fully fledged member of the broader scientific community. By 1920 both the British Ecological Society (founded in 1913) and the Ecological Society of America (ESA; 1915) were growing in membership. But if ecology as a discipline was becoming institutionalized, it had not yet gained internal coherence. Many basic and applied fields of research—limnology, botany, zoology, physiology, geography, fisheries science, soil science, hydrology, food crop agriculture, entomology, ornithology, and forestry—included what could be considered ecological explorations, yet each had been developing separately. The ESA seemed "a polyglot organization made up of botanists, zoologists, etc., but only a handful of ecologists. . . . The Society is not a group of one mind," founder Victor Shelford complained as late as 1939.[5] Signs of increasing cooperation, though, were present among members of different branches of the scientific community. Ecologists were talking with more specialized "economic scientists," who studied nature in relation to resource production problems. Wildlife conservation in particular had taken on a more "ecological flavor," noted another prominent ecologist, in no small part because of the works of Herbert Stoddard (*The Bobwhite Quail*, 1931) and Aldo Leopold (*Game Management*, 1933).[6]

Despite ecology's youth and diversity, if not yet principles, core topics and themes were emerging. Some scientists were probing nature's ongoing changes and were identifying patterns in them. Others were suggesting theories about how nature's parts and processes came to fit together in ways that displayed degrees of balance or equilibrium. Among the most popular ecological notions at the time was the community concept, which incorporated ideas about both patterns of ecological change and conditions of equilibrium.[7] As early as the 1840s aquatic scientists had observed that groups of organisms formed assemblages or communities. In 1877 German zoologist Karl Möbius, after studying marine oyster beds, defined the "biocoenosis," a collection of species living together in community on a given territory, the resources of which determined the number of organisms living there.[8] A seminal article by Stephen Forbes in 1887, "The Lake as a Microcosm," extended the holistic perspective of the organic community to lakes.[9] In 1899 Henry Cowles published a foundational article on the dynamics of terrestrial plant communities as they developed in an apparently orderly series of types.[10] And in 1907 Victor Shelford produced a study tracking animal community changes in relation to plant community dynamics; by 1912 he was arguing for the unity of the plant-animal community, or "biotic association."[11] By the 1920s the study of natural communities had become widespread, although assemblages of plants and animals still were often studied separately. Looking back on four decades of ecology's development, Park and his Chicago colleagues summarized its history, emphasizing the importance of the community concept. "Early in the century," they wrote, "botanists and zoologists began to conceive of biotic groupings as integrated wholes. These they designated 'communities.' The community concept flourished from then on and, for a time, was identified by some as synonymous with ecology."[12]

Although the community idea was popular, not all scientists liked it, and many variations were advanced on what it meant and how it should be used, if at all, in scientific research.[13] By the mid-1930s, too, ecologists were arguing over whether it was helpful to think of assemblages of coexisting plants and animals as being like "complex organisms."[14] In an influential 1935 article in *Ecology*, the ESA's primary journal, British ecologist Arthur Tansley challenged nature-as-organism and even nature-as-community language. He proposed instead the term "ecosystem,"[15] which, he believed, would better represent combined organic and inorganic physical systems as wholes while promoting a sounder mental conception of the "basic units of nature."

Leopold's own understanding of ecological science was maturing alongside that of his colleagues and the discipline itself. In the early 1930s Leopold conceived of game management as a branch of applied ecology that included aspects of forestry, agronomy, mammalogy, ornithology, and other land sciences.[16] By the end of that decade he understood ecology as the science that could help bring all of these approaches together with the common aim of understanding the complexities of the land — its soils, waters, plants, and animals — as a whole.[17] Leopold understood that ecology, still a "new science" in the 1930s, was "an infant just learning to talk."[18] He would ply the field's full range of vocabulary using both organismic and systems terminology as well as creatively adding to its lexicon to make ecological ideas accessible to diverse audiences. "Plants, animals, men, and soil are a community of interdependent parts, an organism,"[19] he wrote. At the same time the land was a system, "a fountain of energy flowing through a circuit of soils, plants, and animals,"[20] as well as a "biotic stream" or "round river."[21] By the 1930s Leopold had begun referring regularly to land as a "biotic community."[22] And it would remain a term he preferred.

The years 1935–1939 were particularly fruitful in Leopold's ongoing effort to understand the basics of the land's functioning. His 1935 trip to Germany, with its opportunities to observe European-style game management and forestry administration, had come shortly after his purchase that spring of land along the Wisconsin River in Sauk County, with a chicken coop soon dubbed "the Shack." Here he and his family would begin restoring some of the worn-out agricultural land about which Leopold had thought and written so much, as dust from the Great Plains drifted eastward. National wildlife planning was in the works, as were the farmer-sportsman cooperative experiments and the Coon Valley Project, which drew his attention and helped stimulate his research and teaching at the University of Wisconsin. In 1936 and 1937 Leopold took two hunting vacation trips in the wilds of Mexico along the Gavilan River.

These, too, would critically shape his evolving thought. In addition to these direct experiences, Leopold was learning a great deal from fellow ecologists. Knowledge about the land, in short, was coming from a variety of sources, and Leopold was at work bringing pieces together in his mind.

Leopold took good advantage of an opportunity in 1939 to present a summary of some of those ideas to his professional colleagues. The occasion was the plenary session of a joint meeting in Milwaukee of the Ecological Society of America and the Society of American Foresters. He used the opportunity to explain his developing concept of the land's functioning and why such a concept was important for conservation efforts. His presentation, quickly published, was titled "A Biotic View of Land."[23] It would be Leopold's most sustained exposition on the subject, providing the foundation for such of his later essays as "The Ecological Conscience"[24] and "The Land Ethic."[25] It also would be his single most important contribution to the science of ecology. In what he considered ecology's most urgent

The "Shack," the only structure standing on a worn-out farm that Leopold acquired in 1935. Leopold bought the Shack so that he and his family could enjoy restoring the land and spending time together outdoors.

task—developing an overall sense of how land worked—Leopold at the moment stood at the forefront of the field.

Before Leopold could draft that presentation, however, he had needed to finish constructing his mental image of land as a dynamic operating system. Piece by piece his understanding came together, and by 1939 he was ready to speak.

ECOLOGY AS THE FUSION POINT FOR THE SCIENCES

During the mid-1930s it was becoming clear to many besides Leopold that successful land management, integrating in one place the full range of conservation values, was far from easy. "The plain lesson," Leopold observed in 1934,

> is that to be a practitioner of conservation on a piece of land takes more brains, and a wider range of sympathy, forethought, and experience, than to be a specialized forester, game manger, range manager, or erosion expert in a college or a conservation bureau. Integration is easy on paper, but a lot more important and more difficult in the field than any of us foresaw.[26]

It was the repeated failure by land managers to succeed in this integration endeavor that led to the persistence of many land-related problems. "Nearly all maladjustments in land," Leopold stated in a report for the Society of American Foresters, "have one thing in common: the difficulty of adjusting two or more simultaneous uses for the same soil."[27] A full solution to the problem would not come easily, but "a part of the remedy," Leopold contended, "seems to lie in the development of a keener ecological perception in foresters and other land technicians."[28] Even in the mid-1930s, decades into the new era of professionally managed public lands, maladjustments remained common:

> Continued overgrazing of public properties which have been under technical administration free from politics can be ascribed only to two things: lack of courage, or lack of ecological perception (ability to "read country"). Of the two, the latter seems by far the most probable. . . . [D]eficiencies in ecological perception are the principal obstacle to the development of game management.[29]

Leopold would return to the point again and again, urging others to keep it in sight. "The last two years," explained Leopold in a 1937 game policy report, "have brought increasing confusion of thought to the entire conservation field. An intellectual revolution seems to be in process, the net effect of which is to vastly expand both the importance and the difficulty of the conservation idea."[30] Coordinating land uses was the elusive goal, and an ecological perception— a clear concept of land—was the necessary precursor:

> One mistake, probably made by us as individuals as often as by others, is the notion that coordination of land uses is easy. In the enthusiasm of trying to get both game management and silviculture started, both professions have adopted the uncritical assumption that they fit beautifully together.
>
> They do fit beautifully, but not always easily. Nor can the fitting be accomplished without mutual concessions. . . . Exactly analogous difficulties and delays are being experienced in fitting together the sciences underlying land uses.[31]

The challenge of understanding the land, Leopold analogized in his 1933 *Game Management*, was much like a "jig-saw puzzle," and the key to its solution was "the science of ecology."[32] Ecology, as he put it later in the decade, could provide "the new fusion point for all the sciences."[33] If ecology could fulfill that task, and if land managers could make effective use of it, they would be "helping to write a new definition of what science is for."[34] Equipped with an ecological concept of land, they would be readied "to harmonize the increasing kit of scientific tools and the increasing recklessness in using them with the shrinking biotas to which they are applied."[35]

A piece-by-piece approach to conservation was not successful because the land's parts were so intricately interwoven. It was therefore critical to conservation, Leopold was coming to see, for people to understand land as an integrated whole. By mid-decade Leopold, drawing from the science of ecology, had collected a number of key pieces of the puzzle, revealing ways in which the land was self-organized and functioned, and he was fitting them together in his own mind. Over the course of his career in conservation, already spanning a quarter of a century, soils, waters, plants, and animals emerged in Leopold's understanding as the interacting parts common to landscapes, or, in other words, the "alphabet of 'natural objects,'" which spelled out an ecological story—a story in which people's actions were playing an increasing role.[36] It was this story—this ecological odyssey—Leopold believed, that needed telling and retelling for conservation to succeed, but first it needed to be understood. Leopold thus set about the challenging work of synthesizing what was so far known about the complex story of land.

AN ORGANIZED TANGLE

For years the issue of fluctuating animal population numbers and the mechanisms behind them had intrigued scientists studying a diversity of organisms and systems, including the scientists gathered at Matamek in 1931. Research into wildlife population cycles was one manifestation of such interest, one that, as we have seen, held Leopold's attention as a game manager concerned about lows in game populations. On the other side of the numbers question was the matter of animal populations that suddenly rose in number to become pests: why did this happen? The irruption of animal pests had drawn increasing notice among land managers since early in the century. In 1917 Leopold's friend P. S. Lovejoy had compiled a useful overview of the mounting pest problems in the forests.[37] Some pests were native species whose numbers had gotten out of control. Tamarack sawflies, for instance, had practically eliminated millions of acres of tamaracks in the Great Lakes states; *Dendroctonus* beetles had killed western yellow pines. Other pest problems were due to species that humans had introduced into new places. These "ecological stowaways"[38] or "exotic" species could also become plaguelike. Gypsy and brown-tail moths were accidentally loosed in the eastern forests; the chestnut blight, a fungus from Asia, left little hope for the American chestnut. In the West and Midwest rodent and insect pests were responsible for large losses to farmers; in the southern cotton fields, the boll weevil caused crop failure and farm devastation. The federal government's principal response to pest complaints was to support efforts to poison or otherwise kill them, but this response was seldom effective in the long term.

Important new information on pest irruptions arose out of work in the Southwest published in 1935 by another of Leopold's colleagues, Walter Taylor of the USDA Biological Survey.[39] In "The Relation of Jack Rabbits to Grazing in Southern Arizona"[40] Taylor concluded that many pest irruptions were less the *cause* of vegetative degradation than they were the *effect* of that degradation. It was on heavily altered lands that populations of grasshoppers, white grubs, and small rodents all tended to rise. Once they became numerous, the pests then contributed further to the land's degradation. Taylor's work with jackrabbits supported the theory. So did research in British Columbia that showed a positive relationship between range depletion and outbreaks of noxious grasshoppers.[41] According to that study, insect pests could be "fenced out" of grasslands simply by fencing out cattle. Insects were seldom troubling when grasslands remained intact. Similarly, in southern Wisconsin, pastures with thick, dense sod, ample fertility, and favorable moisture conditions were relatively free from white grub infestations, whereas grubs were more common in pastures that were not judiciously grazed and where livestock had thinned the turf.

If Taylor's assertions were true, Leopold noted in a December 1935 letter, "then the poisoning problem becomes a problem which cannot be dissociated from the range problem. Rodent pests appear as one of the penalties which we now face as a consequence of fifty-years of land-abuse."[42] A further implication, important in terms of Leopold's understanding, was that such pest irruptions served as useful indicators of ecological degradation, in much the same way as did abnormal erosion and flash floods. For decades scientists and land users had understood that heavy grazing did not merely deplete the vegetation in a place: it actually changed the composition of resident plants. Perennial prairie plants often were reduced or eliminated, replaced by annual grasses, herbs, and weeds of various kinds and qualities.[43] Now it was turning out that heavy grazing could foster not just plant weeds but also animal pests. Taylor drew the parallel directly: "Results of grazing are expressed not only in terms of weeds and annual grasses, but of animal 'weeds' also. Both animals and plants are likely to be different on a grazed area from what they are on an ungrazed or lightly grazed area."[44]

Taylor's work helped Leopold not only in his ecological understanding of pests but also in his continuing struggle with a second ecological issue, the roles of competition and cooperation in shaping the mix of life that inhabited a given place. Leopold's thinking on this subject took place in the context of the widely influential ideas of University of Nebraska plant ecologist Frederic Clements regarding systematic changes in plant communities — assemblies of plants in an area, Clements thought, largely being determined by climate and soil substrates.[45] Clements was intrigued by the processes of change within natural systems, particularly the process of vegetative succession,[46] involving a series of developmental changes in an area's plant composition. Over time (and assuming no disruptions), Clements believed, the process led to a final, particular mix of plant species. Clements named the ultimate mix the climax stage;[47] when it was reached the progress of succession had come to its mature end. Plant communities occurring in the sandy region of north-central Indiana served to illustrate the phenomenon: first cottonwood trees would come in; these typically would give way to jack pine and then black oak, which would be replaced in turn by white oak and then red oak; finally the community would reach a mature state dominated by a nonprogressing association of beech and maple.[48] Succession, Clements admitted, often was disrupted, and it regularly got sidetracked or overshot the mark (he discussed a postclimax stage as well), but it was a discernible process nonetheless and usefully teased out of the larger mix of ongoing vegetation change. Clements' work provided a fruitful research framework for many ecologists, though many found his single "climatic" climax idea either doubtful or unhelpful, given numerous exigencies that often apparently prevented climaxes and the difficulties that arose in identifying them.[49]

While Leopold and other scientists and land managers were at work making sense of population mechanisms, Clements labored with Victor Shelford and others to catalogue the various types of vegetative communities in North America.[50] This was a different, practical kind of ecological work, requiring a holistic view of natural systems. With Shelford's influence Clements amended his ideas of dynamic successional communities to include characteristic animal species — accompanying the cottonwood on sandy Indiana soil was the white tiger beetle, with the jack pine was the tiger beetle, and so on.[51] A full categorization of such biotic communities, Clements and Shelford assumed, would prove helpful to both future scientific studies and land protection. It was urgent, as they saw matters, for the nation to act immediately to preserve prime examples of as many types of communities as possible before they were significantly altered by humans.[52] The climax community idea seemed as useful a guide as any for the classification task, however inexact. Their work continued throughout the 1930s even as Clements and Shelford disagreed endlessly in their attempts to identify types.[53]

Leopold's work in human-altered landscapes, however, did not require him to categorize natural areas in detail by type. For that reason and perhaps others he made less use of Clements' ideas about particular climatic climax stages, even though he embraced the idea of succession.[54] The climax vegetative stage, Leopold knew from his early days in the Southwest, could be perpetually hindered by fire or other natural disturbances. The climax stage also was not necessarily best for humans, nor was it a necessary stage to reach for the land to remain productive.

Of greater personal value for Leopold was Clements' and others' work on the role of competition in shaping plant and animal communities and directing community dynamics, including succession.[55] As vegetative succession progressed, a wide variety of organisms, many with narrow functional specialties, were linked in an intricate arrangement. Typically this arrangement was remarkably efficient in sharing resources and enhancing the land's overall productivity—its issue of plant and animal life. Before he could forge a full concept of land, Leopold had to understand better how this complexity, specialization, and efficiency all came about.

Clements and his coauthors, plant ecologists John Weaver and Herbert C. Hanson, described competition as a give and take between plants and their physical environment.[56] Plants competed with one another when there was a shortage in the local environment of something they needed. The more similar two plants were in terms of needs, the more likely they were to compete;[57] dissimilarity of plant form tended to reduce competition and to allow invasion of new species, altering the community. Each plant affected its habitat, and the habitat in turn affected the plant. As a plant successfully captured nutrients and water, and as that plant's leaf surface increased, for example, it reduced the amount of light and heat available to those near or underneath it. Although competition continued endlessly, its dynamic effects, Clements believed, diminished as a community's successional development progressed toward its climax, making it harder for new plants to displace established ones or otherwise to gain greater light, moisture, and nutrients. Each new season, however, still brought new seedlings and shoots and often changes in the land's physical environment (rainfall, fire episodes, and the like), which would also alter the community's conditions.[58]

According to Clements and his coauthors, "competition plays the basic rôle in the community that food-making does in the plant. No community escapes its effects."[59] "Indeed," asserted the authors, the community "can hardly be said to exist as such until the individuals come into this relation with each other."[60] Only when competition became fierce, though, did the vegetative community gain its full complexity, with the various plants dividing up available resources. When allowed to operate without overriding disruption, competition produced a tightly knit, reasonably stable community of plants, one that, Clements believed, operated with a high level of efficiency. Not unlike Adam Smith's popular capitalist philosophy, some invisible hand seemingly molded the "self-interest" of organisms into a common good. Once the organisms had sorted out their respective spaces the resulting community was characterized by what appeared to be cooperation or coordination among the species. But competition, not any motive to cooperate, was the driving force; it was what largely determined the kinds and numbers of plants in a given place.

Competition, of course, took place among animals as well as among plants. This competition, too, required understanding as Leopold was piecing together his overall concept of land. Competition limited densities of animal populations, determined what kinds of organisms might live in a given place, and supplied a necessary mechanism for balance. As he probed this issue Leopold paid attention to the work of mathematical ecologist Alexander J. Nicholson[61] and even more to the related work of his friend Charles Elton.[62] Competition among animals, Elton believed, centered on their feeding habits. "The primary driving force of all animals," wrote Elton, "is the necessity of finding the right kind of food and enough of it."[63] Animals were thus arranged according to their diets, with herbivores feeding on plants and carnivores on other animals.

The result was a web of life consisting of animals linked together into complex food chains.[64] Two broad generalizations highlighted the central characteristics of this web: "the enemy is larger than the animal upon which it preys,"[65] and the "very existence of food chains is due mainly to the fact that any one animal can only live on food of a certain size."[66] Elton's conclusion, based on this and other evidence, was that "although the actual species of animals are different in different habitats, the ground plan of every animal community is much the same."[67]

As Elton studied the varied roles that animals had in food webs, he found it useful to describe their positions with the term "niche."[68] A niche to Elton was the specific functional position that an animal filled within a community in terms of what it was *doing—"its relations to food and enemies."*[69] A niche was largely determined by an animal's size and food habits. Every community contained animals with certain types of food habits; there were herbivores, seed eaters, pollen gatherers, carnivores, and scavenging animals of various types. The exact species filling the niches varied considerably from place to place, but the food-habit roles remained much the same from community to community. "The importance of studying niches," wrote Elton, "is partly that it enables us to see how very different animal communities may resemble each other in the essentials of organisation."[70]

Like Clements, Shelford, Tansley, and other ecologists, Elton wanted to know how organisms in a given place changed over time and organized themselves. And, ahead of many animal ecologists of the time, Elton emphasized competition. Competition shaped a wide variety of niches over time, generating distinct patterns of organisms bound together in complexes of interdependent relationships. Niches, in a sense, helped turn competition into cooperation, he believed. Through ecological and evolutionary processes organisms in a particular place came to have specialized community roles. As they did they divided limited resources among themselves efficiently, enabling a diversity of species to coexist. Paradoxically, that is, competition for resources apparently produced an arrangement in which competition was reduced or contained.

As Elton and colleagues were studying competition and food

interrelations other ecologists were approaching similar issues of dynamic community organization and functioning by focusing on energy flows through physical inorganic-organic systems, applying fundamentals of physics. The evolutionary trend, some scientists argued, was toward increasing efficiency of energy flows. According to the "law of maximum energy," suggested in 1925 by mathematical population scientist A. J. Lotka, the "net effect" of evolution was to "maximize . . . the energy flux through the system of organic nature."[71] Similarly, Arthur Tansley thought in terms of "whole webs of life," which were the "living nuclei of *systems* in the sense of the physicist," subject to the law of the conservation of energy.[72] There was, Tansley argued, "a kind of natural selection of incipient systems": a system's components through evolutionary processes were shaped to work together with increasing efficiency, maximizing use of the energy flows that sustained its survival.[73]

In the work going on around him Leopold found important pieces to add to his emerging image of the land as a functioning system. Competition and cooperation, Leopold sensed (as did others) were not independent forces; in some way they were parts of a single community-shaping mechanism involving both plants and animals. In a 1937 article Leopold made reference to the jigsaw puzzle of competition and cooperation that characterized communities in nature.[74] By 1939 he was confident enough to use the past tense when talking about species competition and cooperation as separate and distinct functions. They should no longer be thought about that way, Leopold implied; instead they were parts of a single interwoven process that contributed to the "complex biota."[75] That biota—all the living creatures in a given place—was held together by food chains, as stressed by Elton, Shelford, and others. It also could be compared to an unclosed circuit through which energy flowed, as Lotka and Tansley talked about matters.[76] "This interdependence between the complex structure of land and its smooth functioning as an energy circuit," Leopold summarized, "is one of its basic attributes."[77]

As Leopold continued pondering the entire web of life, he found himself drawing upon Elton's work to supply the frame for his own mental concept of land. Leopold borrowed what Elton referred to in his 1927 book as "the pyramid of numbers"[78]—the overall arrangement of animals in predatory interrelationships and characteristic relative population numbers. The foundational principle of the "pyramid" was that "the smaller an animal the commoner it is on the whole."[79] "If you are studying the fauna of an oak wood in summer," Elton explained,

> you will find vast numbers of small herbivorous insects like aphids, a large number of spiders and carnivorous ground beetles, a fair number of small warblers, and only one or two hawks.... To put the matter more definitely, the animals at the base of a food-chain are relatively abundant, while those at the end are relatively few in numbers, and there is a progressive decrease between the two extremes.[80]

The reason for this arrangement, observed Elton, was that small animals were able to increase in number at a very high rate. This high rate of reproduction left ample offspring to feed small carnivorous predators, which in turn produced enough offspring for larger carnivores, and so on, until at the top of the food chain resided a carnivore (such as a lynx or peregrine falcon) whose numbers were too small to support another stage. "This arrangement of numbers in the community," wrote Elton,

> the relative decrease in numbers at each stage in a food-chain, is characteristically found in animal communities all over the world, and to it we have applied the term "pyramid of numbers." It results, as we have seen, from the two facts (a) that smaller animals are preyed upon usually by larger animals and (b) that small animals can increase faster than large ones, and so are able to support the latter.[81]

PLANTS AND ANIMALS TOGETHER

The pyramid of numbers, the idea of niches, the sequential changes of succession, the links between competition and cooperation, energy flows, the tendency of ecological and evolutionary forces to produce diversity and efficiency: these and other concepts all were proving useful. There was, too, the important matter of how plants and animals interacted. Frederic Clements early in the twentieth century had raised the claim that vegetation was the controlling element; the animals in a region, he asserted, were largely determined by the plants there. After further consideration, however, he came more to appreciate the effects of animals on plant distribution and abundance.[82] Animal ecologists were learning more about the important roles animals played in nature's overall dynamical processes, sometimes even dominant ones.[83]

In his 1933 *Game Management* Leopold emphasized plant succession and stressed a controlling role for vegetation in determining the kinds and numbers of animals present in an area. "Each combination of soil, climate, and animal life has its own series of vegetative types,"[84] Leopold wrote. Given this dependence, the art of controlling game populations, by means of manipulating cover and food, was "largely a matter of understanding and controlling plant succession."[85] If the game that a landowner wanted to promote inhabited a given successional plant stage, then the key to elevating game numbers was somehow to arrest the vegetative succession at that stage — just as Indian fires and lightning had done in the Southwest by keeping woody plants from taking over the grasslands.

Even as Leopold wrote his management text, however, he knew that plant-animal interactions were not this simple. As he dug further he was particularly struck by Elton's observations on animal community succession and evidence of how animals altered local plant life rather than merely adapting to it.[86] Elton's work added to the understanding of how the composition of animals in an area could go through developmental stages just as plants did. This possibility, Elton urged, was easily seen in a simple laboratory experiment involving a hay infusion in water, left exposed to air for several weeks.[87] Bacteria were the first organisms to become abundant; then came protozoa. Soon it was possible "to see a whole animal community being gradually built up, as each new species arrives and multiplies and fits into its proper niche."[88] And Elton's work, too, was pointing out how powerful a force animals could be in shaping plant communities. Leopold took particular note of what Elton labeled "Case 8," involving "a typical heather moor in Scotland, with its normal inhabitant, the red grouse."[89] Over a fifteen-year period the heather had converted into rushes and docks, apparently as a result of the arrival of a few pairs of nesting gulls. Protected from harm by the landowner, the gulls had increased to a population of more than 3,000.

The birds manured and trampled the soil, prompting the heather to change to coarse grass and then rushes and docks. Pools of water formed among the plants, attracting large numbers of teal. Meanwhile, the grouse—whose habitat had been so transformed as to make it uninhabitable to them—vanished. At this point the landowner ceased protecting the gulls. Over the next twenty years the nesting gull population diminished to fewer than 60. The teal nearly disappeared and the grouse returned. Ultimately the site became a heather moor again.

What this case and others made clear was that animals, particularly deer, rodents, and other herbivores, could themselves become a controlling factor in vegetational succession. Elton's interpretation was reinforced by the work of Walter Taylor,[90] who offered several examples of how animals affected plant communities. Some changes were beneficial, such as when bees and birds pollinated plants. Other changes, from the human point of view, were destructive, as when human disruptions to landscapes led to outbreaks of species that became pests. Taylor highlighted the matter with the example of what happened when neither natural predators nor hunters were allowed to keep deer herds trimmed. Without such checks deer populations increased, leading to overbrowsing of woody plants, which degraded the regenerative ability of forests.[91] Clearly animals could sometimes control the vegetation.

Elton brought his evidence and theories together into a simple description of how all kinds of life fit together:

> We may perhaps regard the organisms, both plants and animals, occupying any given habitat, as woven into a complex but unstable web of life. The character of the web may change as new organisms appear on the scene and old ones disappear during the phases of succession, but the web itself remains.[92]

Leopold agreed with Elton's view. And as he mulled the supporting evidence from Elton, Taylor, and others he was particularly struck by how the processes of competition and succession, in both plants and animals, seemed to give rise to such complex, interwoven systems, with each species playing its distinct part. Out of nature's dynamic forces apparently came greater efficiencies in the full arrangement, in terms of an ecological system's ability to use and

*With neither native predators nor human hunters to keep herds trimmed,
the deer population in this forest increased. This burgeoning population
overbrowsed herbaceous vegetation and young trees, diminishing forest
reproduction. The horizontal line shows the limit of the deers' reach,
an obvious sign of food shortage.*

cycle nutrient energy. And this ability—building from the ground
up—was directly linked with soil's ability "to receive, store, and
return energy"[93]—its fertility.

WHAT MAKES THINGS GROW

From the beginning of his conservation career Leopold had been
drawn to the fundamental importance of soil. By the time the Dust
Bowl occurred, he already had spent years on efforts to encourage
farmers and ranchers to keep their lands from washing or blowing
away. Now, as he thought about Elton's work and considered earlier
comments of Stoddard and others about soil fertility and animal life,
Leopold tried to figure out how soil was related to ecological communities. Soil, he understood, was not just the medium that allowed
plants to grow and thus animals to live; it was the foundational link
in the entire web of life, the base of the fountain of energy that flowed
through nature's system. Of the pieces that Leopold added to his

image of land in the 1930s, none would take on a bigger role than his growing understanding of soil.

Analysis of soils had long been important to foresters in determining what trees would grow well in a given terrain. A forester recommended proper stocking by comparing soils on different sites, as Leopold had pointed out.[94] On the same soil types in like climates similar trees presumably would grow. From his days in the Southwest he understood painfully that deterioration in soils led, in a kind of retrogressive succession,[95] to changes in an area's array of plants. Plant changes, in turn, could lead both to further deterioration in the soils and to changes in the animals dependent upon them:

> Most of these soils, when grazed, reverted through a successive series of more and more worthless grasses, shrubs, and weeds to a condition of unstable equilibrium. Each recession of plant types bred erosion; each increment to erosion bred a further recession of plants. The result today is a progressive and mutual deterioration, not only of plants and soils, but of the animal community subsisting thereon.[96]

In *Game Management* Leopold explained how the exhaustion of soil fertility could bring about declines in upland game. Soil exhaustion, he said, was the factor that managers should consider whenever a problem could not be attributed to such obvious causes as clean farming (e.g., agricultural methods emphasizing productivity of single crops), lack of proper habitat interspersion (e.g., various mixtures of food and cover at a landscape scale),[97] overkilling, and predation. "There is a remarkable correlation," he observed, "between game supply and soil fertility throughout North America."[98]

Leopold's confidence about soil-animal links would strengthen early in the next decade on the basis of new research being done by William Albrecht in Missouri.[99] Albrecht was finding that soil fertility affected the nutrient qualities of plants and that these nutritional effects cumulatively were passed upward through food chains. Differing plant nutritional conditions, he discovered, affected the distribution and health of wildlife. Leopold noted in a letter to Paul Errington that Albrecht's conclusions called into question the assumption that as long as quantity and composition of food and cover changed little visibly on a game range, there would be "no great changes in environmental carrying capacity." "Albrecht's (Missouri) papers," Leopold noted, "indicate that soil fertility may affect the welfare of animals profoundly, without any visible change in 'food and cover.'"[100]

Adding weight to these generalizations about soil and organism growth was evidence gathered by John Weaver in Nebraska. Weaver was showing that the condition of soils was itself dependent upon plant composition. The interdependence between soils and plants, that is, worked both ways: soils affected plants and plants affected soils.[101] So struck was Leopold by Weaver's evidence that he mentioned it in a number of essays, even the brief manifesto he prepared to announce the purpose of the newly formed Wilderness Society in 1935:

> Weaver at Nebraska finds that prairie soils lose their granulation [the grain structure of soil promoting its porosity and aeration] and their water-equilibrium when too long occupied by exotic crops. Apparently native prairie plants are necessary to restore that biotic stability which we call conservation. It is possible that dust storms, erosion, floods, agricultural distress, and depletion of range in the plains region all hark back fundamentally to degranulation [resulting in poorly draining soils]. Perhaps degranulation also plays a part in these same phenomena elsewhere.[102]

The lesson appeared to be clear. If native species built up fertile soils, as Weaver's work showed, and kept down erosion and pests, as Taylor's and others' research revealed, and if people wanted to prosper enduringly, then farmers and other land users would do well to take cues from nature and mimic its ways.[103]

Not only plants but animals, too, had a direct effect on soil quality, and some of the details of these effects also were emerging from Taylor's work.[104] The excreta, hairs, horns, skin, feathers, and other shed parts of animal bodies, and in the end the bodies themselves, were continually added to soils. The cumulative effect was significant. According to Taylor's calculations, on one southwestern range at any given time approximately forty-three rabbit and rodent bodies (about 8.7 pounds of combined animal flesh) per acre enriched the soil, and that was but a small segment of all the creatures on the range. In an acre of soil at Rothamsted, England, according to another study, the combined weight of protozoa, insects, nematodes, myriapods, and earthworms could be as high as 840 pounds. Decades earlier Charles Darwin had estimated that more than ten tons of dry earth per acre annually passed through the bodies of earthworms in many parts of England. Animals, in fact, affected soils and soil quality in many ways. The continuous packing of soils by large hoofed animals, for instance, tended to exclude air and suffocate plant roots. Other animals physically changed the conditions under which soils developed, such as the beaver with its dam building. Then there were the effects that came from the removal of a species, such as the wolf in large parts of Minnesota. A reduction in wolves permitted beavers and deer to increase greatly. The beavers destroyed aspen near waters, while deer curtailed young pine production in the region. Both changes disturbed the synthesis and decomposition of organic matter and nutrient exchange between plants and soil and thus the soil's normal development.[105] "It is interesting to review," concluded Taylor matter-of-factly, "the extent to which living creatures are intimately connected with soils."[106]

As Leopold considered these many plant–animal–soil interactions he also understood that evolutionary processes were very much at work. The long-term trend of evolution by natural selection apparently was to lengthen food chains, he suggested. Evolution operated so as to elaborate and diversify life forms. As it did so it added "layer after layer, link after link"[107] to the pyramid of numbers, to the web of life, thereby keeping nutrients flowing and conserving the energy circulating through ecological systems.

By 1939 these apparent evolutionary tendencies had assumed an important role in Leopold's emerging view of land.[108] At the time he could state only general conclusions about evolutionary trends, which had not yet been well studied by evolutionary biologists. Within a few years he would fill in more details. A critical fact, as Leopold would express it in his 1944 essay "Conservation in Whole or in Part," was that throughout geologic time until the modern industrial age "the extinction of one species by another occurred more rarely than the creation of new species by evolution." This meant that the "net trend of the original community" was "toward more and more diversity of native forms, and more and more complex relations between them."[109] Such complexity, he thought, was necessary to the sustained flow of energy in an ecological system. A simplified pyramid of numbers lacking diverse species or even entire layers would fail to keep nutrients circulating. In a sense, energy formerly used by other species would spill quickly back into soil, where it easily could erode away or, at best, be picked up by organisms lower in the pyramid—insects, small rodents, and birds—which now had fewer competitors. These lower organisms, by making use of some of the additional energy, could increase in number, transforming into what Walter Taylor called "animal weeds." All in all, without diversity of pyramidal layers and of organisms within them, a landscape would lose nutrients, which would cycle fewer times and potentially erode away faster, leaving whole systems diminished. Weaver's work illustrated a related link between native diversity and efficiency of nutrient use within a plant community. Prairie flora were more drought resistant than farm plants because native species practiced, as Leopold later summarized it, "'team work'[110] underground—by distributing their root-systems to cover all levels," thereby dividing up and sharing available water and nutrient resources maximally. Crop monocultures overdrew one soil level and neglected others, resulting in cumulative deficits.[111] "Any prairie," wrote Leopold by way of contrast,

> is a model cooperative commonwealth. . . . Each prairie species draws its sustenance from a different subterranean level, so that feast and famine are shared by all species alike. The leguminous members of the community (such as prairie clover, trefoil, baptisia, vetch, lupine, and lead-plant) manufacture nitrogen for the rest, and at such a rate as to exceed the annual loss by prairie fires. The prairie community collectively enhances the flocculation of soils [bringing together bits of soil, which can promote soil granulation desirable for growing crops], whereas agricultural plants deplete it. From these two characters, nitrogen-fixation-rate and flocculating capacity, stems that vast savings-bank of fertility which made us a rich nation.[112]

Ecological and evolutionary processes both created and were sustained by biological diversity, as Leopold understood matters. In his

Midwestern home region, native prairie blossoms of pasque flower and blazing star were not only beautiful, but also symbols, to his mind, of land that was whole, complex, and life-giving.[113] These flowers also represented "the greatest mass effort in evolutionary history to create a rich soil for man to live on."[114] And it was conservation's task, believed Leopold, to discover how people could live within nature's riches without depleting them.

Two native prairie plants, Silphium *(featured in "Prairie Birthday" in* A Sand County Almanac*) and* Liatris, *growing in the Faville Grove Prairie, which was "one of the largest and best remnants of unplowed, ungrazed prairie sod" left in Wisconsin in 1937. These two plants, among others, do not withstand grazing well, and because of agricultural practices they had become rare in a region where they once flourished and helped promote the soil's fertility—one reason why Leopold believed that native plant and animal diversity should be maintained.*

A COMMON CONCEPT

It seemed entirely possible, Leopold observed as the 1930s came to a close,

> that prevailing failure of economic self-interest as a motive for better private land use has some connection with the failure of the social and natural sciences to agree with each other, and with the landholder, on a common concept of land.[115]

If landowners were to know how to manage their lands well, Leopold believed, they first had to understand how land worked as a whole. Nature's parts were too numerous and interwoven to manipulate successfully resource by resource. Nature, though, was too complex for humans to comprehend directly in all its detail. What people needed, accordingly, was a coherent way of thinking about land, some image or concept of land that was both scientifically accurate and mentally graspable. Around such an understanding, commonly held, private landowners and public lands administrators might better adjust their land-use practices.

It was such a "common concept of land," derived from ecology, "the fusion point of the sciences and all the land uses,"[116] that Leopold was finally ready to propose in his June 21, 1939, plenary address to the joint meeting of the Society of American Foresters and the Ecological Society of America in Milwaukee, Wisconsin. Leopold's presentation, titled "A Biotic View of Land," was soon published in the *Journal of Forestry* with an accompanying diagram illustrating the structure of his concept and again in condensed form in the National Park Service monthly circular. In modified form the core of the talk later would be incorporated into his essay "The Land Ethic," in *A Sand County Almanac* under the heading "The Land Pyramid."[117]

Leopold's proposed concept of land drew upon his lifetime of personal observation, his own research and that of many others, and his skill in synthesizing a vast accumulation of ideas and facts. It was, he knew, no easy task to draw it all together. "When the human mind deals with any concept too large to be easily visualized," Leopold explained, "it substitutes some familiar object which seems to have similar properties."[118] Some such familiar image was needed to help the human mind grasp what was too large for it—the workings of the land. This image could never be a permanent, static depiction. Rather it was a starting place, to come back to again and again on the perpetual path to understanding the vast and often mysterious workings of nature.

As Leopold began his presentation he first had to set aside one popular concept of land—the "balance of nature." As a "mental image for land and life," explained Leopold, the balance-of-nature idea "grew up before and during the transition to ecological thought."[119] While some laymen seemed to accept it, ecologists did so, he asserted, only with reservations. For ecologists, the balance of nature did have value in the senses that it "conceives of a collective total, that it imputes some utility to all species, and that it implies oscillations when balance is disturbed."[120] To the lay mind, though, Leopold suspected, "balance of nature" probably conveyed an actual image of the familiar weighing scale. "There may even be," Leopold observed, "danger that the layman imputes to the biota properties which exist only on the grocer's counter."[121] The defect in this notion of balance of nature was the implication that there existed "only one point at which balance occurs, and that balance is normally static."[122] On both counts the implication was false.

"If we must use a mental image for land instead of thinking about it directly," Leopold suggested to his professional colleagues in Milwaukee, "why not employ the image commonly used in ecology, namely the biotic pyramid?" With certain additions, which Leopold intended to propose, the pyramid presented "a truer picture of the biota." Armed with such a truer picture "the scientist might take his tongue out of his cheek" when he talked about land as a whole. He could avoid using images that were true only with great qualification. Laypeople guided by a sounder image, moreover, "might be less insistent on utility as a prerequisite for conservation, more hospitable to the 'useless' co-habitants of the earth, more tolerant of values over and above profit, food, sport, or tourist-bait." Not the least, a sound picture of land might enable conservationists to obtain "better advice from economists and philosophers."[123]

Providing the structural framework for Leopold's new concept of land was Charles Elton's biotic pyramid of food levels and food

Vol. I   Washington, D. C., Nov. 13, 1939   No. 12

A BIOTIC VIEW OF LAND

By Aldo Leopold
University of Wisconsin

(Using a pyramid as the symbol of land, Professor Leopold shows the plant and animal community as an "energy circuit." He explains this in detail, as illustrated by the accompanying chart, then presents the following discussion. —Editor's Note.)

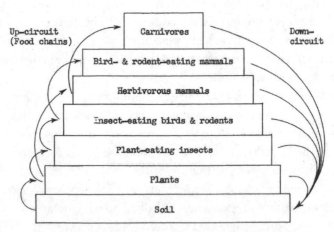

Biotic pyramid, showing plant and animal community
as an energy circuit.

Leopold's "biotic pyramid," which he later called the "land pyramid."
The sketch portrays a plant and animal community organized into
characteristic kinds and numbers of species, based on food habits and
body sizes. The whole community is like an energy circuit, cycling nutrients
upward from the soil to carnivores and then back down to the soil.

chains. In his oral presentation Leopold proposed to "sketch the pyramid as a symbol of land, and later develop some of its implications in terms of land use."[124] In the printed versions he was able to insert a drawing of it, expanded in vision from Elton's 1927 pyramid and integrating research that Leopold and other scientists had conducted since then.

The base of the pyramid rested on and was linked with the soil. Above that were plants, then plant-eating insects, insect-eating birds and rodents, herbivorous mammals, bird- and rodent-eating mammals, and carnivores.[125] The levels of the pyramid were connected not only by food habits but also by energy, including the food itself, and other lines of dependence among organisms.[126] Linking everything was energy from the sun, absorbed by the plants and running through the entire system:

> This energy flows through a circuit called the biota. It may be represented by the layers of a pyramid. The bottom layer is the soil. A plant layer rests on the soil, an insect layer on the plants, and so on up through various groups of fish, reptiles, birds, and mammals. At the top are predators.
>
> The species of a layer are alike not in where they came from, nor in what they look like, but rather in what they eat. Each successive layer depends on those below for food and often for other services, and each in turn furnishes food and services to those above.[127]

The basic elements of Elton's work and subsequent work by others explained why the arrangement formed a pyramid. Leopold continued to describe his concept:

> Each successive layer decreases in abundance; for every predator there are hundreds of his prey, thousands of their prey, millions of insects, uncountable plants.
>
> The lines of dependency for food and other services are called food chains. Each species, including ourselves, is a link in many food chains. Thus the bobwhite quail eats a thousand kinds of plants and animals, i.e., he is a link in a thousand chains. The pyramid is a tangle of chains so complex as to seem disorderly, but when carefully examined the tangle is seen to be a highly organized structure. Its functioning depends on the cooperation and competition of all its diverse links.[128]

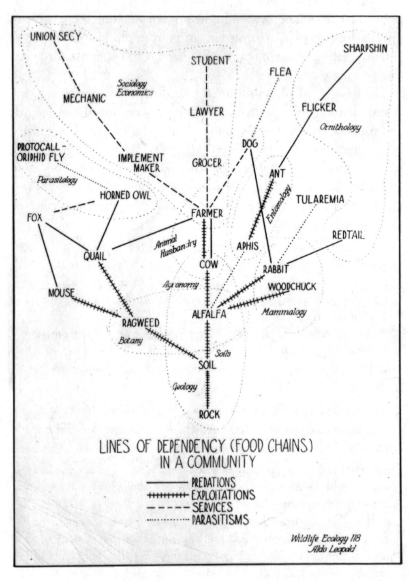

A web of life, sketched by Leopold, showing interdependencies among humans and their agricultural plants and animals and rocks, soils, and wild species.

At this point Leopold moved from merely describing the arrangement to identifying the basic reasons why the arrangement was so central to the land's capacity to maintain itself:

> In the beginning, the pyramid of life was low and squat; the food chains short and simple. Evolution has added layer after layer, link after link. Man is one of thousands of accretions to the height and complexity of the pyramid. Science has given us many doubts, but it has given us at least one certainty; the trend of evolution is to elaborate the biota.
>
> Land, then, is not merely soil; it is a fountain of energy flowing through a circuit of soils, plants, and animals. Food chains are the living channels which conduct energy upward; death and decay return it to the soil. The circuit is not closed; some energy is dissipated in decay, some is added by absorption from the air, some is stored in soils, peats, and forests; but it is a sustained circuit, like a slowly augmented revolving fund of life.[129]

The sustained flow of energy through the system, Leopold explained —upward, from soil to top carnivore and downward back into soil— depended upon a diversity of plant and animal species and the way they were organized into a complex community structure. By "structure" Leopold meant "the characteristic numbers, as well as the characteristic kinds and functions of the component species,"[130] of a system.

The complexity of the system, then—in terms of the numbers of pyramidal levels and the intricate movement of energy among them—was critical to the ability of the entire system to operate normally, Leopold suggested. When the system was disrupted—when pieces in it were added or removed—then the functioning of the system was altered to varying degrees and scales:

> When a change occurs in one part of the circuit, many other parts must adjust themselves to it. Change does not necessarily obstruct the flow of energy; evolution is a long series of self-induced changes, the net result of which has been probably to accelerate the flow; certainly to lengthen the circuit.
>
> Evolutionary changes, however, are usually slow and local. Man's invention of tools has enabled him to make changes of unprecedented violence, rapidity, and scope.[131]

This, then, was a central lesson. The entire system in nature was dynamic. Changes in it, though, were typically slow enough for other parts to make adjustments without materially disrupting the system's ability to cycle nutrients. Man-made changes, however, were often of a radically different order. Substantial alterations of natural systems could easily disrupt energy flows in ways that sapped the land's characteristic fertility. Because the diversity of life in a place was a tightly interwoven complex, Leopold explained, it was therefore virtually impossible to say which native species were useful or harmful and to what degree, as "economic biologists" and land managers had been trying to do for decades. All native species, soils, and waters in a given landscape had places in the biotic pyramid. They all contributed, however modestly, to its efficient functioning.

As Leopold brought his presentation toward a close he distilled his message even further:

> This thumbnail sketch of land as an energy circuit conveys three basic ideas . . . :
> 1. That land is not merely soil.
> 2. That the native plants and animals kept the energy circuit open; others may or may not.
> 3. That man-made changes are of a different order than evolutionary changes, and have effects more comprehensive than is intended or foreseen.[132]

No ecologist before had presented such a comprehensive and comprehensible concept of the land and explained its implications for the broad range of conservation concerns.

Weighing the Pyramid

Leopold's biotic concept of land was hardly a final answer to the question of how land functioned. Gaps remained. Despite the importance of the pyramid concept, no one had yet measured all the populations of a pyramid, let alone studied in whole the localized implications of human changes made to them.[133] Further research was needed. One major project that Leopold sponsored offered particularly clear insights into his thinking at the time. The project, initially submitted on December 10, 1940, as a funding request to the

University of Wisconsin, bore the title "The Animal Pyramid of Prairie du Sac."[134] What Leopold proposed was a detailed study of all animal life in a given place, providing a concrete example of the biotic pyramid and conducted in a way that allowed comparisons of what the pyramid looked like before and after human newcomers altered the land. The place to do it, Leopold thought, was the Prairie du Sac area of Wisconsin, just north of Madison along the Wisconsin River. Leopold and his colleagues had conducted wildlife censuses there for eleven years; it was, Leopold believed, the longest continuous wildlife census in North America. Leopold gave a developed explanation of the project in one of his funding applications:

> One of the basic concepts in ecology is Elton's "Pyramid of Numbers." Elton asserts that each of the species comprising an animal community occurs in characteristic numbers which diminish from the plant-eaters at the bottom to the carnivores at the top. . . . These numbers may be expressed graphically as a pyramid, the successive layers representing dependency for food. The disturbance of the characteristic number in one layer forces readjustment in the others.
>
> Management, the control of numbers by manipulating environment, can hardly be successful unless conducted within this fixed limitations of the elasticity of the pyramid.[135]

In this study Leopold proposed to construct, as no one had yet done, the biotic pyramid of a given area in terms of the weights of organisms present.[136] It would describe, in other words, the interrelationships of animal populations in the Prairie du Sac region by comparing each species' total weight in grams per acre before and after humans had transformed it with modern agriculture.[137] The hope was to learn how far people could go in altering land and in what ways before the land showed symptoms of maladjustment:

> Agriculture is a distortion of the pyramid. There are, presumably, limits of elasticity, within which agricultural manipulations are feasible, but beyond which they are not. It is possible that the irruption of pests, the breakdown of soils, and the disappearance of species without visible cause represent overstrains beyond the elastic limit of the pyramid.[138]

The plan was for Leopold's graduate student Harold Hanson to gather data on livestock and wild animals presently in the region and compare this with historical records on wild animals that had inhabited the place before European settlement.[139] The data comparisons and ensuing deductions, Leopold and Hanson explained in what became a joint proposal, would largely

> revolve around the comparative bulk and composition of the present wild-plus-tame pyramid and the original wild pyramid, and around the present and former food-chains. Agriculture is essentially a stepping up of the metabolic rate of the biota by shortening the food-chains, by increasing the percentage of palatable foods in the plant succession, and by decreasing the impoundment of nutrients in long-lived vegetation such as trees.[140]

In its basic arrangement the study bore striking similarities to the scientific approach that Leopold had used again and again. The main questions having to do with the study site were familiar ones, exploring the organizations and mechanisms behind the workings of the land: What was? What is? And what accounts for ecological change? In the case of Prairie du Sac, an important agricultural region, the study would take into account both nature's ways and human needs and values. And the results would bear on the critical question, how should people be using this land so as to meet their needs and keep its sound functioning—what ought to be?[141]

A number of ecological investigations had taken place in the Prairie du Sac study area over the past years, all focused on "learning the structure of the animal community and trying to deduce mechanisms of population behavior."[142] Among the studies was Paul Errington's research beginning in the 1920s on the bobwhite quail and its predators. After Hanson had completed field data collection, Leopold, Errington, and Hanson prepared a manuscript that synthesized information from their various projects. From their data they developed two figures, each portraying an average square mile of the Prairie du Sac community and giving the numbers and weights of its constituent birds and mammals. Of the first figure[143] one-half was devoted to an Eltonian pyramid of numbers and the other half to a pyramid of weights, for comparison. The second figure[144] showed, side by side in pyramid form, the weights of (1) domestic

animals, (2) present wild animals, and (3) historical, presettlement wild animals.[145]
From the comparison of the present-day wild and present-day domestic animal pyramids, one conclusion was stark: "the domestic animals [including English sparrows, Norway rats, house mice, dogs, chickens, and large livestock][146] outweigh the wild so overwhelmingly that not a single layer is plottable."[147] The wild animal data from the historical landscape, were necessarily crude estimates, the authors admitted. Yet even when the estimates were quadrupled the weight of the historical wild animal community was negligible in comparison with that of domestic animals.[148]

Leopold and his team also took people into account, inserting them into the pyramid as one of the mammals. The logical place for humans, they thought, was near the semicarnivorous raccoon. The present human population, they discovered, was "somewhat heavier than his chickens, and twice as heavy as the entire present wild community."[149] The original Indian population, they surmised (on the basis of the scanty reports of explorer Captain Jonathan Carver from "October 1763"), was "much lighter," and about 1.2 percent of the human density in 1941. Complicating the entire study was the fact that the total present-day animal community was not supported entirely by the square mile on which it lived. The farming community imported livestock feed and food for people while exporting most of the dairy products, pork, and poultry that the imported food helped grow. Even wild animals were supported by imports: if a fox swallowed a mouse or an owl a chicken, it would be eating "not only local produce but also Iowa corn and Dakota wheat."[150]

Rising above the detailed conclusions from Prairie du Sac, though, was a preeminent one. The entire square mile of study area was suffering from a clear nutrient drain. Nutrients were being drawn from the soil at rates far above what could be sustained. "That the land is suffering a net drain," wrote Leopold and his colleagues,

is attested by growing "sandblows," and by a growing number of old fields, once cultivated, but now useable only for pasture. What part of their fertility is carried away as milk, and what part as erosion silt or dust, is hard to determine.

Previous to settlement the only transport capable of importing or exporting fertility consisted of rivers, winds, and migratory birds. The community was substantially self-contained in terms of any time-scale short of a geological one.[151]

The clear evidence of nutrient drain raised serious questions about the wisdom and sustainability of farming methods:

> The overwhelming bulk of the present domestic animals, as compared with either the present or the former wild animals, raises the question: "At what cost are they supported? Is agriculture mining the soil to feed its enormously expanded flocks and herds, or was the original animal community an inefficient expression of the true food-producing capacity of the soil?"
> The answer is, we think, "both."[152]

This troubling evidence brought Leopold back to his biotic view of land and to the need to keep nutrients on the land. A conservation philosophy based on the biotic pyramid, he believed, should seek to use land to its fullest expression of fertility without diminishing it. It would take from nature only what nature could give without reducing its life-promoting capacities. So far as Leopold could tell, present-day land uses were far from achieving that goal.

Reversing the Flow

As Leopold continued developing his concept of land, he incorporated ideas about water and gravity and how erosion could quickly carry away nutrients from ecological systems. He imagined nutrients, under the constant forces of nature, tending to flow downhill from the hills and mountains to land's lowest point—the bottom of the sea. The rate of loss of nutrients from systems depended on many factors, including ecological diversity and complexity, organic content and fertility of soils, and storage capacities of lakes. The more diverse and fertile a system, Leopold suggested, in general, the more efficiently it could retain nutrients and the slower the downhill flow—with nutrient loss tending to balance nutrient uptake from rock decomposition. The work of Frank Fraser Darling, whom Leopold regarded highly as an ecologist and a writer, contributed another idea: how animals themselves played various roles in moving nutrients around a landscape, influencing the amount and rate of nutrient flows and providing an important connection between aquatic and terrestrial food webs. In particular, Darling's research on red deer in the Scottish Highlands showed that animals could sometimes help move nutrients back uphill, counteracting gravity's pull and helping to slow their loss from downhill wash. Nutrients on the Highlands were scarce, Darling had noted in *A Herd of Red Deer*,[153] because the soil was largely derived from "sterile rocks." The red deer needed more calcium and phosphorus to grow his yearly antlers than his Highlands range could supply.[154] But how and from where did the deer get them? How did the upland deer habitat gain nutrients?

Darling's answer to these questions and Leopold's thinking about them in relation to his concept of land showed up in a 1941 paper by Leopold, "Lakes in Relation to Terrestrial Life Patterns."[155] In it Leopold used a flowing-water metaphor [156] and a detailed figure to display the calcium-phosphorus food chain of red deer that Darling had identified. The chain included native herbs and grasses, nutrient-concentrated ashes left behind by heath fires, the deer's velvet horn casings, small rodents, and small aquatic animals. Terrestrial sources did not supply enough of the minerals the deer needed, Darling calculated. But the deer obtained additional minerals by traveling downhill to tap the aquatic food chain of lakes and tarns for frozen salt-rich frogs, duck eggs, and dead fish. Thus nourished with minerals, the deer returned uphill to his terrestrial life, where the minerals eventually were deposited by defecation or death and decomposition. In this way the deer performed the task of moving nutrients back uphill—from a lower place to a higher place in the landscape.

This movement uphill illustrated what Leopold termed "the back-current of the downhill stream."[157] By means of the red deer's feeding behavior, food temporarily impounded in lakes was pulled back into the terrestrial circuit, against the usual downhill "flow of nutrients from the hills to the sea."[158] Many animals merely circulated food within their habitual aquatic circuit (e.g., diving ducks) or terrestrial circuit (e.g., quail). But other animals, like the red deer, also transported nutrients between water and land, some of them in addition carrying nutrients back uphill and over long distances. River ducks, geese, terns, frogs, snakes, and muskrats might eat in or at the edge of water and then die or defecate inland—though they might do the reverse as well, moving nutrients downhill. Eagles, crows, bears, and moose also carried food to and from water, often over long distances, probably with a net uphill gain, Leopold thought. River-spawning salmon dying inland performed a large and long uphill transport of nutrients from the sea. Guano birds, penguins, otters, bats, and certain "water-hatching, land-dying" insects probably performed net uphill transport, but only over a short distance inland. At least two species—humans and beavers—performed predominantly downhill transport, getting most of their food on land and depositing most of it in water. All these creatures and a host of others got caught up in back-currents, eddies, and the regular, ongoing downhill roll through the food chain.

Everything—waters, soils, plants, and animals, including humans —was integrated, Leopold realized, into "one organic system," "one biotic organism."[159] "Soil and water are not two organic systems, but one. Both are organs of a single landscape,"[160] he concluded. "There is a circulatory system of food substances common to both, as well as a circulatory system within each. The downhill flow is carried by gravity, the uphill flow by animals."[161] The overall tendency in eco- logical systems, however, was for nutrients to wash down to the sea. For a system to be self-sustaining, therefore, its downhill nutrient losses needed to be retarded and offset to balance its nutrient intake from rock decomposition. The longer the food chain—the more diverse and complex an ecological community—the longer a system could keep its nutrients cycling, preventing loss. Nutrient storage in fertile soils and lakes and animals doing their uphill "back-current work," too, helped soil-water systems hold on to their nutrients.

Aided by Darling's work and other research, Leopold, by 1941, was ready to try again to explain his concept of land, this time with additional elements more expressly included: water, erosion, and other forces that moved nutrients downhill and uphill within a land- scape. He did so in what he considered one of his most important essays, "Odyssey," first published in 1942 and later included in *A Sand County Almanac.*

In "Odyssey" Leopold portrayed two types of journey taking place in two different dimensions.[162] One journey, occurring over geologic time, was implicit in the essay; it was the voyage that all the various types of the earth's creatures shared as they were shaped by evolution through natural selection, resulting in the development of diversity and complexity of plant and animal communities over long periods of time. The second journey—the ecological odyssey, which evolution sustained—was depicted in the essay directly. Leopold portrayed the land's ecological functioning by telling the story of the travels through the biotic community—through that "never-ending circuit of life"[163]—of "X," which was sucked out of a just-decayed portion of rock by a burr oak root and "helped build a flower, which became an acorn, which fattened a deer, which fed an Indian."[164] From the Indian, atom X was once again returned to the soil, only to be sucked up by a bluestem rootlet. On and on went atom X, working its way through the complex food web and returning, again and again, to the soil. This is the way land worked, Leopold observed, when it was normal. Another story, told side by side with X's tale, was that of nutrient atom Y, revealing what happened in nutrient-cycling terms when modern land use removed native species and the land's functioning was compromised. In a significantly altered landscape, atom Y circulated through the food chain more rapidly and fewer times before being lost to the land community. In brief poetic form Leopold conveyed his common concept of land and provided "a complete summary of the fundamentals of ecological conservation."[165] Ecological conservation was about using land in ways that promoted the flow of nutrients along the path of atom X.

FROM SCIENCE TO WISDOM

Even as Leopold continued to develop his common concept of land, he worked to make as clear as possible for a diversity of audiences some of its practical implications. "If it is possible to manage game upward [in numbers]," wrote Leopold in a typical advisory letter, "it is possible to manage rodents downward,"[166] not with poisoning or any other single-track approach but by making use of an ecological understanding of how the land worked and taking land-use cues from that understanding. In a letter to W. L. Anderson of the Soil Conservation Service, Leopold distilled out of his rich ecological understanding a set of critical recommendations for land use goals:

1. it is desirable to maintain the largest possible variety of plants and animals on the farm,

2. variety in animals automatically follows from variety in plants, that is, food and cover,

3. a very small area devoted to food and cover produces astonishing gains in the diversity of animal life.[167]

Time and again Leopold stressed the importance of the interconnections among plants, animals, soils, and waters to the well-being of the entire ecological system as a whole. Fertile soil not only promoted a diversity of well-nourished plants and animals but also helped keep hydrologic systems intact. And as he observed in another letter, organic content in soil performed a variety of functions: "to create millions of little dams" (thus reducing water runoff and erosion); to anchor plant nutrients so they did not leach down or wash away; and to anchor moisture so the soil did not dry up.[168] These functions of organic matter Leopold had gleaned from his friend the soil scientist W. C. Lowdermilk. Leopold termed the positive relationship between rainwater absorption and plant and animal residues present in and on the soil "Lowdermilk's Law." This law, he believed, was "almost as fundamental to human continuity as the law of gravity."[169]

The biotic or land pyramid showed up also in Leopold's more philosophic musings, providing his observations with a stronger ecological grounding. Among his more polished contemplations was an introductory lecture titled "Ecology and Politics," prepared for students in his Wildlife Ecology 118 class in the spring of 1941. With attention focused on the war in Europe, he believed, too few people were noticing the ecological harms that people were imposing on themselves:

> Ecology tries to understand the interactions between living things and their environment. Every living thing represents an equation of give and take. Man or mouse, oak or orchid, we take a livelihood from our land and our fellows, and give in return an endless succession of acts and thoughts, each of which changes us, our fellows, our land, and its capacity to yield us a further living. Ultimately we give ourselves.

That this collective account between the earth and its creatures ultimately balances is implicit in the fact that both continue to live. It does not follow, however, that each species continues to live. Paleontology is a book of obsequies for defunct species.[170]

Human beings had an internal drive to survive and an inherent fear of their own extinction, Leopold went on. Modern people placed their faith in science to guarantee their continuity. Yet now, he wrote, [t]here remains a doubt whether war, famine, and pestilence are the only horsemen to be feared. A new one, unnamed in holy writ, is now much in the headlines: a condition of unstable equilibrium between soils and waters, and their dependent plants and animals.[171]

War was a disruption of the biotic equation of give and take. "What, if anything, can ecology say about it?" asked Leopold. Perhaps not much. Appraising the right and wrong of wars was beyond his power, Leopold admitted. Yet "[i]f science cannot lead us to wisdom as well as power," Leopold wrote, "it is surely no science at all."[172] He thought that it might be fitting for an ecologist, drawing upon biological analogies of density dependence, carrying capacities, and predacious tendencies of animals, to appraise the soundness of modern technological assumptions leading to increasing human populations and human take from the land. "Every environment carries not only characteristic kinds of animals, but characteristic *numbers* of each," he explained. "That number is the carrying capacity of that land for that species."[173] Perhaps, he mused, "the present world-revolution is the sign that we have exceeded that limit, or that we have approached it too rapidly."[174]

→← ←←

Leopold concluded his 1941 lecture on ecology and politics by suggesting that conservation problems were rooted in modern industrialism's separation of human society from the land. Three years later, in "Post-War Prospects," Leopold stressed again the problems arising from the growth of "economic man" away from "any consciousness of the land."[175] And in his view this was not only an American phenomenon: it was an impending one worldwide. The post-war prospect was largely gloomy, Leopold predicted, yet it was not without glimmers of hope. Among "the most encouraging" glimmers,

Leopold announced in his 1944 essay, was "the recent discovery that the fertility of the soil determines the nutritional value of plants grown on it,"[176] whereas before the only consideration had been the amount of a crop. Though the information at first glance was seemingly irrelevant to conservation, Leopold found in it seeds of a different kind of "revolutionary" meaning. Now it was clear that all crops had not merely quantitative, but also qualitative, values that needed to be taken into account. "Wheat grown on healthy soil," he explained, "carries the potentiality of healthy animals and healthy people: wheat grown on abused soil is something less than wheat."[177] This new understanding placed on people a new obligation to conserve soil and all that went with it, Leopold urged. This would be an obligation that affected living people, and as such it would be more difficult to evade than obligations to future generations: "He who erodes his field," Leopold declared, "now erodes the health of his children and his neighbors. It is ironical that chemistry, the most materialistic of sciences, has thus unwittingly synthesized a conscience for land-use."[178]

Over the years, Leopold synthesized his most important scientific understandings into his concept of land. His "common concept of land" was a critical piece he felt was needed to craft and implement an overall conservation vision that could help make it possible for modern people to live well with the land. As important as science was, Leopold knew it would take more than that to move toward such a vision. People would need to gain consciousness of land—its soils, waters, plants, and animals as a whole, in all their vibrant arrays. The most important matters for conservation, Leopold believed, thus stepped beyond science.[179]

Chapter 7

Ecological Poetry

*The river was cut by the world's great flood and runs over
rocks from the basement of time. On some of the rocks are
timeless raindrops. Under the rocks are the words.*

Norman Maclean, *A River Runs Through It*

In conjunction with his June 1939 talk, "A Biotic View of Land,"
before the joint meeting of the Ecological Society of America and the
Society of American Foresters, Leopold sent a copy of the address to
a respected friend and frequent correspondent, P. S. Lovejoy, asking
for a critique. Lovejoy, an Illinois native three years Leopold's
senior—once a fellow forester and for twelve years chief of the Michigan Conservation Department's Game and Fur Division—wrote
frequently about broad-reaching land-use issues.[1] Like Leopold,
Lovejoy had an ecological mind that was quick to see interconnections on the land. With a firm imagination, he used a quirky vernac-
ular in his letters, which Leopold termed "Lovejoyiana" and which,
for the uninitiated, sometimes required translation.

Lovejoy responded to Leopold's paper on July 12, 1939, acting, as
Leopold had hoped, as both friend and critic. "My prelim notion,"
wrote Lovejoy, using metaphorically their common language of
forestry mapping technique, "is that you have run your lines on several different magnetic variations—which will need to be reduced to
a common base before the traverse will close properly."[2] Lovejoy
thought Leopold had tried to cover too much ground in "A Biotic

View of Land" and perhaps would not be well understood or appreciated for it. "But that is assuming that you are going to shoot at a critical and professional audience—& I'm not sure that's intended," Lovejoy surmised. "In spots you are evidently doing an 'essay' in the Thoreau et al. manner; or even verging on the poetic. Both may be highly OK for given audiences or vehicles, but I'm trying to swing comment on a straight-line professional biologist's stance only."

It was clear to Lovejoy that Leopold's land pyramid included people within it and that Leopold's ultimate objective of developing the land pyramid concept itself extended beyond science. Leopold had a sound grasp of the science, Lovejoy affirmed. But, as to these other human-related issues, he thought Leopold was "sorta fumbling with a very large & important Sumpin"[3] deserving of further thought and research. Leopold had mixed together in one essay two types of work that he might better develop separately, Lovejoy suggested. On the one hand was the scientific data in diagram form—the pyramid and the energy flows through the circuitry of the biota. On the other hand was Leopold's conservation philosophy, which combined ecology with history, sociology, ethics, and general cultural observations. Leopold's synthesis led to "one general deduction": "the less violent the man-made changes, the greater the probability of successful readjustment in the pyramid."[4] Leopold believed that humans should reduce violence to the land; they should keep soils fertile and waters flowing; they should realize that parts of nature viewed by many as mere "aesthetic luxuries"—prairie flowers, cranes and condors, otters and grizzlies—deserved protection as contributing parts of the biota, however small or unknown. "En route" between science and practice, Lovejoy told Leopold, "seems like as if you stray into various other slants & now & then into what is mostly (really?) poetry—i.e. more 'feeling' than 'thinking.' (Of course & why not? Me too. . . .)."[5] Although Lovejoy shared Leopold's ecological mind and his conservationist's heart, he cautioned his friend about combining scientifically wrought ideas with conservation philosophy, particularly where scientific audiences were concerned.

Leopold did typically pay attention to the traits of his audience when speaking and writing. He chose his language and metaphors carefully. He could discuss his central ecological concept—that land was a whole entity expressing properties that went beyond the sum of its parts[6]—from various perspectives and using different words. As Lovejoy put it (as only he could), effective conservation work, in addition to getting scientific facts straight, involved understanding your audience and "'selling' The Dope so it sticks etc."[7] With something of this in mind, Leopold emphasized the *energetic systems* language preferred by Arthur Tansley when communicating with other scientists; he used *organismic* language, the choice of Frederic Clements, particularly when communicating with people as citizens and leaning toward conservation philosophy; and he tended to employ *mechanistic* language when addressing land technicians and farmers who manipulated parts of nature for human benefit and tinkered with tractors.

Often, however, Leopold used more than one metaphorical framework in the same essay, combining scientific with "beyond science" discussions. When choosing language he kept in mind not only his audience but also his multifaceted objectives, striving, though not always successfully, to make convincing conceptual matches. In "A Biotic View of Land," for example, when describing the scientifically grounded land pyramid, he talked about land as energy flowing through "a circuit called the biota." In the same essay, as he moved from synthesizing scientific information to describing harmful human effects on the land pyramid, he switched from the language of physics to that of health, talking about "wastage in the biotic organism" as "similar to disease in an animal." When referring to remediation of land-use harms, he spoke in terms of mechanistic manipulations—"Professor Weaver proposes that we *use* [italics added] prairie flowers to reflocculate the wasting soils of the dust bowl."[8] In "The Farmer as a Conservationist," another 1939 essay, he again used a variety of metaphors. Farmland was like a machine and conservation was "keeping the resource in working order, as well as preventing overuse." "Few realize today," he explained to his tractor-owning audience, "that soil, water, plants, and animals are an engine, subject like any other, to derangement."[9] But in the same essay land also was like a body whose legs or fingers might be

regrettably lost, whose creek was like a face that did not want muti-
lating, and whose "good health" was the fertility of its fields.
Language held rich possibilities, but, Leopold knew, it also was beset
with pitfalls.[10] It often seemed inadequate to express what was most
important to him, which was the vital thing inspiring the words—the
land itself.

Leopold very likely took his friend Lovejoy's critique seriously,
and Leopold's philosophic and poetic bent had made scientists and
land technicians uncomfortable before.[11] Yet rather than develop his
scientific and philosophic theses in separate papers, as Lovejoy had
suggested, Leopold took the opposite route, even for scientific audiences: he tried instead to do a better job of showing how science and
philosophy fit together. He emphasized the importance of linking
science with conservation values in his 1940 presidential address to
the newly formed Wildlife Society: "We are attempting to manage
wildlife," Leopold told his audience,

> but it is by no means certain that we shall succeed, or that this will be
> our most important contribution to the design for living.
>
> For example, we may, without knowing it, be helping to write a
> new definition of what science is for.[12]

Scientific research in America had been aimed "almost exclusively
[at] the creation and exercise of power,"[13] Leopold asserted. Scientists played roles in the American scheme of industrial and economic
progress—emphasizing (and receiving funding for) contributions
towards new technological inventions and ways to enhance wealth
by increasing the efficiency and productivity of resource-rich lands
and factory workers. But why should science be the tool merely of
technological power and economic growth, Leopold asked. Why
should it not also be a tool to promote other important values—
such as "the creation and exercise of wonder, of respect for [nature's]
workmanship"[14]—and for discovering ways to harmonize modern
humans with the biotas of which they were part? These were not
unrelated aims, to Leopold's mind. Understanding land and having
a knowing affection for it were, he believed, the same thing as using
it well, and the only nearly sure guarantee of doing so. Scientists
and land technicians should help remove the "senseless barrier
between science and art,"[15] Leopold declared to his audience of

wildlife scientists. By exploring and describing the "ecological dramas" all around them they could at once promote perception, knowledge, affection, and wonder.

There was an important place in wildlife management and all the land-related disciplines, believed Leopold, for both scientists and poets. Ideally, both ways of perceiving and talking about land— empirical and aesthetic—would be merged in individual men and women. "Land ecology," Leopold wrote two years later, "is putting the sciences and arts together for the purpose of understanding our environment." Who is the land? What are the sciences? What is art? Leopold answered his own questions: humans and no less the "meanest flower that blows" were together co-members of "the land."[16] The sciences were merely systematic ways of thinking about the land. Art was the drama of a land's workings. In terms of language, ecological metaphors were helpful for capturing the mind-boggling complexity of nature, but poetry was perhaps the only way to express with words what humans sensed as meaning and beauty in nature—what was, in other words, to be discovered in the essences or under the surfaces of things.

The beauty of nature—so vital a part of the definition of the "good life" to Leopold, as to many others—was much in need of protection from destruction. But beauty was difficult to talk about, and there were few ecological poets. How could conservationists concerned with protecting beauty make their case without words? Leopold, who could reach lyrical heights of literary expression, like all artists struggled with the challenge, seeking language to convey what went beyond language. As Lovejoy, who had his own way with words, once wrote to his friend, "[H]a-ha I sez ta self, Aldo, he's fuzzy-fumbling, too. . . . Hunching a strong sumpin he can't yet quite see or say."[17]

Constructive critiques similar to those of Lovejoy's reached Leopold from another of his favorite correspondents—a former student, Albert Hochbaum. After reading some of Leopold's essays (intended for what was to become *A Sand County Almanac*) Hochbaum, too, noted the struggle Leopold was having in blending science, aesthetics, and practical conservation ideas. Hochbaum found it difficult at first to identify Leopold's central theme. He challenged

Leopold to find a better balance between his aesthetic "literary effects" and getting across a clear conservation point of view. He found in Leopold's essays "something quite intangible" like music and a second chord having to do with the dialectic reactions between humans and land in America. As best as Hochbaum could tell, Leopold mainly was trying to get across something like a "state of mind," something having to do with the human perception of beauty, something intangible, though probably common to all men.[18] Leopold for his part admitted that he indeed struggled with how to bring together artistry, science, and conservation objectives in his writings. He wanted to convey not merely fragments of an idea but a whole, clear point of view, a comprehensive conservation philosophy; yet, as Leopold wrote to Hochbaum, who was a painter, "[i]f you inserted all of the ideas on your picture, it would spoil it."[19] Leopold's literary talents were obvious to Hochbaum, and Hochbaum's criticisms, like those of Lovejoy, were rooted in deep respect for Leopold's work.[20] Leopold sat, Hochbaum believed, "in a circle which may never hold more than a dozen in the century,"[21] and, in the words of Henry David Thoreau, Leopold could "nail words to their primitive senses," transplanting them "to his page with earth adhering to their roots."[22] But, like farming, writing was hard work. Hochbaum made another perceptive point about Leopold's essays: more than Leopold probably realized or intended, his essays collectively were painting a portrait not only of the land but also of Leopold himself—the scientist, artist, and ordinary man.[23]

Criticisms aside, Leopold's struggles to remove "the senseless barrier between science and art" often produced works of high craftsmanship and powerful effect. One such effort, "Song of the Gavilan," came out barely a year after publication of "A Biotic View of Land." Both addressed the same subject: the circulation of nutrient energy through a species-diverse land pyramid and the need for humans to work in concert with nature's scheme. In "A Biotic View," as we have seen, Leopold portrayed material evidence about the mechanisms of nature, yet he stepped beyond science to express his ideas about how humans should appreciate and use it. In "Song of the Gavilan" Leopold created poetry about the beauty of land yet also conveyed his scientific knowledge in doing so. The domains of scientists and poets, Leopold himself showed time and again, need not be so separate. Each perspective could enrich the other. Enduring, vibrant human societies and healthy rivers like the Gavilan, in fact, might both require that the barrier between them be removed.

THE SPEECH OF HILLS AND RIVERS

In September 1936 Leopold returned to the Southwest with his friend Ray Roark from the engineering department at the University of Wisconsin. They were headed for a two-week bow-hunting vacation in the Sierra Madre Occidental region of northern Mexico and along the Rio Gavilan, its chief river. So much did Leopold enjoy the trip and the region that he returned the next winter for another bow-hunting and "loafing" getaway, flying into Casas Grandes as 1937 waned in the closing days of December. It was here that Leopold first appeared in the introduction to this book as he embarked with his eldest son, Starker, and younger brother, Carl, on this second Gavilan excurson. Leopold's experiences along the Rio Gavilan during each trip greatly affected his thinking and were soon reflected in both the substance of his writing and its poetic tone.

The Sierra Madre reaches its summit in Chihuahua, Mexico, south and west of Casas Grandes and west of Colonia Pacheco, across the border from the lands of New Mexico and Arizona that Leopold had come to know as a young forest ranger. The region was unmapped, so far as Leopold could tell, and comprised about 2 million acres. Who owned the Mexican land Leopold did not know; most of it, he suspected, was public.[24] The Apache Indians had claimed the territory until recently, delaying Mexican settlement of the region and creating a deep contrast with land conditions on the north side of the Mexican-U.S. border. A small number of cattle ranches, accessible only by packing in, were located in the area. Yellow pine forest made up half of the landscape, while scrub oak grew in the foothills. A composite forest of fir and pine spread over some 5 percent of the region; another 5 percent supported grama grass in open parks. The area retained its "full flora and fauna," Leopold surmised, including top predators, with only one known exotic—the wild horse. Grazing of the grasslands had been intermittent and light.[25]

Through this rich, uncharted land the men tramped, rode,

adventured, and chased and schemed for game—snipe, teal, deer, quail, and turkey. Their arrows typically missed the bounding deer and flushing birds, which enjoyed the security of plentiful cover. But enough did strike home to put meat sizzling over the campfire for most meals.[26] There was plenty of time for resting around the campsite. Sometimes members of the group sang their own songs, calling themselves the "glee club." Leopold oftentimes, too, watched quietly, listened, and thought.

Running through the rimrock towering above the men's camp, the song of the river was audible to all who could hear. The rush of water against boulders and mossy tree roots, the flow of the stream over riffles, the splash of trout in cold deeps, the tinkle of rivulets down hillsides. Leopold knew this kind of riverine music. He also knew another, much different kind of music, sung in a language that testified to a realm of existence beyond the surface of things. To hear even a few notes of this more subtle riverine music, Leopold later recorded—the music that rested below, above, and in the midst of the robust physical sounds—"you must first live here a long time, and you must know the speech of the hills and rivers."

> Then on a still night, when the campfire is low and the Pleiades have climbed over rimrocks, sit quietly and listen for a wolf to howl, and think hard of everything you have seen and tried to understand. Then you may hear it—a vast pulsing harmony—its score inscribed on a thousand hills, its notes the lives and deaths of plants and animals, its rhythms spanning the seconds and the centuries.[27]

In the great house of knowledge there is a threshold between science and poetry where physical nature is transformed. So Leopold thought, and for him, food crossed that threshold. At least it did in the Sierra Madre, where food supplied "the continuum in the Song of the Gavilan,"[28] as he explained in his essay of that name, written upon his return. Food kept the land's music humming and pulsing, food for all life, humans included. "Every region has a human food symbolic of its fatness," Leopold observed, and for the particular gastronomic offering of the Gavilan, he composed a mouthwatering recipe in parable form:

> The hills of the Gavilan find their gastronomic epitome in this wise:
> Kill a mast-fed buck, not earlier than November, not later than

January. Hang him in a live-oak tree for seven frosts and seven suns. Then cut out the half-frozen "straps" from their bed of tallow under the saddle, and slice them transversely into steaks. Rub each steak with salt, pepper, and flour. Throw into a Dutch oven containing deep smoking-hot bear fat and standing on live-oak coals. Fish out the steaks at the first sign of browning. Throw a little flour into the fat, then ice-cold water, then milk. Lay a steak on the summit of a steaming sour-dough biscuit and drown both in gravy.

This structure is symbolic. The buck lies on his mountain, and the golden gravy is the sunshine that floods his days, even unto the end.[29]

Leopold, preparing to field dress his "mast-fed" Gavilan buck, hangs the carcass from a tree. This buck, Leopold says in "Song of the Gavilan," represents the land's "fatness" and is to him a symbolic part of the region's nutrient-cycling land pyramid.

The "Song of the Gavilan" also might be called the "Song of the Food Cycle," the "Song of the Nutrient Atom's Odyssey," or the "Song of the Land Pyramid," for Leopold's lyricism was rooted in his ecological concept of land. The biscuit underneath the venison was most likely made of wheat grown on prairie soils and of milk from cows grazed on grama grass, which had captured the hot midday sun and carried nutrients into the cow's belly. The deer had been made fat on acorns from great three-hundred-year-old oaks. The old oak's fallen leaves—after completing their annual task of delivering energy to its seed—had made a soft bed for the panting deer, which was weary from being chased by a cougar or maybe a wolf or bobcat, until finally it fell prey to and fed a man, leaving the leaves to molder alone into soil for another season: "dust to dust."[30] But not only for man was the song sung. The "glee club of the land" sang for all its members, and all the lands' members were its singers, eating and being eaten. It was "food for the oak," from the sun and the soil that sounded their notes in the song,

> which feeds the buck who feeds the cougar who dies under an oak and goes back into acorns for his erstwhile prey. This is one of many food cycles starting from and returning to oaks, for the oak also feeds the jay who feeds the goshawk who named your river, the bear whose grease made your gravy, the quail who taught you a lesson in botany, and the turkey who daily gives you the slip. And the common end of all is to help the headwater trickles of the Gavilan split one more grain of soil off the broad hulk of the Sierra Madre to make another oak.[31]

Leopold the ecologist had learned how to see, hear, and "think hard." Science aided that process by contributing, in addition to material blessings, "the moral blessing" of logical objectivity: "This means doubting everything except facts"[32] and hewing to them. Yet, Leopold observed, few people were open enough to question the prevailing assumption that "every river needs more people, and all people need more inventions," and that the job of science thus is to serve these purposes. And few seriously considered the fact that "the good life"[33] did not necessarily flow automatically from the "good invention"[34] but depended, with or without inventions, on the presence and perception of the song of the Gavilan. Indeed, why should science not serve poetry and beauty at least as well as technological innovation and economic progress? The speech of the hills and rivers, the wholeness of the land, the meaning in the depths of it, the pleasures of being a knowing part of it: all were, to Leopold's mind, realities of priceless worth.

In the Mexican hills Leopold was struck by another "fact," heretofore undiscovered by science, as he put it. He had observed the vital, communal role played by one particular member of the local humming chorus. In its physical features and behavior the thick-billed parrot (*Rhynchopsitta pachyrhyncha*)—in Spanish, "Guacamaja"[35] —was known to naturalists and scientists, though the bird was hardly well studied.[36] The parrot's call resembled that of the piñon jay, only louder and with more "salty enthusiasm."[37] About as big as pigeons, according to Leopold, the birds "wore velvet green uniforms with scarlet and yellow epaulets and black helmets." In spring the Guacamaja made nests in holes; in fall they feasted on ripe acorns and swept noisily from pine to pine, mostly in groups of even numbers, eating seeds from cones.[38] But none of these physical facts was the discovery to which Leopold laid claim. What had never been recorded, until Leopold did so in 1937, was that the Guacamaja was the "numenon" of the Sierra Madre.[39] The bird to him somehow represented the spirit of the region and lent it some form of ecological life that went beyond what was physical.

Leopold unabashedly submitted his discovery to a well-respected ornithological journal, and *The Condor* was willing to publish it. "Everybody knows," Leopold told his American bird-watching audience,

> that the autumn landscape in the north woods is the land, plus a red maple, plus a ruffed grouse. In terms of conventional physics, the grouse represents only a millionth of either the mass or the energy of an acre. Yet subtract the grouse and the whole thing is dead. An enormous amount of some kind of motive power has been lost.[40]

"It is easy to say that the loss is all in our mind's eye," Leopold confessed to his readers, many of them no doubt dubious. "[B]ut is there any sober ecologist who will agree?" "He knows full well," Leopold contended, pressing the scientist-reader to "exercise wonder" that there has been an ecological death, the significance of which is inexpressible in terms of contemporary science. A philosopher has called this imponderable essence the *numenon* of material things. It stands in contradistinction to *phenomenon*, which is ponderable and predictable, even to the tossings and turnings of the remotest star.[41]

The grouse, in other words, held the essence of the woods and the essence of the woods was in the grouse. A woods without its characteristic spirit, without its numenon, was something less than *that* woods. The blue jay was the numenon of the hickory groves; the whisky-jack that of the muskegs; and the piñonero that of the juniper foothills—at least for many ornithologists. In the Sierra Madre it was the Guacamaja that held the character. Not only in terms of its organization but also in its characteristic spirit the land was like an organism. To allow the loss of a landscape's numenon—the grouse or the parrot, the blue jay or the whisky-jack—was to destroy, bringing about a kind of death to the whole.

Leopold had lifted the word "numenon" from the Russian philosopher Piotr Ouspensky's *Tertium Organum*.[42] As mentioned in chapter 2, Leopold first picked up Ouspensky's newly translated work sometime around 1922 or 1923 and seems to have found within it resonant with his own hard-to-verbalize thoughts, returning to the book from time to time. "*Noumenal*," wrote Ouspensky (Leopold reconfigured the spelling when he used it in 1937), "means *perceived by the mind*[,] and the characteristic feature of the *things belonging to the noumenal world* is the fact that *they cannot be perceived by the same method as things of the phenomenal world*."[43] Such talk about things like numena and riverine music, Leopold knew, could make a scientist turn on his heels. He also understood that he was in good company in being drawn to such ideas. Among predecessors sharing a similar perspective Leopold identified a few of those "ecological poets whose lives spanned three millenniums," including the Old Testament's prophet Isaiah, the Old Testament's King David, and John Muir.[44] Prominent on Leopold's list of like-minded nature observers, too, was Muir's contemporary John Burroughs, a poet-naturalist who by reputation "hewed to the facts." Along with Theodore Roosevelt, Burroughs early in the twentieth century had stood up against "nature-fakers" whose imaginations ran away from the truth, fabricating natural history to compose a good story.[45] Burroughs insisted that reports about nature remain true to reliable empirical knowledge. Still there was understanding that was beyond the reach of science, Burroughs believed, following in the footsteps of his mentor Walt Whitman. Good natural-history writing took readers beyond mere words. Into his personal journal Leopold had copied ideas from a Burroughs volume, *Whitman: A Study*:

> [Whitman] thinks natural history, to be true to life, must be inspired, as well as poetry. There ought to be intuitive perception of truth, important conclusions ought to be jumped to—laws, facts, results arrived at by a kind of insight or inspirational foreknowledge, that never could be obtained by mere observation or actual verification. In science—some of the most important discoveries seem inspirations, or a kind of winged, ecstatic reasoning, quite above and beyond real facts.[46]

Unknown Places

To perceive a thing both phenomenally and noumenally, as Leopold had with the thick-billed parrot and Rio Gavilan, was to get a richer understanding of that thing than either form of perception would give by itself. Leopold experienced nature from as many different perspectives as he could and urged others to do likewise. Science could help open up understanding about the physical, phenomenal world. Its discoveries, in turn, could become entryways to the noumenal world, the world of beauty and pleasure, thereby stimulating wonder and respect for nature. Leopold illustrated the kind of scientific endeavor that might yield such fruit in the form of an imagined conversation with a hunting friend: "Dear Judge Botts," he jotted in a never finished, letterlike essay, "How does a hound follow a trail? What is scent? By what alchemy of nose does a dog know backtrail from forward. . . ."[47] These were among the kinds of questions that, unleashed on science, could lead to both knowledge and wonder. "I must tell you first, my specifications of a perfect research enterprise," Leopold continued. First, it should promise to yield no gainful knowledge. Second, it must be so challenging as to hold no assurance of success and should most likely lead to a wider understanding of human ignorance. Third, the quest for knowledge must lie in no single field of science. On the contrary, it should take down such categorical barriers. Only in that way, by removing intellectual frames and filters, could nature be known personally.

The frozen world of January—simple, cold, and peaceful—in Leopold's view was a perfect setting to engage in such idle musings and to open personally to nature, not only asking "who has done what, but [speculating] why."[48] Upon sight of a meadow mouse darting across a skunk track in the snow one sunny day in the first month of the year, Leopold wondered why this critter was so unusually "abroad in daylight." Quite likely the thawing snow, he surmised, had drenched and collapsed his grass tunnels. Then came a hawk sailing over the meadow, dropping like a "feathered bomb" into the marsh and not rising again. Surely he had caught some such unwitting mouse forced out of her formerly safe and dry under-snow world, imagined Leopold. To the mouse, snow meant freedom from want and fear. To the hawk, thaw meant freedom from want and fear. It was a matter of perspective.[49] To see a thing from different viewpoints was to see it more wholly.

Leopold allowed his musings and searches to take him sometimes not only beyond species boundaries but also beyond the usual boundaries of time and space: How did it come to pass, Leopold wondered, that he and his dog on a walk before daybreak in Baraboo, Wisconsin, found all property lines vanish as expanses unknown opened wide—"as far as the dew can reach," but not beyond the drying rays of the sun?[50] Why, he asked himself, did pine trees stimulate his deep imaginations and hopes so and a somber wintry-white dusk infuse him with courage?[51] Who could explain how a sandhill crane could incarnate wildness and in its guttural baying translate millions of years of evolutionary history into one moment?[52]

Leopold felt the values of mystery keenly. There was, to his experience, "a peculiar virtue in the music of elusive birds,"[53] and he knew a "painting so evanescent that it is seldom viewed at all, except by some wandering deer." It was a river that wielded the brush dipped in green *Eleocharis* sod, spangled with blue mimulus, pink dragonhead, and the milk-white blooms of *Sagittaria*. And it was this same river that, before Leopold could bring his friends to view its work, erased the painting forever from human view.[54] The transient aesthetic perception of nature easily merged into an adventurous sensibility, yet another way of knowing the land. Adventure, too, had to do with transcending boundaries, in both time and space. "If we poor three-dimensional humans could be lifted for a moment into the fourth, a lot of mere illusions like time, motion, mortality, and ether would fall like scales from our eyes," a young Leopold mused in "Thoughts on a Map of Liberia,"[55] under the sway of Ouspensky.[56] Leopold, not one to be carried away by mysticism even in youthful exuberance, though, brought things back down to earth:

Thus speak the metaphysicians. But who has extolled those rather more frequent benefactors which lift us out of two dimensions into three? And which of these is more potent than the map? . . . Before we aspire to be lifted into the fourth dimension, it is best to give thanks that these things [unmapped, unknown places] have helped lift us into the third.[57]

"Unknown places" were necessary to the "spiritual and physical welfare of future Americans,"[58] to Leopold's view. Blank spots on a map were fodder for mental creativity and risky adventures. A canoe, ignorance of what was beyond the next bend, powers of vivid imagination, a sense of open time, the freedom to make mistakes and suffer their consequences, and a legendary wild river that sings provided another doorway into nature's experience.[59] To protect such blank spots—opportunities for another way of knowing nature—was part of Leopold's overall conservation vision.

Another entry into the world beyond the physical senses was through the portal of paradox. To find the common ground between apparent contradictions, in other words, was often to find some revelation of understanding. The relation between competition and cooperation in nature was one example Leopold used. Considered individually from a scientific point of view these ideas appeared antagonistic, but viewed together they became parts of a single, interwoven process that created complex biotas. From a philosophic perspective, competition and cooperation were akin to "two spots where the fingers of two equally blind men touch a single elephant."

Leopold paddles into an "unknown place" in the Colorado River delta, following the allure of mystery and the possibility of coming to know nature in new ways.

To touch only one part of the elephant—to look at either competition or cooperation in isolation—gave only a partial truth. "The antagonism between them [competition and cooperation] is the antagonism of opposing interpretations, both true. The truth inheres neither in the one nor in the other, but in the coexistence and interaction of both and perhaps of other interpretations as yet unknown."[60]

Leopold explained this idea as "a close analogy to Goethe's philosophical principle of polarity."[61] Or, as he put it another time, "Paradox is the earmark of valid truth."[62]

THE TEST OF THE RIGHT

"Truth is that which prevails in the long run," Leopold wrote first in a 1921 article arguing for the rightness of wilderness preservation.[63] He repeated the statement in his 1923 article "Some Fundamentals of Conservation in the Southwest,"[64] in which he discussed the rightness of a land-respecting civilization. With this pithy wisdom, Leopold showed his practicality and his willingness to go beyond science. Leopold's assertion paraphrased the writing of the pragmatist Arthur Twining Hadley, president of Yale University while Leopold was in residence, between 1905 and 1909. It is difficult to tell how much of Hadley's philosophic work Leopold knew directly, but on the elusive, vital concepts of truth and rightness, Leopold shared the pragmatist's general view.[65]

From the beginning Leopold's Progressive-era forestry training interjected a long-term perspective into resource arenas where short-term considerations had governed. Looking upon the devastation of the Blue River area he was impressed by nature's power to wipe away human activities that failed to respect basic ecological processes. Home building was about making homes that would endure; in the Blue River settlement the process largely had failed—thousands of acres had eroded away largely because of inept land-use practices, and pioneering settlers had been left without their land and their living. In sensitive landscapes, land-use practices were immediately put to nature's test to see whether they would last. It is not surprising that Leopold saw merit in Hadley's definition of rightness.

Hadley's pragmatic philosophy also held appeal because it complemented the basic reality of evolutionary change, which linked fitness and survival. If there was indeed, as so many people wanted to believe, "a special nobility inherent in the human race—a special cosmic value, distinctive from and superior to all other life,"[66] Leopold argued, would it not at least be evidenced by a similar standard—the test of time and its own endurance? Truth, fitness, and survival were closely linked. Would modern Americans be "a society like that of

John Burroughs' potato bug, which [if left to its own devices] exterminated the potato, and thereby exterminated itself?"[67] Or would it exhibit not merely a prudential but also an ethical form of self-restraint, a token of human nobility, that acknowledged community membership and limited what humans took from the land accordingly? Would Americans, Leopold wondered, prove to be "a society decently respectful of its own and all other life, capable of inhabiting the earth without defiling it?" "As one or the other" — self-defeating potato bug or noble man — Leopold challenged, the human race "shall be judged in 'the derisive silence of eternity'"[68] by the wider reaches of evolutionary time.

In 1937 Leopold produced an extraordinary essay, a meditation on marshlands and the cranes that inhabit them, pouring into poetic form much of his philosophy about truth, beauty, and rightness as it meshed with the standard of endurance and revelations of evolutionary science:

> A dawn wind stirs on the great marsh. . . . A sense of time lies thick and heavy on such a place. Yearly since the ice age it has awakened each spring to the clangor of cranes. . . . This much . . . can be said: our appreciation of the crane grows with the slow unraveling of earthly history. His tribe, we now know, stems out of the remote Eocene. . . . When we hear his call we hear no mere bird. We hear the trumpet in the orchestra of evolution. He is the symbol of our untamable past, of that incredible sweep of millennia which underlies and conditions the daily affairs of birds and men.
>
> And so they live and have their being — these cranes — not in the constricted present, but in the wider reaches of evolutionary time. . . . Amid the endless mediocrity of the commonplace, a crane marsh holds a paleontological patent of nobility, won in the march of eons.[69]

"The cranes stand, as it were, upon the sodden pages of their own history," Leopold wrote. They were voyagers on an evolutionary odyssey through vast reaches of time. And they were among the multitude of creatures taking part in an ongoing ecological odyssey — in their energy-circulating roles; as part of a successional landscape; and as community members:

> These peats [of the marsh] are the compressed remains of the mosses that clogged the pools, of the tamaracks that spread over the moss, of

the cranes that bugled over the tamaracks since the retreat of the ice sheet. An endless caravan of generations has built of its own bones this bridge into the future, this habitat where the oncoming host again may live and breed and die. To what end? Out on the bog a crane, gulping some luckless frog, springs his ungainly hulk into the air and flails the morning sun with mighty wings. The tamaracks re-echo with his bugled certitude. He seems to know.[70]

The endurance of crane marshes through the refining fires of eons-long change had proved something of their "rightness," in Leopold's view. It had patented their "nobility." Cranes gulping frogs and flying into marsh meadows and dying there, their bones crumbling into peat, where nutrient atoms would be recollected by tamaracks and lady's slippers, were playing their roles in opposing gravity and bringing nutrients uphill, helping to sustain the entire developing web of life. Crane and parrot, piñon jay and pine tree, ruffed grouse and human: each in its place was "one of thousands of accretions to the height and complexity of the land pyramid."[71] In the test vial of evolutionary time the rightness of all types of creatures together great and small was proved, and as fellow members of the humming, nutrient-cycling ecological community of life each species was "entitled to continuance." To understand these things, to Leopold's thinking, was to admit the inherent value of species and their inter-relationships and to imply toward them an obligation of moral respect.[72]

There was for humans a practical side to this philosophic wisdom, Leopold recognized: fighting against the land's ways was as destructive and useless as fighting against God. Instead humans needed to watch what endured; learn from nature; heed the forces of nature rather than strive against them. As a young forester in the Southwest, Leopold in 1913 had urged colleagues to measure the success of forest management by "the effect on the forest."[73] By 1921 he was applying the idea of survival to forestry practices. Forestry and farming practices were not "right" if they caused soil, the very capacity of the land for life, to erode down hillsides, waters to rage over their banks and sweep away bottomlands, and cattle to starve, leaving families destitute and communities isolated. And thus, check dams would work only if they did not "oppose natural processes";[74] they were useless if erosive forces were not human-caused, not due to live-stock grazing on surrounding lands.

Something was wrong with human attitudes and behaviors, Leopold believed, when game supplies dwindled close on the heels of heavy human settlement, clean farming, and "vermin" control. As for game management, it was absurd to try to change the timing of dove reproduction in the Rio Grande Valley, Leopold asserted in an early technical paper; it was the hunter who must refrain from shoot-ing in August stubble, while adult birds were rearing their still-dependent young.[75] Game management had sought to understand the land's mechanisms so that they might be manipulated, but that task was turning out nigh impossible. Nature's ways contained enduring, embedded wisdom that humans needed to respect.

Among the Dust Bowl's lessons was that Americans had failed to fit their political organizations and economy with the ways of nature. Nature had responded by rearing her head and raising her dust. The conservation efforts of the New Deal could not be about reforming the ways the land worked. They should have been, or needed to be, about reforming the ways people interacted with the land—and in the process changing "their ideas of what land is for."[76]

If modern industrialized people wanted to survive and thrive in the long term, Leopold concluded, they needed to learn better than they had who they were in relation to the community of life. They needed to draw lessons in survival from the "survivors": from the layers of peat in a crane marsh; from the rich prairie soil; from the age-old junipers and oaks of Mexico; from the cliff dwellers of the Southwest and the testimony of their smiling valleys. The survivors of the eons—the sandhill crane, the song of the Gavilan, the thick-billed parrot, the flowery community of the prairie—all had won a right from that success, a right to *nobility* and their place in the sun. Would humans, too, remain among the survivors?

To Leopold's mind it was not mere survival that was at issue; it was also richness of life—the things that made the odyssey of a human life worth living. For Leopold a life lived in a world devoid of its wild things—devoid, in other words, of full meaning and poetic beauty—was hardly worth living. "If, then, we can live without goose music," Leopold wrote, "we may as well do away with stars, or sunsets, or *Iliads*. But the point is that we would be fools to do away with any of them." "What value has wildlife from the standpoint of morals and religion," he asked.[77] "It just occurs to me," Leopold once explained, "that God started his show a good million years before he had any men for audience . . . and it is just barely possible that God himself likes to hear birds sing and see flowers grow."[78] "I heard of a boy once who was brought up an atheist," Leopold admitted, perhaps with shyness, switching to the second person as he revealed an intimate detail about himself.

> [That boy] changed his mind when he saw that there were a hundred-odd species of warblers, each bedecked like to the rainbow. . . . No "fortuitous concourse of elements" working blindly through any number of millions of years could quite account for why warblers are so beautiful. No mechanistic theory, even bolstered by mutations, has ever quite answered for the colors of the cerulean warbler . . . —or goose music. I dare say this boy's convictions would be harder to shake than those of many inductive theologians.[79]

DIFFERENT CATHEDRALS

Although Leopold's family of origin did not attend an organized church, Leopold's cultural heritage included Christianity, and as a student at Yale he participated in formal Bible study.[80] He was particularly drawn to the Old Testament as a scholarly and historical book as well as a guide and standard.[81] He combed its pages for references to issues of land use, responding to what resonated true. In his personal journal Leopold wrote out six pages of quotations from the Old Testament books of Ecclesiastes, Isaiah, Hosea, Ezekiel, Jonah, and Job, verses dealing with the urgency of seeking wisdom, dependence on and humility before God, the insufficiency of humans in and of themselves before God, active care for those weaker or needier than oneself, respect for the creation of God, and satisfaction with God's provision.[82] Religious texts echoing with philosophic ideas and empirical evidence about nature supported Leopold's developing understanding of the world.

Even as Leopold found the Old Testament a source of wisdom, perhaps a place for glimpsing what Hadley termed "something fixed and permanent,"[83] he was not a churchgoer. In marrying Estella, Leopold became part of a noble, landowning Hispanic family, Catholic by religion and tradition. To honor her beliefs and heritage, Aldo and Estella were married in the "Cathedral" in Santa Fe. One requisite for doing so was Aldo's promise, as a non-Catholic, not to interfere with the religious upbringing of their children. He kept his promise, increasing his reticence to talk directly about his religious beliefs, even at home.[84] While he respected the traditions and beliefs of others, particularly those of his wife and her family, Leopold by all appearances could give himself only to and for what was living and whole. For him the church did not seem that way. Leopold in his younger years copied in his journal an unattributed poem, "Portrait of an Old Cathedral," offering a rare glimpse of what he thought about a religious tradition that had, as far as he could see, "died of its own too much":[85] "What vigor raised those spires; what joyful hand / . . . Making the structure greater than it planned! / . . . What laughter shook the builders . . . / While, laid with love, each stone was made to stand! / And now, . . . / These sober generations, self-deceiving, / Come with perfunctory prayers and every small / Hatred that turns them hard and unforgiving, / Dead worshipping the dead! / . . . Only the stone is living."[86]

Deeply felt spiritual matters are difficult to bring into common words; for such expressions Leopold often quietly turned to creating his poetical essays. Leopold's elder daughter, Nina—affirming the sense of so many of his readers—knew her father as a particularly spiritual person. She remembers feeling the need to be silent beside him when they walked in the woods. As a young man Leopold also had copied into his journal lines from Theodore Winthrop's 1863 book *The Canoe and the Saddle*, perhaps revealing his attitude while on such walks about his forested surroundings:

> The trail took us speedily into a forest temple. Long years of labor by artists the most unconscious of their skill had been given to modeling these columnar firs. Unlike the pillars of human architecture, chipped and chiseled in bustling, dusty quarries and hoisted to their site by sweat of brow and creak of pulley, these rose to fairest proportion by the life that was in them, and blossomed into foliated capitals three hundred feet overhead.[87]

WALKING A POEM

By all appearances Leopold worshiped freely in living, leafy cathedrals and buried prone "in the muck of a muskrat house."[88] One day, Leopold recounted, he buried himself under the springtime sodden ground of a Canadian marsh he had visited hoping "to *see*" a mysterious western grebe mother launch her young into "their watery career." With his eyes at mud level Leopold absorbed the local color and the "lore of the marsh"—a redhead duck with her ducklings, a Virginia rail, a pelican's shadow, a yellowlegs ascending with a whistle to a nearby pool. It occurred to him then, he reported, "that whereas I *write* a poem by dint of mighty cerebration, the yellow-leg *walks* a better one just by lifting his foot."[89] Finally, seemingly out of nowhere a mother grebe with two "pearly-silver young" on her back rounded a bend and moved behind a curtain of reeds. Here she let

Leopold discovered this nest of an eared grebe among some reeds.
In Leopold's view the grebe, a species that had proven itself through
ages of survival, represented evolutionary history and thereby
deserved our respect.

loose her "clear and derisive" bell-like call. "A sense of history should be the most precious gift of science and the arts," Leopold wrote, reflecting on the experience,

> but I suspect that the grebe, who has neither, knows more history than we do. His dim primordial brain knows nothing of who won the Battle of Hastings, but it seems to sense who won the battle of time. If the race of men were as old as the race of grebes, we might better grasp the import of his call. Think what traditions, prides, disdains, and wisdoms even a few self-conscious generations bring to us! What pride of continuity, then, impels this bird, who was a grebe eons before there was a man.
>
> Be that as it may, the call of the grebe is, by some peculiar authority, the sound that dominates and unifies the marshland chorus. Perhaps, by some immemorial authority, he wields the baton for the whole biota.[90]

To respect the grebe, then, was to honor more than a single bird. It was to promote beauty, grace, artistry, history, evolution, enduring truth, and the whole community of life. What might it take, wondered Leopold, for his neighbors and people all over the country—upon whom the cooperative effort of conservation depended and against which so many destructive forces presently were at work—to come to such an understanding? What would it take to establish in society, in other words, a new "understanding of what land is for"?

Chapter 8

The Germ
and the Juggernaut

Have not invention, energy, and discipline consolidated the gains of mankind securely against all danger, excepting our own selfishness and capacity for mutual destruction in time of war and peace?

Paul B. Sears, *Deserts on the March*

Culture is a state of awareness of the land's collective functioning. A culture premised on the destructive dominance of a single species can have but short duration.

Aldo Leopold, "Land-Use and Democracy"

Leopold composed his lyrical descriptions of the great marsh, with its "sense of time . . . thick and heavy" and its noble cranes, "symbol of our untamable past," in the form of a "Marshland Elegy." It was a sad song of past, present, and future loss. After tracking the effects of intensifying, machine-driven human land uses on the marsh, from first settlement to the late 1930s, Leopold offered a bleak prediction:

Some day . . . the last crane will trumpet his farewell and spiral skyward from the great marsh. High out of the clouds will fall the sound of hunting horns, the baying of the phantom pack [of cranes flying overhead], the tinkle of little bells, and then a silence never to be broken, unless perchance in some far pasture of the Milky Way.[1]

The gray tone in "Marshland Elegy," first published in 1937,[2] was appearing in Leopold's other writings also, and sensitive readers noticed it. One who did was his former student, Albert Hochbaum, now a waterfowl ecologist working in the marshes of Manitoba, Canada. Leopold sent Hochbaum, in the early 1940s, several of the pieces he had gathered for his essay collection.[3] The somber tone in several of them, Hochbaum wrote to Leopold, belied one of Leopold's "strongest characteristics": an "unbounded enthusiasm . . . for the future."[4] Perhaps, Hochbaum hinted, Leopold could reveal more of this trait.

Leopold's zeal for good conservation work never waned, even in the gloomiest of times. Alongside it, though, was increasing frustration as he witnessed the man-wrought tragedies then shaping the world and the great, perhaps unstoppable forces behind them. No force brought more darkness than World War II, which gathered rage as Leopold worked on his various essays recounting experiences that had taught him, "gradually and sometimes painfully, that the [conservation] company is out of step."[5] Leopold rarley talked about the war outside his home,[6] though in class lectures ruminations about the conflict emerged as he tried to understand aspects of it in ecological terms.[7] As the war wore on, enrollment dropped at the university—its young men and women were flung across the world, Leopold's students and sons included. Leopold's youngest son, Carl, enlisted with the U.S. Marines and was sent to an undisclosed (and by Carl's accounts badly overgrazed by land-crabs) Pacific island; his middle son, Luna, enlisted with the U.S. Army and trained with the meteorology division; and his eldest son, Starker, on the draft list, continued with his graduate studies at the University of California, Berkeley.

Compounding these war worries were personal setbacks that Leopold suffered. In August 1943 Leopold, now fifty-six, wanted to begin writing a new conservation ecology textbook,[8] in addition to the collection of his literary essays. Instead he was laid up with sciatica, only the start of a series of painful and debilitating neurological episodes.[9] And that November, during deer season, Leopold was forced to put down his beloved German shorthaired pointer Gus, badly injured on a hunting trip by the kick of a wounded deer. It

*A photograph in Leopold's collection of his daughter Estella's tame crow
perched on his beloved dog Gus, whom he had to put down.*

was a sad, guilt-burdening accident for Leopold, more so because
Wisconsin state law banned deer hunting with dogs.[10] Meanwhile,
Leopold, recently appointed to the Wisconsin Conservation Commission, took part in a heated battle over deer management in the
state. Northern Wisconsin's burgeoning deer population had been
eating up its food supply, leaving nothing but leafless sapling stalks,
a high browse line on trees, and a damaged capacity for forest
regrowth. In some areas deer now were starving to death, particularly in the hard winter months. To trim the herd Leopold supported
a management plan that included killing does and fawns, for the good
of the herd and the forest.[11] But this plan met with misunderstanding
and hostile public resistance. The open season on female and young
deer was branded the "crime of '43" and resulted in a smear campaign
against Leopold by the Save Wisconsin's Deer Committee.[12] On
Christmas Day 1944 Leopold wrote soberly to his son Starker and
family in California, "The war has us all worried"; and things overall
were "not so good."[13]

A pile of forty-five starved deer, most of them fawns, collected in March 1943 in one northern Wisconsin county. An excess of deer relative to food supply was a problem in many areas of the country.

Meanwhile, though, Leopold found warm support at home in Madison from his wife, Estella, and his younger daughter, also Estella, then a teenager. Nina, Leopold's elder daughter, was married to zoologist Bill Elder and lived not far away, in Chicago. More distant encouragement came to Leopold from "round-robin letters" — packets of correspondence that gathered in bulk as they circulated from military post to post among his war-dispersed students. The letters were filled with personal news, developing wildlife research ideas and questions, warm humor, and good-natured jabs the soldiers aimed at one another. On September 1, 1943, Leopold took a turn, writing, "In the year since our round-robin 'got global' there has been a heavy consumption of brass buttons by the wildlife group. Only 4 of us left now [in Madison]." After giving brief accounts of what he had seen or heard of common friends, Leopold concluded, "So you see that if somebody had banded wildlifers, there would be many far-flung returns, and great mobility would be indicated. The most cheerful thing I have to report is that there are no 'recoveries' so far."[14]

One of the round-robin entries in May of the next year was a unique graphic contributed by Leopold's former student Douglas

Wade, now teaching at Dartmouth College. Wade had drawn a diagram revealing something of the realism and hopefulness, as well as the content, of what Leopold had taught him over the years. Wade's aim, he explained, was "to work out a pictorial presentation of a philosophy that will help the ecologists attain a mature place in this world." Yet he felt that some pieces still were missing from his understanding. "That's why," Wade explained in a small appended note, "we need the Professor's book or books [i.e., his ecology text and book of essays] soon. He can help us all so much."[15]

Wade's diagram took off from one that had appeared in Leopold's 1933 game management text.[16] Leopold's original depicted the naturally rising curve of an animal population as it was pulled down by various limiting factors (hunting, predators, starvation, disease, etc.) and affected negatively or positively by more generalizable influences (including weather, fire, grazing, cutting, and drainage). In Wade's rendering the rising curve was labeled "Unimpeded Curve of Life of Truth and Enjoyment (Idealist Attainment)." Factors pulling down the curve included "hypocrisy, ignorance, apathy, jealousy, selfishness, hate, fear." Negative or positive influences affecting it included the "physical, mental and aesthetic nature of an individual; economic set-ups; scientific method and ecological viewpoint; and philosophy, religion, art, and drama," which "provide a moral code which holds in check the 'pressure' of the anti-social factors which present economic organization fosters." "Our personal lives," Wade explained, "are strangely separated from our business life, political life, and economic relationships, generally." "What," Wade asked, could "the ecological viewpoint do to put an end to all of this so-called separation of personal and so-called practical life?"[17] What might unify, in Leopold's words, the "economic and esthetic, public and private" aspects of people's lives so as to achieve a *universal symbiosis with land*"—the ultimate goal of conservation?[18] Wade had learned from Leopold that conservation was not merely a scientific problem; it was also a cultural and social one. It was a problem that eluded an easy solution. Whatever the knowledge and wisdom of scientists and poets, if people could not, or did not want to, adjust their land uses to fit a land's characteristics and limitations, then conservation would not succeed.

The Germ of Hope

There was much for which a conservationist could be regretful in an industrialized and war-torn world. And Leopold often was, deeply so. But, as Hochbaum observed, Leopold believed even in dark times that there lay within human nature at least the "germ of a better order of things."[19] If well nourished, this seed might one day yield better fruits for humankind and the whole community of life.

Leopold called this germ of hope by different names, including the "decent opinion of mankind," the "essence of civilization," the human conscience, and "that something"[20] so deeply and commonly felt by humankind. It was the wellspring of what was noble in humans, something intuitive, something touching some "sub-economic stratum of the human intelligence." It made humans break their backs tilling the land to feed their families and buy them shoes. It made a neighbor help a neighbor rebuild a burned-down barn. It also, Leopold thought, distinguished people from potato bugs or burgeoning deer, which lacked the capacity to intentionally limit their appetites. It was this germ, if anything, that set humans apart from other creatures, enabling them to practice respectful, ethical behavior toward others. This seed of decency, Leopold believed, was related to what people felt as "love of nature."[21] From it emerged the inner sensibility that thrilled to the trumpeting of a crane overhead or gently appreciated billowing prairie grass—wanting to keep and protect them or mourning their loss, should that come to pass.[22] For conservation to take hold, Leopold believed, this germ of human decency would need to grow into what Leopold later would call an "ecological conscience," expressing itself in ethical behavior not only toward other people but also toward land itself.[23]

Leopold optimistically noted the budding of such a conscience whenever he saw it. The cultural soil of the time, he knew too well, was often inhospitable to its development, and he often found it in what seemed unlikely places. He discovered it hidden within 1920s-era "Boosterism" or "Babbittry," for instance, which he had criticized for its "bigger and better" mentality, narrow economic measures of success, and sprawling road systems jammed with traffic and lined with billboards. Yet, Leopold recognized, underneath the urge for more roads and more moneyed tourists visiting Booster's towns and cities resided the "decent" motive to build better communities and better places to live.[24] The ongoing problem of ruined "submarginal lands" also contained hidden seeds of hope. Amid the land degradation were signs of public dissatisfaction with merely economic rationales for land use. Farmers had long been overproducing staple crops, and the government was already spending millions of tax dollars to pay farmers to retire excess croplands. It made economic sense, then, for government to take no remedial action on the submarginal lands that farmers had "skinned . . . for profit" and left in ruins. It made more practical sense to address crop surplus problems by allowing erosion to wash away the sodless, damaged, economically useless soil. Yet *"no man has so spoken,"* Leopold pointed out.[25] No one had promoted such public disregard for damaged lands. Just the opposite, in fact: government programs were designed to restore and resettle them. Americans could stomach the burning or plowing under of overproduced cotton, coffee, or corn, Leopold pointed out. "But the destruction of mother-earth, however 'submarginal,' touches something deeper"—the germ, perhaps, of an ecological conscience.

Years later Leopold would identify similar signs of budding conscience in another unlikely situation. Market hunters by the turn of the century had slaughtered to extinction the passenger pigeon, a species that once numbered in the billions.[26] In 1947 the Wisconsin Society for Ornithology marked the loss with a monument to the last pigeon of its kind shot in the state, near Babcock, in 1899. Leopold spoke at the dedication, held in Wyalusing State Park, along the Mississippi River. Standing by the fieldstone monument with its engraved plaque—"This species became extinct through the avarice and thoughtlessness of man"—Leopold found hope in the act of dedication:

> We have erected a monument to commemorate the funeral of a species. It symbolizes our sorrow. . . . For one species to mourn the death of another is a new thing under the sun. . . . To love what *was* is a new thing under the sun, unknown to most people and to all pigeons. To see America as history, to conceive of destiny as a becoming, to smell a hickory tree through the still lapse of ages—all

these things are possible for us, and to achieve them takes only the free sky, and the will to ply our wings. In these things, and not in Mr. Bush's bombs and Mr. DuPont's nylons, lies objective evidence of our superiority over the beasts.[27]

If there were anything distinctively noble in the human species, Leopold had asked rhetorically years earlier—anything setting human beings apart from other life-forms—by what would it be known? Might it be manifest, he answered, "by a society decently respectful of its own and all other life, capable of inhabiting the earth without defiling it?"[28]

THE WAR FOR VALUES

The growth of any seed is a mysterious and uncertain thing. Sprouts of ecological conscience, Leopold realized, would require particularly careful tending in modern America because factors opposing their growth were strong. Rumbling below the surface of things was a war of values between the prevailing philosophy of market individualism and a developing philosophy of conservation. Socialism, communism, fascism, capitalism, and what Leopold called "technocracy" all shared the same virtually unquestioned end: "[t]he distribution of more machine-made commodities to more people." The underlying theory for all was "*salvation by machinery.*"[29] Land in this view was "merely an economic commodity," and economic land development, especially with the force of mechanization behind it, was deemed inherently good.[30] Industrial advocates talked often about adjusting humans and machinery to the production of goods. They had little to say about adjusting humans and machines to the land. It was a mentality that, harnessed to powerful technologies, was running roughshod over the very earth out of which humans had hammered their civilization in the first place. And it was crushing under its wheels those qualities that encouraged people to value not only material comfort but also natural beauty; not only wealth but also health and wholeness; not only their individual welfare but also that of their neighbors.[31]

Sometime earlier (probably in the late 1920s) Leopold had tried to capture in verse something of the modern threats to that positive impulse he sometimes termed the "germ of a better order."[32] Even though it may have stumbled as poetry, Leopold's expression was insightful, displaying his sense of fundamental cultural conflict. His writing drew upon the *Nibelungenlied*,[33] a thirteenth-century epic drama involving an Icelandic queen, Brunhild, who was renowned for her strength and sporting skill as well as her beauty. In the drama, men who wooed Brunhild were required to compete with her in physical contest, and all but one met death. What unfolded thereafter was a complicated tale of magic, betrayal, and lost power.[34] In his personal journal Leopold composed an updated version of this Germanic myth, set in the modern era of mechanization and industrial culture. In Leopold's version the reborn Brunhild lost her beauty and wild strength, not to a man but to the lure of "yellow wheels" and a smooth, inviting road, which distracted, subdued, and ultimately won her. Once a daughter of the gods, Leopold's Brunhild lived as if born of Sinclair Lewis' Mr. Babbitt, enthralled by emerging technology and rising physical comfort. Could she have forgotten who she really was? Leopold wondered: "Life chained you / To a tan automobile / With a gold monogram on the door / And yellow wheels . . . / As you sweep up the avenue / In robins-egg blue silk . . . / I wonder if you know / Who you are."[35] Strength, beauty, vigor— the attributes necessary to a vibrant, enduring human civilization— were being sapped by the materialism and technological powers of the modern age. If even Brunhild could fall victim to an industrial culture, who would be strong enough to resist? How could society restrain this juggernaut of its own making so that the values it was crushing might grow again and thrive?

Leopold raised these questions repeatedly, seeking different ways to address them. In his 1933 essay "The Conservation Ethic," for example, he proposed that "the ultimate issue in conservation as in other social problems" "is whether the mass-mind *wants* to extend its powers of comprehending the world in which it lives [in order to adjust its wants and ways to the world], or, granted the desire, *has the capacity to do so*."[36] Leopold did not know the answers, but some geneticists, he pointed out, were attempting to probe the latter question.[37] And, Leopold felt, Spanish philosopher José Ortega y Gasset, in his newly translated best-seller *The Revolt of the Masses*, had addressed the first question "with devastating lucidity."[38]

Ortega's thesis—which captured Leopold's attention—was that a tripling of the population of Europe and America over the past two centuries and the spread of material comforts to broader classes of people (the more recent national and worldwide economic depressions aside) had allowed "mass-man" to usurp "complete social power" from the elite. This had occurred even though "mass-man" was incompetent to rule well. Set free by technology and relative material ease, Ortega argued, the masses felt independent from the sources of their prosperity, unencumbered by limitations and dependencies, and without obligation to any higher authority or principle than themselves. Without objective standards, he asserted, there could be no basis for reason and no moral foundation upon which a mature culture might develop.[39] As Ortega characterized the situation, the ascendancy of the masses had precipitated a crisis that threatened the cultural and political achievements of the West.

Ortega's definition of "the masses" was not merely a quantitative one; it was also a condition of quality. Humankind for Ortega was divided into two groups: the "noble men," who made demands on themselves in terms of excellence and duty, and the masses, who made little or no effort to pursue ideals. "Strictly speaking," wrote Ortega,

> the mass, as a psychological fact, can be defined without waiting for individuals to appear in mass formation. In the presence of one individual we can decide whether he is "mass" or not. The mass is all that which sets no value on itself—good or ill—based on specific grounds, but which feels itself "just like everybody," and nevertheless is not concerned about it; is, in fact, quite happy to feel itself as one [and the same] with everybody else.[40]

Ortega's sense of conflict in society—between the more narrow-minded, self-interested understandings of the masses and the more far-seeing, socially responsible views of the noble minded—resonated with Leopold. He could see these two mentalities at odds in the context of land use and conservation. To the "mass-mind," wrote Leopold in 1933—connecting Ortega's terminology with conservation—the relationship between people and land was still "strictly economic, entailing privileges but not obligations."[41] Land was simply a means to personal comfort and economic wealth, nothing more. There was no more a moral right and wrong in relation to land than there was a moral right and wrong in relation to any other commodity or thing. Bathtubs, food, cars, timber, and soil: all held the same moral status, and all could be traded freely in the marketplace. To counter this fragmented view of the world, ecologists needed to step out of their "cloistered sequestration"[42] and play their part as responsible, if not noble-minded, community members, Leopold urged. They needed to promote an understanding of land based on ecological knowledge, and this needed somehow to lead to a broader than economic relation with and valuation of nature.

Leopold had once believed that if people were told how much harm arose from ecologically insensitive land use, they would change their ways. Over time he came to see that more was needed.[43] Conservation indeed required ecological knowledge, but it also entailed a struggle over America's cultural values and priorities, over what people thought right and most *wanted* in life. "It is increasingly clear," Leopold wrote sometime in the early 1940s, "that there is a basic antagonism between the philosophy of the industrial age and the philosophy of the conservationist."

> What are necessities to [the conservationist] are luxuries to his neighbors, and vice versa. How shall he live in a world whose scale of values are, in important respects, inverse to his own? What are those values? Why the difference in viewpoint? What can be done about it? I am not competent to answer these questions, but it is time for somebody to try to answer them.[44]

The philosophy of industrialism harnessed technology and economic power and drove the automobile of American civilization toward its goal of individual prosperity—toward an ideal of an ever more profitable and comfortable future for all. Within this philosophy, "industry is the end and conservation the means." "Commodity conservation," in other words, "assumes as a matter of course that man-built power is more desirable than salmon, or any other thing that grows of its own accord."[45] A profit-driven, machine-run culture gained more Fords, roads, bathtubs, and radios in the short term. But its triumph, Leopold believed, was merely a "Pyrrhic victory."[46] It came at the cost of maladjustments in organization and functioning of the land community, including troubling losses in landscape diversity, beauty, and soil fertility.[47] The philosophy of "ecological" conservation, in contrast, reversed these matters: "the thrift and beauty of the resource is the end, and industry merely the means of preparing and distributing its fruits."[48] A culture of ecological conservation valued its native landscape as a priority[49] and its Fords, roads, bathtubs, and radios as they were consistent with the land's well-adjusted condition.

Pyrrhic Victory

To conquer some of the country's land, converting it to intensive economic use, was necessary for civilization. But to say that because some conversion was necessary, conversion of all lands was therefore good made little sense and ran against the grain of other important values—including aesthetic, historical, recreational, scientific, and moral ones. Ultimately, this mentality was also self-defeating.[50] The Dust Bowl illustrated these truths dramatically.

The Dust Bowl and the conquering mentality that stimulated it received an unusually probing critique in a report issued by the federal government in 1937 titled *Future of the Great Plains*.[51] The report was prepared by the Great Plains Committee, appointed by Franklin D. Roosevelt, with members including some of the nation's leading land planning intellects.[52] The group was to identify how the nation could help people maintain reasonable standards of living in a geographic area in which climatic conditions made special land-use considerations necessary. Like Leopold the committee blamed the Dust Bowl mainly on the failure of humans to adapt to nature, rather than simply some misbehavior by nature itself.[53] Many Americans, leading up to the crisis, had believed that there were no restrictions in nature that could not be overcome with human energy. And rain would follow the plow, they thought.[54] Thus, not only with plows but also with new tractors and other powerful farm machinery, millions of enterprising neighbors had torn up the semi-arid short-grass prairie on their homesteads and replaced it with wheat—which came to total nearly 33 million acres, or one-third of the Dust Bowl region[55]—intending to turn the wheat into money and more comfortable personal lives in the future. Underlying this land-use pattern were some cultural assumptions that, in light of the disaster, needed reevaluation, the report claimed.[56] One of these was the belief that natural resources were inexhaustible. Another was the belief in an owner's unquestioned right to use private land without regard for nature's ways, without limits, and without regard for the public interest in the future condition of such land. And implied underneath these beliefs, also calling for closer scrutiny, was the dominating American pro-expansionary, free-enterprise, fast-cash-generating ethos that had been turning farms into factories and that, in addition to its ills elsewhere, was devastatingly ill suited to conditions on the Great Plains:

> The Plainsman cannot assume that whatever is for his immediate good is also good for everybody. . . . [H]e cannot assume the right always to do with his own property as he likes — he may ruin another man's property if he does; he cannot assume that the individual action he can take on his own land will be sufficient, even for the conservation and best use of that land. He must realize that he cannot "conquer Nature" — he must live with her on her own terms, making use of and conserving resources which can no longer be considered inexhaustible. . . . In this new point of view . . . the whole Nation has more than a sentimental stake.[57]

The report's most powerful cultural critique came in chapter 5, "Attitudes of Mind." In it the authors drew extensively upon Leopold's 1933 article "The Conservation Ethic." "[I]n a deeper sense," the report intoned, "modern science has disclosed that fundamentally Nature is inflexible and demands conformity. On this point Aldo Leopold has well said" that

> [c]ivilization is not . . . the enslavement of a stable and constant earth. It is a state of *mutual interdependent cooperation* between human animals, other animals, plants, and the soils, which may be disrupted at any moment by the failure of any of them. Land despoliation has evicted nations, and can on occasion do it again. . . . It thus becomes a matter of some importance, at least to ourselves, that our dominion, once gained, be self-perpetuating, rather than self-destructive.[58]

The Great Plains offered a test case of America's ability to see its faults and remedy them, nurturing to growth the germ of a better order. Could citizens of such an individualistic nation come together to address common concerns? "We now know," the report asserted, "that it is essential to adjust agricultural economy on the Plains" to the region's characteristic periods of drought and severe winds rather than to a temporarily high price for wheat or beef.[59] A "purely individualistic system of pioneering"[60] would simply not suffice.

The cultural critique of the Great Plains Committee and Leopold's criticisms of countrywide land-use trends were similar. Its recommendations, however, did not press for the kind of deep cultural changes Leopold believed were necessary to bring about successful conservation. Instead, the committee's report expressed confidence that problems of the plains would respond to institutional adjustments—an "altered system which will invoke the power of voluntary cooperation without sacrificing any of the virtues of local initiative and self-reliance."[61] The committee's suggested remedies included government purchases of submarginal private lands, cooperative grazing arrangements, creation of larger farm units, new soil conservation districts and protective zoning, farm loans tied to improved land practices, drought tax relief, and conservation education. While likely to improve the land-use situation for the short term, none could be expected to get to the root causes of land problems, Leopold believed. None would require reform of hard-pushing economic priorities,[62] nor would they address other underlying cultural values that had so visibly clashed with ecological realities. Modern, prevailing trends would be allowed to continue fundamentally unchecked.

As industrial culture—with its ideals of efficiency, quick profit, and powerful technology—gained momentum during the 1940s, Leopold began to question whether a balance between industrial culture and conservation was even possible. Perhaps, he mused, industrialism needed to be discarded entirely.[63] Conservation's deepest challenge—to change cultural values—was so large and complex and the industrial juggernaut had so much momentum that restraining it seemed virtually impossible. It was destroying what he loved, however, and he would not stop trying. Leopold expressed his intensifying doubt as well as offering his idea of what it would take to moderate industrialism—a new culture-of-conservation ethos—in a 1946 letter to his close friend William Vogt, who was at the time working on what was to become a best seller, *Road to Survival*:[64]

The only thing you have left out is whether the philosophy of industrial culture is not, in its ultimate development, irreconcilable with ecological conservation. I think it is.

I hasten to add, however, that the term industrialism cannot be used as an absolute. Like "temperature" and "velocity" it is a question of degree. Throughout ecology all truth is relative: a thing becomes good at one degree and ceases to be so at another.

Industrialism might theoretically be conservative if there were an ethic limiting its application to what does not impair (a) permanence and stability of the land (b) beauty of the land. But there is no such ethic, nor likely to be. . . .

That the situation is hopeless should not prevent us from doing our best.[65]

WHY CONSERVATION WAS FALTERING

A year after his letter to Vogt, Leopold reiterated publicly his somber assessment of conservation's overall ineffectiveness over the previous half century: "Everyone ought to be dissatisfied with the slow spread of conservation to the land." "Our 'progress,'" he explained, "still consists largely of letterhead pieties and convention oratory. The only progress that counts is that on the actual landscape of the back forty, and here we are still slipping two steps backward for each forward stride."[66]

By this time, too, Leopold had a pretty clear idea in mind of why the backward slipping so often came about. It was related to the same "conquering" attitudes that the Great Plains Committee blamed for the Dust Bowl disaster. Three key elements in American culture were at work cutting across the realities of ecological interdependencies.[67] Conservation that left these attitudes unchecked—no matter how well meaning—would inevitably encounter problems,[68] Leopold understood. One element had to do with how Americans viewed themselves, another with what they used as a yardstick of success, and a third with how they conceived of nature. Most Americans, Leopold observed, understood themselves as isolated individuals free to act in their own self-interest, they commonly understood short-term economic profit (i.e., cash wealth) as the yardstick of their success, and they tended to view land as readily and properly divisible into products or commodities destined for the market. In contrast with these three prevailing attitudes, ecology and evolutionary science were revealing that humans were interdependent members of ecological communities. Landscapes overall were most productive and stable in the long term when their native species occurred in characteristic kinds and numbers. And each of the land's parts[69] was connected to a host of others forming an integrated whole.

Conservationists clearly cared about nature, Leopold readily admitted; the germ of ecological conscience was budding within them. But their cultural assumptions too often went unexamined, sometimes causing conservation efforts to do more harm than good. One example Leopold used was that of zealous deer protectors who desired abundant deer to hunt, to enjoy watching, and to show to tourists. What they failed to see was that focusing on only one species led to policies that harmed the larger landscape, eventually boomeranging to harm the deer themselves. "These people call themselves conservationists," Leopold complained, "and in one sense they are, for in the past we have pinned that label on anyone who loves wildlife, however blindly." But, he explained,

> [t]he basic fallacy in this kind of "conservation" is that it seeks to conserve one resource by destroying another. These "conservationists" are unable to see the land as a whole. They are unable to think in terms of community rather than group welfare, and in terms of the long as well as the short view. They are conserving what is important to them in the immediate future, and they are angry when told that this conflicts with what is important to the state as a whole in the long run.[70]

Leopold's critique of deer conservationists applied to other single resource–minded conservationists. Truly "ecological conservationists,"[71] he urged, needed to rise above prevailing perceptions of land as consisting of distinct parts and needed also to view it as an integrated whole. Valuing nature was vital to conservation, but the love of nature needed to be informed by ecological understanding. Ecological conservation was "an affair of the mind as well as the heart."[72]

Another obvious conservation "muddle," as Leopold called it, resulted from conservation efforts that failed to align economic policies with ecological understanding. Confusion regularly occurred when well-meaning conservationists told landowners that good land use was economically profitable while at the same time government administrators promoted subsidies on the ground that conservation was *not* profitable. In Leopold's view the matter was clear: conservation sometimes made economic sense but often it did not. Wildflowers and songbirds offered little conceivable economic profit. Entire biotic communities—bogs, dunes, deserts, marshes—could also lack economic value in the market sense. Some tree species were not worth growing economically because they matured too slowly or brought low prices. Beyond that, an action that made economic sense for one landowner could harm the landscape as a whole. Landowners who killed the hawks hovering over their fields might make their chickens safer, but the entire neighborhood would decline physically and aesthetically by losing a community member. Conservation might often require a landowner to forgo an individually profitable act. Finally, there was the common situation in which

A fencerow of Osage orange trees planted as a windbreak to help keep soils in place and create wildlife habitat in an agricultural area otherwise cleared of trees. For both goals to be met across a landscape, neighbors needed to agree to establish and maintain the windbreaks.

a conservation action made sense economically only when all land-owners in a region engaged in it—for example, when all landowners planted windbreaks and established fencerows to help keep a land-scape's soils in place. Whether an individual profited from conserva-tion, that is, could depend on the behavior of neighbors. The profit motive, in short, would accomplish "a few, but only a few" of the things that needed to be done on the land, Leopold instructed his wildlife ecology students.[73] The bottom line was that "a system of conservation based solely on economic self-interest is hopelessly lopsided. It tends to ignore and thus eventually to eliminate, many elements in the land community that lack commercial value, but that are (as far as we know) essential to its healthy functioning."[74] When viewing the conservation problem on the whole, Leopold explained, "we see one common denominator: regard for community welfare is the keystone to conservation."[75]

By the late 1930s it was clear to Leopold that economic and educa-tional incentives for better conservation practices did not necessarily motivate landowners to pick up on and practice new methods on their own, nor did they stimulate landowners to awaken to commu-nity obligations. When landowners stopped getting government help they generally continued only those activities that yielded visible economic gain for themselves, such as liming (to reduce soil acidity and improve fertility) and strip-cropping (growing alternat-ing strips of two or more crops, following the land's contours and at right angles to prevailing wind patterns to prevent water and wind erosion). They did not tend to continue practices that were good only for their communities or good only in the longer term, such as planting fencerows and windbreaks and excluding cows from steep slopes. When the Wisconsin legislature gave citizens the opportunity to write their own counties' rules for land use, various counties organized to receive state help. Yet over the next ten years no conser-vation district self-imposed legal restrictions on how landowners used their lands. Payment programs and other government efforts alone simply did not change the dominant land culture.[76]

Relying heavily on the "Let Uncle Sam do it" formula was, Leopold feared, ineffective. Although government ownership and management of land was vital in some cases, most often "husbandry of land," he wrote, "is inherently an action calling for continuous synthesis of the ideal and the practical. The government can not furnish the one ingredient while the owner furnishes the other. The government is not around while the things that matter happen."[77] If decent land use had to be bought by government intervention on an ever-increasing scale, projected Leopold, it would mean "the end of private landownership, the end of government solvency, and the end of the present economic system."[78] From an ecological perspective an owner of a land parcel really owned not a distinctly bounded piece of nature but "a stock certificate in a common biota."[79] Landowners were co-owners of a larger, integrated whole. Unless they understood that and accepted responsibility for community welfare, conservation would falter and so would the human enterprise.

Socially Responsible Individualism

Conservation depended ultimately upon individuals taking greater personal responsibility for community welfare, Leopold concluded. "The real substance of conservation," he wrote in 1937, began not with the "physical projects of government" but "in the mental processes of citizens"[80] and had to be built up from there. "The basic defect" in conservation, as Leopold put it a decade later, was that it had "not asked the citizen to assume any real responsibility."[81] It had not yet called for private effort or sacrifice to meet its challenges, nor had it pushed hard to change the prevailing philosophy of cultural values. The "current doctrine of private-profit and public-subsidy" did not demand a sense of community obligation from the private landowners. It expected buyouts and subsidies to do more and private owners to do less for the community than they were capable of doing. "We rationalize these defects as individualism," Leopold pointed out, "but they imply no real respect for the landowner as an individual."[82] They reflected instead a "bogus individualism."[83]

Leopold returned to the issue repeatedly. "Is the individual landowner capable of dedicating private land to uses which profit the community," he asked, "even though they may not so clearly profit him?" The assumption was that the owner would not, but "we may be overhasty in assuming that he is not,"[84] Leopold suggested. What seemed to stand in the way was a set of cultural assumptions that stood at cross-purposes to ecologically sensitive land use:

> I doubt if there exists today a more complete regimentation of the human mind than that accomplished by our self-imposed doctrine of ruthless utilitarianism [bred of the dream of sudden economic affluence]. The saving grace of democracy is that we fastened this yoke upon our own necks, and we can cast it off when we want to, without severing the neck. Conservation is perhaps one of the many squirmings which foreshadow this act of self-liberation.[85]

If they chose, American democrats could cast off the yoke of a merely industrial philosophy.[86] The question was, as Leopold had asked a few years earlier, does the mass mind *want* to extend its powers of comprehending the world in which it lives and adjust its goals and ways accordingly? "A sufficiently enlightened society," he believed, could "by changing its wants and tolerances" change "the economic factors bearing on land."[87]

As Leopold surveyed the trends of individualistic, economically motivated land use it became clear that landscapes across the country were heading rapidly toward monotypes—large areas dominated by one species—or separate fragments of community types, the antithesis of diversity in a landscape and the antithesis of conservation.[88] Just as Ortega's mass men were becoming "just like everybody" else, so were their various landscapes becoming more alike. Economic efficiency in agriculture—not only in the Great Plains but across the country—called for the use of ever bigger machines that worked best on large, uniform sweeps of land. This created factorylike farms specializing in single crops. Contributing to the trend toward land simplification, too, was the American "pioneer" enthusiasm to thoroughly conquer land, made manifest in the ideal of "clean farming," which cut down woodlots and tree rows, straightened streams, and drained marshes. Public conservation, which set aside large tracts for forests, parks, and other particular purposes, also tended to relegate nature into blocks of types at the landscape scale. Simplification came, too, by killing off some species and introducing to the landscape other non-native, invasive species, thereby reducing native diversity.[89]

Leopold recognized that it was not necessary (and probably not possible) to reverse all of these trends, nor indeed did he think they should all be reversed.[90] But his position was clear as to what was needed: "Kill the economic doctrine which makes for monotypes"[91] and replace it with an ecologically informed philosophy for land use, he suggested. Modify the prevailing trends by combining the task of meeting human needs with ecological awareness. And go beyond the ideal of economic profit to create a new motive for conservation—the good of the community. This would express real individualism, Leopold believed. And this would be reflected on the land itself. The landscape of any landowner, Leopold asserted, "is the owner's portrait of himself."[92] Landowners who revolted would show on their lands the signatures of their unique personalities. They would create appealing self-portraits by the particular good ways in which they used and cared for their lands. Some would get started by a desire to hunt and would provide ample wildlife habitat. Others might begin by emphasizing ecologically sound forestry or a love of wildflowers or songbirds. As neighbors expressed their interests, one thing would be discovered to connect with another and the more the collective total could add up to a beautiful, productive, and prosperous landscape.[93] The harmonious growth of "bread and beauty" could make farming "not only a business but an art; the land not only a food-factory but an instrument for self-expression."[94]

Landowners of the new order would be proud of their unique ecological self-portraits, Leopold hoped. In seeing themselves as caring community members rather than merely self-interested individuals, they would be embarrassed by ecological land-use misjudgments. Landowner-conservationists would understand that waters, soils, plants, and animals were shared community responsibilities, just as were roads and schools. Going even further, they would extend their understanding of community membership to the land itself and see themselves as humble members of it, respecting the rights of all its members to continuance regardless of economic advantage to humans.[95] You cannot hurry your soil down the hill or "your water down the creek," the conservation-minded individual would recognize, "without hurting the creek, the neighbors, and yourself."[96]

A landowner's livestock grazing on a steep slope broke down the sod and allowed the soil to erode. This caused the formation of a spreading gully that encroached on this neighbor's land.

AN ECOLOGICAL CONSCIENCE

"All ethics begin with taboos,"[97] Leopold taught his wildlife ecology class. "An ethic, philosophically," he explained, "is a differentiation of social from anti-social conduct."[98] Leopold hoped that socially responsible private landowners would begin creating ecological land-use taboos and that the trend would spread. The first step was "*to throw your weight around* on matters of right and wrong in land-use."[99] Criteria of societal rights and wrongs were not lacking in

America; indeed, they were plentiful. But they had not yet been extended to the land community. On occasion particular conservation norms had arisen, as when at the turn of the century thousands of citizens had become concerned about declining songbird populations and joined together to boycott the use of birds for millinery ornaments. By making their collective disapproval known they succeeded in turning around an entire industry and protecting songbirds. Leopold asked: Might not similar social pressures be effective in improving private land use? What if American society began to see land use as a reflection of the qualities of the landowner? What if citizens offered praise to their neighbors who used land well and somehow dispensed disapproval to those who did not? What if a social stigma attached to farm gullies and landowners who allowed them to happen, whereas creating a "fertile, stable, and beautiful farmstead" was viewed as a great and difficult achievement?[100] That was the operation for any ethic: "[s]ocial approbation for right actions: social disapproval for wrong actions."[101]

What was needed for conservation in addition to economic yardsticks was a shared understanding—a shared *conviction*[102]—regarding what was ecologically and aesthetically right in land use.[103] The aggregate of conservation problems, Leopold declared in 1947, shows one common need for conservation success: "an ecological conscience,"[104] which was an "ethics of community life" built upon "the positive conviction that cohabitation of the land by wild and tame things is good."[105] This was a matter both of valuing or expressing love for land and of doing so knowingly: "The citizen who aspires to something more than milk-and-water conservation must first of all be aware of land and all its parts," Leopold explained.

He must feel for soil, water, plants, and animals the same affectionate solicitude as he feels for family and friends. Family and friends are often useful, but affection based on utility alone leads to the same pitfalls and contradictions in land as in people.[106]

For conservation to be successful, Leopold believed, a new kind of people with this kind of understanding and conscience would need to carry it out.

In a letter written barely a month before his death, in 1948, Leopold admitted his own limits in understanding. To Morris Cooke, a friend and former member of the Great Plains Committee, Leopold confessed that he lacked "a completely logical [conservation] philosophy all thought out, in fact on the contrary, I am deeply disturbed and do not myself know the answer to the conflicting needs with which we are faced."[107] Yet though pieces may have been missing and his understandings incomplete, Leopold had come a great distance.[108]

In the past, with low human densities and simpler tools, industrialist-capitalist human civilization had progressed by using economic yardsticks as measures for using land, Leopold reasoned. With rising population density and increasingly powerful technology those same measures had proven insufficient for balancing take from the land with its ecological capacities.[109] Destructive land effects arising from intensifying economic development by a still-expanding civilization eventually led to the institutions of land-use restrictions, widespread predator control, public preserves, artificial restocking of resources, and game farming.[110] None of these efforts went far enough to control the juggernaut. Next there came scientific land management—forestry, game management, and the like.[111] Now this, too, proved insufficient, given nature's vast complexity. A new approach was needed. The time had come, Leopold was seeing, for civilization to nurture a widely shared, ecologically informed land ethic.[112]

To Douglas Wade's honest challenges about his political and social philosophies Leopold had responded in 1944, "[F]rom my realization . . . nothing can be done about [conservation problems] without creating a new kind of people"[113]—a "new kind of farmer, banker, voter, consumer," and the like.[114] More conservation education was needed, Leopold could see, but it was not quantity alone that was of issue. Conservation education needed to improve its content as well, and it needed to include both science and teachings that went beyond science to nurture a full range of land values and land-use responsibilities.[115] The germ of a better order was present in people, Leopold believed. Perhaps if the seed of love of nature were well watered by personal exposure to land and ecological knowledge it would spring to life in the field of land use. Leopold had no illusions as to how quickly this might occur. Defining "decent man-to-man conduct" was a many centuries old and ongoing endeavor. The same would be true, Leopold could imagine, in developing an ethical code for a decent man-to-land relationship.[116] What mattered for now was to move in the right direction. Tree roots over time could crack boulders; perhaps then, too, a germ could grow to obstruct a juggernaut.

Chapter 9

Wildlife and the New Man

We learned that you can't conserve game by itself; to rebuild the game resource you must first rebuild the game range [i.e., the land], and this means rebuilding the people who use it, and all of the things they use it for.

Aldo Leopold, "A Survey of Conservation"

Once you learn to read the land, I have no fear of what you will do to it, or with it. And I know many pleasant things it will do to you.

Aldo Leopold, "Wherefore Wildlife Ecology?"

For Leopold, by the late 1930s it had become a regular drumbeat: Conservation was not chiefly about restoring and protecting land. It was about improving people and transforming culture, rebuilding values from the ground up. It was about making "a new kind of people," as he said in his letter to former student Douglas Wade;[1] it was about "rebuilding *Homo sapiens*" and producing a "new kind of farmer, banker, voter, consumer, etc.," as he phrased it for Morris Cooke.[2] How could we change the ways we use land, Leopold asked, without "an internal change in our intellectual emphases, our loyalties, our affections, and our convictions"?[3] How could we "improve the face of the land without improving ourselves"?[4]

This issue of cultural reform, as we have seen, had appeared early in Leopold's writings. In 1923 he speculated that conservation would succeed only if people saw it as a moral issue; for that to occur, there had to be a transformation in their perceptions and values.[5] In the same year he sharply criticized the "booster spirit" he was finding so prevalent in New Mexico: "The booster seems almost proud of the ugliness and destruction that accompany industrialism," Leopold wrote. "The typical booster is entirely out of contact with the most fundamental of his boasted resources, the soil."[6]

By the mid-1930s Leopold was directing his efforts toward creating positive examples of connecting land and people. When he began work at the University of Wisconsin in game management, Leopold also was appointed research director of the university's newly created arboretum—he turned the job into an opportunity to practice land restoration, which he hoped would help promote "a harmonious relationship between men and land." Leopold submitted a management plan for the area in October 1933, recommending it be administered as a research area for university students, a game management demonstration site, and a refuge for the region's dwindling native game species. By June 1934 he had conceived of a new vision for the place—a site to restore native plant and animal communities. In so doing, he hoped to cultivate in students and visitors an awareness of and an interest in land history and future land possibilities.[7]

A few years later, in 1936, Leopold corresponded with a University of Wisconsin colleague, P. E. McNall, about a university-related plan to dedicate a tract of land to benefit students. Leopold was quick to express his support for the land dedication, but more than that would be needed, he stressed, to get to what he deemed vital: "What the young people need most," Leopold wrote, "is not buildings or tracts to facilitate their contact with nature, but rather those inner qualities which enable them to enjoy nature wherever they go."[8] The land involved was a privately owned five-acre tract called Milford Meadows. It was adjacent to other lands included in the Faville Grove Wildlife Area east of Madison, near the small town of Lake Mills—a pooled area of ten farms established by Leopold and octogenarian farmer Stoughton Faville and managed by Leopold's student Art Hawkins to promote wildlife and land restoration.[9] Milford

Meadows was one of the few tracts of land in the area that, ungrazed and unfarmed, remained diverse in its native flora and fauna. It was, to the nature lover, beautiful: "[I]ts value lies in the satisfaction it brings to that inner something—call it what you may—that makes man appreciate nature. Is not the appreciation of the beauty of nature as much culture as Music of the Masters, or beautiful paintings, or classical literature? All of these feed the soul but not the pocket book."[10]

Leopold agreed with McNall that it was a good idea to gain the tract of land. But he also stressed the extra effort it would require to make it truly worthwhile for students. "As I have told you," Leopold wrote to McNall,

> I think the Faville Grove and Lake Mills community would be an excellent place to make a really serious test of the idea of re-connecting people with land. The facile extension and uplift work we have heretofore done along those lines is much too superficial and spread over too much ground to be successful. I would like to see the University start a 25-year experiment to see whether the human mind in this (or some other) *one* community can be put back into vital connection with natural beauty. If and when this is done, conservation will be a reality.[11]

The long-term experiment Leopold had in mind would entail, in addition to wildlife management demonstrations, natural history surveys, a planting program to restore native vegetation, a number of special ongoing studies, a variety of nature classes, nature clubs for children and adults, an advisory council made up of community leaders, a weekly newspaper column, involvement by Scout and 4-H groups, and opportunities for individuals to hike and explore the area. Many of these activities were already under way as part of the Faville project, led by Hawkins and other students of Leopold.[12] To reconnect people with land would require even more than dedicated land and ongoing financial support, as necessary as these were.

Leopold was interested in doing more than merely protecting acres of land by fiat, though that work was critical. He sought to awaken in people awareness and appreciation of the land and of their social responsibilities to it as community members. If public awareness could arise, fewer fiats would be required. Conservation needed

A pair of Leopold's students move imperiled white lady's slippers from the
Faville Grove prairie, recently opened to grazing, to a small nearby area
where they could be preserved. The act was an expression of a caring connection
between people and land as well as a way to further strengthen that bond,
which became Leopold's main objective in his university work.

to reach deep, helping to nurture within people the seed of "love of nature"[13] and of their neighbors. It should "not stop at teaching techniques of biology and land use," which was good, Leopold explained in 1939, "but should likewise bridge the gap between land use and human culture."[14] This was the very goal that Leopold had set for himself, as he made clear in a 1939 letter to a friend in Germany: "[T]he task of bridging this gap is the real objective of all my present work at this university."[15] "Land, to the average citizen, means the people on the land," Leopold observed, as he worked out his thoughts about education:

> There is no affection for or loyalty to the land as such, or to its non-
> human cohabitants. The concept of land as a community, of which
> we are only members, is limited to a few ecologists. Ninety nine per-
> cent of the world's brains and votes have never heard of it.[16]

"The mass mind," Leopold noted in the mid-1930s, using José Ortega y Gasset's phrase, "is devoid of any notion that the integrity of the land community may depend on its wholeness."[17] And it did not see that "this wholeness is needlessly destroyed by present modes of land-use."[18] An effective conservation program had to be "premised first of all on a revision of the national attitude toward land, its life, and its products."[19] This was why, he told conference organizer Seth Gordon in 1935, the first North American Wildlife Conference ought to have as its aim "the enrichment of the national life through contacts with nature." That goal required not just "the preservation of nature" but also a significant enhancement in "the capacity of the individual to observe and appreciate."[20] "The latter capacity," he lamented, "is, in comparison with what it might be, almost as impoverished as the present remnants of nature are in comparison with what they once were."[21]

In light of these inadequacies, Leopold concluded, the wildlife movement as a whole ought to have two objectives: "Perpetuating 'outdoor America'" and "[b]uilding citizens able to appreciate it."[22] The objectives were essential for the earth to remain habitable and civilization to endure.[23] This, then, was conservation's chief challenge: fostering within people an ability to see and value nature as a complex whole. It was a daunting challenge, Leopold knew—the work not of years but of decades and generations. As he would put it just before his death, in his foreword to *A Sand County Almanac*, what was needed was "a shift of values."[24] For successful conservation people simply had to view land as a community to which they belonged, not as a commodity to exploit. Only then could land and society survive the energies of mechanized man.

ECOLOGICAL PERCEPTION

Leopold's own awakening to nature had come largely through contact with wildlife, as a young birder in Burlington, as a hunter along the Mississippi River, and on family vacations on Marquette Island in Lake Huron. Given these beginnings and given his post as professor of wildlife management at the University of Wisconsin, it was natural for him to think a lot about wildlife and wildlife experiences when he considered the possible ways in which people could be inspired by nature. Perhaps widespread experiences with wildlife might combat the industrial mind-set and stimulate an ecological conscience. In the final section of his 1933 *Game Management* Leopold had hinted at this possibility. A game manager's specific job was to manipulate land, but this was "only a superficial indication of his social significance." "What he really labors for," explained Leopold, "is to bring about a new attitude toward land." The love of game and sport, hoped Leopold, would expand "with time into that new social concept toward which conservation is groping."[25]

At the university Leopold pushed to get wildlife study viewed in a new way. It was not merely an academic field that professionals alone needed to learn, he contended. Wildlife study could help students of all sorts see how the land worked, how they fit within the land community, and why they ought to respect nature's processes. The time had come, Leopold told his academic colleagues, to "cease teaching land ecology only to budding professionals" and to start teaching it "to whomever will listen":

> If it be true that ecology offers a new view of the land, then it is unthinkable that its teaching be relegated to ecologists alone. Nothing less than the full educational machine can do the job, and nothing short of a generation or two can get the job well-started.[26]

Leopold expanded his argument in a paper prepared for the seventh North American Wildlife Conference in 1942. The aim of wildlife study, he urged, should be "to teach citizens the function of wildlife in the land organism," leading in turn to a more wide-ranging personal transformation:

> The objective is to teach the student to see the land, to understand what he sees, and enjoy what he understands. I say land rather than wildlife, because wildlife cannot be understood without understanding the landscape as a whole. Such teaching could well be called land ecology rather than wildlife, and could serve very broad educational purposes.[27]

By "very broad" purposes Leopold meant realignment in the ways people perceived land and the human role within it. To see land wholly, as Leopold urged, was to challenge academic dogma and the intellectual fragmentation that characterized the big research university. It was to remove barriers from between not only science and art, but from between the sciences themselves:

What is the land? We are, but no less the meanest flower that blows.
Land ecology discards at the outset the fallacious notion that the
wild community is one thing, the human community another.

What are the sciences? Only categories of thinking. Sciences can
be taught separately, but they can't be used separately, either for seeing land or doing anything with it.[28]

Leopold wanted wildlife ecology to be part of the education program of as many students as possible. He understood, though, that
not all students were interested in it. The seed of interest was perhaps
"a racial inheritance,"[29] he suggested, which not all students possessed. Among students who did possess it the curiosity about wildlife could take various forms:

The individual may express his interest in a wide variety of ways:
hunting and fishing, nature study, photography, biological research,
artificial propagation, literary or artistic description, or even the
training of dogs and perfecting of equipments. These alternative
channels of expression, while often regarded as mutually antagonistic, are actually individualistic elaborations of an identical impulse.
They have as their common denominator the inherited interest in
wild things. For present purposes they may be regarded as all good,
or capable of becoming so.[30]

At the university Leopold attempted to teach wildlife ecology in
just this way, as a point of entry into a new perspective on land,
science, and the values of land as a whole. Not long before he died he
composed a two-page explanation of what he sought to accomplish
in his introductory course, Wildlife Ecology 118. "The object,"
Leopold explained to his undergraduate students, "is to teach you
how to read land."[31] The parts of the land community often had
meaning and value as separate resources, but they had "a much larger
meaning as the component parts of the organism":

No one can understand an animal by learning only its parts, yet
when we attempt to say that an animal is "useful," "ugly," or "cruel"
we are failing to see it as part of the land. We do not make the error
of calling a carburetor "greedy." We see it as part of a functioning
motor.[32]

Leopold's plain aim was to heighten his students' interest in
studying wildlife within the context of the land community. He

wanted them to view ecological research as an outdoor sport; to engage in "amateur exploration, research for fun, in the field of land."[33] Ultimately he was interested, of course, in conservation.[34] Without it, "our economy will ultimately fall apart."[35] Without it, "many plants, animals, and places of entrancing interest to me as an explorer will cease to exist."[36] On these prospects Leopold commented, "I do not like to think of economic bankruptcy, nor do I see much object in continuing the human enterprise in a habitat stripped of what interests me most."[37]

TRAINING PERCEPTION

Wildlife ecology as Leopold understood it was no easy subject to teach. In truth, few were qualified to teach the kind of wide-ranging courses that he had in mind. If ecologically minded instructors were to be had, they must be cultivated. To begin with they would need to emerge from wildlife-training programs that somehow produced graduates who in their breadth of understanding rose above the individual faculty members who taught them. A well-constructed program would do more than transmit information on wildlife and wildlife-research techniques, as important as both were. It would also develop ecological perception and an ecological conscience in people who in turn could help cultivate these virtues in others.

Leopold saw an opportunity to promote this kind of professional-training interest when at the 1936 wildlife conference a new organization of wildlife professionals was formed, tentatively called The Society of Wildlife Specialists.[38] In the minds of the leading wildlife experts who formed the society, the emerging professional field needed its own journal and a clear set of professional guidelines, including standards for the training of the next generation of wildlife leaders.[39] A year later, in St. Louis, the society adopted a constitution and a new name, The Wildlife Society.[40] Membership was open to any person professionally engaged in the practice or teaching of wildlife management, wildlife administration, or wildlife research. It also was open to graduate students and to anyone else who possessed in-depth understanding of wildlife work.[41]

Leopold was actively involved in the new organization from its inception, taking particular interest in educational philosophies and

*One of Leopold's wildlife students prepares to release a pheasant he has
just banded to learn more about its habits and survival.*

in developing a set of professional standards. Along with Herbert
Stoddard (joined later by Joseph Grinnell and Ralph King) he was
named a society advisor at the initial meeting.[42] The next year he was
urged to take on the job of president. "The Society is going to need a
President with a wiser and steadier head than most of us possess,"[43]
Leopold was told by Rudolf Bennitt, the first president. Leopold
admitted the need but demurred:

> Your argument is good and I am willing to do what I can but—quite
> bluntly—need I shoulder the *mechanics* of the presidency in order
> to make my contribution? . . . My predicament is very simple: it
> stretches me to the limit to make even partial success of my Wis-
> consin job. I'm even beginning to fear I might flunk it. Hence I nec-
> essarily look on other duties with apprehension.[44]

Unburdened for the time being by presidential duties, Leopold, beginning in April 1938, instead took charge of the subcommittee assigned to draft a statement of qualifications for wildlife professionals.[45] It was a task he had begun in the final chapter of *Game Management*. Among those aiding him in the work were Herbert Stoddard, Paul Errington, Walter Taylor, and fisheries biologist Carl Hubbs. Despite a capable committee, the drafting job took Leopold much of the year. By the time the final version appeared in print, in April 1939, Leopold had consented to his election as the society's third president.[46]

As he worked on devising the professional standards Leopold turned for help to various colleagues and to his own graduate students,[47] in addition to fellow committee members.[48] Charles Elton was among those he first contacted. "I agree with all you say!" wrote Elton, with an offer to elaborate later.[49] Elton particularly approved the controversial main thrust of Leopold's proposal, which was to focus professional standards not on a required course of formal education but instead on what a well-trained professional ought to know and be. The focus, Leopold urged, should be on "what a student is, what he knows, what he can do, and how he thinks."[50] University courses were merely a means. The desired end was an ecologically minded person, one who could promote true conservation by studying wildlife, managing land, and instructing students of all types in the ecological perspective.

Leopold hoped that his own graduate students at Wisconsin would become just such people. Fresh from a visit to Madison in 1938, Elton wrote enthusiastically to Leopold: "It was a real experience to meet all those men [Leopold's students] and talk about wild life questions. This place [Oxford University] is good and sound and grand, but it is not quite *alive* in the way that you have kept your research and your young men."[51] Leopold was quick to relay to Bennitt Elton's favorable view of his professional-training vision: "I have talked with Elton about the present idea of defining a wildlife manager in terms of what he is rather than what schooling he has had. He was pleased with the proposal."[52]

Predictably, Leopold's professional-standards proposal encountered resistance. A prescribed menu of training courses struck many colleagues as more typical and preferable. Leopold countered that attitude by quoting Herbert Stoddard, the pioneering American wildlife researcher. "Are we not making an undue showing of our immaturity as a profession," Stoddard had asked, "by all this talk of courses, universities and so forth, as though they were the aim of wildlife management, rather than a desirable transitory period in the life of a wildlife manager?"[53] The final iteration of the standards document, submitted on November 30, 1938, retained Leopold's focus on the wildlife student himself.[54] It included comments on minimum educational requirements only by way of emphasizing the knowledge and temperament expected of a top-quality wildlife manager.

In terms of formal education, the subcommittee's proposed standards were nevertheless demanding. Four undergraduate years and one graduate year leading to a master's degree was the minimum academic standard. A three-year period of graduate training, the document noted, was already commonplace in the better schools. More important as a training standard was the matter of what a student was, what the student knew, how he thought, and what he could do.[55] These would be measured and judged at two stages in the educational process: at the time of selecting an undergraduate major and again at the time of completing professional training. Leopold's educational criteria give a good sense of his ideal conservation professional.

What he is. At the undergraduate level, the subcommittee proposed, a wildlife student should be physically healthy and personally cooperative. Upon completion of graduate studies the student should have developed "an intense conviction of the need for and usefulness of science as a tool for the accomplishment of conservation."[56]

What he knows. An undergraduate student selecting a wildlife-related major should display a better-than-average scholastic record. His specific choice of a major should take into account which biological field offered "the best 'gateway' to professional training." A student should avoid narrow specialties, given the breadth of the land-management task, and should choose a subject of focus based more on departmental quality than on any particular departmental label. Also at this educational stage, the subcommittee asserted,

> the student should have attained, by his own efforts, considerable knowledge and field skill in some field of natural history (such as

ornithology, mammalogy, or botany). Animals, plants, and soils are the alphabet of wildlife management; a good school can in five years teach a student to spell words with it, but he must in some degree know his alphabet from the start.[57] Upon completion of graduate study the student should possess the foundational skill of all wildlife management, which was "to diagnose the landscape, to discern and predict trends in its biotic community, and to modify them where necessary in the interests of conservation."[58] The graduate should be able, in evaluating land, to deduce

(1) its original condition and recent history, (2) the present status of its principal wildlife species and the population trend and behavior of each, (3) the status of its economic uses and their effects on wildlife, (4) the modifications of economic use needed in the interest of wildlife, [and] (5) the rough outlines of researches needed to refine and verify his diagnosis.[59]

"To diagnose the landscape," Leopold wrote in the proposal, required an ecological viewpoint:

the student must know [the land's] component parts and something of their interrelationships. That is to say, he must know its plants and animals, its soils and waters, and something of their interdependences, successions, and competitions. He must know the industries dependent on that landscape, their effect upon it, and its effect upon them. He must know and habitually use visible "indicators" of those slow landscape changes which are invisible but nevertheless real.[60]

What he can do. At the stage of selecting an undergraduate major, a student should display "more than average ability to express thoughts in writing and in speech."[61] He should also have some pre-existing skill in woodsmanship, hunting, and fishing as well as familiarity with field operations in farming, forestry, or some other land industry. Upon graduation the student should know the basics of taxonomy and statistics and possess a full toolbox of technical skills in field, laboratory, and office operations: environmental inventories and mapmaking, census taking, trapping, nest searching, vegetative measuring, artificial propagation, sign reading, analysis of food habits, the making of study skins, and technical photography. A student should habitually read current professional literature and know something about the personalities represented in that literature, so as to recognize how individual human perceptions color even objective fields of science.[62]

How he thinks. The undergraduate student starting serious wildlife study should already display a scholarly habit of mind, the all-important trait of "habitual self-teaching."[63] The lure of the outdoors, however strong, was insufficient in itself. Indeed, in the hands of an unprofessional mind, technical skills attained in wildlife training could be useless or even dangerous. It was this final category—the professional mind—that Leopold considered most important. It was also the hardest to put into words. To create a professional mind that combined both care and skill was "the aim of all education, including wildlife," Leopold explained, yet "to define such a mind defies the best efforts of all committees, including this one."[64]

Beyond these particular points were more general requirements of professional maturity. A newly minted graduate should be able to talk sensibly in public about basic questions of wildlife policy. He should have developed some "appreciation of the ethics and esthetics as well as economics of wildlife."[65] He should be able to seek out and use scientific advice. When viewing a landscape the student should habitually raise the broad questions of conservation science: "He should think in terms, not of plant and animal species alone, but of communities; not of types alone, but of successions."[66] Last and foremost, "he should have developed in some degree that imponderable combination of curiosity, skepticism, and objectivity known as 'the scientific attitude.'"[67]

Having assembled its list of qualifications, Leopold's committee confessed that few students would score high on all criteria. Nonetheless, modern schools should labor to raise the professional bar and attempt to turn out graduates more competent overall than the faculty who taught them.[68]

CREATING THE NOBLE HUNTER

For many graduates of wildlife programs, their professional lives would involve the management of game and fish populations for hunters and anglers. Nongame species, to be sure, were as important, and Leopold urged as much attention to them. Conservation implied promoting not only game species but "all the varied forms" of indigenous wildlife, Leopold believed, and, moreover, "the greatest possible variety of them [should] exist in each community."[69] But hunting and fishing were culturally popular and well funded; they drew millions of people into contact with wild species and wild places.[70] It was thus essential for the ecologically minded professional to consider whether and how hunting might promote appreciation of land ecology. Did hunting stimulate ecological awareness? Did it breed an ethical attitude toward nature?

Hunting had been one of Leopold's formative activities. His thinking about wildlife and outdoor ethics began during his youth as he went hunting for ducks on the Illinois River at his father's side. In the 1920s Leopold took up archery and came to prefer a handmade bow over a gun and nature observation to a full game bag. Once in Wisconsin, he hunted regularly in the fields and forests around Madison. Well into his adult years he found longer hunting trips restorative. Among other forays he enjoyed a long canoe hunting expedition with his brother in 1922 along the Colorado River—the subject later of the essay "The Green Lagoons" in *A Sand County Almanac*. Additional hunting and fishing trips took him into Missouri, Minnesota, and Canada. He enjoyed hunting in the mixed landscapes of Germany and Silesia in 1935 and, as we have seen, relished his time in the wilds of the Sierra Madre Occidental in 1936 and 1937. Long pack trips, in particular, addressed his yearning for adventure.

From early in his adult hunting career Leopold linked the sport of hunting with the fieldwork of the naturalist. While on outings he routinely kept a detailed journal of nature observations, intermingled with the results of his hunting exploits. From his field observations he prepared several brief contributions to the scientific literature, including some of his first published writings from the Southwest.[71] Leopold commented on this link between hunting and nature observation in an early unpublished manuscript—a proposed article on the advantages and satisfactions of keeping a hunting and fishing journal. The hunter who looked beyond the kill itself and recorded his nature observations, Leopold suggested, enriched not only science but himself:

Leopold collects data about a woodcock after returning from a hunt.
From early in his adult hunting career Leopold linked the sport of
hunting with the fieldwork of the naturalist.

[K]eeping such a journal entails very little labor, and may be made to take rank with family, dog, gun, old coat, and old memories as one of the possessions beyond price. In fact the Journal is the old memories, but put down so that they can be classified, correlated, and made the basis for conclusions that the owner never even dreamed of as he gradually collected the seemingly insignificant observations on which they are based.[72]

At the core of hunting was the sporting element, Leopold believed. Hunting in a rapidly developing America was no longer about putting food on the table. It had become a test of outdoor skills and hardihood, a form of enjoyable outdoor sport. Repeatedly Leopold sought to put into words the essence of sportsmanship. The sportsman, Leopold wrote, was a "civilized" hunter.[73] He was "a hunter with a heart," one who realized that "his power to destroy carries with it [or] places upon him the responsibility to conserve." The sportsman "respects himself as his"; "has respect for the land and its owner"; "has respect for the game"; "has respect for nature"; "has respect for the future."[74] A sportsman was "a hunter or fisherman who combines his intense enthusiasms for—the hunt, game, wild things, the chase"—with "a decent respect for man and nature."[75] As his skill increased, the good hunter reduced his armament rather than enlarging his bag. Game laws and their restrictions provided merely the minimum standard of ethical restraint for the true sportsman.[76]

Among the cultural benefits that hunters could gain from their sport was what Leopold called "split-rail values."[77] To engage in the hunt was to reenact the process by which America was settled, reminding the hunter of the "distinctive national origins and evolution"[78] of American society. Hunting was closest to this historical practice when the hunter deliberately traveled "light," using as few gadgets and as few bullets as possible.[79] To the extent that the hunter did so, Leopold wrote during World War II, he was "culturally prepared to face the dark and bloody realities of the present."[80] When hunting was conducted as a sport it allowed the hunter to engage in a variety of ethical restraints. When he hunted alone these were tested by his own conscience, not by peer pressure, giving him an opportunity to build up his self-respect and moral character.[81] Sportsmanship, then, was "a voluntary limitation,"[82] not just in what one killed and how the killing took place but also in the use of the new mechanical weaponry. When hunting abided by this sporting ethic, it strengthened the "distinctively American tradition of self-reliance, hardihood, woodcraft, and marksmanship."[83]

Leopold expressed his support for hunting in his wildlife ecology classes at the University of Wisconsin. One way he did so was by openly questioning the anti-hunting sentiments expressed by Wisconsin-born political economist Thorstein Veblen. In *The Theory of the Leisure Class*[84] Veblen had condemned hunting as an undesirable carryover of the barbaric tendencies of "ferocity and astuteness."[85] These tendencies were well suited to help the individual thrive in battle, Veblen asserted, but were ill suited to foster cooperative social arrangements in modern America.

First published in 1899, during the Spanish-American War,

Veblen's book lambasted the militaristic attitude of the "leisure class." Only the wealthy leisure class and "lower-class delinquents"[86] thought that fighting was the way to resolve conflict. The leisure class, with its robber barons, preyed upon the average citizen and disrupted domestic habits of life. Individuals who displayed an aggressive mentality into adulthood pulled down the community, Veblen contended. Predaceous leanings were normal in people, especially young males, but maturity brought or should bring them to an end. Too often, though, individuals never emerged from the "fighting temper" stage of development, often with detrimental consequences for society.[87] People could enjoy physical fitness, general good health, and contact with nature, Veblen argued; all could be had without the predatory and exploitive elements.

Leopold had many reasons to agree with Veblen's cultural criticism, particularly his complaint against aggressive individualism and his call for greater attention to communitarian values. Nonetheless, he regularly asked his students in Wildlife Ecology 118, after reading a survey of hunting history and game management, to answer the leading question "What is the weakness in Veblen's demolition of sports?"[88]

Leopold's own answer included several parts even as he became increasingly aware that hunting often did little to elevate the mass mind. Properly undertaken, hunting could instill sound cultural values of both the split-rail variety and the more elevated, ethical type, he believed. Hunting was also a form of useful rebellion against the exaggerated tendencies of the day, particularly its "ruthless utilitarianism."[89] As a way of putting food on the table hunting was highly inefficient—and all the better because of it, Leopold thought. In 1931, the year Veblen's book was republished by Viking Press, Leopold commented upon the intangible benefits of reenacting the hunt:

> Most of our atavistic instincts, including hunting, find their exercise only through the frank acceptance of illusion. It isn't really necessary to see the lady home—in most communities she is quite safe anyhow. To keep a dog to guard the "castle" expresses our love for dogs, not our solicitude for the family. To kill a mess of game "by strength of hound" or quickness of trigger, and bring it home to the

family, is just about as necessary to most grown Americans as for their very young sons to go fishing in the family washtub. And that, in my opinion, is very necessary indeed.[90]

Leopold expanded this line of thought in a 1935 talk before the Parent-Teacher Association of the Randall School in Madison. His chosen topic was "Hobbies."[91] "What is a hobby anyway?" Leopold asked the school group. On the surface a hobby was a recurring activity that was largely "useless, inefficient, laborious, or irrelevant."[92] It was, that is, a calculated act in "defiance of the contemporary," an "assertion of those permanent values which the momentary eddies of social evolution have contravened or overlooked."[93] If he was right on this point, Leopold asserted, "then we may also say that every hobbyist is inherently a radical, and that his tribe is inherently a minority."[94] Like other hobbies, hunting was not a means to an end: The means itself, the act of recreation, was the central value.

Leopold's defense of hunting, though, went still deeper. The urge to hunt had roots deep in the human psyche, or so it seemed. It was embedded by forces of evolution and had withstood the test of time. If so, "rightness" of some sort was therefore contained within it, even if people could not understand it. To view the impulse dismissively, as Veblen had, was to show misunderstanding of a time-proven truth. There were dangers involved in the exercise of the impulse, of course. It could be vented in distinctly antisocial ways. Yet this danger merely heightened the need for hunting as a socially accepted outlet.

Leopold hoped that the urge to hunt could be harnessed and turned into something even more socially valuable. A hunter could connect to nature, gaining respect for it and developing an ecological understanding. Linked to hunting as expressions of this ingrained urge were the related hobbies of falconry, archery, and bow-making, all of which the Leopold family enjoyed.[95] These related sports, as he saw them, similarly involved self-limitation, skill, craft, and adventure. And they contained the element of predation: "The hawk, as a lethal agent," wrote Leopold, "is the perfect flower of that still utterly mysterious alchemy—evolution. No living man can, or possibly ever will, understand the instinct of predation which we share with our raptorial servant."[96]

Even as Leopold was quick to rise to hunting's defense, however, his worries about it continued to grow. If his own hunting experiences had proven useful in building his character, all around him were signs that hunting did not similarly affect everyone. Too many hunters failed to display the ethics that marked the true sportsman. Records of dead deer left on hunting grounds, does in particular, offered painful evidence that many hunters shot any animal in sight, whether it was legal or not. Too many hunters were addicted to the latest mechanical gadgets of the day—steel boats with "put-put motors," "canned heat," factory-made duck callers and decoys—which separated them, step by step, from split-rail cultural values.[97] Duck hunters lined up side by side, competing with one another to shoot incoming birds as quickly as possible. Automobiles roared hunters to crowded counties where they hardly needed to leave their

Hunters' cars line the highway near a waterfowl refuge. The hunters stood beside their cars or attempted to hide behind fence posts to watch for geese leaving the refuge. This kind of hunting was antithetical to the sportsmanship Leopold promoted.

cars to do their shooting. Information about good hunting spots was now for sale in the form of paid guides or hunting books. No longer did hunters and anglers need to learn the land themselves, adventuring through "unknown places," and gaining appreciation of the habits and territories of their prey. They could buy their way to the front with everyone else.[98]

Linked to these problems of fascination with gadgetry, questionable ethics, and mindless slaughter was the American cultural value of individual liberty, which too expressed itself as a "free-for-all exploitation" of nature.[99] If the split-rail values that Leopold applauded were part of America's cultural inheritance, so too was this related, intertwined strand of democratic vigor. It was hard to promote one without promoting the other. Free-for-all exploitation had brought great devastation to the land. It also undergirded the idea that in America hunting ought to be free and open to the public, on private as well as public lands—contributing to increasing posting by owners distraught over onslaughts of trespassers with guns. It was this free-hunting attitude that almost had slowed the embrace of the 1931 American Game Policy, authored by Leopold, which viewed control over access as an essential step in giving landowners incentive to manage their lands to promote wild game.

In contrast with the free-for-all, industrial approach to hunting was Leopold's own approach, described in his lyrical essay "Red Lanterns."[100] In it he recorded the sights, sounds, and smells of the sand counties of central Wisconsin in October, brought particularly to life as he watched his sensitive dog respond eagerly to them. More than a dozen species played roles in this hunt, yet Leopold left unmentioned whether he ever fired his gun. In "Red Legs Kicking,"[101] another brief essay in his *Sand County Almanac*, Leopold recalled a hunt he undertook as a youth with a single-barreled shotgun presented by his father. With the shotgun had come a paternal admonition not to shoot partridges from trees. It was a stern ethical limitation, Leopold felt. "Compared with a treed partridge, the devil and his seven kingdoms was a mild temptation."[102] His second hunting season was coming to an end, Leopold reported in the essay, again without feathers in his bag, when by chance a big partridge roared in front of him, towering over the aspens. He brought it down with a single swinging shot. His success was all the sweeter and his memory made more vivid because of his ethical restraint.[103]

As Leopold surveyed the various ways that people interacted with wildlife, though, he came to see that hunting as often practiced rated low in terms of cultivating an ecological attitude. Hunting done only to return the kill was merely a form of trophy collecting. Focused on the trophy itself and the taking of it, the collector often learned nothing about the land or even about the living creature being taken. Trophy hunting was the "prerogative of youth," and the hunter of this type was merely "the caveman reborn."[104] While "nothing to apologize for," it was an activity that a maturing adult ought to outgrow.

One problem with this form of nature interaction, relevant directly to the wildlife professional, was that the aesthetic quality of trophy taking diminished in response to overly intensive land management. The more artificial hunting or fishing became, the less valuable it was in terms of cultivating ecological perception and responsible behavior.[105] The hatchery-raised trout, newly released into a stream, was less valuable in aesthetic terms than a wild trout. Artificiality, of course, was a question of degree, "but as mass-use increases it tends to push the whole gamut of conservation techniques toward the artificial end, and the whole scale of trophy-values downward."[106] Artificial management for game, Leopold complained, also tended to harm the surrounding natural community, including its plant life. Particularly damaging in many settings was predator control, which could indirectly harm land while often failing to increase game populations. Predator control, killing carnivores that appeared to threaten game or livestock, was doubly troubling because the thrill of seeing a hawk or wolf in action could be just as satisfying, in terms of wild experience, as the hunt itself.[107]

Before the 1940s Leopold had turned away from land management aimed at elevating single populations. Only when land was managed as a community would trophy collecting bring its full gains; even then ethical restraint was required. Only when artificiality was avoided or minimized would the land retain its fullest ecological vigor.

Leopold was clearly troubled late in his life by the ways modern hunting was changing. Hunting was required, he knew, to deal with excessive game populations, deer in particular, when human-caused landscape changes disrupted nature's population-control mechanisms. But as a method of nurturing an ecological conscience, hunting could be problematic. Even when hunting helped people engage with nature, the hunter needed to go beyond hunting to reach higher levels of thinking and action. One of the wildlife professional's important jobs, Leopold therefore concluded, given the costs of unnaturally elevated game populations, was to provide hunters opportunities to mature. Indeed, this was the true heart of the wildlife manager's job—not merely to manage wildlife but to help people grow in ecological perception and responsibility.

RECREATIONAL ENGINEERING

In Leopold's view, well-trained wildlife managers could not merely promote game populations and then open the land to public hunting. Far more was needed if conservation was to achieve its goal. In "Conservation Esthetic," written in 1938 and incorporated into *A Sand County Almanac*, Leopold drove home his main message. Far better than trophy collecting was the ability to perceive nature, ecologically, aesthetically, and ethically. Perception had to do with "the natural processes by which the land and the living things upon it have achieved their characteristic forms (evolution) and by which they maintain their existence (ecology)."[108] One characteristic of this form of interacting with nature was that the enjoyment of it by one person did not diminish the ability of others to enjoy it. Unlike trophy collecting and unlike activities that required solitude, an unlimited number of people could learn to perceive ecologically. Here, then, was a way that the professional wildlife manager could increase human benefits from the land. Indeed, Leopold emphasized, promoting this type of perception was "the only truly creative part of recreational engineering."[109]

Many people, of course, did not possess a clear perception of nature. The engineering job was therefore formidable. The "first embryonic groping of the mass-mind toward perception," Leopold asserted—the early germination of the seed of love of nature—

was perhaps "that thing called 'nature study.'"[110] It was merely a beginning, to be sure, but it could get people heading down the path. Full success would plainly take time. "Recreational development," Leopold reiterated, "is a job not of building roads into lovely country, but of building receptivity into the still unlovely human mind."[111] It was, as his good friend P. S. Lovejoy put it, "to take the public where it will be glad to be when it gets there."[112] Leopold returned to the issue in his important 1943 essay "Wildlife in American Culture." Among the benefits of contact with wildlife, he urged, was that it could remind us that we were interdependent co-travelers with other species in the ecological and evolutionary odysseys of life—eating and being eaten, dust to dust, evolving over many generations.[113] Recognition of this reality was a central element of insightful land perception and thus a central goal for conservationists.

As Leopold assessed how people interacted with nature, how they made contact with wildlife, and how they gained truer ecological perception, his thoughts turned more and more toward another activity from which he had gained so much personally: wildlife research. Perhaps wildlife research itself could be presented to ordinary citizens as a new form of outdoor sport, he suggested. Whether undertaken by professional or amateur, research could cultivate positive cultural values while respecting the individual's desire for liberty. Like other forms of wildlife observation (and unlike hunting), wildlife research could accommodate an unlimited number of people, and affirmative planning could promote it. It was, Leopold asserted, a totally new form of sport, "which does not destroy wildlife." Wildlife research, he continued, is that which

> uses gadgets without being used by them, which outflanks the problem of posted land, and which greatly increases the human carrying capacity of a unit area. This sport knows no bag limit, no closed season. It needs teachers, but not wardens.[114]

Saving the best for last, Leopold added, "It calls for a new woodcraft of the highest cultural value."[115]

Supported mainly in universities, scientific wildlife research retained the aura of priesthood,[116] and some problems, Leopold understood, might properly remain in professional hands. But there were plenty of questions suitable for citizens of all sorts to take on—doctors, factory workers, farmers, housewives, and businessmen alike. Ecological perception did not require a doctorate in ecology or, in fact, any degree. "The real game," wrote Leopold, "is decoding the messages written on the face of the land."[117] And the outcome of that game, Leopold hoped more deeply, was not only a more accurate reading of the land but also a growth of ecological perception in the people engaged in exploring nature.

In 1940, ending his term as president of The Wildlife Society, Leopold summarized his thoughts about the state of the wildlife movement. The unfolding of professional wildlife management, he proclaimed, was "a story of almost romantic expansion in professional responsibilities."[118] The profession had begun with "the job of producing something to shoot." In a few years it had recognized the true breadth of its task: "to write a new definition of what science was for",[119] to find a way to harmonize human life with the rest of the biota. Somehow, using science, wildlife professionals and their conservation colleagues needed to nurture ecological perception and ecological conscience. Conservation required the inculcation of a new cultural attitude toward land—no small thing, Leopold emphasized, for to "change ideas about what land is for is to change ideas about what anything is for."[120]

"Thus we started to move a straw," he concluded soberly in his assessment of the profession, "and end up with the job of moving a mountain."[121]

Chapter 10

Knowing Nature

[T]here is also drama in every bush, if you can see it. When enough men know this, we need fear no indifference to the welfare of bushes or birds, or soil or trees. We shall then have no need of the word "conservation," for we shall have the thing itself.

Aldo Leopold, "The Farmer as a Conservationist"

"Dawn on the Delta was whistled in by Gambel quail. . . . When the sun peeped over the Sierra Madre, it slanted across a hundred miles of lovely . . . wilderness rimmed by jagged peaks,"[1] Leopold vividly recalled in his 1940s essay "The Green Lagoons." The essay recounts the story of a "voyage of discovery"[2] that Aldo and his brother Carl had taken twenty years earlier into the unknowns of the Colorado River delta at its confluence with the Gulf of California.[3] A sketchy map shows the delta "bisected by a river"; in reality, however, "the river was nowhere and everywhere"; it twisted and meandered through "awesome jungles" and "lovely groves"[4]—and so did the adventurers. Discovering the hazards of spearlike *cachinilla* plants; learning the hard way where to find potable water; and feeling, though never seeing, the presence of *el tigre*, the great jaguar, the two journeymen enjoyed all the more the land's cornucopia of culinary rewards—feasts of roasted goose, mallard, quail, dove, and teal, fat and tender from feeding on mesquite, tornillo seeds, and wild melons. All along Aldo and Carl shared with the delta's abundant

*Some of the wilderness Leopold enjoyed on his 1922 Delta Colorado
adventure, which inspired his essay, "Green Lagoons."*

wildlife "their evident delight in this milk-and-honey wilderness."
"Their festival mood became our mood," Leopold recounted; "we all
reveled in a common abundance and in each other's well-being."[5]

Some of the most authentic and engaging land-human experiences, to Leopold's thinking, were made possible by wide stretches
of untrammeled, unpeopled places, like the Colorado delta. Yet he
knew it was not only such vast, ecologically intact expanses that
could inspire people. A single blossom of the tiniest of flowers,
"weeds" growing in the crack of an urban parking lot, birds visiting

a cow pasture, a small suburban garden—all had stories to tell of nature's ecological and evolutionary odysseys, stories available to any person with ears to hear and eyes to see.[6] Coming to know the land, Leopold believed, would require getting off sidewalks and out of automobiles, perhaps paddling a canoe rather than running a motorboat or learning how to make an effective duck call rather than buying a factory-made gadget.

Many people agreed, Leopold wrote, that it was "a good thing for people to get back to nature." But, he pressed his readers further, "wherein lies the goodness?" And in an industrialized, mechanized world, "what can be done to encourage its pursuit?"[7] How could people be inspired to seek out such goodness? Leopold raised these questions and pondered answers to them. As he did so he struggled to identify not only ways in which human culture shaped the land but also ways in which the land shaped people. Many of Leopold's interactions with land had positively transformed his own perceptions and enlightened his values. What could be done for others, he wondered, to encourage such land encounters, ones that might encourage love of nature to bloom, transform values, and nurture an ecological conscience? Contact with wildlife was one valuable form of engagement that Leopold believed sound management could promote, as we have seen. Visits to wilderness areas offered another opportunity. Farming, too, particularly offered chances for landowners to grow in ecological perception and to gain respect for the whole of nature.

As Leopold considered these options he refined his thinking about wilderness—what it was and why it was valuable—as well as his ideas about good farming. Out of Leopold's concern over how to bring people and the rest of nature together emerged his collection of essays, *A Sand County Almanac*. One of Leopold's veiled hopes for the book was that, by sharing his personal experiences and awakenings, he might entice readers to undergo their own transformative engagements with land.

THE ILLUSION OF REALITY

Leopold's thinking about people–and–nature interactions was affected in important ways by his trip to Europe in the fall of 1935.

Although he arrived in Germany as Adolf Hitler was consolidating his power, which complicated and compromised matters, new forestry ideas had been gaining influence in the country. As he traveled Leopold learned not only about farm game, but also about these forestry ideas and he inspected landscapes where the ideas were being tried out. His sense, as he did so, was that he was glimpsing not where land conservation in the United States was or had been but where it might be heading.

The ideal of sustained-yield forest management emerged in Germany a full century before Gifford Pinchot's 1889 arrival in Europe to study its practice.[8] The idea was an advance on the more vague economic concept of *Nachhaltigkeit*—meaning "endurance" of the forest resource.[9] As Georg Ludwig Hartig had summarized the new thinking in 1795, "not more and not less may be taken annually [from state forests] than is possible on the basis of good management by permanent sustained yield."[10] Increasing demands for timber in the country immediately conflicted with limits dictated by the principle of sustained yield, however. Financial considerations competed with biological ones in management calculations. German liberal economist Robert Pressler, promoting what he termed *Weiserprozent*—indicating percent or "money yield"—called for harvesting trees as soon as a stand's financial value reached its peak, paying little attention to the future welfare of the woods. As the theoretical battles waged, clear-cutting and forest monocultures spread.[11]

Germany's most profitable cash tree crop was spruce. Planting it in solid blocks, acre after acre, became the rage.[12] By the end of the nineteenth century the downside of this *Fichtenomania* (spruce mania) was becoming apparent. The high yields of spruce monocultures lasted only a single generation; over second and third rotations they progressively declined. In addition, the closed stands of trees shaded out underbrush, reducing timber regeneration. Litter failed to decay and piled up on the forest floor, creating a dry, sterile blanket. Roots could not penetrate the hardening soil, which became acidic, bleached, and separated from the subsoil. What developed was a form of soil sickness termed podsolization.[13] Neither trees nor much else could grow well in such soils. Spruce monocultures also held only half as many bird species as natural pine forests.[14] With the

Examples of late nineteenth-century Germany's "spruce mania": on the left is pure mature spruce on "sick" soil; on the right, a strip that was clear-cut and replanted in spruce with some birches also growing; all other hardwoods are kept down by browsing deer.

understory almost gone, many other animals had little to eat. Hungry deer browsed anything they could reach, ultimately eradicating their food supply.[15] Foresters responded by eliminating top predators and setting out hay and salt in winter (and often in summer, too), thus keeping alive deer that would otherwise starve and sustaining the forest-destructive cycle. "It's a love affair"[16] between Germans and their deer, a forester explained to Leopold when asked about the irrational feeding. The result was a shockingly artificial landscape—the spruce monocultures, dead soil, lack of underbrush, low wildlife diversity, overbrowsing, and fat, tame deer.

While in Germany Leopold also took particular note of the ways people responded to such contrived landscapes. For many Germans

the landscapes were now deficient as places for much real engagement with nature. Germans from all walks of life instead flocked on
holidays to the Carpathian Mountains, one of the last nearby areas
with rugged terrain, uncut forests, and large predators.[17] A hunt in
many German forests was something more like a catered picnic compared with one in the Carpathians or with the typical experience in
American forests. Germany still had tall forests, visible game, and
clear streams and lakes; all the elements were there. "But yet to the
critical eye, there is something lacking that should not be lacking in a
country which actually practices, in such abundant measure, all of
the things we in America preach in the name of 'conservation,'"[18]
Leopold wrote. With its artificially crowded trees, soil sickness, and
cowlike deer, the forest landscape was "deprived of a certain exuberance which arises from a rich variety of plants fighting with each
other for a place in the sun,"[19] Leopold observed. "It is almost as if the
geological clock had been set back to those dim ages when there were
only pines and ferns."

> I never realized before that the melodies of nature are music only
> when played against the undertones of evolutionary history. In the
> German forest—that forest which inspired the *Erlkönig*—one
> now hears only a dismal fugue out of the timeless reaches of the
> carboniferous.[20]

This clash between authenticity and artificiality ran throughout
Leopold's German journey. He was a guest on hunts; toured forest
schools, lumber mills, and marketplaces; and enjoyed performances
in concert halls and theaters. One outing took him to Schorfheide, a
national park once used by the kaiser for hunting and now set aside
to preserve the "European buffalo," moose, wild horses ("no longer
genuine"), cranes, the black stork, and other species. In a letter home
Leopold also noted another experience. "[Dr. Hardy] Shirley was
here in Berlin till yesterday," he wrote. "We heard *Lohengrin* and
Madame Butterfly. I enjoyed Butterfly, but Siegfried was too fat to
hug his girl and I can't preserve the illusion of reality under such
circumstances."[21]

The deer in the spruce, the controlled national park, fat Siegfried
and his girl: they were not, in Leopold's mind, unrelated dramas.[22]
All involved attempts to create an aura of beauty and native

authenticity that fell short because of the artificiality they entailed. And the quality of aesthetic experience one got from it, the perceptions one gained, all diminished as artificiality crept in.

If Leopold departed Germany in November 1935 with criticisms of conventional land-management methods there (and grave fear about the rise of German militarism and oppression),[23] he also left with considerable respect for the willingness of German land managers to learn from their mistakes. In response to spruce mania and soil sickness came a new forest-management philosophy, *Dauerwald*, or "permanent woods." *Dauerwald* was a form of sustainable forestry that attended not only to the productivity of forests but also to their quality as vibrant communities. According to Alfred Möller, who had written the 1920 "manifesto" of the movement, "the most beautiful [e.g., naturally complex] forests will also be the most productive." Möller promoted the health of forests as dynamic organisms and called for the natural regeneration of native species, leading to mixed, uneven-aged stands.[24] Arising also at this time in Germany was the *Naturschutz* movement, which included an aggressive plan to restore wildlife.[25]

The lands of Germany, though much altered, continued to support wild flora and fauna. Their land was strong and resistant, particularly compared with that of the American Southwest, and many Germans appeared willing to adapt themselves to nature's ways.[26] Still, the German record was full of warnings for the younger American nation, Leopold recognized. Land management could quickly become too demanding of land, leading to unexpected ecological problems. In addition, overmanagement could lead to artificiality, reducing the land's ability to inspire ecological perception and a love of nature. A genuine land relationship had to build upon authenticity rather than artificiality. People obviously could come to know nature only to the extent that it was allowed to flourish.

THE RAW MATERIAL OF WILDERNESS

Leopold's observations in Germany served to fuel his long-standing desire to protect remaining wilderness areas in America. They also gave him new or at least clearer reasons for doing so. To protect wilderness within increasingly peopled landscapes was a land-use choice. Wilderness was, in this sense, "a form of land use" potentially yielding not only raw physical materials but also various social and cultural values.[27] As Leopold thought about wilderness he posed the same questions that he was also asking about wildlife. In what way could wilderness, as place and experience, foster love and responsibility for the land? How could it help trigger the cultural changes that true conservation required?

The United States still contained large areas of wild nature, unbroken places possessed of Whitman's "vast Something." But these had been much reduced over the past century. Wild places contained "the raw material out of which man has hammered the artifact called civilization."[28] So anxious had early European settlers been to build their ideal of civilization in America that they paid little attention to what, in aggregate, they were losing. Leopold lamented the excesses of land clearing in a brief manifesto written to introduce the new Wilderness Society, an organization that he had helped found in 1934 and actively shape:[29]

> This country has been swinging the hammer of development so long and so hard that it has forgotten the anvil of wilderness which gave value and significance to its labors. The momentum of our blows is so unprecedented that the remaining remnant of wilderness will be pounded into road-dust long before we find its values.[30]

Did it not make profound sense to preserve the stuff of which the American nation had been created in the first place? Was it not insolent for the created thing to turn against its creator?[31] And yet the American nation, riding on "yellow wheels" and smooth highways, was doing just that. Wilderness preservation involved a change in this philosophy of land use, Leopold believed.[32] It proposed a qualitative versus a merely economic conception of progress.[33] It demanded an "intelligent humility toward man's place in nature."[34] Wilderness was the one thing *Homo sapiens* could not create or build, for the very essence of wilderness lay in its "will of its own," its independence from human design.[35]

Leopold had been a leader in the rise of America's wilderness preservation movement.[36] Indeed, he proposed the term "wilderness area"[37] as a federally designated land classification and was among the first to issue a public plea for official protection of wilderness in national forests for recreational purposes, beginning with a seminal article in 1921.[38] In his early arguments Leopold justified wilderness areas as places for people to undertake forms of solitary recreation that were not possible elsewhere. "By wilderness," Leopold wrote in 1921, "I mean a continuous stretch of country preserved in its natural state, open to lawful hunting and fishing, big enough to absorb a two weeks' pack trip, and kept devoid of roads, artificial trails, cottages, or other works of man."[39]

In wilderness experience Leopold saw clear opportunities for at least a minority of people to awaken to their connection with nature and the value of conservation. He described that possibility in a brief essay written late in his life, "Flambeau,"[40] a lament for a wilderness "on its last legs"[41] as development encroached upon one of Wisconsin's few remaining wild rivers. Yet it was an essay, too, about a more promising vision and how that stretch of fast-flowing water could promote healthy cultural values. "Flambeau" described a canoe trip taken by Leopold and a small group of friends. On their second day out on the river the group met two young men who were enjoying a brief interlude of freedom between a regimented campus life and the even stricter army life soon to come. Living by "suntime"[42] and depending on their wits for food, shelter, and warmth, the journeyers were coming alive through their immersion in the wild:

> The elemental simplicities of wilderness travel were thrills not only because of their novelty, but because they represented complete freedom to make mistakes. The wilderness gave them their first taste of those rewards and penalties for wise and foolish acts which every woodsman faces daily, but against which civilization has built a thousand buffers. These boys were "on their own" in this particular sense.[43]

"Flambeau" distilled several of Leopold's reasons for protecting wilderness. Not all wilderness visitors, of course, but many of them might be awakened to a more intimate perception of nature by coming to it in the raw. They might be reminded of their ultimate dependence on the land community[44] or take pleasure in listening to the "speech of hills and rivers."[45] Wilderness provided an opportunity for contemplative solitude and a chance to be revived apart from the modern workaday life.[46]

There was a paradoxical limitation on wilderness experience as an opportunity for authentic interactions with nature, however. This had to do with the sensitivity of wilderness areas to overuse. High numbers of visitors could quickly degrade a landscape's native wild qualities. High use could both alter wilderness physically and reduce its value as a place to find solitude. "[A]ll conservation of wildness is self-defeating," Leopold wrote in his essay on marshlands, "for to cherish we must see and fondle, and when enough have seen and fondled, there is no wilderness left to cherish."[47]

The governing standard for wilderness management should not be the number of visitors who came but rather the quality of the experience they enjoyed, Leopold urged.[48] An authentic wilderness adventure necessarily required time and effort. It should not be made too easy.[49] It should be full of risk and intrigue to stimulate the explorer's curiosity and awareness of interdependencies between humans and nature. "Of what avail are forty freedoms without a blank spot on the map?" Leopold asked.[50]

Remnant Values

Because even large, isolated wilderness areas could withstand only small numbers of people, not everyone could visit such places successfully. Mass visits were simply not an effective tool for connecting people with nature, yet many opportunities existed outside untrammeled wilderness areas. As early as the mid-1920s Leopold began explaining that wilderness and wilderness values existed at many scales and in various conditions. "Wilderness exists in all degrees," he wrote in 1925, "from the little accidental wild spot at the head of a ravine" in a farmer's corn-belt woodlot or a home owner's yard to vast expanses of virgin country. "What degree of wilderness, then, are we discussing?" he asked readers. "The answer is *all degrees*. Wilderness is a relative condition."[51]

Leopold extended his argument the next year in a talk before the National Conference on Outdoor Recreation.[52] In it he challenged those who thought that true wilderness areas could not be established in the eastern half of the country.[53] It was wrong to assume, Leopold responded, that wilderness existed only in large blocks or "that an area is either wild or not wild, that there is no place for intermediate degrees of wildness":

> All land-planning must deal in intermediate degrees and especially in the skillful dovetailing of many uses in a single area. If this were not true, even the generous proportions of America would be already outgrown as a container for this nation. The wilderness idea is merely a proposition in good land-planning.
>
> What, now, would the land-planner do to supply New England with wilderness? All absolute wilderness areas of large size have disappeared long ago. The small remaining wild spots should be kept as such, but could not a larger area be devised by skillful combination with other uses? I think so.[54]

The more or less pristine remnants of wildlands that were so valuable for typical recreational pursuits such as hunting, fishing, swimming, and hiking also were valuable as living museums. In them people could explore "the origins of their cultural inheritance." They could experience some of the wild nature out of which America had been developed, Leopold suggested.[55] Moreover, "tag-ends of wilderness" were important for ecological research,[56] as places to study the workings of normal (or as nearly so as possible) lands. Good representative types of natural areas were rapidly disappearing. By the 1930s Leopold was among the many ecologists urging hastened efforts to protect remaining samples of all biotic communities for scientific study.[57] Such samples—large or small—could also serve as places where people could engage in ecological research as a hobby or a new kind of outdoor sport, thereby gaining awareness and broadening their values.[58] This last rationale—wilderness as a place for ecological sport—straddled the land protection interests of The Wilderness Society and those of the Ecological Society of America and thus, Leopold hoped, offered a way to unite the groups' efforts.[59] "Many members of the Wilderness Society probably think the Ecological Society seeks mainly small areas for scientific study," Leopold explained in a 1940 Wilderness Society document, while "many ecologists probably think the Wilderness Society seeks mainly large areas for recreation." What both groups should realize, he continued, was that only a nation-wide system of both large and small areas, will serve the needs of the future. Both should realize that ecological observation is one of the highest forms of recreation, while ecological studies without an esthetic appreciation of the biota are dull and lifeless.[60]

While promoting wilderness as a place for research and cultural change, Leopold did not lose sight of its value as game and other wildlife habitat.[61] Through the late 1930s and the 1940s he promoted a national system of wilderness remnants based on an inventory of the immediate needs of particular species in particular places.[62] Some of the areas protected would necessarily be large, but not all of them. Remnants for spruce partridges, Sonora deer, California condors, wolverines, wolves, migratory songbirds, and otters, among many others, should be covered in the plan. Particularly in need of protection was habitat for the "miracle of evolution" known as the grizzly bear, a vital component of a healthy ecological community and the fear-inspiring numenon of the places it lived.[63] "Permanent grizzly ranges and permanent wilderness areas," as Leopold saw things, "are of course two aspects of one problem."[64] Wilderness was needed, Leopold believed, not just to protect this remarkable species but also to protect the aura the bears created and the essential human experiences they made possible.[65] Even more value could come from such wild habitats if local citizens were to help monitor and manage them as volunteer custodians of particular remnants.[66] Such involvement with nature could benefit the people participating along with the wildlife. What better way to learn about land and develop an affection for it?

HUSBANDRY

Ironically, perhaps no group of citizens was more in need of "getting back to nature," given the importance of their work, than the private landowners who tended the land. Most of America's lands were in the hands of farmers,[67] and thus much of conservation's success depended upon them. The farmer, Leopold put it, was the "key man in the national wild life conservation movement."[68] Moreover, the work of food production offered a natural opportunity to nurture ecological perception and affection for to till the land was already to encounter it to some degree; it was to participate in man–earth dramas, of domesticated, though potentially authentic forms. One of the highest expressions of land engagement, in Leopold's view, was a caring way of farming—land husbandry. Done well it entailed an "art of management applied to land by some person of perception."[69] And a "sense of husbandry exercised in the production of crops," Leopold wrote, "may be quite as important as the crops themselves."[70]

During the 1930s and 1940s Leopold considered numerous means to promote opportunities for ecological awakening in farmers, for he was well aware that much agriculture was not done well. It was with the aim both of restoring land and of inspiring farmers, as well as urban sportsmen and other citizens, to interact with more of nature that Leopold had organized local farmer-sportsman cooperatives such as the Riley game cooperative in Dane County, Wisconsin,[71] and nearby Faville Grove. "[O]ne can get a big kick out of building up the wild life which lives, or would like to live, in our marshes, woodlots, and fencerows," Leopold appealed. "It is a game which preserves that tradition of woodsmanship which seemed to die with the passing of the frontier, but which still lies dormant in thousands of land-loving Americans, of both sexes and all ages. We envy Daniel Boone his job of conquering the wild; what we should do is get busy on our job of preserving the wild."[72] Husbandry of not only live-stock, grains, and vegetables, but also of wildlife, offered farmers a reminder of the interdependent man-earth relation, Leopold sug-gested. This was especially true when farmers embraced "ethical restraints" such as managing game without resorting merely to predator control. Participants in this new outdoor sport of wildlife husbandry necessarily learned about the interconnections among members of the land community. To manage land for a variety of wild species called for restraint, high skill, and a "lively and vital curiosity" about the workings of nature.[73]

Leopold repeatedly emphasized to farm audiences the living dra-mas playing out around them, hoping to awaken their sensibilities. On Wisconsin farms that retained a little undrained marshland there often grew a small bush, "mousy, unobtrusive, inconspicuous, unin-teresting," Leopold wrote in "The Farmer as a Conservationist." It carried the name "bog-birch." "It bears no flower that you would recognize as such, no fruit which bird or beast could eat. It doesn't grow into a tree which you could use. It does no harm, no good, it doesn't even turn color in the fall."[74] In the spring and summer, if allowed to grow, the little bush shaded out white lady's slippers. But on some snowy winter morning, Leopold recommended to readers, follow the animal tracks around the bush. Starving deer, flocks of sharp-tailed grouse, and rabbits all came to munch on it. When rabbits reached a high in their population cycle and enough such browsing took place, the formerly shade-suppressed flower was given its place in the sun the next season. And so the bog birch was eaten down and grew up as rabbits and lady's slippers came and went and the sun continued shining on bog birches, lady's slippers, and rabbits alike.

Here, Leopold explained to readers, "I have translated one little scene out of the life-drama of one species. Each of the 500 [species native to Wisconsin farmland] has its own drama. The stage is the farm. The farmer walks among the players in all his daily tasks, but he seldom sees any drama, because he does not understand their language." "Neither do I," Leopold added humbly, "save for a few lines here and there." "Would it add anything to farm life if the farmer learned more of that language?"[75] "All I am saying," he explained, "is that there is . . . drama in every bush, if you can see it. When enough men know this, we need fear no indifference to the welfare of bushes or birds, or soil, or trees."[76] A farmer who perceived that he was part of an unfolding drama of vibrant life would in time care deeply for his fellow protagonists, or at least for the pleasure he got from them.

Like much modernized hunting, however, mechanized farming did not tend to breed within farmers an ecological perspective or even a curiosity about wild nature. Indeed, Leopold realized, it often did just the opposite. Agricultural schools taught modern farmers how to push the land harder for crop productivity and how to use bigger and more efficient machines. Both practices had an artificializing effect on agriculture and on man-earth relations. Farmers and agricultural advisors who aided them regularly categorized species by their direct value to humans; a few species were valuable, but the vast majority, such as bog birches and lady's slippers, were not. A particularly biting critique of this mentality appeared in "Illinois Bus Ride,"[77] an essay included in *A Sand County Almanac*. In it Leopold portrayed the narrow-mindedness of farmers and of "State College" advisors who dismissed native species in their self-appointed jobs "to make Illinois safe for soybeans."[78] Leopold had worked with farmers enough to know that most of them embraced prevailing cultural ideas and values, which were far different from his own—ideas and values that distracted farmers from perceiving the land as a whole and ultimately harmed the land and the people living on it.[79]

From his days in the Southwest Leopold knew the ecological dangers of farming based on prevailing values and thus poorly done. The Midwest was less arid and fragile, but many farmers there had cut forests to gain pasturage for cows, even on steeply sloping lands. Steep lands denuded of their primary vegetation and grazed by livestock held up in the Midwest little better than in the Southwest. The problem had been the "epic cycle," as Leopold put it, of competitive industrialization: "More cows, more silos to feed them, then machines to milk them, then more pasture to graze them."[80] The irony, of course, was that while the individual farmer in the 1930s felt pushed economically to squeeze all he could out of the land, the nation itself was enjoying a food surplus that pushed prices down and made farmers even more desperate. Abuse of the soil, wrote Leopold, had not only "filled the national dinner pail" but also "created the Mississippi flood problem, the navigation problem, the overproduction problem, and the problem of its own future continuity."[81]

Leopold was well aware that farmers had to alter land to grow their crops. Nevertheless, there must be limits. Just as he had criticized artificiality in German spruce monocultures and winter-fed deer, it was in the Midwest that Leopold came to complain against the drastic artificializing effects of "slick-and-clean" farming, first on game and then on all forms of wildlife. "The physical manifestations of the covert shrinkage," wrote Leopold of this style of farming, "are plain to any one who can look out of a train window":

> [W]oodlots are grazed clean of reproduction and undergrowth, there is less and less cover on fencerows and drainage channels, hedges are uprooted to make room for metal fences, swamps are increasingly drained or burned to make new pasture or tillage, and in many regions corn is no longer left standing over winter, but shocked or gathered in fall.[82]

This devegetation and dewatering of the land adversely affected every species of game bird and mammal. The ill consequences also extended "into fields of conservation even more important than game. A part of the erosion which is undermining the fertility of farm lands and choking rivers and harbors with silt is due to the same devegetation of gullies, creek banks, and drainage channels which is undermining the game crop."[83] Many intensive land managers even mowed roadsides in the name of weed and insect pest control. This disturbing practice, Leopold commented in 1931, provided a "withering indictment of current public taste and morals" even as it did little to reduce noxious weeds.[84] It was a circular problem: the more land was degraded, the more the man-earth relation was artificialized; the less people came to know about and participate in the land's authentic dramas, the less they understood and cared about land; the less they knew about land, the more they degraded it, pushed by prevailing economic forces.[85] Leopold found this thoughtless attitude predominating—there was in the general farming population, as yet, "no sense of pride in the husbandry of wild plants and animals, no sense of shame in the proprietorship of a sick landscape"[86] lacking native diversity and beauty. There was no difference, Leopold believed, between growing crops well and promoting native beauty:

> We may postulate that the most complex biota is the most beautiful. I think there is much evidence that it is also the most useful. Certainly it is the most permanent, i.e., durable. Hence there is no distinction between esthetics and utility in respect of biotic objective. . . . In actual practice esthetics and utility are completely interwoven. To say we do a thing to land for either reason alone is prima facie evidence that we do not understand what we are doing, or are doing it wrong.[87]

To Leopold these conclusions seemed clear. To the average farmer they seemed not. And therein lay a problem, among the most grave of problems that conservation faced as World War II came to a close.[88] Here and there one saw signs of change in the agricultural landscape, the rumblings, at least, of a new cultural perspective. In Wisconsin, for instance, some farmers with whom Leopold worked became serious about restoring trees and wildflowers on their lands rather than cutting them down or plowing them under as they had in the past. But the overall trends were not encouraging. Farmer-sportsman setups, so promising in 1931, rarely lasted more than a few years and typically did little to promote nongame species.[89] Economic incentives, also holding promise when the New Deal began, did little to improve land use once the flow of money stopped. What was needed, Leopold had concluded by the mid-1930s, was a "new conception of agriculture," one based on a relationship with the land that went deeper than an economic one. "The [farm] problem is ethical and social as well as economic," Leopold wrote. Yet he had found that "the average voter or political leader is as yet unconscious of a land-ethic."[90] If conservation was to be successful—if the good condition of the land was to be protected and restored—farmers had to adjust their values; farmers had to become more aware of ecological processes and interconnections and develop an ecological conscience. Leopold did not know how to achieve this, but he experimented with various land-engaging activities on his own worn-out farm. People could not be forced to love land, he knew, but one thing he could offer was the testimony of his own encounters with nature.

Curiosity and Positive Skill

Leopold's thoughts about conservation and the need to cultivate close farmer-earth relationships were considerably influenced by his own experiences as a landowner. His farm-owning days began early in 1935 when a friend, Ed Ochsner,[91] a taxidermist from Sauk County who dealt in real estate, showed him an abandoned farm in poor condition on the Wisconsin River about fifty miles north of Madison—only sandburs grew on its spent soil.[92] The farm's single structure was a small, sturdy chicken coop containing a year's worth of livestock manure—donation of the former tax-delinquent landowner. The parcel adjoined a neighbor's stand of tall pines—the last remnant of pine along the river. Leopold needed to see nothing else.[93] Here was his chance to practice much of what he had been thinking and talking about: to know and care intimately for a piece of land, particularly to nurture back to thriving life a formerly misused one—a restoration effort. In time the coop became "the Shack" and the original 80-acre tract expanded to 120 acres. So pleased was he with his newly purchased land that through that fall, while far away in Germany, Leopold's mind kept returning to it. "I am more than ever enthusiastic about our project of building a little forest for ourselves up there," he wrote in a letter to his eldest son, Starker, "and I hope you and Luna are also still keen about it."[94]

Spring 1936 at the Shack saw the first of several years of numerous tree plantings—a family activity involving two thousand pine trees and dozens of shrubs, including mountain ash, Juneberry, raspberry, and plum[95]—many of which failed, thus providing one lesson of many that good land use would come only by trying ideas out and learning from mistakes. Leopold and his family—perhaps inspired by a small surviving prairie remnant on the side of the road between Madison and the Shack, blooming in season with sprays of native pink geraniums, man-high stalks of bright yellow *Silphium*, and blue asters[96]—also initiated efforts to restore the former prairie to their land.[97] Bird banding, for ecological study of bird survival and behavior and to stoke natural curiosity, began in 1938. By 1940 Leopold was referring to the Shack as his "'experimental farm' where everything from pines to woodcocks" was being played with[98] and where the world was a stage and all the members of the community of life its players.[99]

Among the activities Leopold and his family undertook at the Shack was the new "sport" of phenology. This was the study of nature's timing, the detailed recording of the first flower to break out in the spring, the order of arriving migrant songbirds, the date on which skunk tracks were first seen in late winter snow. To record this unfolding order of nature was to know the land more closely than ever.[100] Phenology was "a very personal sort of science." "Once he learns the sequence of events," explained Leopold, "the phenologist falls easily into the not-very-objective role of successful seer and prophet. He may even fall in love with the plants and animals which so regularly fulfil his predictions, and he may harbor the pleasant illusion that he is 'calling shots' for the biota, rather than vice versa."[101]

Phenology was precisely the kind of activity Leopold hoped that other landowners would find appealing, and that through it they might gain an enhanced ecological perception. "The phenology of crops and livestock is the farmer's own profession," Leopold wrote, "and needs no elaboration from me, but the phenology of wild plants and animals furnishes me with so much sport and recreation that I would like to share it with others."[102] Some of his students and visiting friends got caught up in the game, which family members still continue at the Shack, long after Leopold's death.

Along with phenology Leopold paid special attention to how the work of land restoration, particularly tree planting and prairie growing, might be a way of engaging people with the workings of nature. And sometimes others did catch on. "One Saturday night not long ago," Leopold reported,

> two middle-aged farmers set the alarm clock for a dark hour of what proved to be a snowy, blowy Sunday. Milking over, they jumped into a pick-up and sped for the sand counties of central Wisconsin. . . . In the evening they returned with a truck full of young tamarack trees and a heart full of high adventure. The last tree was planted in the home marsh by lantern-light. There was still the milking.[103]

Game management, tree planting, phenology, natural history observation, ecological research: any farm family could engage in at least some of such pleasures, as Leopold did on his own farm and with his own family. Widely practiced, the activities could enhance perception, help shift values, and improve and restore the land. The key was to get landowners to engage with nature. There was no easy way to do that, Leopold knew. What he could and did do was describe possibilities to those who would listen. And he could show how they gave him joy.

As Leopold thought about his work at the Shack property, which differed so much from the work of other Wisconsin farm owners, he was writing his unique signature on the land. So similar were practices of market-driven slick-and-clean agriculture that landscapes became increasingly more uniform. Row upon row of monocultures, whether of corn, wheat, or spruce trees, reflected a lack of variation among the people as well as among lands. How free could rural landowners be if, because of economic forces, they saw no choice but to use lands precisely as their neighbors did? Driving the land hard in a rush for short-term profits resulted too often in land degradation, harming the owner in the long term, the land, and the surrounding community. It displayed, Leopold believed, as we saw earlier, merely "a bogus individualism"[104] at work, based on selfishness and short-sightedness. Poor land use was an exercise of license, not true liberty. Good land use was an exercise of curiosity and positive skill.

An Exemplar

Leopold's vision for the ecologically land-engaged farmer was most distinctly summarized in his essay "The Farmer as a Conservationist," published in 1939, the same year as his "Biotic View of Land" — his first public articulation of his ecological "common concept of land." Conservation on private farms was "not merely a negative exercise of abstinence or caution" but "a positive exercise of skill and insight." It was oriented toward maintaining fertile soils and keeping the land organism in working order. It promoted "a certain wholeness" in the landscape, in terms of keeping its natural parts. Wholeness implied "a certain pepper-and-salt pattern in the warp and woof of the land use fabric."[105] Conservation, which in its principles could be extended from rural to suburban and urban areas, Leopold explained, was "harmony between men and land."[106]

With a burning fire of curiosity about land and an affection for it, Leopold's ideal conservationist-farmer tried to learn all he could about the land's natural mechanisms and to use his land in tune with them. He threw off the ideas that had become "dictators" — particularly the "self-imposed doctrine of ruthless utilitarianism" in land use — and made his business a personal and creative act of growing agricultural crops, native diversity, and land beauty. He would no more mutilate his creek by straightening it or denuding its banks than he would mutilate "his own face."[107] Were he to inherit a straightened creek he would be embarrassed by it and would want to explain it to visitors. The farmer was proud that his farm had no soil erosion check dams or terraces, and no need for any, and that the fertility of his soil was on an upward trend. He was proud also of his woods, with its varied species, its "sprinkling of hollow-limbed veterans left for the owls and squirrels," and its "down logs left for the coons and fur-bearers."[108] An attentive naturalist generally, Leopold's farmer was a particularly avid birder, keeping track of the multitude of species attracted to his land. The farm pond supplied "our farmer's special badge of distinction," wrote Leopold, so full was it of diverse plant and animal life that the farmer refused to drain it, whatever the engineers and agricultural colleges might think.[109] And, too, the farmer's knowledge of nature extended beyond biology to geology. In his clover field "a huge glacial erratic of pink granite" was allowed to remain in place. "Every year, when the geology teacher brings her class out to look at it, our farmer tells how once, on a vacation trip, he matched a chip of the boulder to its parent ledge, two hundred miles to the north."[110]

With these details and others, Leopold gave flesh to his ideal Wisconsin farmer, his exemplar of the developed ecological conscience. Good land use was not a matter of knowledge alone, though detailed knowledge was indispensable. It was about values, about affections and enthusiasms, and about a holistic understanding of land. "Ruthless utilitarianism" had been set aside in favor of scales of value more enduring and less selfish. The farmer had a sense of belonging, to the land community and to the human social community. And when wound up the farmer would entertain listeners by telling stories about the bad old days, when "everybody worried about getting his share; nobody worried about doing his bit."[111]

ASCENDING THE MOUNTAIN

Leopold's life at his own farm helped inspire yet another project—the collection of essays he was gathering for a new book.[112] The project was challenging because the essays varied in length and tone. As the work progressed, new pieces were added and the ordering changed; still potential publishers had trouble identifying its unifying theme. With the particular help of his friend Albert Hochbaum and several others Leopold worked hard to clarify it. After a couple of rejections and further revisions and a reorganization, as well as help from his son Luna in negotiating with publishers, Leopold landed a contract with Oxford University Press in April 1948, just one week before he died.[113]

A Sand County Almanac was not a sustained argument on *why* an ecological conscience was necessary or about *how* it might be stimulated, though Leopold hoped to communicate both. His book was not an academic study or a manual for fellow professionals about where their work should head. It was instead a book intended to win people to the need for a shift of perception and values, with ordinary citizens as its audience. With words, Leopold tried to stimulate in readers just the kind of awareness that he deemed so essential to the task. He told many ecological stories, portrayed the land's dramas, raised questions about nature's mysteries, and looked at things from multiple perspectives. He tugged at readers' hearts, appealed to their sense of beauty, teased their natural curiosity, disturbed and warned them with signs of loss and degradation, challenged them to contemplate their own and their society's values, urged them to an understanding of social responsibility as it extended to land, drew them into the land's history, and displayed the many ways in which humans and wild creatures were, after all, parts of the same community.

Although many themes would run through the essays in the book, one rose above the rest: the need for awakening to the values of things "natural, wild, and free" and for reappraising society in terms of these values. Leopold began part I of the book quietly, tracking the skunk in the January snow, leading the reader to follow him and his family through a calendar year of representative human-land dramas and ecological lessons taking place at the Shack.[114] The Shack, he explained to readers, was his family's refuge from modernity. It was where they came to be reminded that their sustenance arose from the land. Part II—intended to show the ways modern culture was "out of step" with conservation—would end in Manitoba, with Leopold lying prone in the muskrat muck, once again inviting the reader to come to see, know, love, and respect the land. Part III was not for the fainthearted. It was Leopold's rational exposition of the philosophical justifications for conservation, including the relationship of his ecological "common concept of land"—the mental image of the dynamic land pyramid that had become central to his understanding—to an overall goal for conservation: a vision for land, including people, that he came to call "land health." There was a considerable way to go in opening people's eyes to the land, Leopold observed. "Education, I fear," began Leopold wryly in his part II essay "Clandeboye," "is learning to see one thing by going blind to

Leopold followed these skunk tracks in the snow and invited readers of "January Thaw," the first essay in A Sand County Almanac, *to come along and see where they headed.*

another."[115] And so it had been for the American people. The pioneers who stepped off the boats from Europe had no choice but to attend to the natural world. The educated moderns of Leopold's day, though, not only could ignore nature but did so. If they did not turn the tide soon, Leopold feared, wild things would be so lost and degraded that little would be left to live for.[116]

There was the Illinois farmer's lack of awareness of what made prairie soil fertile, for example.[117] There was the moral confusion that came from failing to perceive one's dependence on nature.[118] There were the rushing motorists, very few of whom noticed the roadside

Silphium and "hardly one" of a hundred thousand passing by annually who would record its demise.[119] There were people of all backgrounds who saw no virtue in dead trees or wild bees.[120] But then there was the whole world of nature known only to those who rose before dawn, who sat in silence, who looked closely at forest floors, and who knew the first signs of spring and could read drama in a bush.[121] Expert naturalists, Leopold suggested, must be the most humble of the lot, for with their greater knowledge came recognition of their vast ignorance. Who knew about animal home ranges[122] or about the behavioral motivations of the woodcock?[123] Who knew why one chickadee outlasted all others?[124] In essay after essay Leopold would show the dangers of our blindness, the lessons we might learn from nature but have not, and the beauties that lie too often unseen and unappreciated.

Leopold's essay "Thinking Like a Mountain" was about seeing into such hidden ecological beauties. It was inspired by Hochbaum's urgings to be more honest about his own personal journey toward ecological perception. Coming to agree that this might be helpful to readers, Leopold wrote this piece, admitting some of the mistakes he had made along the way.[125] The essay seemed almost to take on a life of its own as Leopold shared his inner awakening when, upon killing a wolf and seeing the "green fire"[126] in its dying eyes, he sensed something wrong in the loss of wolves on the mountain.

"Thinking Like a Mountain" was a story of awakening—that much was clear. But in what ways had Leopold awakened, and in what ways did he hope that his readers might similarly wake up?

Leopold's essay can be read as a personal story leading to his awareness of the role wolves played in keeping deer populations in check. But Leopold knew this fact from the beginning, as did everyone else; indeed, it was the role of wolves in reducing deer populations that prompted efforts to kill them. Closer to the truth and significant in appeal was his recognition that deer themselves were a threat to the mountain. An overpopulation of deer could prove as destructive to land as too many cows. Density-dependent animals and seed eaters posed no problems to their home ranges; browsers such as deer certainly did.[127] Leopold's awakening included this simple ecological truth, and yet there was even more to it.

To Leopold as an ecologist, the wolf was at the top of the food pyramid, a vital link in keeping energy flowing through the food web and in retaining nutrients in the landscape. In its position it was a symbol of wholeness and native beauty. The wolf was a voice in the speech of river and hills. An interdependent member of the ecological community and a noble survivor of evolutionary processes, the wolf was also the preeminent symbol of wildness in the land. As its "numenon" it was full of mystery and power, and its presence was a reminder to be humble—to reflect that in nature there is much that people do not know and may never know. The wolf was quintessentially nonhuman, yet when Leopold looked into the "green fire" in the wolf's eyes something in him stirred—a sense of recognition, of creaturely kinship rooted in the deep reaches of time. Humans, too, were survivors of geologic ages and evolutionary change; they, too, were members of the land community, and indeed humans, too, were full of mystery and wildness. As a brother or sister and a fellow community member, the wolf was a creature due respect, and to respect the wolf was to honor the proper relations of the parts of the land to the whole, the evolutionary processes that produced it, and the ecological forces that sustained it—and us.

As Leopold wrote his essay he was no doubt mindful of the imagery in it. There was the wolf, long the literary symbol of nature's savagery and now, he hoped, of things far different. Indeed, his essay was all the more confrontational in its challenge to his readers precisely because the wolf had played such a symbolic role through centuries of literature.

And then there was the symbol of the mountain itself, just as richly suggestive. The mountain was the place where spiritual leaders long had gone to receive ultimate wisdom. It was the place from which pilgrims glimpsed promised lands just across the river. From the mountaintop one could see the land as a whole and sense its timelessness. Do not think, then, merely like the wolf, Leopold intimated, however embedded the wolf might be in the land around it. The wolf lived only for itself, as all creatures did. Think instead like a mountain. Rise to the mountaintop. When the land community was knocked down, when the wolf was removed, the mountain had reason to fear. And so, too, did its people. When the land community was whole the mountain was nourished, and so, too, were its people. Perhaps after all the job of wildlife management, which had started with the job of producing something to shoot, ended with the job not of moving a mountain but of encouraging people to climb one.

Chapter 11

A New Kind of Conservation

We were sawing firewood when we picked up an elm log and gave a cry of amazement. It was a full year since we had chopped down the trunk . . . and yet this elm log had still not given up! A fresh green shoot had sprouted from it with a promise of a thick leafy branch, or even a whole new elm tree.

We placed the log on the sawing horse, as though on an executioner's block, but we could not bring ourselves to bite into it with our saw. How could we? That log cherished life as dearly as we did; indeed its urge to live was even stronger than ours.   Alexandr Solzhenitsyn, "The Elm Log"

By the time Leopold wrote "The Farmer as a Conservationist" and "A Biotic View of Land," his important essays from 1939, he was ready to face again the question he had struggled with since 1913: what was conservation's object? He was also ready to speak directly about land use in moral terms, a matter he had first broached in 1923.

Leopold addressed both of these issues repeatedly in his final years. On the moral question his late writings exuded finality and confidence. He had reached bedrock, or so he sensed. In the case of an overall conservation goal, his late writings were focused in their content but less certain in tone. His most extended pieces on what he termed "land health" remained in his desk drawer "cooler," apparently in his view unready for publication (three would appear in print many years later, in 1991 and 1999).[1] When he died, in April 1948, Leopold had not offered his colleagues anything resembling the full exposition on land health he had hoped to give. Still, he had introduced the concept in numerous published writings and summarized its main elements in three essays in *A Sand County Almanac*, published posthumously.[2] Human needs and values came into play, as did ecological understanding.

Leopold's writings leave no doubt about the importance to him of land health as a concept (the term itself was of less significance). They demonstrate also how his now famous "land ethic," the term he increasingly used as a shorthand way to talk about a moral relationship to land, was directly tied to it. Land health became conservation's vision, and his land ethic, a guide to help people find their ways there.

FUNDAMENTAL LESSONS

Leopold's conservation focus was on the land as a whole—not just wilderness but entire landscapes, including those with people in them. Nor did he lose sight of the nation's democratic vision, even as he worried that human numbers were too high for the land to sustain.[3] The humans who occupied his landscape visions were themselves part of the cycle of life that he conceived of as a land pyramid, which functioned and evolved over time according to the principles of his common concept of land. Soils were the foundation of the pyramid of life, with native plants, insects, fish, birds, and mammals in their characteristic numbers and kinds building upward in interconnecting layers to the largest and fewest in number, the carnivorous predators, at the pinnacle. Energy flowed upward through the food chains of the pyramids and back down to the soil, ready to be reused in promoting a richness of life. For Leopold, life—"a rich variety" of native plants and animals and the "exuberant" landscapes of which they were members—was inherently good.[4]

The science of ecology supplied the chief means for understanding the land's interconnections. It was ecology, Leopold said, that accounted for "the outstanding discovery of the 20th century": the immense complexity of the collective interactions and organizations of nature.[5] No part of nature was independent of the other parts, *Homo sapiens* included.[6] When the land was studied over time, the forces of evolution could be seen to provide a motive power. Over geologic time, to Leopold's understanding, the general trend was for floras and faunas to become more elaborate and diverse[7] as the emergence of new species outran the extinction of old ones.

In the land's evolutionary drama humans were kin and "fellow-voyagers with other creatures in the odyssey of evolution."[8] Evolution and ecology were two ways of studying the odyssey of life. Evolution revealed the flow of life over time, whereas ecology cut against the flow at a right angle,[9] exposing life at a given moment. Ecology revealed the land pyramids with their fountains of energy flowing upward and downward through webs of dependence. Evolutionary science revealed that these pyramids tended over time to increase in dimension and complexity as life-forms became more diverse. "Ecology," wrote Leopold, "is a science that attempts this feat of thinking in a plane perpendicular to Darwin":

> A rock decays and forms the soil. In the soil grows an oak, which bears an acorn, which feeds a squirrel, which feeds an Indian, who ultimately lays him down to his last sleep in the great tomb of man — to grow another oak. . . . Ecology calls this sequence of stages in the transmission of energy a food chain, but it can be more accurately envisioned as a pipe line. It is a fixed route or channel, established by evolution. . . . Thus we see each animal and each plant is the "intersection" of many pipe lines; the whole system is cross-connected. Nor is food the only thing transmitted from one species to another. . . . [C]hains of plants and animals are not merely "food chains," but chains of dependency for a maze of services and competitions, of piracies and cooperations. This maze is complex; no efficiency engineer could blueprint the biotic organization of a single acre. It has grown more complex with time.[10]

Land was "a slowly augmented revolving fund of life," Leopold said in "The Land Pyramid."[11] The more diverse the flora and fauna became over time, the more complex, vast, and well organized their interactions became, thus promoting, he believed, the retention of nutrient energy in the system and the endurance and life-promoting capacity of the whole. It was not just nonhuman nature, Leopold knew, that was subject to the forces of evolution. Humans, too, were being pushed along by it, in ways that they understood little better than did other evolving life-forms.

The practice of conservation, in Leopold's view, was not about promoting some parts of nature—natural resources—at the expense of other parts, given nature's interconnections. It was about promoting the functioning and endurance of the whole. As Leopold had put it earlier, "there is only one soil, one flora, one fauna, one people, and hence only one conservation problem."[12] "If the components of land," he explained in a 1944 essay, "have a collective as well as a separate welfare,"

> then conservation must deal with them collectively as well as separately. Land-use cannot be good if it conserves one component and injures another. Thus a farmer who conserves his soil but drains his marsh, grazes his woodlot, and extinguishes the native fauna and flora is not practicing conservation in the ecological sense. He is merely conserving one component of land at the expense of another.[13]

Resource exhaustion was an important consideration, Leopold knew; human life depended upon continued production of the elements that sustained them. But land often failed because its mechanisms were disrupted, well before its human-desired products were used up.[14] Moreover, given nature's complexity it was often impossible to predict degradation until it was too late, until soils started eroding and species disappeared, perhaps forever. Grazing in one place could cause soils miles downriver to wash away; a monocultural tree plantation could ruin soil fertility, diminish plant and animal species, and increase diseases and pests as timber production slowly declined. Conservation needed to consider the condition of the integrated natural whole, humans included, in terms of its collective functioning and organization.

A Culminating Concept

Leopold's preferred ways of thinking about nature as a whole were as a community and, more loosely, as an organism or as a living, biotic mechanism. These concepts struck him as more apt than any other, and they put a face on land. "We can be ethical," Leopold explained in "The Land Pyramid," "only in relation to something we can see, feel, understand, love, or otherwise have faith in."[15] It was impossible to love a collection of natural resources thought about in strictly economic terms. The land pyramid itself was a descriptively rich scientific concept of land, and Leopold made frequent use of it. But the land pyramid image had something of a factory aspect, its parts functioning like the parts of a machine. It lacked the full connotation of a system that was brimming with life forces and able to replenish and develop itself over time. Machines also lacked inherent moral value; it was often prudent to care for them, but not morally obligatory. Far better were the images of community and organism, with their living, self-directed, morally valuable connotations. These concepts put a living face on the land pyramid. Thinking about land in this way, Leopold believed, encouraged people to consider their actions toward land as a whole as well as toward its members, in both moral and prudential terms.

When land was conceived of as a community (or, even more, as an organism) it made sense to consider its well-being in terms of health and sickness. Both organisms and communities had parts working together as wholes and could be variously healthy (i.e., objectively normal) or deranged or ill (i.e., objectively abnormal). Leopold was hardly the first to speak of nature in terms of its health. Such language had figured prominently, for instance, in the important Governors Conference held in 1908.[16] Health connoted a desirable state; it was a condition productive of life, and life itself was inherently good.[17] The goal of conservation, then, focused as it should be on the whole rather than the parts, was appropriately considered in terms of the health of the land community, or land health.

By the early 1920s Leopold was talking publicly about land's good condition in terms of its overall health or normality. He increasingly made reference to land sickness and to ecological health in talks and writings during the 1930s, his meaning becoming more detailed as his ecological concept of land developed. It was only around 1940, however, that Leopold embraced the term "land health" (or, as an adjective and sometimes as compound noun, "land-health") with regularity, as a term of choice, to capture his emerging overarching conservation idea.[18]

Based on decades of synthetic intellectual work—bringing together ecological knowledge and practical wisdom—Leopold's land health concept became his culminating vision of enduring prosperity and ecological harmony among humans and the entire community of life.[19] Land health became for Leopold a yardstick for evaluating the ways people lived on land. It became, in other words, the much-needed standard for judging conservation's "effect on the forest," which he had called for in 1913.[20] It provided the on-the-ground "conservation standard" or "ultimate goal" that Leopold had sought in his 1922 "Standards of Conservation."[21] It was the moral standard that he had called for in "The Conservation Ethic" in 1933.[22] It was the framework for building a "workable criterion of good vs. bad land use" that he had struggled to identify in his 1934 "Conservation Economics."[23] Land health was conservation's sought-after "collective purpose," which Leopold talked about as such in the early 1940s.[24] Land health provided the touchstone for a needed "shift of values," as he put it in A Sand County Almanac—a way of "reappraising things unnatural, tame, and confined in terms of things natural, wild, and free."[25] The condition of land health became the responsibility of people with an ecological conscience, Leopold believed. It was the expression of Leopold's famous land ethic well practiced on the land itself.[26]

For years Leopold had considered the land's healthful physical condition in terms of its functioning. In his 1923 Watershed Handbook he observed, for instance, that land in good or normal condition had "[self]-healing power" after being "injured."[27] He carried this understanding[28] into his final work. Land health, Leopold explained in the final pages of A Sand County Almanac, "is the capacity of the land for self-renewal."[29] As his concept of land developed through the 1930s, Leopold's understanding of the "self-healing" or regenerative processes of land became more directly linked with the composition and organization of land's native elements: diverse forests in Germany were ecologically healthier than spruce monocultures, he recognized in 1936; the Mexican side of the Sierra Madre Occidental, with its wildflowers and trout, Leopold recognized in 1937, was healthier than America's eroding lands just across the border, which were "spangled with snakeweed"; and the midwestern farmer who grew tamaracks and lady's slippers alongside cows and corn, to Leopold's 1939 thinking, promoted healthier landscapes than did the conventional slick-and-clean farmer who grew only cows and corn.[30] Land health, he wrote in 1941—bringing together scientific evidence with his more sweeping observations of land—was expressed in "the cooperation of the interdependent parts: soil, water, plants, animals, and people"; it implied "collective self-renewal and collective self-maintenance."[31] And again, three years later:

> The land consists of soil, water, plants, and animals, but health is more than a sufficiency of these components. It is a state of vigorous self-renewal in each of them, and in all collectively. Such collective functioning of interdependent parts for the maintenance of the whole is characteristic of an organism. In this sense land is an organism, and conservation deals with its functional integrity, or health.[32]

The land health concept had become, by the early 1940s, the centerpiece of Leopold's thinking about conservation, building directly upon his common concept of land and his holistic moral vision. In nearly every major essay from 1941 on, Leopold brought in the idea of land health if it was at all relevant to the topic at hand, whether he spoke about wildlife, wilderness, conservation education, or philosophy. Land health was a condition of land in which wild nature was given free play apart from human trammeling. It was also a condition, to Leopold's mind, of human-inhabited land that had kept its regenerative capacities.

ODYSSEY

Leopold's concept of land health arose directly out of his carefully crafted concept of land—the nutrient-cycling biotic pyramid[33]— which he had continued to develop after its 1939 unveiling. Nutrients rose upward through food webs—from soil at the base of the pyramid to plants and animals, with large carnivores at the pinnacle—and they spilled back down into the soil through organisms' wastage and death. In the soil, nutrients from such spillage and from rock decomposition remained until picked up by some other organism, the start of another upward trip. Moving animals, too, Leopold had observed, carried nutrients from place to place, while forces of gravity and water worked to transport nutrients downward across a landscape—from hills and mountains, eventually into the sea.

Land was a kind of circulatory system, Leopold observed. There was a constant tension in the land between the pull of gravity on nutrients and the resistance of plants and animals sucking nutrients from the soil, eating and being eaten, temporarily impounding the nutrients in their bodies. These processes of ever-present pull and intermittent resistance created what Leopold described as a continuous rolling movement of nutrients downhill. The speed of this downhill roll was linked to the complexity of the land community and to the soil fertility: the more complex the community, Leopold believed, the longer the nutrients could be kept within it. As the whole trend of evolution had been to make food chains longer and more complex, as he understood matters, the general effect had been to slow the speed of the downhill motion, holding nutrients within the system. When the downhill pull on nutrients was no faster than the speed at which the landscape system gained them from decay of rocks—land had continuity and was healthy. When nutrients washed away faster than they were gained, on the other hand, the land began to show signs of sickness.[34]

Modern humans were reversing long-term ecological and evolutionary trends, and therein lay the main source of land sickness, in Leopold's view. When modern agriculture and other industrial land uses came on the scene, domesticated plants and animals were substituted for native ones and the complexity of food webs was often drastically reduced.[35] Downhill nutrient roll became faster and faster as fewer (and shorter-lived) species were present to keep nutrients circulating within the community, soil, organic matter, and fertility declined, and all manner of disorganizations and maladjustments in the land pyramid began to occur. It was that simple, and yet that complicated, for the dynamic land pyramid was endlessly intricate. Human activities inevitably affected it and could easily disrupt it. Moreover, disruptions in one place could show up as signs of sickness in a distant place. Keeping the land healthy was no easy task.

Nowhere did Leopold tell the story of land health in contrast with land sickness more vividly and lyrically than in his essay "Odyssey"—the dramatic representation of his "common concept of land" and his most succinct statement of what ecological conservation was all about.[36] The essay was a prose poem about Wisconsin's land-use history: about the transformation of native prairie to the wheat epoch and then to the intensive dairying epoch, and about the effects these changes had on the land. The first part of Leopold's story recounted the journey of nutrient atom "X" through the circulatory system of the prairie, before the wheat epoch and before the era of slick-and-clean farming. In the second half of the story, nutrient atom "Y" journeyed through the same landscape after the arrival of industrial farming. Like X, nutrient atom Y was released from a limestone ledge and sucked up by a root, which had nosed into a crack in the rock. But because so many species had been removed from the land—everything from prairie flowers to passenger pigeons to predators—Y's journey through the food chain was much speedier than X's—its route from soil through biota back to soil took one year, not a decade or century. Nutrient Y also made far fewer trips through the food chain before being washed downhill and lost to the land community.

An oxteam turned the prairie sod, and Y began a succession of dizzy annual trips through a new grass called wheat. The old prairie lived by the diversity of its plants and animals, all of which were useful because the sum total of their co-operations and competitions achieved continuity. But the wheat farmer was a builder of categories; to him only wheat and oxen were useful. He saw the useless pigeons settle in clouds upon his wheat, and shortly cleared the skies of them. He saw the chinch bugs take over the stealing job, and fumed because here was a useless thing too small to kill. He failed to see the downward wash of over-wheated loam, laid bare in spring against the pelting rains. When soil-wash and chinch bugs finally put an end to wheat farming, Y and his like had already traveled far down the watershed.

When the empire of wheat collapsed, the settler took a leaf from the old prairie book: he impounded his fertility in livestock, he augmented it with nitrogen-pumping alfalfa, and he tapped the lower layers of the loam with deep-rooted corn.

But he used his alfalfa, and every other new weapon against wash, not only to hold his old plowings, but also to exploit new ones which, in turn, needed holding.

So, despite alfalfa, the black loam grew gradually thinner.[37]

On X's prairie landscape, "for every atom lost to the sea, the prairie pulls another out of the decaying rocks."[38] The system's nutrient losses were offset by its gains. On Y's landscape, nutrient atoms were being lost more quickly than they could be sucked out of rocks. The system was losing fertility, sapping the land's "capacity for self-renewal." In a 1943 unpublished draft, "Land as a Circulatory System," Leopold commented, "Conservation is a matter of the size of the deficit in the circulatory system. Land is healthy when its nutrient deficit is met by 'new earnings.'"[39]

Conservation, in short, thus was about keeping nutrients within ecological systems, cycling through long food chains and repeating their cycles enduringly before being washed to the sea. Lands were degraded when and to the extent that human changes in the land disrupted this process. In a landscape the most obvious sign of nutrient loss took the form of direct soil erosion. The loss of fertility—soil's ability to "receive, store, and return energy"and to produce life—provided another sure indication. But even without such direct evidence it was possible to know that land was sick. Nutrient cycling was altered when species were removed and new ones added.[40] Changes in hydrologic systems could disrupt nutrient cycling as well, while signaling that nutrient cycles had already been disrupted. Then there were, for Leopold, the telltale signs—overbrowsed deer ranges, damaged forests, irrupting insect and rodent populations—that often appeared particularly when predators at the top of the land pyramid were removed.

From his early days in the Southwest Leopold had been in the habit of identifying and cataloguing the signs that lands might be deranged or sick. Soil erosion and flash floods provided the most stark evidence. His first list of symptoms appeared in his 1923 *Watershed Handbook*,[41] derived by his comparison of current conditions of the land with those of its "normal" past. The problem, he could see already, was not merely that too much grass had been eaten or too many trees cut. It was that the foundation upon which grass and trees grew was disappearing. The matter involved the degradation of the land's "self-healing power." Siltage problems, abnormal floods, gullies, loss of soil fertility and plant and animal productivity: these were the signs that land's regenerative capacity had declined. In ensuing years Leopold returned to his list of symptoms, refining it and adding to it.[42] In 1946 he drafted a comprehensive list.[43] In his essay "Wilderness for Science," which would appear in *A Sand County Almanac*, Leopold summarized the symptoms again, now categorizing them according to what he considered the land's four fundamental parts or organs: soils, waters, plants, and animals—loss of soil fertility and soil erosion; abnormal floods and water shortages; "the disappearance of plant and animal species without visible cause despite efforts to protect them; and the irruption of others as pests despite efforts to control them."[44]

Leopold's definition of healthy land and his signs of sickness were based on his assumption of the goodness of life and hence the goodness of basic diversity, fertility and self-renewal. His judgment was thus not a matter of science alone. Evolution had something to do with it; to preserve fertility and the complexity of food pyramids was

Leopold approvingly labeled this photograph "Picturebook Country"—
a landscape found along Route 33 in Vernon County, Wisconsin.

to move with rather than against evolution's long-term trends. The writings of Piotr Ouspensky, Arthur Twining Hadley, José Ortega y Gasset, and many others had contributed to his thinking about the importance and moral goodness of healthy communities. The parts were linked to the welfare of the whole, and the whole depended in the long run on the maintenance of the land's nutrient cycles. A healthy system was not one that was static. It was a dynamic one that retained its local fertility, slowly building on it. When fertility remained and nutrient cycles were flowing through a diverse community, plant life could flourish. When plant life flourished, so, too, did animal life. When the land as a whole was healthy, it was a good place for people to live.

A NEW SCIENCE

Despite his confidence in listing signs of sickness and proposing definitions of health, Leopold knew that there was much to learn about the whole matter. Research was called for, and he was anxious to promote it. What was needed was a new science of land health.[45] The science would probe the health of lands in various terrains and climates, finding out more about the land's regenerative capacities. The science would identify symptoms of unhealthy land, diagnose the causes of land derangements, and prescribe remedies for land illness.

In the summer of 1943 Leopold had begun work on a new conservation-oriented textbook, but illness of his own and work demands kept him from completing it.[46] As his text *Game Management* had ten years earlier, this work, he hoped, would help lay the groundwork for a new kind of conservation science—this new science of land health. Draft notes for an introduction explained what he had in mind for the text's orientation: "Ecological conservation," or the science of land health, Leopold wrote, was "a *positive* proposal" for conservation. Rather than focusing on the threat of deficit in various natural resources, as conservationists had done in the past, the new conservation science would look at the whole "biotic stream" and attempt to learn "the attributes or properties of the whole [land] mechanism: as it was; as it is; as it might be."[47] It would be an attempt to find out more about the "collective functioning of

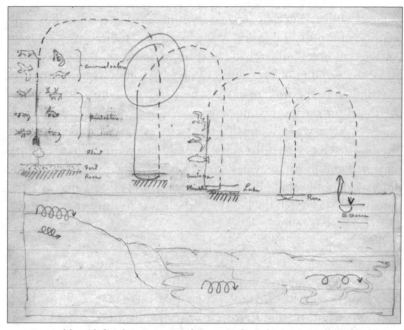

*Leopold used this diagram to explain to students his concept of the land's
nutrient cycling. From left (uphill) to right (downhill), nutrients spiral from
the soil upward through the food chain—plants, insects, herbivores, carnivores—
and back down again to the soil. In a diverse community the downhill
movement of nutrients is gradual; the community can keep nutrients cycling
within it for a long time, holding out against the force of gravity. When species
are removed from a community, however, nutrient cycles are shortened and
downhill nutrient flow is quickened as gravity gains the upper hand.*

[the land's] interdependent parts for the maintenance of the whole"[48]
and how humans could promote it.

In the draft for chapter 1, "Land as a Circulatory System," Leopold set out, as he put it, to "enlarge the conventional concept of a
landscape" and to describe the land's "capacity for self-renewal."[49]
As in "Odyssey," he portrayed the land in terms of a biotic pyramid
and energy flows. Here Leopold likened the land to the vessels and
organs in an organism; the landscape system was best understood as
"nutrients in motion": "The plant-animal community, then, is a kind
of circulatory system for nutrients, and food-chains are the channels
of flow."[50]

Leopold also planned to discuss the general effects of modern land use on the organization and functioning of land and the ecological readjustments that had taken place as a result. "Regarded collectively, the adjustments in flora and fauna consequent to civilization are prolonged, radical, and complex," Leopold wrote:

> The conservationist knows them as facts, but previous attempts to explain those facts have been unsatisfactory, because our ecology was too rudimentary to cope with them. Attempts to guide these adjustments (conservation) have been largely unsuccessful for the same reason.[51]

His new ecology text was to be "an attempt to explain and guide these adjustments in the light of recent advances in ecological knowledge."[52] In the following chapter he planned to develop "what happens to wild animals and plants when they are no longer needed as links in the human food-chain."[53] In later sections Leopold intended to "describe the workings of land by following the known history of a series of landscapes or communities."[54] For illustration he apparently intended to describe a series of case studies that he and his

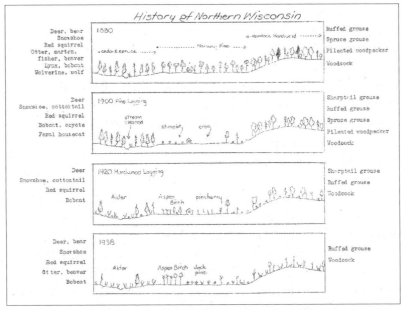

Leopold used this diagram in his wildlife ecology class to show land-use history and changes in species over time in northern Wisconsin since European-American settlement.

wildlife students at the University of Wisconsin used for class assignments.[55] These case studies traced the histories over time of particular places, differing widely in size: a ragweed patch, a roadside, a fencerow, a marsh, the vast landscape of northern Wisconsin, and others. What had these areas been like when European settlers arrived, and what were they like over the decades as humans developed the land? What were the possible ecological mechanisms behind the changes that took place? Leopold also asked his students to project land conditions into the future—fodder for further observation and hypothesis testing.[56]

The big conservation question for people everywhere had to do with human changes to the land. How far could people go in altering it, and in what ways, before they compromised its capacity for self-renewal? For the new science of ecological conservation or land health, it was a central challenge. Related to that were more specific questions: What plant and animal species were needed to keep the land's regenerative abilities? How many species could the land lose, and which ones, before its health declined? Which would be needed to restore sick land to health?

By the 1940s Leopold had developed several approaches to use in addressing these questions. One approach was to pay close attention to lands that humans had altered little, if at all. Areas in native wilderness condition provided a standard by which to measure how much humans had changed land, particularly when a nearby area still in untrammeled condition was similar to a human-altered area except for the human change—the undeveloped Mexican and developed American sides of the Sierra Madre Occidental in the Southwest being such an example.[57] A second approach, one that Leopold habitually used in studying land health was to go back in time, comparing current conditions in a given place with conditions in the same place before significant human change, to the extent that historical conditions could be surmised. For Leopold the past, like a wilderness area, could be "a laboratory."[58] What had lands looked like and how had they functioned before industrial man arrived? Human-caused changes in the land, particularly in nutrient cycling, might be abnormal if they were noticeably out of character with past conditions.[59] To reconstruct historical conditions Leopold frequently used the records of trappers, explorers, and early agrarian settlers. The land itself also provided evidence. The tools of observation, which he had used since his early efforts to sort out the grass-timber-fire-grazing-erosion story in Arizona and New Mexico, were many: tree-ring studies, evidence of vegetative succession, fire scarring, archaeological remains, geologic observations, and pollen analyses.

A third approach, Leopold concluded, was to pay particular attention to lands that people had long occupied yet that had maintained their overall health despite alterations. These lands could provide special local and general insights into a land's ability to withstand human-caused change. Further knowledge could come by contrasting healthy, human-inhabited lands with lands that humans had used in similar ways but that had not endured as well. A prime target for study was northwestern Europe,[60] where water systems and soil fertility had apparently remained largely normal despite centuries of human occupation, as he had observed in parts of Germany.

Leopold's historical work had begun in the Southwest with his study of normal and abnormal erosion. From his travels for the game survey in the late 1920s and early 1930s Leopold gained a sense of how farming had affected the Midwest, again by studying the land and consulting as many historical records as he could find. Particularly helpful was his work in Iowa on quail, which gave him insight into the land's functioning as a whole. The "golden age" for quail and men had occurred between 1860 and 1890, he noted. Before then natural prairie conditions had provided plenty of cover but scant food. Earlier settlers had improved conditions for quail by adding food in the form of nourishing seed crops and better cover in the form of hedgerows. But after 1890 agricultural methods became increasingly intense, reducing both food and cover. So rapidly did quail decline that even with a hunting ban the bird's recovery was uncertain.[61]

In Wisconsin, too, in the marshlands along the state's rivers, Leopold identified a "golden age" or "optimum conditions" for both game and humans. The "Arcadian age"[62] for many wildlife populations came after European settlers arrived.[63] Only after the new agriculturists began burning openings in the tamaracks for hay meadows did ideal conditions for many kinds of animals arise. "The open haymeadows," wrote Leopold, separated by stringers of grass, oak, and popple, and by occasional remnants of tamarack, were better crane, duck, and sharptail range than the primeval bogs. The grain and weeds on the farms abutting the marsh acted as feeding stations for prairie chickens, which soon became so abundant as to take a considerable part of any grain left in the fields. These were the golden days of wildlife abundance. Fires burned parts of the marsh every winter, but the water table was so high that the horses had to wear "clogs" at mowing times, hence no fire ever "bit" deep enough to do any lasting harm.[64]

The Arcadian age, though, soon gave way as "the March of Empire"[65] arrived in the marsh, bringing its drainage dredges and machine mind. Deep ditches lowered water tables and dried out the land. During times of drought, fires burned the peat until most of it was gone. For a time many plants and animals thrived on the nutrients released by fires, but the ashes soon leached or blew away. Plant species disappeared, and many animals disappeared, too. Aspens, able to survive the new conditions, took over but provided poor conditions for many species. The land had found a new equilibrium, but at a lower level of energy, plant and animal productivity, and biological diversity. It would be a generation or longer before new soils could build and an army of plant and animal species could return.[66] The downfall of the marsh could be seen in the loss of soils, the loss of species, the emerging dominance of just a few plant species, and the land's inability to produce things needful to humans.[67]

Supplementing these studies was a more detailed look at land change in Wisconsin. Here Leopold was able to draw upon the latest advance in historical ecology—pollen analysis,[68] which used microscopy to identify the plants and animals that had coexisted in past ages.[69] The primary lessons that Leopold learned from these paleontological studies were revealing. Before 1840 it appeared that Wisconsin's lands had slowly increased in species diversity and complexity. For thousands of years native floral and faunal communities had remained generally "intact." After 1840 many species began to disappear and communities became deranged.[70] This reversal of trends, Leopold believed, was a symptom of sickening land.[71]

For a lecture on land health within the southwestern Wisconsin region, first given in 1943 and repeated in tightened form the following year, Leopold probed the region's history, seeking insights into human land-use options.[72] He divided the region's land-use history into four overlapping epochs and then evaluated each in terms of whether or not downhill losses of nutrients during the era tended to exceed natural gains from decaying rocks. During the first era—the fur epoch, 1680–1832—furbearing mammals had withstood heavy exploitation, but there were few signs that the land itself had become deranged. Some furbearers, particularly the beaver, had "bounced back" when excessive trapping pressure was relieved. Some, like the otter, were reduced to persistently lower densities than before the trapping. Some became extinct (e.g., martin, fisher, wolverine), but extinctions were a direct result of trapping pressure, not of any indirect organic cause. Buffalo and elk endured for a time under heavy exploitation before disappearing, again because of hunting pressure rather than any derangement in the land. As Leopold put it in 1944, southwestern Wisconsin had "lost some fingers" during the fur epoch but was not sick.[73]

The fire epoch, 1750–1850, overlapped with the fur epoch and was characterized by deliberate annual burning of prairies by the "Winnebago (Ho-Chunk)" Indians, who had driven out the Sioux by 1750. Burned and unburned areas in the region obviously differed in the plant and animal species that inhabited them; to various degrees burned forests changed into prairie. But as in the fur epoch the land had not been deranged. There was "[n]o evidence," Leopold wrote,

> that Winnebago fires hurt either soil, fauna, or flora (except as they replaced forest flora with prairie flora). As to soil, the old prairies are our richest farm lands. As to fauna, we have already seen how "tough" the fur mammals were to resist the exploitations of the fur trade, both with and without fire. As to flora, the forest "bounced back" when the fire pressure was removed. All these facts indicate that there was no organic derangement which could be called sickness.[74]

A far different story unfolded during the ensuing wheat epoch, 1832–1878. Small farms expanded in size and were planted in wheat year after year. Timber was taken down for fencing. In a brief span

the prairies and oak openings of southern Wisconsin were transformed into fields of billowing grain. Much of this was exported,
carrying away many of the land's nutrients, thus creating a fast-
leaking nutrient-cycling deficit. The ecological effects were drastic.
Early signs of trouble came in the irruption of the native chinch bug
as a pest and in the widely spreading wheat diseases rust and smut.
Declining crop yields provided evidence that soils were being exhausted. Then came wheat gullies and sheet erosion on slopes. When
the wheat boom subsided—as it did, as a result of competition from
farmers on land farther west—pests and erosion subsided as well. A
general healing began to take place.[75]

From these three epochs Leopold drew several conclusions.
Plowing and the export of nutrients with the wheat crop did organic
damage to land, whereas fire and the decimation of some mammals
had not. The damage caused by nutrient export diminished when
large-scale wheat export ceased, even though farming and plowing
continued. Leopold's conclusion: when erosion was not a problem a
nutrient deficit was more dangerous than plowing as such.[76] The
wheat epoch, in summary, had left scars on the land, but changes in
farm practices had halted the disease process enough for the land to
begin healing.

Then came the dairy epoch, in the end the worst, to Leopold's
understanding. Cows gradually replaced wheat, and at first all went
well, even beautifully. Manure replaced a good portion of the nutrients exported via butter, cheese, milk, and meat. Pastures and hay
lands on flatlands were resistant to erosion. Soils in general retained
the humus built up by centuries of wilderness vegetation. Trout
streams ran clear, deep, narrow, and full, seldom overflowing. Even
the steepest fields and pastures had few gullies.[77] But soon, owing to
economic pressures, more cows were added and more machines
arrived. Marshes were drained and woods were cleared from sloping
lands. Cows in woodlots inhibited tree reproduction, killing the
sprouting stumps and compacting soil. The resulting conditions
encouraged pests and diseases. Hillsides began to erode, gullies
formed anew, and the intensified flooding of rivers carried away
more soil. Wildlife declined radically.

Southwestern Wisconsin land history allowed Leopold to draw

important if tentative conclusions: "the land-health which withstood animal exploitation and fire broke down under continuous wheat, healed under general farming, then broke down again under [intensive] cow pressure."[78] The lesions of the wheat era had been reopened; the land's health again declined. As sickness progressed more soils, plants, and animals were lost, pests and diseases became more prevalent, and watercourses were flooded and silted. And the land's fundamental capacity for self-healing had declined. To effect a cure society had to address the root land-use causes.

The lessons from southwestern Wisconsin, like those from the Southwest, Iowa, and the Wisconsin marshlands, suggested that humans could live on land in ways consistent with its continued health. But if they were not sensitive to the land as a whole they could degrade it, and economic forces, which made adding more cows and planting more crops profitable in the short run, too readily pushed them to do so.

Leopold's lessons from regions of America were supplemented by important data from Europe, some that he collected personally, much that he got secondhand. While in Germany in 1935, Leopold had witnessed obvious signs of forest "soil-sickness"[79] taking place after the German bout with "spruce mania," which had ripple effects throughout forestry. Solid spruce plantings had led to podsolization, which led to poor vegetative reproduction in the understory, to artificial feeding of deer, to deer overpopulation and overbrowsing, and to the loss of native flora and fauna. It was in the mid-1930s, around the time he was talking about German forest soils, that Leopold began regularly using the term "sickness" in relation to land. The opposite of soil sickness, Leopold said then, was "ecological health," which Germans were hoping to restore by encouraging a return to permanent mixed forests.[80] Leopold was impressed by the German readjustment.[81] In addition to a cultural willingness to make such changes, Leopold believed that the endurance of German civilization was due to the climate, flexibility, and strength of the land itself. Northwestern Europe seemed to be "resistant to abuse" and "to possess extraordinary recuperative capacity, i.e., capacity, when disturbed, to establish new and stable equilibria between soil, plants, and animals."[82] "European civilization," Leopold concluded, developed on a landscape extraordinarily resistant to disorganization, i.e., one which endures very rough usage and severe modification without derangement of function. Thus the oak forests of England became closely grazed sheep downs without losing their soil. The fauna and flora shifted, but did not disintegrate.[83]

Because lands varied significantly in their ability to withstand human land use,[84] land users had to be attentive to the particular capabilities and limitations of their locales.[85] The signs and principles of health and the symptoms of illness might be fundamentally universal; the land-use practices to maintain health clearly were not.

Yet another geographic region that drew Leopold's attention for studying land health was the Sierra Madre Occidental region of Mexico, which had impressed him so favorably during his two visits along the Gavilan in the late 1930s. It was a splendid example of a whole landscape particularly because it offered such a stark comparison with American lands just to the north.[86] "[O]ur southwestern mountains," Leopold wrote in 1937, "are now badly gutted by erosion, whereas the Sierra Madre range across the line still retains the virgin stability of its soils and all the natural beauty that goes with that enviable condition."[87] Despite every kind of well-meaning and scientific conservation effort, the American side was "so badly damaged that only tourists and others ecologically color-blind, can look upon them without a feeling of sadness and regret,"[88] whereas the Mexican side, even without national parks or national forests, presented a most lovely "picture of ecological health."[89] "It was here," Leopold reported, "that I first clearly realized that land is an organism, that all my life I had seen only sick land, whereas here was a biota still in perfect aboriginal health."[90] The entire Mexican region, Leopold believed, cried out for protection, and Americans ought to get involved. "The preservation and study of the Sierra Madre wilderness, by an international experiment station, as a norm for the cure of sick land on both sides of the border, would be a good-neighbor enterprise well worthy of consideration."[91]

SHREWD GUESSES

As Leopold thought about land health through the 1940s and looked over the relatively meager evidence collected about it, he was impressed as much by his ignorance as by any knowledge that he had obtained. Nature was extraordinarily complex, not just around the world but also in any given place. The science of land health, in contrast, was in its infancy. It would take many years for the science to gain maturity. In the meantime, land-use decisions were proceeding briskly and conservation programs were being framed. It was simply not possible to delay all action until science could mature.

"The land mechanism is too complex to be understood," Leopold observed in 1944, "and probably always will be. We are forced to make the best guess we can from circumstantial evidence."[92] Ecologists had no choice but to offer their predictions about how lands worked and how people could use them while still keeping them in normal condition. To make best guesses, ecologists needed to supplement their knowledge in some way by taking into account their ignorance. The time was not ripe, Leopold wrote in "The Land-Health Concept and Conservation," for ecologists to speak with confidence. Still, it was essential for them to present their "shrewd guess[es]" about keeping land healthy. When lands were resilient, mistakes might be corrected.[93] When lands were more sensitive, caution was even more essential.

It was no easy task to come up with workable, practical yardsticks by which to measure land health. To propose land health as an overall conservation goal was to call for a new type of conservation, aimed at the integrated whole of nature rather than the parts singly. The new conservation would need to stress prevention of problems, while calling for remediation if they arose. In his first major writing about land health, the essay "Biotic Land-Use," Leopold offered his own best guess about ways of measuring the land's health.[94] He prefaced his observation by noting two basic characteristics of "new" land—land not yet dominated by humans. The first characteristic was what he called stability: "Undisturbed communities change their composition and their internal economy only in geological time," he observed. "Within the time-scale of human affairs, they are stable."[95] The second characteristic, he wrote, was diversity: "The biotic community is diverse in composition, complex in organization, and tends to become more so."[96]

These two characteristics of new land, added to Leopold's existing understanding of nature and culture, led him to offer readers two "yardsticks" that might be used to produce crude measures of a landscape's condition. The first was as obvious as it was essential: soil fertility. "That the maintenance of at least the original fertility is essential to land-health is now a truism, and needs no further discussion."[97] The best way to judge the land's condition was to look at its soil, in terms of what was normal for a given landscape and climate. The second yardstick, related to the first, had to do with the land's "diversity of fauna and flora."[98] The more a landscape retained its original fauna and flora, the more likely it was to be healthy.

As Leopold thought about these yardsticks—as he thought about land health—his mind focused on the soil and on the biotic circulatory system that kept it intact. Soil fertility was the foundational element of land health. This was the base measure of land's condition. Land was healthy when it retained over long periods of time its ability to cycle nutrients efficiently and continuously. When land could accomplish this feat it was, in Leopold's vocabulary, stable. "Stability," Leopold explained in "Biotic Land-Use," "is the continuity of this organized circulatory system. Land is stable when its food chains are so organized as to be able to circulate the same food an indefinite number of times."[99] Erosion, floods, pest irruptions, species loss, and other land symptoms without directly visible cause were expressions of instability. They provided evidence of breakdowns in the circulatory system; they emerged because of simplification and derangement of the land pyramid, or degradation of the land's capacity to sustain and renew itself over time.

Land stability as Leopold defined it appeared to be connected to the maintenance of the land pyramid, and thus to the many native species of plants and animals that lived in an area. Undeveloped land, as he had noted, tended toward diversity in composition and complexity in organization,[100] whereas the arrival of industrial civilization typically led to the reverse—the loss of many native species and to organizational simplification and land problems. From his many studies Leopold came to believe that the loss of species was both a cause and an effect of declining land health.[101]

To get at this issue Leopold returned to his land pyramid and to the principles upon which it was based. "Stability implies," Leopold stated, "not only characteristic kinds, but also characteristic numbers of each species in the food chains."[102] This idea was not new; it had been a premise of food web analysis for years. So far as Leopold could tell it was sound. Particular species might come and go in a land community, but the function of a departing species in the pyramid had to be taken over by another species or the system as a whole would suffer, with nutrient cycles becoming shorter. "The circumstantial evidence" provided by history, Leopold stressed, "is that stability and diversity in the native community were associated for 20,000 years, and presumably depended on each other."[103] The connection here was not entirely clear; some lands remained healthy despite significant changes in species composition. Still, plentiful evidence supported the typical existence of a strong positive connection. Both stability and diversity in many places were "now partly lost, presumably because the original community [had] been partly lost and greatly altered."[104] This observation led logically to another: "Presumably the greater the losses and alterations, the greater the risk of impairments and disorganizations."[105]

The apparent link between stability (as thus defined) and diversity was not one that Leopold thought he could prove, despite the historical correlation; indeed, he believed, it never would be proven, and, in fact, debates about it would continue within the ecological community.[106] Evidence Leopold knew about from his studies of the land, however, tended to support the connection between diversity and stability. Parts of northwestern Europe demonstrated the only cases known to Leopold in which a material loss of diversity had not resulted in major derangements in the land pyramid and depleted soil fertility.[107] All other lands that had lost substantial diversity, to Leopold's knowledge, had displayed serious symptoms of sickness. In terms of the land mechanism itself, the land's circulatory system was dependent upon its complexity and organization. "The question in hand," he wrote in "Biotic Land-Use," "is whether other parts of the globe can remain stable without the deliberate retention of diversity. All I can say is that I doubt it."[108]

"Diversity" as Leopold used the term meant simply the variety of native plants and animals that resided in a given place. As he continued working on land health he began to find it helpful to use a word that captured more precisely the kind of diversity that he deemed important. The term he seized upon was "integrity." An early use of the term came in a 1939 lecture, "Basis of Conservation Education." In the lecture he explained the fallacy underlying the old kind of conservation, which viewed as sufficient the coordination of single resource–use practices:

> [The] fallacy in this is to regard any plant or animal as a "separate" thing. There are plenty of parts of your industrial plant "of no economic importance." Do you tear them out? No—not if they are parts of the organism. In conservation we don't yet realize that every living thing is part of the organism. To the conservationist, the spar of a dying tamarack [in a drained marshland] is not merely a dead tree—it is the symbol of a countryside which is losing its wholeness, its integrity as an organism.[109]

As Leopold put it, integrity had to do with the parts of nature, but it meant more particularly the parts of nature that were necessary for land to keep its stability and its health. But what parts were necessary? If land maintained its integrity when it kept the parts that it had possessed before humans changed the land, given human ignorance, it was wise to keep all of them.[110] As a prudential matter, this was the integrity that ought to be maintained. Integrity, then, had for Leopold two overlapping meanings, which came together by means of his rule of caution in using land: it meant the species needed to keep land stable, and it meant the full range of native plants and animals that had inhabited a place before industrial civilization arrived. A third implication was that all member species of the land community had value as such and were entitled to continuance as a matter of "biotic right,"[111] and, "at least in spots," their right to "continued existence in a natural state."[112]

One of Leopold's most extended treatments of integrity would appear in his final major writing on land health, "The Land-Health Concept and Conservation." "It is necessary to suppose," he concluded from all the evidence, "that a high degree of interdependence exists between the capacity for self-renewal and the integrity of the native communities."[113] Leopold admitted that it might not be worth debating the removal of some species from some landscapes, which was perhaps necessary for civilization—for example, the extirpation of buffalo and pigeons from settled regions of the corn belt—and which did not necessarily preclude some habitable degree of land health. But in other cases—for example, the extirpation of wolves across most of the West and the Great Lakes states, leading to deer irruptions—the removal of species could have more ecologically drastic effects. Likewise, exotic species, which often spread to the detriment of native species, could cause serious land maladjustments and generally were undesirable. It was thus important to take the likely relationship between integrity and stability as well as human ignorance seriously and to be careful about altering communities unduly:

> We must assume, therefore, that some causal connection exists between the integrity of the native communities and their ability for self-renewal. To assume otherwise is to assume that we understand the biotic mechanisms. The absurdity of such an assumption hardly needs comment, especially to ecologists.[114]

As Leopold wrote about land health he continually searched for better ways to express his ideas.[115] In "Conservation: In Whole or in Part?" he offered a definition for the new conservation and land health, phrased in terms of "collective functioning" and "functional integrity":

> The land consists of soil, water, plants, and animals, but health is more than a sufficiency of these components. It is a state of vigorous self-renewal in each of them, and in all collectively. Such collective functioning of interdependent parts for the maintenance of the whole is characteristic of an organism. In this sense land is an organism, and conservation deals with its functional integrity, or health.[116]

In both "A Biotic View of Land" from 1939 and its condensed version incorporated in "The Land Ethic," Leopold used the words "complexity" and "structure" to talk about "normal circulation" through the pyramidal land community:

> The velocity and character of the upward flow of energy depend on the complex structure of the plant and animal community, much as the upward flow of sap in a tree depends on its cellular organization. Without this complexity, normal circulation presumably would not occur. Structure means the characteristic numbers, as well as the characteristic kinds and functions, of the component species. This

interdependence between the complex structure of the land and its smooth functioning as an energy unit is one of its basic attributes.[117] In retrospect Leopold might have been wiser to employ less variety in his terms, just as he might wisely have used his metaphors with greater care. Nonetheless, one can see through the words to the ideas that he meant to capture. Land health was the goal of conservation. Land health depended on soil that received nutrients at least at the rate it released them and on the normal structure and functioning of the land pyramid. The land pyramid, in turn, depended upon the self-organization of its full complement of native species. It was wise to keep nature's parts. It was wise to use the land gently, avoiding violent changes whenever possible. It made sense to remember the gradual pace at which nature worked, particularly the forces of evolution, and attempt to work in concert with them. Evolutionary changes were "slow and local."[118] Industrial changes, by contrast, often occurred with "unprecedented violence, rapidity, and scope."[119] "We are remodeling the Alhambra with a steam-shovel," Leopold observed in the closing paragraph of his section "The Outlook" in *A Sand County Almanac*. "We shall hardly relinquish the shovel, which after all has many good points, but we are in need of gentler and more objective criteria for its successful use."[120]

In his final major writing on land health Leopold included as a possible "requisite" or rule of thumb for sound land use that people attempt to foster land beauty. Much as did the other terms he used, "beauty" had for Leopold a particular and rich meaning. The land's beauty, Leopold said, was not separable from its usefulness; utility and beauty went side by side. Both utility and beauty in turn depended upon the health of the land as a whole.

> The biota is beautiful collectively and in all its parts, but only a few of its parts are useful in the sense of yielding a profit to the private landowner. Healthy land is the only permanently profitable land, but if the biota must be whole to be healthy, and if most of its parts yield no salable products, then we cannot justify ecological conservation on economic grounds alone. To attempt to do so is sure to yield a lop-sided, and probably unhealthy, biotic organization.[121]

Beauty, then, was an attribute of lands that were healthy, particularly lands that retained their native integrity. Beauty was not a mere subjective choice of the viewer; it was an objective ecological attribute of lands that could endure. It was a characteristic that arose when the parts of nature were linked harmoniously into a whole promoting the land's stability and long-term flourishing—its "capacity for self-renewal." Beauty could not be separated from ecological functioning, from the land's enduring productivity, and from the prosperity of human civilization:

> The divorcement of things practical from things beautiful, and the relegation of either to specialized groups or institutions, has always been lethal to social progress, and now it threatens the land-base on which the social structure rests. . . . Tomorrow we shall find out that no land unnecessarily mutilated is useful (if, indeed, it is still there). The true problem of agriculture and all other land-use, is to achieve both utility and beauty, and thus permanence.[122]

Year by year Leopold probed more deeply the conservation predicament of the age, gaining greater wisdom about it. The more he progressed, however, the more he distanced himself from his generation, even from many other conservation professionals. He had traveled far enough that his words, he suspected, were making less and less sense to other people. All around him, conservation work as most other people understood it had to do almost entirely with particular resources and specific technologies to address merely the symptoms of land misuse. As farm fields deteriorated fertilizers were added, or at most a leguminous rotation was added to a cropping system, with little to no thought of the wild plants and animals that had built the soil to begin with. Poisons were spread to deal with agricultural pests, with no search for the organic causes of the irruptions or invasions. Foresters who faced declining yields looked for new tree species to plant, paying little attention to the disturbed microflora of the soil. Flood-control dams for flooding, check dams and terraces for erosion control: none of them touched the true causes or proposed any lasting cure. Wildlife refuges and fish hatcheries did not address the reasons behind widespread declines in game and fish populations. Such treatments, wrote Leopold, were not cures. They were merely "local alleviations of biotic pain."[123]

Leopold inspects the tamarack seedlings he and his family planted at the Shack sometime in the mid-1940s. For decades farmers in Wisconsin had been destroying tamaracks—burning and chopping them down and draining the bogs in which they grew—to gain more land for crops and pastures. Partly through Leopold's influence, a few farmers enthusiastically planted young tamaracks and restored their marshes and bogs, reintroducing sphagnum moss, lady's slippers, and other characteristic wildflowers.

YET THE TREES GROW

Leopold's mature thinking about conservation would do more than take him further from the world as he knew it, further even from his conservation and research colleagues. What became clear to him was that nothing short of fundamental cultural change was needed for lands to keep or regain their health. More powerfully than before, he recognized how the industrial-economic-individualist mind, so dominant in his age, was leading the nation in precisely the opposite direction. The conservation movement, now several decades old, had done little to improve land-use practices. And the destructive technologies coming along, symbolized for Leopold by DDT and the atomic bomb, were terrifying in what they portended.[124] Industrialism as a mode of living, economic determinism as a cultural ideology, and individualism as an ethical doctrine were gradually destroying the land. In the long run they would very likely destroy the people as well.

As the United States' entry into a second world war approached, Leopold drafted in late 1941 a somber commentary on the modern cultural landscape, "Yet the Trees Grow."[125] Never published, it stayed in his desk drawer, an expression of his inner thoughts, not of his outer persona. It bore witness to Leopold's mournful perception of the inherent conflict between the industrial and ecological minds and of the far greater power that the industrial one presently possessed. On came the slick-and-clean farming, Leopold wrote; on came the plant and animal pest irruptions and the new chemical poisons; away blew the soils and, with them, the native floras and faunas and human homesteads; on came more roads and ever larger machines; on came advertisers and assembly-line trinkets; on came war and weapons of terror. The juggernaut of industrial civilization was having its way.

Yet even then the life forces and seasons of nature continued to exert themselves. The oaks continued to make wood, responding not to human follies but to the fundamental forces of nature.

Empires spread over the continents, destroying soils, the floras and faunas, and each other. Yet the trees grow.

Philosophies spread over the empires, teaching the good life with tank and bomb. Machines crawl over the empires, hauling goods. Goods are plowed under, or burned. Goods are hawked over the ether, and along the lanes where Whitman smelled locust blossoms morning and evening. Quarrels over goods are planted thick as trees along the rivers of America. . . . Yet the trees grow.[126]

Walt Whitman's dream had been that the west-flowing settlers might "plant companionship as thick as trees along all the rivers of America."[127] Looking back at America's actual record, knowing as well as anyone what had come to pass, Leopold could not help but be saddened. The trees, rivers, prairies, wild creatures—all had been too often viewed as obstacles on the road to progress, or as raw material whose primary reason to exist was to be transformed into commodities and consumed. Companionship as Americans understood it had little to do with nature and far more to do with disposable manufactured "goods," the production and exchange of which bred competition, strife, and destruction. And yet the trees grew.

This was a somber side of Leopold's imagination, a vivid portrait of a world gone gravely awry. Here growing within the nation was an undiagnosed cultural disease, lying face-up on the land while its root causes lay in the hard-to-reach deep within the minds and hearts of people. In essay after essay, particularly in part II of his *Sand County Almanac*, Leopold would plumb the sources of his sorrow, his profound, aching sense of loss. He would mention some of his losses specifically, in terms of the plants, animals, and places that he held so dear. And in speaking of them he would offer a vision of what was taking place overall and of what seemed to lie ahead. It was wildness itself that was under assault, wildness itself that was on the verge of being crushed. For Leopold, for the Wisconsin in which he lived, the crane was a symbol of that "wildness incarnate,"[128] a representation of the land's persistent inner force and its time-tested wisdom. To fear for the crane was to fear for much more, as we read earlier:

> Some day, perhaps in the very process of our benefactions, perhaps in the fullness of geologic time, the last crane will trumpet his farewell and spiral skyward from the great marsh. High out of the clouds will fall the sound of hunting horns, the baying of the phantom pack, the tinkle of little bells, and then a silence never to be broken, unless perchance in some far pasture of the Milky Way.[129]

In the silence never to be broken wildness would be gone, and with it the world that Leopold so cherished.

RIGHTNESS

In his literary masterwork, written for all citizens, especially the landowner, Leopold took his concept of land health and transformed it into a moral duty.[130] It was a moral duty placed not only on society as a whole but also on the individual as a member of society. As Leopold stated plainly, it reflected an "individual responsibility for the health of the land"[131] and an ecological conscience toward the community.

Leopold's proposed ethic admonished the individual to "[e]xamine each [land-related] question in terms of what is ethically and aesthetically right, as well as what is economically expedient." "A thing is right," Leopold said in his now famous summation, "when it tends to preserve the integrity, stability, and beauty of the biotic community. It is wrong when it tends otherwise."[132] This was the core of

Leopold's land ethic. It was the distillation of his guidance, for those who could interpret it, on right and wrong living on the land.

The "biotic community" as such, not any concept of human needs or of resource flows, was what this land ethic sought to promote. It was a holistic vision linked to the entire community of life, people included. By "stability," as we have seen, Leopold meant the capacity of the land to cycle nutrients efficiently and continuously because its biotic pyramid was intact and its food circuits were open. By "integrity" Leopold meant that the land possessed all the parts needed to maintain its stability. Given biotic rights and human ignorance about what it took to maintain stability, integrity in practical terms meant keeping the biotic parts that the land had possessed before humans changed it, or as many of them as possible. As for "beauty," it was, in Leopold's view, an attribute of lands that possessed stability and integrity. Integrity, stability, and beauty: they were three ways of describing one object—healthy land—in terms of its interrelated parts, its nutrient cycling, and its pleasing appearance to the eye, ear, and soul.

With these key words Leopold gave his land ethic both an ecological and a moral orientation, linked to his concept of land and to the overall goal of land health. Leopold also situated his ethic in an evolutionary context. Evolution had no ultimate goal, nor was it morally based or purpose driven, but it had apparently produced historical trends toward increasingly diverse, and complexly organized biotic communities. Humans as fellow objects of evolutionary processes might expect to be included with other species on that trajectory. In any event, historically the extension of human ethics had so far embraced relationships between individuals and between individuals and society. Perhaps, Leopold thought, if he was "read[ing] the evidence correctly," a next possibility would be a biological extension of ethical behavior to the relationship between humans and land.[133] From past trends Leopold thought it at least possible—particularly if people preserved and interacted with some of the natural environment out of which they had been shaped—that the human species might evolve toward increasingly intuitive cooperative interactions with the land community.[134]

In recent generations particularly, though, humans had embraced modes of living that cut against nature's enduring ways, in evolutionary as well as ecological terms. They had exercised their unique powers to reason and make deliberate choices in ways that seemingly hampered their own and others' long-term welfare. In the final section of "The Land Ethic" Leopold sketched the chief ways in which humans were cutting against evolution's trends. "Perhaps the most serious obstacle impeding the evolution of a land ethic," he wrote, "is the fact that our educational and economic system is headed away from, rather than toward, an intense consciousness of land."[135] This was the obstacle that affected the vast majority of people, those who no longer made their living on the land. "Almost equally serious" as an obstacle to evolution was "the attitude of the farmer, for whom the land is still an adversary."[136] This was the leading obstacle for landowners who did possess a consciousness of land but who did not perceive it ecologically.

"One of the requisites" for the removal of both obstacles was the development of "an understanding of ecology"[137]—a matter of the right kind of education, including face-to-face interactions with nature. For ordinary citizens Leopold suggested that ecological knowledge and direct experience with land would foster the kind of "intense consciousness"[138] of land that landowners presently lacked; it would help promote "a vital relation to it" and ongoing awakenings in people that would enable them to see, know, understand, love, and respect the land. For farmers and other land managers, an ecological comprehension of nature would help them shift from an oversimplified, resource-oriented view of land to seeing it as an integrated whole.

If a land ethic was only "an evolutionary possibility," it was nevertheless an "ecological necessity."[139] Until such a time as it might become instinctual, caring for the land, Leopold urged, required people to consciously "improve themselves" in the sense of improving their ecological comprehension of land, improving their "social conduct,"[140] and learning and practicing an "ethics of community life" extended to soils, waters, plants, and animals as well as people.[141] "I have no illusions about the speed or accuracy with which an ecological conscience can become functional," Leopold wrote in 1947.

It has required 19 centuries to define decent man-to-man conduct and the process is only half done; it may take as long to evolve a code of decency for man-to-land conduct. In such matters we should not worry too much about anything except the direction in which we travel. The direction is clear, and the first step is to *throw your weight around* on matters of right and wrong in land-use. Cease being intimidated by the argument that a right action is impossible because it does not yield maximum profits, or that a wrong action is to be condoned because it pays. That philosophy is dead in human relations, and its funeral in land-relations is overdue.[142]

In the short term, Leopold suggested, a land ethic might help people broaden their ideals and bring themselves into line with nature's forces. Until that distant day when harmonious living with land became ingrained, the land ethic could provide an interim land-use guide. It could serve as a placeholder or outward standard, "a kind of community instinct in-the-making,"[143] providing a practical guide for confronting the tangle of ecological situations so complex and intricate that no human mind could determine how to act.[144]

In hoping to cut through that complex tangle to clearer understanding, Leopold phrased his land ethic in general terms, connecting it with a comprehensible mental image of dynamic land grounded in the most up-to-date ecological research. Leopold's guiding land ethic and the goal of land health could be applied to the use and conditions of all lands. On the other hand, no two land parcels were alike. Even at the smallest scale lands were unique. Some were more resilient than others because of climate or other factors. On some lands the organization of the land pyramid appeared to be more flexible and able to adjust to change without becoming deranged. A particular action on one landscape might be right while the same action elsewhere might be wrong.

In the end Leopold was able to address with his land ethic nearly the full range of tasks that had drawn his attention during his professional life. It pointed toward the overall goal of conservation—land health—offering the prospect of redressing the fragmentation that so afflicted the conservation cause. It provided the means to protect the public interest in private land, an issue for Leopold from his first days in the Southwest. It offered a remedy for the excessive individualism of the day. It provided the ecological base for a new understanding of private landownership, giving content to the individual's duty, as he put it, "to manage his land in the interest of the community, as well as in his own interest."[145] And it addressed, finally, the need to respect the moral value that he believed infused the natural world, the "biotic right"[146] of species and biological communities to exist as long as evolutionary forces allowed. A land ethic "affirmed the right of community members to exist, and, at least in spots," as mentioned earlier, "to exist in a natural state."[147] Even creatures with no conceivable value to humans were members of the biotic community and entitled as such to a chance to endure.

"All history," Leopold wrote as he closed his final writing on wilderness, "consists of successive excursions from a single starting-point, to which man returns again and again to organize yet another search for a durable scale of values."[148] For Leopold this search for values began and ended with the land. The land itself provided the guiding lessons, available to all who would open themselves to them. The land—"things natural, wild, and free"—provided a standard for reappraising things "unnatural, tame, and confined," for reappraising progress and the meaning of "the good life."[149]

→→ ←←

Aldo Leopold died of a heart attack on April 21, 1948, while helping a neighbor in Sauk County fight an accidental grass fire. He had suffered health problems over the previous two years but was nonetheless at the height of his professional powers. His death caught him in mid-stride. As outgoing president of the Ecological Society of America, Leopold looked forward to the customary address that he would deliver that September. He apparently planned a major talk on land health, viewed from the perspective of wilderness. In his desk lay a stack of unfinished manuscripts, mostly having to do with land health and with the conservation challenge that Leopold deemed most important: getting private landowners to use their lands better. Included in Leopold's files was the first chapter of his planned textbook on ecology. Attached to it were the detailed ecological case studies that he had put together for use in his wildlife ecology class and planned to develop for his ecology text. Just a week earlier

Leopold had received word from Oxford University Press of its desire to publish his collection of essays, so there was revising and editing that would need doing. His graduate students were in the thick of important research projects. Returning soldiers meant overflowing undergraduate classes and thus fresh educational possibilities. For the land itself pressures toward an ever more industrialized way of life were forming darker clouds on the horizon. In the meantime, though, spring was in full swing at the Shack. There was planting to do, and there were phenology notes to record. Overhead were the migratory birds; underfoot there was "draba, the smallest flower that blows." And then, as in Aprils past, there was the "drama of the sky dance"—the nightly entertainment of the male woodcock, offered to those who lived by the land and not merely on it. For ages humans had watched the woodcock in joy, yet its ways remained largely its own. People could pose their questions, as Leopold and his family did. But many answers would remain elusive. They would linger within the timeless mists, as did so many of nature's ways, veiled amid the "mysteries of the deepening dusk."[150]

The evening before his death, Leopold recorded a final dusk-time "sky-dance" in his journal: "Woodcock 7:10 p.m."

Notes

Frequently cited works are identified by the following abbreviations:

AL Aldo Leopold

ALSW D. E. Brown and N. B. Carmony, eds., *Aldo Leopold's Southwest* (Albuquerque: University of New Mexico Press, 1990).

FHL J. B. Callicott and E. T. Freyfogle, eds., *Aldo Leopold: For the Health of the Land; Previously Unpublished Essays and Other Writings* (Washington, DC: Island Press, Shearwater Books, 1999).

LP Leopold Papers (series number followed by box number), University of Wisconsin–Madison Archives.

RAMC R. A. McCabe Collection of the Writings of Aldo Leopold, University of Wisconsin–Madison Libraries.

RMG S. L. Flader and J. B. Callicott, eds., *The River of the Mother of God and Other Essays by Aldo Leopold* (Madison: University of Wisconsin Press, 1991).

RR L. Leopold, ed., *Round River: From the Journals of Aldo Leopold, Author of "A Sand County Almanac"* (New York: Oxford University Press, 1993).

SCA A. Leopold, *A Sand County Almanac and Sketches Here and There* (New York: Oxford University Press, 1987).

USFS USDA Forest Service

UW University of Wisconsin–Madison

UWDWE University of Wisconsin Department of Wildlife Ecology

For a full listing of Aldo Leopold's publications, the reader is referred to the following:

S. L. Flader and J. B. Callicott, eds., *The River of the Mother of God and Other Essays by Aldo Leopold* (Madison: University of Wisconsin Press, 1991).

C. D. Meine, *Aldo Leopold: His Life and Work* (Madison: University of Wisconsin Press, 1988).

Preface

1. Albert Hochbaum, letter to AL, 11 March 1944. See also S. Flader, *Thinking Like a Mountain: Aldo Leopold and the Evolution of an Ecological Attitude toward Deer, Wolves, and Forests* (Madison: University of Wisconsin Press, 1974), p. 271: "Leopold wrote, 'A prophet is one who recognized the birth of an idea in the collective mind, and who defines and clarifies, with his life, its meanings and its implications.'" In that sentence taken from Leopold's tribute to his colleague, "Charles Knesal Cooperrider, 1889–1944," *Journal of Wildlife Management* 12, no. 3 (July 1948): 337–339, writes Flader, "Aldo captured the essence of his own ecological odyssey." See also C. Meine, *Aldo Leopold: His Life and Work* (Madison: University of Wisconsin Press, 1988), p. 521. In his epilogue Meine states, "Aldo Leopold's odyssey ended where it began, in the limestone bluffs above the Mississippi River at Burlington, Iowa," where Leopold was both born and buried.
2. AL, SCA, p. 200.
3. AL, letters to Estella Leopold, 15 August 1935 and 16 September 1935, LP 10-8, 9.
4. AL, "Professional Training in Wildlife Work," 30 November 1938, LP 10-2, 9, p. 6.

Introduction: Launching Out

1. *Guttierrezia*, or snakeweed (also known as fireweed and turpentine weed), was a plant native to the southwestern plains region. Green and lovely to the eye, it nonetheless was a plant that no animal was known to eat. It often spread in livestock-grazed regions when competition from palatable plants was removed.
2. AL, "Conservationist in Mexico," RMG, p. 240; AL, "The Community Concept," SCA, p. 204.
3. Leopold and his companions took turns writing daily journal accounts by which to remember their trip. See AL, RR, pp. 130–141.
4. "Song of the Gavilan" appeared first in *Journal of Wildlife Management* 4, no. 3 (July 1940): 329–332.
5. AL, SCA, p. 154.
6. See also S. Flader, *Thinking Like a Mountain: Aldo Leopold and the Evolution of an Ecological Attitude toward Deer, Wolves, and Forests* (Madison: University of Wisconsin Press, 1974), p. 5.
7. AL, "The Arboretum and the University," *Parks and Recreation* 18, no. 2 (October 1934): 59–60, also in RMG, p. 209; A. Tansley, "The Use and Abuse of Vegetational Concepts and Terms," *Ecology* 16 (1935): 284–307.
8. AL, "The Ecological Conscience," RMG, p. 340.
9. AL, "A Survey of Nature," RR, p. 146, SCA, p. 204.
10. AL, "The Round River: A Parable," RR, p. 158.
11. Ibid., p. 159.
12. AL, "On a Monument to the Pigeon," SCA, p. 109. See also AL, "A Biotic View of Land," RMG, p. 268, and AL, "The Land Pyramid," SCA, p. 215.
13. AL, "On a Monument to the Pigeon," SCA, p. 109.
14. Donald Worster identifies an essentially similar triadic cultural ethos of land

use in his *Dust Bowl: The Southern Plains in the 1930s* (New York: Oxford University Press, 1979), p. 6.

15. AL, "The Conservation Ethic," RMG, p. 181; AL, "The Land Ethic," SCA, p. 201.

16. AL, SCA, p. 203.

17. AL, "Engineering and Conservation," RMG, p. 254. See C. Meine, "The Oldest Task in Human History," in *Correction Lines: Essays on Land, Leopold, and Conservation* (Washington, DC: Island Press, 2004), pp. 1–44.

18. AL, "Defenders of Wilderness," SCA, pp. 200–201.

Chapter 1: Seed Plots

1. C. A. Beard and M. R. Beard, *The Rise of American Civilization* (New York: Macmillan, 1930); J. Bronowski and E. J. Hobsbawm, *The Age of Revolution, 1789–1848* (New York: New American Library, 1962); S. P. Hays, *The Response to Industrialism, 1885–1914* (Chicago: University of Chicago Press, 1957); H. D. Croly, *The Promise of American Life*, edited by A. M. Schlesinger Jr. (Cambridge, MA: Harvard University Press, Belknap Press, 1965).

2. U.S. Department of Commerce, Bureau of the Census, *Statistical Abstract of the United States: 1908* (Washington, DC: Government Printing Office, 1909), pp. 21–22.

3. Ibid., pp. 44–45; *Statistical Abstract: 1910*, pp. 48–49. Density ranged from 0.7 people per square mile in Nevada to 5,517.8 people per square mile in the District of Columbia. Arizona and New Mexico, where Leopold worked, held populations of 204,354 and 327,301 people and densities of 1.8 and 2.7 people per square mile (1910 figures), respectively.

4. *Statistical Abstract: 1909*, p. 23.

5. Ibid., p. 734.

6. *Statistical Abstract: 1917*, pp. 125–126, 247–257. Farmers numbered nearly 6 million out of 38 million, or 16 percent, of the gainfully employed.

7. *Statistical Abstract: 1909*, p. 32.

8. *Statistical Abstract: 1917*, pp. 247–257. There were about 10.5 million Americans working in manufacturing and mechanical industries by 1910.

9. Ibid., p. 744.

10. *Statistical Abstract: 1910*, p. 715.

11. *Statistical Abstract: 1911*, p. 279.

12. Ibid., pp. 308–314.

13. Ibid., p. 278.

14. R. A. Long, in *Proceedings of a Conference of the Governors of the United States, 1908, White House, May 13–15* (Washington, DC: Government Printing Office, 1909), p. 89.

15. *Statistical Abstract: 1910*, p. 161.

16. Ibid., pp. 163–164.

17. Ibid., p. 165.

18. An M ft. is 1,000 feet, board measure, and a board foot of timber is one foot long, one foot wide, and one inch or less thick.

19. *Statistical Abstract: 1910*, p. 165. Up from 18 million M ft. milled annually in the 1880s.

20. Ibid., p. 162.

21. J. J. Berger, *Understanding Forests* (San Francisco: Sierra Club Books, 1998), p. 29.

22. Ibid.

23. *Statistical Abstract: 1909*, pp. 159–160. Also see the Forest History Society's Web site, http://www.lib.duke.edu/forest/Research/usfscoll/people/Pinchot/Pinchot.html (accessed 8 December 2005); these figures include national forests established in Alaska (1909) and Puerto Rico (1903). The first installments of forest conservation are recounted in R. W. Judd, "A Wonderfull Order and Ballance: Natural History and the Beginnings of Forest Conservation in America, 1730–1830," *Environmental History* 11, no. 1 (2006): 8–36, and D. Pisani, "Forests and Conservation, 1865–1890," in *American Forests: Nature, Culture, and Politics*, edited by C. Miller (Lawrence: University Press of Kansas, 1997), pp. 15–34.

24. The Forest Reserve Act of 1891 had given the president power to proclaim national forest reserves. The Fulton Amendment of 1907 would disallow the president's setting aside of additional national forests in the six northwestern states. On the eve of this bill's signing Roosevelt, with assistance from Gifford Pinchot and his assistant Arthur Ringland, mapped out millions of acres of new reserves in these six states, and Roosevelt signed a proclamation establishing them. On the first forest reserves, see H. K. Steen, "The Beginning of the National Forest System," in *American Forests: Nature, Culture, and Politics*, edited by C. Miller (Lawrence: University Press of Kansas, 1997), pp. 49–68, and H. K. Steen, ed., *The Origins of the National Forests* (Durham, NC: Forest History Society, 1992).

25. *Statistical Abstract: 1909*, pp. 159–160.

26. Ibid., p. 156.

27. U.S. Department of Commerce, Bureau of the Census, *Historical Statistics of the United States: Colonial Times to 1970*, Forests and Forest Products Series L 1-223 (Washington, DC: Government Printing Office, 1976), p. 534.

28. *Statistical Abstract: 1909*, p. 156.

29. *Statistical Abstract: 1917*, p. 247. The U.S. Bureau of the Census counted about 4,332 professional foresters in 1910. But fewer than that number had been trained in the nation's only two college forestry programs, which existed at Cornell and Yale. In 1909 only 91 foresters received bachelor's and master's degrees. In 1939, however, the numbers had risen to more than twenty colleges graduating a total of 1,200 foresters. See D. W. MacCleery, *American Forests: A History of Resiliency and Recovery*, 3rd ed. (Durham, NC: Forest History Society, 1994), p. 28, and G. W. Williams, *The USDA Forest Service—the First Century*, Publication No. FS-650 (Washington, DC: U.S. Department of Agriculture, Forest Service, 2000).

30. C. D. Meine, *Aldo Leopold: His Life and Work* (Madison: University of Wisconsin Press, 1988), p. 80.

31. G. Pinchot, "An American Fable," *National Geographic* 19, no. 5 (May 1908): 347.

32. Leopold quoted this estimate in 1904; see AL, "The Maintenance of the Forests," RMG, p. 37.

33. Ibid. See D. W. MacCleery, *American Forests: A History of Resiliency and Recovery*, 3rd ed. (Durham, NC: Forest History Society, 1994). Logged lands not converted to other uses regenerated, MacCleery claims, with net annual wood growth rebounding nationally beginning around 1920. But even in regrown areas a legacy remained of important differences in forest distributions, ages, and species compositions, between regrown forest and pre-logged forest, the former becoming predominant in the country. In the final decade of the twentieth century, the United States had about the same forest area as in 1920, but 55 percent of the nation's forests were fewer than 50 years old and only 6 percent were 175 years old or older. U.S. Department of Agriculture, Forest Service, *U.S. Forest Facts and Historical Trends*, FS-696-M (Washington, DC: U.S. Department of Agriculture, Forest Service, 2001).

34. An overview of conservation in the first half of the twentieth century is provided in C. R. Koppes, "Efficiency, Equity, Esthetics: Shifting Themes in American Conservation," in *The Ends of the Earth: Perspectives on Modern Environmental History*, edited by D. Worster (Cambridge: Cambridge University Press, 1988), pp. 230–251.

35. F. J. Turner, "The Problem of the West," *Atlantic Monthly* 78, no. 467 (1896): 290.

36. Ibid., p. 294.

37. Ibid., p. 293.

38. Ibid., p. 294.

39. Ibid., pp. 294–295.

40. C. Richter, *The Trees* (New York: Alfred A. Knopf, 1940), pp. 5–7. The reaction of settlers to new land and its healthfulness, though with little attention to forests and vegetative communities as such, is explored in C. B. Valencius, *The Health of the Country: How American Settlers Understood Themselves and Their Land* (New York: Basic Books, 2002).

41. Meine, *Aldo Leopold*, pp. 87–105. See AL, "Escudilla," SCA, pp. 133–136.

42. F. H. Olmstead, *Gila River Flood Control*, 65th Cong., 3rd sess., Document No. 436 (Washington, DC: Government Printing Office, 1919), pp. 7–8.

43. G. P. Winship, *Why Coronado Went to New Mexico in 1540* (Washington, DC: Government Printing Office, 1896).

44. The annual average amount and value of mine timbers extracted from forests between 1912 and 1921 was close to 300 million cubic feet and $57 million. *Statistical Abstract: 1924*, p. 690. Before 1850 the United States mined an inconsequential amount of copper; by 1906 it was mining 58 percent of the world's production of that mineral. *Proceedings of a Conference of Governors*, p. 46. In 1909 more than 1 billion pounds was being mined, with a total value of $142,083,711.

45. AL, letter to Clara Leopold, 7 October 1909, LP 10-8, 7. See Meine, *Aldo Leopold*, p. 94.

46. AL, letter to Clara Leopold, 13 January 1911, LP 10-8, 7; Meine, *Aldo Leopold*, p. 103. See also AL, "Maintenance of the Forests," pp. 37–39.

47. See Meine, *Aldo Leopold*, pp. 106–123.

48. Meine, *Aldo Leopold*, pp. 119–121.

49. Ibid.

50. AL, letter to Estella Bergere, 2 February 1912, LP 10-8, 8. See Meine, *Aldo Leopold*, p. 120.

51. M. Lorbiecki, *Aldo Leopold: A Fierce Green Fire* (New York: Oxford University Press, 1996), pp. 66–67.

52. Copied down in Aldo Leopold's personal journal, p. 50, LP 10-7, 1 (15).

53. AL, letter to Clara Leopold, 17 November 1909, LP 10-8, 7. See Meine, *Aldo Leopold*, p. 95.

54. AL, "A Man's Leisure Time," address to the University of New Mexico Assembly, 15 October 1920, p. 4, LP 10-6, 16 (4). A revised version appears in RR, pp. 3–8.

55. Meine, *Aldo Leopold*, p. 108; AL, letter to Clara Leopold, 3 June 1911, LP 10-8, 7.

56. Meine, *Aldo Leopold*, pp. 121–122; AL, letter to Estella Bergere, 21 May 1912, LP 10-8, 8.

57. W. Whitman, "America's Characteristic Landscape," in *Walt Whitman: Complete Poetry and Collected Prose*, edited by Justin Kaplan (New York: Library of America, 1982), pp. 853, 864.

58. Ibid.

59. W. Whitman, "The Prairies," Ibid., p. 853.

60. D. Worster, "John Muir and the Modern Passion for Nature," *Environmental History* 10, no. 1 (2005): 8–19.

61. Marsh's book was revised and republished in 1874 with the new title *The Earth as Modified by Human Action*. See D. Lowenthal, *George Perkins Marsh: Prophet of Conservation* (Seattle: University of Washington Press, 2000); M. Williams, *Deforesting the Earth: From Prehistory to Global Crisis* (Chicago: University of Chicago Press, 2003); and M. Williams, *Americans and Their Forests* (New York: Cambridge University Press, 1988).

62. W. deBuys, ed., *Seeing Things Whole: The Essential John Wesley Powell* (Washington, DC: Island Press, Shearwater Books, 2001); D. Worster, *A River Running West: The Life of John Wesley Powell* (New York: Oxford University Press, 2001).

63. H. Adams, quoted in Turner, "Problem of the West," p. 4.

64. The Organic Act of 1897 was passed "to improve and protect the forest within the boundaries, or for the purpose of securing favorable conditions of water flows, and to furnish a continuous supply of timber for the use and necessities of the citizens of the United States."

65. T. Roosevelt, "Opening Address by the President," in *Proceedings of a Conference of Governors*, p. 3.

66. Ibid., p. 6.

67. R. A. Long, "Forest Conservation," in *Proceedings of a Conference of Governors*, p. 83.

68. T. C. Chamberlin, "Soil Wastage," in *Proceedings of a Conference of Governors*, p. 77.

69. Ibid.

70. Ibid., p. 78.
71. C. R. Van Hise, "Address," in *Proceedings of a Conference of Governors*, p. 45.
72. Ibid., p. 48.
73. Ibid., p. 47.
74. J. M. Carey, "Address," in *Proceedings of a Conference of Governors*, p. 149.
75. Ibid.
76. W. J. McGee, "The Relations among the Resources," in *Proceedings of the National Conservation Congress*, vol. 1 (Washington, DC: U.S. Congress, 1909), p. 100.
77. Ibid.
78. Chamberlin, "Soil Wastage," p. 76.
79. Also at this time Hardy Webster Campbell popularized dry farming—an agricultural technique that called for plowing and planting practices intended to keep moisture in the soil in areas with rainfall insufficient for crops.
80. T. Roosevelt, "The New Nationalism," 1910 campaign speech, http://www.edheritage.org/1910/pridocs/1910roosevelt.htm (accessed 18 February 2006).
81. Roosevelt, "Opening Address," p. 10. The idea of greater coordination and more forceful national leadership was not confined to the United States at the time. Great Britain, too, could see the benefits of societal unity and centralized, science-based guidance at the national level. Winston Churchill expressed this new orientation in *Liberalism and the Social Problem*, also published in 1909. See Croly, *Promise of American Life*, p. xi.
82. Roosevelt, "New Nationalism."
83. See Croly, *Promise of American Life*, and D. Worster, *The Dust Bowl: The Southern Plains in the 1930s* (New York: Oxford University Press, 1979).
84. In addition to population growth from reproductively expanding families, immigration numbers were rising—from 387,203 in 1870 to more than a million annually by 1905. *Statistical Abstract: 1909*, 91.
85. Turner, "Problem of the West," p. 297.
86. C. J. Blanchard, "The Call of the West: Homes Are Being Made for Millions of People in the Arid West," *National Geographic* 20, no. 5 (1909): 403–436.
87. Ibid., p. 403.
88. Ibid.
89. Ibid.
90. Roosevelt, "New Nationalism."
91. Ibid.
92. Pinchot, "American Fable," pp. 348–349.
93. Ibid., p. 349.
94. McGee, "Relations among the Resources," p. 100.
95. Chamberlin, "Soil Wastage," p. 77.
96. Long, "Forest Conservation," p. 84.
97. See G. Pinchot, *The Use of the National Forests: Regulations and Instructions for the Use of the National Forests*, U.S. Department of Agriculture, Forest Service (Washington, DC: Government Printing Office, 1907). And see H. S. Graves, *The Use Book: A Manual of Information about the National Forests*,

U.S. Department of Agriculture, Forest Service (Washington, DC: Government Printing Office, 1918). Leopold summarized the purposes of the national forests under the Organic Act in his *Watershed Handbook* (Albuquerque: U.S. Department of Agriculture, Forest Service, District 3, December 1923 [revised and reissued October 1934]), p. 10, LP 10-11, 1.

98. AL, "The Maintenance of Forests," RMG, p. 38.
99. Meine, *Aldo Leopold*, pp. 122–125.
100. Ibid., p. 128.
101. AL, "To the Forest Officers of the Carson," *Carson Pine Cone* (15 July 1913); also in RMG, pp. 41–46.
102. Ibid., p. 43.
103. Ibid.
104. Ibid.
105. Ibid.
106. AL, letter to Carl A. Leopold, 1 October 1914, LP 10-8, 8. See Meine, *Aldo Leopold*, p. 132.

Chapter 2: Written on the Hills
1. C. D. Meine, *Aldo Leopold: His Life and Work* (Madison: University of Wisconsin Press, 1988), p. 136.
2. Meine, *Aldo Leopold*, p. 145. A thoughtful survey of the interactions of Americans with wildlife in the West is offered in D. Worster, *An Unsettled Country: Changing Landscapes of the American West* (Albuquerque: University of New Mexico Press, 1994), pp. 55–90.
3. AL, personal journal, p. 5, LP 10-7, 1 (15); this was a quote from Alexandre Dumas' *Three Musketeers*.
4. W. Wilson, "Neutrality of Feeling," presidential proclamation, 18 August 1914, in *Selected Addresses and Public Papers of Woodrow Wilson*, edited by A. B. Hart (New York: Boni and Liveright, 1918), p. 45.
5. W. Wilson, "Foreign Trade and Ship Building," address to Congress, 8 December 1914, in Hart, *Selected Addresses and Public Papers*, p. 56.
6. J. W. Chambers II, ed., *The Tyranny of Change: America in the Progressive Era, 1890–1920* (New Brunswick, NJ: Rutgers University Press, 2000), p. 234; W. E. Leuchtenburg, *The Perils of Prosperity, 1914–1932* (Chicago: University of Chicago Press, 1993), p. 15.
7. Wilson, "Foreign Trade," p. 57.
8. W. Wilson, "A New President's Principles," first inaugural address, 4 March 1913, p. 2.
9. Meine, *Aldo Leopold*, p. 133; AL, letter to Carl A. Leopold, 19 December 1914, LP 10-8, 8.
10. AL, "The Maintenance of the Forests," RMG, pp. 38–39; AL, "The Popular Wilderness Fallacy: An Idea That Is Fast Exploding," RMG, p. 49.
11. AL, "The Popular Wilderness Fallacy: An Idea That Is Fast Exploding," RMG, pp. 47, 52.
12. G. Pinchot, *The Use of the National Forests*, U.S. Department of Agriculture, Forest Service (Washington, DC: Government Printing Office, 1907), p. 15.
13. W. B. Greeley, *Forests and Men* (Garden City, NY: Doubleday, 1951), p. 87.

14. Ibid., p. 92.
15. Ibid., p. 93. The lingering effects of the war on U.S. forest policy, particularly in the national forests, is assessed in A. J. West, "Forests and National Security: British and American Forestry in the Wake of World War I," *Environmental History* 8, no. 2 (2003): 270–293.
16. U.S. Department of Commerce, Bureau of Foreign and Domestic Commerce, *Statistical Abstract of the United States: 1920* (Washington, DC: Government Printing Office, 1921), p. 180; U.S. Department of Commerce, Bureau of Foreign and Domestic Commerce, *Statistical Abstract of the United States: 1930* (Washington, DC: Government Printing Office, 1930), p. 730. By the end of the decade, the number of cattle grazing on the national forests had been reduced to 1,322,465.
17. *The Pine Cone: Official Bulletin of the Albuquerque Game Protective Association* (Christmas 1915), LP 10-6, 1.
18. Meine, *Aldo Leopold*, p. 159.
19. Ibid., p. 144.
20. Ibid., p. 156.
21. Ibid., p. 157. Leopold and Tusayan supervisor Don P. Johnston in the fall of 1916 drafted the "Grand Canyon Working Plan," the first comprehensive recreational plan for this national wonder; LP 10-11, 1. It suggested establishing a zoning system for uses and called for a crackdown on "repugnant" business practices.
22. Ibid., p. 159.
23. Ibid., p. 165.
24. Meine, *Aldo Leopold*, p. 94; AL, letter to Clara Leopold, 7 October 1909, LP 10-8, 7.
25. Ibid., p. 165; AL, "The Civic Life of Albuquerque," speech, 27 September 1918, p. 5, LP 10-8, 9. Also see Leopold's 1917 "Progressive Cattle Range Management," *Breeder's Gazette* 71, no. 18 (3 May 1917): 919, in which he pointed out the benefit of stock growers' associations made up of groups of neighboring landowners who cooperated in maintaining range standards and regulated many of their own range activities.
26. Meine, *Aldo Leopold*, p. 167; AL, "What about Drainage?" *Bernalillo County Farm Bureau News* 1, no. 1 (June 1918): 2. In later years, Leopold would view indiscriminate wetland draining as harmful to wildlife and other land values.
27. AL, "City Tree Planting," *American Forestry* 25, no. 308 (August 1919): 1295.
28. AL, "Relative Abundance of Ducks in the Rio Grande Valley," *Condor* 21, no. 3 (1919): 122; AL, "Notes on the Weights and Plumages of Ducks in New Mexico," *Condor* 21, no. 3 (1919): 128; AL, "Notes on the Behavior of Pintail Ducks in a Hailstorm," *Condor* 21, no. 2 (1919): 87, also in RMG, p. 60.
29. AL, "Are Red-headed Woodpeckers Moving West?" *Condor* 20, no. 3 (1918): 122. Supporting this thesis, Leopold had spotted within a quarter mile of the main line of the Santa Fe railroad yet another adult red-headed woodpecker on 18 August 1918. See AL, "Notes on Red-headed Woodpecker and Jack Snipe in New Mexico," *Condor* 21, no. 1 (1919): 40.

30. AL, "A Breeding Record for the Red-headed Woodpecker in New Mexico," *Condor* 21, no. 4 (1919): 173–174. The birders had watched as parents fed their young in a dead cottonwood tree five miles south of Albuquerque.

31. Leopold wrote several articles on the business aspects of the Forest Service. See, e.g., AL, "The National Forests: The Last Free Hunting Grounds of the Nation," *Journal of Forestry* 17, no. 2 (1919): 150–153. In this article Leopold asserts that the demand for hunting on the national forests exceeds supply and that it is not only practical but also a public duty and responsibility of foresters to help develop a practice of scientific game management to promote an abundant game supply. He also predicts that widespread game farming will lead to commercialization of hunting privileges on private lands, which he believes would be the end of free hunting and a crime against democracy in America unless public lands could provide hunting opportunities. As the demand for hunting on national forests increased with population, ease of transportation, and the cost of hunting elsewhere, Leopold suggested, it also would be good business sense for the Forest Service to develop species on which they would have a practical monopoly—in other words, on those species (e.g., mountain sheep, wild turkeys, javelinas, white goats) that were more sensitive to human disruption or required a wider range or more rugged territory than most private lands were likely to provide. In another article, "Forest Service Salaries and the Future of the National Forests," *Journal of Forestry* 17, no. 4 (1919): 398–401, he complained that low wages for Forest Service employees were lowering the public prestige of the Service and discouraging competent men from joining it. Without sufficient salaries, the Service would be demoralized, efficiency would decrease, public support would be alienated, and the whole structure of technical national forestry would be undermined, with widespread and profound effects rippling through other fields of conservation. He argued for the organization of public opinion regarding the whole "great cause of national forestry" in order to pressure Congress for higher salaries. He also recommended that foresters themselves promote the idea of political action on behalf of forestry in their interactions with influential private landowners and organize federal employee unions. For a discussion of Leopold's Forest Service legacy see S. Flader, "Aldo Leopold's Legacy to Forestry," *Forest History Today* (1998): 2–5.

32. Meine, *Aldo Leopold*, p. 167.

33. Ibid., p. 175.

34. AL, "Topic #60, The D-3 Notebook Tally Sheet: A Combination Inspection Outline and Report Talk Given at Special Fire Conference," 10 November 1921, LP 10-6, 2; AL, letter to Frank Pooler, District Forester, 2 February 1925, subject "Supervision, Inspection, D-3."

35. AL, "Tonto Inspection Report," handwritten notebook, 1923, p. 106, LP 10-11, 3.

36. AL, "To the Forest Officers of the Carson," *Carson Pine Cone* (15 July 1913); also in RMG, pp. 41–46.

37. J. Baird Callicott draws attention to Leopold's interest in soil in "Standards of Conservation: Then and Now," *Conservation Biology* 4 (1990): 229–232,

as does Susan Flader in "Let the Fire Devil Have His Due: Aldo Leopold and the Conundrum of Wilderness Management," in *Managing America's Enduring Wilderness Resource*, edited by D. Lime (St. Paul: Minnesota Extension Service, 1990).

38. In 1922 and 1923 he returned to the Prescott, Manzano, and Santa Fe national forests. In August 1923 Leopold carefully inspected for the first time the Tonto National Forest, site of Roosevelt Dam; Meine, *Aldo Leopold*, p. 217.

39. The term "oecology" had been coined by German zoologist Ernst Haeckel in 1866. Ecology did not become a formal science with its own professional organizations until the twentieth century, however. In 1913 the British Ecological Society was founded; in 1915 the Ecological Society of America was formed. Leopold had become familiar with the new discipline of ecology by at least 1920 and thereafter referred to ecological science and ideas with increasing frequency and familiarity. See, e.g., AL, "The Forestry of the Prophets," *Journal of Forestry* 18, no. 4 (April 1920): 412–419, also in RMG, p. 76 ("Isaiah seems to have had some knowledge of . . . the ecological relations of species"); AL, "Report of General Inspection of Prescott National Forest," 31 July–1 September 1922, LP 10-11, 1, section on fire, p. 1; AL, "Ecology of Brush Type"; AL, "Erosion as a Menace to the Social and Economic Future of the Southwest," speech read at the meeting of the New Mexico Association for Science in 1922 and later published, with an introduction by H. H. Chapman, in *Journal of Forestry* 44, no. 9 (September 1946): 627–633 and 630, on ecological balance. Chapman uncovered the article and submitted it to the journal. See also AL, "Tonto Inspection Report," p. 3: "Southern Arizona ecology."

40. Greeley, *Forests and Men*, p. 106.

41. AL, *Watershed Handbook* (Albuquerque: U.S. Department of Agriculture, Forest Service, District 3, December 1923 [revised and reissued October 1934]), p. 10, LP 10-11, 1. Leopold inspected the Prescott from 31 July to 1 September 1922; AL, "Inspection Report: Prescott NF 1922," n.d., approved by District Forester Frank Pooler ca. 6 October 1922, p. 1, LP 10-11, 3 (10); AL, "A Plea for Recognition of Artificial Works in Forest Erosion Control Policy," *Journal of Forestry* 19, no. 3 (1921): 267.

42. AL, "A Plea for Recognition of Artificial Works in Forest Erosion Control Policy," *Journal of Forestry* 19, no. 3 (1921): 269.

43. In addition to soils disappearing, Leopold also chronicled the disappearance of wildlife and wilderness in the area. AL, "Escudilla," SCA, pp. 133–136.

44. F. H. Olmstead, *Gila River Flood Control*, 65th Cong., 3rd sess., Document No. 436 (Washington, DC: Government Printing Office, 1919), pp. 16–17.

45. Ibid., p. 65; AL, "Erosion and Prosperity," 18 January 1921, p. 4, LP 10-8, 9. "Erosion and Prosperity" was a talk given during the observation of Farmers' Week at the University of Arizona. Olmstead, *Gila River Flood Control*, p. 68; W. Barnes, *Western Grazing Grounds and Forest Ranges: A History of the Live-Stock Industry as Conducted on the Open Ranges of the Arid West* (Chicago: Breeder's Gazette, 1913), pp. 226–245.

46. Olmstead, *Gila River Flood Control*, p. 65.

47. Ibid., p. 68.

48. Ibid.; AL, "Plea for Recognition," p. 270.
49. AL, "Erosion and Prosperity."
50. Ibid., p. 1. See also Meine, *Aldo Leopold*, p. 188.
51. The figures, which do not seem to add up, were Leopold's calculations. AL, "Pioneers and Gullies," *Sunset* 52, no. 5 (1924): 15–16, 91–95; also in RMG, p. 107. See also AL, "Plea for Recognition," pp. 270–271; AL, "Erosion as a Menace," p. 628.
52. AL, "Pioneers and Gullies," RMG; AL, "Erosion as a Menace."
53. AL, "Erosion as a Menace," p. 628.
54. Ibid., p. 627.
55. AL, "Erosion and Prosperity," p. 3.
56. AL, *Watershed Handbook*, December 1923, p. 9.
57. Ibid.
58. AL, "Pioneers and Gullies," RMG, p. 106.
59. AL, "Some Fundamentals of Conservation in the Southwest," RMG, p. 97. See J. Burroughs, *Accepting the Universe* (New York: Russell and Russell, 1920) pp. 35–36.
60. AL, "Pioneers and Gullies," RMG, p. 107.
61. AL, "Some Fundamentals of Conservation in the Southwest," RMG, p. 89; AL, "Skill in Forestry," unfinished manuscript, ca. 1922, p. 178, LP 10-6, 17. See also AL, "Some Fundamentals of Conservation in the Southwest," RMG, p. 95: "Possibly in our intuitive perceptions, which may be truer than our science and less impeded by words than our philosophies, we realize the indivisibility of the earth—its soils, mountains, rivers, forests, climate, plants, and animals, and respect it collectively not only as a useful servant but as a living being."
62. Ibid., p. 94.
63. Ibid.
64. H. S. Canby, "Redwood Canyon," *Atlantic Monthly* (June 1914), in AL, personal journal, p. 1.
65. AL, "Some Fundamentals of Conservation in the Southwest," RMG, pp. 86–97.
66. AL, "Erosion and Prosperity," p. 5.
67. P. W. Gates, *History of Public Land Law Development* (Washington, DC: William W. Gaunt and Sons, 1987), p. 567.
68. Leopold commented in a 14 November 1913 letter titled "To the Boys on the Job," written while he was recuperating from nephritis in Burlington and published in the December 1913 issue of *Carson Pine Cone*: "In the endeavor to find a satisfactory substitute for something to do, I have found the nearest approach to satisfaction in browsing around in books. It's pretty poor pickin' without the salt of reality, but so be it. . . . A new book of great interest to Forest Officers is Inspector Will C. Barnes 'Western Grazing Grounds and Forest Ranges.'" LP 10-11, 1. Leopold reported results of a grazing experiment on the Manti forest in his *Watershed Handbook* (December 1923), p. 6. In 1912 two small watersheds on the Utah forest had been fenced for study and placed under continuous observation to determine comparative effects of various degrees of grazing on forage cover and water flow.

Heavy grazing reduced and reconfigured vegetation; compacted soil; increased stormwater runoff, erosion, and silting; and increased soil nutrient leaching. Leopold noted that most of the conclusions from Utah were true of the Southwest as well.

69. Barnes, *Western Grazing Grounds*, p. 230.
70. Pinchot, *Use of the National Forests*, p. 9.
71. Ibid., p. 7.
72. Ibid., p. 12.
73. Ibid., p. 13.
74. Ibid. For a discussion of how surveying affected the settlement and use of land see C. Meine, "Inherit the Grid," in *Correction Lines: Essays on Land, Leopold, and Conservation* (Washington, DC: Island Press, 2004), pp. 188–209.
75. Under the 1906 Forest Reserve Homestead Act settlers were allowed to purchase approved agricultural lands for $2.50 per acre. In 1862 the regular Homestead Act had been approved as an act of land reform. It entitled any head of a family at least twenty-one years old to claim up to 160 acres (a quarter section) of surveyed land declared open to entry. If the homesteader paid the filing fees and established and cultivated the land for five years, he could "prove up" and gain title to it. The act was intended to help ward off monopoly and speculation in landownership. Until then a relatively few wealthy individuals who could afford to amass great shares of public land often had done so, reselling it later for a profit. The act was also intended to promote the historic Jeffersonian agrarian ideal that every man had a right to a share of the soil and that cultivation of the soil was virtue-building work—a way of life that yielded good for the whole nation. And the act, reformers hoped, also would help ameliorate overcrowding in the industrial centers of the East and help draw settlers to the newer lands of the West. Settlers on unsurveyed land who intended to preempt it (the special right of squatters to purchase 160 acres of land they occupied for $1.25 per acre) might instead wait until it was surveyed to file a homestead application. More than 400 million acres of western lands granted by the federal government to railroads, states, and Indians were excluded from homesteading, as were millions of acres held at high prices by successful 1850s speculators. See Gates, *History of Public Land Law Development*, pp. 291–395, 397.
76. Greeley, *Forests and Men*, p. 24.
77. Gates, *History of Public Land Law Development*, p. 512.
78. Pinchot, *The Use of the National Forests*, p. 10.
79. By 1878 explorer and scientist John Wesley Powell had tried to explain what was becoming increasingly evident through widespread land-use failure—that successful agricultural settlement on dry western lands was a tricky business. Powell had explained decades earlier that success would require irrigation, which in turn would require cooperative communal practices. Furthermore, 160 acres was far too little land on which to make a living where it may take 35–50 acres to graze one head of cattle. The need for irrigation was obvious, and the federal government had responded in due course with the Reclamation Act of 1902. The need to share limited resources would

make it increasingly obvious that cooperation would be necessary among community landowners and between public and private interests. The Forest Service's mission to control private use in the public interest was a model of such recognition. In the 1920s a few modest experiments in voluntary land-use cooperation took place, and Leopold would in fact urge the necessity of such efforts in many of his forestry-related publications. The government did establish ways in which citizens could possess greater areas, such as the 1916 Stock-Raising Homestead Act, which allowed 640-acre applications, but this still fell far short of the large allotments Powell had called for. Overall, the government denied outright the harsh evidence that successful agriculture in arid lands could be sustained only if it was spread out over thousands of acres of land, not mere hundreds. See W. deBuys, ed., *Seeing Things Whole: The Essential John Wesley Powell* (Washington, DC: Island Press, Shearwater Books, 2001), and Gates, *History of Public Land Law Development*, p. 514. See D. Worster, *A River Running West: The Life of John Wesley Powell* (New York: Oxford University Press, 2001). The continuation of homesteading in the arid parts of the West into the 1920s is considered in E. L. Peffer, *The Closing of the Public Domain* (Stanford, CA: Stanford University Press, 1951), pp. 134–180.

80. AL, *Watershed Handbook*, December 1923, p. 3.
81. AL, "Erosion as a Menace," p. 632.
82. AL, "Inspection Report: Prescott NF 1922," p. 1 of section titled "General Appraisal of Prescott Forest."
83. AL, "Inspection Report: Prescott NF 1920," 15 May 1920, p. 1, LP 10-11, 3 (4).
84. Ibid.
85. AL, "Plea for Recognition," p. 267.
86. AL, "Inspection Report: Prescott NF 1920," p. 1.
87. Ibid., p. 2.
88. AL, "Plea for Recognition," pp. 267–273.
89. Ibid., p. 267.
90. AL, letter to Clara Leopold, 15 May 1920, LP 10-8, 9. See also Meine, *Aldo Leopold*, p. 186.
91. AL, *Watershed Handbook*, December 1923, p. 6.
92. AL, "Some Fundamentals of Conservation in the Southwest," RMG, p. 93.
93. AL, "Pioneers and Gullies," RMG, p. 111.
94. AL, "Grass, Brush, Timber, and Fire in Southern Arizona," RMG, p. 114.
95. AL, "Some Fundamentals of Conservation in the Southwest," RMG, p. 89.
96. Ibid., pp. 89–90.
97. AL, "Inspection Report: Prescott NF 1922."
98. Ibid.
99. Ibid., handwritten notes; no page number.
100. Ibid. See also AL, "Standards of Conservation," RMG, p. 83.
101. AL, "Standards of Conservation," RMG, p. 83.
102. Ibid.
103. AL, "Plea for Recognition," p. 268.
104. AL, *Watershed Handbook*, December 1923, p. 8.
105. AL, "Tonto Inspection Report," LP 10-11, 3; AL, "Grass, Brush, Timber,

and Fire in Southern Arizona," RMG, p. 115. These types characterized the greater parts of the Prescott, Tonto, Coronado, and Crook national forests, as well as much range outside the public lands.

106. Leopold's discussion of this process in his "Grass, Brush, Timber, and Fire in Southern Arizona" (RMG) included the use of terms popularized by the well-known plant ecologist Frederic Clements, who was famous for his work on vegetational succession. The woodland type was, in Clements' terminology, the "climax type." For a similar discussion of the Southwest's ecological grazing and erosion story, see also A. Leopold, J. S. Ligon, and R. F. Pettit, "Southwestern Game Fields," first draft of chap. 2, "The Virgin Southwest and What White Man Has Done to It," pp. 18–20, unpublished draft, 1927–1929, 10 April 1927, LP 10-6, 10.

107. At the same time that Leopold was piecing together the part fire played in the erosion story of the Southwest—that is, that fire had kept brush and trees from encroaching on grass and that grass was a better conserver of soil than trees in the watersheds of the region—he wrote an article titled "Wild Followers of the Forest: The Effect of Forest Fires on Game and Fish—the Relation of Forests to Game Conservation," which appeared in the September 1923 issue of *American Forestry*. Fire suppression was an internal mandate and unquestioned principle of the Forest Service, perhaps an importation from German forestry to American forestry. Leopold himself wrote in 1923 about the destruction fires caused not only to trees but also to wild animals: "[F]ire," he wrote, "is the enemy of the wild"—in the forest, prairie, and on the farm—though his understanding would change. See AL, "The Virgin Southwest," RMG, pp. 173–180. Game scientist Herbert Stoddard, a strong influence on Leopold, discussed the importance of fire in game systems in *The Bobwhite Quail: Its Habits, Preservation, and Increase* (New York: Charles Scribner's Sons, 1931), pp. 401–414. See also AL, "Conservationist in Mexico," p. 240; various 1939 *Wisconsin Agriculturalist and Farmer* articles by AL, FHL, pp. 105–157; and Susan Flader, *Thinking Like a Mountain*.

108. AL, "Grass, Brush, Timber, and Fire in Southern Arizona," RMG, p. 118.

109. It had become clear to Leopold by this time, however, that using grazing to control brush fire hazard was virtually impossible; to try to do so was to ignore "the plain story written on the face of Nature" (AL, "Grass, Brush, Timber, and Fire in Southern Arizona," RMG, p. 118). The brush consisted of numerous species of varied palatability. Grazing the brush, as a number of foresters suggested, was a prescription dangerous to the land. It would merely result in unpalatable species gaining ground while the fire and erosion hazards remained.

110. AL, "Standards of Conservation," RMG, pp. 82–85.

111. J. Baird Callicott proposes that it was never finished because Leopold realized that his own argument implied grazing, which was causing erosion problems in the first place. See Callicott, "Standards of Conservation: Then and Now," pp. 230–231. See also S. L. Flader, "Aldo Leopold and the Evolution of Ecosystem Management," in *Sustainable Ecological Systems: Implementing an Ecological Approach to Land Management*, edited by W. W. Covington and L. F. DeBano (Fort Collins, CO: U.S. Department of

Agriculture, Forest Service, Rocky Mountain Forest and Range Experiment Station, 1993), pp. 15–19.

112. AL, "Standards of Conservation," RMG, p. 82.

113. Ibid., p. 83.

114. AL, *Watershed Handbook*, December 1923, p. 3.

115. AL, "Standards of Conservation," RMG, pp. 83–84.

116. Unsigned letter to AL, 17 April 1923, p. 1, LP 10-6, 17.

117. Years later, in 1935, Leopold would diagram the dynamics of the natural erosion cycle in the Southwest, showing in more detail a possible mechanism for erosion related to grazing pressure. His theory was strongly criticized by Kirk Bryan, a prominent geologist and Harvard University professor. Of importance to Leopold as a land manager were human-related problems in human time and spatial scales. Different scalar perspectives may have had something to do with the differences between the ideas of Leopold and Bryan, though Bryan did find evidence of trends in meteorologic conditions more conducive to erosion at the same time that grazing was promoting erosion. See K. Bryan, "Date of Channel Trenching (Arroyo Cutting) in the Arid Southwest," *Science* 62 (1925): 228–344, and K. Bryan, "Change in Plant Associations by Change in Ground Water Level," *Ecology* 9 (1928): 474–478. Luna Leopold's work supported some of Bryan's evidence. Luna, who studied under Brian, found that fewer small rains and more frequent large rains, which were conducive to weak vegetal cover and greater incidence of erosion, occurred in the mid- to late nineteenth century in the Southwest: "Thus there is established concrete evidence of a climatic factor operating at the time of initiation of Southwestern erosion which no doubt helped to promote the initiation of that erosion." See L. Leopold, "Rainfall Frequency: An Aspect of Climatic Variation," *Transactions of the American Geophysical Union* 32, no. 3 (1951): 347–357. Luna continued to study the subject even into his later years (personal communication, 19 August 2005). See L. Leopold, "Geomorphology: A Sliver off the Corpus of Science," *Annual Review of Earth and Planetary Sciences* 32 (2004): 1–12.

118. AL, "Standards of Conservation," RMG, p. 89; AL, *Watershed Handbook*, December 1923, p. 5.

119. AL, *Watershed Handbook*, December 1923, pp. 4–5.

120. Ibid., p. 4.

121. Ibid.

122. Ibid.

123. Ibid.

124. AL, "Erosion as a Menace," p. 630.

125. AL, *Watershed Handbook*, December 1923, p. 5.

126. AL, "A Plea for Artificial Works," p. 271; AL, *Watershed Handbook*, December 1923, p. 10.

127. AL, "Erosion as a Menace," p. 630. The "balance of nature" Leopold recognized in "Some Fundamentals of Conservation in the Southwest" (RMG, p. 91) "compresses into three words an enormously complex chain of phenomena." He associated the complex idea with that of "stability," by which he meant the ability of the land to resist or withstand human abuse. Stable

land was, in this sense, land that could tolerate intensive human use without becoming fundamentally deranged.

128. AL, "Erosion as a Menace," p. 631. In 1905 President Theodore Roosevelt, at a meeting of the American Forestry Association, reportedly declared, in a thunder of emotion, "I am against the man who skins the land." Greeley, *Forests and Men*, p. 64. In 1910 Roosevelt declared: "That farmer is a poor creature who skins the land and leaves it worthless to his children. The farmer is a good farmer who, having enabled the land to support himself and to provide for the education of his children leaves it to them a little better than he found it himself. I believe the same thing of a nation." T. Roosevelt, "The New Nationalism," 1910 campaign speech, http://www.edheritage. org/1910/pridocs/1910roosevelt.htm (accessed 18 February 2006).

129. AL, *Watershed Handbook*, December 1923, p. 27.

130. Ibid.

131. AL, "Skill in Forestry," LP, 10–6, 16.

132. Ibid., p. 1.

133. Ibid., p. 2.

134. Ibid., p. 3. Leopold in this draft makes an interesting self-disclosure: "The writer," he commented, "who has made some pretense at helping to develop the science of wild life management, is keenly aware of an entire absence of 'natural skill' in dealing with game animals. What he may know in this field must always be a forced knowledge that can never get more than about so far or so deep. The point is that 'natural skill' seems to occur in very small pieces, of which no man ever has very many, and usually only one. Many men are successful and useful foresters without possessing natural skill in anything relating to natural objects. Such men may, however, possess the conservation viewpoint and such organizing ability that their lack of natural skill is offset by their ability to use that possessed by others. I incline to believe that some of the big work in forestry has been done by such men" (p. 4).

135. AL, "Some Fundamentals of Conservation in the Southwest," RMG, p. 88.

136. Ibid., p. 91.

137. Ibid., p. 94.

138. AL, "The Forestry of the Prophets," *Journal of Forestry* 18, no. 4 (April 1920): 412–419; also in RMG, pp. 71–77 (74). The biblical passage is Ezekiel 34:18–19.

139. AL, "Some Fundamentals of Conservation in the Southwest," RMG, p. 94.

140. P. D. Ouspensky, *Tertium Organum: The Third Canon of Thought; a Key to the Enigmas of the World*, revised translation by E. Kadloubovsky and the author (New York: Alfred A. Knopf, 1981).

141. AL, "Some Fundamentals of Conservation in the Southwest," RMG, p. 94.

142. Ibid., p. 95.

143. Ibid.

144. Ibid.

145. Ibid.

146. Ibid.

147. Ibid., p. 96.

148. Ibid., p. 94.

Chapter 3: The Middle Border

1. W. Wilson, "The Farmers' Patriotism," 31 January 1918, in *Selected Addresses and Public Papers of Woodrow Wilson*, edited by A. B. Hart (New York: Boni and Liveright, 1918), p. 254.

2. U.S. Department of Commerce, Bureau of Foreign and Domestic Commerce, *Statistical Abstract of the United States: 1920* (Washington, DC: Government Printing Office, 1921), pp. 146–180; U.S. Department of Commerce, Bureau of Foreign and Domestic Commerce, *Statistical Abstract of the United States: 1930* (Washington, DC: Government Printing Office, 1930), pp. 675–730. In 1875 close to 58 million acres were planted in wheat and corn, the two top staple crops. That figure had jumped to nearly 158 million acres by 1915 and 168 million by 1921, dropping back down a bit by 1929 to around 159 million. Farmers were not merely plowing more land but were pushing it for productivity, too. In 1914 land was producing on average 16.6 bushels per acre of wheat and 25.8 bushels per acre of corn. By 1920 productivity had risen to 18.8 and 30.9 bushels for wheat and corn, respectively. By 1929 productivity had dropped to near or below 1914 levels, at 13.2 bushels per acre of wheat and 26.8 for corn.

3. In D. Brinkley, *Wheels for the World: Henry Ford, His Company, and a Century of Progress* (New York: Viking Penguin, 2003), p. 264.

4. U.S. Department of Commerce, Bureau of Foreign and Domestic Commerce, *Statistical Abstract of the United States: 1921* (Washington, DC: Government Printing Office, 1922), p. 142.

5. Ibid., p. 53.

6. Ibid., p. 349.

7. Ibid., p. 103.

8. Quoted in W. E. Leuchtenburg, *The Perils of Prosperity, 1914–1932* (Chicago: University of Chicago Press, 1993), p. 6.

9. J. Reed, "Almost Thirty," in "Fortieth Anniversary Issue: 1914–1954," *New Republic* (22 November 1954): 34. Originally published in the issues of 15 and 29 April 1936.

10. H. D. Croly, *The Promise of American Life*, edited by A. M. Schlesinger Jr. (Cambridge, MA: Harvard University Press, Belknap Press, 1965), pp. 3, 6. The war raised questions about how much control people had whether they planned or not.

11. Quoted in Leuchtenburg, *Perils of Prosperity*, p. 268.

12. Ibid., p. 143.

13. Quoted in Brinkley, *Wheels for the World*, p. 376.

14. AL, "A Criticism of the Booster Spirit," RMG, p. 105.

15. AL, "The Popular Wilderness Fallacy: An Idea That Is Fast Exploding," RMG, pp. 49–50.

16. Ibid., p. 49.

17. Ibid., p. 52.

18. J. F. Reiger, *American Sportsmen and the Origins of Conservation* (New York: Winchester Press, 1975), pp. 44, 53.

19. "The Fate of Our Waterfowl," *The Pine Cone: Official Bulletin of the Albuquerque Game Protective Association* (Christmas 1915), LP 10-6, 1.

20. AL, "The Popular Wilderness Fallacy: An Idea That Is Fast Exploding," RMG, pp. 49–50.
21. C. D. Meine, *Aldo Leopold: His Life and Work* (Madison: University of Wisconsin Press, 1988), pp. 19–20.
22. Ibid., p. 37.
23. AL, letter to Clara Leopold, 21 March 1904, LP 10-8, 4. See also ibid., p. 38.
24. Quoted in S. Flader, *Thinking Like a Mountain: Aldo Leopold and the Evolution of an Ecological Attitude toward Deer, Wolves, and Forests* (Madison: University of Wisconsin Press, 1994), p. 13. (From "For the 1908S. Class Record, Yale University," holograph, ca. 1916, 5 pp., Aldo Leopold folder, Sheffield Scientific School, Yale University.)
25. Quoted in Meine, *Aldo Leopold*, p. 158. T. Roosevelt, letter to AL, 18 January 1917, copy in LP 10-8, 2.
26. AL, "Address before the Albuquerque Rotary Club on Presentation of the Gold Medal of the Permanent Wild Life Protection Fund," 1–2 July 1917, LP 10-8, 8.
27. AL, "Forestry and Game Conservation," *Journal of Forestry* 16 (April 1918): 404–411; also in ALSW, p. 83.
28. AL, "Wild Lifers vs. Game Farmers: A Plea for Democracy in Sport," *The Pine Cone: Official Bulletin of the Albuquerque Game Protective Association* 8, no. 2 (April 1919): 6–7; also in RMG, pp. 62–67 and ALSW, pp. 54–62.
29. AL, "Wild Lifers vs. Game Farmers: A Plea for Democracy in Sport," ALSW, p. 56.
30. Ibid., p. 57.
31. W. T. Hornaday, *Thirty Years War for Wild Life* (New York: Charles Scribner's Sons, 1931), p. 3. According to Hornaday, there were 1,486,228 licensed hunters in 1911; 4,495,007 in 1922; and 6,493,454 in 1929.
32. Meine, *Aldo Leopold*, p. 149.
33. W. T. Hornaday, *Wild Life Conservation in Theory and Practice: Lectures Delivered before the Forest School of Yale University* (New Haven, CT: Yale University Press, 1914), pp. 2–3.
34. W. T. Hornaday, "The Seamy Side of the Protection of Wild Game," *New York Times*, 8 March 1914, p. SM3 (ProQuest Historical Newspapers, *The New York Times*, 1857–current file).
35. Hornaday, *Wild Life Conservation*, pp. 40–43; W. T. Hornaday, *Our Vanishing Wild Life: Its Extermination and Preservation* (New York: New York Zoological Society, 1913), p. 267.
36. Hornaday, *Wild Life Conservation*, p. 179.
37. W. T. Hornaday, *The Extermination of the American Bison* (Washington, DC: Smithsonian Institution Press, 1889, 2002), pp. 492–498.
38. G. J. Dehler, "An American Crusader: William Temple Hornaday and Wildlife Protection in America: 1840–1940," PhD diss., Lehigh University, 2001, p. 66.
39. One professional market hunter, who kept exceptionally good records over his forty years of late nineteenth-century business, had killed 6,250 game birds in a three-month's shoot in Iowa and Minnesota and 4,450 ducks in one winter's hunting in the South. His forty-year total was 139,628 game birds

representing twenty-nine species. Highlights included 61,752 ducks, 5,291 prairie chickens, 8,117 blackbirds, 5,291 quail, 5,066 snipe, and 4,948 plovers. The first state to ban market hunting was New York, which in 1911 led the way to reform with the Bayne law, which Hornaday helped push through. See Hornaday, *Wild Life Conservation*, pp. 32–33.

40. Hornaday, *Vanishing Wild Life*.
41. Meine, *Aldo Leopold*, p. 128.
42. Along with Hornaday's later *Wild Life Conservation in Theory and Practice*, GPA members were urged to buy discounted copies for themselves and as Christmas gifts for their friends. "A Christmas Suggestion," *The Pine Cone: Official Bulletin of the Albuquerque Game Protective Association* (Christmas 1915), LP 10-6, 1.
43. Hornaday, *Vanishing Wild Life*, p. x.
44. Ibid., p. 2.
45. O. E. Rölvaag, *Giants in the Earth* (New York: Harper and Brothers, 1929).
46. Ibid., p. 112.
47. AL, personal journal, pp. 72–73, LP 10-7, 1 (15).
48. AL, "Address before the Albuquerque Rotary Club," p. 6.
49. AL, "Game Conservation: A Warning, Also an Opportunity," ALSW, p. 20.
50. Leopold's hope was to encourage all forest officers to keep good game records. He also kept records of prosecutions for the breaking of game laws initiated by forest officers and of fish requisitions throughout his district. AL, *Game and Fish Handbook* (Albuquerque, NM: U.S. Department of Agriculture, Forest Service, District 3, 15 September 1915), UWDWE.
51. C. Richter, *The Trees* (New York: Alfred A. Knopf, 1940), p. 3.
52. H. Garland, ed., *A Son of the Middle Border* (New York: Penguin Books, 1995).
53. Ibid., p. 117.
54. Hornaday, *Vanishing Wild Life*, pp. 10–16.
55. Ibid., p. 7.
56. Ibid., p. 8.
57. Ibid., p. 393.
58. From AL, *Game and Fish Handbook*, p. 9, UWDWE. Chap. 3 of Hornaday's *Vanishing Wild Life* is titled "The Next Candidates for Oblivion."
59. Hornaday, *Vanishing Wild Life*, p. x.
60. Meine, *Aldo Leopold*, p. 260.
61. Ibid., p. 154; Flader, *Thinking Like a Mountain*, p. 61. Refuge legislation failed repeatedly, though Congress did establish a number of large game sanctuaries, among them the Grand Canyon National Game Preserve in 1906, which included the Kaibab Plateau. In any event, Leopold forged ahead in planning a refuge system for his own forest district. To his dismay, after the failure of the Chamberlain-Hayden Bill, which incorporated the "Hornaday Plan," Arizona established several large state sanctuaries on national forest lands. Hunting was restricted on some entire mountain ranges there, including on the Blue Range—his old stomping grounds. Flader, *Thinking Like a Mountain*, p. 63.
62. Meine, *Aldo Leopold*, p. 154. AL, "Wanted—National Forest Game Ref-

uges," *The Pine Cone: Official Bulletin of the Albuquerque Game Protective Association* 9, no. 1 (1920): 8–10, 22.

63. AL, "The Essentials of the Game Refuge," *Literary Digest* (15 January 1921): 14, LP 10-6, 1.

64. AL, "Stinking Lake," *The Pine Cone: Official Bulletin of the Albuquerque Game Protective Association* (Christmas 1915): 1, LP 10-6, 1.

65. AL, "The Why and How of Game Refuges" (cartoon), *The Pine Cone: Official Bulletin of the Albuquerque Game Protective Association* (July 1920), LP 10-6, 1.

66. AL, "The National Forests: The Last Free Hunting Grounds of the Nation," *Journal of Forestry* 17, no. 2 (1919).

67. AL, "Forestry and Game Conservation," pp. 404–411; also in RMG, pp. 53–59.

68. RMG, p. 54.

69. Ibid.

70. Ibid.

71. Ibid.

72. Ibid., p. 55.

73. Ibid., p. 56.

74. AL, "Determining the Kill Factor for Blacktail Deer in the Southwest," *Journal of Forestry* 18, no. 2 (February 1920): 131–134; also in ALSW, pp. 87–91.

75. Meine, *Aldo Leopold*, p. 224.

76. A. Leopold, J. S. Ligon, and R. F. Pettit, "Southwestern Game Fields," unpublished draft, 1927–1929, LP 10-6, 10.

77. Ibid., chap. 1, 5 May 1927, p. 46.

78. Ibid., chap. 2, 10 April 1927, p. 28.

79. Ibid., chap. 3, n.d., p. 4. The authors' intent was to include sections on a number of game species. The ambitious nature of this project may have been one reason why it was never completed.

80. Ibid., p. 9.

81. Ibid., pp. 9–10.

82. Ibid., p. 10. In his 1933 *Game Management* (New York: Charles Scribner's Sons), p. 388, Leopold put the process of conservation science this way: "To see merely what a range is or has is to see nothing. To see *why* it is, how it *became*, and the direction and velocity of its changes—this is the great drama of the land, to which 'educated' people too often turn an unseeing eye and a deaf ear. The stumps in a woodlot, the species age and form of fencerow trees, the plow-furrows in a reverted field, the location and age of an old orchard, the height of the bank of an irrigation ditch, the age of the trees or bushes in a gully, the fire scars on a sawlog—these and a thousand other roadside objects spell out words of history . . . of the recent past and the trend of the immediate future."

83. Leopold, Ligon, and Pettit addressed this issue in "Southwestern Game Fields," chap. 4, "Normal Deer Stocking and Productivity," n.d.

84. Ibid., p. 1.

85. Ibid.

86. Ibid., chap. 1, p. 15.
87. Ibid., pp. 15–16.
88. Ibid., chap. 4, p. 2.
89. Ibid.
90. Ibid., p. 3.
91. Ibid., chap. 5, n.d., p. 11.
92. Ibid., chap. 8, n.d. (signed "by Ligon"), p. 1.
93. Greeley had offered Leopold a position at the Forest Products Laboratory three years earlier, in 1921, and Leopold had then turned it down. See Meine, *Aldo Leopold*, p. 191.
94. W. B. Greeley, *Forests and Men* (Garden City, NY: Doubleday, 1951), pp. 144–145; Greeley, letter to Frank Pooler, 18 March 1924, in Meine, *Aldo Leopold*, p. 225.
95. Meine, *Aldo Leopold*, p. 225.
96. Ibid.
97. The Forest Products Laboratory experimented with different preservative solutions for railroad ties.
98. F. J. Turner, "The Problem of the West," *Atlantic Monthly* 78, no. 467 (1896): 296–297.
99. Garland, *A Son of the Middle Border*, p. 355.
100. W. T. Hornaday, "Hunters Menace All Birds," *New York Times*, 29 March 1925, p. XX11.
101. G. Bennett, "Our Game Protectors at War," *New York Times*, 18 October 1925, p. X14.
102. AL, "The Varmint Question," RMG, p. 47.
103. AL, "The Popular Wilderness Fallacy: An Idea That Is Fast Exploding," RMG, p. 49.
104. AL, "Forestry and Game Conservation," RMG, p. 53.
105. AL, "'Piute Forestry' vs. Forest Fire Prevention," RMG, p. 68.
106. AL, "Wild Followers of the Forest: The Effect of Forest Fires on Game and Fish—the Relation of Forests to Game Conservation," *American Forestry* (September 1923): 518.
107. Ibid., p. 568.
108. Ibid.
109. Ibid.; see also AL, "A Criticism of the Booster Spirit," RMG, p. 103.
110. Leuchtenburg, *Perils of Prosperity*, p. 188.
111. D. P. Thelen, *Robert La Follette and the Insurgent Spirit* (Boston: Little, Brown, 1976), p. 181.
112. Meine, *Aldo Leopold*, p. 239.
113. Thelen, *La Follette and the Insurgent Spirit*, p. 81.
114. AL, "The Posting Problem," *Outdoor Life* 49, no. 3 (March 1922): 187.
115. AL, "Natural Reproduction of Forests," *Parks and Recreation* 9, no. 2 (1925): 366–372; AL, "The Utilization Conference," *Journal of Forestry* 23, no. 1 (1925): 98–100; AL, "Wastes in Forest Utilization—What Can Be Done to Prevent Them," address abstracted in *Southern Lumberman* 121 (1925): 1574; AL, "Short Lengths for Farm Buildings," *United States Forest Products Laboratory Report* (8 November 1926); AL, "Wood Preservation and

Forestry," *Railway Engineering and Maintenance* 22, no. 2 (1926): 60–61, and a shorter version in *Railway Age* 80, no. 5 (1926): 346; AL, "Forest Products Research and Profitable Forestry," *Journal of Forestry* 25, no. 5 (1927): 524–548 (in this article Leopold complained that "President Coolidge's famous aphorism: 'Reduce wood waste—a tree saved is a tree grown,'" missed important facets of promising research objectives); AL, "The Home Builder Conserves," *American Forests and Forest Life* 34, no. 413 (1928): 267–278, 297, also in RMG, pp. 143–147; AL, "Glues for Wood in Archery," *United States Forest Products Laboratory Technical Note*, no. 226 (1929): 4; AL, "Some Thoughts on Forest Genetics," *Journal of Forestry* 27, no. 6 (1929): 708–713.

116. Meine, *Aldo Leopold*, p. 256.

117. Ibid., p. 261.

118. Anonymous, "Forestry Worker Retires," *New York Times*, 8 July 1928, p. 38 (ProQuest Historical Newspapers, *The New York Times*, 1857–current file).

119. AL, "Game Survey, Report No. 1, Covering Preliminary Trip, June 4–5, 1928," LP 10-6, 11. See Meine, *Aldo Leopold*, pp. 261–262.

120. Hornaday, "Hunters Menace All Birds"; W. T. Hornaday, "Game Protection," letter to the editor, *New York Times*, 18 December 1927, p. E5 (ProQuest Historical Newspapers, *The New York Times*, 1857–current file).

121. Meine, *Aldo Leopold*, pp. 262, 279.

122. AL, "Fires and Game," *Journal of Forestry* 24, no. 6 (1926): 727.

123. AL, "Quail Production: A Remedy for the 'Song Bird List,'" *Outdoor America* 3, no. 4 (1924): 42; AL, "Posting Problem," p. 187; AL, "Report of the Quail Committee," ALSW; *The Pine Cone: Official Bulletin of the Albuquerque Game Protective Association* (March 1924).

124. *Transactions of the 15th National Game Conference* (3–4 December 1928), pp. 128–132. The report was later reprinted in *American Game* 18 (April–May 1929): 45–47.

125. Ibid., p. 129.

126. Meine, *Aldo Leopold*, p. 265.

127. AL, "Progress of the Game Survey," *Transactions of the 16th American Game Conference* (2–3 December 1929), pp. 64–71; see Meine, *Aldo Leopold*, p. 266.

128. AL, "Progress of the Game Survey," p. 64.

129. Ibid., p. 65. Earlier writings by Leopold had already connected overgrazing with game losses. AL, "Report of the Quail Committee," ALSW, p. 109; AL, "Pineries and Deer on the Gila," *New Mexico Conservationist* (March 1928), p. 3.

130. AL, "Progress of the Game Survey," p. 69; AL et al., "Report to the American Game Conference on an American Game Policy," *Transactions of the 17th American Game Conference* (1–2 December 1930): 303, also in RMG, pp. 150–155. Leopold believed similarly in terms of a preference for native fish species. See AL, "Mixing Trout in Western Waters," Transactions of the American Fisheries Society 47 No. 3 (June 1918), pp. 101–102.

131. AL, "Environmental Controls: The Forester's Contribution to Game Conservation," *The Ames Forester* 17 (1929): 25–26.

132. AL, "Progress of the Game Survey," pp. 64–65.

133. AL et al., "Report to the American Game Conference," pp. 284–309.

134. AL, "The American Game Policy in a Nutshell," *Transactions of the 17th American Game Conference* (1–2 December 1930): 281–282.

135. Editor, "American Game Policy, Discussion," *Transactions of the 17th American Game Conference* (1–2 December 1930): 143–145.

136. Meine, *Aldo Leopold*, p. 278. See D. Allen et al., "Report on the Committee on North American Wildlife Policy," *Transactions of the 38th North American Wildlife and Natural Resources Conference*, 18–21 March 1973, Washington, DC.

137. AL et al., "Report to the American Game Conference," p. 288.

138. Ibid., pp. 143–145; pp. 288–289.

139. AL, "American Game Policy in a Nutshell," p. 281.

140. AL, *Report on a Game Survey of the North Central States* (Madison, WI: Democrat Printing Company for the Sporting Arms and Ammunition Manufacturers' Institute, 1931). Made available by the American Game Association for one dollar.

141. AL, "A History of Ideas in Game Management," *Outdoor America* 9, no. 9 (April 1931): 22–24, 38–39, 47.

142. Through 1931 Leopold submitted *Game Management* to various publishers, who were reluctant to take on the manuscript because of the hard economic times. Finally, in December 1931, Charles Scribner's Sons offered to publish it if Leopold would help reduce costs and contribute $500 himself. Leopold signed to their terms on 11 January 1932—his forty-fifth birthday. Meine, *Aldo Leopold*, p. 285.

143. AL, "American Game Policy in a Nutshell," p. 283.

144. AL, *Report on a Game Survey*, p. 5. In 1930, 986,771,000 acres of U.S. land area, or 51.8 percent of the country's 1,903,217,000 acres of land area, was in farms. *Statistical Abstract: 1940*, p. 634.

145. AL, "Progress of the Game Survey," p. 65; AL et al., "Report to the American Game Conference," p. 284.

146. AL, "The River of the Mother of God," RMG, p. 125.

147. AL et al., "Report to the American Game Conference," p. 284; also in RMG, p. 150.

148. AL, *Report on a Game Survey*, p. 268.

Chapter 4: Interpreting Pharaoh's Dream

1. W. E. Leuchtenburg, *The Perils of Prosperity: 1914–1932* (Chicago: University of Chicago Press, 1993), p. 252.

2. J. Hjort, "Whales and Whaling," in Anonymous, *Matamek Conference on Biological Cycles: Full Proceedings* (Matamek Factory, Canadian Labrador, 1932), together with E. Huntington, *Matamek Conference on Biological Cycles: Report by Ellsworth Huntington, Yale University* (Matamek Factory, Canadian Labrador, 1932), p. 112.

3. C. Amory, "Inaugural Meeting," in Anonymous, *Full Proceedings*, pp. 8, 10.

4. Ibid., p. 11.

5. Huntington, *Report*, p. 4.

6. Ibid.
7. E. Huntington, "The Matamek Conference on Biological Cycles, 1931," *Science* 74, no. 1914 (1931): 229–235.
8. Anonymous, *New York Times*, 13 August 1931, p. 4N.
9. Anonymous, *American Weekly*, 1 November 1931, p. 5.
10. Anonymous, *Full Proceedings*, p. 139.
11. R. G. Green, "Tularemia: A Disease of Wild Life," discussion, in Anonymous, *Full Proceedings*, pp. 57–72.
12. R. DeLury, "Astronomical Periods," discussion, in Anonymous, *Full Proceedings*, pp. 207–225.
13. Green, "Tularemia," p. 65.
14. C. Elton, "Cycles in the Fur Trade of Canada," discussion, in Anonymous, *Full Proceedings*, p. 83.
15. P. Crowcraft, *Elton's Ecologists: A History of the Bureau of Animal Population* (Chicago: University of Chicago Press, 1991).
16. C. Elton, "Cycles in the Fur Trade of Canada," in Anonymous, *Full Proceedings*, p. 76.
17. E. Huntington, comment, in Anonymous, *Full Proceedings*, p. 149.
18. R. G. Green, comment, in Anonymous, *Full Proceedings*, p. 22.
19. AL, comment, in Anonymous, *Full Proceedings*, p. 25. Leopold gave a talk at Matamek titled "Grouse Cycles and Conservation," published in Anonymous, *Full Proceedings*, pp. 50–56.
20. AL and J. N. Ball, "The Quail Shortage of 1930," *Outdoor America* 9, no. 9 (April 1931): 14–15, 67; AL and J. N. Ball, "Grouse in England," *American Game* 20, no. 4 (July–August 1931): 57–58, 63.
21. AL, letter to John Olin, 4 May 1931, LP 10-2, 4.
22. John Olin, letter to AL, 7 May 1931, LP 10-2, 4.
23. AL, letter to John Olin, 9 May 1931, LP 10-2, 4.
24. AL, letter to John Olin, 8 August 1931, LP 10-2, 4.
25. Ibid.
26. Ibid.
27. AL, letter to Copley Amory, 6 August 1934, LP 10-2, 4.
28. AL, letter to Copley Amory, 3 October 1934, LP 10-2, 4.
29. AL, letter to Ellsworth Huntington, 15 March 1943, LP 10-2, 4. Leopold eventually signed off on this paper, which Paul Errington and graduate students eventually published in pieces.
30. AL, "Deer, Wolves, Foxes, and Pheasants," *Wisconsin Conservation Bulletin* 10, no. 4 (April 1945): p. 5. Also see AL, "Round-Table Discussion: Game and Fur Population Mechanisms" (31 December 1947), prepared for ESA symposium, p. 5 ("Clues to Mechanisms" section), LP 10-2, 2 (12).
31. Through May, the state of Iowa also paid him a consulting fee to do a new survey of that state. AL, letter to Charles Elton, 5 January 1932, LP 10-3, 10.
32. C. D. Meine, *Aldo Leopold: His Life and Work* (Madison: University of Wisconsin Press, 1988), pp. 288–292.
33. Quoted in W. E. Leuchtenburg, *Franklin D. Roosevelt and the New Deal, 1932–1940* (New York: Harper and Row, 1963), p. 18.
34. F. D. Roosevelt, nomination address at the Democratic National Convention

in Chicago, 2 July 1932, http://newdeal.feri.org/speeches/1932b.htm (accessed 31 December 2005).

35. Ibid.

36. Meine, *Aldo Leopold*, p. 306. See AL, "Vegetation for Erosion Control in the CCC Camps of Southwestern Wisconsin," pp. 1–10, LP 10-6, 16.

37. AL, letter to William T. Hornaday, 1 March 1933, LP 10-6, 4. See also Meine, *Aldo Leopold*, p. 301.

38. Anonymous, "Book Notes," *New York Times*, 28 April 1933, p. 20 (ProQuest Historical Newspapers, *The New York Times*, 1837–current file).

39. Anonymous, "Wisconsin to Aid in Raising Game," *New York Times*, 27 August 1933, p. E6 (ProQuest Historical Newspapers, *The New York Times*, 1837–current file).

40. William T. Hornaday, letter to AL, 17 August 1922, LP 10-8, 9; see Meine, *Aldo Leopold*, p. 307.

41. Leuchtenburg, *Roosevelt and the New Deal*, p. 23.

42. Ibid.

43. Ibid.

44. Ibid., p. 34.

45. Ibid., p. 35.

46. AL, "Game Restoration by Cooperation on Wisconsin Farms: Where Farmers and Sportsmen Plan Together," *Wisconsin Agriculturalist and Farmer* 59, no. 16 (18 April 1931): 5, 16.

47. AL, "How Research and Game Surveys Help the Sportsman and Farmer," *Proceedings New England Game Conference* (Cambridge: Samuel Marcus Press, for the Massachusetts Fish and Game Association, 11 February 1933), p. 54.

48. J. Burroughs, "Hit-and-Miss Method of Nature," *Summit of the Years* (New York: William H. Wise, 1924), p. 86. See AL, "Ecology and Politics," RMG, p. 281.

49. AL, "Science Attacks the Game Cycle," *Outdoor America* 10, no. 2 (September 1931): 25.

50. Ibid.

51. Several studies around this time proposed that even "wars and periods of war activity may have a rhythmic periodicity in the affairs of men." See E. R. Dewey and E. F. Dakin, *Cycles: The Science of Prediction* (New York: Henry Holt, 1947), p. 200.

52. See T. Malthus, *Parallel Chapters from the First and Second Editions of "An Essay on the Principle of Population," by T. R. Malthus: 1798; 1803* (New York: Macmillan, 1895). "It is an obvious truth, which has been taken notice of by many writers, that population must always be kept down to the level of the means of subsistence; but no writer that the Author recollects, has inquired particularly into the means by which this level is effected: and it is a view of these means, which forms, to his mind, the strongest obstacle in the way to any very great future improvement of society," Malthus wrote (1798, p. xii). "Population, when unchecked," he posited, "increases in a geometrical ratio. Subsistence only increases in an arithmetical ratio" (1798, p. 7). Malthus' reasoning provided a competitive, struggle-for-existence rationale

upon which Darwin's theory of evolution by natural selection drew and set the stage for future population and demographic studies on human and non-human species.

53. A. Leopold, J. S. Ligon, and R. F. Pettit, "Southwestern Game Fields," chap. 3, "Breeding Habits of Deer," and chap. 4, "Decimating Factors and Their Control," unpublished draft, 1927–1929, LP 10-6, 10.

54. AL, *Watershed Handbook* (Albuquerque: U.S. Department of Agriculture, Forest Service, District 3, December 1923 [revised and reissued October 1934]), LP 10-11, 1.

55. The idea that there were limiting or controlling factors on population numbers was not a new one. See C. Darwin, *The Origin of Species* (London: John Murray, 1872; London: Guernsey Press, 1995), p. 53. Darwin acknowledged the subject of checks on reproductive increase as among the most obscure and complex subjects and discussed the idea at greater length in his chapter "Struggle for Existence." H. Spencer, *The Principles of Biology*, vol. 1 (New York: D. Appleton, 1896), pp. 411–431. Spencer discussed external factors (astronomic, geologic, meteorologic, and organic) and internal factors (including molecular, mechanical, and physiological) that influence the functions of organisms. See V. Shelford, "Physiological Animal Geography," *Journal of Morphology* 22 (1911): 551–618, and V. Shelford, *Animal Communities in Temperate America* (Chicago: University of Chicago Press, 1913)—Shelford included a section on the importance of environmental factors (climate, geology, vegetation, topography, etc.) in the control of animals and elaborated on German chemist Justin von Liebig's "law" that the rate of any process is limited by the least or slowest factor affecting it. See also C. Elton, *Animal Ecology* (London: Sidgwick and Johnson, 1927; Chicago: University of Chicago Press, 2001), pp. 33–49, 118–120. Elton discussed the environmental factors that limit species to particular habitats, influence animal numbers, and are involved in community organization. H. L. Stoddard, in *Report on Cooperative Quail Investigation: 1925–1926: With Preliminary Recommendations for the Development of Quail Preserves*, U.S. Department of Agriculture, Biological Survey, Division of Food Habits Research (Washington, DC: Committee Representing the Quail Study Fund for Southern Georgia and Northern Florida, 1926), and *The Bobwhite Quail: Its Habits, Preservation, and Increase* (New York: Charles Scribner's Sons, 1931), promoted the idea of treating quail like an agricultural crop and manipulating environmental factors in their interest.

56. Leopold, Ligon, and Pettit, "Southwestern Game Fields," chap. 1 (5 May 1927), pp. 23–25, 44. Also see AL, *Game Management* (New York: Charles Scribner's Sons, 1933), pp. 26–32.

57. Leopold, Ligon, and Pettit, "Southwestern Game Fields," drafting notes, n.d., p. 26.

58. Ibid., chap. 4, "Decimating Factors and Their Control," p. 1.

59. AL, *Game Management*, p. 24. Leopold's work on wildlife populations in "Southwestern Game Fields" and *Game Management* showed the apparent influence of R. Pearl's *The Biology of Population Growth* (New York: Alfred A. Knopf, 1925). Pearl and his colleague L. J. Reed derived a mathematical

equation for the same population growth pattern they observed for a diverse array of organisms, describing its graphic form as that "which would be obtained if one first fashioned a letter S out of fairly stiff but flexible wire" and stretched it out until "the upper and lower limbs of the letter were practically straight and parallel to a horizontal base, and the curve at the middle of the S had been straightened and inclined to the right instead of the left" (p. 5). Belgian mathematician P. F. Verhulst as early as 1838 had described the same pattern in a single-species model, calling it the "logistic curve." Then, in 1925 and 1926, A. J. Lotka (who had worked with Pearl) and Italian mathematician V. Volterra independently published a similar dual-species model based on predator-prey relations, which predicted cyclic fluctuations in both populations. The Lotka-Volterra model would become increasingly important in wildlife management. E. R. Dewey and E. F. Dakin, in *Cycles: The Science of Prediction* (New York: Henry Holt, 1947), applied models of biological population growth to economics and other human institutions, such as corporations or industries, predicting trends in terms of dollars rather than individuals.

60. AL, *Game Management*, pp. 22–27, 182.

61. Ibid., p. 26, and Leopold, Ligon, and Pettit, "Southwestern Game Fields," chap. 1, p. 24. The balance-of-nature idea was no static concept to Leopold's mind, and he realized there were strengths and weaknesses of the phrase. As Charles Elton explained, the picture of a natural community living in "a certain harmony," with "regular and essentially predictable" changes taking place, which were "nicely fitted into the environmental stresses without," had the advantage of intelligibility and apparent logic but the disadvantage of being untrue. See C. Elton, *Animal Ecology and Evolution* (London: Humphrey Milford, 1930), cited in P. L. Errington and F. N. Hamerstrom, "The Northern Bob-white's Winter Territory," Research Bulletin 201 (Ames: Iowa State College of Agriculture and Mechanical Arts, Agricultural Experiment Station, 1936), p. 399. Yet, as Paul Errington and Leopold's student Frances Hamerstrom pointed out: though "'the balance of nature'" may not be everything it has been thought to be, the fact should not be overlooked that biotic equilibria of some sorts do exist" (Errington and Hamerstrom, "Northern Bob-white's Winter Territory," p. 399). Leopold would later, drawing from Elton's work, suggest another picture of nature as an alternative to the "balance of nature"—the "biotic pyramid" or the "land pyramid." See AL, "A Biotic View of Land," RMG, p. 267, and SCA, p. 214. For further discussion see chap. 6 of this book.

62. Leopold, Ligon, and Pettit, "Southwestern Game Fields," chap. 1, p. 13.

63. Ibid.

64. Stoddard, *Bobwhite Quail*, p. xxi.

65. Stoddard, *Bobwhite Quail*. Two preliminary reports also were published: H. L. Stoddard, *Progress on Cooperative Quail Investigation* (Washington, DC: Committee on the Cooperative Quail Investigation, 1925), and H. L. Stoddard, *Report on Cooperative Quail Investigation: 1925–1926: With Preliminary Recommendations for the Development of Quail Preserves*, U.S. Department of Agriculture, Biological Survey, Division of Food Habits Research (Washington, DC: Committee Representing the Quail Study Fund

for Southern Georgia and Northern Florida, 1926). Leopold also worked with, and his game management ideas were influenced by, Wallace B. Grange, the first superintendent of game for the Wisconsin Conservation Department. Stoddard, Grange, and Leopold worked together after 1928 supervising SAAMI's research fellowships. See Flader, *Thinking Like a Mountain*, p. 24, and Meine, *Aldo Leopold*, pp. 268, 286.

66. Stoddard discussed fire as a management tool, noting the effect of burning on quail food and plants. "To sum up," he wrote, "we consider fire a convenient, though not always a vitally necessary, tool for occasional use in cover control, and as a sterilizing agent on the Southern quail preserves, but recognize that it is capable of doing vastly more harm than good if not intelligently handled." Stoddard, *Bobwhite Quail*, pp. 410–411. As he learned more about fire's natural roles, from his observations on the relationships between grazing, fire, and grass in the Southwest and forward, Leopold's thinking about it shifted away from the Forest Service's maxim that fire was always an enemy of management. See also S. Flader, *Thinking Like a Mountain: Aldo Leopold and the Evolution of an Ecological Attitude toward Deer, Wolves, and Forests* (Madison: University of Wisconsin Press, 1994).

67. Anonymous, "Milwaukee Taxidermist Turned Down Snug Berth Here to Become Leading Game Management Expert in South," *Sunday Milwaukee Journal*, 9 February 1941. Stoddard's work in Georgia, the article stated, "has made history of a kind that is as important in its field as the history made by Babcock with the milk tester."

68. Stoddard recognized the importance of soil fertility to the quail crop: "It may be stated as a demonstrated fact that any area where the fertility of the soil has been exhausted to a point where it can not produce a vigorous growth of weeds and leguminous plants will not support quail in abundance even with ideal thicket cover and effective control of quail enemies. This fact must be considered when 'worn out' cotton and tobacco lands are being developed into quail preserves." Stoddard, *Bobwhite Quail*, p. 351.

69. Ibid., p. 357.

70. Ibid., pp. 339–348.

71. Ibid., pp. 226, 341–342.

72. Ibid., pp. 226, 415. The reassessment of hawks, owls, and other birds of prey during the 1920s and 1930s is recounted in M. V. Barrow Jr., "Science, Sentiment, and the Specter of Extinction," *Environmental History* 7, no. 1 (2002): 69–98. See also, Flader, *Thinking Like a Mountain* and Meine, *Aldo Leopold* for discussions of Leopold's changing ideas about top predators.

73. P. Errington, "The Northern Bobwhite: Environmental Factors Influencing Its Status," PhD diss., University of Wisconsin–Madison, 1932.

74. Ibid., p. b. For a discussion of the relations between Stoddard, Errington, and Leopold, see also T. R. Dunlap, *Saving America's Wildlife: Ecology and the American Mind, 1850–1990* (Princeton, NJ: Princeton University Press, 1988), pp. 70–74, and Flader, *Thinking Like a Mountain*, pp. 24–25.

75. Errington, "Northern Bobwhite," p. c. Leopold also cited "Stoddard and Errington jointly" as "probably responsible for the discovery of the food sequence, a concept unknown to the economic ornithologists with their composite cross-sections of stomachs gathered at diverse times and places.

The daily menu of quail in winter was found to follow a sequence representing a descending scale of palatability. Winter survival was found to be a question of how low on the scale the last blizzard came. That low-scale foods do not sustain weight and fitness was experimentally verified." Undated draft, c. 1935, of "Wild Life Research in Wisconsin," p. 4, LP 10-6, 14. Leopold and his students in Wisconsin kept up research on wildlife palatability sequences.

76. Errington, "Northern Bobwhite," p. 53.
77. Ibid., pp. 183, 198. See also P. Errington, "What Is the Meaning of Predation?" annual report of the board of regents of the Smithsonian Institution, Publication 3405 (Washington, DC: Government Printing Office, 1937).
78. Errington, "Northern Bobwhite," pp. 198–200. Errington developed two explanatory theories relating population densities and predation: the "threshold of security" and "inversity." "Threshold of security" became Errington's replacement term for "carrying capacity," a phrase he believed was so diversely used as to have lost its original meaning. A. Leopold, P. Errington, and H. Hanson, "Animal Populations at Prairie du Sac, Wisconsin, 1929–1942," 18 January 1943, corrected draft 18 February 1943, p. 15, LP 10-6, 13; P. L. Errington, "Some Contributions of a Fifteen-Year Local Study of the Northern Bobwhite to a Knowledge of Population Phenomena," *Ecological Monographs* 15, no. 1 (1945): 11. When population numbers were below the threshold, not security predator loss in winter was negligible; when above it, predators would take even strong, healthy birds until the prey population declined. "Inversity," later termed "density dependence," reflected the idea that when a population was low numerically it tended to show high rates of increase in summer, whereas reproduction declined as a population approached the threshold of security or carrying capacity. The practical implication of these ideas for quail was that their survival was best promoted by providing plenty of food and cover, particularly in winter. Leopold stressed that the mechanistic theories behind this conclusion were as good as could be had, given the known facts, but that they were merely theories. Still unsure on key points, Leopold admitted in a January 1944 letter that he did not yet grasp Errington's notion of the threshold mechanism. More research was needed, and more thinking.

Errington moved on from Wisconsin to a position at Iowa State College, but he and Leopold (along with a number of Leopold's graduate students) continued a working relationship over the years, studying possible mechanisms behind game population fluctuations at Prairie du Sac, Wisconsin, from 1929 to the early 1940s. By the mid-1940s Leopold was "neck-deep in courses," at work on what would become his final and best-known book, and having trouble communicating with Errington over geographic distance. Leopold eventually turned over to Errington authorship of the paper resulting from the Prairie du Sac population studies. AL, letter to Paul Errington, 8 January 1944, LP 10-5, 5. See also A. Leopold and P. Errington, "Limits of Summer Gain and Winter Loss in Bobwhite Populations at Prairie du Sac, Wisconsin 1929–1943," 1 December 1943 and 13 December 1943 drafts, p. 1, LP 10-5, 5; and Errington, "Some Contributions." See also C. Kabat, D. Thompson, and R. Hine, eds., "Wisconsin Quail, 1834–1962: Population Dynamics and Habitat Management," *Technical Bulletin of the*

Wisconsin Department of Natural Resources, no. 30 (Madison: Wisconsin Conservation Department, Game Management Division, 1963).

79. Close to $1,000,000 was appropriated annually in the mid-1930s for predator control. See Ecological Society of America Committee for the Study of Plant and Animal Communities, "Confidential Memorandum on Sanctuaries to Include Predatory Animals," unpublished, c. 1935, which Leopold kept in his files, LP 10-2, 2. See W. T. Hornaday, *Wild Life Conservation in Theory and Practice: Lectures Delivered before the Forest School of Yale University* (New Haven, CT: Yale University Press, 1914), p. 41; W. T. Hornaday, *Our Vanishing Wild Life: Its Extermination and Preservation* (New York: New York Zoological Society, 1913), p. 267.

80. Errington noted that between the mid-1930s and the 1940s wildlife was adjusting itself to three particular changes: soil depletion, modification of plant life, and the spread of exotic species. In the case of bobwhite quail, these changes coincided with and possibly caused a depression in carrying capacity to half that of a decade earlier. See Errington, "Northern Bobwhite," pp. 205–219, and Leopold, Errington, and Hanson, "Animal Populations," pp. 44–45.

81. Charles Elton, letter to AL, 9 September 1931, LP 10-3, 10.

82. AL, letter to Charles Elton, 12 November 1931, LP 10-3, 10.

83. Charles Elton, letter to AL, 9 October 1933, LP 10-3, 10.

84. Ibid.

85. Leopold and some of his students made studies of food habits and palatability sequences one strand of their ecological investigations; LP 10-4, 7, and 10-4, 8. See L. H. Kelso, "Food Habits of Prairie Dogs," USDA Circular 529 (Washington, DC: U.S. Department of Agriculture, 1939), and C. S. Robinson, "Observations and Notes on the California Condor from Data Collected on Los Padres National Forest" (Santa Barbara, CA: U.S. Department of Agriculture, Forest Service, 1939).

86. Elton, *Animal Ecology*, pp. 55–70, 117. The matter of organization was, of course, much more complex than any one factor. Even Malthus' fundamental ideas were subjected to reconsideration in light of these new understandings. Both Elton in *Animal Ecology* (p. 117) and Errington in "What Is the Meaning of Predation?" (p. 243) noted that animal populations rarely approached the limit of their food supplies. Often some other factor came in as a check before starvation took place. Also see W. L. McAtee, "The Malthusian Principle in Nature," *Scientific Monthly* 42 (1936): 444–456, and Errington and Hamerstrom, "Northern Bob-white's Winter Territory," p. 380: "It is quite apparent that the 'Malthusian Principle' is not the principal factor in determining animal populations in nature, although it unquestionably is not without application."

87. AL, *Game Management*, pp. 232–241.

88. Elton, *Animal Ecology*, p. 102.

89. Ibid.

90. Ibid., p. 106.

91. Ibid., pp. 107–108.

92. Ibid., pp. 110–111.

93. Ibid., p. 111.

94. Ibid., p. 112.
95. AL, *Watershed Handbook*, December 1923, p. 5.
96. AL, "Ecology of Jack Rabbits," review of C. T. Vohries and W. P. Taylor, "The Life Histories and Ecology of Jackrabbits, *Lepus alleni* and *Lepus californicus* spp., in Relation to Grazing in Arizona," *Technical Bulletin* 49 (1933): 471–583 (Tucson: University of Arizona College of Agriculture Agricultural Experiment Station).
97. Elton, *Animal Ecology*, pp. 113–114.
98. AL, "Theories of Population," unpublished, n.d., LP 10-6, 14. "Banding" wildlife was a common field experimental technique.
99. Ibid. The Elton group was "grappling with the still unexplained rhythmic oscillations of population density called cycles." The Errington-Stoddard group was trying to "decipher the upper and lower limits of density called carrying capacity and saturation point" and relating these to predation. The Chapman-Nicholson group was attempting "mathematical expression" of breeding potential, mortality, cycles, predation, and census problems. The Lorenz group was exploring the "psychological interactions of individual animals." Nice and Howard were relating these interactions "to (space) territory"; Allee, "to physiology and to the social order." The Rowan-Bissonnette group was exploring the "physiological basis of reproductive and migratory rhythms." Finally there were groups studying food (McAtee), diseases (Green), and "the beginnings of a study of weather" (Baldwin, Kendeigh, Gerstell).
100. In a 28 May 1940 letter to Morris Cooke, president of Friends of the Land, Leopold mentioned "one little stunt that grew up of its own accord. . . . We have a faculty group representing land economics, law, philosophy, agronomy, and wildlife which meets quietly and is slowly attempting a synthesis of these fields bearing on land conservation." LP 10-2, 4 (006).
101. Leopold's strength was not in math, but he respected the value of sound quantitative studies. In addition to integrating parts of the work of R. N. Chapman (in *Game Management*, pp. 26, 172; see R. N. Chapman, "The Quantitative Analysis of Environmental Factors, *Ecology* 9, no. 2 [1928]: 111–122) and A. J. Nicholson into his thinking, Leopold had interactions with the well-known quantitative ecologist D. Lack (AL, letter to Charles Elton, 30 January 1947, LP 10-1, 1), and his university class assignments included works by quantitative population ecologists Chapman, Nicholson, and G. F. Gause. AL, "List of References: Questions for Discussion" for Game Management 118, 1937, p. 2, UWDWE.
102. AL, letter to Charles Elton, 22 January 1934, LP 10-3, 10.
103. A. J. Nicholson, "The Balance of Animal Populations," *Journal of Animal Ecology* 2 (1933): 132–178. Nicholson's ideas were similar to Errington's concepts of saturation points, thresholds of security, and inversity. Nicholson emphasized the roles of population densities and competition in controlling populations. And Errington cited Nicholson's work on p. 244 of "What Is the Meaning of Predation?"
104. Ibid., p. 133.
105. Ibid., pp. 140–141.
106. See also William Howard, letter to AL, 24 October 1946, LP 10-2, 9, request-

ing AL to accept the position of "summarizer" for the upcoming Twelfth North American Wildlife Conference, to be held in Texas in February 1947.

107. V. Shelford, "The History of Ecology," lecture, University of Illinois, History of Science Society, 6 October 1958, p. 7.

108. These included Shelford, *Animal Communities in Temperate America*; C. Adams, *Guide to the Study of Animal Ecology* (New York: Macmillan, 1913); J. Murray and J. Hjort, *The Depths of the Ocean* (London: Macmillan, 1912); and D. S. Jordan and V. L. Kellogg, *Evolution and Animal Life* (New York: D. Appleton, 1907).

109. R. Pearl, *The Biology of Population Growth* (New York: Alfred A. Knopf, 1925). Pearl introduced his work by declaring that there was in the 1920s a "great recrudescence of public interest in the problem of population." He tied the 1920s revival of interest in population theories (after earlier popularity of the work of Thomas Malthus) to the consequences of war. Wars, according to some theories, Pearl suggested, were a result of human population pressure and often led people to feel that there were too many people in the world.

110. Elton, *Animal Ecology*, p. viii.

Chapter 5: An American System

1. W. E. Leuchtenburg, *Franklin D. Roosevelt and the New Deal, 1932–1940* (New York: Harper and Row, 1963), p. 53.

2. The total U.S. population between 1920 and 1935 rose from 105,710,620 to 127,152,000. About 25 percent of the national population lived on farms in 1935, down from 29.9 percent in 1920; in 1935, 43.1 percent of the nation's people were rural dwellers, down from 48 percent in 1920 (and 60 percent in 1900). In 1920, 51 percent of the population lived in cities, rising to 57 percent by 1935. U.S. Department of Commerce, Bureau of the Census, *Statistical Abstract of the United States: 1940* (Washington, DC: Government Printing Office, 1941), pp. 634–637.

3. Ibid. By 1935, 1,054,515 acres, or 55.4 percent, of the continental U.S. land area was in farms, up from 955,884 acres, or 50.2 percent, in 1920.

4. D. Worster, *The Dust Bowl: The Southern Plains in the 1930s* (New York: Oxford University Press, 1979), p. 123. Worster reasserted his main conclusions about the Dust Bowl and its cultural origins in "Grassland Follies: Agricultural Capitalism on the Plains," in *Under Western Skies: Nature and History in the American West* (New York: Oxford University Press, 1992), pp. 93–105.

5. Worster, *Dust Bowl*, pp. 11, 123.

6. *Statistical Abstract: 1940*, p. 638; The nation's top ten crops were corn, wheat, oats, barley, rye, buckwheat, potatoes, hay, tobacco, and cotton, which made up 90 percent of total planted crops. *Statistical Abstract: 1934*, p. 595.

7. AL, "Conservation Economics," *Journal of Forestry* 32, no. 5 (May 1934): 537–544; also in RMG, p. 193.

8. The New Deal–era efforts to use resource-use programs to promote social welfare are considered in S. T. Phillips, "Acres Fit and Unfit: Conservation and Rural Rehabilitation in the New Deal Era," PhD diss., Boston University, 2004. A classic work on the subject is R. S. Kirkendall, *Social Scientists*

and Farm Politics (Columbia: University of Missouri Press, 1966). Farm policy during the Hoover years is considered in D. E. Hamilton, *From New Day to New Deal: American Farm Policy from Hoover to Roosevelt, 1928–1933* (Chapel Hill: University of North Carolina Press, 1991).

9. L. C. Gray, "The Resettlement Land Program," *American Forests* 42, no. 8 (August 1936): 348.

10. By the summer of 1933 more than 10 percent of the nation's working population was receiving federal unemployment relief funds, rising to 17 percent by the start of 1935. By the summer of 1933 more than 200,000, and by the next winter more than 300,000, were enrolled in the CCC program. *Statistical Abstract: 1935*, pp. 326–327.

11. An invitation to speak at an erosion symposium in December 1935 gave Leopold occasion to sort out his thoughts on the mechanisms behind soil erosion. See AL, "The Erosion Cycle in the Southwest," unpublished manuscript, ca. 1935 (including notes with slides by the same title for "Erosion Symposium," dated 17 December 1935), p. 1, LP, 10-6, 12.

12. AL, "Conservation Economics," RMG, p. 197.

13. Ibid., pp. 193–202. ESA president Walter Taylor repeated Leopold's examples of lack of conservation coordination in "What is Ecology and What Good Is It?" *Ecology* 17 no. 3 (July 1936), p. 338.

14. Ibid., p. 198.

15. Ibid.

16. Eric Freyfogle describes a thoughtfully wrought modern version of landownership grounded in ecological knowledge; his work emphasizes the need for fundamental changes in prevailing cultural values to bring about conservation and is based on many of Leopold's ideas. See E. T. Freyfogle, *The Land We Share: Private Property and the Common Good* (Washington, DC: Island Press, Shearwater Books, 2003). See also his *Bounded People, Boundless Lands: Envisioning a New Land Ethic* (Washington, DC: Island Press, Shearwater Books, 1998), and "Battling over Leopold's Legacy" (Washington, DC: Georgetown Environmental Law and Policy Institute, Georgetown University Law Center, 2004). Also see R. L. Knight, "Aldo Leopold: Blending Conversations about Public and Private Lands," *Wildlife Society Bulletin* 26 (Winter 1998): 725–731, and R. L. Knight and S. Riedel, eds., *Aldo Leopold and the Ecological Conscience* (New York: Oxford University Press, 2002), chap. 2.

17. AL, "Conservation Economics," RMG, p. 200. See also AL et al., "The University and the Erosion Problem," *Bulletin of the University of Wisconsin* series no. 2097, general series no. 1881, Science Inquiry (ca. 1936): 15–17.

18. AL, "Conservation Economics," RMG, p. 196.

19. As early as 1930, during Herbert Hoover's administration, the idea of buying up many of the increasing number of America's unprofitable and degraded "submarginal" farms had been proposed by the U.S. Department of Agriculture. A year later, after the USDA-sponsored National Conference on Land Utilization had been held, the USDA prepared a report suggesting that government undertake buyouts for suffering farm families. See Gray, "Resettlement Land Program," p. 347.

20. AL, "Conservation Economics," RMG, p. 194.

21. Ibid.
22. Ibid., p. 196.
23. One of the few historians to comment on Leopold's growing disillusionment with individualism (particularly economic) and the failure of conservation to confront it has been Donald Worster, in *An Unsettled Country: Changing Landscapes of the American West* (Albuquerque: University of New Mexico Press, 1994), pp. 85–87.
24. AL, "Some Fundamentals of Conservation in the Southwest," RMG, p. 94.
25. AL, "The Conservation Ethic," *Journal of Forestry* 31, no. 6 (October 1933): 634–643. Reprinted as "Racial Wisdom and Conservation" in *Journal of Heredity* 37, no. 9 (September 1946); also in RMG, pp. 181–182.
26. AL, "A Proposed Survey of Land-Use for the Farm Foundation," ca. 1934, p. 2, LP 10-2, 4.
27. AL, "Some Thoughts on Recreational Planning," *Parks and Recreation* 18, no. 4 (1934): 137.
28. Leuchtenburg, *Roosevelt and the New Deal*, p. 163.
29. A. Brinkley, *The End of Reform: New Deal Liberalism in Recession and War* (New York: Alfred A. Knopf, 1995), p. 10.
30. Ibid.
31. B. Frank, "Foresters and Land Planning," *Journal of Forestry* 34, no. 3 (March 1936): 263.
32. In the 1890s a new technique called "dry farming" was popularized, with Hardy Campbell its most prominent spokesman. Campbell thought he had worked out a "climate-free" farming system: deep plowing in fall, packing subsoil, frequently stirring up a dust mulch, and summer fallowing to restore moisture. In 1909, in part to satisfy enthusiasm wrought by the dry farming idea, the Enlarged Homestead Act was passed, allowing settlers 320 acres apiece, and between 1910 and 1930 thousands rushed to get their share. See Worster, *Dust Bowl*, p. 87.
33. Ibid., p. 78.
34. Tractors on Oklahoma farms, for instance, increased by 25 percent between 1929 and 1936. Some farm owners used government subsidies to make machinery purchases, rather than to employ workers. Ibid., p. 58.
35. Ibid., p. 61; T. Egan, *The Worst Hard Time: The Untold Story of Those Who Survived the Great American Dust Bowl* (New York: Houghton Mifflin, 2006).
36. The centrality of soil issues in the 1930s is considered in R. S. Beeman and J. A. Pritchard, *A Green and Permanent Land: Ecology and Agriculture in the Twentieth Century* (Lawrence: University Press of Kansas, 2001), pp. 9–34. The primacy of soil as a natural resource continued to draw adherents after the dust storms calmed. See W. C. Lowdermilk, "Conservation of Soil as a Natural Resource," in *The Foundations of Conservation Education*, edited by H. B. Ward ([Washington, DC]: National Wildlife Federation, 1941), pp. 15–31.
37. Worster, *Dust Bowl*, pp. 13–14.
38. Ibid., p. 15.
39. AL, "Land Pathology," RMG, p. 214.
40. Ibid., p. 212.

41. Ibid., p. 215.
42. C. G. Bates and O. R. Zeasman, "Soil Erosion—a Local and National Problem," Research Bulletin 99 (Madison: U.S. Department of Agriculture and University of Wisconsin, Agricultural Experiment Station, August 1930), p. 1: "The loss of fertile surface soil from the farms of the country alone represents an enormous economic loss, so that the problem becomes a 'conservation' problem of the first magnitude. But this is only one of the injuries. . . ."; others included an increase in occurrence of large, damaging floods.
43. "The Grasslands," *Fortune* 12 (November 1935): 35.
44. D. Helms, "Coon Valley, Wisconsin: A Conservation Success Story," in *Readings in the History of the Soil Conservation Service* (Washington, DC: Soil Conservation Service, 1992), pp. 51–53.
45. Ibid., p. 52.
46. AL, "Coon Valley: An Adventure in Cooperative Conservation," *American Forests* 41, no. 5 (May 1935): 205–208; also in FHL, p. 49, RMG, p. 221. Hugh Bennett, chief of the Soil Erosion Service, wrote to Leopold on 22 May 1935: "Dear Mr. Leopold: Let me express my very great appreciation of your article in the May number of *American Forests Magazine*, under the title, 'Coon Valley.' You have certainly packed into this brief article a great deal of profound thought, and you have expressed these thoughts in a way that will appeal to the people. The article is so pertinent, so well written and otherwise so pleasing to us that we have procured from *American Forests Magazine* 500 reprints. These we are giving wide distribution. First a reprint goes to every Regional Director in our Service with special request that the article be passed around for careful reading and for comments." LP 10-2, 8.
47. AL, "Abandonment of Game Management on the Soil Erosion Projects," 2 July 1934, p. 1, LP 10-2, 8.
48. AL, "Coon Valley," RMG, p. 219. The breadth of the Coon Valley project was threatened in 1934 when Secretary of the Interior Harold Ickes ordered a halt to game management work on all erosion projects, presumably for jurisdictional and financial reasons. Leopold responded by writing to Ickes (AL, letters to Harold Ickes, 19 June 1934, 2 July 1934, and 5 July 1934, LP 10-2, 8) and by circulating to various conservation periodicals a three-page statement expressing his opposition to the move (AL, letter to S. B. Locke, Izaak Walton League of America, with attached statement, "Abandonment of Game Management on the Soil Erosion Projects," 2 July 1934, LP 10-2, 8). The project, Leopold asserted, was of "greater immediate consequence to game conservation work" than anything else taking place in Wisconsin (AL, "Memorandum for Mr. Darling: Re: Game Management Demonstration Work," 15 June 1934, p. 1, LP 10-2, 8). Whether Ickes agreed or not is unclear, but under threat of bad press he soon revoked his order. Harold Ickes, letter to AL, 29 June 1934, LP 10-2, 8.
49. Helms, "Coon Valley, Wisconsin," p. 53.
50. AL, "The Ecological Conscience," RMG, p. 340.
51. See also AL, "Improving the Wildlife Program of the Soil Conservation Service," 3 May 1940, LP 10-6, 16, in which Leopold works from the premise that justifying the SCS work in terms "of individual profit economics is

false and should be discontinued." Most of what should be done for and with wildlife on Wisconsin farms would not "pay." But promoting wildlife on farms could be justified by the pleasure to be derived from the wild animals, their benefit or profit to the community (vs. the individual), and "an appreciation of benefits which are usually indirect, often small, often long deferred, and always interlaced with farming, forestry, and other activities."

52. LP 10-6, 12. Leopold wondered if conservation's economic problems could be solved within the educational framework of the university's "existing limitations as a social unit." He urged integration of conservation and social sciences departments and held up the University of Wisconsin's "Science Inquiry" project, with which he had been involved and which he thought showed promise but had "petered out." See AL et al., "The University and Conservation of Wisconsin Wildlife: Science Inquiry Publication III," *Bulletin of the University of Wisconsin* series no. 2211, general series no. 1995 (February 1937).

53. AL, "To Determine Methods of Inducing Landowners to Follow Land Use Practices That Will Conserve the Public Interest," 12 September 1934, LP 10-6, 12.

54. Leopold in 1934 also was asked by a university colleague, soil scientist George Wehrwein, for help in outlining a comprehensive survey of the entire land utilization field as it affected Wisconsin. G. Wehrwein, letter to Aldo Leopold, 7 March 1934, LP 10-6, 12. Leopold responded in half a page, listing, in order of importance, what he considered Wisconsin's present conservation needs. The first was again to move conservation onto private lands. The second was to reorganize public lands administration so as to get a better integration of uses. Third, Leopold suggested some solution of the marginal farm problem that would not shift the population to industry. "A more conjectural need," Leopold concluded, "in the event the public area gets so large that the private tax-base cannot support it, is to develop a system of allotting public lands, in trust, to private users." AL, letter to G. Wehrwein, 23 March 1934, LP 10-6, 12. For a discussion of possible ways to put rural people to work, see H. A. Wallace (U.S. secretary of agriculture), "The Restoration of Rural Life," *American Forests* 39, no. 12 (1933): 486, 527.

55. Leopold resubmitted his proposal in 1938: AL, "Conservation Economics Study," 7 November 1938, LP 10-6, 12. Although his larger hopes for the program seemed to stall, finally in 1943 Leopold and one of his students, Joseph Hickey, produced a manuscript on a study addressing some of these questions: What could be done once the system of federal subsidies had shrunk, free CCC labor was gone, and AAA was left paying for crops no matter the technique used for growing them on eroding, hilly farms in southwestern Wisconsin? See A. Leopold and J. J. Hickey, "The Erosion Problem of Steep Farms in Southwestern Wisconsin: A Report Prepared for the Wisconsin State Soil Conservation Committee," 1943, LP 10-6, 12. The tension among economists at the University of Wisconsin at the time Leopold submitted his proposal is described in J. Gilbert and E. Baker, "Wisconsin Economists and New Deal Agricultural Policy: The Legacy of Progressive Professors," *Wisconsin Magazine of History* (Summer 1997): 281–312. The disinterest of most economists in Leopold's conservation ideas was linked to

a profound shift within economics as a discipline. The shift was from an empirically and historically based, inductive approach toward greater reliance on models, deductive reasoning, and a lessened interest in reform. The shift is recounted in Y. P. Yonay, *The Struggle over the Soul of Economics: Institutional and Neoclassical Economists in America between the Wars* (Princeton, NJ: Princeton University Press, 1998). The early years of resource economics, influenced by conservation thought and aimed at improving land uses, is considered in G. A. Smith, "Natural Resource Economic Theory of the First Conservation Movement (1895–1927)," *History of Political Economy* 14, no. 4 (1982): 483–495.

56. AL, "Proposed Survey of Land-Use."

57. AL, "The Conservation Ethic," RMG, p. 192. Leopold would revisit the issue at greater length in "Land-Use and Democracy," *Audubon* 44, no. 5 (September–October 1942): 259–265, also in RMG, pp. 295–300. And see AL, "Armament for Conservation," 23 November 1943, LP 10-6, 16.

58. J. N. Darling, letter to AL, 22 September 1934, LP 10-1, 1: "Dear Aldo— Your article on Economics of Conservation in the May issue of the *Journal of Forestry* is the finest thing I have ever read, seen or heard on the subject. It ought to make you President. Sincerely, Jay."

59. AL, "Proposed Conservation Economics Study," 7 November 1938, p. 3, LP 10-6, 12.

60. AL, "Proposed Survey of Land-Use," p. 5.

61. AL, "Conservation Economics," RMG, p. 201.

62. Ibid., p. 200.

63. Ibid., p. 201.

64. Ibid. See also AL, letter to Roger Baldwin, 21 June 1944, LP 10-2, 5: "Sometimes I wonder whether we all begin to organize at the wrong end. Perhaps we should throw away all our blueprints and simply look for outstanding people, then let them build their own jobs."

65. AL, "Conservation Economics," RMG, pp. 201–202.

66. On 19 December 1930, Leopold prepared a memorandum for the U.S. Senate Committee on Wildlife Conservation, "The Role of the Federal Government in Game Conservation," LP 10-12, 6. He set forth three guiding principles for federal work in game management: help states and private landowners work out better cropping methods through research and demonstration, conduct their own management operations on federal lands, and take part in management of migratory birds, which cross state boundaries.

67. C. D. Meine, *Aldo Leopold: His Life and Work* (Madison: University of Wisconsin Press, 1988), p. 298.

68. Anonymous, "Roosevelt Recommends a Department of Conservation," *American Forests* 43, no. 2 (February 1937): 74. In January 1937, FDR had recommended to Congress a sweeping reorganization of the federal government framework, which would have converted the U.S. Department of the Interior into a Department of Conservation, because conservation represented a major purpose of the government. Its role would have been to advise the president "with regard to the protection and use of the natural resources

of the nation and the Public Domain." The conservation community was speculating about whether this change also would imply transferring USDA conservation agencies, including the Forest Service, Soil Conservation Service, and Biological Survey, into the Department of the Interior (Department of Conservation) or whether those agencies would be split between Interior and the USDA. Gifford Pinchot also came out vigorously against making Interior the Department of Conservation, declaring that it would split up and "hamstring" government forest work. Nor did he think that conservation could be housed in a single department, being as "universal as the air we breathe" and related to everything. See G. Pinchot, "It Can Happen Here," *American Forests* 43, no. 4 (1937): 282–283, 321; Anonymous, "Pinchot Opposes Department of Conservation," *American Forests* 43, no. 4 (1937): 196–197.

69. AL, letter to John H. Baker, 9 December 1937, LP 10-2, 5.

70. See AL, "Conservation Blueprints," *American Forests* 43, no. 12 (December 1937): 596, 608.

71. Anonymous, "Wallace Appoints Three to Aid Wild Life Plan," editorial, *New York Times*, 3 January 1934, p. 8 (ProQuest Historical Newspapers, *The New York Times*, 1837–current file); V. Van Ness, untitled, "Rod and Gun," *New York Times*, 16 January 1934, p. 27 (ProQuest Historical Newspapers, *The New York Times*, 1837–current file).

72. Anonymous, "Wallace Appoints Three."

73. Anonymous, "Wild Life Project Calls for U.S. Aid," *New York Times*, 24 January 1934, p. 24 (ProQuest Historical Newspapers, *The New York Times*, 1837–current file).

74. Ibid.

75. T. H. Beck, J. N. Darling, and A. Leopold, "A National Plan for Wild Life Restoration" (Washington, DC: President's Committee on Wild Life Restoration, 8 February 1934), p. 4, UWDWE.

76. Anonymous, "Map Aid to Wild Life as a Works Project," *New York Times*, 11 May 1934, p. 16 (ProQuest Historical Newspapers, *The New York Times*, 1837–current file).

77. Ibid.

78. G. Greenfield, untitled, "Rod and Gun," *New York Times*, 7 June 1934, p. 34 (ProQuest Historical Newspapers, *The New York Times*, 1837–current file). It appears that the source used by the *Times* was the organization More Game Birds, established around 1930 by a wealthy American, Joseph P. Knapp. Leopold encouraged the use of private resources for the advancement of game conservation and Knapp's "fundamental idea of a big-scale program." But he criticized Knapp's plan as unduly narrow and restricting. Knapp apparently sought to dictate what he considered the best kind of game management—an importation of the European system of private game ownership. Leopold favored commercializing the shooting privilege in some cases but not the game. There was plenty to learn from European game management, Leopold admitted, but what America needed was to try out on the land a system of its own. This had not yet been done. This system needed to be flexible, to fit various locales, and would involve the need for ongoing

experimentation. A rigid line of thinking, in any case, would not do. See AL, letter to Joseph P. Knapp, 18 September 1930; Ovid Butler, letter to AL, 25 September 1930; and AL, letter to Ovid Butler, 30 September 1930; LP 10-2, 1.

79. Anonymous, "New Deal Sought for Our Wild Life: Conservation Leaders Urge a National Plan at Session of Audubon Societies," *New York Times*, 30 October 1935, p. 23 (ProQuest Historical Newspapers, *The New York Times*, 1837–current file).

80. G. Greenfield, untitled, "Wood, Field, and Stream," *New York Times*, 31 October 1935, p. 25 (ProQuest Historical Newspapers, *The New York Times*, 1837–current file).

81. FDR did sign the Duck Stamp Bill on 6 March 1934, however, and Jay Darling used his artistic talent to draw scenes for the stamps, which hunters were required to buy. The stamps sold well and helped raise money to establish a national system of waterfowl refuges. A federal duck stamp program continues into the twenty-first century.

82. By then Leopold had little good to say about the federal effort except that it made funds available (albeit in small amounts) for biological research and did achieve gains in the federal migratory bird program. See National Research Council, "Report of the Committee on Wild Life Studies," 22 May 1935, LP 10-2, 6 (2). There is also evidence that the committee did not always agree and struggled to create a report that was mutually acceptable. See also AL, letters to J. N. Darling, 16 January 1934 and 29 January 1934: "The more I think about the Committee's job," Leopold wrote, "the more I am convinced that our success depends not on the report that we write, but on the man who is chosen to execute the program." Leopold put a premium on finding "a qualified administrator, with . . . [a] broad conception of his duties." Then Leopold "would not care what the report said, or whether we submitted any at all."

83. FDR, "Remarks of Hon. Henry A. Wallace" (Wallace read a letter from FDR, who was unable to attend), 3 February 1936, *Proceedings of the North American Wildlife Conference (Taking the Place of the Twenty-second American Game Conference)* (Washington, DC: Government Printing Office, 1936), p. 5. Efforts during the 1930s to promote wildlife conservation are outlined in J. B. Trefethen, *An American Crusade for Wildlife* (New York: Winchester Press, 1975), pp. 195–236. A personal memoir of FDR and wildlife issues by one of his informal advisors appears in I. Brandt, *Adventures with Franklin D. Roosevelt* (Flagstaff, AZ: Northland Publishing Company, 1988), pp. 37–52.

84. The Oberlaender Trust of the Carl Schurz Memorial Foundation, Inc., was founded in 1931 by Gustav Oberlaender of Reading, Pennsylvania, to stimulate appreciation of cultural achievements of German-speaking populations. Members of the group included L. F. Kneipp, head of the USDA Forest Service's Division of Land, with a focus on "utilization of forest for the local community," and W. N. Sparhawk, senior forest economist, looking at "social relationships of forestry." See Anonymous, "Study Grants Given to Forestry Experts," *New York Times*, 5 August 1935, p. 13 (ProQuest

Historical Newspapers, *The New York Times*, 1837–current file). Each team member was assigned a research topic according to his specialty; Leopold's was game management in relation to forestry. Upon returning to the United States Leopold published six articles based on his observations. Several dealt with specific forestry methods used in the country, yet he was inclined to dwell also upon social organization in Germany and its stronger sense of national cohesion. AL, "Notes on Wild Life Conservation in Germany," *Game Research News Letter* 6 (16 September 1935 and 21 October 1935): 1–3, 7, and 1–3; AL, "*Naturschutz* in Germany," *Bird-Lore* 38, no. 2 (March–April 1936): 102–111; AL, "Deer and *Dauerwald* in Germany: I. History," *Journal of Forestry* 34, no. 4 (April 1936): 366–375; AL, "Deer and *Dauerwald* in Germany: II. Ecology and Policy," *Journal of Forestry* 34, no. 5 (May 1936): 460–466; AL, "Farm Game Management in Silesia," *American Wildlife* 25, no. 5 (September–October 1936): 67–68, 74–76, also in FHL, pp. 54–69; AL, "Notes on Game Administration in Germany," *American Wildlife* 25, no. 6 (November–December 1936): 85, 92–93.

85. AL, "Suggestions for American Wildlife Conference," attachment to a letter from AL to Seth Gordon dated 27 October 1935, p. 2, LP 10-6, 17 (6).

86. Ibid.

87. Ibid. See also AL, "Land Pathology," RMG, pp. 212–217.

88. Jay Darling, letter to AL, 20 November 1935, LP 10-2, 8.

89. Compare the postmechanization landscapes of the American Great Plains and the agricultural lands of collectivist Ukraine in the mid- to late 1930s. View Pare Lorentz' *The Plow That Broke the Plains* (1936) along with Alexandr Dovzhenko's *Earth* (1930).

90. AL, "Suggestions for American Wildlife Conference," p. 1.

91. Jay Darling, letter to AL, 20 November 1935, LP 10-2, 8.

92. Ibid.

93. AL, "Notes on Game Administration in Germany," p. 93. As Leopold put it against the background of World War II in 1942: "War has defined the issue: we must prove that democracy can use its land decently. . . . We deal with bureaus, policies, laws, and programs which are the *symbols* of our problem, instead of with the resources, products, and landusers, which *are* the problem." AL, "Land-Use and Democracy," *Audubon* 44, no. 5 (September–October 1942): 259–265; also in RMG, p. 295. See C. Meine, "Home, Land, Security," in *Correction Lines: Essays on Land, Leopold, and Conservation* (Washington, DC: Island Press, 2004), pp. 222–246.

94. Leopold and the rest of the American Game Policy Committee objected to the option of ceding title of game to private landowners, giving the reason that it was the English system and incompatible with American tradition and thought. AL et al., "Report to the American Game Conference on an American Game Policy" and "Discussion of the American Game Policy," *Transactions of the 17th American Game Conference* (1–2 December 1930), pp. 284–309, 142, 146–147; AL, "Game Methods: The American Way," RMG, pp. 156–163; and see AL, review of W. Shepard, *Notes on German Game Management Chiefly in Bavaria and Baden, Journal of Forestry* 32, no. 7 (1934): 774–775.

95. Leopold continued to ponder the question of human population density. In the early decades of the twentieth century, when he began his career, America was trying to fill up its frontier lands with people. By the time of World War II, national concerns about overpopulation were increasingly serious. Leopold wrestled with the issue in a written lecture in 1941, "Ecology and Politics" (RMG, pp. 281–286). There were no easy answers, he recognized, and he wondered aloud about both the practical and the moral facets of the issue. By 1946 Leopold, in an unpublished manuscript, "The Land-Health Concept and Conservation" (FHL, pp. 218–226), included stabilizing human population density as one of the conditions requisite to achieving land health. Leopold's elder daughter, Nina Leopold Bradley, remembers the influence William Vogt's thinking had on her father (see W. Vogt, *Road to Survival* [New York: William Sloan Associates, 1948], which argues that human numbers exceeded the earth's carrying capacity, yet numbers were continuing to rise, with real and potentially increasingly dire consequences in store). Nina recalls that Leopold once mentioned that perhaps he and his wife, Estella, should have had two children instead of five (though many people are glad they had the five they had).

96. AL, Review of *Notes on German Game Management Chiefly in Bavaria and Baden* (by Ward Shepard, Senate Committee on Wild Life Resources, 1934) *Journal of Forestry* 32, no. 7 (October, 1934), p. 775.

97. Ibid.

98. Leopold's visit took place three years into Nazi Party rule, yet letters home are filled with observations focused on his forestry and game-hunting observations and experiences and trips to the theater, not politics. LP 10-8, 9. Leopold was deeply disturbed from his observations of the rise of German Militarism and oppression. See Meine, *Aldo Leopold*, pp. 358, 360.

99. Douglas Wade, letter to AL, 30 September 1944, pp. 1–2, LP 10-8, 1.

100. Ibid., p. 2.

101. AL, letter to Douglas Wade, 23 October 1944, LP 10-8, 1.

102. AL, "Ecology as an Ethical System," ca. 1940s, p. 1, LP 10-6, 17.

103. Ibid., p. 1.

104. AL, "Land-Use and Democracy," RMG, p. 300.

105. AL, "Proposed Game Survey" prepared for the Wild Life Committee, National Research Council, 30 December 1931, p. 2, LP 10-2, 6. Leopold, still in the first blush of a national career, was initially hopeful about the work this committee might accomplish, which included the likes of prominent ecologist Victor Shelford, the Audubon Society's T. Gilbert Pearson, Paul Redington of the USDA Biological Survey, and A. B. Howell of the American Society of Mammalogists. See AL, letter to Charles Elton, 2 March 1932, LP 10-3, 10; AL, "Function of the Wild Life Committee: National Research Council," 20 February 1932, p. 1, LP, 10-2, 6 (1).

106. G. Greenfield, untitled, "Wood, Field, and Stream," *New York Times*, 1 February 1936, p. 12 (ProQuest Historical Newspapers, *The New York Times*, 1837–current file).

107. F. A. Silcox, "Remarks," 3 February 1936, *Proceedings of the North American Wildlife Conference (Taking the Place of the Twenty-second*

American Game Conference) (Washington, DC: Government Printing Office, 1936), p. 3.

108. The new wildlife federation did emerge (now the National Wildlife Federation), replacing the former American Game Association, but its formation did not end the disagreements. Another new organization was formed at the 1936 conference—the Wildlife Institute, which would collect and allocate "some $200,000 in industrial funds." See AL, letter to Ivey F. Lewis, 2 March 1936, LP 10-2, 6.

109. AL, in *Proceedings of the North American Wildlife Conference*, p. 156.

110. AL, "Farmer-Sportsmen Set-Ups in the North Central Region," *Proceedings of the North American Wildlife Conference*, pp. 279–284.

111. In particular, Leopold was active in and wrote about the Riley Cooperative, supported by the new Wisconsin Shooting Preserve Law, which allowed a generous open season to those who raised pheasants on their land. In the cooperative, an intimate group of farm and town members shared shooting privileges equally, with town members paying dues in cash to farmers for management expenses and farmers paying "dues" by contributing the use of their land and grain. The Riley experiment continued throughout the decade, producing longer-term results that were for the most part discouraging, however. The cooperative was hard to maintain without the personal involvement of Leopold and his graduate students; when the students left for the war, the experiment largely folded.

The Faville Grove project, near Lake Mills, east of Madison, was a "farmer pool" type of organization wherein farmers managed game for their own shooting and outsiders were allowed in only as guests. This project, which Leopold advised, included restoration of prairie and marsh flora as well as game and nature education for schoolchildren. It was operated by Leopold's graduate student Art Hawkins and made possible by farmer-conservationist Stoughton Faville, owner of the farmland.

Leopold began requiring each of his professional game students to live on and operate his own game setup for at least a year, to give the student experience and research opportunities and to aid various farmers. Leopold and his students were also actively involved in game management and other restoration projects at the University of Wisconsin Arboretum. See also AL, "The Arboretum and the University," RMG, p. 209. See also B. Sibernagel and J. Sibernagel, "Tracking Aldo Leopold through Riley's Farmland," *Wisconsin Magazine of History* (Summer 2003): 34–45. The issue and possibilities of farmer-sportsman cooperation continued to draw attention after Leopold's death. Durward Allen explored the matter at length with particular attention to the public's ownership of the wildlife itself in *Our Wildlife Legacy*, rev. ed. (New York: Funk and Wagnalls, 1962), pp. 309–336.

112. AL, "Helping Ourselves," RMG, pp. 203–208; AL, "Farmer-Sportsmen Set-Ups," p. 283.

113. AL, "Farmer-Sportsman Set-Ups," p. 284; see also AL, "Vertical Planning for Wild Life," address to Rural Regional Planning group, 25 March 1936, LP 10-6, 14.

114. AL, "Suggestions for American Wildlife Conference," p. 4. Earlier that

month Leopold had received a letter from Seth Gordon asking him for ideas on the upcoming American Wildlife Conference, called by FDR. This was a portion of Leopold's response, sent from the Savoy Hotel in Breslau.

115. Darling also would encourage national management and wilderness planning work at the Biological Survey, starting with the needs of various species and working up to provide for those needs at appropriate spatial scales, which Leopold viewed as so important. The grizzly bear was being given some particular attention. See the discussion in various letters between Leopold and Darling: AL to Jay Darling, 27 November 1939; Darling to AL, 23 November 1939; Darling to AL, 21 November 1939; LP 10-4, 8. See also AL, "Proposal for a Conservation Inventory of Threatened Species," undated draft, LP 10-2, 6; AL, "Wildlife in Land-Use Planning," 20 March 1942, UWDWE; and AL, "The Grizzly—a Problem in Land-Planning," 6 April 1942, LP 10-6, 16.

116. Jay Darling, letter to AL, 14 January 1935, LP 10-1, 1.

117. AL, letter to Jay Darling, 21 January 1935, LP 10-1, 1.

118. AL, "The Research Program," *Transactions of the 2nd North American Wildlife Conference*, 1937, p. 104. Reprinted in *American Wildlife* 26, no. 2 (March–April 1937): 22.

119. Ibid.

120. AL, "Proposed Conservation Economics Study," p. 6.

Chapter 6: A Common Concept of Land

1. Frederick Clements, letter to Victor Shelford, 19 December 1936, Shelford Papers, University of Illinois–Champaign-Urbana (hereafter SP), 15/24/20, box 1. Clements believed that the demand for ecologists who could advise federal bureaus and projects was threefold the supply.

2. For an overview of the history of ecology see works including W. C. Allee et al., *Principles of Animal Ecology* (Philadelphia: W. B. Saunders, 1949); A. Bramwell, *Ecology in the 20th Century: A History* (New Haven, CT: Yale University Press, 1989); F. N. Egerton, "History of Ecology: Achievements and Opportunities, Part I," *Journal of History of Biology* 16, no. 2 (1983): 259–310; F. N. Egerton, "History of Ecology: Achievements and Opportunities, Part II," *Journal of the History of Biology* 18, no. 1 (1985): 103–143; F. B. Golley, *A History of the Ecosystem Concept in Ecology* (New Haven, CT: Yale University Press, 1994); R. P. McIntosh, *The Background of Ecology: Concept and Theory* (Cambridge: Cambridge University Press, 1985); H. N. Scheiber, "From Science to Law to Politics: An Historical View of the Ecosystem Idea and Its Effect on Resource Management," *Ecology Law Quarterly* 24, no. 631 (1997): 631–651; M. G. Barbour, "Ecological Fragmentation in the Fifties," in *Uncommon Ground: Rethinking the Human Place in Nature*, edited by W. Cronon (New York: W. W. Norton, 1996), pp. 233–255; and D. Worster, ed., *Nature's Economy: A History of Ecological Ideas* (Cambridge: Cambridge University Press, 1994).

3. McIntosh, *Background of Ecology*, p. 86.

4. T. Park, "Analytical Population Studies in Relation to General Ecology," in *Plant and Animal Communities*, edited by T. Just (Notre Dame: University

Press, 1939), reprinted in *The American Midland Naturalist* 21, no. 1 (1939): 250. See also W. Allee and T. Park, "Concerning Ecological Principles" (abstract), *Bulletin of the Ecological Society of America* 18 (1937).

5. Victor Shelford, letter to Warder C. Allee, 30 November 1939, SP 15/24/20, box 1.

6. Allee et al., *Principles of Animal Ecology*, p. 68.

7. Alongside the strand of community ecology there developed a quantitative strand related to scientific interest in fluctuating animal population numbers and productivity of natural resource flows, as described in chap. 4.

8. K. Möbius, *Die Auster und die Austernwirtschaft* (Berlin, 1877); translated and reprinted by the U.S. Fish Commission, 1880, as "The Oyster and Oyster-Culture," pp. 683–751.

9. S. Forbes, "The Lake as a Microcosm," *Bulletin of the Scientific Association of Peoria, Illinois* (1887): 77–87; reprinted, with emendations, in *Illinois Natural History Survey Bulletin* 15 (1925): 537–550.

10. H. C. Cowles, "The Ecological Relations of the Vegetation on the Sand Dunes of Lake Michigan," *Botanical Gazette* 27 (1899): 95–118, 167–202, 281–308, 361–391.

11. V. E. Shelford, "Preliminary Note on the Distribution of the Tiger Beetles (*Cicindela*) and Its Relation to Plant Succession," *Biological Bulletin* 15 (1907): 9; V. Shelford, "Ecological Succession: IV, Vegetation and the Control of Land Animal Communities," *Biological Bulletin* 23 (1912): 59–99; V. Shelford, "Principles and Problems of Ecology as Illustrated by Animals," *Journal of Ecology* 3, no. 1 (1915): 1–23.

12. Allee et al., *Principles of Animal Ecology*, p. 68.

13. See A. Tansley, "The Use and Abuse of Vegetational Concepts and Terms," *Ecology* 16 (1935): 295–296. Of the scientists gathered at the 1938 Conference on Plant and Animal Communities, Henry Gleason, well known for his "Individualistic Concept of the Plant Association," was strongest in his objection to the entire vocabulary of "community." See *American Midland Naturalist* 21, no. 1, special conference issue (January 1939): 92–110.

14. Plant ecologist Frederic Clements was among those most forcefully pushing the organismic notion. The idea was strongly disliked by plant scientists Henry Chandler Cowles, Arthur Tansley, and Henry Gleason, among others.

15. Tansley, "Use and Abuse of Vegetational Concepts," p. 299.

16. AL, "The Forester's Role in Game Management," *Journal of Forestry* 29, no. 1 (1931): 30.

17. AL, "A Biotic View of Land," RMG, pp. 266, 273.

18. AL, "The Round River: A Parable," RR, p. 159.

19. AL, "The Arboretum and the University," *Parks and Recreation* 18, no. 2 (October 1934): 59–60; also in RMG, p. 209.

20. AL, "A Biotic View of Land," RMG, p. 268.

21. AL, "Round River," p. 159.

22. At the first meeting of the ESA in 1916, Frederic Clements used the term "biotic community," by which he meant the complete, interrelated collection of plants and animals that inhabited a particular place. F. E. Clements,

"The Development and Structure of Biotic Communities," printed program for New York meeting of the Ecological Society of America, 27–29 December 1916, pp. 1–5; abstract reprinted in *Journal of Ecology* 5 (1916): 120–121. It may have been C. C. Adams who first used "biotic community," on p. 159 of "An Ecological Study of Prairie and Forest Invertebrates," *Bulletin of the Illinois State Laboratory of Natural History* 11 (1915): 33–280, but by the term he seemed to have meant only animals. See W. P. Taylor, "Significance of the Biotic Community in Ecological Studies," *Quarterly Review of Biology* 10, no. 3 (1935): 292.

23. AL, "A Biotic View of Land," *Journal of Forestry* 37, No. 9 (September 1939): 727-30. Condensed in *The Council Ring* (National Park Service monthly mimeographed publication) 1, No. 12 (November 1939): 1-4; RMG, pp. 266–273.

24. AL, "The Ecological Conscience," *Bulletin of the Garden Club of America*, September 1947, pp. 45–53.

25. AL, "The Land Ethic," SCA, pp. 201–226.

26. AL, "Conservation Economics," *Journal of Forestry* 32, no. 5 (May 1934): 537–544; also in RMG, p. 197. Walter Taylor cites Leopold in, "What is Ecology and What Good is it?" p. 338.

27. AL, "Preliminary Report of Forestry and Game Management," *Journal of Forestry* 33, no. 3 (March 1935): 274.

28. Ibid.

29. Ibid., pp. 274–275.

30. AL, "Second Report of the Game Policy Committee," *Journal of Forestry* 32, no. 2 (February 1937): 228.

31. Ibid. In a letter dated 17 June 1936 Leopold wrote to W. S. Cooper of the ESA, "What I mean is that biologists in general are not building any foundations for conservation, and we technologists are trying to erect a structure on a base which exists only in spots. The base needed is mostly ecological." LP 10-2, 2.

32. AL, *Game Management* (New York: Charles Scribner's Sons, 1933), p. 39.

33. AL, "A Biotic View of Land," RMG, pp. 266, 273.

34. AL, "The State of the Profession," *Journal of Wildlife Management* 4, no. 3 (July 1940): 343–346; also in RMG, p. 276.

35. Ibid., pp. 276–277.

36. AL, "Wherefore Wildlife Ecology?" RMG, p. 337.

37. P. S. Lovejoy, "Forest Biology," *Journal of Forestry* 15, no. 2 (1917): 203–214.

38. AL, "Cheat Takes Over," SCA, p. 158.

39. Walter Taylor was 1935 president of the Ecological Society of America and a member of Leopold's game policy committee. See S. Flader, *Thinking Like a Mountain: Aldo Leopold and the Evolution of an Ecological Attitude toward Deer, Wolves, and Forests* (Madison: University of Wisconsin Press, 1974), p. 151.

40. W. P. Taylor et al., "The Relation of Jack Rabbits to Grazing in Southern Arizona," *Journal of Forestry* 33, no. 5 (May 1935): 490–498.

41. Taylor et al., "Relation of Jack Rabbits," p. 493.

42. AL, letter to John H. Baker (National Association of Audubon Societies), 17 December 1935, LP 10-2, 5.

43. This ecological process was summarized in J. E. Weaver and W. W. Hansen, "Native Midwestern Pastures: Their Origin, Composition, and Degeneration," *Nebraska Conservation Bulletin*, no. 22 (1941).

44. Taylor et al., "Relation of Jack Rabbits," p. 496.

45. F. E. Clements, *Plant Succession*, Publication 242 (Washington, DC: Carnegie Institution, 1916).

46. F. E. Clements, "The Relict Method in Dynamic Ecology," *Journal of Ecology* 22 (1934): 39–68; F. E. Clements et al., *The Nature and Role of Competition*, Year Book 23 (Washington, DC: Carnegie Institution, 1924); Clements, *Plant Succession*; F. Clements, "Development and Structure of Vegetation," *Report of the Botanical Survey of Nebraska 7* (1904). Clements was not the first plant ecologist to study processes of succession. See also Cowles, "Ecological Relations," and E. Warming, *Plantesamfund: Grundtrak af den Okologiska Plantegeografi* (Copenhagen: Philipsen, 1895), English version (modified), *Oecology of Plants: An Introduction to the Study of Plant Communities* (Oxford: Clarendon Press, 1909).

47. Clements, *Development and Structure of Vegetation*; Clements, *Plant Succession*; F. E. Clements et al., "Climate and Climaxes," *Carnegie Institution Washington Year Book* 31 (1932); F. E. Clements, "Nature and Structure of the Climax," *Journal of Ecology* 24 (1936): 252–284.

48. F. E. Clements and V. E. Shelford, *Bio-ecology* (New York: John Wiley and Sons, 1939), pp. 231–232.

49. Clements, "Nature and Structure of the Climax." Clements had also catalogued by 1936 a thorough and somewhat terminologically mind-boggling list "to meet *nearly* every exigency." For a summary discussion of various perspectives, including comments on Clements' 1936 article such as the one above, see S. A. Cain, "The Climax and Its Complexities," *American Midland Naturalist* 21, no. 1 (1939): 147–182 (150).

50. F. E. Clements and V. E. Shelford, "Bio-ecology," *Carnegie Institution of Washington Year Book* 25–33 (1926–1934); Clements and Shelford, *Bio-ecology*.

51. Clements and Shelford, *Bio-ecology*, p. 232.

52. Like Leopold, Shelford was an advocate as well as a scientist. Since his term in 1916 as the first president of the Ecological Society of America, Shelford had led efforts to protect natural areas for scientific study and served as chairman of the organization's Committee on the Preservation of Natural Conditions for the United States from its establishment in 1917–1936. V. Shelford, "Ecological Society of America: A Nature Sanctuary Plan Unanimously Adopted by The Society, December 28, 1932," *Ecology* 14, no. 2 (April 1933): 240–245; V. Shelford, "Nature Sanctuaries—a Means of Saving Natural Biotic Communities," *Science* 77, no. 1994 (17 March 1933): 281–282; V. Shelford, "International Preservation of Nature," *Ecology* 16, no. 4 (October 1935): 662–663; and V. Shelford, "The Preservation of Natural Conditions," *Science* 51, no. 1312 (1920): 316–317 were all found in AL's files; LP 10-2, 2. See R. Croker, *Pioneer Ecologist: The Life and Work of Victor Ernest Shelford: 1877–1968* (Washington, DC: Smithsonian Institution Press, 1991); D. Philippon, *Conserving Words: How American Nature Writers Shaped the Environmental Movement* (Athens: University of

Georgia Press, 2004); and J. L. Newton, "Science, Recreation, and Leopold's Quest for a Durable Scale," in *Wilderness Debate*, vol. 2, edited by M. Nelson and J. B. Callicott (Athens: University of Georgia Press, 2006).

53. Croker, *Pioneer Ecologist*, pp. 70–90.

54. Leopold, like Shelford, promoted the preservation of representative biotic types for scientific purposes. See AL, "Wilderness as a Land Laboratory," RMG, pp. 288-289 and "Wilderness for Science," SCA, p. 196. Leopold understood succession as a foundational ecological concept. In his 1923 *Watershed Handbook* (Albuquerque: U.S. Department of Agriculture, Forest Service, District 3, December 1923 [revised and reissued October 1934]), p. 5, LP 10-11, 1, he noted that settlement was more likely to upset the "equilibrium" in the Southwest than in other regions of the country because "for one thing, our plant successions are different." "The kind of vegetation on any piece of land does not remain unchanged from year to year if left to itself. . . . Control of game cover or food," he explained in his 1933 *Game Management* (pp. 304–305), "is largely a matter of understanding and controlling succession," and the successional process was toward an "inexorable" climax, though a vegetative type might be "fixed" by human or nonhuman forces (e.g., by fire: AL, "Grass, Brush, Timber, and Fire in Southern Arizona," RMG, p. 118; by "buffer" species: AL, *Game Management*, pp. 237-238, 304-305; by farmers: AL, "Marshland Elegy," SCA, pp. 98–99). In his 1933 "The Conservation Ethic" (RMG, p. 185), Leopold explained that in "all climates the plant succession determines what economic activities can be supported." In 1938 he lectured on biotic sequences: "Every soil has a fixed sequence of plant communities, each of which carries a characteristic animal community. Agriculture is the art of arranging 'desirable' combinations of these three: it is ecological engineering. . . . The first law of intelligent tinkering is to keep all the parts" (AL, "Economics, Philosophy, and Land," lecture, 23 November 1938, p. 2, LP 10-6, 14). Reflections upon overgrazing moved Leopold to comment on "the immense power of plant succession" in his 1944 "Review" (RMG, p. 215). In his essay "The Land Ethic" (SCA, p. 205), Leopold asks readers to consider how dependent American history has been on plant succession.

55. F. E. Clements, J. E. Weaver, and H. C. Hanson, *Plant Competition: An Analysis of Community Function* (Washington, DC: Carnegie Institution, 1929).

56. Ibid., pp. 10–11.

57. Ibid., p. 21.

58. Ibid.

59. Ibid., p. 327.

60. Ibid.

61. A. J. Nicholson, "The Balance of Animal Populations," *Journal of Animal Ecology* 2 (1933): 135.

62. C. Elton, *Animal Ecology* (New York: Macmillan, 1927; Chicago: University of Chicago Press, 2001), p. 28: "Succession brings the ecologist face to face with the whole problem of competition among animals."

63. Ibid., p. 56. Victor Shelford noted in 1931 ("Some Concepts of Bioecology,"

Ecology 12, no. 3:455–467) that "Weaver and Clements ('29) hold that *food* rather than physical factors, controls animals, and, since plants are the direct food of all animals, the biotic community has unity through food relations" (p. 455). See J. E. Weaver and F. E. Clements, *Plant Ecology* (New York: McGraw-Hill, 1929). V. Shelford, "Animal Communities in Temperate America," *Bulletin of the Geographical Society of Chicago* 5 (1913): 70–72, 166–168; see also Croker, *Pioneer Ecologist*, pp. 35–37.

64. Elton, *Animal Ecology*, p. 56. C. Elton, *Animal Ecology* (New York: Macmillan, 1927; Chicago: University of Chicago Press, 2001). In 1942 Raymond Lindeman of Yale University, building upon the works of Hutchinson, Clements, Shelford, Elton, and other community ecologists, published "The Trophic-Dynamic Aspect of Ecology" (*Ecology* 23, no. 4:399–418), which "emphasizes the relationship of trophic or 'energy-availing' [food-cycle] relationships within the community-unit to the process of succession." Also see H. Stoddard, *The Bobwhite Quail: Its Habits, Preservation, and Increase* (New York: Charles Scribner's Sons, 1931), p. 350.

65. Elton, *Animal Ecology*, p. 62.

66. Ibid., p. 61.

67. Ibid., p. 63.

68. Ibid., pp. 63–68.

69. Ibid., p. 64.

70. Ibid, p. 64. In a typed lecture draft from 17 February 1945, "Plant Patterns: Interspersion Theory; Patterns" (the lecture was noted as not given; LP 10-6, 14), Leopold defined an ecologist as "a person who recognizes niches and studies animal responses to variations in them" and a wildlife manager as "a person who improves niches, and thus regulates population."

71. See McIntosh, *Background of Ecology*, p. 200, and A. J. Lotka, *Elements of Physical Biology* (Baltimore: Williams and Wilkins, 1925). Drawing on Lotka's law, R. N. Chapman, in his 1931 *Animal Ecology*, used electrical metaphors such as environmental "potential" and "resistance" to describe population growth and natural productivity. Leopold cited Chapman in *Game Management*, p. 26. See R. N. Chapman, "The Quantitative Analysis of Environmental Factors," *Ecology* 9, no. 2 (1928): 111–122. Walter Taylor also argued that "The *biotic community* and its environment may be regarded as the internal and external portions of a single system of material and energy." See Taylor, "Significance of the Biotic Community," p. 294.

72. Tansley, "Use and Abuse of Vegetational Concepts," p. 297. The total inflow of energy into a system must equal the total outflow from a system plus any changes of energy within a system. In other words, energy can be converted in form, but not created or destroyed.

73. Tansley, "Use and Abuse of Vegetational Concepts," pp. 299–300.

74. AL, "Teaching Wildlife Conservation in Public Schools," *Transactions of the Wisconsin Academy* 30 (1937): 80.

75. AL, "A Biotic View of Land," RMG, pp. 266–267, and AL, "Conservation: In Whole or in Part?" RMG, p. 312: "It is hard for the layman, who sees plants and animals in perpetual conflict with each other, to conceive of them as cooperating parts of an organism."

76. AL, "A Biotic View of Land," RMG, pp. 268–269.
77. Ibid., p. 269.
78. Elton, *Animal Ecology*, p. 68.
79. Ibid., p. 69.
80. Ibid.
81. Ibid., pp. 69–70.
82. Croker, *Pioneer Ecologist*, p. 68.
83. Adams, "Ecological Study of Prairie and Forest Invertebrates." See also Shelford, "Principles and Problems."
84. AL, *Game Management*, pp. 304–305.
85. Ibid, p. 305. See also AL, "The Conservation Ethic," RMG, p. 183; AL, "The Land Ethic," SCA, p. 205.
86. Elton, *Animal Ecology*, pp. 22–34.
87. Elton, *Animal Ecology*, p. 25.
88. Ibid.
89. AL, letter to Carl O. Sauer, 29 December 1938, LP 10-3, 3; Elton, *Animal Ecology*, pp. 23–24.
90. W. P. Taylor, "Some Effects of Animals on Plants," *Scientific Monthly* 43 (1936): 262–271. Leopold cites this work in his "Second Report of the Game Policy Committee," pp. 228–232.
91. Taylor, "Some Effects of Animals on Plants," p. 266. In later years Leopold would become preoccupied with deer population problems in Wisconsin. See, for example, AL, "The Excess Deer Problem," *Audubon* 45, no. 3 (May–June 1943): 156–157; AL, "Deer Irruptions," *Wisconsin Conservation Bulletin* 8, no. 8 (August 1943): 1–11; AL, "What Next in Deer Policy?" *Wisconsin Conservation Bulletin* 9, no. 6 (June 1944): 3–4, 18–19; AL, "The Deer Dilemma," *Wisconsin Conservation Bulletin* 11, nos. 8–9 (August–September 1946): 3–5; AL, "Mortgaging the Future Deer Herd," *Wisconsin Conservation Bulletin* 12, no. 9 (September 1947): 3. Susan Flader tells the story of Leopold's evolving understanding of deer ecology and management in *Thinking Like a Mountain*. See also D. Binkley et al., "Was Aldo Leopold Right about the Kaibab Deer Herd?" *Ecosystems* 9 (2006): 227–241.
92. This was a quote from R. H. Yapp, "The Concept of Habitat," *Journal of Ecology* 10 (1922): 1, in Elton, *Animal Ecology*, p. 23.
93. AL, "A Biotic View of Land," RMG, p. 269.
94. A. Leopold, J. S. Ligon, and R. F. Pettit, "Southwestern Game Fields," first draft of chap. 4, "Normal Deer Stocking and Productivity," unpublished, n.d., p. 2, LP 10-6, 10.
95. Leopold did not perceive retrogressive succession as inherently negative, however, as we saw in his opinion about watershed-forest-grazing management in the Southwest. Sometimes going from a more to a less mature state could be highly productive for both humans and wildlife. For example, Leopold asked in 1934, "At what stage of the retrogression from forest to meadow is the marsh of greatest use to the animal community?" See AL, "The Arboretum and the University," RMG, p. 210.
96. AL, "The Conservation Ethic," pp. 634–643; also in RMG, pp. 183–184.
97. In his *Game Management* Leopold emphasized not only the composition of

habitat but also the size, geometry, and interspersion of various habitat types throughout a landscape and in relation to animal mobility. One of the few "laws" Leopold ever proposed was his "Law of Interspersion": "The potential density of game of low mobility requiring two or more [habitat] types is, within ordinary limits, proportional to the sum of the type peripheries. . . . Texts on ecology all recognize that certain species are associated with certain types, but I have found few which recognize the need for diverse types in juxtaposition, and none which state clearly that the frequency of such juxtaposition depends on interspersion, or that interspersion determines population density" (p. 132). This is a particularly important concept today in the field of conservation biology, as expanded and applied to continental- and national-scale reserve designs and "rewilding." See D. Foreman, *Rewilding North America: A Vision for Conservation in the 21st Century* (Washington, DC: Island Press, 2004). Many landscapes today have been highly fragmented so that in many places edge species are thriving while those requiring larger blocks of habitat are suffering.

98. AL, *Game Management*, p. 307; AL, "Report of the Iowa Game Survey," "Chapter One: The Fall of the Iowa Game Range" and "Chapter Two: Iowa Quail," *Outdoor America* 2, no. 1 (1932): 7–9, and 2, no. 2:11–13, 30–31; A. Leopold et al., "Animal Populations at Prairie du Sac, Wisconsin, 1929–1942" (draft corrected 18 February 1943, unpublished), pp. 44–45, LP 10-6, 13. See also AL, "A biotic view of land," RMG, p. 271 on nutrition and soil fertility.

99. W. Albrecht, "Pattern of Wildlife Distribution Fits the Soil Pattern," *Missouri Conservationist* 4, no. 3 (June 1943): 1–3, 16; W. Albrecht, "Sound Horses Are Bred on Fertile Soils," *Percheron News,* July 1942, pp. 15, 20–22. See AL, "A Biotic View of Land," RMG, p. 271 on nutrition and soil fertility.

100. AL, letter to Paul Errington, 4 September 1943, p. 2, LP 10-5, 5.

101. J. E. Weaver, "Plant Production as a Measure of Environment: A Study in Crop Ecology," *Journal of Ecology* 12, no. 2 (July 1924): 205. See also J. E. Weaver and E. L. Flory, "Stability of Climax Prairie and Some Environmental Changes Resulting from Breaking," *Ecology* 15, no. 4 (October 1934): 333–347; J. E. Weaver et al., "Relation of Root Distribution to Organic Matter in Prairie Soil," *Botanical Gazette* 96, no. 3 (March 1935): 389–420.

102. AL, "Why the Wilderness Society?" *Living Wilderness* 1, no. 1 (September 1935): 6; AL, "Wilderness for Science," SCA, pp. 195, 197.

103. Weaver and Flory, "Stability of Climax Prairie," pp. 345–346. Weaver's work also suggested a definition of stability on the prairie: "The relative constancy of the numbers of plants over a long period of time and the ordinary fluctuations within relatively narrow limits indicate the high degree of balance or stabilization" (p. 334). Native prairies, in comparison with cropped fields, experienced far less erosion and gullying and greater resistance to pest invasion and generally used water, light, and other resources much more efficiently and productively. See also W. C. Lowdermilk, "The Role of Vegetation in Erosion Control and Water Conservation," *Journal of Forestry* 32, no. 5 (May 1934): 553. See also Lowdermilk's earlier article, "Influence of Forest Litter on Run-off, Percolation, and Erosion," *Journal of Forestry* 28,

no. 4 (April 1930): 474–491. Weaver cited C. T. Vorhies and W. P. Taylor, "The Life Histories and Ecology of Jackrabbits, *Lepus alleni* and *Lepus californicus* spp., in Relation to Grazing in Arizona," *Technical Bulletin— University of Arizona, College of Agriculture, Agricultural Experiment Station* 49 (1933): 541, 563–564.

104. W. Taylor, "Some Animal Relations to Soils," *Ecology* 16, no. 2 (April 1935): 127–136.

105. C. E. Kellogg, "The Place of Soil in the Biological Complex," *Scientific Monthly* 39, no. 1 (1934): 46–51.

106. Taylor, "Some Animal Relations to Soils," p. 130.

107. AL, "A Biotic View of Land," RMG, p. 268; See also AL, "Economics, Philosophy, and Land," unfinished manuscript, 23 November 1938, LP 10-6, 16: "Evolution strives to lengthen food chains . . . complicates the pyramid."

108. Leopold's thinking was undergirded by evolutionary science, yet he chose primarily to speak in the language of ecology. He did so because he believed that ecology provided a particularly good "window from which to view the world." Ecology could lead to lifelong opportunities for observational study and even experimentation for students and citizens. It was more difficult to add to one's evolutionary knowledge outside the academic classroom. See AL, "The Role of Wildlife in a Liberal Education," *Transactions of the 7th North American Wildlife Conference* (8–10 April 1942): 485–489; also in RMG, p. 305.

109. See AL, "Conservation: In Whole or in Part?" RMG, p. 312.

110. AL, "Wilderness for Science," SCA, p. 197.

111. See J. E. Weaver, *Root Development of Field Crops* (New York: McGraw-Hill, 1926); Weaver and Flory, "Stability of Climax Prairie"; J. E. Weaver and T. J. Fitzpatrick, "The Prairie," *Ecological Monographs* 4, no. 2 (April 1934): 111–295.

112. AL, "Roadside Prairies," FHL, pp. 138–139.

113. Ibid., p. 138.

114. Ibid.

115. AL, "A Biotic View of Land," RMG, p. 273.

116. Ibid., pp. 266, 273.

117. AL, "The Land Pyramid," SCA, pp. 214–220.

118. AL, "A Biotic View of Land," RMG, p. 267.

119. Ibid.

120. AL, "A Biotic View of Land," RMG, p. 267.

121. Ibid.

122. Ibid.

123. Ibid., pp. 267–268. Leopold believed, too, that ecology was the only "language" by which the land mechanism could be adequately portrayed: "A language is imperative, for if we are to guide land-use we must talk sense to the farmer and economist, pioneer and poet, stockman and philosopher, lumberjack and geographer, engineer and historian. The ecological concept is, I think, translatable into common speech." See AL, "Biotic Land-Use," FHL, p. 204.

124. AL, "A Biotic View of Land," RMG, p. 267, and AL, "The Land Pyramid," SCA, p. 214.

125. In 1943, soil scientist William Albrecht complimented Leopold on his "biotic pyramid" idea and urged him to include microbes in it, writing, "I do not recall whether you had bacteria in the pyramid between soil and plants. I should like to emphasize the place of microbes because these minute life forms have been harassed so thoroughly that like snakes they seldom get favorable attention . . . we are learning that microbes in decomposition are synthesizing many of the essentials, particularly vitamins . . . it is high time that we put microbes near the foundation of our biotic pyramid." William Albrecht, letter to AL, 6 July 1943, LP 10-5, 5.

126. AL, "The Role of Wildlife in a Liberal Education," fig. 1; RMG, p. 304. Also see Leopold's typed lecture for Wildlife Ecology 118, "Definitions of Food Chain Relationships," LP 10-6, 15.

127. AL, "A Biotic View of Land," RMG, p. 268. See also an updated version in AL, "The Land Pyramid," SCA, p. 215.

128. Ibid., p. 268. See also an updated version in AL, "The Land Pyramid," SCA, p. 215.

129. Ibid., pp. 268–269. See also an updated version in AL, "The Land Pyramid," SCA, pp. 215–216.

130. Ibid., p. 269. See also an updated version in AL, "The Land Pyramid," SCA, p. 216.

131. Ibid. See also an updated version in AL, "The Land Pyramid," SCA, pp. 216–217.

132. Ibid., p. 270. See also an updated version in AL, "The Land Pyramid," SCA, p. 218.

133. E. C. Williams published an example of an Eltonian pyramid based on the "floor fauna" of the Panama rain forest. See "An Ecological Study of the Floor Fauna of the Panama Rain Forest," *Bulletin of the Chicago Academy of Sciences* 6 (1941): 63–124.

134. AL, "Request for Grant-in-Aid: The Animal Pyramid of Prairie du Sac," 10 December 1940, LP 10-5, 5.

135. AL, "Request for Grant-in-Aid, 1941–42: The Animal Pyramid of Prairie du Sac," n.d., LP 10-5, 5. This proposal was supplemented on 23 September 1941 by a statement by Leopold's student Harold Hanson.

136. This was a follow-up to the work of Elton, Nicholson, and others emphasizing the importance of animal numbers in community organization and functioning.

137. H. Hanson and A. Leopold, "The Prairie du Sac Project," 23 September 1941, LP 10-5, 5. Of note, too, is that R. L. Lindeman, in his 1942 "Trophic-Dynamic Aspect of Ecology," also suggested that "the Eltonian Pyramid may be expressed in terms of biomass" (p. 408). See also F. S. Bodenheimer, *Problems of Animal Ecology* (London: Oxford University Press, 1938).

138. A. Leopold and H. Hanson, "Request for Grant-in-Aid, 1942–43: The Animal Pyramid at Prairie du Sac," 30 December 1941, LP 10-5, 5.

139. Obtained from A. W. Schorger and N. C. Fasset at UW.

140. Leopold and Hanson, "Request, 1942–43," p. 2.

141. See, too, AL, "The Arboretum and the University," RMG, p. 210: "If civilization consists of cooperation with plants, animals, soil, and men, then a university which attempts to define that cooperation must have, for the use of its faculty and students, places which show what the land was, what it is, and what it ought to be."

142. Leopold et al., "Animal Populations at Prairie du Sac, Wisconsin, 1929–1942," p. 1.

143. Ibid. Captioned "Figure 3: Wild Pyramid of Numbers and Weights for an Average Square Mile."

144. Ibid. Captioned "Figure 4: Wild Pyramid [right] Compared with Tame Pyramid [left], in Terms of Per Cent of Their Combined Weight for an Average Square Mile. At the Extreme Right an Estimate of the Former Wild Layers Added—Dashed Lines."

145. Ibid., pp. 6–7.

146. The authors included exotic species in the category of domestic animals.

147. AL et al., "Animal Populations at Prairie du Sac, Wisconsin, 1929–1942," p. 7.

148. Ibid., pp. 7–8.

149. Ibid., p. 8.

150. Ibid., p. 9.

151. Ibid., p. 9. The manuscript also included a winter bird pyramid ("Winter Bird Pyramid of Numbers and Weights on Seven Square Miles"), noting that the exotic species, English sparrow, "outnumbered all other birds combined, and [outweighed] any other single species except pheasant."

152. Ibid., p. 10.

153. F. F. Darling, *A Herd of Red Deer: A Study in Animal Behavior* (London: Oxford University Press, 1937).

154. Ibid., p. 160.

155. AL, "Lakes in Relation to Terrestrial Life Patterns," in J. G. Needham et al., *A Symposium on Hydrobiology* (Madison: University of Wisconsin Press, 1941), pp. 17–22.

156. Ibid., pp. 17–18. Leopold presented this paper to a group of hydrobiologists, consciously choosing "a language" appropriate to soil-water nutrient interactions.

157. Ibid., pp. 19–20.

158. Ibid., p. 18.

159. Ibid., pp. 17, 22.

160. Ibid, p. 17.

161. Ibid., p. 22.

162. AL, "Odyssey," *Audubon* 44, no. 3 (May–June 1942): 133–135; also in SCA, pp. 104–108. For an interesting comparison see P. Levi, "Carbon," in *The Periodic Table*, translated by R. Rosenthal (New York: Schocken Books, 1984).

163. AL, "Round River," p. 158.

164. AL, "Odyssey," SCA, p. 104.

165. AL, "Foreword," revision of 31 July 1947, LP 10-6, 16. Printed in J. B. Callicott, ed., *Companion to "A Sand County Almanac": Interpretive and Critical Essays* (Madison: University of Wisconsin Press, 1987), pp. 281–290.

In this lengthy foreword, later replaced with a shorter one, Leopold invites readers to pay particular attention to "Odyssey," which a colleague had told him captured so much.

166. AL, letter to Ernest Holt (Soil Conservation Service), 2 October 1939, LP 10-2, 8.
167. AL, letter to W. L. Anderson, 21 May 1940, LP 10-2, 8.
168. AL, letter to Jay Darling, 31 October 1944, LP 10-2, 3.
169. In a 12 July 1943 draft of "Land as a Circulatory System," unpublished, LP 10-6, 16; this document was apparently intended as the first chapter in a new ecology text that Leopold had planned.
170. AL, "Ecology and Politics," RMG, p. 281.
171. Ibid., p. 282.
172. Ibid., p. 284.
173. Ibid., p. 282.
174. Ibid., p. 284. See also Leopold's earlier *Game Management*, pp. 391–395. Leopold understood that an expanding human population was a major force pushing the need for management. The denser the human population, the more intense was the management needed. He recommended "regulating our future human population density by some qualitative standard."
175. AL, "Post-War Prospects," *Audubon* 46, no. 1 (January–February 1944): 27–29.
176. Ibid., p. 29.
177. Ibid.
178. Ibid. Leopold was exposed to the work of a number of scientists studying the relationship between soil fertility, plant and animal nutrition, and human health. Of particular note are two articles published in the journal *Land*, reprinted in N. P. Pittman, ed., *From the Land* (Washington, DC: Island Press, 1988): W. Albrecht, "Health Depends on Soil," 1942 (Pittman, *From the Land*, pp. 312–318); and J. Forman, M.D., "The Trace Elements in Nutrition," 1943 (Pittman, *From the Land*, pp. 305–311). Elmer McCollum, a chemist who had worked on nutrition next door to Leopold at the University of Wisconsin (see R. Lord, "The Newer Knowledge of Elmer V. McCollum," in Pittman, *From the Land*, pp. 295–301), codiscovered vitamin A in 1907 and made other important discoveries related to nutrition and soil fertility.
179. AL, "The Land-Health Concept and Conservation," FHL, p. 226.

Chapter 7: Ecological Poetry

1. See AL, "Obituary: P. S. Lovejoy," *Journal of Wildlife Management* 7, no. 1 (1943): 125–128.
2. P. S. Lovejoy, letter to AL, 12 July 1939, p. 1, UWDWE.
3. Ibid., p. 7.
4. AL, "A Biotic View of Land," RMG, p. 270.
5. P. S. Lovejoy, letter to AL, 12 July 1939, p. 7.
6. In ecological science, holists and reductionists have been perhaps most commonly distinguished by whether or not they understand the whole (a community or ecosystem, for instance) to be equal to more than the sum of its

parts, that is, to have emergent properties. Scientists who recognize emergent properties, in turn, may divide the properties into those that arise out of scientific ignorance, so that the trait disappears upon further study of the parts, and those that are truly and inherently not reducible to parts, so that the characteristic must be examined at the appropriate unit level. Differences among ecologists come largely from their position with regard to reductionism, holism, and emergence. See R. P. McIntosh, *The Background of Ecology: Concept and Theory* (Cambridge: Cambridge University Press, 1985). P. S. Lovejoy in letters to Leopold referred several times to the work of social-insect ecologist William Morton Wheeler's "emergent evolution" thesis: Lovejoy wrote that Wheeler said, in *Emergent Evolution and the Development of Societies* (New York: W. W. Norton, 1928), "that no amount of study as to 'steam' or 'water,' will pre-determine the properties of 'ice' . . . & mebby likewise as genes get shuffled etc. [we cannot predict outcomes of interactions of parts just by knowing something of the parts]." See, for example, P. S. Lovejoy, letters to AL, 10 May 1941 and 4 August 1941, UWDWE. I have not been able to find a response of Leopold's to this particular idea. Leopold assigned to his wildlife ecology class readings on ecological social organization that included a number of works by University of Chicago social ecologist W. C. Allee on the "evolution of communities," including Allee's *Animal Life and Social Growth* (Baltimore: Williams and Wilkins, 1932) and *Animal Aggregations* (Chicago: University of Chicago Press, 1931). See also AL, "Of Mice and Men," p. 5, LP 10–6, 16.

7. P. S. Lovejoy, letter to AL, 7 January 1937, UWDWE.
8. AL, "A Biotic View of Land," RMG, p. 271.
9. AL, "The Farmer as a Conservationist," FHL, pp. 164–165.
10. AL, "Some Fundamentals of Conservation in the Southwest," RMG, p. 94.
11. For example, see comments to Leopold on his draft of "Skill in Forestry," UWDWE.
12. AL, "The State of the Profession," *Journal of Wildlife Management* 4, no. 3 (July 1940): 343–346; RMG, p. 276.
13. Ibid.
14. Ibid., pp. 276–277.
15. Ibid., p. 277.
16. AL, "The Role of Wildlife in a Liberal Education," RMG, pp. 302–303.
17. P. S. Lovejoy, letter to AL, 10 May 1941, p. 3, UWDWE. Lovejoy was writing to Leopold about a phrase the latter had used in his 1940 "Wisconsin Wildlife Chronology" (*Wisconsin Conservation Bulletin* 5, no. 11:8–20): "Each [trivial event in the following chronology of wildlife events] marks the birth or death of an aspiration, the beginning or the end of an experience, a loss or a gain in the vitality of that great organism: Wisconsin." Lovejoy apparently didn't believe that this was Leopold at his finest.
18. Albert Hochbaum, letter to AL, 4 February 1944, LP 10-2, 3.
19. AL, letter to Albert Hochbaum, 1 March 1944, LP 10-2, 3.
20. P. S. Lovejoy, letter to AL, 31 October 1940, UWDWE: "I still like the Gavilan job very well . . . & I make another bow for you."
21. Albert Hochbaum, letter to AL, 22 January 1944, LP 10-2, 3.

22. Albert Hochbaum, letter to AL, 4 February 1944, LP 10-2, 3.
23. Albert Hochbaum, letter to AL, 11 March 1944, LP 10-2, 3.
24. AL, "Request for Information on Existing and Needed Reserves of Natural Conditions" for the Sierra Madre, submitted to C. Kendeigh of the Ecological Society of America Committee for the Study of Plant and Animal Communities, ca. 1941, LP 10-3, 10.
25. Ibid.
26. AL, RR, pp. 131–132.
27. AL, "Song of the Gavilan," *Journal of Wildlife Management* 4, no. 3 (July 1940): 343–346; also in SCA, p. 149.
28. Ibid., p. 152.
29. Ibid., pp. 151–152.
30. Ibid., p. 151.
31. Ibid., pp. 152–153.
32. Ibid., pp. 153–154.
33. Ibid., p. 154.
34. AL, "The State of the Profession," RMG, p. 276.
35. This was Leopold's spelling.
36. AL, "The Thick-Billed Parrot in Chihuahua," *Condor* 39, no. 1 (January–February 1937): 74–75; also in SCA (as "Guacamaja"), pp. 137–141.
37. AL, "Guacamaja," p. 140.
38. While abundant on the Mexico side, this species appeared only on the hypothesis list of the 1931 American Ornithologists' Union checklist for the U.S. side of the Sierra Madre (partly because of Leopold's careful identification and reporting of the bird), wandering only occasionally across the border in search of mast; LP 10-3,10. See also F. Bailey, *Birds of New Mexico* (Santa Fe: New Mexico Department of Game and Fish, 1928), pp. 306–307. The thick-billed parrot appeared not at all in J. L. Peters' *Check-List of Birds of the World.*
39. AL, "Guacamaja," p. 138.
40. Ibid., p. 137.
41. Ibid., p. 138.
42. "Numenon" was Leopold's spelling. The word is taken from P. D. Ouspensky, *Tertium Organum: The Third Canon of Thought; a Key to the Enigmas of the World,* revised translation by E. Kadloubovsky and the author (New York: Alfred A. Knopf, 1981). It is like in meaning to "numen": "a spiritual force or influence often identified with a natural object, phenomenon, or locality" (*Webster's New Collegiate Dictionary,* 1976) and "noumenon": "a ground of phenomena that according to Kant cannot be experienced, can be known to exist, but to which no properties can be intelligibly ascribed." Scattered throughout Leopold's writings are indications that Leopold continued to think of Ouspensky's work and perhaps returned to it from time to time. Although most entries in his personal journal are undated, it is likely that his first entry from Ouspensky was written sometime in the early to mid-1920s: "The aim of art is the search for beauty, just as the aim of religion is the search for God and truth. And exactly as art stops, so religion stops as soon as it ceases the search for God and truth, thinking it

has found them" (AL, personal journal, p. 22). What Ouspensky conveyed in the remainder of the text from which this passage is quoted was similar to Leopold's urge to break down "senseless barriers." Science, art, religion, and philosophy were all different approaches to the same end of gaining knowledge about the world, the truest of which was to discover the inner qualities of things. "Science," Ouspensky had written, should be an *"investigation of the unknown"* (p. 99). But in getting to the essences of things, religion and art had an upper hand. And it somehow seemed that it was in the seeking, as opposed to the finding, that a person came closest to truth and beauty. Ouspensky, *Tertium Organum*, pp. 193–194. More than forty pages after the first reference to Ouspensky in Leopold's pocket-sized journal, indicating a passage of some time (though probably still recorded in the mid- to late 1920s), are two more small quotes from Ouspensky: "But life belongs not alone to separate, individual organisms—anything indivisible is a living being," and "All cultural conquests in the realm of the material are double-edged, may equally serve for good or for evil. A change of consciousness can alone be a guarantee of the surcease of misuses of the powers given by culture, and only thus will culture cease to be a 'growth of barbarity.'" AL, personal journal, p. 69. See also AL, "Land Pathology," 15 April 1935, p. 1, LP 10-6, 16, in which he wrote "Ouspensky" in the margin next to the paragraph beginning "Philosophers have long since claimed that society is an organism."

43. Ouspensky, *Tertium Organum*, p. 146.

44. AL, "Introduction," unpublished notes, LP 10-6, 16. Isaiah: " . . . upon the cedars of Lebanon that are high and lifted up, and upon all the oaks of Bashan"; David: "The trees of the Lord are full of sap"; John Muir: "Every cell is in a swirl of enjoyment, humming like a hive, singing the old-new song of creation." Leopold wrote, "An even more impelling reason [than pest control for desiring a diverse landscape, composed as far as possible of native species] is that we like it. This liking is not economic; it is compounded of ecology and poetry."

45. For instance, see T. Roosevelt, "Nature Fakers," *Everybody's Magazine* 17, no. 3 (September 1907): 427–430. The controversy is considered in detail in R. H. Lutts, *The Nature Fakers: Wildlife, Science, and Sentiment* (Charlottesville: University of Virginia Press, 1990). See R. Nash, "Aldo Leopold's Intellectual Heritage," in J. B. Callicott, ed., *Companion to "A Sand County Almanac": Interpretive and Critical Essays* (Madison: University of Wisconsin Press, 1987), pp. 63–90.

46. AL, personal journal, p. 28, LP 10-7, 1 (15). See J. Burroughs, *Whitman: A Study* (Boston: Houghton Mifflin, 1896).

47. AL, "Dear Judge Botts," unpublished, n.d., LP 10-6, 16.

48. AL, "January Thaw," SCA, p. 4.

49. Ibid.

50. AL, "Great Possessions," SCA, pp. 41–42; "Pines above Snow," SCA, p. 87.

51. AL, "Axe-in-Hand," SCA, p. 70.

52. AL, "Marshland Elegy," *American Forests* 43, no. 10 (October 1937): 472–474; also in SCA, p. 101.

53. AL, "The Choral Copse," SCA, p. 53.
54. AL, "The Green Pasture," SCA, p. 51.
55. AL, "Thoughts on a Map of Liberia," unpublished, n.d., LP 10-6, 16. This draft was a precursor to "The River of the Mother of God," RMG, pp. 123–127.
56. See Ouspensky, *Tertium Organum*, pp. 11, 21, 51–52, 93–94. Ouspensky drew from C. H. Hinton's *The Fourth Dimension* (London, S. Sonnenschein, 1904), which had to do with the spatial perception of humans and, more broadly, with how humans might enhance their apprehension of the world.
57. AL, "Thoughts on a Map of Liberia."
58. AL, "The River of the Mother of God," RMG, p. 127. This manuscript was written in the early 1920s and submitted to and rejected by the *Yale Review*.
59. See AL, "Flambeau," SCA, pp. 112–116.
60. AL, "Ecology, Philosophy, and Conservation," ca. late 1930s, p. 1, LP 10-6, 16. Truth, suggested Ouspensky, putting it another way, could be expressed only in the form of a paradox. Ouspensky, *Tertium Organum*, p. 226.
61. AL, "Ecology, Philosophy, and Conservation," p. 1.
62. AL, review of A. E. Parkins and J. R. Whitaker, eds., *Our National Resources and Their Conservation* (New York: John Wiley and Sons, 1936), in *Bird-Lore* 39, no. 1 (January–February 1937): 74–75.
63. AL, "The Wilderness and Its Place in Forest Recreational Policy," *Journal of Forestry* 19, no. 7 (November 1921): 718–721; also in RMG, p. 79. Leopold, it seems, had turned a phrase from A. T. Hadley's *Some Influences in Modern Philosophic Thought* (New Haven, CT: Yale University Press, 1913): "That which will prevail in the long run," Hadley had written, "must be right" (p. 129). Hadley distilled this philosophy in a lecture included in this book, titled "Politics and Ethics": "The criterion which shows whether a thing is right or wrong is its permanence. Survival is not merely the characteristic of right; it is the test of right" (p. 71).
64. AL, "Some Fundamentals of Conservation in the Southwest," RMG, p. 96.
65. The influence of Ouspensky and Hadley on Leopold has been noted and discussed in B. G. Norton, "The Constancy of Leopold's Land Ethic," *Conservation Biology* 2, no. 1 (1988): 93–102; B. G. Norton, personal communication, 2004.
66. AL, "Some Fundamentals of Conservation in the Southwest," RMG, p. 97. In an unpublished and undated draft titled "Ecology, Economics, and Land Use" (LP 10-6, 16) Leopold makes an effort to reason through his conservation viewpoint, noting that the assumption that the biota was all built for humans is "an arrogance hardly compatible with the theory of evolution" and that respect for the value of the biota as a whole "probably precludes an ethical society from exterminating its constituent parts. It certainly precludes their needless extermination. Conservation is respect for biotic values."
67. Ibid. See also J. Burroughs, *Accepting the Universe* (NY: Russell & Russell, 1920), pp. 35–36.
68. Ibid.

69. AL, "Marshland Elegy," SCA, pp. 95–96.
70. Ibid., p. 96.
71. AL, "The Land Ethic," SCA, p. 216.
72. Land community membership gave species a "right to continued existence, and, at least in spots, their continued existence in a natural state" (AL, "The Community Concept," SCA, p. 204; see also AL, "Substitutes for a Land Ethic," SCA, p. 210). "[B]irds" and other creatures "should continue as a matter of biotic right, regardless of the presence or absence of economic advantage to us" ("Substitutes for a Land Ethic," SCA, p. 211). "We should have been better off to assert, in the first place, that good and bad are attributes of numbers, not of species; that hawks and owls are members of the native fauna, and as such are entitled to share the land with us; that no man has the moral right to kill them except when sustaining injury" (AL, "What Is a Weed?" RMG, p. 309, FHL, p. 212). "We have no right to exterminate any species of wildlife. I stand on this as a fundamental principle" (AL, "Deer, Wolves, Foxes, and Pheasants," *Wisconsin Conservation Bulletin* 10, no. 5 [1945]: 4). "Mr. Hayden concludes, I think rightly, that the only sure foundation for wildlife conservation is 'the right of things to exist for their own sake'" (AL, "Review of S. S. Hayden, *The International Protection of Wildlife*," in *Geographical Review* 33, no. 2 [April 1943]: 341). "Soil built the flora and fauna and was in turn rebuilt by them. Conservation must consider the biota as a whole, not as separate parts." Second, "Man must assume that the biota has value in and of itself, separate from its value as human habitat" (AL, "Ecology and Economics in Land Use," unpublished, n.d., LP 10-6, 16).
73. AL, "To the Forest Officers of the Carson," RMG, p. 44.
74. See AL, "The Erosion Cycle in the Southwest," unpublished manuscript, ca. 1935 (including notes with slides by the same title for "Erosion Symposium," dated 17 December 1935), p. 1, LP, 10-6, 12.
75. AL, "A Hunter's Notes on Doves in the Rio Grande Valley," *Condor* 23, no. 1 (January–February 1921): 19–21; also in ALSW, p. 96.
76. AL, "The State of the Profession," RMG, p. 280.
77. AL, "Goose Music," RR, p. 171.
78. AL, "Some Fundamentals of Conservation in the Southwest," RMG, p. 96.
79. AL, "Goose Music," RR, p. 171.
80. C. D. Meine, *Aldo Leopold: His Life and Work* (Madison: University of Wisconsin Press, 1988), p. 65.
81. The final sentences of AL, "The Forestry of the Prophets," *Journal of Forestry* 18, no. 4 (April 1920): 412–419 (also in RMG, p. 77), were as follows: "In closing, it may not be improper to add a word on the intensely interesting reading on a multitude of subjects to be found in the Old Testament. As Stevenson said about one of Hazlitt's essays, 'It is so good that there should be a tax levied on all who have not read it.'" In his personal journal (p. 7) AL copied down these lines: "If I were appointed a committee of one to regulate the much debated question of college entrance examinations in English, I should . . . erase every list of books that has been thus far suggested, and I should confine the examination wholly to the Authorized Version of the Bible. —Wm. Lyon Phelps." See Meine, *Aldo Leopold*, p. 64.

82. AL, personal journal, pp. 36–42.
83. A. T. Hadley, *Baccalaureate Addresses: And Other Talks on Kindred Themes* (New York: Charles Scribner's Sons, 1907), p. 91.
84. Nina Leopold Bradley, Leopold's elder daughter, personal communication, 2003.
85. Leopold used this line from Shakespeare's *Hamlet* (Act IV, scene 7) a number of times: "For goodness, growing like a pleurisy, / Dies in his own too much"; see, e.g., AL, "Conservation Economics," RMG, p. 196, and AL, "Wilderness," RMG, p. 229.
86. AL, personal journal, p. 46. The poem, by Louis Untermeyer, was published in the July 1919 *Yale Review*.
87. AL, personal journal, p. 26.
88. AL, "Clandeboye," SCA, p. 160.
89. Ibid.
90. Ibid., p. 161.

Chapter 8: The Germ and the Juggernaut

1. AL, "Marshland Elegy," *American Forests* 43, no. 10 (1937): 472–474, and later in SCA, pp. 95–100; quote from p. 101. For a discussion of this essay, see C. Meine, "Giving Voice to Concern," in *Correction Lines: Essays on Land, Leopold, and Conservation* (Washington, DC: Island Press, 2004), pp. 132–147.
2. AL, "Marshland Elegy," SCA.
3. The essays ultimately formed parts of *A Sand County Almanac*.
4. Albert Hochbaum, letter to AL, 11 March 1944, LP 10-2, 3.
5. AL, SCA, p. viii.
6. C. D. Meine, *Aldo Leopold: His Life and Work* (Madison: University of Wisconsin Press, 1988), p. 467.
7. AL, "Ecology and Politics," RMG, pp. 281–286; See, too, Chapter 6.
8. AL, round-robin letter titled "Mobility of Wildlifers, 2nd Progress Report," 1 September 1943, LP 10-1, 3. See also AL, letter to William Vogt, 12 August 1942, LP 10-1, 3: "I had planned to write my 'Conservation Ecology' during the coming year," and AL, letter to William Vogt, 8 July 1943, LP 10-1, 3: Vogt had been urging Leopold to visit him in South America. Leopold responded, "I am somewhat in doubt about putting off my book for two years," Doug Wade to the Gang letter, 5 May 1944: I still lay into the professor about his ecology book . . ." LP 10-1, 3.
9. See also Meine, *Aldo Leopold*, p. 486. Two years later Leopold began experiencing symptoms of what would be diagnosed as tic douloureux, which required strong pain medication and ultimately brain surgery at the Mayo Clinic's St. Mary's Hospital in Rochester, Minnesota, in September 1947.
10. Meine, *Aldo Leopold*, pp. 451–452.
11. For an extensive discussion of Leopold's understanding of the deer overpopulation issue, see S. Flader, *Thinking Like a Mountain: Aldo Leopold and the Evolution of an Ecological Attitude toward Deer, Wolves, and Forests* (Madison: University of Wisconsin Press, 1974).
12. For a discussion of the Crime of '43 and Leopold's work as a Wisconsin conservation commissioner, highlighting Leopold's concern over the public

interest in deer management, see Flader, *Thinking Like a Mountain*, pp. 193–203; see also Meine, *Aldo Leopold*, pp. 452–455.

13. Ibid., p. 467; AL, letter to Starker Leopold and Betty Leopold, 25 December 1944, LP 10-1, 2.

14. AL, round-robin letter to "The Gang," 1 September 1943.

15. Douglas Wade, round-robin letter to "The Gang," 5 May 1944, LP 10-1, 3.

16. AL, *Game Management* (New York: Charles Scribner's Sons, 1933), fig. 2, p. 25. See also Chapter 4, p. 132.

17. Douglas Wade, round-robin letter to "The Gang," 5 May 1944.

18. AL, "The Conservation Ethic," RMG, p. 188.

19. AL, "A Criticism of the Booster Spirit," RMG, p. 104.

20. AL, "The Conservation Ethic," RMG, p. 189; AL, "The Ecological Conscience," RMG, pp. 338–346. See also AL, "Review of Farrington, *The Ducks Came Back*," RMG, p. 328.

21. AL, "The Conservation Ethic," RMG, p. 190.

22. The German system of game administration, according to Leopold, arose in part as "a manifestation of that intense love of the soil which is found throughout Germany." What impressed Leopold more than anything else as he observed German forests and game in 1935 was a "surging interest in nature." Germans wanted to spend time outdoors—walking, hiking, hunting, and farming—they seemed to want "to get their feet in the soil." See "Every Farm in Wisconsin to Be a Game Preserve: Professor Leopold Finds German Methods Practical Here," *Milwaukee Journal*, 5 January 1936, LP 10-3, 10. In 1940 Leopold summarized a similar hope for Americans: "Our profession [of wildlife management] began with the job of producing something to shoot. However important this may seem to us, it is not very important to the emancipated moderns who no longer feel soil between their toes." See AL, "The State of the Profession," *Journal of Wildlife Management* 4, no. 3 (July 1940): 343–346, also in RMG, p. 280; AL, "On a Monument to the Pigeon," SCA, pp. 108–112.

23. Leopold's ecological and ethical ideas have influenced several academic fields in the humanities, including ethics, law, history, and philosophy. For example, J. Baird Callicott has worked out and promoted a formal moral theory for land use based on some of Leopold's ideas. He argues that it is the holism of Leopold's ethic that sets it apart from dominant strands of ethical philosophy—its focus on the community as such rather than the particular living parts of it. Callicott argues that Leopold's worldview evolved to become one that was ecocentric, versus anthropocentric, while still acknowledging that Leopold never left off advocating for human-nature symbiosis. He also emphasizes a paradigm shift in ecology away from a balance-of-nature to a flux-of-nature view, arguing that Leopold's land ethic is adaptable to the new paradigm. See J. B. Callicott, "Whither Conservation Ethics?" *Conservation Biology* 4 (1990): 15–20. See also his "Elements of an Environmental Ethic: Moral Considerability and the Biotic Community," *Environmental Ethics* 1 (1979): 71–81; "Hume's *Is/Ought* Dichotomy and the Relation of Ecology to Leopold's Land Ethic," *Environmental Ethics* 4, no. 2 (1982): 163–174; "The Conceptual Foundations of the Land Ethic," in

Companion to "A Sand County Almanac": Interpretive and Critical Essays (Madison: University of Wisconsin Press, 1987), pp. 186–217; *In Defense of the Land Ethic* (Albany: State University of New York Press, 1989); *Beyond the Land Ethic: More Essays in Environmental Philosophy* (Albany: State University of New York Press, 1999); and "From the Balance of Nature to the Flux of Nature: The Land Ethic in a Time of Change," in *Aldo Leopold and the Ecological Conscience*, edited by R. L. Knight and S. Reidel (New York: Oxford University Press, 2002), pp. 90–105.

Also drawing heavily from Leopold's work, Bryan Norton, in building his ethical philosophy for land use, on the other hand, argues that Leopold's changing views on management arose not from a conversion from anthropocentrism to ecocentrism but from increasing knowledge and experience that better informed the values he already held: "Leopold believed throughout his career that long-sighted anthropocentrism provides an adequate basis for conservation practices." Norton also emphasizes that Leopold took into account both ecological change and ecological stability and constancy by thinking holistically in terms of different spatial and temporal scales. See also Norton's "The Constancy of Leopold's Land Ethic," *Conservation Biology* 2, no. 1 (1988): 93–102; "Context and Hierarchy in Aldo Leopold's Theory of Environmental Management," *Ecological Economics* 2 (1990): 119–127; *Toward Unity among Environmentalists* (New York: Oxford University Press, 1991); *Searching for Sustainability: Interdisciplinary Essays in the Philosophy of Conservation Biology* (Cambridge: Cambridge University Press, 2003); "Change, Constancy, and Creativity: The New Ecology and Some Old Problems," *Duke Environmental Law and Policy Forum* 7, no. 49 (1996): 49–70; and *Sustainability: A Philosophy of Adaptive Management* (Chicago: University of Chicago Press, 2005).

For further comments on Leopold's ethical philosophy, see others including M. P. Nelson, "A Defense of Environmental Ethics: A Reply to Janna Thompson," *Environmental Ethics* 15, no. 3 (1993): 147–160; M. P. Nelson, "Aldo Leopold, Environmental Ethics, and the Land Ethic," *Wildlife Society Bulletin* (Winter 1998): 741–744; H. Ralston III, *Environmental Ethics: Duties to and Values in the Natural World* (Philadelphia: Temple University Press, 1988); H. Ralston III, *Conserving Natural Value* (New York: Columbia University Press, 1994); and K. J. Warren, "Leopold's Land Ethic, Ecofeminist Philosophy, and Environmental Ethics," in *Aldo Leopold's Land Ethic: A Legacy for Public Land Managers*, proceedings of conference, 14–15 May 1999, National Conservation Training Center, Shepherdstown, WV.

In law and conservation thinking, see the work of Eric Freyfogle, e.g., "The Land Ethic and Pilgrim Leopold," *University of Colorado Law Review* 61 (1990): 217–256, and *Bounded People, Boundless Lands: Envisioning a New Land Ethic* (Washington, DC: Island Press, Shearwater Books, 1998).

In history, see, e.g., D. Worster, "Restoring Natural Order," in *The Wealth of Nature: Environmental History and the Ecological Imagination* (New York: Oxford University Press, 1993), pp. 171–183; D. Worster,

"Transformations of the Earth: Toward an Agroecological Perspective in History," *Journal of American History* 76, no. 4 (1990): 1087–1106; W. Cronon, "Modes of Prophecy and Production: Placing Nature in History," *Journal of American History* 76, no. 4 (1990): 1122–1131; and D. Worster, "Seeing beyond Culture," *Journal of American History* 76, no. 4 (1990): 1142–1147.

24. AL, "A Criticism of the Booster Spirit," RMG, p. 105.
25. AL, "The Conservation Ethic," RMG, p. 189.
26. The last recorded observation of a wild passenger pigeon was in Ohio in 1900; the last captive specimen died in 1914.
27. AL, "On a Monument to the Pigeon," SCA, pp. 108–112. In 1940 Vannevar Bush was FDR's chief advisor on wartime military research, promoting the idea that technical innovation was the key to national security. He took control of America's secret research on the atomic bomb and pushed for greater use of scientists and engineers in military planning. See G. P. Zachary, "Vannevar Bush Backs the Bomb," *Bulletin of the Atomic Scientist* 48, no. 10 (1942): 24–31.
28. AL, "Some Fundamentals of Conservation in the Southwest," RMG, p. 97.
29. AL, "The Conservation Ethic," RMG, p. 188.
30. AL, "Suggestions for American Wildlife Conference," attachment to a letter from AL to Seth Gordon dated 27 October 1935, p. 2, LP 10-6, 16.
31. AL, "Wilderness," SCA, p. 188; AL, "Wildlife in American Culture," SCA, pp. 177–187.
32. AL, "A Criticism of the Booster Spirit," RMG, p. 104.
33. Leopold's progenitors, the Leopolds, Runges, and Starkers, emigrated to America from Germany in the 1830s and 1840s. His mother, Clara Starker Leopold, privately educated in German culture, gardening, and the fine arts (she was especially fond of grand opera), exposed her children to the homemaking skills, literature, and music of their European heritage. German was the household language of Aldo's family until he was enrolled at age five in Prospect Hill School in Burlington. His reading list included German literature, philosophy, and poetry, perhaps including some version of the *Nibelungenlied*. See Meine, *Aldo Leopold*, pp. 3–16.
34. R. Lichtenstein, trans., *The Nibelungenlied* (New York: Edwin Mellen Press, 1991).
35. AL, personal journal, p. 51, LP 10-7, 1 (15).
36. AL, "The Conservation Ethic," RMG, p. 192.
37. Leopold's 1933 "Conservation Ethic" was reprinted in September 1946 in the *Journal of Heredity* (37, no. 9:275–279) under the title "Racial Wisdom and Conservation." It is uncertain whether Leopold gave permission for the publication; he held a copy in his scrapbook of reprints. The introduction to the 1946 publication, written anonymously by someone other than Leopold, urged readers to consider what it might take to stimulate a "general constructive interest in eugenics and the conservation of our race," noting that Leopold's "'Conservation Ethic' is envisioned as an emerging stage in the evolution of ethical concepts."

Also, in 1947 Leopold's close friend William Vogt urged him to read a book on semantics by Alfred Korzybski, founder of the Institute of General Semantics. The institute was dedicated to fostering human potential and building a new, more exacting science of man, promoting research and education. Vogt bought for Leopold a subscription to *ETC*, the institute's periodical, and Leopold stated that he had "got a great deal out of" Korzybski's book and would "certainly examine [the periodical] with care and with interest"; AL, letter to William Vogt, 8 January 1947, LP 10-1, 3; AL, letter to William Vogt, 8 February 1946, LP 10-1, 3.

38. AL, "The Conservation Ethic," RMG, p. 192; see J. Ortega y Gasset, ed., *The Revolt of the Masses* (New York: W. W. Norton, 1957).

39. Ibid., pp. 61–74.

40. Ibid., pp. 14–15.

41. AL, "The Conservation Ethic," RMG, p. 182.

42. Ibid., p. 185.

43. AL, "Conservation Education: A Revolution in Philosophy," unpublished fragment, LP 10-6, 17.

44. AL, "A Modus Vivendi for Conservationists," unfinished manuscript, n.d. (ca. 1941?), p. 1, LP 10-6, 16.

45. Ibid.

46. Ibid., p. 2.

47. See AL, "Motives for Conservation," class lecture for Wildlife Ecology 118, ca. 1940s, LP 10-6, 14.

48. Ibid.

49. AL, "Armament for Conservation," 23 November 1943, p. 1, LP 10-6, 16.

50. AL, "The Community Concept," SCA, p. 204.

51. Great Plains Committee, *The Future of the Great Plains*, 75th Cong., 1st sess., Document No. 144 (Washington, DC: Government Printing Office, 10 February 1937).

52. Committee participants included engineer Morris Cooke, head of the Rural Electrification Administration; economist and land planner Lewis C. Gray; collectivist brain truster Rexford Tugwell; and social scientist Hugh H. Bennett.

53. Great Plains Committee, *Future of the Great Plains*, p. 1.

54. D. Worster, *The Dust Bowl: The Southern Plains in the 1930s* (New York: Oxford University Press, 1979), p. 82.

55. Ibid., p. 94.

56. Great Plains Committee, *Future of the Great Plains*, pp. 64–65.

57. Ibid., p. 6. Also see Worster, *Dust Bowl*, p. 195.

58. Quoted in Great Plains Committee, *Future of the Great Plains*, p. 63.

59. Ibid., pp. 63–64.

60. Ibid., p. 11.

61. Ibid. See also Worster, *Dust Bowl*, p. 195.

62. Worster, *Dust Bowl*, pp. 195–196.

63. AL, "Ecology as an Ethical System," (unfinished), ca. 1940s, LP 10-6, 17.

64. Vogt's book stirred up both controversy and concern nationally with its thesis that a rising population of machine-equipped humans was well on its way

to pushing past the earth's resource limits. (See "Eat Hearty," *Time*, 8 November 1948—a controversial commentary on Vogt's book and *Our Plundered Planet* by Fairfield Osborn.) Vogt's publisher asked Leopold for comment on the book, which Leopold gladly provided, writing: "I have, of course, not seen Bill's book, but I have followed his thoughts with intense interest.... I notice the trend of Bill's thinking is distinctly visible in the thinking of many other ecological people who are deeply concerned with the land.... In other words, Bill has beaten them to it, and that is the makings of a book because the appetite for it will exist before hand. I am willing to bet it will have a large sale." AL, letter to Eric Swenson, 9 March 1948, LP 10-1, 3.

65. AL, letter to William Vogt, 25 January 1946, LP 10-1, 3. See W. Vogt, *Road to Survival* (New York: William Sloan Associates, 1948).

66. AL, "The Ecological Conscience," RMG, p. 338. For a thorough and modern treatment of problems within the conservation movement, also drawing on many of Leopold's ideas, see E. T. Freyfogle, *Why Conservation Is Failing and How It Can Regain Ground* (New Haven, CT: Yale University Press, 2006).

67. For a similar assessment see Worster, *Dust Bowl*, p. 6.

68. AL, "The Ecological Conscience," RMG, pp. 338–346; AL, SCA, pp. 207–210.

69. Leopold included "aerial space" along with soils, waters, plants, and animals in his list of what "land" includes in "Ecology as an Ethical System," p. 1.

70. AL, "The Ecological Conscience," RMG, p. 342.

71. AL, "Conservation: In Whole or in Part?" RMG, p. 315.

72. AL, "The Ecological Conscience," RMG, p. 343.

73. AL, "Motives for Conservation," p. 2, LP 10-6, 14.

74. AL, SCA, p. 214.

75. AL, "Motives for Conservation," p. 2.

76. AL, "The Ecological Conscience," RMG, pp. 340–341.

77. AL, "The Farm Wildlife Program: A Self-Scrutiny," ca. 1937, p. 7, LP 10-6, 14.

78. AL, "Conservation and Politics," ca. 1941, p. 3, LP 10-6, 14.

79. AL, "Motives for Conservation," p. 2.

80. AL, "Conservation Blueprints," *American Forests* 43, no. 12 (December 1937): 596.

81. AL, "The Ecological Conscience," RMG, p. 338.

82. AL, "Farm Wildlife Program," pp. 7–8.

83. Ibid.

84. AL, "The Farmer as a Conservationist," FHL, p. 168. Leopold in 1938 also suggested a detailed land management policy to the Huron Mountain Club for land use that promoted together wilderness, scientific, wildlife, and timber values on their lands. Not only could this be done, he argued, but it was also the club members' obligation as private landowners to do so in the public interest. Wilderness recreational and timber values might belong to the private club, but wildlife values were shared with neighbors because animals ranged across ownership boundaries. The club also had an obligation, Leopold believed, to preserve the public scientific values of one of the last

remaining large remnants of old-growth maple-hemlock forest, which was under its care as landowners. AL, "Report on Huron Mountain Club" (1938), printed by Huron Mountain Club, Michigan; reprinted in *Report of Huron Mountain Wildlife Foundation, 1955–1966* (n.p., 1967), pp. 40–57. See also Flader, *Thinking Like a Mountain*, pp. 156–163, and Meine, *Aldo Leopold*, pp. 385–386.

85. AL, "The Farmer as a Conservationist," FHL, p. 167.
86. Ibid.
87. AL, "The Conservation Ethic," RMG, p. 192.
88. AL, "Motives for Conservation," p. 1; AL, "Farm Wildlife Program," p. 7; AL, "The Farmer as a Conservationist," FHL, p. 168.
89. AL, "Motives for Conservation," p. 1.
90. Ibid.
91. AL, "Farm Wildlife Program," p. 7.
92. AL, "The Farmer as a Conservationist," FHL, p. 172.
93. AL, "Farm Wildlife Program," p. 8.
94. AL, "The Conservation Ethic," RMG, p. 191.
95. AL, SCA, pp. 210–211; AL, "The Farmer as a Conservationist," FHL, pp. 172–175.
96. AL, "The Farmer as a Conservationist," FHL, p. 174.
97. AL, "Motives for Conservation," p. 3.
98. AL, SCA, p. 202.
99. AL, "The Ecological Conscience," RMG, p. 346.
100. AL, "Conservation Blueprints," p. 596. See also AL, "Armament for Conservation," p. 1; AL, SCA, p. 225.
101. AL, SCA, p. 225. See also AL, "Conservation Blueprints," pp. 596, 608; AL, "Armament for Conservation," p. 1.
102. AL, "The Ecological Conscience," RMG, p. 345.
103. See AL, "The Conservation Ethic," RMG, p. 181; AL, "The Ecological Conscience," RMG, p. 345; AL, SCA, pp. 201–202, 224.
104. AL, "The Ecological Conscience," RMG, p. 345.
105. AL, "Farm Wildlife Program," p. 1.
106. Fragment, ca. 1940s, LP 10-6, 16.
107. AL, letter to Morris L. Cooke, 17 March 1948, 10-1, 1. The letter concerned a recent disagreement between Leopold and Cooke about a "Conservation Credo" that Morris was circulating for signatures of support. Leopold had not signed the document and criticized it for supporting what he believed were prospects in opposition to ecological conservation—"comprehensive development of river basins for flood control" and FDR's brand of "democratically managed river and power control." See also AL, letter to William Vogt, 24 February 1948, LP 10-1, 3.
108. See "Ecology and Economics in Land Use," unfinished, unpublished, ca. 1940s, LP 10-6, 17. Leopold was working out his conservation philosophy in this manuscript. "Conservationists of ecological viewpoint," he wrote, seemed to have "tacitly agreed upon a set of premises from which they measure the phenomena of land-use." No one person was entitled to write a conservation movement "constitution," he acknowledged, but he believed it

was necessary for someone to make a start. He ventured five progressive premises: First, "Soil built the flora and fauna and was in turn rebuilt by them. Conservation must consider the biota as a whole, not as separate parts." Second, "Man must assume that the biota has a value in and of itself, separate from its value as human habitat. The only alternative is to assume it was all built for him, an arrogance hardly compatible with the theory of evolution." Third, "Respect for this value probably precludes an ethical society from exterminating its constituent parts. It certainly precludes their needless extermination. Conservation is respect for biotic values." Fourth, "Self interest, on the other hand, requires any society to alter and manage the biota on the areas needed for habitation. The motivation for such alterations and management is referable to economics; the technique to agriculture; but the obligation to restrain these alterations and to respect biotic values underlies both, and is referable to ethics. The basic motivation for conservation is therefore not economic, but ethical." Finally, "Science facilitates alteration of the biota, but this is not its sole function. It also explains the biotic mechanism, and thus should enhance both respect for and appreciation of that mechanism. In the elaboration of machines there are indications that scientific effort may be subject to a law of diminishing returns, but in the illumination of the universe, returns are still proportional to achievement."

109. AL, "Motives for Conservation," pp. 4–5; AL, SCA, p. 202.
110. AL, *Game Management*, pp. 4–5.
111. Ibid., pp. xxxi, 21, 391–392. Game management and to some degree ecology were, in the first place, responses to needs associated with rising human population density and uses of increasingly powerful technology.
112. AL, "Motives for Conservation," pp. 3–6; AL, SCA, pp. 202–203.
113. AL, letter to Douglas Wade, 23 October 1944, LP 10-8, 1.
114. AL, "State of the Profession," RMG, p. 280. AL, letter to Morris Cooke, 30 September 1940, 10-2, 4. Leopold wrote to his friend Morris Cooke in 1940 commenting on a manuscript of Cooke's titled "Total Conservation": "I take issue with you on one point. You assume, by implication at least, that the 'total job' [of conservation] can be done without rebuilding Homo sapiens, or, to put it conversely, by government initiative alone. I do not believe it can. . . . The steps [taken by the Soil Conservation Service) are *toward* this end, but they will not reach it until we have a new kind of farmer, banker, voter, consumer, etc."
115. AL, "The Ecological Conscience," RMG, p. 338.
116. Ibid., pp. 345–346.

Chapter 9: Wildlife and the New Man
1. AL, letter to Douglas Wade, 23 October 1944, LP 10-8, 1.
2. AL, letter to Morris L. Cooke (Friends of the Land), 30 September 1940, LP 10-2, 4. See also "The State of the Profession," RMG, p. 280.
3. AL, "The Ecological Conscience," RMG, p. 338.
4. Ibid., p. 340.
5. AL, "Some Fundamentals of Conservation in the Southwest," RMG, pp. 94–97.
6. AL, "A Criticism of the Booster Spirit," RMG, pp. 102, 103.

7. See AL, "The Arboretum and the University," *Parks and Recreation* 18, no. 2 (October 1934): 59–60; also in RMG, pp. 209–211. See C. Meine, "Reimagining the Prairie: Aldo Leopold and the Origins of Prairie Restoration," in *Recovering the Prairie*, edited by R. F. Sayre (Madison: University of Wisconsin Press, 1999), pp. 144–160. The story of the founding of the University of Wisconsin Arboretum is told in N. Sachse. *A Thousand Ages: The University of Wisconsin Arboretum* (Madison: University of Wisconsin Press, 1965). See also J. B. Callicott, "The Arboretum and the University: The Speech and the Essay," *Transactions of the Wisconsin Academy of Sciences, Arts, and Letters* 87 (1999): 5–22.

8. AL, letter to P. E. McNall, 27 February 1936, LP 10-5, 2.

9. N. A., "Plan for Utilization of Milford Meadows Disconnected 5 Acre Tract," p. 2, LP 10-5, 2 (2).

10. Ibid., p. 1.

11. AL, letter to P. E. McNall, 27 February 1936. It remains uncertain what happened to the plan to dedicate the five-acre Milford Meadows tract (Betty Hawkins, personal communication, 2006). But in May 1940, the nearby Faville Grove Prairie was turned into a pasture. See AL, "Exit Orchis," 15 May 1940, LP 10-5, 2, and in *Wisconsin Wildlife* 2, no. 2 (August 1940): 17.

12. Ibid.; McNall, "Plan for Utilization"; see, too, one-page collage of news clippings and photos of "wildlifers club" (27 March 1936), "the nature class," (early spring 1936), and other related events, LP 10-5, 2.

13. AL, "The Conservation Ethic," RMG, p. 190; AL et al., "The University and Conservation of Wisconsin Wildlife: Science Inquiry Publication III," *Bulletin of the University of Wisconsin* series no. 2211, general series no. 1995 (February 1937): 35.

14. AL, letter to W. K. Thomas, 24 April 1939, LP 10-2, 7.

15. Ibid.

16. AL, "The Role of Wildlife in Education," unfinished, n.d., p. 1, LP 10-6, 16.

17. Ibid.

18. Ibid.

19. AL, "Suggestions for American Wildlife Conference," unpublished, 27 October 1935, p. 2, LP 10-6, 16.

20. Ibid., p. 1.

21. Ibid.

22. Ibid.

23. AL, "The Arboretum and the University," RMG, p. 210. See AL, "Role of Wildlife in Education," p. 3, and AL, *Game Management* (New York: Charles Scribner's Sons, 1933), p. 423.

24. AL, SCA, p. ix.

25. AL, *Game Management*, pp. 420, 423.

26. AL, "Role of Wildlife in Education," pp. 1, 3.

27. AL, "The Role of Wildlife in a Liberal Education," *Transactions of the 7th North American Wildlife Conference* (8–10 April 1942): 485–489; also in RMG, pp. 301, 302.

28. AL, "The Role of Wildlife in a Liberal Education," RMG, p. 303. See also Chapter 7, p. 221.

29. AL et al., "The University and Conservation of Wisconsin Wildlife: Science

Inquiry Publication III," *Bulletin of the University of Wisconsin* series no. 2211, general series no. 1995 (February 1937), p. 26.

30. Ibid.

31. AL, "Wherefore Wildlife Ecology?" RMG, p. 336. See also J. B. Callicott, "Aldo Leopold on Education, as Educator, and His Land Ethic in the Context of Environmental Education," *Journal of Environmental Education* 14 (1982): 34–41, and W. Kessler and A. Booth, "Professor Leopold, What Is Education For?" *Wildlife Society Bulletin* (Winter 1998): 707–712.

32. Ibid.

33. Ibid.

34. Ibid.

35. Ibid.

36. Ibid.

37. Ibid., pp. 336–337.

38. Anonymous, "Preliminary Organization of a Society of Wildlife Specialists" (taking place at the North American Wildlife Conference, Washington, DC, February 1936); Anonymous, "The Wildlife Society: A General Statement," 1937, p. 1, LP 10-2, 9.

39. As the organization developed, members of the Ecological Society of America raised the question of formal affiliation of the new Wildlife Specialists with the ESA. Walter Taylor (on the executive committee of the ESA) wrote to Leopold on 25 May 1936, asking: "Do you think it necessary to form a new society and thereby promote the continued disintegration of biologists and their organizations? Would it not be possible for us to form a section on wildlife of some such organization as the Ecological Society of America? You have most eloquently and effectively urged the integration of conservation as related to activities. Why should we not, like the chemist, work toward the better co-ordination and integration of biological organizations?" Leopold came to favor the idea, but the merger never took place. See P. Errington, letter to W. L. McAtee, 23 November 1936, LP 10-2, 9. See also J. L. Newton, "Science, Recreation, and Leopold's Quest for a Durable Scale," in *Wilderness Debate*, vol. 2, edited by M. Nelson and J. B. Callicott (Athens: University of Georgia Press, 2006). In a 1939 letter from E. V. Komarek to Gardiner Bump of the NYS Conservation Department is found evidence regarding the impression the ESA had given: it had been accused publicly at a meeting in St. Louis of "intellectual snobbery." LP 10-2, 2.

40. Anonymous, "Wildlife Society: A General Statement," p. 1; "The Constitution and By-laws of The Wildlife Society," 1937, LP 10-2, 9.

41. Anonymous, "Constitution and By-laws," p. 1.

42. Anonymous, "Wildlife Society: A General Statement," p. 2.

43. Rudolf Bennitt, letter to AL, 1 November 1937, LP 10-2, 9.

44. AL, letter to Rudolf Bennitt, 4 November 1937, LP 10-2, 9.

45. Victor Calahane, letter to AL, 16 April 1938, LP 10-2, 9.

46. See *Journal of Wildlife Management* 3, no. 2 (April 1939).

47. Douglas Wade sent a thoughtful response (ca. 1938, LP 10-2, 9) to Leopold's earliest draft (May 1938, titled "What a Wildlife Manager Should Be and Know") with thoughtful comments. Leopold incorporated Wade's

comments in following drafts, including changing the title, which Wade thought was redundant. LP 10-2, 9.

48. AL, letter to Rudolf Bennitt, 24 September 1938, LP 10-2, 9.
49. Charles Elton, letter to AL, 28 September 1938, LP 10-2, 9.
50. AL, "Professional Training in Wildlife Management," 6 September 1938 draft, p. 2, LP 10-2, 9.
51. Charles Elton, letter to AL, 28 September 1938, LP 10-2, 9.
52. AL, letter to Rudolf Bennitt, 24 September 1938, LP 10-2, 9.
53. AL, letter to Rudolf Bennitt, 8 September 1938, LP 10-2, 9.
54. AL et al., "Professional Training in Wildlife Work," 30 November 1938, pp. 1–9, LP 10-2, 9. Incidentally, Leopold graduated from his program at the University of Wisconsin one of the first women in the field—Frances Hamerstrom.
55. Ibid., pp. 1–3.
56. Ibid., pp. 3, 5.
57. Ibid., p. 4.
58. Ibid., p. 5.
59. Ibid.
60. Ibid.
61. Ibid., p. 4.
62. Ibid., p. 6.
63. Ibid., p. 4.
64. Ibid., p. 7.
65. Ibid., p. 8.
66. Ibid.
67. Ibid.
68. Ibid. To test the plausibility of the standards in 1939, Leopold conducted a mental experiment using his own graduate students: "I have tested the standards as now revised on my own mental picture of four of my best students—Hawkins, Frederick and Frances Hamerstrom, and Hochbaum. Unless my picture is altogether distorted, they could score on all of the points listed. On the other hand, I admit that no such average could reasonably be expected in any considerable number of students." See AL, letter to Rudolf Bennitt, 16 January 1939, LP 10-2, 9.
69. See AL, *Game Management*, pp. 211, 403: "In the long run, no system is satisfactory which does not conserve the rich variety of our game fauna, as distinguished from merely its most resistant and 'shootable' species. . . . The objective of a conservation program for non-game wild life should be exactly parallel [to game management]: to retain for the average citizen the opportunity to see, admire and enjoy, and the challenge to understand, the varied forms of birds and mammals indigenous to his state. It implies not only that these forms be kept in existence, *but that the greatest possible variety of them exist in each community.*" Paul Errington noted in his dissertation ("The Northern Bobwhite: Environmental Factors Influencing Its Status," University of Wisconsin, Madison, 2 May 1932, p. a) that "[t]he term 'wild life' now has an accepted meaning, embracing fishes, birds, mammals, and the related association of fields, forests, and waters. Report of Special

Committee on Conservation of Wild Life Resources to U.S. Senate, Jan. 21, 1931." And in AL et al., "Professional Training in Wildlife Work," 30 November 1938, p. 2, it is noted that "[w]ildlife . . . includes both animals and plants, both terrestrial and aquatic. Where the illustrative material implies a narrower scope, the reader is asked to interpolate to the broader one."

In 1936 Leopold urged his colleagues to attend particularly to threatened forms of wildlife, calling them the "crux of conservation policy." "The new organizations which have now assumed the name 'wildlife' instead of 'game,'" he argued, "are I think obligated to focus a substantial part of their effort on these threatened forms." AL, "Threatened Species," RMG, pp. 231–232. See also C. D. Meine, *Correction Lines: Essays on Land, Leopold, and Conservation* (Washington, DC: Island Press, 2004), p. 127. Leopold also served on the Committee on Bird Protection of the American Ornithologists' Union in the early 1940s, and beginning in the mid-1930s he urged the creation of conservation inventories of threatened species. See also AL, "Proposal for a Conservation Inventory of Threatened Species," unpublished, unfinished, UWDWE; AL, letters to Jay Darling, 21 and 23 November 1939, LP 10-4, 8.

70. Game management, Leopold wrote, "proposes a motivation—the love of sport—narrow enough actually to get action from human beings as now constituted, but nevertheless capable of expanding with time into that new social concept toward which conservation is groping." AL, *Game Management*, p. 423.

71. AL, "Notes on the Weights and Plumages of Ducks in New Mexico," *Condor* 21, no. 3 (May–June 1919): 128–129; AL, "Relative Abundance of Ducks in the Rio Grande Valley," *Condor* 21, no. 3 (May–June 1919): 122; AL, "A Hunter's Notes on Ducks in the Rio Grande Valley," *Condor* 23, no. 1 (January–February 1921): 19–21; AL, "Weights and Plumages of Ducks in the Rio Grande Valley," *Condor* 23, no. 3 (May–June 1921): 85–86.

72. AL, "The Sportsman-Naturalist: Some Commonly Overlooked Opportunities for Real Contributions to Natural History and Game Management," unfinished, n.d., UWDWE, vol. 2, p. 329, and LP 10-6, 17, p. 169. The statement was intended to introduce an article that Leopold apparently never finished.

73. AL, "What Is a Sportsman?" unfinished, n.d., UWDWE, vol. 1, and LP 10-6, 17, p. 166.

74. Ibid.

75. Ibid.

76. Ibid.

77. AL, "Wildlife in American Culture," *Journal of Wildlife Management* 7, no. 1 (January 1943): 1–6; also in SCA, p. 177.

78. AL, "Wildlife in American Culture," SCA, p. 177.

79. Ibid., p. 179.

80. Ibid., p. 177.

81. Ibid., p. 179; On the other hand, voluntary disregard of hunting ethics could work to degenerate and deprave him.

82. Ibid., p. 178.
83. Ibid., p. 179.
84. T. B. Veblen, *The Theory of the Leisure Class: An Economic Study of Institutions* (New York: Modern Library, 1934). Leopold used in class the 1931 edition (New York: Viking Press). With Charles Beard, James Harvey Robinson, and John Dewey, Veblen, after teaching at the University of Chicago and Stanford University, helped found in 1919 the New School for Social Research in New York City.
85. Ibid., p. 275.
86. Ibid., p. 247.
87. Ibid., pp. 253–256.
88. AL, "List of References/Questions for Discussion" for Game Management 118 (1937), p. 2, UWDWE. AL assigned his class chap. 10 ("Modern Survivals of Prowess") of Veblen's book.
89. AL, "The Farmer as a Conservationist," FHL, p. 167.
90. AL, "Game Methods: The American Way," *American Game* 20, no. 2 (March–April 1931): 20, 29–31; also in RMG, p. 163.
91. AL, "Hobbies," address to the Parent-Teacher Association, Randall School, Madison, Wisconsin, 10 April 1935, p. 1, UWDWE, vol. 1.
92. Ibid.
93. Ibid.
94. Ibid., p. 2. See, too, AL, "A Man's Leisure Time," address to the University of New Mexico Assembly, 15 October 1920, LP 10-6, 16 (4), and in RR, p. 8: "A good hobby may be a solitary revolt against the commonplace, or it may be the joint conspiracy of a congenial group. That group may, on occasion, be the family. In either event it is a rebellion, and if a hopeless one, all the better. I cannot imagine a worse jumble than to have the whole body politic suddenly 'adopt' all the foolish ideas that smolder in happy discontent beneath the conventional surface of society. There is no such danger. Nonconformity is the highest evolutionary attainment of social animals, and will grow no faster than other new functions. Science is just beginning to discover what incredible regimentation prevails among the 'free' savages, and the freer mammals and birds. A hobby is perhaps creation's first denial of the 'peck-order' that burdens the gregarious universe, and of which the majority of mankind is still a part."
95. Leopold was proud when his wife, Estella, was women's archery champion in the state of Wisconsin for five years running and placed 4th at the nationals in 1930. See C. D. Meine, *Aldo Leopold: His Life and Work* (Madison: University of Wisconsin Press, 1988), p. 269.
96. AL, "Hobbies," p. 2.
97. AL, "Wildlife in American Culture," SCA, p. 180.
98. AL, "Smoky Gold," SCA, p. 56.
99. AL, "Wildlife in American Culture," SCA, p. 183.
100. AL, "Red Lanterns," SCA, pp. 62–65.
101. AL, "Red Legs Kicking," SCA, pp. 120–122.
102. Ibid., p. 121.
103. Ibid.

104. AL, "Conservation Esthetic," SCA, p. 176.
105. See Olaus J. Murie, letter to AL, 30 October 1931, LP 10-3, 10. Murie had just read Leopold's "Game Methods: The American Way" (RMG, pp. 156–163) and was intrigued by Leopold's second theorem, which conditioned American game matters: the recreational value of game is inversely related to the artificiality of its origin. "I think you have struck a very fine note," wrote Murie. "I have felt that in recent times hunting has lost much of its old time flavor, some of the esthetic 'aura' is vanishing from our sport. I do not mean to say that the fine type of sportsman is gone, for I meet one every once in a while. But in the grand scramble for one's own share of game in many places the result is mere killing and our so called recreational values are not felt."
106. AL, "Conservation Esthetic," SCA, p. 170.
107. In 1937 Leopold exchanged remarks with T. D. Peffley, a car dealer in Dayton, Ohio, who was a member of the local chapter of the Izaak Walton League of America: "I am intensely interested in your situation, because the scientific idea of predation, if it can be 'sold' to sportsmen at all, should be salable to the I.W.L.A. I say this as a sportsman and a long-time member. The information you ask for is voluminous. . . . I will, however, attempt to give you a comprehensive summary of why we game managers think that 'vermin campaigns' are ordinarily not only useless, but actually harmful to conservation." AL, letter to T. D. Peffley, 11 May 1937, in response to T. D. Peffley, letter to AL, 5 May 1937, LP 10-2, 5. Leopold followed with nine points of scientific argument regarding the matter, concluding: "All of the foregoing propositions are supportable by physical evidence. It should be admitted, though, that the game manager's view is in part determined by personal conviction on certain questions of abstract principle, not easily proven either pro or con.

    "One of these is that the opportunity to see predators has just as high sport value as the opportunity to see game, and if we can have a reasonable amount of game without blanket vermin control, then those who practice it are, wittingly or unwittingly, disregarding the rights and interests of others. . . . No game manager has ever said that all predator-control is useless or wrong. Most game managers agree, however, that 'campaigns' (i.e., the artificial whipping up of control activities by bounties, prizes or competition) are inherently devoid of discrimination in what, where, when, or how much to control."
108. AL, "Conservation Esthetic," SCA, p. 173.
109. Ibid.
110. Ibid.
111. Ibid., pp. 176–177.
112. AL, "Obituary: P. S. Lovejoy," *Journal of Wildlife Management* 7, no. 1 (1943): 126. The full passage from the text, quoting Lovejoy: "Our [ecological engineer] will bear in mind that *Homo sapiens* is still considerably sap. The normal function of the politician is to take the public where he thinks it wants to go; the function of our engineer is to take the public where it will be glad to be when it gets there."

113. AL, "Wildlife in American Culture," SCA, p. 178.

114. Ibid., p. 184.

115. Ibid. See, too, AL, "Dear Judge Botts," unpublished, n.d., LP 10-6, 16; AL, "A Man's Leisure Time," RR, p. 5.

116. AL, "Wildlife in American Culture," SCA, p. 185.

117. AL, "Wildlife in American Culture," *Journal of Wildlife Management* 7, no. 1 (January 1943): 5.

118. AL, "The State of the Profession," *Journal of Wildlife Management* 4, no. 3 (July 1940): 343–346; also in RMG, p. 280.

119. AL, "The State of the Profession," RMG, pp. 276, 280.

120. Ibid.

121. Ibid. See, too, AL, letter to Charles W. Collier, 12 March 1940, LP 10-2, 9.

Chapter 10: Knowing Nature

1. AL, "The Green Lagoons," SCA, p. 141.

2. AL, "The Delta Colorado," RR, p. 10.

3. C. D. Meine, *Aldo Leopold: His Life and Work* (Madison: University of Wisconsin Press, 1988), p. 207.

4. AL, "The Green Lagoons," SCA, p. 142.

5. Ibid., p. 146.

6. AL, "Conservation Esthetic," SCA, p. 174.

7. Ibid., p. 165.

8. See F. Heske, *German Forestry* (New Haven, CT: Yale University Press, 1938). This volume was published for the Oberlaender Trust, which supported Leopold's trip to Germany.

9. See H. Rubner, "Sustained-Yield Forestry in Europe and Its Crisis during the Era of Nazi Dictatorship," in *History of Sustained-Yield Forestry: A Symposium; Western Forestry Center, Portland, Oregon, October 18–19, 1983*, edited by H. K. Steen (Santa Cruz, CA: Forest History Society, 1984), p. 171.

10. Ibid., p. 171.

11. Ibid., p. 172.

12. Science Service, "Forest Mistakes of Germans Now Being Corrected," 28 September 1936, interview with AL, LP 10-3, 10.

13. AL, "Deer and *Dauerwald* in Germany: I. History," *Journal of Forestry* 34, no. 4 (April 1936): 374.

14. AL, "*Naturschutz* in Germany," *Bird-Lore* 38, no. 2 (March–April 1936): 109.

15. For a discussion of Leopold's thoughts on deer and overbrowsing in Germany see S. Flader, *Thinking Like a Mountain: Aldo Leopold and the Evolution of an Ecological Attitude toward Deer, Wolves, and Forests* (Madison: University of Wisconsin Press, 1994), pp. 139–144.

16. AL, "Deer and *Dauerwald* in Germany: II. Ecology and Policy," *Journal of Forestry* 34, no. 5 (May 1936): 463.

17. AL, letter to Herbert A. Smith, 20 December 1935, LP 10-2, 9. See also AL, "*Naturschutz* in Germany," p. 102.

18. AL, "Wilderness," RMG, p. 226.

19. Ibid., pp. 228, 229.
20. Ibid., p. 229.
21. AL, letter to Estella Leopold, 9 October 1935, LP 10-8, 9.
22. See AL, "Conservation Esthetic," SCA, p. 168.
23. Meine, *Aldo Leopold*, pp. 358, 360.
24. AL, "Deer and *Dauerwald* in Germany: I," p. 374, and "Deer and *Dauerwald* in Germany: II," p. 464. Leopold, though, emphasized the conflict between German forestry and deer management and the "difficulties and delays which impeded [the] realization [of *Dauerwald*]" ("Deer and *Dauerwald* in Germany: II," p. 460). See, too, Leopold's caption to a photograph of a spruce thicket in Tharandterwald, Saxony: "The Germans talk 'Dauerwald' but plant spruce" (dated 29 September 1935, photograph G66, UWDWE). Also see Adalbert Ebner, letter to AL, 31 July 1936, LP 10-3, 10. Ebner noted that the "Dauerwald Idea" predated the "Dauerwald movement" in Germany and that he, as a professional forester, did not "quite agree with this [new official] policy." The *Dauerwald* movement's future beyond the mid-1930s was complicated and compromised as the Nazi movement strongly supported it and then linked it to ardent nationalism. See Rubner, "Sustained-Yield Forestry in Europe," pp. 173–174. See also C. Meine, "A Lesson in Naturalism," unpublished manuscript. For other discussions on Aldo Leopold in Germany see S. Flader, "Leopold on Wilderness: Aldo Leopold on Germany's Landscape," *American Forests* (May–June 1991); H. G. Schabel, "Deer and Dauerwald in Germany: Any Progress?" *Wildlife Society Bulletin* 29 (2001): 888–898; H. G. Schabel and S. L. Palmer, "The Dauerwald: Its Role in the Restoration of Natural Forests," *Journal of Forestry* 97 (1999): 20–25; and M. Wolfe and F. C. Berg, "Deer and Forestry in Germany Half a Century after Aldo Leopold," *Journal of Forestry* 86, no. 5 (1 May 1988): 25–31.
25. The *Naturschutz* movement is considered in detail in T. M. Lekan, *Imagining the Nation in Nature: Landscape Preservation and German Identity, 1885–1945* (Cambridge, MA: Harvard University Press, 2004).
26. AL, "Sketches of Land Use in Germany," address to the Taylor-Hibbard Club, 22 January 1936, p. 2, LP 10-6, 14.
27. AL, "Wilderness as a Form of Land Use," RMG, pp. 134–142.
28. AL, "Wilderness," SCA, p. 188.
29. Leopold was one of ten organizing members of the society in October 1934. The members promptly asked him to serve as first president. After a few exchanges, Leopold made clear his reluctance to serve in a letter to Robert Marshall on 3 April 1935, LP 10-2, 9: "Unless you have already taken action, I want to express the opinion that my taking the presidency of the Wilderness Society would simply be an absurdity." In Leopold's view, the society needed a president who resided in Washington, DC, where the society's headquarters were located. Marshall himself was unavailable because of an apparent conflict with his role as head of the Department of Interior's Office of Indian Affairs. Robert Marshall, letter to AL, 14 March 1935, LP 10-2, 9. Leopold did serve as council member from 1935 on and as vice president from 1945 until his death. AL, letter to A. N. Marquis, 23 May 1947, LP 10-2, 9.

30. AL, "Why the Wilderness Society?" *Living Wilderness* 1, no. 1 (1935): 6.
31. Leopold also warned that humans, with their great powers to alter their environment, might be thus directing their own evolution: "Is it to be expected that [wilderness] shall be lost from human experience without something likewise being lost from human character?" See AL, "The River of the Mother of God," RMG, p. 124; AL, "Wilderness as a Form of Land-Use," *Journal of Land and Public Utility Economics* 1, no. 4 (October 1925): 398–404, also in RMG, pp. 137, 142; AL, "Ecology and Politics," RMG, pp. 281–286.
32. AL, letter to Benton MacKaye, 1 May 1946, LP 10-2, 9: "I am thoroughly convinced of one basic point: that wilderness is merely one manifestation of a change of philosophy of land use."
33. AL, "Wilderness as a Form of Land Use," RMG, p. 142.
34. AL, "Why the Wilderness Society?" p. 6.
35. AL, "Wilderness Conservation," address delivered at National Conference on Outdoor Recreation, Washington, DC, 20 January 1926, p. 3, LP 10-4, 8. Wilderness, Leopold wrote, was a "category of outdoor things which are God-made, but also absolutely self-destructive under any unguided economic system." See D. Foreman, *Rewilding North America: A Vision for Conservation in the 21st Century* (Washington, DC: Island Press, 2004), p. 1. The term "wilderness" arose from the Old English word "wildeor," meaning "wild beasts." "[T]he ancient meaning of wilderness [was] 'self-willed land.'"
36. Leopold's wilderness advocacy is considered in R. F. Nash, *Wilderness and the American Mind* (New Haven, CT: Yale University Press, 2001), pp. 182–199; M. Oelschlaeger, *The Idea of Wilderness: From Prehistory to the Age of Ecology* (New Haven, CT: Yale University Press, 1991), pp. 205–242; S. L. Flader, "Aldo Leopold and the Wilderness Idea," *Living Wilderness* 43, no. 147 (December 1979): pp. 4–8; W. Cronon, "A Voice in the Wilderness," *Wilderness* (Winter 1998): 8; and C. W. Allin, "The Leopold Legacy and American Wilderness," in *Aldo Leopold: The Man and His Legacy*, edited by T. Tanner (Ankeny, IA: Soil Conservation Society of America, 1987), pp. 25–38. The influence of the "good roads" movement in stimulating the wilderness protection effort, by Leopold and others, is considered in P. S. Sutter, *Driven Wild: How the Fight against Automobiles Launched the Modern Wilderness Movement* (Seattle: University of Washington Press, 2002). Leopold's role in promoting an ecological perspective on wilderness within The Wilderness Society is considered in D. J. Philippon, *Conserving Words: How American Nature Writers Shaped the Environmental Movement* (Athens: University of Georgia Press, 2004), pp. 159–218. A brief review of Leopold's wilderness writings, in the context of his larger conservation thought, is offered in RMG, pp. 24–27. The heightened protection of federal lands, particularly as national parks, inevitably disrupted existing patterns of land use by rural dwellers. This cost—referred to by one historian as the "hidden history" of conservation—is elaborated in K. Jacoby, *Crimes against Nature: Squatters, Poachers, Thieves, and the Hidden History of American Conservation* (Berkeley: University of California Press, 2001).
37. See Robert Yard, letter to AL, 9 May 1940, LP 10-2, 9: "It is you who invented the title wilderness areas, making practical certain ideals which had

been in men's minds for many years, and had occasionally crept timidly into print." And see Philippon, *Conserving Words*, pp. 173–174.

38. AL, "The Wilderness and Its Place in Forest Recreational Policy," *Journal of Forestry* 19, no. 7 (November 1921): 718–721; also in RMG, pp. 79–81. See also AL, "Origin and Ideals of Wilderness Areas," *Living Wilderness* 5, no. 5 (July 1940): 7. Prominent ecologist G. A. Pearson supportively cited Leopold's 1921 article in his "Preservation of Natural Areas in the National Forests," *Ecology* 3, no. 4 (1922): 286.

39. AL, "The Wilderness and Its Place in Forest Recreational Policy," RMG, p. 79. Leopold was not against roads per se, but rather roads in the wrong places. As he explained in his 1925 article "The Pig in the Parlor" (*USFS Bulletin* 9, no. 23 [8 June 1925]: 1–2, also in RMG, p. 133), the "wilderness area idea" had to do with the distribution of roads: "Roads and wilderness are merely a case of the pig in the parlor. We now recognize that the pig is all right—for bacon, which we all eat. But there no doubt was a time, soon after the discovery that many pigs meant much bacon, when our ancestors assumed that because the pig was so useful an institution he should be welcomed at all times and places. And I suppose that the first 'enthusiast' who raised the question of limiting his distribution was construed to be uneconomic, visionary, and anti-pig." See also Sutter, *Driven Wild*.

40. AL, "Flambeau," SCA, pp. 112–116.

41. Ibid., p. 113.

42. Ibid., p. 112.

43. Ibid., p. 113.

44. AL, "Wildlife in American Culture," SCA, p. 178.

45. AL, "Song of the Gavilan," SCA, p. 149.

46. AL, Wildlife in American Culture," SCA, p. 181.

47. AL, "Marshland Elegy," SCA, p. 101. Also see AL, "Conservation Economics," RMG, p. 196.

48. Even the roadless area of the Superior National Forest and Quetico Provincial Park was already showing signs of overcrowding by recreationists. See H. H. Chapman, letter to William P. Wharton, 25 July 1946, LP 10-2, 9, and Olaus Murie, letter to The Councillors of The Wilderness Society, 31 July 1946, LP 10-12, 9. See also AL, "Discussion on the Park Executive and Landscaper," unpublished fragment, n.d., UWDWE, vol. 1, p. 131.

49. See "Thoughts on a Map of Liberia," unfinished, n.d., UWDWE, vol. 1.

50. AL, "The Green Lagoons," SCA, p. 149.

51. "As a form of land use [wilderness] cannot be a rigid entity of unchanging content, exclusive of all other forms. On the contrary, it must be a flexible thing, accommodating itself to other forms and blending with them in that highly localized give-and-take scheme of land-planning which employs the criterion of 'highest use.'" AL, "Wilderness as a Form of Land Use," RMG, pp. 135–136.

52. In the same talk (pp. 1–4) Leopold also described three categories of outdoor recreational contexts, which varied in terms of their responsiveness to economic forces. There were man-made things, such as roads, trails, and other modern conveniences, which responded automatically to market forces of

supply, demand, and advertising. The second category was of "God-made but man-fostered things," such as "forests, waters, scenery, and wild life." Both economic and aesthetic demands existed for these things, and they could be produced as crops in response to market forces. The danger of allowing the market alone to govern them was that the unprofitable parts of nature would be sacrificed. Moreover, the man of moderate means could lose access to the profitable parts as prices for them rose. Finally, there was the third category of outdoor things, wilderness most prominently, which were "God-made" and vulnerable to destruction under "any unguided economic system." Wilderness was "the fundamental recreational resource," and its preservation was nothing short of a radical act against a merely economic mind-set.

53. AL, "Wilderness Conservation," address delivered at the National Conference on Outdoor Recreation, Washington, DC, 20 January 1926, p. 8, LP 10-4, 8. In this address and later, including in a letter to Robert Marshall dated 1 February 1935, LP 10-2, 9, Leopold also countered the idea that only aesthetically pleasing places deserved wilderness protection. "I have only one important suggestion," Leopold wrote in response to a draft essay by Marshall. "[U]nder 'Extensive wilderness areas,' add: 'marsh or desert.' We are fighting not only mechanization of country, but the idea that wild landscapes must be 'pretty' to have value."

54. AL, "Wilderness Conservation," p. 8.

55. AL, "Wilderness," SCA, p. 188.

56. See Pearson, "Preservation of Natural Areas": natural areas were "places where plant and animal life and natural features in general may remain undisturbed by human activities"—for ecological study. Pearson cited Leopold's earlier work (p. 286) and discussed the need for recreationists, scientists, and custodians of public lands to work together. Victor Shelford later wrote, "A nature sanctuary is a community or community fragment covering a certain area within which the fluctuations in abundance and other natural changes are allowed to go on unmodified and uncontrolled [by humans]. Such areas afford opportunity for the study of the dynamics of natural biotic communities." V. Shelford, "Nature Sanctuaries: A Means of Saving Natural Biotic Communities," *Science* 77, no. 1994 (17 March 1933) p. 281, LP 10-2, 2.

57. AL, "Wilderness for Science," SCA, pp. 194–197. It was too late, Leopold realized in the 1940s, "to salvage more than a lopsided system of wilderness study areas, and most of these remnants are far too small to retain their normality in all respects" (p. 196). AL, "Wilderness as a Land Laboratory," *The Living Wilderness* 6 (July 1941): 3; also in RMG, p. 289.

58. AL, "Dear Judge Botts," unpublished, n.d., LP 10-6, 16; AL, "Wherefore Wildlife Ecology?" RMG, p. 336; AL, "Conservation Esthetic," SCA, pp. 173–175.

59. By 1940 conversations were under way among the leaders of both the Ecological Society of America and The Wilderness Society to bring their work together. Leopold and The Wilderness Society's president, Robert Yard, interacted with Victor Shelford from the University of Illinois, first president of the ESA and chairman of the ESA's Committee for the Study of

Plant and Animal Communities and of the Committee on the Preservation of Natural Conditions (AL, letter to Robert Yard, 4 June 1940, LP 10-2, 9). Shelford had been the intellectual leader behind the ESA's nature sanctuary plans. Shelford, "Nature Sanctuaries." Direct cooperation between the two organizations did not come to pass. When the ESA was in turmoil over its role in land protection work, however, it turned to Leopold for leadership. The organization elected him vice president in 1946 and president in 1947, even though he had failed to show up at the ESA meetings (see AL, letter to William Dreyer, 11 January 1947, LP 10-2, 2). Leopold continued to stress the importance of cooperation in land protection work. It is likely that he drafted his essay "Wilderness" as his formal talk as outgoing ESA president (see AL, letter to Wallace Grange, 3 January 1948, LP 10-1, 1), and his plan also was to end *A Sand County Almanac* with the essay, which stressed "the cultural value of wilderness" (see AL, "Great Possessions," unpublished manuscript, LP 10-6, 16). However, Leopold died before he could deliver the talk, and those helping to see Leopold's essay book to publication rearranged the order of the writings so that it ended with "The Land Ethic" instead. See J. L. Newton, "Science, Recreation, and Leopold's Quest for a Durable Scale," in *The Great Wilderness Debate*, vol. 2, edited by M. Nelson and J. B. Callicott (Athens: University of Georgia Press, 2006).

60. AL, "Resolution," 1940, LP 10-2, 9.

61. One of Leopold's detailed efforts to get private landowners to manage lands in the public interest for timber, wildlife, scientific, and wilderness values was in response to the request of the Huron Mountain Club, which owned a fifteen-thousand-acre tract of near-virgin maple-hemlock forest near Lake Superior: "The size-scale of a wilderness area for scientific study greatly affects its value. A small area may be 'natural' in respect of its plants, but wholly unnatural in respect of its mobile animals or water. However, mobile animals greatly affect plant life, so that a small virgin forest may *appear* to be natural when actually it has been profoundly affected by forces applied to animals, waters, or climate at points far distant. . . . In general, a small area is valuable for studies of vegetation and soils. Birds, mammals, and waters require larger areas by region of their mobility." Although many of Leopold's suggestions were well ahead of the curve, he was not entirely satisfied with his plan. See Flader, *Thinking Like a Mountain*, pp. 159–163; Meine, *Aldo Leopold*, pp. 385–386; W. P. Harris, letter to AL, 16 June 1938, and AL, letter to W. P. Harris, 17 June 1938, LP 10-2, 4. See, too, AL, "Report on Huron Mountain Club" (1938), printed by Huron Mountain Club, Michigan; reprinted in *Report of Huron Mountain Wildlife Foundation, 1955–1966* (n.p., 1967), pp. 40–57.

62. AL, "Threatened Species: A Proposal to the Wildlife Conference for an Inventory of the Needs of Near-Extinct Birds and Mammals," *American Forests* 42, no. 3 (March 1936): 116–119; AL, "Threatened Species," RMG, p. 233. Also see rough draft of "Threatened Species": "Proposal for a Conservation Inventory of Threatened Species," UWDWE. The idea of a national system based on wildlife inventories was promoted by Jay Darling. See Jay Darling, letter to AL, 23 November 1939, LP 10-4, 8: "I inaugurated

this study [of the wilderness area project] in order that we might have a picture before us of the areas needed thruout the United States, so that none of the major species (including the grizzly bear) might be neglected. I showed that map to the President [FDR] and received a thoro and enthusiastic endorsement of the program." Darling's ideas also included acreages of various sizes: "[W]e will waste a lot of energy chipping away at the log without any great progress toward a final solution if we do not establish the principle of wilderness areas in the beginning, even tho it be a small acreage." Leopold responded, "It is welcome news that such a project is under way, and it immediately occurs to me that if the USBS [United States Biological Survey] already has it in hand, our [The Wilderness Society's] best bet is to stand at their elbow rather than to try to take over the job." AL, letter to Jay Darling, 27 November 1939, LP 10-4, 8.

63. AL, "Escudilla," SCA, pp. 133–137.
64. AL, "The Grizzly—a Problem in Land Planning," *Outdoor America* 7, no. 6 (April 1942): 11–12; AL, "Threatened Species," RMG, p. 231; AL, "Escudilla," SCA, pp. 133–137. See Olaus Murie, letter to The Councillors of The Wildlife Society, 31 July 1946, LP 10-2, 9, on the need for large wilderness areas to support large wildlife predators like the wolf.
65. See AL, letter to Howard Zahniser (The Wilderness Society), 5 June 1946, LP 10-2, 9: "It is gratifying to me that you are convinced we must broaden our definition of wilderness. I look forward to talking over the question of how to define the broadening." In the late 1940s, largely by Leopold's initiative, The Wilderness Society's objectives were revised to include "the conservation of soil, water, forests, and wildlife, and the conservation of all these resources is essential to the survival of our civilized culture" (The Wilderness Society, "Purpose and Program," ca. 1947, LP 10-2, 9). Leopold emphasized this wildlife protection role of wilderness in a 1948 letter to Roberts Mann, head of forest preserves in Cook County, Illinois: "[W]ilderness is not only acres, but also organisms. There are processes and laws of the wild to be guarded from extermination as well as wilderness areas." AL, letter to Roberts Mann, 31 January 1948, LP 10-1, 2.
66. AL, "Threatened Species," RMG, p. 233.
67. U.S. Department of Commerce, Bureau of the Census, *Statistical Abstract of the United States: 1944–1945* (Washington, DC: Government Printing Office, 1945), p. 597. In 1940, 55.7 percent of America's land area was in farms, while 23.2 percent of America's population lived on farms.
68. AL, "Preserving Wisconsin's Game Supply," College of the Air radio broadcast, 17 February 1936. In the 1930s Leopold participated in teaching short courses for farmers on game management techniques, and he addressed speeches to farmers on the University's College of the Air broadcasts.
69. AL, "Conservation Esthetic," SCA, p. 175.
70. Ibid.
71. AL, "History of the Riley Game Cooperative, 1931–1939," FHL, pp. 175–192.
72. AL, "New Methods for Game Cropping," College of the Air radio broadcast, 10 February 1936.

73. AL, "The Farmer as a Conservationist," FHL, p. 165.
74. Ibid., p. 169.
75. Ibid., p. 171.
76. Ibid., p. 172.
77. AL, "Illinois Bus Ride," SCA, pp. 117–119.
78. Ibid., p. 117. See, too, AL, "What Is a Weed?" FHL, pp. 207–212.
79. Leopold's grave concerns about modern agriculture are noted in D. Fleming, "Roots of the New Conservation Movement," *Perspectives in American History* 6 (1972): 24–26.
80. AL, "Coon Valley: An Adventure in Cooperative Conservation," *American Forests* 41, no. 5 (May 1935): 205–208; also in FHL, quote on p. 50.
81. Ibid.
82. AL, "Progress of the Game Survey," *Transactions of the 16th American Game Conference* (2–3 December 1929), p. 65.
83. Ibid.
84. AL, "Vegetation and Birds," *Report of the Iowa State Horticultural Society*, 66th Annual Convention (12–14 November 1931), p. 204.
85. AL, "Cheat Takes Over," SCA, pp. 154–158.
86. Ibid., p. 158.
87. AL, "Economics, Philosophy, and Land," unfinished, 23 November 1938, p. 6, LP 10-6, 16, and UWDWE, vol. 2, p. 33. Here, too, Leopold was echoing observations from Germany. See AL, "Lecture on Deer and Forestry," 19 December 1935, LP 10-6, 14. Leopold criticized the average scientific land manager for assuming uncritically that technology would automatically achieve good. For Germans, "the term 'wood factory' as applied to a forest, is now a term of opprobrium. With us [Americans] it is still a term of honor. The German now speaks of all conservation not as economic, but as 'transeconomic' in motivation. The American still proudly justifies his particular cult in the esperanto of 'dollars and cents.' I doubt whether either knows exactly what he means by these terms—I certainly do not. But I can see one thing clearly emerging which is applicable to land-use the world over: the deep interdependence of interests heretofore considered separate. One cannot divorce esthetics from utility, quality from quantity, present from future, either in deciding what is done to or for the soil, or in educating the persons delegated to do it. All land-uses and land-users are interdependent, and the forces which connect them follow channels still largely unknown."
88. For a discussion of Leopold's "fine line" between utility and beauty, see "Leopold's Fine Line," in C. D. Meine, *Correction Lines: Essays on Land, Leopold, and Conservation* (Washington, DC: Island Press, 2004), pp. 89–116.
89. AL, "Story of the Riley Game Cooperative, 1931–1939," *Journal of Wildlife Management* 4, no. 3 (1940): 291. The Riley and Faville Grove cooperatives lasted longer than most. Of some 350 started in the north-central region since 1931, only five survived in 1936. Riley was kept going largely thanks to Leopold's efforts; the effort fizzled after his death. See B. Sibernagel and J. Sibernagel, "Tracking Aldo Leopold through Riley's Farmland," *Wisconsin Magazine of History* (Summer 2003): 35–45.

90. AL, "A Proposed Survey of Land-Use for the 'Farm Foundation,'" ca. 1934, pp. 2–3, LP 10-2, 4.
91. Meine, *Aldo Leopold*, p. 341.
92. Ibid.
93. Nina Leopold Bradley and Estella Leopold, personal communication, 2004.
94. AL, letter to Starker Leopold, 21 September 1935, LP 10-8, 9.
95. Meine, *Aldo Leopold*, p. 364.
96. AL, "Prairie Birthday," SCA, pp. 44–50.
97. See C. Meine, "Reimagining the Prairie: Aldo Leopold and the Origins of Prairie Restoration," in *Recovering the Prairie*, edited by R. F. Sayre (Madison: University of Wisconsin Press, 1999), pp. 144–160. Of course, Leopold was particularly free to experiment, not depending on the outcomes for his livelihood.
98. AL, letter to Victor Cahalane (president of The Wildlife Society), 5 April 1940, LP 10-2, 9.
99. AL, "Sky Dance," SCA, p. 32.
100. A. Leopold and S. Jones, "A Phenological Record for Sauk and Dane Counties, Wisconsin, 1935–45," *Ecological Monographs* 17 (January 1947): 81.
101. Ibid.
102. AL, "Farm Phenology—a New Sport," unfinished, n.d., p. 116, LP 10-6, 16.
103. AL, "Natural History: The Forgotten Science," RR, p. 57.
104. AL, "The Farm Wildlife Program: A Self-Scrutiny," ca. 1937, p. 7, LP 10-6, 14.
105. AL, "The Farmer as a Conservationist," FHL, pp. 164, 168. See also E. T. Freyfogle, *Why Conservation Is Failing and How It Can Regain Ground* (New Haven, CT: Yale University Press, 2006), chap. 5.
106. Ibid., p. 161.
107. Ibid., p. 172.
108. Ibid.
109. Ibid., p. 174.
110. Ibid.
111. Ibid., p. 175.
112. For discussions of the genesis, development, and interpretation of *A Sand County Almanac* see J. B. Callicott, ed., *Companion to "A Sand County Almanac": Interpretive and Critical Essays* (Madison: University of Wisconsin Press, 1987), and C. D. Meine, "Moving Mountains" and "The *Secret* Leopold," in *Correction Lines*, pp. 148–160, 161–183.
113. See Meine, *Aldo Leopold*, pp. 460–461, 485–486, 505, 509–511, 512, 517, 523–526, and J. B. Callicott, ed., *Companion to "A Sand County Almanac": Interpretive and Critical Essays* (Madison: University of Wisconsin Press, 1987). Friends and family helped see the book through to publication with Oxford, and the book appeared in the fall of 1949.
114. AL, "January Thaw," SCA, p. 3. Also see A. Leopold and S. E. Jones, "A Phenological Record for Sauk and Dane Counties, Wisconsin, 1935–1945," draft dated 5 November 1946, p. 1, LP 10-6, 8.
115. AL, "Clandeboye," SCA, p. 158.
116. AL, "The Geese Return," SCA, p. 18.

117. AL, "Illinois Bus Ride," SCA, pp. 117–119.
118. AL, "Good Oak," SCA, p. 6.
119. AL, "Prairie Birthday," SCA, pp. 44–50.
120. AL, "A Mighty Fortress," SCA, pp. 73–77.
121. AL, "Clandeboye," SCA, pp. 158–164.
122. AL, "Home Range," SCA, pp. 78–80.
123. AL, "Sky Dance," SCA, pp. 30–33.
124. AL, "65290," SCA, pp. 87–94.
125. Albert Hochbaum, letter to AL, 11 March 1944, LP 10-2, 3. Hochbaum also urged Leopold to reveal that his "way of thinking is not that of an inspired genius, but that of any other ordinary fellow trying to put two and two together. Because you have added up your sums better than most of [us], it is important that you let fall a hint that in the process of reaching the end result of your thinking you have sometimes followed trails like anyone else that lead you up the wrong alleys. That is why I suggested the wolf business." This note was part of the discussion that led Leopold to write "Thinking Like a Mountain" (SCA, pp. 129–133).
126. AL, "Thinking Like a Mountain," SCA, p. 130.
127. See Flader, *Thinking Like a Mountain*. Leopold's understanding of the deer-predator-mountain relationships evolved over time. See, too, AL's "confession," in his "Foreword," unpublished revision of 31 July 1947, LP 10-6, 16 (4), and in Callicott, *Companion to "A Sand County Almanac,"* pp. 281–290.

Chapter 11: A New Kind of Conservation

1. AL, "Conservation: In Whole or in Part?" RMG, pp. 310–319; AL, "Biotic Land-Use," FHL, pp. 198–207; AL, "The Land-Health Concept and Conservation," FHL, pp. 218–226.
2. AL, "Odyssey," SCA, pp. 104–108; AL, "Wilderness for Science," SCA, pp. 194–198; AL, "The Land Pyramid," SCA, pp. 214–220. Susan Flader, in *Thinking Like a Mountain: Aldo Leopold and the Evolution of an Ecological Attitude toward Deer, Wolves, and Forests* (Madison: University of Wisconsin Press, 1994), traces Leopold's thinking about deer ecology to the concept of land health (including pp. 172, 268–269) and links its substance with Leopold's land ethic (p. 270). Flader also notes the direct links between Leopold's land ethic and land health in "Aldo Leopold and the Evolution of a Land Ethic," in *Aldo Leopold: The Man and His Legacy*, edited by T. Tanner (Ankeny, IA: Soil Conservation Society of America, 1987), p. 21. J. Baird Callicott emphasizes the importance of land health to Leopold's thinking in "Standards of Conservation: Then and Now," *Conservation Biology* 4 (1990): 229–232, and "Whither Conservation Ethics?" *Conservation Biology* 4 (1990): 15–20. Eric Freyfogle draws attention to the centrality of Leopold's land health concept in "A Sand County Almanac at 50: Leopold in the New Century," *Environmental Law Reporter* 30 (2000): 10058–10068. Curt Meine also traces the evolution of Leopold's land health idea in *Correction Lines: Essays on Land, Leopold, and Conservation* (Washington, DC: Island Press, 2004), chap. 5. See also J. B. Callicott and E. T. Freyfogle, eds., *Aldo Leopold: For the Health of the Land; Previously*

Unpublished Essays and Other Writings (Washington, DC: Island Press, Shearwater Books, 1999). For discussions of health as metaphor and its usefulness for conservation, see J. B. Callicott, "Aldo Leopold's Concept of Ecosystem Health" and "The Value of Ecosystem Health," in *Beyond the Land Ethic: More Essays in Environmental Philosophy* (Albany: State University of New York Press, 1999), pp. 333–364.

3. AL, "Ecology and Politics," RMG, p. 284; AL, "The Land-Health Concept and Conservation," FHL, p. 225.

4. AL, "Wilderness," RMG, p. 229; AL, "The Farm Wildlife Program: A Self-Scrutiny," unfinished, n.d., p. 1, UWDWE, vol. 2, pp. 362–370; AL, "Ecology and Economics in Land Use," unfinished, unpublished, ca. 1940s, p. 1, LP 10-6, 17; AL, "Substitutes for a Land Ethic," SCA, pp. 210–211.

5. AL, "A Survey of Conservation," RR, p. 146.

6. AL, "The Arboretum and the University," *Parks and Recreation* 18, no. 2 (October 1934): 59–60; also in RMG, p. 209, and AL, "The Community Concept," SCA, p. 204.

7. AL, "A Biotic View of Land," RMG, pp. 268, 269; AL, "The Round River," p. 162; AL, "Conservation: In Whole or in Part," RMG, p. 312; AL, "The Land Pyramid," SCA, p. 216.

8. AL, "On a Monument to the Pigeon," SCA, p. 109.

9. AL, "The Round River: A Parable," RR, p. 159.

10. Ibid., pp. 159–162.

11. AL, "The Land Pyramid," SCA, p. 216; also in AL, "A Biotic View of Land," RMG, p. 269.

12. AL, "Land Pathology," RMG, p. 213.

13. AL, "Conservation: In Whole or in Part?" RMG, p. 316.

14. AL, "The Farmer as a Conservationist," FHL, p. 162. See also AL, "The Role of Wildlife in a Liberal Education," *Transactions of the 7th North American Wildlife Conference* (8–10 April 1942): 485–489; also in RMG, p. 303.

15. AL, "The Land Pyramid," SCA, p. 214.

16. Even back at least to Plato and Moses. See R. A. Long, "Forest Conservation," in *Proceedings of a Conference of the Governors of the United States, 1908, White House, May 13–15* (Washington, DC: Government Printing Office, 1909), pp. 87–88: "The effect and influence of forests on the climate, health, and water conditions of the country is evidenced by the chronicles of the Mosaic, the Roman and the Greek writers, and many of their far-seeing priests prevented the destruction of the forests. . . . Plato writes that the consequence of deforestation is the 'sickening of the country.'"

17. The foundation for Leopold's conservation ideas, upon which grew the concepts of land health and the land ethic, can be summarized as "the positive conviction that cohabitation of the land by wild and the tame things is good." He believed in "the fundamental goodness of men living on land with plants and animals." AL, "Farm Wildlife Program," p. 1.

18. Leopold's first major writing directly on land health dated from October 1940, his initial draft of a paper titled "Biotic Land-Use" (draft attached to AL, letter to Rudolf Bennitt, 22 October 1940, LP 10-1, 1). Sometime around

1942 he expanded the essay, but he still left it unpublished (it was published in 1999 in FHL, pp. 198–205). Leopold's first major published work on land health was the piece he contributed in 1941 to a symposium on hydrobiology: "Soil health and water health are not two problems, but one," he asserted. AL, "Lakes in Relation to Terrestrial Life Patterns," in J. G. Needham et al., *A Symposium on Hydrobiology* (Madison: University of Wisconsin Press, 1941), pp. 17–22. Also appearing in 1941, discussing land health, was a piece on wilderness as "a base-datum of normality, a picture of how healthy land maintains itself as an organism." AL, "Wilderness as a Land Laboratory," *Living Wilderness* 6 (July 1941): 3; also in RMG, p. 288, and appearing almost in full as part of "Wilderness for Science," SCA, pp. 194–198. Important, brief discussions of land health appeared in two 1942 essays, AL, "Land-Use and Democracy," *Audubon* 44, no. 5 (September–October 1942): 218, also in RMG, p. 300; and AL, "The Role of Wildlife in a Liberal Education," RMG, p. 303. Most significant from 1942 was an essay describing land health in story form: AL, "Odyssey," *Audubon* 44, no. 3:133–135; also in SCA, pp. 104–108. In later essays Leopold again used the land health concept in brief, important ways. See AL, "The Outlook for Farm Wildlife," *Transactions of the 10th North American Wildlife Conference*, 26–28 February 1945, pp. 165–168, also in FHL, p. 217; and AL, "The Ecological Conscience," *Bulletin of the Garden Club of America*, September 1947, pp. 45–53, also in RMG, p. 345: "A thing is right only when it tends to preserve the integrity, stability, and beauty of the community, and the community includes the soil, waters, fauna, and flora, as well as people." These lines, with some modifications, occur in "The Land Ethic," SCA, p. 224. It was in two essays from the middle of the decade, however, that Leopold placed land health in the center of his writing, overtly proposing the concept as the much-needed overall goal for conservation. AL, "Conservation: In Whole or in Part?" RMG, pp. 310–319, in which he explains in detail the scientific bases for land health. In abbreviated form ideas from this essay showed up in AL, "Land-Health and the A-B Cleavage," SCA, pp. 221–223, and AL, "The Land-Health Concept and Conservation," FHL, pp. 218–226, in which he considers the conservation implications of the concept, what it would take to achieve the goal, and the importance of professional ecologists in better grounding the idea.

19. Land health was a culminating concept in Leopold's thinking, bringing together as it did scientific and moral matters. Yet Leopold plainly understood the concept as a work in progress. It was an idea that would need continual fleshing out as science revealed new information and culture evolved. See AL, "The Land-Health Concept and Conservation," FHL, p. 220. Leopold's uncertainty about the details of the concept—and his intent to keep working on them—seem the most reasonable explanation for why he left so many key writings in his desk drawer. Leopold's principal writings on land health were thus known only to Leopold scholars until they were published in edited volumes of Leopold's work in the 1990s. These include AL, "Biotic Land-Use," FHL, pp. 198–206; AL, "Conservation: In Whole or in Part?" RMG, pp. 310–319; and AL, "The Land-Health Concept and Conservation," FHL, pp. 218–226. Still unpublished writings of substance

include AL, "Land-Health in Southwest Wisconsin," unpublished lecture drafts of 3 November 1943 (for the American Society of Civil Engineers) and 7 April 1944 (for the Garden Club of America), LP 10-6, 14, and AL, "Land as a Circulatory System" (draft of chap. 1, 12 July 1943, LP 10-6, 16), apparently intended as the first chapter of his proposed text on ecology, which remained unfinished. This may explain why Leopold's readers over the years have underappreciated the importance he attached to the concept.

20. AL, "To the Forest Officers of the Carson," *Carson Pine Cone* (15 July 1913); also in RMG, pp. 41–46.

21. AL, "Standards of Conservation," RMG, p. 84. See Callicott, "Standards of Conservation: Then and Now."

22. AL, "The Conservation Ethic," *Journal of Forestry* 31, no. 6 (October 1933): 634–643; also in RMG, p. 182.

23. AL, "Conservation Economics," *Journal of Forestry* 32, no. 5 (May 1934): 537–544; also in RMG, p. 202.

24. AL, "Biotic Land-Use," FHL, p. 202.

25. AL, "Foreword," SCA, p. ix.

26. AL, "Land Health and the A–B Cleavage," SCA, p. 221. "A land ethic, then, reflects the existence of an ecological conscience, and this in turn reflects a conviction of individual responsibility for the health of the land."

27. AL, *Watershed Handbook* (Albuquerque: U.S. Department of Agriculture, Forest Service, District 3, December 1923 [revised and reissued October 1934]), p. 8, LP 10-11, 1.

28. E.g., in his 1935 lecture "Land Pathology," society and land regarded together as an organism had "suddenly developed pathological symptoms, i.e. self-accelerating rather than self-compensating departures from normal functioning." AL, "Land Pathology," RMG, p. 217.

29. AL, SCA, p. 221.

30. In his report from Germany titled "Deer and *Dauerwald*," "soil sickness" was described as a troubling condition in artificialized forests, whereas more natural, diverse forests exhibited signs of "ecological health." AL, "Deer and *Dauerwald* in Germany: I. History," *Journal of Forestry* 34, no. 4 (April 1936): 374. In Leopold's major early writing about the Sierra Madre, "Conservationist in Mexico," he remarked that the Chihuahua presented "so lovely a picture of ecological health." AL, "The Conservationist in Mexico," *American Forests* 43, no. 3 (March 1937): 118–120, 146; also in RMG, p. 239. And in his 1939 "The Farmer as a Conservationist," Leopold declared that the fields and pastures of an ecologically diverse farm were all "built on a foundation of good health," which he linked with soil fertility. AL, "The Farmer as a Conservationist," FHL, p. 173.

31. AL, "Land-Use and Democracy," RMG, p. 300.

32. AL, "Conservation: In Whole or in Part?" RMG, p. 310. For similar definitions of land health, see AL, "The Role of Wildlife in a Liberal Education," RMG, p. 303, and AL, "Land Health and the A-B Cleavage," SCA, p. 221. Leopold used an alternative phrasing in his 1941 "Wilderness as a Land Laboratory," RMG, p. 287: Health was the "capacity for internal self-renewal."

33. See also S. Flader, *Thinking Like a Mountain*, pp. 31–32.

34. AL, unpublished manuscript, 12 July 1943; AL, "Land as a Circulatory System," p. 1. In thinking this way, it was possible to speak in terms of general principles of health while recognizing that particular measures of health—e.g., fertility and diversity—would be relative conditions in relation to unique locales.

35. Leopold also pointed out that in human-dominated landscapes much of the land system's energy was rerouted directly to humans as the new top animal in the land pyramid. Modern humans rarely returned their nutrient intake to the soil; it ended up in rivers and lakes via sewers, in which case "the circulatory system suffers a short-circuit which must ultimately impoverish the land." See AL, "Land as a Circulatory System," p. 5.

36. See AL, "Foreword," SCA, unpublished, 31 July 1947, p. 7, LP 10-6, 16 (4), published in *Companion to "A Sand County Almanac": Interpretive and Critical Essays*, edited by J. B. Callicott (Madison: University of Wisconsin Press, 1987), p. 287.

37. AL, "Odyssey," SCA, pp. 107–108.

38. Ibid., p. 107.

39. AL, "Land as a Circulatory System," p. 2. Leopold collected a data set (incomplete at his writing) from an actual scientific experiment comparing the downhill wash of nutrients on six different landscapes, ranging from continuous corn to ungrazed woods. He found, for instance, that downhill wash was twenty times as rapid in corn as in ungrazed grass.

40. Ibid., p. 6.

41. AL, *Watershed Handbook*, December 1923, p. 11. In a 1946 letter to Bill Vogt, Leopold admitted that he maintained "only a casual contact with the erosion field and have been able to do less and less contact with the erosion field." AL to Bill Vogt, 12 August 1946, LP 10-1, 3.

42. See W. P. Taylor, "Some Effects of Animals on Plants," *Scientific Monthly* 43 (1936): 262. Taylor, too, noted that large numbers of people with powerful tools had disturbed "natural equilibria," resulting in temporary bursts of productivity of some species; "accelerated erosion . . . shrinking water supplies . . . forest, range, and wildlife depletion; and soil exhaustion."

43. AL, "The Land-Health Concept and Conservation," FHL, p. 219.

44. AL, "Wilderness for Science," SCA, p. 194.

45. Ibid., p. 196.

46. See Douglas Wade, round-robin letter to "The Gang," 5 May 1944, p. 2, LP 10-1, 3; AL, letter to "Wildlifers" titled "Mobility of Wildlifers: 2nd Progress Report," 1 September 1943, LP 10-1, 3; AL, letters to William Vogt, 12 August 1942 and 8 July 1943, LP 10-1, 3.

47. AL, introduction to unpublished manuscript, ca. 1943, p. 5, LP 10-6, 17.

48. AL, "Conservation in Whole or in Part?" RMG, p. 310.

49. Ibid., p. 318.

50. AL, unpublished manuscript, 12 July 1943; AL, "Land as a Circulatory System," p. 1.

51. AL, "Land as a Circulatory System," p. 6.

52. Ibid.

53. Ibid., p. 5.

54. AL, "Land as a Circulatory System," p. 1. See AL, unpublished fragment, ca.

1930s, "Social Consequences Material," LP 10-6, 16; and AL, "Land-Health in Southwest Wisconsin." Leopold's approach to time scales in conservation science was influenced by several works of history, including C. Beard and M. Beard, *The Rise of American Civilization* (New York: Macmillan, 1930) (Leopold appreciated the Beards' dialectic approach); B. De Voto, *The Year of Decision, 1846* (Boston: Little, Brown, 1943), which was, according to Leopold, a "slow-motion picture of the year 1846 in America"; H. G. Wells, *The Outline of History* (New York: Garden City, 1920), which begins in geologic time with ages of rocks, reptiles, mammals, and man and human society and ends with a chapter that projects into a hopeful future of progressing unity among mankind (which Leopold said had "photographed the unfolding of the so-called human race from Cro-Magnon to the Jazz age"); and W. P. Webb, *The Great Plains* (Boston: Ginn and Company, 1931), which Leopold called an outstanding work that viewed "all aspects of land from a long time-scale." Leopold modeled his historical study of southwestern Wisconsin on Webb's work, the purpose of which was to show how the Great Plains landscape "affected the various peoples, nations as well as individuals, who came to take and occupy it, and was affected by them" (Webb, *The Great Plains*, p. 8). Leopold was also fascinated with the history of ideas, or "idea succession," about which he and P. S. Lovejoy corresponded at some length. P. S. Lovejoy, letters to AL, e.g., 1 May 1941, 10 May 1941. See also AL, "Wildlifers and Game Farmers," RMG, p. 63; AL, *Game Management*, chap. 1, "A History of Ideas"; AL, "Wisconsin Wildlife Chronology," *Wisconsin Conservation Bulletin* 5, no. 11 (1940): 8–20; AL, "Obituary: P. S. Lovejoy," *Journal of Wildlife Management* 7, no. 1 (1943): 127. See also Flader, *Thinking Like a Mountain*, pp. 54, 122, 170–172.

55. AL, "Suggestions for Individual Projects," class handout for Wildlife Ecology 118, 1942, UWDWE. Students were assigned "Interpretation of Case Studies." See also C. Meine, "Reading the Landscape: Aldo Leopold and Wildlife Ecology 118" *Forest History Today* (Fall 1999): 35–42.

56. AL, "Case Studies for Wildlife Ecology 118 Class," Cases 1–8, respectively, ca 1940s: "Recent History of Roadsides" (1948); "History of a Prairie Coulee" (n.d.); "History of the Ragweed Patch, Faville Grove" (n.d.); "History of Central Wisconsin Marshes" (n.d.); "History of Northern Wisconsin" (n.d.); "Evolution of the Fencerow" (n.d.); "History of a Tussock Marsh" (n.d.); "History of Gilbert Creek, Dunn County, Wisconsin" (n.d., compiled by student Irven O. Buss).

57. AL, "Conservationist in Mexico," RMG, pp. 239–244. See also AL, letter to Carl O. Sauer, 29 December 1938, LP 10-3, 3: "I was much pleased to learn . . . that you are interested in deciphering the ecology of the northern Sierra Madre . . . before the terrain is manhandled and before the opportunity is lost. . . . To my mind, the most important item is to decipher the soil-water-streamflow relation and compare it with the 'modified' terrain of similar geologic formation on this side of the line [using historical records]. . . . By comparing the ecology of an unspoiled terrain with the known history of a similar spoiled terrain, some important deductions would probably result" about how to better use the land.

58. AL, "Report of the Iowa Game Survey," "Chapter Two: Iowa Quail,"

Outdoor America 2, no. 2 (1932): 11: "The known past is, in fact, a laboratory, in which quail have been successively exposed to four sets of conditions."

59. This idea bears similarity to the concept termed today historic range of variability (HRV), which requires the identification of variables in nature and an estimation of how those variables have fluctuated at various scales in the past, particularly before European-American land use affected an area. The suggestion is that if management promotes conditions that are within the HRV, it is more likely to be promoting forms of sustainable land use. See T. Veblen, "Historic Range of Variability of Mountain Forest Ecosystems: Concepts and Applications," *Forest Chronicle* 79 (2003): 223–226, and P. Landres, P. Morgan, and F. Swanson, "Overview of the Use of Natural Variability Concepts in Managing Ecological Systems," *Ecological Applications* 9 (1999): 1179–1188.

60. It seems likely that "northeastern Europe" in "Wilderness as a Land Laboratory" (reprinted as "Wilderness for Science" in SCA) is a typographical error and that Leopold intended to say "northwestern Europe." Leopold had already claimed in an earlier writing that northwestern Europe might have provided the only such example. See "Biotic Land-Use," FHL, p. 204.

61. AL, "Report of the Iowa Game Survey," "Chapter Two: Iowa Quail," pp. 11–13, 30–31.

62. AL, "Marshland Elegy," SCA, p. 99.

63. AL, "The Wisconsin River Marshes," *National Waltonian* 2, no. 3 (September 1934): 59–60; also in FHL, p. 40.

64. Ibid., pp. 41–42. Leopold retold the story in "Marshland Elegy," SCA, p. 99.

65. Ibid., p. 42.

66. Also see J. L. Dupouey et al., "Irreversible Impact of Past Land Use on Forest Soils and Biodiversity," *Ecology* 83, no. 11 (2002): 2978–2984.

67. Also see AL, "Case Studies for Wildlife Ecology 118 Class," Case 4: "History of Central Wisconsin Marshes," n.d., UWDWE, and "Bogs, Swamps, and Marshes in Relation to Wisconsin Game Animals," by Franklin Schmidt (a top student of Leopold's who died tragically in 1935), LP 10-5, 7.

68. Leopold likely drew on works of Edward Deevey and Stanley Cain, who were prominent in this field and remained so until the 1980s. Estella Leopold, personal communication.

69. S. Cain, *Foundations of Plant Geography* (New York: Harper and Brothers, 1944). Techniques of analysis improved in the following decades, and not all claims made via this technique have held. In Leopold's time it was believed that pollen evidence indicated a floral and faunal composition in Wisconsin that remained intact geographically throughout changing climatologic and geologic eras over 20,000 years. Paleontologist Linda Brubaker more recently (1988) sketched a picture of communities seldom persisting intact for more than 2,000–5,000 years; see J. B. Callicott, "Do Deconstructive Ecology and Sociobiology Undermine the Leopold Land Ethic?" in *Beyond the Land Ethic: More Essays in Environmental Philosophy* (Albany: State University of New York Press, 1999), p. 125. Whether 2,000 or 20,000 years,

however, the point holds that radical changes in landscape trends occurred after European settlement in Wisconsin around 1840. See AL, "Conservation: In Whole or in Part?" RMG, pp. 310–319.

70. AL, "Conservation: In Whole or in Part?" RMG, pp. 311–312.

71. See also AL, "Sick Trout Streams" (unpublished, 14 April 1944, LP 10-6, 16), which linked dried-up and silted Wisconsin trout streams to land misuse, including overgrazing and exhaustion of soil organic matter.

72. AL, "Land-Health in Southwest Wisconsin," 1943 and 1944.

73. Ibid., 1944, p. 1.

74. Ibid., 1943, p. 5.

75. Ibid., p. 7.

76. Ibid.

77. AL, "Coon Valley: An Adventure in Cooperative Conservation," *American Forests* 41, no. 5 (May 1935): 273–275; also in RMG, p. 220, and FHL, p. 49.

78. AL, "Land-Health in Southwest Wisconsin," 1943 draft, p. 10.

79. AL, "Deer and *Dauerwald* in Germany: I," p. 374; AL, "Deer and *Dauerwald* in Germany: II. Ecology and Policy," *Journal of Forestry* 34, no. 5 (May 1936): 460.

80. AL, "Deer and *Dauerwald* in Germany: I," p. 374.

81. AL, "Sketches of Land Use in Germany," address to the Taylor-Hibbard Club, 22 January 1936, pp. 2, 5, LP 10-6, 14. Leopold pointed out in a photograph a dead tree "snag left for woodpeckers—a revolutionary change in the mental habit of foresters, unthinkable a decade ago. In short, the Germans do not cease and desist from conflicting uses; they fit, modify, and adjust, realizing that the whole organic universe is a process of adjustment."

82. AL, "Land Pathology," RMG, p. 213.

83. AL, "Conservation: In Whole or In Part?" RMG, p. 311. Leopold cited E. P. Farrow, *Plant Life on East Anglian Heaths* (Cambridge: Cambridge University Press, 1925). Leopold was interested in international conservation. He undertook an informal comparative study of the historical effects of human occupancy on land pyramids of England and Arizona, concluding that plant succession provided a key to the differences in land's resistance to human alteration. He also comparatively considered land pyramids of southern Arizona, South Africa, and land and marine environments of the Arctic tundra. See AL, informal class lecture notes for Wildlife Ecology 118 at the University of Wisconsin, ca. 1940, LP 10-6, 14, and AL, "A Biotic View of Land," RMG, p. 270.

84. AL, "Land Pathology," RMG, pp. 213–214.

85. See, too, AL, "Vertical Planning for Wild Life," address to Rural Regional Planning group, 25 March 1936, LP 10-6, 14: "As an antidote for the recent errors [in land use]: go to the local area (group of men as versatile as possible). Forget all the isms, manuals, bureaus, abstractions and ask: 1. What is this land good for? 2. What is on it? 3. What could be on it? 4. How can its resources be used with least damage to each other?"

86. AL, "Wilderness as a Land Laboratory," RMG, p. 289; AL, "Foreword," in Callicott, *Companion to "A Sand County Almanac,"* pp. 285, 286.

87. AL, "Conservationist in Mexico," RMG, p. 239.

88. Ibid.
89. Ibid.
90. AL, "Foreword," in Callicott, *Companion to "A Sand County Almanac,"* pp. 285, 286.
91. AL, "Wilderness for Science," SCA, p. 197. See also AL, "Wilderness as a Land Laboratory," RMG, p. 289. Leopold had no time to study the Sierra Madre, but he hoped others would do so. His particular hope was to interest prominent geographer Carl Sauer of the University of California to take up the task. Leopold's eldest son, Starker, was in contact with Sauer and raised the prospect with him. Leopold proposed for the region the kind of comparative historical inquiry that he had undertaken elsewhere, looking not just at both sides of the border but at present conditions in comparison with past ones. AL, letter to Carl Sauer, 29 December 1938, LP 10-3, 3. Leopold also tried to get the Ecological Society of America involved in studying the region, but it lacked the leadership and resources at the time to undertake the task. Additionally, Mexico's political landscape was changing, which dimmed the prospects further. See AL, letter to Harvey Broome, 7 August 1940, LP 10-2, 9.
92. AL, "Conservation: In Whole or in Part?" RMG, p. 315.
93. AL, "The Land-Health Concept and Conservation," FHL, p. 220.
94. Draft attached to AL, letter to Rudolf Bennitt, 22 October 1940, LP 10-1, 1; later draft in FHL, pp. 198–207.
95. AL, "Biotic Land-Use," FHL, p. 200.
96. Ibid. See also Flader, *Thinking Like a Mountain*, p. 31, and C. D. Meine, *Aldo Leopold: His Life and Work* (Madison: University of Wisconsin Press, 1988), p. 404.
97. Ibid., p. 203.
98. Ibid.
99. Ibid., p. 205. In Leopold's lexicon, in short, stability ranked as a fundamental characteristic of healthy land. Indeed, so linked was the land's health to its stability—to its sustained ability to recycle nutrients and maintain soil fertility—that Leopold several times treated the words "health" and "stability" as if they were synonyms. In "Biotic Land-Use" he would talk about the goal of "stabilization or land-health" (FHL, p. 202). In "Planning for Wildlife" he would talk of "stable (i.e., healthy) land" (FHL, p. 194); in "Conservation: In Whole or in Part?" he would explain that "land was stable, i.e., it retained its health" (RMG, p. 311). The words were not synonyms, though: "stability" had a more narrow, particular meaning, whereas "health" was a broader concept, not yet well grasped. As Leopold understood land health, however, stability was a defining element; if stable land was not fully healthy, it was very close.
100. AL, "Biotic Land-Use," FHL, p. 205.
101. AL, "Substitutes for a Land Ethic," SCA, p. 210.
102. AL, "Biotic Land-Use," FHL, p. 205.
103. AL, "Conservation: In Whole or in Part?" RMG, p. 315.
104. Ibid.
105. Ibid. For an interesting discussion of the recent emphasis within the field of

ecology on flux and change in nature in relation to ideas of stability, predictability, and conditions of equilibrium in nature and how we understand good land use and define healthy land, see Callicott, "Deconstructive Ecology and Sociobiology," pp. 117–139. See also B. Norton,. "Change, Constancy, and Creativity: The New Ecology and Some Old Problems," *Duke Environmental Law and Policy Forum* 7, no. 49 (1996): 49–70; B. Norton, "The Constancy of Leopold's Land Ethic," *Conservation Biology* 2, no. 1 (1988): 93–102; D. Worster, "The Ecology of Order and Chaos," in *The Wealth of Nature: Environmental History and the Ecological Imagination* (New York: Oxford University Press, 1993), pp. 156–170; and D. Worster, ed., *Nature's Economy: A History of Ecological Ideas* (Cambridge: Cambridge University Press, 1994). Leopold intended the land pyramid concept to replace the balance-of-nature idea of land as an ecologically "truer image"—one that tried to incorporate the limits and flexibilities of self-organization and dynamism in nature. See AL, "The Land Pyramid," SCA, p. 214.

106. Work exploring possible relationships between diversity and stability has continued. See, e.g., D. Goodman, "The Theory of Diversity-Stability Relationships in Ecology," *Quarterly Review of Biology* 30 (1975): 237–266; D. Tilman and J. A. Downing, "Biodiversity and Stability in Grasslands," *Nature* 367, no. 6461 (January 1994): 363–365; and S. Naeem et al., "Declining Biodiversity Can Alter the Performance of Ecosystems," *Nature* 369, no. 6473 (April 1994): 734–737.

107. AL, "Wilderness for Science," SCA, p. 196.

108. AL, "The Land-Health Concept and Conservation," FHL, p. 204.

109. AL, "The Basis of Conservation Education," unpublished address to Kiwanis Club, Racine, Wisconsin, 20 July 1939, p. 3, LP 10-6, 14.

110. AL, "Economics, Philosophy, and Land," unpublished manuscript, 23 November 1938, p. 5, LP 10-6, 16: "The first law of intelligent tinkering is to keep all the parts. We might need them." See also AL, "The Land-Health Concept," FHL, pp. 221–222, and AL, "The Community Concept," SCA, pp. 204–205.

111. AL, "Substitutes for a Land Ethic," SCA, pp. 210–211.

112. AL, "The Community Concept," SCA, p. 204.

113. AL, "The Land-Health Concept and Conservation," FHL, p. 221.

114. Ibid.

115. Along with the terms "stability" and "integrity," which he used with particular meanings of his own, he also drew on words and phrases such as "continuity," "structure," "capacity for self-renewal," "complexity," "beauty," "wholeness," and "collective functioning" to define health.

116. AL, "Conservation: In Whole or in Part?" RMG, p. 310.

117. AL, "The Land Pyramid," SCA, p. 216; AL, "A Biotic View of Land," RMG, p. 269.

118. AL, "The Land Pyramid," SCA, p. 217.

119. Ibid.

120. AL, "The Outlook," SCA, p. 226.

121. AL, "The Land-Health Concept and Conservation," FHL, p. 224.

122. Ibid.

123. AL, "Wilderness for Science," SCA, pp. 195–196. See also AL, "The Meaning of Conservation," unpublished address, Milwaukee, 10 September ca. 1942, LP 10-6, 17. Also see AL, "Scientific Uses of Wilderness," unpublished address to the Get-Away Club, 17 January 1942, LP 10-6, 14.

124. See AL, "Ticks and Deer," unpublished manuscript, 5 December 1944; AL, "On a Monument to the Pigeon," SCA, p. 110.

125. AL renamed the essay "Yet Come June" in a subsequent draft. Both drafts dated 23 December 1941, LP 10-6, 17.

126. AL, "Yet the Trees Grow"/"Yet Come June," p. 1.

127. Quoted in AL, "The Conservation Ethic," RMG, p. 191.

128. AL, "Marshland Elegy," SCA, p. 101.

129. Ibid.

130. AL, "Conservation," unpublished manuscript stapled to letter from Horace Fries (member of the National Educational Committee for a New Party), 8 August 1946, LP 10-1, 1.

131. AL, "Land Health and the A-B Cleavage," SCA, p. 221.

132. AL, "The Outlook," SCA, pp. 224–225. For further discussion of Leopold's use of "beauty" in his land ethic, see C. D. Meine, "Building the Land Ethic," in Callicott, *Companion to "A Sand County Almanac,"* p. 184, and C. D. Meine, "Building 'the Land Ethic': A History of Aldo Leopold's Most Important Essay," master's thesis, University of Wisconsin–Madison, 1983, p. 67. On Leopold and aesthetics, see also J. B. Callicott, "The Land Aesthetic," in *Companion to "A Sand County Almanac,"* pp. 157–171.

133. AL, "The Ethical Sequence," SCA, p. 203.

134. Ibid.

135. AL, "The Land Ethic," SCA, pp. 224–225.

136. Ibid., p. 224.

137. Ibid.

138. Ibid., p. 223.

139. AL, "Ethical Sequence," SCA, p. 203.

140. Ibid., p. 202.

141. AL, "The Ecological Conscience," RMG, p. 340.

142. Ibid., pp. 345–346.

143. AL, "Ethical Sequence," SCA, p. 203.

144. Ibid.

145. AL, "Conservation," unpublished manuscript stapled to letter from Horace Fries (member of the National Education Committee for a New Party), 8 August 1946, LP 10-1, 1.

146. AL, "Community Concept," SCA, p. 204; AL, "Substitutes for a Land Ethic," SCA, p. 211.

147. AL, "Community Concept," SCA, p. 204.

148. AL, "Defenders of Wilderness," SCA, p. 200.

149. See AL, "Foreword," SCA, pp. vii–ix.

150. AL, "Sky Dance," SCA, p. 34.

Bibliography

Ahlers, J. "Thinking Like a Mountain: Toward a Sensible Land Ethic." *Christian Century* 107 (1990): 433–434.

Albrecht, W. A. "Pattern of Wildlife Distribution Fits the Soil Pattern." *Missouri Conservationist* 4, no. 3 (1943): 1–16.

———. "Sound Horses Are Bred on Fertile Soils." *Percheron News*, July 1942.

Aldo Leopold Papers. University of Wisconsin Archives. Madison, Wisconsin.

Allee, W. C., A. Emerson, O. Park, T. Park, and K. Schmidt. *Principles of Animal Ecology*. Philadelphia: W. B. Saunders, 1949.

Allen, A. W. "Victorian Hypocrisy." *Atlantic Monthly*, August 1914, 174–188.

Allen, D. "Leopold: The Founder." *American Forests* 93, no. 10 (October 1987): 26–29, 69–70.

———. *Our Wildlife Legacy*, rev. ed. New York: Funk and Wagnalls, 1962.

Allen, D., et al. "Report on the Committee on North American Wildlife Policy." *Transactions of the 38th North American Wildlife and Natural Resources Conference*. 18–21 March 1973, Washington, DC.

Anderson, L. *Benton MacKaye: Conservationist, Planner, and Creator of the Appalachian Trail*. Baltimore: Johns Hopkins University Press, 2002.

Anonymous. "An American Game Policy." *American Forests* 37, no. 1 (1931): 41.

———. "The Changing Bases of Public Forest Policy." *Journal of Forestry* 33, no. 5 (1935): 457–459.

———. "Conservation of Our Natural Resources." *National Geographic* 19, no. 5 (1908): 384–740.

———. "Danger Ahead." *American Forests* 43, no. 1 (1937): 21.

———. "Editorial: The Copeland Report." *American Forests* 39, no. 5 (1933): 211.

———. "Forest Industry Charts Conservation Course." *American Forests* 39, no. 12 (1933): 540–573.

———. "A House Divided." *American Forests* 39, no. 1 (1933): 27.

———. "An Issue That Will Not Down." *Journal of Forestry* 34, no. 6 (1936): 551–553.

———. *Matamek Conference on Biological Cycles: Full Proceedings*. Matamek Factory, Canadian Labrador, 1932.

———. "Pinchot Opposes Department of Conservation." *American Forests* 43, no. 4 (1937): 196–197.

———. "Roosevelt Recommends a Department of Conservation." *American Forests* 43, no. 2 (February 1937): 74, 92.

———. "The Value of the United States Forest Service." *National Geographic* 20, no. 1 (1909): 29–40.

———. "A Wasteful Nation." *National Geographic* 20, no. 2 (1909): 203–206.

Aubrey, J. R. "Aldo Leopold: A Bio-bibliography." U.S. Air Force Academy, Colorado, 1990.

Babbitt, B. "The Fierce Green Fire." *Audubon* 95, no. 3 (1994): 120–123.

Badger, A. J. 1989. *The New Deal: The Depression Years, 1933–1940.* New York: Hill and Wang.

Bailey, L. H. *The Holy Earth.* New York: Charles Scribner's Sons, 1915.

Baillie, F., and W. A. Grohman. *Master of Game: Edward of Norwich, Second Duke of York.* London: Chalto and Windres, 1909.

Bakken, P. W. "The Ecology of Grace: Ultimacy and Environmental Ethics in Aldo Leopold and Joseph Sittler." PhD diss., University of Chicago, 1991.

Barnes, W. C. "Herds in San Simon Valley: What Has Happened to the Promised Land of Arizona's Oldtime Cattlemen." *American Forests* 42, no. 10 (1936): 456–457, 481.

Barrow, M., Jr. "Science, Sentiment, and the Specter of Extinction." *Environmental History* 7, no. 1 (2002): 69–98.

Bates, C. G., and O. R. Zeasman. "Soil Erosion—a Local and National Problem." Research Bulletin 99. Madison: U.S. Department of Agriculture and University of Wisconsin, Agriculture Experiment Station, August 1930.

Beck, T. H., J. N. Darling, and A. Leopold. 1934. "A National Plan for Wild Life Restoration." Washington, DC: President's Committee on Wild Life Restoration, 8 February 1934.

Beeman, R. S., and J. A. Pritchard. *A Green and Permanent Land: Ecology and Agriculture in the Twentieth Century.* Lawrence: University Press of Kansas, 2001.

Behre, E. "The Place of Forestry in the New Agricultural Conservation Program." *Journal of Forestry* 34, no. 7 (1936): 674–681.

von Behring, E., et al. "Manifesto of the Ninety-three German Intellectuals to the Civilized World." 1914. Brigham Young University, Harold B. Lee Library, World War I Document Archive. http://www.lib.byu.edu/~rdh/wwi/1914/93intell.html (accessed November 2005).

Bellamy, E., ed. *Looking Backward: 2000–1887.* New York: Modern Library, 1942.

Bennett, H. H. "Wild Life and Erosion Control." *Bird-Lore*, March–April 1936, 115–121.

Berger, J. J. *Understanding Forests.* San Francisco: Sierra Club Books, 1998.

Berry, D. K. *The Uneasy State: The United States from 1915 to 1945.* Chicago: University of Chicago Press, 1983.

Berry, W. "Amplifications: Continuing Notes on the Land Ethic—Preserving Wildness." *Wilderness* (Spring 1987): 39–40, 50–54.

Binkley, D., M. M. Moore, W. H. Romme, and P. M. Brown. "Was Aldo Leopold Right about the Kaibab Deer Herd?" *Ecosystems* 9 (2006): 227–241.

Blanchard, C. J. "The Call of the West: Homes Are Being Made for Millions of People in the Arid West." *National Geographic* 20, no. 5 (1909): 403–436.

——. "Home-making by the Government: An Account of the Eleven Immense Irrigating Projects to Be Opened in 1908." *National Geographic* 19, no. 4 (1908): 258–287.

Botkin, D. B. *Discordant Harmonies: A New Ecology for the Twenty-first Century.* New York: Oxford University Press, 1990.

Bradley, C. C. "The Leopold Memorial Reserve." In *Aldo Leopold: The Man and His Legacy*, edited by T. Tanner, 161–164. Ankeny, IA: Soil and Conservation Society of America, 1987.

Bradley, N. L. "Aldo Leopold: Reflections of a Daughter." *Journal of Soil and Water Conservation* 46 (1991): 404–405.

Bradley, N. L., A. C. Leopold, J. Ross, and W. Huffaker. "Phenological Changes Reflect Climate Change in Wisconsin." *Proceedings of the National Academy of Sciences* 96, no. 17 (August 1999): 9701–9704.

Bradley, N. L., et al. "Great Possessions." *Wisconsin Academy Review* 26, no. 1 (1979): 3–9.

Bramwell, A. *Ecology in the 20th Century: A History.* New Haven, CT: Yale University Press, 1989.

Brandt, I. *Adventures in Conservation with Franklin D. Roosevelt.* Flagstaff, AZ: Northland, 1988.

Brinkley, A. *The End of Reform: New Deal Liberalism in Recession and War.* New York: Random House, 1995.

Bronowski, J., and B. Mazlish. *The Western Intellectual Tradition: From Leonardo to Hegel.* New York: Harper and Brothers, 1960.

Brooks, P. *Speaking for Nature: How Literary Naturalists from Henry Thoreau to Rachel Carson Have Shaped America.* Boston: Houghton Mifflin, 1980.

——. "The Wilderness Ideal: How Aldo Leopold and Robert Marshall Articulated the Need for Preservation." *The Living Wilderness* 44 (1980): 150.

Brown, D. E., and N. B. Carmony, eds. *Aldo Leopold's Southwest.* Albuquerque: University of New Mexico Press, 1990.

Bryan, K. "Change in Plant Associations by Change in Ground Water Level." *Ecology* 9 (1928): 474–478.

——. "Date of Channel Trenching (Arroyo Cutting) in the Arid Southwest." *Science* 62 (1925): 338–344.

Burroughs, J. *Accepting the Universe.* New York: Russell & Russell, 1920.

——. *Whitman: A Study.* New York: William Wise, 1924.

Buss, I. O. "Wisconsin Pheasant Populations: Progress Report of Pheasant Investigations Conducted from 1936–1943." Federal Aid in Wildlife Restoration Project No. 9R. Madison: Wisconsin Conservation Department, 1946.

Butler, O. "Conservation at the Forks." *American Forests* 43, no. 3 (1937): 109–110, 143.

——. "Forest Situation Exposed." *American Forests* 39, no. 5 (1933): 204–206.

Cain, S. A. *Foundations of Plant Geography.* New York: Harper Brothers, 1944.

Cain, S. A., and G. M. de Oliveira Castro. *Manual of Vegetation Analysis.* New York: Harper and Brothers, 1959.

Callicott, B. "Aldo Leopold: An Annotated Secondary Bibliography." Master's thesis, University of South Carolina, 1996.

Callicott, J. B. "Aldo Leopold and the Foundations of Ecosystem Management." *Journal of Forestry* (May 2000): 5–13.

——. "Aldo Leopold on Education, as Educator, and His Land Ethic in the Context of Environmental Education." *Journal of Environmental Education* 14 (1982): 34–41.

——. "Aldo Leopold's Metaphor." In *Ecosystem Health: New Goals for Environmental Management*, edited by R. Costanza, B. G. Norton, and B. D. Haskell, 42–56. Washington, DC: Island Press, 1992.

——. "The Arboretum and the University: The Speech and the Essay." *Transactions of the Wisconsin Academy of Sciences, Arts, and Letters* 87 (1999): 5–22.

——. *Beyond the Land Ethic: More Essays in Environmental Philosophy*. Albany: State University of New York Press, 1999.

——. "A Brief History of American Conservation Philosophy." In *Sustainable Ecological Systems: Implementing an Ecological Approach to Land Management*, edited by W. W. Covington and L. F. DeBano. Fort Collins, CO: U.S. Department of Agriculture, Forest Service, Rocky Mountain Forest and Range Experiment Station, 1993.

——. "A Critical Examination of 'Another Look at Leopold's Land Ethic.'" *Journal of Forestry* 96, no. 1 (1998): 20–26.

——. "Elements of an Environmental Ethic: Moral Considerability and the Biotic Community." *Environmental Ethics* 1 (1979): 71–81.

——. "Hume's *Is/Ought* Dichotomy and the Relation of Ecology to Leopold's Land Ethic." *Environmental Ethics* 4, no. 2 (1982): 163–174.

——. *In Defense of the Land Ethic*. Albany: State University of New York Press, 1989.

——. "The Land Aesthetic." *Environmental Review* 7 (1983): 345–358.

——. "Leopold's Land Aesthetic." *Journal of Soil and Water Conservation* 38, no. 4 (1983): 329–332.

——. "Non-anthropocentric Value Theory and Environmental Ethics." *American Philosophical Quarterly* 21 (1984): 299–309.

——. "Standards of Conservation: Then and Now." *Conservation Biology* 4 (1990): 229–232.

——. "Whither Conservation Ethics?" *Conservation Biology* 4 (1990): 15–20.

——. "The Wilderness Idea Revisited: The Sustainable Development Alternative." *The Environmental Professional* 13 (1991): 235–247.

——, ed. *Companion to "A Sand County Almanac": Interpretive and Critical Essays*. Madison: University of Wisconsin Press, 1987.

Callicott, J. B., and E. T. Freyfogle, eds. *Aldo Leopold: For the Health of the Land; Previously Unpublished Essays and Other Writings*. Washington, DC: Island Press, Shearwater Books, 1999.

Carter, L. "The Leopolds: A Family of Naturalists." *Science* 207 (1980): 1051–1055.

Chambers, J. W., II, ed. *The Tyranny of Change: America in the Progressive Era, 1890–1920*. New Brunswick, NJ: Rutgers University Press, 2000.

Chapman, H. H. "Forestry and Game Management." *Journal of Forestry* 34, no. 2 (1936): 104–106.

Chapman, R. N. "The Quantitative Analysis of Environmental Factors." *Ecology* 9, no. 2 (1928): 111–122.

Chapple, C. K. *Ecological Prospects: Scientific, Religious, and Aesthetic Perspectives*. Albany: State University of New York Press, 1994.

Chase, S. *Rich Land, Poor Land: A Study of Waste in the Natural Resources of America*. New York: Whittlesey House, 1936.

———. *The Tragedy of Waste*. New York: Macmillan, 1925.

Chisholm, A. "The Leopolds: An Ecological Family." In *Philosophers of the Earth: Conversations with Ecologists*, 54–66. London: Sidgwick and Jackson, 1972.

Clark, E. B. "Real Naturalists on Nature Faking." *Everybody's Magazine* 17, no. 3 (1907): 423–430.

———. "Roosevelt on the Nature Fakirs." *Everybody's Magazine* 16, no. 6 (1907): 770–774.

Clements, F. E. *Plant Succession*. Publication 242. Washington, DC: Carnegie Institution, 1916.

Clements, F. E., and V. E. Shelford. *Bio-ecology*. New York: John Wiley and Sons, 1939.

Clements, F. E., J. E. Weaver, and H. C. Hanson. *Plant Competition: An Analysis of Community Function*. New York: Arno Press, 1977.

Clements, K. A. *Hoover, Conservation, and Consumerism: Engineering the Good Life*. Lawrence: University Press of Kansas, 2000.

Costanza, R., B. G. Norton, and B. D. Haskell, eds. *Ecosystem Health: New Goals for Environmental Management*. Washington, DC: Island Press, 1992.

Cowan, C. S. *The Enemy Is Fire!* Seattle: Superior Publishing, 1961.

Cozzens, S. W. *The Ancient Cibola: The Marvellous Country; or, Three Years in Arizona and New Mexico*. Boston: Lee and Shepard, 1876.

Croker, R. A. *Pioneer Ecologist: The Life and Work of Victor Ernest Shelford: 1877–1968*. Washington, DC: Smithsonian Institution Press, 1991.

Croly, H. D. *The Promise of American Life*. Edited by A. M. Schlesinger Jr. Cambridge, MA: Harvard University Press, Belknap Press, 1965.

Cronon, W. "Modes of Prophecy and Production: Placing Nature in History." *Journal of American History* 76, no. 4 (1990): 1122–1131.

———, ed. *Uncommon Ground: Rethinking the Human Place in Nature*. New York: W. W. Norton, 1996.

Curtis, J. T. *The Vegetation of Wisconsin: An Ordination of Plant Communities*. Madison: University of Wisconsin Press, 1959.

Cutright, P. R. *Theodore Roosevelt: The Making of a Conservationist*. Urbana: University of Illinois Press, 1985.

Darling, F. F. *A Herd of Red Deer: A Study in Animal Behavior*. London: Oxford University Press, 1937.

Darwin, C. *The Descent of Man and Selection in Relation to Sex*. London: John Murray, 1871.

———. *The Formation of Vegetable Mould through the Action of Worms*. London: John Murray, 1881.

———. *The Origin of Species*. London: John Murray, 1859.

Davis, T. "Aldo Leopold, 1887–1987." Part I, "Aldo Leopold's Forgotten Book

[*Game Survey of the North Central States*]." *Wisconsin Sportsman* 16, no. 1 (1987): 25–28.

Deevey, E. S. "Biogeography of the Pleistocene." *Bulletin of the Geological Society of America* 60, no. 9 (1949): 1315–1416.

———. *Living Record of the Ice Age.* San Francisco: W. H. Freeman, 1949.

Detweiler, F. B. "Better Acorns from a Heavily Fertilized White Oak Tree." *Journal of Forestry* 41, no. 12 (1943): 915–916.

De Voto, B. "The West against Itself." *Harpers* 194 (1947): 1–13.

———. *The Year of Decision: 1846.* Boston: Little, Brown, 1943.

Dewey, E. R., and E. F. Dakin. *Cycles: The Science of Prediction.* New York: Henry Holt, 1947.

Dickinsen, V. L. "The Trend of Conservation." *Wisconsin Conservation Bulletin* 8, no. 7 (July 1943): 1–10.

Diner, S. J. *A Very Different Age: Americans of the Progressive Era.* New York: Hill and Wang, 1998.

Douglas, H. *Dreamers and Defenders: American Conservationists.* Lincoln: University of Nebraska Press, 1988.

Dumenil, L. *Modern Temper: American Culture and Society in the 1920s.* New York: Hill and Wang, 1995.

Dunlap, J. *Aldo Leopold: Living with the Land* (children's book). New York: Twenty-First Century Books, 1993.

Dupouey, J. L., et al. "Irreversible Impact of Past Land Use on Forest Soils and Biodiversity." *Ecology* 83, no. 11 (2002): 2978–2984.

Egan, T. *The Worst Hard Time: The Untold Story of Those Who Survived the Great American Dust Bowl.* New York: Houghton Mifflin, 2006.

Egerton, F. N. "History of Ecology: Achievements and Opportunities, Part I." *Journal of the History of Biology* 16, no. 2 (1983): 259–310.

———. "History of Ecology: Achievements and Opportunities, Part II." *Journal of the History of Biology* 18, no. 1 (1985): 103–143.

Elton, C. *Animal Ecology.* New York: Macmillan, 1927.

———. *Animal Ecology and Evolution.* London: Humphrey Milford, 1930.

———. *The Ecology of Invasions by Animals and Plants.* London: Methuen, 1958.

———. *Matamek Conference on Biological Cycles: Abstract of Papers and Discussions.* Matamek Factory, Canadian Labrador, 1933.

———. *Voles, Mice, and Lemmings: Problems in Population Dynamics.* Oxford: Clarendon Press, 1942.

Errington, P. L. "In Appreciation of Aldo Leopold." *Journal of Wildlife Management* 12, no. 4 (1948): 341–350.

———. "The Northern Bobwhite: Environmental Factors Influencing Its Status." PhD diss., University of Wisconsin–Madison, 1932.

———. "Some Contributions of a Fifteen-Year Local Study of the Northern Bobwhite to a Knowledge of Population Phenomena." *Ecological Monographs* 15, no. 1 (1945): 1–34.

———, ed. *Of Men and Marshes.* Ames: Iowa State University Press, 1996.

Errington, P. L., and F. N. Hamerstrom. "The Northern Bob-white's Winter Territory." Research Bulletin 201. Ames: Iowa State College of Agriculture and Mechanical Arts, Agricultural Experiment Station, 1936.

Errington, P. L., et al. "The Great Horned Owl and Its Prey in North-central U.S." Research Bulletin 277, 817–831. Ames: Iowa State College of Agricultural and Mechanical Arts, Agricultural Experiment Station, 1940.

Ferré, F. "Persons in Nature: Toward an Applicable and Unified Environmental Ethics." *Zygon* 28 (1993): 441–453.

Flader, S. L. "Aldo Leopold and the Evolution of Ecosystem Management." In *Sustainable Ecological Systems: Implementing an Ecological Approach to Land Management*, edited by W. W. Covington and L. F. DeBano, 15–19. Fort Collins, CO: U.S. Department of Agriculture, Forest Service, Rocky Mountain Forest and Range Experiment Station, 1993.

———. "Aldo Leopold's Legacy to Forestry." *Forest History Today* (1998): 2–5.

———. "Leopold on Wilderness: Aldo Leopold on Germany's Landscape." *American Forests* 97 (May–June 1991).

———. "Leopold's 'Some Fundamentals of Conservation': A Commentary." *Environmental Ethics* 1, no. 2 (1979): 143–148.

———. "Let the Fire Devil Have His Due: Aldo Leopold and the Conundrum of Wilderness Management." In *Managing America's Enduring Wilderness Resource*, edited by David Lime. St. Paul: Minnesota Extension Service, 1990.

———. "Thinking Like a Mountain: A Biographical Study of Aldo Leopold." *Forest History* 17, no. 1 (1973): 14–28.

———. *Thinking Like a Mountain: Aldo Leopold and the Evolution of an Ecological Attitude toward Deer, Wolves, and Forests*. Madison: University of Wisconsin Press, 1994.

Flader, S. L., and J. B. Callicott, eds. *The River of the Mother of God and Other Essays by Aldo Leopold*. Madison: University of Wisconsin Press, 1991.

Flader, S. L., and C. Steinhacker. *The Sand County of Aldo Leopold*. San Francisco: Sierra Club Books, 1973.

Fleming, D. "Roots of the New Conservation Movement." *Perspectives in American History* 6 (1972): 24–26.

Forbes, S. A. "The Lake as a Microcosm." *Bulletin of the Scientific Association of Peoria, Illinois* (1887): 77–87.

Foreman, D. *Rewilding North America: A Vision for Conservation in the 21st Century*. Washington, DC: Island Press, 2004.

Fox, S. *The American Conservation Movement: John Muir and His Legacy*. Madison: University of Wisconsin Press, 1981.

Frank, B. "Foresters and Land Planning." *Journal of Forestry* 34, no. 3 (1936): 262–271.

Freyfogle, E. T. "Battling over Leopold's Legacy." Washington, DC: Georgetown Environmental Law and Policy Institute, Georgetown University Law Center, 2004.

———. *Bounded People, Boundless Lands: Envisioning a New Land Ethic*. Washington, DC: Island Press, Shearwater Books, 1998.

———. "Conservation and the Four Faces of Resistance." In *Reconstructing Conservation: Finding Common Ground*, edited by B. A. Minteer and R. E. Manning, 145–164. Washington, DC: Island Press, 2003.

———. "Conservation and the Lure of the Garden." *Conservation Biology* 18, no. 4 (2004): 995–1003.

——. "Ethics, Community, and Private Land." *Ecology Law Quarterly* 26 (1996): 631–661.

——. "The Evolution of Property Rights: California Water Law as a Case Study." In *Property Law and Legal Education: Essays in Honor of J. E. Cribbet*, edited by M. H. Hoeflich and P. Hay, 73–107. Urbana: University of Illinois Press, 1988.

——. *Justice and the Earth: Images for our Planetary Survival.* Urbana: University of Illinois Press, 1993.

——. "The Land Ethic and Pilgrim Leopold." *University of Colorado Law Review* 61 (1990): 217–256.

——. "Land Use and the Study of Early American History." *Yale Law Journal* 94 (1985): 717–742.

——. *The Land We Share: Private Property and the Common Good.* Washington, DC: Island Press, Shearwater Books, 2003.

——. "Ownership and Ecology." *Case Western Reserve Law Review* 43 (1993): 1269–1297.

——. "The Owning and Taking of Sensitive Lands." *UCLA Law Review* 43 (1995): 77–138.

——. "Owning Land: Four Contemporary Narratives." *Land Use and Environment Law Review* 13 (1998): 279–307.

——. "Private Lands Made (Too) Simple." *Environmental Law Reporter* 33 (2003): 10155–10169.

——. "A Sand County Almanac at 50: Leopold in the New Century." *Environmental Law Reporter* 30 (2000): 10058–10068.

——. *Why Conservation Is Failing and How It Can Regain Ground.* New Haven, CT: Yale University Press, 2006.

Fritzell, P. A. "Aldo Leopold's 'A Sand County Almanac' and the Conflicts of Ecological Conscience." *Transactions of the Wisconsin Academy of Sciences, Arts, and Letters* 64 (1976): 22–46.

Gabrielson, I. N. "The Correlation of Forestry and Wildlife Management." *Journal of Forestry* 34, no. 2 (1936): 98–103.

Garland, H., ed. *A Son of the Middle Border.* New York: Penguin Books, 1995.

Gilbert, J., and E. Baker. "Wisconsin Economists and New Deal Agricultural Policy: The Legacy of Progressive Professors." *Wisconsin Magazine of History* (Summer 1997): 281–312.

von Goethe, J. W., ed. *The Sorrows of Young Werther and Novella.* New York: Vintage Classics, 1990.

Goldberg, D. J. *Discontented America: The United States in the 1920s.* Baltimore: Johns Hopkins University Press, 1999.

Golley, F. B. *A History of the Ecosystem Concept in Ecology.* New Haven, CT: Yale University Press, 1994.

Goodman, D. "The Theory of Diversity-Stability Relationships in Ecology." *Quarterly Review of Biology* 30 (1975): 237–266.

Goodwyn, L. *The Populist Moment: A Short History of the Agrarian Revolt in America.* New York: Oxford University Press, 1978.

Goschen, E. "Origin of the Term 'A Scrap of Paper.'" 4 August 1914. Brigham

Young University, Harold B. Lee Library, World War I Document Archive. http://www.lib.byu.edu/~rdh/wwi/1914/paperscrap.html (accessed November 2005).

Graham, O. L., Jr. *An Encore for Reform: The Old Progressives and the New Deal.* New York: Oxford University Press, 1967.

Grange, W. B. "Must Public Conservation Eliminate Private Initiative." *Game Breeder and Sportsman* (October 1936): 215–219.

———. *The Way to Game Abundance, with an Explanation of Game Cycles.* New York: Charles Scribner's Sons, 1949.

Grange, W. B., and W. L. McAtee. *Improving the Farm Environment for Wildlife.* Washington, DC: Government Printing Office, 1942.

Graves, H. S. "Comments on the Copeland Report." *American Forests* 39, no. 6 (1933): 258–259.

———. *Instructions for Making Timber Surveys in the National Forests, Including Standard Classification of Forest Types.* U.S. Department of Agriculture, Forest Service. Washington, DC: Government Printing Office, 1917.

———. *The Use Book: A Manual of Information about the National Forests.* U.S. Department of Agriculture, Forest Service. Washington, DC: Government Printing Office, 1918.

Gray, L. C. "The Resettlement Land Program." *American Forests* 42, no. 8 (August 1936): 346–349.

Great Plains Committee. *The Future of the Great Plains.* 75th Cong., 1st sess. Document No. 144. Washington, DC: Government Printing Office, 10 February 1937.

Greeley, W. B. *The Use Book: A Manual of Information about the National Forests: Grazing Section.* U.S. Department of Agriculture, Forest Service. Washington, DC: Government Printing Office, 1921, 1926.

Green, S. W. "Relation between Winter Grass Fires and Cattle Grazing in the Longleaf Pine Belt." *Journal of Forestry* 33, no. 3 (1935): 338–341.

Greene, R. A., and C. Reynard. "The Influence of Two Burrowing Rodents, *Dipodomys spectabilis spectabilis* (Kangaroo Rat) and *Neotoma albigula albigula* (Pack Rat) on Desert Soils in Arizona." *Ecology* 13, no. 1 (1932): 73–80.

Greene, R. A., and G. H. Murphy. "The Influence of Two Burrowing Rodents: Kangaroo Rat and Pack Rat on Desert Soils in Arizona: II Physical Effects," *Ecology* 13, no. 4 (1932): 359–363.

Hack, R. K. "The Case for Humility." *Atlantic Monthly*, February 1918, 222–231.

Hadley, A. T. *Baccalaureate Addresses: And Other Talks on Kindred Themes.* New York: Charles Scribner's Sons, 1907.

———. "The Influence of Charles Darwin upon Historical and Political Thought." *Psychological Review* 16, no. 3 (1909): 143–151.

———. *The Relations between Freedom and Responsibility in the Evolution of Democratic Government.* New Haven, CT: Yale University Press, 1903.

———. *Some Influences in Modern Philosophic Thought.* New Haven, CT: Yale University Press, 1913.

Hall, A. D. *The Soil: An Introduction to the Scientific Study of the Growth of Crops.* New York: E. P. Dutton, 1907.

Hamilton, D. E. *From New Day to New Deal: American Farm Policy from Hoover to Roosevelt, 1928–1933*. Chapel Hill: University of North Carolina Press, 1991.

Hamsun, K., ed. *Growth of the Soil*. New York: Modern Library, 1921.

Hanson, H. C. "Small Mammal Censuses near Prairie du Sac, Wisconsin." *Transactions of the Wisconsin Academy of Sciences, Arts and Letters* 36 (1944): 105–129.

Hargrov, E. C., and J. B. Callicott. "Leopold's Means and Ends in Wild Life Management: A Brief Commentary." *Environmental Ethics* 12 (1990): 333–337.

Hart, A. B., ed. *Selected Addresses and Public Papers of Woodrow Wilson*. New York: Boni and Liveright, 1918.

Haskins, C. H. *Studies in the History of Mediaeval Science*. Cambridge, MA: Harvard University Press, 1927.

Hawley, E. W. *The Great War and the Search for a Modern Order: A History of the American People and Their Institutions, 1917–1933*. New York: St. Martin's Press, 1992.

Hays, S. P. *The Response to Industrialism: 1885–1914*. Chicago: University of Chicago Press, 1957.

———, ed. *Conservation and the Gospel of Efficiency*. Pittsburgh, PA: University of Pittsburgh Press, 1999.

Heasley, L. *A Thousand Pieces of Paradise: Landscape and Property in the Kickapoo Valley*. Madison: University of Wisconsin Press, 2005.

Heffernan, J. D. "The Land Ethic: A Critical Appraisal." *Environmental Ethics* 4 (1982): 235–247.

Helms, D. "Coon Valley, Wisconsin: A Conservation Success Story." In *Readings in the History of the Soil Conservation Service*, edited by D. Helms, 51–53. Washington, DC: Soil Conservation Service, 1999.

Herbert, P. A. "Review of Proceedings of Land Use Symposium, American Association for the Advancement of Science." *Journal of Forestry* 31, no. 5 (1933): 605–606.

Heske, F. *German Forestry*. New Haven, CT: Yale University Press, 1938.

Hickey, J. "Preliminary Bibliography of Aldo Leopold." *Wildlife Research News Letter* 35 (1948): 4–19.

Hinchman, L. P. "Aldo Leopold's Hermeneutic of Nature." *Review of Politics* 57 (1995): 225–249.

Hine, R. V., and J. M. Faracher. *The American West: A New Interpretive History*. New Haven, CT: Yale University Press, 2000.

Hobswam, E. J. *The Age of Revolution, 1789–1848*. New York: New American Library, 1962.

Hochbaum, A. *Canvasback on a Prairie Marsh*. Washington, DC: American Wildlife Institute, 1944.

Hofstadter, R. *The Age of Reform*. New York: Vintage Books, 1955.

———. *The Progressive Movement, 1900–1915*. Englewood Cliffs, NJ: Prentice-Hall, 1963.

Hopkins, C. G. *Soil Fertility and Permanent Agriculture*. Boston: Ginn and Company, 1910.

Hornaday, W. T. *Our Vanishing Wild Life: Its Extermination and Preservation.* New York: New York Zoological Society, 1913.

———. *Wild Life Conservation in Theory and Practice: Lectures Delivered before the Forest School of Yale University.* New Haven, CT: Yale University Press, 1914.

Howard, A., ed. *The Soil and Health: A Study of Organic Agriculture.* New York: Schocken Books, 1975.

Huntington, E. "The Matamek Conference on Biological Cycles, 1931." *Science* 74, no. 1914 (1931): 229–235.

———. *Matamek Conference on Biological Cycles: Report by Ellsworth Huntington, Yale University.* Matamek Factory, Canadian Labrador, 1932.

Jacks, G. V., and R. O. Whyte. *Vanishing Lands: A World Survey of Soil Erosion.* New York: Doubleday, Doran and Company, 1939.

Jacoby, K. *Crimes against Nature: Squatters, Poachers, Thieves, and the Hidden History of American Conservation.* Berkeley: University of California Press, 2001.

Jordan, D. S., and V. L. Kellogg. *Evolution and Animal Life.* New York: D. Appleton, 1907.

Jordon, W. R., III. "Restoration: Shaping the Land, Transforming the Human Spirit [on the Curtis Prairie Restoration Project]." *Whole Earth Catalog* 66 (1990): 22–23.

Judd, R. W. *Common Lands, Common People: The Origins of Conservation in Northern New England.* Cambridge, MA: Harvard University Press, 1997.

———. "A Wonderfull Order and Ballance: Natural History and the Beginnings of Forest Conservation in America, 1730–1830." *Environmental History* 11, no. 1 (2006): 8–36.

Just, T., ed. *Plant and Animal Communities.* Notre Dame: University Press, 1939. Reprinted in *The American Midland Naturalist* 21, no. 1 (1939): 1–255.

Kabat, C., D. Thompson, and R. Hines, eds., "Wisconsin Quail, 1834–1962: Population Dynamics and Habitat Management." *Technical Bulletin of the Wisconsin Department of Natural Resources*, no. 30. Madison: Wisconsin Conservation Department, Game Management Division, 1963.

Karp, J. P. "Aldo Leopold's Land Ethic: Is an Ecological Conscience Evolving in Land Development Law?" *Environmental Law* 19 (1989): 737–765.

Kazin, M. *The Populist Persuasion: An American History.* Ithaca, NY: Cornell University Press, 1995.

Kellogg, C. E. *The Soils That Support Us: An Introduction to the Study of Soils and Their Use by Men.* New York: Macmillan, 1941.

Kelso, L. H. "Food Habits of Prairie Dogs." USDA Circular No. 529. Washington, DC: U.S. Department of Agriculture, 1939.

Kendeigh, S. C. "The Role of Environment in the Life of Birds." *Ecological Monographs* 4, no. 3 (1934): 299–411.

Kennedy, D. M. *Freedom from Fear: The American People in Depression and War, 1929–1945.* New York: Oxford University Press, 1999.

Kennedy, J. J. "Understanding Professional Career Evolution—an Example of Aldo Leopold." *Wildlife Society Bulletin* 12 (1984): 215–226.

Kirkendall, R. S. *Social Scientists and Farm Politics.* Columbia: University of Missouri Press, 1966.

Klein, M. *The Flowering of the Third America: The Making of an Organizational Society, 1850–1920.* Chicago: Ivan R. Dee, 1993.

Kneipp, L. F. "Land Utilization and Planning." *Journal of Forestry* 34, no. 3 (1936): 257–262.

Knight, R. L. "Aldo Leopold, the Land Ethic, and Ecosystem Management." *Journal of Wildlife Management* 60, no. 3 (1996): 471–474.

———. "Introduction to the Commemorative Issue Celebrating the 50th Anniversary of *A Sand County Almanac* and the Legacy of Aldo Leopold." *Wildlife Society Bulletin* 26, no. 4 (1998): 695–697.

Knight, R. L., and S. Riedel, eds. *Aldo Leopold and the Ecological Conscience.* New York: Oxford University Press, 2002.

Kolko, G. *The Triumph of Conservation: A Reinterpretation of American History, 1900–1916.* New York: Free Press, 1963.

Komroff, M., ed. *Travels of Marco Polo.* New York: Boni and Liveright, 1926.

Kortright, F. H. *The Ducks, Geese, and Swans of North America.* Washington, DC: American Wildlife Institute, 1942.

Landres, P., P. Morgan, and F. Swanson, "Overview of the Use of Natural Variability Concepts in Managing Ecological Systems." *Ecological Applications* 9 (1999): 1179–1188.

Lears, T. J. J., ed. *No Place of Grace: Antimodernism and the Transformation of American Culture.* Chicago: University of Chicago Press, 1994.

Lekan, T. M. *Imagining the Nation in Nature: Landscape Preservation and German Identity, 1885–1945.* Cambridge, MA: Harvard University Press, 2004.

Leopold, A. *Game Management.* New York: Charles Scribner's Sons, 1933.

———. *Report on a Game Survey of the North Central States.* Madison, WI: Democrat Printing Company for the Sporting Arms and Ammunition Manufacturers' Institute, 1931.

———. *A Sand County Almanac and Sketches Here and There.* New York: Oxford University Press, 1987.

Leopold, L. "The Erosion Problem of Southwestern United States." PhD diss., Harvard University, 1950.

———. "Geomorphology: A Sliver off the Corpus of Science." *Annual Review of Earth and Planetary Sciences* 32 (2004): 1–12.

———. "Rainfall Frequency: An Aspect of Climatic Variation." *Transactions, American Geophysical Union* 32, no. 3 (1951): 347–357.

———. "Vegetation of Southwestern Watersheds in the Nineteenth Century." *Geographical Review* 41 (1951): 295–316.

———, ed. *Round River: From the Journals of Aldo Leopold, Author of "A Sand County Almanac."* New York: Oxford University Press, 1993.

Leopold, L., W. W. Emmett, and R. M. Myrick. "Channel and Hillslope Processes in a Semiarid Area, New Mexico." U.S. Geological Survey Professional Paper 352-G. Washington, DC: U.S. Department of the Interior, U.S. Geological Survey, 1966.

Leopold, L., and T. Maddock. *The Flood Control Controversy: Big Dams, Little Dams, and Land Management.* New York: Ronald Press, 1954.

Leopold, L., and J. P. Miller. "A Postglacial Chronology." U.S. Geological Survey Water Supply Paper 1261. Washington, DC: U.S. Department of the Interior, U.S. Geological Survey, 1954.

Leopold, L., and C. T. Snyder. "Alluvial Fills Near Gallup, New Mexico." U.S. Geological Survey Water Supply Paper 410A. Washington, DC: U.S. Department of the Interior, U.S. Geological Survey, 1951.

Leopold, S. *Wildlife of Mexico: The Game Birds and Mammals.* Berkeley: University of California Press, 1959.

Leuchtenburg, W. E. *Franklin D. Roosevelt and the New Deal, 1932–1940.* New York: Harper and Row, 1963.

———. *The Perils of Prosperity.* Chicago: University of Chicago Press, 1993.

Lewis, S. *Babbitt.* New York: P. F. Collier, 1922.

Lime, D., ed. *Managing America's Enduring Wilderness Resource.* St. Paul: Minnesota Extension Service, 1990.

Lindeman, R. L. "The Trophic-Dynamic Aspect of Ecology." *Ecology* 23, no. 4 (1942): 399–418.

Link, A. S. *Woodrow Wilson and the Progressive Era: 1910–1917.* New York: Harper and Row, 1954.

Lissauer, E. "The Hasslied." 1914. Brigham Young University, Harold B. Lee Library, World War I Document Archive. http://www.lib.byu.edu/~rdh/wwi/1914/hasslied.html (accessed November 2005).

Little, C. E. "Has the Land Ethic Failed in America? An Essay on the Legacy of Aldo Leopold." *University of Illinois Law Review* 1986, no. 2 (1986): 313–318.

Lorbiecki, M. *Aldo Leopold: A Fierce Green Fire.* New York: Oxford University Press, 1996.

Lord, R., and K. Lord, eds. *Forever the Land.* New York: Harper and Brothers, 1950.

Lotka, A. J. *Elements of Physical Biology.* Baltimore: Williams and Wilkins, 1925.

Lovejoy, P. S. "Concepts and Contours in Land Utilization." *Journal of Forestry* 31, no. 5 (1933): 381–391.

———. "Correspondence: Dear Mr. Silcox." *Journal of Forestry* 36, no. 6 (1938): 628–634.

———. "Forest Biology." *Journal of Forestry* 15, no. 2 (1917): 203–214.

Lowdermilk, W. C. "Conservation of Soil as a Natural Resource." In *The Foundations of Conservation Education,* edited by H. B. Ward, 15–31. [Washington, DC]: National Wildlife Federation, 1941.

———. "Influence of Forest Litter on Run-off, Percolation, and Erosion." *Journal of Forestry* 28, no. 4 (April 1930): 474–491.

———. "The Role of Vegetation in Erosion Control and Water Conservation." *Journal of Forestry* 32, no. 5 (May 1934): 529–536.

Lowenthal, D. *George Perkins Marsh: Prophet of Conservation.* Seattle: University of Washington Press, 2000.

Lutts, R. H. *The Nature Fakers: Wildlife, Science, and Sentiment.* Charlottesville: University of Virginia Press, 1990.

Lynn, W. M., et al. "Tobacco Following Rare and Natural Weed Fallow and Pure Stands of Certain Weeds." *Journal of Agricultural Research* 59, no. 11 (1939): 829–846.

Lyon, T. L., and H. O. Buckman, eds. *The Nature and Property of Soils: A College Text of Edaphology.* New York: Macmillan, 1938.

MacCleery, D. W. *American Forests: A History of Resiliency and Recovery.* Durham, NC: Forest History Society, 1992.

Malthus, T. R. *Parallel Chapters from the First and Second Editions of "An Essay on the Principle of Population," 1798, 1803.* New York: Macmillan, 1909.

Mann, R. "Aldo Leopold: Priest and Prophet." *American Forests* 60, no. 8 (1954): 23, 42–43.

May, H. F., ed. *The End of American Innocence: A Study of the First Years of Our Own Time, 1912–1917.* Chicago: Quadrangle Books, 1964.

McCabe, R. *Aldo Leopold: The Professor.* Madison, WI: Rusty Rock Press, 1987.

——, ed. *Aldo Leopold: Mentor.* Madison: University of Wisconsin, Department of Wildlife Ecology, 1988.

McCabe, R. A., Collection of the Writings of Aldo Leopold, University of Wisconsin–Madison Libraries.

McClintock, J. I. *Nature's Kindred Spirits: Aldo Leopold, Joseph Wood Krutch, Edward Abbey, Annie Dillard, and Gary Snyder.* Madison: University of Wisconsin Press, 1994.

McConkey, D. "Why the Plains Are Treeless: Geology Scans Prehistory to Explain Why Prairies Grow No Trees, Discovers an American Mediterranean, and a Range of Mountains Called Rocky." *American Forests* 39, no. 11 (1933): 483–485, 526.

McGerr, M. *A Fierce Discontent: The Rise and Fall of the Progressive Movement in America, 1870–1920.* New York: Free Press, 2003.

McIntosh, R. P. *The Background of Ecology: Concept and Theory.* Cambridge: Cambridge University Press, 1985.

McMath, R. C., Jr. *American Populism: A Social History, 1877–1898.* New York: Hill and Wang, 1993.

Meine, C. D. *Aldo Leopold: His Life and Work.* Madison: University of Wisconsin Press, 1988.

——. "Building 'the Land Ethic': A History of Aldo Leopold's Most Important Essay." Master's thesis, University of Wisconsin–Madison, 1983.

——. *Correction Lines: Essays on Land, Leopold, and Conservation.* Washington, DC: Island Press, 2004.

——. "The Farmer as Conservationist: Aldo Leopold on Agriculture." *Journal of Soil and Water Conservation* 42 (1987): 144–149.

——. "Giving Voice to Concern: Aldo Leopold's 'Marshland Elegy.'" In *Marshland Elegy: With an Interpretive Essay by Curt Meine*, 13–24. Madison: Wisconsin Center for the Book, Wisconsin Academy of Sciences, Arts and Letters, 1999.

——. "Keepers of the Cogs." *Defenders* 67, no. 6 (1992): 9–17.

——. "Reading the Landscape: Aldo Leopold and Wildlife Ecology 118." *Forest History Today* (Fall 1999): 35–42.

———. "Reimagining the Prairie: Aldo Leopold and the Origins of Prairie Restoration." In *Recovering the Prairie*, edited by R. F. Sayre, 144–160. Madison: University of Wisconsin Press, 1999.

Meine, C., and R. L. Knight. *The Essential Aldo Leopold: Quotations and Commentaries.* Madison: University of Wisconsin Press, 1999.

Miller, C. *Gifford Pinchot and the Making of Modern Environmentalism.* Washington, DC: Island Press, Shearwater Books, 2001.

Miller, N. *New World Coming: The 1920s and the Making of Modern America.* New York: Charles Scribner's Sons, 2003.

Mills, S. "The Leopolds' Shack." In *In Service of the Wild: Restoring and Reinhabiting Damaged Land*, 93–112. Boston: Beacon Press, 1995.

Moline, J. N. "Aldo Leopold and the Moral Community." *Environmental Ethics* 8 (1986): 99–120.

Moore, K. D. "An Ethic of Care." *Inner Voice* (March–April 1999): 15–16.

Morrell, F. "Men, Trees, and Game." *American Forests* 42, no. 8 (1936): 363–365, 385–386.

Morris, E. *Theodore Rex.* New York: Random House, 2001.

Mullen, F. E. "A 'New Deal' in Conservation." *Outdoor America*, April–May 1933, 4–6.

Murie, O. "Amplifications: Continuing Notes on the Land Ethic" (reprinted address from 1945 *Journal of Wildlife Management*). *Wilderness* (Summer 1985): 54–55.

Naeem, S., L. J. Thompson, S. P. Lawler, J. H. Lawton, and R. M. Woodfin. "Declining Biodiversity Can Alter the Performance of Ecosystems." *Nature* 369, no. 6473 (April 1994): 734–737.

Nash, R. F. *Wilderness and the American Mind.* New Haven, CT: Yale University Press, 1982.

Needham, P., et al. *A Symposium on Hydrobiology: Addresses Given at an Institute Held at the University of Wisconsin: September 4–6, 1940.* Madison: University of Wisconsin Press, 1941.

Nelson, M. P. "A Defense of Environmental Ethics: A Reply to Janna Thompson." *Environmental Ethics* 15, no. 3 (1993): 147–160.

———. "Environmental Ethics and the Land Ethic." *Wildlife Society Bulletin* (Winter): 741–744.

Nelson, M. P. and J. B. Callicott, eds. *The Great Wilderness Debate*, vol. 2 Athens: University of Georgia Press, 2006.

Nicholson, A. J. "The Balance of Animal Populations." *Journal of Animal Ecology* 2 (1933): 132–178.

Norton, B. G. "Change, Constancy, and Creativity: The New Ecology and Some Old Problems." *Duke Environmental Law and Policy Forum* 7, no. 49 (1996): 49–70.

———. "The Constancy of Leopold's Land Ethic." *Conservation Biology* 2, no. 1 (1988): 93–102.

———. "Context and Hierarchy in Aldo Leopold's Theory of Environmental Management." *Ecological Economics* 2 (1990): 119–127.

———. *Searching for Sustainability: Interdisciplinary Essays in the Philosophy of Conservation Biology.* Cambridge: Cambridge University Press, 2003.

——. "Seeking Common Ground for Environmental Change." *Forum for Applied Research and Public Policy* 10 (1995): 100–102.

——. *Sustainability: A Philosophy of Adaptive Management.* Chicago: University of Chicago Press, 2005.

——. *Toward Unity among Environmentalists.* New York: Oxford University Press, 1991.

——. *Why Preserve Natural Variety?* Princeton, NJ: Princeton University Press, 1987.

Odum, E. P. *Fundamentals of Ecology.* Philadelphia: W. B. Saunders, 1953.

Oelschlaeger, M. *The Idea of Wilderness: From Prehistory to the Age of Ecology.* New Haven, CT: Yale University Press, 1991.

Olmstead, F. H. *Gila River Flood Control.* 65th Cong., 3rd sess. Document No. 436. Washington, DC: Government Printing Office, 1919.

Ortega y Gasset, J. *Meditations on Hunting.* New York: Charles Scribner's Sons, 1972.

——, ed. *The Revolt of the Masses.* New York: W. W. Norton, 1957.

Osborn, F. *Our Plundered Planet.* Boston: Little, Brown, 1948.

Ouspensky, P. D. *Tertium Organum: The Third Canon of Thought; a Key to the Enigmas of the World,* revised translation by E. Kadloubovsky and the author. New York: Alfred A. Knopf, 1981.

Palmer, T. S. "Chronology and Index of American Game Protection, 1776–1911." USDA Bulletin 41. Washington, DC: U.S. Department of Agriculture, Biological Survey, 1912.

Parrish, M. E. *Anxious Decades: America in Prosperity and Depression, 1920–1941.* New York: W. W. Norton, 1992.

Partridge, E. "Are We Ready for an Ecological Morality?" *Environmental Ethics* 4 (1982): 175–190.

Patterson, J. T. *The New Deal and the States: Federalism in Transition.* Princeton, NJ: Princeton University Press, 1969.

Pearl, R. *The Biology of Population Growth.* New York: Alfred A. Knopf, 1925.

Pearson, G. A. "Preservation of Natural Areas in the National Forests." *Ecology* 3, no. 4 (1922): 284–287.

Peattie, D. C. *Flowering Earth.* New York: G. P. Putnam's Sons, 1939.

Peffer, E. L. *The Closing of the Public Domain.* Stanford, CA: Stanford University Press, 1951.

Pfeiffer, E. *The Earth's Face: Landscape and Its Relation to the Health of the Soil.* London: Faber and Faber, 1947.

Philippon, D. J. *Conserving Words: How American Nature Writers Shaped the Environmental Movement.* Athens: University of Georgia Press, 2004.

Phillips, S. T. "Acres Fit and Unfit: Conservation and Rural Rehabilitation in the New Deal Era." PhD diss., Boston University, 2004.

Pinchot, G. "An American Fable." *National Geographic* 19, no. 5 (May 1908): 345–350.

——. *Breaking New Ground.* Introduction by C. Miller and V. A. Sample. Washington, DC: Island Press, 1998.

——. *The Green Book: Instructions and Record for Official Accounts.* U.S. Department of Agriculture, Forest Service. Washington, DC: Government Printing Office, 1907.

———. "It Can Happen Here." *American Forests* 43, no. 4 (1937): 282–283, 321.

———. *The Use of the National Forests: Regulations and Instructions for the Use of the National Forests*. U.S. Department of Agriculture, Forest Service. Washington, DC: Government Printing Office, 1907.

Pisani, D. J. "Forests and Conservation, 1865–1890." In *American Forests: Nature, Culture, and Politics*, edited by C. Miller, 15–34. Lawrence: University Press of Kansas, 1997.

Pittman, N. P., ed. *From the Land*. Washington, DC: Island Press, 1988.

Pool, R. J., et al. "Further Studies in the Ecotone between Prairie and Woodland." Botanical Seminar, n.s., No. 2, 1–47. Reprinted from *University of Nebraska Studies* 18 (1918): 1–2.

Potter, V. R. "Aldo Leopold's Land Ethic Revisited: Two Kinds of Bioethics." *Perspectives in Biology and Medicine* 30 (1987): 157–169.

Proceedings of a Conference of the Governors of the United States, 1908, White House, May 13–15. Washington, DC: Government Printing Office, 1909.

Real, L. A., and J. H. Brown, eds. *Foundations of Ecology: Classic Papers with Commentaries*. Chicago: University of Chicago Press, 1991.

Reiger, J. F. *American Sportsmen and the Origins of Conservation*. New York: Winchester Press, 1975.

Reynolds, J. M. "On the Inheritance of Food Effects in a Flour Beetle, *Tribolium destructor*." *Proceedings of the Royal Society of London*. Series B, *Biological Sciences* 132, no. 869 (1945): 438–451.

Ribbons, D. "Making of a Title: *A Sand County Almanac*." *Wisconsin Academy Review* (1982): 8–10.

Richter, C. *The Trees*. New York: Alfred A. Knopf, 1940.

Ripple, W. J., and R. L. Beschta. "Linking Wolves and Plants: Aldo Leopold on Trophic Cascades." *Bioscience* 55, no. 7 (2005): 1–9.

Roe, M. "The Ideas of Aldo Leopold." *Landscape Design* 175 (1988): 15–26.

Rolston, H., III. *Environmental Ethics: Duties to and Values in the Natural World*. Philadelphia: Temple University Press, 1988.

Rölvaag, O. E. *Giants in the Earth*. New York: Harper and Brothers, 1927.

Romasco, A. U. *The Poverty of Abundance: Hoover, the Nation, the Depression*. London: Oxford University Press, 1965.

Roosevelt, T. "Letter from Theodore Roosevelt to Sir Edward Grey." 22 January 1915. Brigham Young University, Harold B. Lee Library, World War I Document Archive. http://www.lib.byu.edu/~rdh/wwi/1915/roosgrey.html (accessed November 2005).

———. "The New Nationalism." 31 August 1910. Public Broadcasting Service, *American Experience: The Presidents*. http://www.pbs.org/wgbh/amex/presidents/26_t_roosevelt/psources/ps_national.html (accessed December 2005).

Rubner, H. "Sustained-Yield Forestry in Europe and Its Crisis during the Era of Nazi Dictatorship." In *History of Sustained-Yield Forestry: A Symposium; Western Forestry Center, Portland, Oregon, October 18–19, 1983*, edited by H. K. Steen, 170–175. Santa Cruz, CA: Forest History Society, 1984.

Sachse, N. *A Thousand Ages: The University of Wisconsin Arboretum*. Madison: University of Wisconsin Press, 1965.

Sauer, C. O., et al. "Preliminary Recommendations of the Land-Use Committee

Relating to Soil Erosion." Confidential report. Washington, DC: National Research Council, Science Advisory Board, 26 April 1934.

Sayre, R. F. "Aldo Leopold's Sentimentalism: A Refined Taste in Natural Objects." *North Dakota Quarterly* 59 (1991): 112–125.

———. *Recovering the Prairie.* Madison: University of Wisconsin Press, 1999.

Schabel, H. G., and S. L. Palmer. "The Dauerwald: Its Role in the Restoration of Natural Forests." *Journal of Forestry* 97 (1999): 20–25.

Scheiber, H. N. "From Science to Law to Politics: An Historical View of the Ecosystem Idea and Its Effect on Resource Management." *Ecology Law Quarterly* 24, no. 631 (1997): 631–651.

Schlesinger, A. M., Jr. *The Cycles of American History.* Boston: Houghton Mifflin, 1986.

———, ed. *The Age of Roosevelt: The Politics of Upheaval.* Boston: Houghton Mifflin, 1966.

Schmitt, P. J. *Back to Nature: The Arcadian Myth in Urban America.* Baltimore: Johns Hopkins University Press, 1990.

Schoenfeld, C. "Aldo Leopold." *Wisconsin Natural Resources* (January–February 1987): 4–10.

Schorger, A. W. "Aldo Leopold." *Wisconsin Conservation Bulletin* 39, no. 1 (January–February 1974): 16.

———. Obituary [for Aldo Leopold]. *Auk* 65, no. 4 (1948): 648–649.

Scott, W. E. "Does Inbreeding Cause the Cycle on Game Animals?" *Wisconsin Conservation Bulletin* 9, no. 2 (1944): 6–10.

Sears, P. B. *Deserts on the March.* Norman: University of Oklahoma Press, 1947.

———. "Postglacial Climate in Eastern North America." *Ecology* 13, no. 1 (1932): 1–6.

Sellars, R. W. *Preserving Nature in the National Parks: A History.* New Haven, CT: Yale University Press, 1997.

Shaw, G. B. "Common Sense about the War." *New York Times,* 15, 22, 29 November 1914. Arizona State University Libraries, ProQuest Historical Newspapers: The New York Times 1851–2003, p. SM1. http://www.asu.edu/lib/resources/db/pqhisnyt.htm (accessed December 2005).

Shelford, V. E. *Animal Communities in Temperate America.* Chicago: University of Chicago Press, 1913.

———. "The History of Ecology." Lecture, University of Illinois, History of Science Society, 6 October 1958.

———. "Principles and Problems of Ecology as Illustrated by Animals." *Journal of Ecology* 3, no. 1 (1915): 1–23.

Shepard, W. "The Purpose of the European Forestry Tour." *Journal of Forestry* 33, no. 1 (1935): 5–8.

Sibernagel, B., and J. Sibernagel. "Tracking Aldo Leopold through Riley's Farmland." *Wisconsin Magazine of History* (Summer 2003): 34–45.

Silcox, F. A. "Correspondence: Dear Lovejoy." *Journal of Forestry* 36, no. 6 (1938): 634–638.

———. "Foresters Must Choose." *Journal of Forestry* 33, no. 3 (1935): 198–204.

Silcox, F. A., W. C. Lowdermilk, and M. L. Cooke. *The Scientific Aspects of Flood Control.* Occasional publications of the American Association for the

Advancement of Science No. 3, supplement to *Science* 84. New York: Science Press, 1936.

Smith, F. E. *Conservation in the United States: A Documentary History; Land and Water, 1900–1970*. New York: Chelsea House, 1971.

Smith, G. A. "Natural Resource Economic Theory of the First Conservation Movement, 1895–1927." *History of Political Economy* 14, no. 4 (1982): 483–495.

Smith, R. C. "Upsetting the Balance of Nature, with Special Reference to Kansas and the Great Plains." *Science* 75, no. 1956 (1932): 649–654.

Special Committee on Conservation of Wildlife Resources. *Wildlife Restoration and Conservation: Proceedings of the North American Wildlife Conference Called by President Franklin D. Roosevelt*. Washington, DC: Government Printing Office, 1936.

Spencer, H. *The Principles of Biology*. 2 vols. New York: D. Appleton, 1896, 1897.

Steen, H. K. "The Beginning of the National Forest System." In *American Forests: Nature, Culture, and Politics*, ed. C. Miller, 49–68. Lawrence: University Press of Kansas, 1997.

———. *The Conservation Diaries of Gifford Pinchot*. Durham, NC: Forest History Society and the Pinchot Institute for Conservation, 2001.

———. *The U.S. Forest Service: A History*. Seattle: University of Washington Press, 1976.

———, ed. *The Origins of the National Forests*. Durham, NC: Forest History Society, 1992.

Stegner, W. *Wolf Willow: A History, a Story, and a Memoir of the Last Plains Frontier*. Lincoln: University of Nebraska Press, 1955.

Stegner, W., and C. E. Little. "The Once and Future Land Ethic: Aldo Leopold's Classic Statement, with Commentary from Wallace Stegner and Charles E. Little." *Wilderness* 48, no. 168 (1985): 5–30.

Steinhacker, C., and S. Flader. *The Sand County of Aldo Leopold: A Photographic Interpretation*. San Francisco: Sierra Club Books, 1973.

Stettner, E. A. *Shaping Modern Liberalism: Herbert Croly and Progressive Thought*. Lawrence: University Press of Kansas, 1993.

Stoddard, H. L. *The Bobwhite Quail: Its Habits, Preservation, and Increase*. New York: Charles Scribner's Sons, 1931.

———. *Report on Cooperative Quail Investigation: 1925–1926: With Preliminary Recommendations for the Development of Quail Preserves*. U.S. Department of Agriculture, Biological Survey, Division of Food Habits Research. Washington, DC: Committee Representing the Quail Study Fund for Southern Georgia and Northern Florida, 1926.

———. *The Use of Controlled Fire in Southeastern Game Management*. Thomasville, GA: Cooperative Quail Study Association, 1939.

———. "Use of Controlled Fire in Southeastern Upland Game Management." *Journal of Forestry* 33, no. 3 (1935): 346–351.

Sutter, P. S. *Driven Wild: How the Fight against Automobiles Launched the Modern Wilderness Movement*. Seattle: University of Washington Press, 2002.

Swain, D. C. *Wilderness Defender: Horace M. Albright and Conservation*. Chicago: University of Chicago Press, 1970.

Tanner, T., ed. *Aldo Leopold: The Man and His Legacy*. Ankeny, IA: Soil Conservation Society of America, 1987.

Tansley, A. G. 1947. "The Early History of Modern Plant Ecology in Britain." *Journal of Ecology* 35, nos. 1/2 (December 1947): 130–137.

———. "Frederic Edward Clements, 1874–1945." Obituary notice. *Journal of Ecology* 34, no. 1 (1945): 194–196.

———. *Practical Plant Ecology*. New York: Dodd, Mead, 1923.

———. "The Use and Abuse of Vegetational Concepts and Terms." *Ecology* 16 (1935): 284–307.

Taylor, W. P. "The Biological Side of the Business of Forest and Forage Production." *Journal of Forestry* 25, no. 4 (1927): 386–414.

———. *The Deer of North America*. Harrisburg, PA: Stackpole Company and Wildlife Management Institute, 1956.

———. "Significance of the Biotic Community in Ecological Studies." *Quarterly Review of Biology* 10, no. 3 (1935): 291–307.

———. "Some Animal Relations to Soils." *Ecology* 16, no. 2 (April 1935): 127–136.

———. "Some Effects of Animals on Plants." *Scientific Monthly* 43 (1936): 262–270.

———. "What Is Ecology and What Good Is It?" *Ecology* 17, no. 3 (1936): 333–346.

Taylor, W. P., et al. "The Relation of Jack Rabbits to Grazing in Southern Arizona." *Journal of Forestry* 33, no. 5 (May 1935): 490–498.

Thelen, D. P. *Robert La Follette and the Insurgent Spirit*. Boston: Little, Brown, 1976.

Tilman, D., and J. A. Downing. "Biodiversity and Stability in Grasslands." *Nature* 367, no. 6461 (January 1994): 363–365.

Trefethen, J. B. *An American Crusade for Wildlife*. New York: Winchester Press, 1975.

Treherne, R. C., and E. R. Buckell. "Grasshoppers of British Columbia." *Canada Department of Agriculture Bulletin* 39 (1924).

Trombulak, S. *So Great a Vision: The Conservation Writings of George Perkins Marsh*. Hanover and London: Middlebury College Press and University Press of New England, 2001.

Turner, F. J. *The Frontier in American History*. New York: Henry Holt, 1920.

———. "The Problem of the West." *Atlantic Monthly*, September 1896. http://www.theatlantic.com/issues/95sep/ets/turn.htm.

University of Wisconsin–Madison, Department of Wildlife Ecology Library.

U.S. Department of Commerce, Bureau of the Census. *Statistical Abstract of the United States*. Various years. Washington, DC: Government Printing Office, 1901–1950.

Valenčius, C. B. *The Health of the Country: How American Settlers Understood Themselves and Their Land*. New York: Basic Books, 2002.

Vanderwall, E. J. "Wise Use." *Wisconsin Conservation Bulletin* 8, no. 7 (July 1943): 11.

Van Hise, C. R. *The Conservation of Natural Resources in the United States*. New York: Macmillan, 1910.

Veblen, T. "Historic Range of Variability of Mountain Forest Ecosystems: Concepts and Applications." *Forest Chronicle* 79 (2003): 223–226.

Veblen, T. B. *The Theory of the Leisure Class: An Economic Study of Institutions.* New York: Modern Library, 1934.

Vogt, W. *Road to Survival.* New York: William Sloan Associates, 1948.

Vohries, C. T., and W. P. Taylor. "The Life Histories and Ecology of Jackrabbits, *Lepus alleni* and *Lepus californicus* spp., in Relation to Grazing in Arizona." *Technical Bulletin—University of Arizona, College of Agriculture, Agricultural Experiment Station* 49 (1933): 471–583.

Wahlenberg, W. J. "Effect of Fire and Grazing on Soil Properties and the Natural Reproduction of Longleaf Pine." *Journal of Forestry* 33, no. 3 (1935): 331–338.

Wallace, H. A. "The Restoration of Rural Life." *American Forests* 39, no. 12 (1933): 486, 527.

Ward, H. B., ed. *The Foundations of Conservation Education.* [Washington, DC]: National Wildlife Federation, 1941.

Warren, H. G. *Herbert Hoover and the Great Depression.* New York: Oxford University Press, 1959.

Warren, K. J. "Leopold's Land Ethic, Ecofeminist Philosophy, and Environmental Ethics." In *Aldo Leopold's Land Ethic: A Legacy for Public Land Managers.* Proceedings of conference. 14–15 May 1999, National Conservation Training Center, Shepherdstown, WV.

Watkins, T. H. *The Great Depression: America in the 1930s.* Boston: Little, Brown, 1993.

———. "Untrammeled by Man: The Making of the Wilderness Act of 1964." *Audubon* 91 (1989): 74–81.

Waugh, F. A. "Wilderness to Keep." *Review of Reviews* 81 (1939): 146.

Weaver, J. E. *The Ecological Relations of Roots.* Washington, DC: Carnegie Institution of Washington, 1919.

———. "Plant Production as a Measure of Environment: A Study in Crop Ecology." *Journal of Ecology* 12 (July 1924): 205–235.

———. *Prairie Plants and Their Environment: A Fifty-Year Study in the Midwest.* Lincoln: University of Nebraska Press, 1968, 1991.

———. *Root Development of Field Crops.* New York: McGraw-Hill, 1926.

Weaver, J. E., and F. E. Clements. *Plant Ecology.* New York: McGraw-Hill, 1938.

Weaver, J. E., and T. J. Fitzpatrick. "The Prairie." *Ecological Monographs* 4, no. 2 (April 1934): 111–295.

Weaver, J. E., and E. L. Flory. "Stability of Climax Prairie and Some Environmental Changes Resulting from Breaking." *Ecology* 15, no. 4 (October 1934): 333–347.

Weaver, J. E., and W. W. Hansen. "Native Midwestern Pastures: Their Origin, Composition, and Degeneration." *Nebraska Conservation Bulletin*, no. 22 (1941).

Weaver, J. E., and G. W. Harmon. "Quantity of Living Plant Materials in Prairie Soils in Relation to Run-off and Soil Erosion." *Bulletin* 8 (1935): 1–53. Lincoln: University of Nebraska, Conservation Department of the Conservation and Survey Division.

Weaver, J. E., and A. F. Thiel. "Ecological Studies in the Tension Zone between

Prairie and Woodland." *Botanical Seminar*, n.s., no. 1 (1917): 1–60. Lincoln: University of Nebraska.

Weaver, J. E., et al. *Development and Activities of Roots of Crop Plants: A Study in Crop Ecology*. Washington, DC: Carnegie Institution of Washington, 1922.

———. "Relation of Root Distribution to Organic Matter in Prairie Soil." *Botanical Gazette* 96, no. 3 (March 1935): 389–420.

Webb, W. P. *The Great Plains*. Boston: Ginn and Company, 1931.

———. "Presidential Address: History as High Adventure." *American Historical Review* 64, no. 2 (January 1959): 265–280.

Wehrein, G. S. "The Economist's Approach to Ecology." *Journal of Forestry* 37, no. 9 (1939): 731–734.

———. "A Social and Economic Program for the Sub-marginal Areas of the Lake States." *Journal of Forestry* 29, no. 10 (1931): 915–924.

Wells, H. G. *The Outline of History: Being a Plain History of Life and Mankind*. New York: Garden City Publishing, 1920.

Wenz, P. S. *Environmental Ethics Today*. New York: Oxford University Press, 2001.

West, A. J. "Forests and National Security: British and American Forestry in the Wake of World War I." *Environmental History* 8, no. 2 (2003): 270–293.

Westra, L. *An Environmental Proposal for Ethics: The Principle of Integrity*. Lanham, MD: Rowman and Littlefield, 1994.

Wheeler, W. M. *Emergent Evolution and the Development of Societies*. New York: W. W. Norton, 1928.

White, C. "The Working Wilderness: A Call for a Land Health Movement." In W. Berry, *The Way of Ignorance: And Other Essays*, 159–180. Emeryville, CA: Shoemaker and Hoard, 2005.

Whitman, W. *Walt Whitman: Complete Poetry and Collected Prose*. Edited by J. Kaplan. New York: Library of America, 1982.

Wiebe, R. H. *The Search for Order: 1877–1920*. New York: Hill and Wang, 1967.

Wilkinson, C. F. "Aldo Leopold and Western Water Law: Thinking Perpendicular to the Prior Appropriation Doctrine." *Land and Water Law Review* 24 (1989): 1–38.

Williams, G. W. *The USDA Forest Service—the First Century*. Publication No. FS-650. Washington, DC: U.S. Department of Agriculture, Forest Service, 2000.

Wing, L. W. "Naturalize the Forest for Wildlife." *American Forests* 42, no. 6 (June 1936): 260–261, 293.

Winship, G. P. *Why Coronado Went to New Mexico in 1540*. Washington, DC: Government Printing Office, 1896.

———, trans. and ed. *The Journey of Coronado: 1540–1542*. New York: A. S. Barnes, 1904.

Wolf, M., and F.-C. von Berg. "Deer and Forestry in Germany: Half a Century after Aldo Leopold." *Journal of Forestry* 8, no. 5 (1988): 25–31.

Worster, D. *The Dust Bowl: The Southern Plains in the 1930s*. New York: Oxford University Press, 1979.

———. *A River Running West: The Life of John Wesley Powell*. New York: Oxford University Press, 2001.

———. "Seeing beyond Culture." *Journal of American History* 76, no. 4 (1990): 1142–1147.

———. "Transformations of the Earth: Toward an Agroecological Perspective in History." *Journal of American History* 76, no. 4 (1990): 1087–1106.

———. *Under Western Skies: Nature and History in the American West.* New York: Oxford University Press, 1992.

———. *An Unsettled Country: Changing Landscapes of the American West.* Albuquerque: University of New Mexico Press, 1994.

———. *The Wealth of Nature: Environmental History and the Ecological Imagination.* New York: Oxford University Press, 1993.

———., ed. *The Ends of the Earth: Perspectives on Modern Environmental History.* Cambridge: Cambridge University Press, 1988.

———. *Nature's Economy: A History of Ecological Ideas.* Cambridge: Cambridge University Press, 1994.

Wrench, G. T. *The Wheel of Health.* London: C. W. Daniel, 1938.

Yapp, R. H. "The Concept of Habitat." *Journal of Ecology* 10, no. 1 (1922): 1–17.

Yonay, Y. P. *The Struggle over the Soul of Economics: Institutional and Neoclassical Economists in America between the Wars.* Princeton, NJ: Princeton University Press, 1998.

Zeide, B. "Another Look at Leopold's Land Ethic." *Journal of Forestry* 96, no. 1 (1998): 13–19.

Zimmerman, M. E., et al. *Environmental Philosophy: From Animal Rights to Radical Ecology.* Englewood Cliffs, NJ: Prentice-Hall, 1998.

Sources of Illustrations and Excerpts

Image courtesy of the Aldo Leopold Foundation: Frontispiece, Aldo Leopold recording the morning's observations at the "Shack," c. 1942. Photo by Irving Buss.

Images courtesy of the University of Wisconsin Department of Wildlife Ecology and the Aldo Leopold Foundation (photographs attributed to Aldo Leopold unless noted otherwise):

Page number	Reference number
6	81
8	86
20	2295 (photographer unknown)
23	1838
53	484
85	2271 (H. H. Bennett)
125	501
156	746 (E.G. Holt)
157	744 (by "Fassett")
164	Drawing by Jay N. Darling in Thomas Beck, Jay N. Darling, Aldo Leopold, "A National Plan for Wild Life Restoration," Report Submitted Washington, D.C., 8 February, 1934, p. 2.
173	884
194	1716
199	937
204	1882
239	229 (Albert Hochbaum)
244	1793 (by "Reese")
257	380

262	1376
269	959
274	1073
284	2269
294	G3S
312	1285
326	1355
329	Leopold's class notes for Wildlife 118

Images courtesy of the University of Wisconsin-Madison Archives and the Aldo Leopold Foundation:

Page number	*Reference number*
13	X25 1854
24	X25 1073
27	X25 2949
50	X25 2950
88	LP 9/25/10-7, 2
103	3/1 file 11
127	X25 1260
132	LP 10-6, 10
137	NA
181	X25 0681
202	LP 10-6, 1
225	X25 1699
232	X25 3214
243	LP 9/25/10-7, box 2
280	X2 0194N (Photo by Robert McCabe)
291	X25 3213
328	LP 10-6, 16
344	X25 197N

Image courtesy of Steven Brower: page 41, Aldo Leopold's childhood home in Burlington, Iowa.

Quotations from *A Sand County Almanac* reprinted by permission of Oxford University Press, Inc.

Excerpt from *Land of the Free* by Archibald MacLeish. Copyright © 1938 and renewed 1966 by Archibald MacLeish. Reprinted by permission of Houghton Mifflin Company. All rights reserved.

Index